6th Edition

Strategic Management

Competitiveness and Globalization

Concepts

Michael A. Hitt
Texas A&M University

R. Duane Ireland
University of Richmond
and
Texas A&M University

Robert E. Hoskisson
The University of Oklahoma

P9-DCV-320

THOMSON
SOUTH-WESTERN

Australia · Canada · Mexico · Singapore · Spain · United Kingdom · United States

THOMSON

SOUTH-WESTERN

Strategic Management: Competitiveness and Globalization (Concepts) 6e
Michael A. Hitt, R. Duane Ireland, and Robert E. Hoskisson

VP/Editorial Director:
Jack W. Calhoun

VP/Editor-in-Chief:
Michael P. Roche

Senior Publisher:
Melissa Acuña

Executive Editor:
John Szilagyi

Senior Developmental Editor:
Mardell Toomey

Marketing Manager:
Jacque Carrillo

Senior Production Editor:
Kara ZumBahlen

Media Developmental Editor:
Kristen Meere

Media Production Editor:
Karen Schaffer

Manufacturing Coordinator:
Rhonda Utley

Production House:
Lachina Publishing Services, Inc.

Printer:
QuebecorWorld
Versailles, KY

Internal and Cover Designer:
Anne Marie Rekow

Cover Photograph:
Image 100

Photography Manager:
John Hill

Photo Researcher:
Jan Siedel

Brief Contents

Contents

Chapter 7

Chapter 8

Chapter 9

Part 3 *Strategic Actions: Strategy Implementation* 302

Chapter 10

Chapter 11

Chapter 12

Chapter 13

Preface

Our goal in writing this book was to establish a new standard in the presentation of current and up-to-date concepts in strategic management. We believe that this goal has been realized and is fully evident in this 6th edition of our market-leading book. Written in a lively and user-friendly manner, this text presents a rich and comprehensive examination of strategic management concepts and tools. Following are some of the most important features of our book and this edition.

- This text offers the most comprehensive and thorough coverage of strategic management available in the market.
- The research presented in our text is the most up-to-date in the field and most current in practice compared to all other strategic management books. Although the text is grounded in the current research, it is also strongly application oriented with more examples and applications of strategic management concepts, techniques, and tools than any other competitor on the market.
- We integrate two of the most popular and well-known theoretical concepts in the field of strategic management, industrial organization economics through the writings of such authors as Michael Porter and the resource-based view of the firm from the work of such authors as Jay Barney. No other book integrates these two theoretical perspectives to explain the process of strategic management.
- We use the ideas of prominent scholars (e.g., Michael Porter, Richard Rumelt, Kathy Eisenhardt, Gary Hamel, C. K. Prahalad, David Teece, Oliver Williamson, Don Hambrick, Dan Schendel, Richard Bettis, Sumantra Ghoshal, Kathy Harrigan, Rosabeth Kanter, and Costas Markides as well as numerous others) and prominent executives and practitioners (e.g., Carly Fiorina, John Chambers, Andy Grove, Herb Kelleher, Steven Jobs, Meg Whitman, Jeffrey Immelt, and Anne Mulcahy as well as many others) to provide an effective understanding of the theoretical base of strategic management and its application in organizations.
- We (the authors of this book) are also highly active scholars in the conduct of strategic management research and the application of the concepts derived from that research. Thus, our own research is integrated in the appropriate chapters as well.
- In this edition, we offer examples of over 100 companies' actions in the chapters' Opening Cases and Strategic Focus segments. Furthermore, the application of strategic management concepts is shown in more than 600 different companies in the book's chapters. There is no strategic management book on the market that has both the up-to-date research and the application orientation shown by this number of company examples.

Some of the highlights of our new edition include:

- **New Opening Cases and Strategic Focus Segments:** We continue our tradition of providing new Opening Cases and Strategic Focus segments and many other new examples in each chapter to describe actions companies take within the context of a chapter's topic.
- **An Exceptional Balance** between current research and applications of it in actual organizations. The content has not only the best research documentation

but also the largest amount of effective firm examples to help students understand the strategies discussed.

- **Enhanced Experiential Exercises** to support learners' efforts to understand the use of strategic management in organizations of all types.
- **Lively, Concise Writing Style** to hold readers' attention and to increase their interest in the subject matter.
- **Continuing, Updated Coverage** of vital strategic management topics such as competitive rivalry and dynamics, strategic alliances, mergers and acquisitions, international strategies, corporate governance and ethics, and strategic entrepreneurship.
- **Full Four-Color Format** to enhance readability by attracting and maintaining readers' interest.
- **New Content in Chapter 12, Strategic Leadership:** "Effectively Managing the Firm's Resource Portfolio"; "Developing Human Capital and Social Capital"; and "Emphasizing Ethical Practices." Also, expanded discussion of the **Balanced Scorecard** used by *many* corporations today.
- **New Content in Chapter 13, Strategic Entrepreneurship:** This chapter presents a discussion of social entrepreneurship that is unique to this edition and not found in any competitor. The discussion is fully developed within the text and also features a Strategic Focus segment on this increasingly important and timely topic.

Supplements

Instructors

IRCD (0-324-20387-X)
Key ancillaries [Instructor's Case Notes, Instructor's Resource Manual, Test Bank, ExamView™, PowerPoint®, Case Analysis Spreadsheets, and CNN Video Guide (integrates cases and videos)] are provided on CD-ROM, giving instructors the ultimate tool for customizing lectures and presentations.

INSTRUCTOR'S RESOURCE MANUAL WITH VIDEO GUIDE AND TRANSPARENCY MASTERS (0-324-20382-9)
Prepared by Leslie E. Palich, Baylor University. The Instructor's Resource Manual, organized around each chapter's knowledge objectives, includes ideas about how to approach each chapter and how to reinforce essential principles with extra examples. The support product includes lecture outlines, detailed answers to end-of-chapter review questions, instructions for using each chapter's experiential exercises, guides to all available videos, and additional assignments.

TEST BANK (0-324-20383-7)
Prepared by Janelle Dozier. Thoroughly revised and enhanced, Test Bank questions are linked to each chapter's knowledge objectives and are ranked by difficulty and question type. We have increased the number of application questions throughout, and we have also retained scenario-based questions as a means of adding in-depth problem-solving questions to exams (these were new to the last edition). The Test Bank material is also available in computerized ExamView™ format for creating custom tests in both Windows and Macintosh formats.

EXAMVIEW™ (0-324-23621-2)
Computerized testing software contains all of the questions in the printed Test Bank. This program is an easy-to-use test creation software compatible with Microsoft

Windows. Instructors can add or edit questions, instructions, and answers, and select questions by previewing them on the screen, selecting them randomly, or selecting them by number. Instructors can also create and administer quizzes online, whether over the Internet, a local area network (LAN), or a wide area network (WAN).

TRANSPARENCY ACETATES (0-324-20384-5)

Key figures from the main text have been re-created as colorful and attractive overhead transparencies for classroom use.

POWERPOINT® DISCUSSION SLIDES (0-324-20386-1)
POWERPOINT® LECTURE SLIDES (0-324-20385-3)

Prepared by Dennis Middlemist, Colorado State University. An all-new PowerPoint® presentation, created for this edition, provides configurations both for lecture-based teaching formats and for discussion-based teaching formats. Slides can also be used by students as an aid to note-taking

Students and Instructors

WEBTUTOR™ TOOLBOX (0-324-23172-5—WEBCT; 0-324-23171-7—BLACKBOARD)

WebTutor™ ToolBox provides instructors with links to content from our book companion websites. WebTutor™ ToolBox also provides rich communication tools to instructors and students including a course calendar, chat, and e-mail.

WEBSITE

This edition's website offers students and instructors access to a wealth of helpful support and learning materials. Included are Instructor Resources, Student Resources, Interactive Study Center, Interactive Quizzes, links to Strategy Suite, e-Coursepacks, and Careers in Management. You will find continually updated case information, a section on how to write a case analysis along with the case analyses for this edition's applicable cases, and a new feature—interactive spreadsheets that help students understand the importance of case analyses and how to perform them. We have provided an Internet index with important strategy URLs and PowerPoint® slide presentations. We have also included additional experiential exercises, Strategic Focus applications, Ethics questions, Internet exercises, and Global Resources. Finally, for quickly finding new terms, we offer an online glossary. The *Strategic Management* website provides information about the authors and allows you to contact the authors and the publisher.

CNN VIDEO (0-324-20389-6)

"Management and Strategy" is a 45-minute video of short news clips from CNN, capitalizing on the resources of the world's first 24-hour all-news network. The 6th edition features videos that are closely linked with current case and text content for a truly integrative approach, assuring particular relevance to students of strategic management and a fresh perspective on text content. A resource guide accompanies the video, and further support is offered in the Instructor's Resource Manual.

ENTREPRENEURSHIP AND STRATEGY VIDEO (0-324-26131-4)

This is a 45-minute video based on the remarkable resources of *Small Business School*, the series on PBS stations, Worldnet, and the Web. The video features seven firms that capitalized on their beginnings and used strategic management to grow market share and create competitive advantage. A resource guide within the Instructor's Resource Manual describes each segment and provides discussion questions.

CORPORATE STRATEGY VIDEO (0-324-20390-X)

This is a 45-minute video featuring corporate strategy situations for classroom viewing. Corporate strategy and strategic planning perspectives are analyzed at an up-and-coming company, Caribou Coffee; strategy and leadership are examined at CVS; and organizational structure is studied through Student Advantage. A resource guide within the Instructor's Resource Manual describes each segment and provides discussion questions.

E-COURSEPACK

Current, interesting, and relevant articles are available to supplement each chapter of *Strategic Management* in an e-Coursepack—the result of a joint effort between the Gale Group, a world leader in e-information publishing for libraries, schools, and businesses, and South-Western. Full-length articles to complement *Strategic Management* are available 24 hours a day over the Web, from sources such as *Fortune, Across the Board, Management Today,* and the *Sloan Management Review.* Students can also access up-to-date information on key individuals, companies, and text-book cases through predefined searches of Gale databases. For more information, contact your South-Western/Thomson Learning sales representative or call Thomson Custom Publishing at 1-800-355-9983.

INFOTRAC COLLEGE EDITION

InfoTrac College Edition gives students access—anytime, anywhere—to an online database of full-text articles from hundreds of scholarly and popular periodicals, including *Newsweek* and *Fortune.* Fast and easy search tools help you find just what you're looking for from tens of thousands of articles, updated daily, all at a single site. For more information, contact your South-Western/Thomson Learning sales representative or call Thomson Custom Publishing at 1-800-355-9983.

Acknowledgments

In the words of Carly Fiorina, "We have hit our stride" in this edition. We are indebted to the following people who worked on and developed several ancillary materials to support this edition of the book:

Charles M. Byles, *Virginia Commonwealth University*
Janelle Dozier
Timothy R. Mayes, *Metropolitan State College of Denver*
R. Dennis Middlemist, *Colorado State University*
Leslie E. Palich, *Baylor University*
Jude Rathburn, *University of Wisconsin—Milwaukee*
Craig VanSandt, *Augustana College*

We also express our appreciation to the following people who reviewed chapters and offered comments to help us develop this edition:

Karen Bilda, *Cardinal Stritch University*
James Bronson, *University of Wisconsin, Whitewater*
Lowell Busenitz, *University of Oklahoma*
Charles M. Byles, *Virginia Commonwealth University*
Bruce Clemens, *James Madison University*
Refik Culpan, *Pennsylvania State University at Harrisburg*
Wade Danis, *Marquette University*
Tamela D. Ferguson, *University of Louisiana at Lafayette*
Charles Gates, *Northern Illinois University*

Ted Herbert, *Rollins College*
Mike Hergert, *San Diego State University*
Phyllis Holland, *Valdosta State University*
Carol Jacobson, *Purdue University*
Franz Kellermanns, *University of Connecticut*
David J. Ketchen, *Florida State*
Haiyang Li, *Texas A&M University*
Roman Nowacki, *Northern Illinois University*
Annette L. Ranft, *Wake Forest University*
Mark Sharfman, *University of Oklahoma*
Tony W. Tong, *Ohio State University*
Henry Van Buren, *University of Northern Iowa*
Robert Wiseman, *Michigan State University*

We also express our appreciation for the excellent support received from our editorial and production team at South-Western. We especially wish to thank John Szilagyi, our editor; Mardell Toomey, the developmental editor; and Kara ZumBahlen, the production editor. We are grateful for their dedication, commitment, and outstanding contributions to the development and publication of this book and its package of support materials.

Michael A. Hitt

R. Duane Ireland

Robert E. Hoskisson

Dedications

To Rebecca and Joe. We love you both. For you, it is certainly true that "two hearts are better than one."
—R. Duane Ireland

To my children, Robyn, Dale, Becky, Angela, Joseph, and Matthew, who have supported me throughout my career.
—Robert E. Hoskisson

Michael A. Hitt

Michael A. Hitt is a Distinguished Professor and holds the Joseph Foster Chair in Business Leadership and the C. W. and Dorothy Conn Chair in New Ventures at Texas A&M University. He received his Ph.D. from the University of Colorado. He has authored or coauthored several books and book chapters and numerous articles in such journals as the *Academy of Management Journal, Academy of Management Review, Strategic Management Journal, Journal of Applied Psychology, Organization Science, Organization Studies, Journal of Management Studies*, and *Journal of Management*, among others. His publications include several books: *Downscoping: How to Tame the Diversified Firm* (Oxford University Press, 1994); *Mergers and Acquisitions: A Guide to Creating Value for Stakeholders* (Oxford University Press, 2001); and *Competing for Advantage* (South-Western College Publishing, 2004). He is Coeditor of several recent books: *Managing Strategically in an Interconnected World* (1998); *New Managerial Mindsets: Organizational Transformation and Strategy Implementation* (1998); *Dynamic Strategic Resources: Development, Diffusion and Integration* (1999); *Winning Strategies in a Deconstructing World* (John Wiley & Sons, 2000); *Handbook of Strategic Management* (2001); *Strategic Entrepreneurship: Creating a New Integrated Mindset* (2002); *Creating Value: Winners in the New Business Environment* (Blackwell Publishers, 2002); and *Managing Knowledge for Sustained Competitive Advantage* (Jossey Bass, 2003). He has served on the editorial review boards of multiple journals including the *Academy of Management Journal, Academy of Management Executive, Journal of Applied Psychology, Journal of Management, Journal of World Business*, and *Journal of Applied Behavioral Sciences*. Furthermore, he has served as Consulting Editor (1988–90) and Editor (1991–93) of the *Academy of Management Journal*. He serves on the Board of the Strategic Management Society and is a Past President of the Academy of Management, an international organization with 13,000-plus members dedicated to the advancement of management knowledge and practice. He received the 1996 Award for Outstanding Academic Contributions to Competitiveness and the 1999 Award for Outstanding Intellectual Contributions to Competitiveness Research from the American Society for Competitiveness. He is a Fellow in the Academy of Management and a Research Fellow in the National Entrepreneurship Consortium, and received an honorary doctorate from the Universidad Carlos III de Madrid for his contributions to the field. He is a member of the *Academy of Management Journal*'s Hall of Fame. He received awards for the best article published in the *Academy of Management Executive* (1999) and *Academy of Management Journal* (2000). In 2001, he received the Irwin Outstanding Educator Award and the Distinguished Service Award from the Academy of Management.

R. Duane Ireland

R. Duane Ireland holds the W. David Robbins Chair in Strategic Management in the Robins School of Business, University of Richmond. Beginning in July 2004, he will hold the Foreman R. and Ruby S. Bennett Chair in Business Administration in the Mays Business School, Texas A&M University. He is currently serving a three-year term as a Representative-at-Large on the Board of Governors of the Academy of Management. He teaches courses at all levels (undergraduate, masters, doctoral, and

executive). His research, which focuses on diversification, innovation, corporate entrepreneurship, and strategic entrepreneurship, has been published in a number of journals including *Academy of Management Journal, Academy of Management Review, Academy of Management Executive, Administrative Science Quarterly, Strategic Management Journal, Journal of Management, Human Relations,* and *Journal of Management Studies,* among others. His published books include *Competing for Advantage* (South-Western College Publishing, 2004) and *Mergers and Acquisitions: A Guide to Creating Value for Stakeholders* (Oxford University Press, 2001). He is Coeditor of *The Blackwell Entrepreneurship Encyclopedia* (Blackwell Publishers, 2004) and *Strategic Entrepreneurship: Creating a New Mindset* (Blackwell Publishers, 2001). He is serving or has served as a member of the editorial review boards for a number of journals such as *Academy of Management Journal, Academy of Management Review, Academy of Management Executive, Journal of Management, Journal of Business Venturing, Entrepreneurship Theory and Practice, Journal of Business Strategy,* and *European Management Journal,* among others. He has coedited special issues of *Academy of Management Review, Academy of Management Executive, Journal of Business Venturing, Strategic Management Journal,* and *Journal of High Technology and Engineering Management.* He received awards for the best article published in *Academy of Management Executive* (1999) and *Academy of Management Journal* (2000). In 2001, his coauthored article published in *Academy of Management Executive* won the Best Journal Article in Corporate Entrepreneurship Award from the U.S. Association for Small Business & Entrepreneurship (USASBE). He is a Research Fellow in the National Entrepreneurship Consortium. He received the 1999 Award for Outstanding Intellectual Contributions to Competitiveness Research from the American Society for Competitiveness and the USASBE Scholar in Corporate Entrepreneurship Award (2004) from USASBE.

Robert E. Hoskisson

Robert E. Hoskisson received his Ph.D. from the University of California–Irvine. Professor Hoskisson's research topics focus on international diversification, privatization and cooperative strategy, product diversification, corporate governance, and acquisitions and divestitures. He teaches courses in corporate and international strategic management, cooperative strategy, and strategy consulting, among others. Professor Hoskisson has served on several editorial boards for such publications as the *Academy of Management Journal* (including Consulting Editor and Guest Editor of a special issue), *Strategic Management Journal, Journal of Management* (including Associate Editor), and *Organization Science.* He has coauthored several books including *Strategic Management: Competitiveness and Globalization,* 5th Edition (South-Western/Thomson Learning); *Competing for Advantage* (South-Western/Thomson Learning); and *Downscoping: How to Tame the Diversified Firm* (Oxford University Press). Professor Hoskisson's research has appeared in over 85 publications including the *Academy of Management Journal, Academy of Management Review, Strategic Management Journal, Organization Science, Journal of Management, Academy of Management Executive,* and *California Management Review.* He is a Fellow of the Academy of Management and a charter member of the Academy of Management Journal's Hall of Fame. He also served for three years as a Representative-at-Large on the Board of Governors of the Academy of Management. He is also a member of the Academy of International Business and the Strategic Management Society.

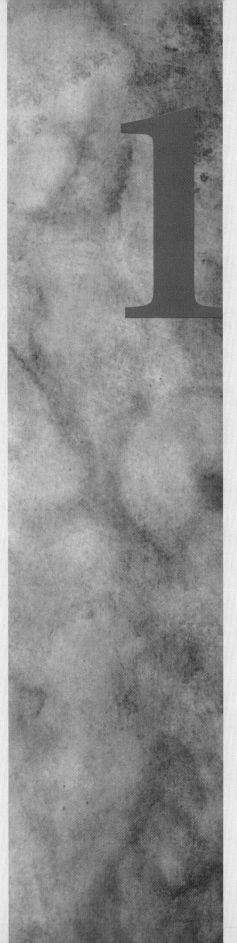

Part One

Chapter 1
Strategic Management and Strategic Competitiveness

Chapter 2
The External Environment: Opportunities, Threats, Industry Competition, and Competitor Analysis

Chapter 3
The Internal Environment: Resources, Capabilities, and Core Competencies

Strategic Management Inputs

Strategic Management and Strategic Competitiveness

Chapter One

1

Knowledge Objectives

Studying this chapter should provide you with the strategic management knowledge needed to:

1. Define strategic competitiveness, competitive advantage, and above-average returns.

2. Describe the 21st-century competitive landscape and explain how globalization and technological changes shape it.

3. Use the industrial organization (I/O) model to explain how firms can earn above-average returns.

4. Use the resource-based model to explain how firms can earn above-average returns.

5. Describe strategic intent and strategic mission and discuss their value.

6. Define stakeholders and describe their ability to influence organizations.

7. Describe the work of strategic leaders.

8. Explain the strategic management process.

Corel Corporation

Research and development is critical to the success of innovative companies such as Samsung, Sony, and Verizon. Continuous development of new products—although costly and sometimes difficult to achieve—is an important aspect of strategic competitiveness.

The Innovation Pipeline: A Lifeline of Survival in Business

Conventional wisdom says to get back to the basics. Conventional wisdom says to cut costs. Conventional wisdom is doomed. The winners are the innovators who are making bold thinking an everyday part of doing business.

—Gary Hamel, 2002

Innovation has become an absolute necessity to survive and perform well in almost every industry. The current competitive landscape demands innovation. Gary Hamel, a well-known writer and management consultant, argues that firms cannot rely on past successes to perform well today. Furthermore, he suggests that current success will not carry firms into the future. Managers must have the foresight and courage to continuously innovate. Thus, a firm's strategy must include continuous innovation.

DuPont, once known as a highly innovative company, lost its way. As one author noted, the company has mostly "shot blanks" in the last decade. Analysts suggest that too many resources have been diverted from developing innovative products to focus on increasing the productivity of its current businesses. Furthermore, the firm's managers have been criticized for failing to evaluate the market effectively and thereby missing primary opportunities, such as in the agricultural biotechnology field. It had to sell off its pharmaceutical business because it could no longer compete against the larger and more innovative companies in the industry. Top executives are also considering divesting some of DuPont's other businesses, accounting for a major portion of its sales, because of poor market performance. Its R&D must be shifted from improving existing products to emphasizing the development of new products. DuPont executives are now in the process of changing the mix of R&D dollars spent from about one-third on creating new products and two-thirds on improving existing ones to two-thirds invested in developing innovative new market entries.

Interestingly, the large conglomerate Samsung has continued its success, largely through innovation. The conventional wisdom was that large, highly diversified firms could not be innovative and most are not. But Samsung has been very innovative and is among the leaders in many markets in which it competes. For example, it is the market leader in big-screen TVs, microwave ovens, LCD displays, and DRAM chips. It is number two in the flash memory market and number three in cell phones, MP3 players, and DVD players. Unlike many other large conglomerates, it places a high priority on investments in R&D. To remain a leader in the markets listed above requires a steady stream of innovative products.

Innovation is important in many industries, as noted above. For example, Clear Channel Communications, the largest owner of radio stations, recently announced that it would market a CD of live recordings from concerts within five minutes of the conclusion of a show. Verizon recently introduced phone booths where people can gain access to the Internet. The firm's intent is to become the market leader in providing broadband services. Sony, the current market leader in video games, is not resting on its current product line. In 2003 it announced a powerful handheld player designed to beat one of its primary competitors, Nintendo. These firms are using innovation to obtain or maintain market leadership. Without it, they would risk even survival.

While innovation is important, it is difficult and costly to achieve. For example, large pharmaceutical competitors are now considering cooperating to develop certain types of drugs because of the costs and risks involved. In fact, an industry task force has recommended establishing a research consortium of pharmaceutical companies similar to Sematech in the semiconductor industry. Sematech allowed U.S. semiconductor companies to regain competitiveness in that industry. Such a research consortium could encourage cooperation in the development of cancer fighting drugs. The costs and risks involved in R&D make some firms take a conservative approach and focus on improving current products. Such research usually has short-term payoffs but is costly in the longer term when there is a deficit of new products to market. Internal dissension exists at Hewlett-Packard (HP) because of the pressure to reduce costs in R&D, which HP scientists argue is hurting the company's level of innovation. The tight market for computer hardware and the high costs of the Compaq acquisition have caused reductions in HP's R&D budgets. Over time, HP will learn if these pressures will harm its competitiveness.

SOURCES: C. Edwards, M. Ihlwan, & P. Engardio, 2003, The Samsung way, *Business Week*, June 16, 56–64; B. J. Feder, 2003, Verizon sets up phone booths to give access to the Internet, *New York Times*, May 14, http://www.nytimes.com; Sony takes on Nintendo with new player, 2003, *New York Times*, May 14, http://www.nytimes.com; A. Pollack, 2003, Companies may cooperate on cancer drugs, *New York Times*, May 14, http://www.nytimes.com; J. Markoff, 2003, Innovation at Hewlett tries to evade the ax, *New York Times*, May 5, http://www.nytimes.com; M. Mirapaul, 2003, Concert CDs sold on the spot by a radio giant, *New York Times*, May 5, http://www.nytimes.com; G. Hamel, 2002, Innovation now! *Fast Company*, December, http://www.fastcompany.com.

Samsung and DuPont's performances are in sharp contrast. DuPont, a once highly innovative company, lost its competitive edge. Clearly, DuPont changed its strategy to emphasize productivity and improve its current product line rather than introduce innovative new products. Such actions probably improved the firm's profits in the short term. But in the long term, it had to sell off divisions that were no longer competitive and is experiencing major problems because of the lack of innovation. In contrast, Samsung is investing in innovation to remain among the leaders in multiple product markets. Again, these are outcomes of its strategy. Samsung's strategy formulation and implementation actions helped it gain an advantage over many of its competitors. Other firms operating in diverse industries are using innovation as a competitive weapon. Examples include Verizon's new telephone booths for access to the Internet, the concert CDs offered by Clear Channel Communications, and Sony's new handheld player.

The actions taken by these firms are intended to achieve strategic competitiveness and earn above-average returns. **Strategic competitiveness** is achieved when a firm

Strategic competitiveness *is achieved when a firm successfully formulates and implements a value-creating strategy.*

successfully formulates and implements a value-creating strategy. When a firm implements such a strategy and other companies are unable to duplicate it or find it too costly to imitate,[1] this firm has a **sustained** (or **sustainable) competitive advantage** (hereafter called simply *competitive advantage*). An organization is assured of a competitive advantage only after others' efforts to duplicate its strategy have ceased or failed. In addition, when a firm achieves a competitive advantage, it normally can sustain it only for a certain period.[2] The speed with which competitors are able to acquire the skills needed to duplicate the benefits of a firm's value-creating strategy determines how long the competitive advantage will last.[3]

Understanding how to exploit a competitive advantage is important for firms to earn above-average returns.[4] **Above-average returns** are returns in excess of what an investor expects to earn from other investments with a similar amount of risk. **Risk** is an investor's uncertainty about the economic gains or losses that will result from a particular investment.[5] Returns are often measured in terms of accounting figures, such as return on assets, return on equity, or return on sales. Alternatively, returns can be measured on the basis of stock market returns, such as monthly returns (the end-of-the-period stock price minus the beginning stock price, divided by the beginning stock price, yielding a percentage return). In smaller new venture firms, performance is sometimes measured in terms of the amount and speed of the growth (e.g., in annual sales) because they may not have returns early or the asset base is too small to evaluate the returns received.[6]

Firms without a competitive advantage or that are not competing in an attractive industry earn, at best, average returns. **Average returns** are returns equal to those an investor expects to earn from other investments with a similar amount of risk. In the long run, an inability to earn at least average returns results in failure. Failure occurs because investors withdraw their investments from those firms earning less-than-average returns.

Dynamic in nature, the **strategic management process** (see Figure 1.1) is the full set of commitments, decisions, and actions required for a firm to achieve strategic competitiveness and earn above-average returns.[7] Relevant strategic inputs derived from analyses of the internal and external environments are necessary for effective strategy formulation and implementation. In turn, effective strategic actions are a prerequisite to achieving the desired outcomes of strategic competitiveness and above-average returns. Thus, the strategic management process is used to match the conditions of an ever-changing market and competitive structure with a firm's continuously evolving resources, capabilities, and core competencies (the sources of strategic inputs). Effective strategic actions that take place in the context of carefully integrated strategy formulation and implementation actions result in desired strategic outcomes.[8] (See Figure 1.1.)

In the remaining chapters of this book, we use the strategic management process to explain what firms should do to achieve strategic competitiveness and earn above-average returns. These explanations demonstrate why some firms consistently achieve competitive success while others fail to do so.[9] As you will see, the reality of global competition is a critical part of the strategic management process.[10]

Several topics are discussed in this chapter. First, we examine the challenge of strategic management. This brief discussion highlights the fact that strategic actions taken to achieve and then maintain strategic competitiveness demand the best efforts of managers, employees, and their organizations on a continuous basis.[11] Second, we describe the 21st-century competitive landscape, created primarily by the emergence of a global economy and rapid technological changes. This landscape provides the context of opportunities and threats within which firms strive to meet today's competitive challenges.

We next examine two models that suggest the strategic inputs needed to select strategic actions necessary to achieve strategic competitiveness. The first model (industrial

A **sustained** or **sustainable competitive advantage** *occurs when a firm implements a value-creating strategy and other companies are unable to duplicate it or find it too costly to imitate.*

Above-average returns *are returns in excess of what an investor expects to earn from other investments with a similar amount of risk.*

Risk *is an investor's uncertainty about the economic gains or losses that will result from a particular investment.*

Average returns *are returns equal to those an investor expects to earn from other investments with a similar amount of risk.*

The **strategic management process** *is the full set of commitments, decisions, and actions required for a firm to achieve strategic competitiveness and earn above-average returns.*

Figure 1.1 — The Strategic Management Process

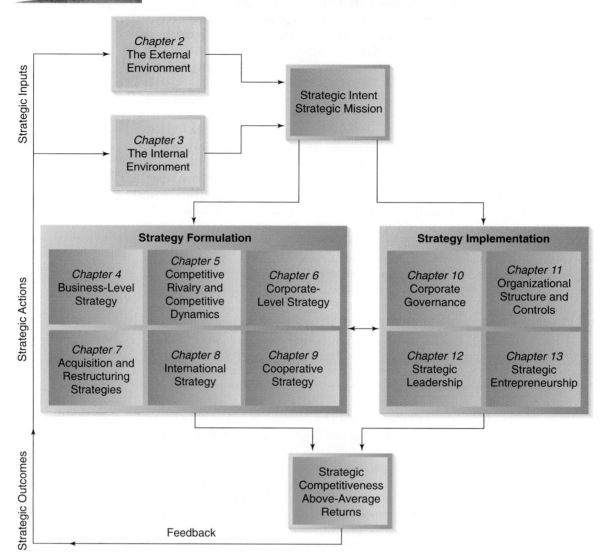

organization) suggests that the external environment is the primary determinant of a firm's strategic actions. The key to this model is identifying and competing successfully in an attractive (i.e., profitable) industry.[12] The second model (resource based) suggests that a firm's unique resources and capabilities are the critical link to strategic competitiveness.[13] Comprehensive explanations in this chapter and the next two chapters show that through the combined use of these models, firms obtain the strategic inputs needed to formulate and implement strategies successfully. Analyses of its external and internal environments provide a firm with the information required to develop its strategic intent and strategic mission (defined later in this chapter). As shown in Figure 1.1, strategic intent and strategic mission influence strategy formulation and implementation actions. The chapter's discussion then turns to the stakeholders that organizations serve. The degree to which stakeholders' needs can be met increases directly with enhancements in a firm's strategic competitiveness and its ability to earn above-average returns. Closing the chapter are introductions to strategic leaders and the elements of the strategic management process.

The goals of achieving strategic competitiveness and earning above-average returns are challenging—not only for large firms such as IBM, but also for those as small as a local computer retail outlet or dry cleaner. As suggested in the Opening Case, the performances of some companies, such as Samsung, have more than met strategic management's challenges to date.

For other firms, the challenges are substantial in the dynamic competitive landscape. Evidence the rapid changes experienced by Cisco Systems. During the 1990s, Cisco's overall performance was among the best—it was among the top ten firms whose stock price increased over 10,000 percent in that decade. However, in 2001, the firm experienced significant reductions in its stock price. One writer referred to Cisco as a fractured fairy tale.[14] Cisco's top management argued that their new strategic actions would, over time, regain the high performance once enjoyed by the firm.[15] In Spring 2003, Cisco announced that it had recovered from the substantial loss suffered in 2001. In fact, Cisco reported a profit of almost $1.9 billion for 2002, and its stock price was beginning to increase.[16]

Business failure is rather common. In 2002, for example, 38,540 U.S. businesses filed for bankruptcy, down approximately 4 percent from the number filed in 2001. But the total value of the assets reached a record in 2002. The bankruptcies filed represented $375.2 billion in assets compared to $258.5 billion in 2001.[17] These statistics suggest that competitive success is transient.[18] Thomas J. Watson, Jr., formerly IBM's chairman, once cautioned people to remember that "corporations are expendable and that success—at best—is an impermanent achievement which can always slip out of hand."[19]

As described in a Strategic Focus later in this chapter, both US Airways and United Airlines filed for bankruptcy, and American Airlines narrowly averted bankruptcy by gaining major wage concessions from its employee unions. In the Opening Case, several companies were noted to be introducing innovative new products while others' capabilities to produce innovation were questioned by knowledgable industry analysts. Without innovations, firms in most industries will not be able to survive over time. And, the innovation must be a part of an effective strategy developed to navigate in the competitive landscape of the 21st century. It is interesting to note that a survey showed CEOs did not place "strong and consistent profits" as their top priority; in fact, it was ranked fifth. A "strong and well-thought-out strategy" was regarded as the most important factor to make a firm the most respected in the future. Maximizing customer satisfaction and loyalty, business leadership and quality products and services, and concern for consistent profits followed this factor.[20] These rankings are consistent with the view that no matter how good a product or service is, the firm must select the "right" strategy and then implement it effectively. In a 2003 survey of the top 100 growth companies, *Business Week* noted that these firms thrive in a tough economy because of their risk taking (e.g., innovation) and use of smart strategies.[21]

Suggesting strategic management's challenge, Andrew Grove, Intel's former CEO, observed that only paranoid companies survive and succeed. Firms must continuously evaluate their environments and decide on the appropriate strategy. **Strategy** is an integrated and coordinated set of commitments and actions designed to exploit core competencies and gain a competitive advantage. By choosing a strategy, a firm decides to pursue one course of action over others. The firm's executives are thus setting priorities for the firm's competitive actions. Strategies are organic in that they must be adapted over time as the external environment and the firm's resource portfolio change.[22]

Firms can select effective or ineffective strategies. For example, the choice by Xerox to pursue a strategy other than the development and marketing of the personal

Strategy *is an integrated and coordinated set of commitments and actions designed to exploit core competencies and gain a competitive advantage.*

computer and laser printers was likely an ineffective one. The purpose of this book is to explain how firms develop and implement effective strategies. Partly because of Grove's approach described above, Intel continuously strives to improve in order to remain competitive. For Intel and others that compete in the 21st century's competitive landscape, Grove believes that a key challenge is to try to do the impossible—namely, to anticipate the unexpected.[23]

The Current Competitive Landscape[24]

The fundamental nature of competition in many of the world's industries is changing.[25] The pace of this change is relentless and is increasing. Even determining the boundaries of an industry has become challenging. Consider, for example, how advances in interactive computer networks and telecommunications have blurred the definition of the television industry. The near future may find companies such as ABC, CBS, NBC, and HBO competing not only among themselves, but also with AT&T, Microsoft, Sony, and others.

Other characteristics of the 21st-century competitive landscape are noteworthy as well. Conventional sources of competitive advantage, such as economies of scale and huge advertising budgets, are not as effective as they once were. Moreover, the traditional managerial mind-set is unlikely to lead a firm to strategic competitiveness. Managers must adopt a new mind-set that values flexibility, speed, innovation, integration, and the challenges that evolve from constantly changing conditions. The conditions of the competitive landscape result in a perilous business world, one where the investments required to compete on a global scale are enormous and the consequences of failure are severe.[26] Developing and implementing strategy remains an important element of success in this environment. It allows for strategic actions to be planned and to emerge when the environmental conditions are appropriate. It also helps to coordinate the strategies developed by business units in which the responsibility to compete in specific markets is decentralized.[27]

Hypercompetition is a term often used to capture the realities of the 21st-century competitive landscape. Hypercompetition results from the dynamics of strategic maneuvering among global and innovative combatants. It is a condition of rapidly escalating competition based on price-quality positioning, competition to create new know-how and establish first-mover advantage, and competition to protect or invade established product or geographic markets.[28] In a hypercompetitive market, firms often aggressively challenge their competitors in the hopes of improving their competitive position and ultimately their performance.[29]

Several factors create hypercompetitive environments and the 21st-century competitive landscape. The two primary drivers are the emergence of a global economy and technology, specifically rapid technological change.

As explained in the Strategic Focus, the global automobile market is highly competitive. The U.S. auto market is the largest and perhaps the most important, but most auto manufacturers compete in markets around the world. Both GM and Ford are headquartered in the United States, but sell their products globally. Likewise, BMW is headquartered in Germany, but considers the United States a critically important market. In fact, many of the new BMW autos were designed specifically for the U.S. market. BMW is performing well, and GM's overall performance is improving. But Ford is in trouble and may encounter challenges to turn around the firm's fortunes. Interestingly, in the mid-1990s, Ford was considered the best U.S. auto manufacturer. But poor strategic decisions and a lack of focus on creating innovative new designs have reversed its fortunes. The change in Ford exemplifies the impermanence of success, especially with global markets and competition.

Gliding above the Water, Treading Water, and Drowning

The global automobile market is highly competitive. The autos compete in market segments but performance, design, and quality are important competitive factors in all market segments. In an annual quality survey conducted by J.D. Power and Associates, some autos fared well and others performed badly. For example, the bottom five performers in quality were Hummer, Land Rover, Kia, MINI, and Saab, whereas the top five performers were Lexus, Cadillac, Infiniti, Acura, and Buick. Performance on such surveys can greatly affect sales, so it is quite important. BMW performed well above average with a score that ranked eighth, whereas two Ford products (Ford and Lincoln) and several GM products (Oldsmobile, Pontiac, GMC, and Saturn) had below-average quality scores. These outcomes are the result of differing strategies followed by these firms in past years.

BMW has developed and implemented a strategy for growth that entails designing and manufacturing a number of different autos targeted for multiple different market segments. BMW is especially targeting the large U.S. auto market, and its goal is to increase BMW's sales in the United States by 40 percent by 2008. This would be total sales of 300,000 cars annually, the largest number of luxury autos sold in one market globally, and would overtake Lexus, the current leader. This is a bold strategic move at a time when many of BMW's competitors are cutting R&D and production. However, the time may be correct for just such a move. When the economy rebounds, BMW will be in a strong position to take advantage of the enhanced market. BMW's actions have already been winning customers and converts from its primary competitor, Lexus.

In contrast, GM is "treading water" and Ford may be "drowning." For a number of years, GM's market share was declining because of multiple past strategic mistakes. The current CEO is providing reasons to believe that GM may turn around its fortunes. Rick Wagoner, CEO, is changing the culture, placing renewed emphasis on new product development and introducing competitive tactics such as zero percent financing to regain a competitive advantage. GM has also reduced both the time and cost of building its automobiles. For example, the number of labor hours required to produce a Malibu has been reduced by 25 percent, and the engineering costs on several of its autos have been reduced by one-third.

Ford, on the other hand, is in deep trouble and faces major challenges to turn around its fortunes. It lost a total of $6.4 billion in 2001–2002 and the outcomes for 2003 were not bright. The year 2003 marked Ford's 100th anniversary, but it was one of the firm's most challenging times since the early years of its existence. Ford's competitors have been relentless in developing advantages that Ford is challenged to overcome. Ford's autos were ranked last in reliability by *Consumer Reports* in 2003. Ford and GM both have substantial pension funding requirements, but much of Ford's obligations have been funded by debt. As a result, Ford's debt rating is only slightly above "junk status." Rumors suggest that there are conflicts among the top management team with turnover likely by some team members. One informed observer stated that "if it didn't have the name Ford, it would be in bankruptcy." Ford's competitors have been building and marketing vehicles that better meet customers' needs and desires. Ford managers somehow lost touch with the market over time

A 2004 BMW on display at a U.S. auto show. BMW has maintained a global sustained competitive advantage through its reputation in automobile engineering as well as its innovations in design. Its long-term strategic plan entails a 40 percent increase in U.S. sales by 2008 and greater attention to market segments especially intended for the U.S.

©Gary Conner/PhotoEdit

and did not invest in new product development while its competitors were designing new models. Currently, it is just trying to catch up to GM's lower costs and speedier production (but still using existing designs).

SOURCES: G. Edmondson, C. Palmeri, B. Grow, & C. Tierney, 2003, BMW: Will Panke's high-speed approach hurt the brand? *Business Week*, June 9, 57–60; N. Shirouzu, 2003, Ford's new development plan: Stop reinventing its wheels, *Wall Street Journal*, April 16, A1, A4; K. Kerwin, 2003, Can Ford pull out of its skid? *Business Week*, March 31, 70–71; D. Hakim, 2003, Long road ahead for Ford, *New York Times*, March 14, http://www.nytimes.com; D. Welch & K. Kerwin, 2003, Rick Wagoner's game plan, *Business Week*, February 10, 52–60; G. L. White, 2003, GM's deep-discounting strategy helps auto maker regain ground, *Wall Street Journal*, January 17, A1, A4; B. Breen, 2002, BMW: Driven by design, *Fast Company*, September, 121–134; D. Welch, 2002, A hit parade for BMW? *Business Week*, September 23, 64–65.

The Global Economy

A global economy is one in which goods, services, people, skills, and ideas move freely across geographic borders.

A **global economy** is one in which goods, services, people, skills, and ideas move freely across geographic borders. Relatively unfettered by artificial constraints, such as tariffs, the global economy significantly expands and complicates a firm's competitive environment.[30] Interesting opportunities and challenges are associated with the emergence of the global economy. For example, Europe, instead of the United States, is now the world's largest single market with 700 million potential customers. The European Union and the other Western European countries also have a gross domestic product that is over 35 percent higher than the GDP of the United States.[31] In addition, by 2015, China's total GDP will be greater than Japan's, although its per capita output will likely be lower.[32] In recent years, as the competitiveness rankings in Table 1.1 indicate, the Japanese economy has lagged behind that of the United States and a number of other countries. In fact, Japanese managers once heralded for their approach have been forced to change their style of operation in order to compete in global markets.[33] A few Asian countries, in particular Malaysia and Taiwan, have maintained their rankings, which is commendable considering the Asian financial crisis of the latter part of the 1990s.[34] Australia and Canada have also ranked highly in recent years.

Achieving improved competitiveness allows a country's citizens to have a higher standard of living. Some believe that entrepreneurial activity will continue to influence living standards during the 21st century. The role of entrepreneurship is discussed further in Chapter 13. A country's competitiveness is achieved through the accumulation of individual firms' strategic competitiveness in the global economy. To be competitive, a firm must view the world as its marketplace. For example, Procter & Gamble believes that it still has tremendous potential to grow internationally because the global market for household products is not as mature as it is in the United States. Recently, U.S. midsize and small firms are demonstrating a strong commitment to competing in the global economy as well as their larger counterparts. For example, 60 percent of U.S. firms now exporting goods are defined as small businesses.

Ikea (discussed further in Chapter 4) has benefited from competing in the global economy. It has annual sales exceeding $11 billion and employs 70,000 workers. It first moved outside its home market in Sweden in 1963 and entered the U.S. market in the mid-1980s. Currently, Ikea has over 150 stores in more than 20 countries. Much of the firm's growth and success have come from sales in international markets.[35]

The March of Globalization

Globalization is the increasing economic interdependence among countries as reflected in the flow of goods and services, financial capital, and knowledge across country bor-

Country	2003	2002
United States	1	1
Australia	2	3
Canada	3	2
Malaysia	4	6
Germany	5	4
Taiwan	6	7
United Kingdom	7	5
France	8	9
Spain	9	8
Thailand	10	13
Japan	11	11
China (mainland)	12	12
Brazil (Sao Paolo)	13	—
China (Zeijiang)	14	—
Korea	15	10
Colombia	16	20
Italy	17	14
South Africa	18	16
India (Maharashtra)	19	—
India	20	17
Brazil	21	15
Philippines	22	18
Romania	23	—
Mexico	24	19
Turkey	25	23
Russia	26	21
Poland	27	22
Indonesia	28	25
Argentina	29	26
Venezuela	30	24

SOURCE: From *World Competitiveness Yearbook 2003*, IMD, Switzerland. http://www.imd.ch.wcy.esummary, April. Reprinted by permission.

ders.[36] In globalized markets and industries, financial capital might be obtained in one national market and used to buy raw materials in another one. Manufacturing equipment bought from a third national market can then be used to produce products that are sold in yet a fourth market. Thus, globalization increases the range of opportunities for companies competing in the 21st-century competitive landscape.

Wal-Mart, for instance, is trying to achieve boundaryless retailing with global pricing, sourcing, and logistics. Most of Wal-Mart's original international investments were in Canada and Mexico, in proximity to the United States. However, the company

©Sergio Dorantes/CORBIS

Although other discount department stores have failed to thrive, Wal-Mart currently enjoys success as the largest retailer in the world through global pricing, sourcing, and logistics. Here a shopper loads his trunk with items purchased at the largest Wal-Mart store in the world in Mexico City, Mexico.

has now moved into Europe, South America, and Asia. Wal-Mart is the largest retailer in the world and changes the structure of business in many countries it enters. In 2003, Wal-Mart had 1,295 stores in international locations representing about 27 percent of its total stores.[37]

The internationalization of markets and industries makes it increasingly difficult to think of some firms as domestic companies. For example, Daimler-Benz, the parent company of Mercedes-Benz, merged with Chrysler Corporation to create DaimlerChrysler. DaimlerChrysler has focused on integrating the formerly independent companies' operations around the world. In a similar move, Ford acquired Volvo's car division. Ford now has six global brands: Ford, Lincoln, Mercury, Jaguar, Mazda, and Aston Martin. It uses these brands to build economies of scale in the purchase and sourcing of components that make up 60 percent of the value of a car.[38]

Neither of these companies has been performing well since the turn of the 21st century. Problems with the integration of Chrysler into the Daimler organization have been blamed for the performance problems of DaimlerChrysler. The problems experienced by Ford were enumerated in the Strategic Focus. The U.S. auto market continues to change, as suggested in the Strategic Focus. In fact, it is predicted that foreign brands will control about 50 percent of this market by 2007.[39] However, auto manufacturers should no longer be thought of as European, Japanese, or American. Instead, they can be more accurately classified as global companies striving to achieve strategic competitiveness in the 21st-century competitive landscape. Some believe that because of the enormous economic benefits it can generate, globalization will not be stopped. It has been predicted that genuine free trade in manufactured goods among the United States, Europe, and Japan would add 5 to 10 percent to the three regions' annual economic output, and free trade in their service sectors would boost aggregate output by another 15 to 20 percent. Realizing these potential gains in economic output requires a commitment from the industrialized nations to cooperatively stimulate the higher levels of trade necessary for global growth. In 2001, global trade in goods and services accounted for approximately 25 percent of the world's GDP and has remained relatively constant since that time.[40]

Global competition has increased performance standards in many dimensions, including quality, cost, productivity, product introduction time, and operational efficiency. Moreover, these standards are not static; they are exacting, requiring continuous improvement from a firm and its employees. As they accept the challenges posed by these increasing standards, companies improve their capabilities and individual workers sharpen their skills. Thus, in the 21st-century competitive landscape, only firms capable of meeting, if not exceeding, global standards typically earn strategic competitiveness.[41]

The development of emerging and transitional economies also is changing the global competitive landscape and significantly increasing competition in global markets.[42] The economic development of Asian countries—outside Japan—is increasing the significance of Asian markets. Firms in the emerging economies of Asia, such as South Korea, however, are becoming major competitors in global industries. Companies such as Cemex are moving more boldly into international markets and are making important investments in Asia. Cemex, a cement producer headquartered in Mexico, also has significant investments in North America and Latin America. Thus, international investments come from many directions and are targeted for multiple regions of the world. However, firms' ability to compete is affected by the resources and institutional environments (e.g., government regulations, access to financial capital, culture) in their country. Firms from emerging market countries often are resource poor and must access resources (often through alliances with resource rich firms) to compete in global markets.[43] Thus, the different institutional frameworks in countries cause firms to follow different strategies. As a result, there are different strategies across countries, and firms entering markets will vary their strategies according to the institutional environments in those countries.[44]

There are risks with these investments (a number of them are discussed in Chapter 8). Some people refer to these risks as the "liability of foreignness."[45] Research suggests that firms are challenged in their early ventures into international markets and can encounter difficulties by entering too many different or challenging international markets. First, performance may suffer in early efforts to globalize until a firm develops the skills required to manage international operations.[46] Additionally, the firm's performance may suffer with substantial amounts of globalization. In this instance, firms may overdiversify internationally beyond their ability to manage these diversified operations.[47] The outcome can sometimes be quite painful to these firms.[48] Thus, entry into international markets, even for firms with substantial experience in them, first requires careful planning and selection of the appropriate markets to enter followed by developing the most effective strategies to successfully operate in those markets.

Global markets are attractive strategic options for some companies, but they are not the only source of strategic competitiveness. In fact, for most companies, even for those capable of competing successfully in global markets, it is critical to remain committed to and strategically competitive in the domestic market.[49] In the 21st-century competitive landscape, firms are challenged to develop the optimal level of globalization that results in appropriate concentrations on a company's domestic and global operations.

In many instances, strategically competitive companies are those that have learned how to apply competitive insights gained locally (or domestically) on a global scale.[50] These companies do not impose homogeneous solutions in a pluralistic world. Instead, they nourish local insights so that they can modify and apply them appropriately in different regions of the world.[51] Moreover, they are sensitive to globalization's potential effects. Firms with strong commitments to global success evaluate these possible outcomes in making their strategic choices.

Technology and Technological Changes

There are three categories of trends and conditions through which technology is significantly altering the nature of competition.

INCREASING RATE OF TECHNOLOGICAL CHANGE AND DIFFUSION

Both the rate of change of technology and the speed at which new technologies become available and are used have increased substantially over the last 15 to 20 years. Consider the following rates of technology diffusion:

> It took the telephone 35 years to get into 25 percent of all homes in the United States. It took TV 26 years. It took radio 22 years. It took PCs 16 years. It took the Internet 7 years.[52]

Perpetual innovation is a term used to describe how rapidly and consistently new, information-intensive technologies replace older ones. The shorter product life cycles resulting from these rapid diffusions of new technologies place a competitive premium on being able to quickly introduce new goods and services into the marketplace. In fact, when products become somewhat indistinguishable because of the widespread and rapid diffusion of technologies, speed to market may be the primary source of competitive advantage (see Chapter 5).[53] While some people became disenchanted with information technology because of the "bubble years" when the Internet was overvalued, the information technology industry comprises 10 percent of the U.S. economy and 60 percent of its capital spending. Thus, the waves of innovation it produces will continue to be highly important.[54]

There are other indicators of rapid technology diffusion. Some evidence suggests that it takes only 12 to 18 months for firms to gather information about their competitors' research and development and product decisions.[55] In the global economy, competitors can sometimes imitate a firm's successful competitive actions within a few days. Once a source of competitive advantage, the protection firms possessed previously through their patents has been stifled by the current rate of technological diffusion. Today, patents are thought by many to be an effective way of protecting proprietary technology only for the pharmaceutical and chemical industries. Indeed, many firms competing in the electronics industry often do not apply for patents to prevent competitors from gaining access to the technological knowledge included in the patent application.

The other factor in technological change is the development of disruptive technologies that destroy the value of existing technology and create new markets.[56] Some have referred to this concept as Schumpeterian innovation, from the work by the famous economist Joseph A. Schumpeter. Others refer to this outcome as radical or breakthrough innovation.[57] While disruptive or radical technologies generally harm industry incumbents, some are able to adapt based on their superior resources, past experience, and ability to gain access to the new technology through multiple sources (e.g., alliances, acquisitions, and ongoing internal basic research).[58]

THE INFORMATION AGE

Dramatic changes in information technology have occurred in recent years. Personal computers, cellular phones, artificial intelligence, virtual reality, and massive databases (e.g., Lexis/Nexis) are a few examples of how information is used differently as a result of technological developments. An important outcome of these changes is that the ability to effectively and efficiently access and use information has become an important source of competitive advantage in virtually all industries.

Companies are building electronic networks that link them to customers, employees, vendors, and suppliers. These networks, designed to conduct business over the Internet, are referred to as e-business,[59] and e-business is big business. Internet trade has exceeded expectations with business-to-business trade reaching $2.4 trillion and business-to-consumer trade reaching $95 billion in 2003. Productivity gains from business use of the Internet are also expected to reach $450 billion by 2005.[60]

Both the pace of change in information technology and its diffusion will continue to increase. For instance, the number of personal computers in use is expected to reach 278 million by 2010. The declining costs of information technologies and the increased accessibility to them are also evident in the 21st-century competitive landscape. The global proliferation of relatively inexpensive computing power and its linkage on a global scale via computer networks combine to increase the speed and diffusion of information technologies. Thus, the competitive potential of information technologies is now available to companies of all sizes throughout the world, not only to large firms in Europe, Japan, and North America.

The Internet provides an infrastructure that allows the delivery of information to computers in any location. Access to significant quantities of relatively inexpensive information yields strategic opportunities for a range of industries and companies. Retailers, for example, use the Internet to provide abundant shopping privileges to customers in multiple locations. The pervasive influence of electronic commerce or e-business is creating a new culture, referred to as e-culture, that affects the way managers lead, organize, think, and develop and implement strategies.[61]

INCREASING KNOWLEDGE INTENSITY

Knowledge (information, intelligence, and expertise) is the basis of technology and its application. In the 21st-century competitive landscape, knowledge is a critical organizational resource and is increasingly a valuable source of competitive advantage.[62] As a result, many companies now strive to translate the accumulated knowledge of individual employees into a corporate asset. Some argue that the value of intangible assets, including knowledge, is growing as a proportion of total shareholder value.[63] The probability of achieving strategic competitiveness in the 21st-century competitive landscape is enhanced for the firm that realizes that its survival depends on the ability to capture intelligence, transform it into usable knowledge, and diffuse it rapidly throughout the company.[64] Therefore, firms must develop (e.g., through training programs) and acquire (e.g., by hiring educated and experienced employees) knowledge, integrate it into the organization to create capabilities, and then apply it to gain a competitive advantage.[65] Thus, firms must develop a program whereby they learn and then integrate this learning into firm operations. And, they must build routines that facilitate the diffusion of local knowledge throughout the organization for use everywhere it has value.[66] To earn above-average returns, firms must be able to adapt quickly to changes in their competitive landscape. Such adaptation requires that the firm develop strategic flexibility. **Strategic flexibility** is a set of capabilities used to respond to various demands and opportunities existing in a dynamic and uncertain competitive environment. Thus, it involves coping with uncertainty and the accompanying risks.[67]

Firms should develop strategic flexibility in all areas of their operations. To achieve strategic flexibility, many firms have to develop organizational slack—slack resources that allow the firm some flexibility to respond to environmental changes.[68] When larger changes are required, firms may have to undergo strategic reorientations to change their competitive strategy. Strategic reorientations often result from a firm's poor performance. For example, when a firm earns negative returns, its stakeholders (discussed later in this chapter) are likely to pressure top executives to make major changes.[69]

To be strategically flexible on a continuing basis, a firm has to develop the capacity to learn. Continuous learning provides the firm with new and up-to-date sets of skills, which allow the firm to adapt to its environment as it encounters changes.[70] As illustrated in the Strategic Focus, most of the airlines, especially US Airways and United Airlines, have been unable to adapt to a turbulent and negative economic environment. They followed flawed strategies too long and failed. As these firms realized, being flexible, learning, and making the necessary changes are difficult, but they are necessary for continued survival.

Next, we describe two models used by firms to generate the strategic inputs needed to successfully formulate and implement strategies and to maintain strategic flexibility in the process of doing so.

Strategic flexibility is a set of capabilities used to respond to various demands and opportunities existing in a dynamic and uncertain competitive environment.

The I/O Model of Above-Average Returns

From the 1960s through the 1980s, the external environment was thought to be the primary determinant of strategies that firms selected to be successful.[71] The industrial organization (I/O) model of above-average returns explains the dominant influence of the external environment on a firm's strategic actions. The model specifies that the industry in which a firm chooses to compete has a stronger influence on the firm's performance than do the choices managers make inside their organizations.[72] The firm's performance is believed to be determined primarily by a range of industry properties, including economies of scale, barriers to market entry, diversification, product differentiation, and the degree of concentration of firms in the industry.[73] These industry characteristics are examined in Chapter 2.

Grounded in economics, the I/O model has four underlying assumptions. First, the external environment is assumed to impose pressures and constraints that determine the strategies that would result in above-average returns. Second, most firms competing within a particular industry or within a certain segment of it are assumed to control similar strategically relevant resources and to pursue similar strategies in light of those resources. The I/O model's third assumption is that resources used to implement strategies are highly mobile across firms. Because of resource mobility, any resource differences that might develop between firms will be short-lived. Fourth, organizational decision makers are assumed to be rational and committed to acting in the firm's best interests, as shown by their profit-maximizing behaviors.[74] The I/O model challenges firms to locate the most attractive industry in which to compete. Because most firms are assumed to have similar valuable resources that are mobile across companies, their performance generally can be increased only when they operate in the industry with the highest profit potential and learn how to use their resources to implement the strategy required by the industry's structural characteristics.

The five forces model of competition is an analytical tool used to help firms with this task. The model (explained in Chapter 2) encompasses several variables and tries to capture the complexity of competition. The five forces model suggests that an industry's profitability (i.e., its rate of return on invested capital relative to its cost of capital) is a function of interactions among five forces: suppliers, buyers, competitive rivalry among firms currently in the industry, product substitutes, and potential entrants to the industry.[75] Firms can use this tool to understand an industry's profit potential and the strategy necessary to establish a defensible competitive position, given the industry's structural characteristics. Typically, the model suggests that firms can earn above-average returns by manufacturing standardized products or producing standardized services at costs below those of competitors (a cost leadership strategy) or by manufacturing differentiated products for which customers are willing to pay a price premium (a differentiation strategy, described in depth in Chapter 4).

As shown in Figure 1.2, the I/O model suggests that above-average returns are earned when firms implement the strategy dictated by the characteristics of the general, industry, and competitor environments. Companies that develop or acquire the internal skills needed to implement strategies required by the external environment are likely to succeed, while those that do not are likely to fail. Hence, this model suggests that external characteristics, rather than the firm's unique internal resources and capabilities, primarily determine returns.

Research findings support the I/O model. They show that approximately 20 percent of a firm's profitability can be explained by the industry. In other words, 20 percent of a firm's profitability is determined by the industry or industries in which it chooses to operate. This research also shows, however, that 36 percent of the variance in profitability could be attributed to the firm's characteristics and actions.[76] The results of the research suggest that both the environment and the firm's characteristics play a role in determining the firm's specific level of profitability. Thus, there is likely a reciprocal relationship between the environment and the firm's strategy, thereby affecting the firm's performance.[77]

A firm is viewed as a bundle of market activities and a bundle of resources. Market activities are understood through the application of the I/O model. The develop-

1. Study the external environment, especially the industry environment.

The External Environment
- The general environment
- The industry environment
- The competitor environment

2. Locate an industry with high potential for above-average returns.

An Attractive Industry
- An industry whose structural characteristics suggest above-average returns

3. Identify the strategy called for by the attractive industry to earn above-average returns.

Strategy Formulation
- Selection of a strategy linked with above-average returns in a particular industry

4. Develop or acquire assets and skills needed to implement the strategy.

Assets and Skills
- Assets and skills required to implement a chosen strategy

5. Use the firm's strengths (its developed or acquired assets and skills) to implement the strategy.

Strategy Implementation
- Selection of strategic actions linked with effective implementation of the chosen strategy

Superior Returns
- Earning of above-average returns

ment and effective use of a firm's resources, capabilities, and core competencies are understood through the application of the resource-based model. As a result, executives must integrate the two models to develop the most effective strategy.

Profitability in the airline industry has been exceptionally low since we moved into the 21st century. In fact, it is an unattractive industry except for Southwest Airlines and a few other innovative carriers, such as JetBlue in the United States and Virgin Atlantic in the United Kingdom. The industry might become more efficient over time if opened to international competition, but this would undoubtedly lead to consolidation and fewer airlines globally. As shown in the Strategic Focus, however, the key to success is building a portfolio of valuable resources. Southwest Airlines has done so and performed much better than the other large airlines in the industry. Resources are Wal-Mart's key to success as well. Therefore, we must attempt to integrate the I/O model discussed above with the resource-based model explained next.

How Do Firms Succeed in a Highly Challenging Economic Environment with Strong Competition? It Is Resources, Stupid!

Airlines exist in one of the most challenging economic environments since the depression of the 1930s in the United States. This industry is reeling from the poor economic environment in the United States and beyond, the terrorist attack on September 11, 2001, the SARS outbreak in Asia, and war in the Middle East. Because of decreased demand and overcapacity in the industry, most airlines have had substantial net losses since the turn of the century. In fact, two major airlines, US Airways and United Airlines, had to file for bankruptcy, and others, such as American Airlines, have narrowly averted it. These major airlines are searching for new strategies and business models. As in the past, several large airlines have stated publicly that they were going to start a low-cost airline (e.g., United, Delta), while others have proclaimed that they will become a low-cost airline. Of course, these decisions are designed to emulate Southwest Airlines. (These actions are described further in Chapter 5's Opening Case.) Several airlines have tried to imitate Southwest in the past and have failed. The primary problem is that the major airlines have had cost structures substantially higher than Southwest's (from 60 percent higher to more than 100 percent higher). One industry analyst called for a relaxation of the regulations to allow foreign competition. The analyst suggested that this would lead to a more efficient industry. While correct, there are significant forces against this proposal.

Southwest Airlines has been the nemesis of the major airlines for many years. It has made a profit every year of its existence, the only airline to do so. Certainly, strategic decisions made early in its history (such as the use of only one type of aircraft) have helped it maintain a low cost structure. But many now believe that the primary reason for the phenomenal success of Southwest Airlines is its resources. Southwest has two important resources not possessed by other major airlines—substantial human capital and a positive corporate culture. Because of its positive work environment and caring culture, Southwest is able to hire outstanding employees who are loyal and productive. An example of the reason for this ability is that Southwest refused to lay off employees with the major downturn in demand after September 11. It was able to do so because it had amassed a major cache of cash in a contingency fund for use in emergencies. All other airlines had substantial employee layoffs. In *Fortune*'s 2003 annual survey of the most admired companies, Southwest Airlines was ranked number two out of all possible companies. Southwest Airlines has been ranked among the top ten companies on this survey since 1999, and it ranked number two in both 2002 and 2003. We further discuss Southwest's uses of its resources in a Strategic Focus in Chapter 4.

The number one ranked firm in *Fortune*'s 2003 survey was Wal-Mart, the largest company in the world. Warren Buffett provided the following description of the firm: "Wal-Mart . . . hasn't lost a bit of its dynamism that it had back when Sam Walton started it . . . I think that's enormously impressive." To be ranked number one, it had to fare well in evaluations of its financial soundness, quality of management, quality of products and services, employee talent, use of corporate assets, and innovation, among other criteria. Thus, many evaluators believe that Wal-Mart has more than economic

An airline "graveyard" shown in the Arizona desert. With few successes, and many bankruptcies or near-bankruptcies, the airline industry has experienced substantial losses for decades. Turning the industry around may depend on increasing international competition.

Airphoto—Jim Wark

power due to its size; it must have substantial resources in its human capital, ability to be innovative, etc. Resources are the key to maintaining strategic flexibility and, thus, the ability to respond to major changes in the environment. They also allow firms to develop and implement the strategies needed to gain and sustain a competitive advantage. Southwest and Wal-Mart have performed so well over time because of the resources they have and the way in which they have managed those resources.

SOURCES: M. Maynard, 2003, United shifts focus on low-cost airline, *New York Times*, http://www.nytimes.com, May 30; W. Zellner & M. Arndt, 2003, Can anything fix the airlines? *Business Week*, April 7, 52–53; K. L. Alexander, 2003, US Airways CEO talks shop, *Washington Post*, http://www.washingtonpost.com, April 4; N. Stein, 2003, America's most admired companies, *Fortune*, March 3, 81–94; W. Zellner & M. Arndt, 2003, Holding steady: As rivals sputter, can Southwest stay on top? *Business Week*, February 3, 66–68; S. McCartney, 2003, U.S. airlines would benefit from foreign competition, *Wall Street Journal*, http://www.wsj.com, January 22.

The Resource-Based Model of Above-Average Returns

The resource-based model assumes that each organization is a collection of unique resources and capabilities that provides the basis for its strategy and that is the primary source of its returns. This model suggests that capabilities evolve and must be managed dynamically in pursuit of above-average returns.[78] According to the model, differences in firms' performances across time are due primarily to their unique resources and capabilities rather than the industry's structural characteristics. This model also assumes that firms acquire different resources and develop unique capabilities. Therefore, not all firms competing within a particular industry possess the same resources and capabilities. Additionally, the model assumes that resources may not be highly mobile across firms and that the differences in resources are the basis of competitive advantage.

Resources are inputs into a firm's production process, such as capital equipment, the skills of individual employees, patents, finances, and talented managers. In general, a firm's resources can be classified into three categories: physical, human, and organizational capital. Described fully in Chapter 3, resources are either tangible or intangible in nature.

Individual resources alone may not yield a competitive advantage.[79] In general, competitive advantages are formed through the combination and integration of sets of resources. A **capability** is the capacity for a set of resources to perform a task or an activity in an integrative manner. Through the firm's continued use, capabilities become stronger and more difficult for competitors to understand and imitate. As a source of competitive advantage, a capability "should be neither so simple that it is highly imitable, nor so complex that it defies internal steering and control."[80]

The resource-based model of superior returns is shown in Figure 1.3. Instead of focusing on the accumulation of resources necessary to implement the strategy dictated by conditions and constraints in the external environment (I/O model), the resource-based view suggests that a firm's unique resources and capabilities provide the basis for a strategy. The strategy chosen should allow the firm to best exploit its core competencies relative to opportunities in the external environment.

Not all of a firm's resources and capabilities have the potential to be the basis for competitive advantage. This potential is realized when resources and capabilities are valuable, rare, costly to imitate, and nonsubstitutable.[81] Resources are *valuable* when they allow a firm to take advantage of opportunities or neutralize threats in its external environment. They are *rare* when possessed by few, if any, current and potential competitors. Resources are *costly to imitate* when other firms either cannot obtain them or are at a cost disadvantage in obtaining them compared with the firm that

Resources *are inputs into a firm's production process, such as capital equipment, the skills of individual employees, patents, finances, and talented managers.*

A **capability** *is the capacity for a set of resources to perform a task or an activity in an integrative manner.*

Figure 1.3 — The Resource-Based Model of Above-Average Returns

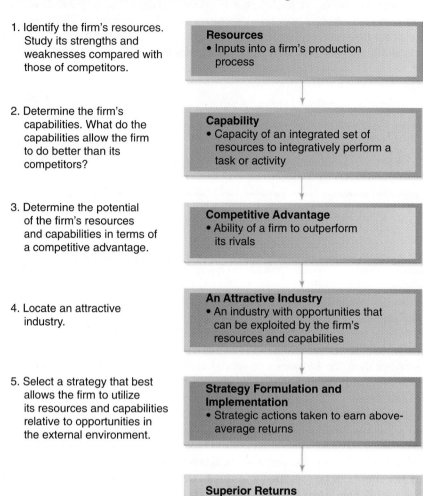

1. Identify the firm's resources. Study its strengths and weaknesses compared with those of competitors.

Resources
• Inputs into a firm's production process

2. Determine the firm's capabilities. What do the capabilities allow the firm to do better than its competitors?

Capability
• Capacity of an integrated set of resources to integratively perform a task or activity

3. Determine the potential of the firm's resources and capabilities in terms of a competitive advantage.

Competitive Advantage
• Ability of a firm to outperform its rivals

4. Locate an attractive industry.

An Attractive Industry
• An industry with opportunities that can be exploited by the firm's resources and capabilities

5. Select a strategy that best allows the firm to utilize its resources and capabilities relative to opportunities in the external environment.

Strategy Formulation and Implementation
• Strategic actions taken to earn above-average returns

Superior Returns
• Earning of above-average returns

already possesses them. And, they are *nonsubstitutable* when they have no structural equivalents. Many resources can either be imitated or substituted over time. Therefore, it is difficult to achieve and sustain a competitive advantage based on resources.[82] When these four criteria are met, however, resources and capabilities become core competencies. **Core competencies** are resources and capabilities that serve as a source of competitive advantage for a firm over its rivals. Often related to a firm's functional skills (e.g., the marketing function is a core competence of Philip Morris, a division of the Altria Group, Inc.), core competencies, when developed, nurtured, and applied throughout a firm, may result in strategic competitiveness.

Managerial competencies are important in most firms. For example, managers often have valuable human (education and experience) and social capital (ties to important customers or critical external organizations such as suppliers).[83] Such competencies may include the capability to effectively organize and govern complex and diverse operations and the capability to create and communicate a strategic vision.[84] Managerial capabilities are important in a firm's ability to take advantage of its resources. Firms must also continuously develop their competencies to keep them up

Core competencies are resources and capabilities that serve as a source of competitive advantage for a firm over its rivals.

to date. This development requires a systematic program for updating old skills and introducing new ones. Dynamic core competencies are especially important in rapidly changing environments, such as those that exist in high-technology industries. Thus, the resource-based model suggests that core competencies are the basis for a firm's competitive advantage, its strategic competitiveness, and its ability to earn above-average returns.

Recent research shows that both the industry environment and a firm's internal assets affect that firm's performance over time.[85] Thus, both are important in the development and implementation of firm strategy.[86] As a result, we integrate analysis of the external environment (Chapter 2) with the evaluation of the firm's internal resources and capabilities (Chapter 3) in the development of the most effective strategy for the firm.

Strategic Intent and Strategic Mission

Resulting from analyses of a firm's internal and external environments is the information required to form a strategic intent and develop a strategic mission (see Figure 1.1). Both intent and mission are linked with strategic competitiveness.

Strategic Intent

Strategic intent is the leveraging of a firm's resources, capabilities, and core competencies to accomplish the firm's goals in the competitive environment.[87] Strategic intent exists when all employees and levels of a firm are committed to the pursuit of a specific (and significant) performance criterion. Some argue that strategic intent provides employees with the only goal worthy of personal effort and commitment: to unseat the best or remain the best, worldwide.[88] Strategic intent has been effectively formed when employees believe strongly in their company's product and when they are focused on their firm's ability to outperform its competitors.

It appears as if Apple Computer is changing its strategic intent. While Steven Jobs has been able to steady a rapidly deteriorating firm after becoming CEO again in the late 1990s, Apple's market share in the computer market has decreased to 2.3 percent, down from 9.3 percent in 1993. Thus, Jobs has turned the company toward development of digital entertainment with a new online music service. His contacts in the entertainment industry have helped him obtain the agreements to offer the music of popular performers such as the Eagles through Apple's new service. The competition will be stiff; however, the change in strategic intent may be a matter of survival for Apple.[89]

It is not enough for a firm to know its own strategic intent. Performing well demands that the firm also identify its competitors' strategic intent. Only when these intentions are understood can a firm become aware of the resolve, stamina, and inventiveness (traits linked with effective strategic intents) of those competitors.[90] For example, Apple must now identify and understand not only Dell Inc.'s strategic intent but also that of Vivendi's Universal Music Group. A company's success may also be grounded in a keen and deep understanding of the strategic intent of its customers, suppliers, partners, and competitors.[91]

Strategic intent is the leveraging of a firm's resources, capabilities, and core competencies to accomplish the firm's goals in the competitive environment.

Apple is currently attempting to increase its market share through digital entertainment. Its success will depend on how well this change in strategic intent will carry them in an already highly competitive industry.

©Bill Aron/PhotoEdit

Strategic Mission

As the preceding discussion shows, strategic intent is internally focused. It is concerned with identifying the resources, capabilities, and core competencies on which a firm can base its strategic actions. Strategic intent reflects what a firm is capable of doing with its core competencies and the unique ways they can be used to exploit a competitive advantage.

Strategic mission flows from strategic intent. Externally focused, **strategic mission** is a statement of a firm's unique purpose and the scope of its operations in product and market terms.[92] A strategic mission provides general descriptions of the products a firm intends to produce and the markets it will serve using its core competencies. An effective strategic mission establishes a firm's individuality and is inspiring and relevant to all stakeholders.[93] Together, strategic intent and strategic mission yield the insights required to formulate and implement strategies.

The strategic mission of Johnson & Johnson focuses on customers, stating that the organization's primary responsibility is to "the doctors, nurses, and patients, mothers and fathers and all others who use our products and services."[94] An effective strategic mission is formed when the firm has a strong sense of what it wants to do and of the ethical standards that will guide behaviors in the pursuit of its goals.[95] Because Johnson & Johnson specifies the products it will offer in particular markets and presents a framework within which the firm operates, its strategic mission is an application of strategic intent.[96]

Research has shown that having an effective intent and mission and properly implementing them have a positive effect on performance as measured by growth in sales, profits, employment, and net worth.[97] When a firm is strategically competitive and earning above-average returns, it has the capacity to satisfy stakeholders' interests.

Stakeholders

Every organization involves a system of primary stakeholder groups with whom it establishes and manages relationships.[98] **Stakeholders** are the individuals and groups who can affect, and are affected by, the strategic outcomes achieved and who have enforceable claims on a firm's performance.[99] Claims on a firm's performance are enforced through the stakeholders' ability to withhold participation essential to the organization's survival, competitiveness, and profitability.[100] Stakeholders continue to support an organization when its performance meets or exceeds their expectations. Also, recent research suggests that firms effectively managing stakeholder relationships outperform those that do not. Stakeholder relationships can therefore be managed to be a source of competitive advantage.[101]

Although organizations have dependency relationships with their stakeholders, they are not equally dependent on all stakeholders at all times; as a consequence, not every stakeholder has the same level of influence. The more critical and valued a stakeholder's participation is, the greater is a firm's dependency on it. Greater dependence, in turn, gives the stakeholder more potential influence over a firm's commitments, decisions, and actions. Managers must find ways to either accommodate or insulate the organization from the demands of stakeholders controlling critical resources.[102]

Cisco changed from being a star to most of its stakeholders to displeasing many of them. In particular, its substantial reduction in stock price concerned shareholders. Its employee layoffs created concern and displeasure among Cisco's workforce, particularly because the need to cut costs was caused by poor strategic decisions that produced large inventories. However, as noted in the Strategic Focus, Cisco has survived the dot-com crash and its performance is improving. While Cisco's stock price is still much lower than in the heady times of the late 1990s, its future looks bright with a

Is Cisco a Survivor?

In the decade of the 1990s, Cisco Systems created more wealth for its shareholders than any other firm. Its stock price increased by 124,825 percent—a $100 investment in Cisco stock in 1990 was worth $1,248,250 by the end of the decade. Cisco was able to satisfy many of its stakeholders during the decade, but with the downturn in the U.S. economy and the poor performance of Internet-based and telecommunications firms (Cisco's major customers), its fortunes turned sour. Its stock price declined by almost 78 percent, from a high of over $71 in 2000 to below $16 in 2001, and Cisco had to lay off employees.

During the earlier strong economy, Cisco experienced delays in obtaining supplies and was unable to meet customers' orders for its systems. As a result, it signed long-term contracts with suppliers to ensure supply. When sales declined significantly, Cisco was faced with large inventories. One analyst suggested that Cisco managers did not know what to do when the economy slowed. Neither shareholders nor employees were pleased with the results.

During this slowdown, CEO John Chambers remained optimistic and vowed to stay the course. But, he compared the Internet slump to a 100-year flood that had not been anticipated by his team. Such a flood causes considerable destruction, so his analogy was appropriate. Chambers suggested that the firm's focus had changed from revenue growth to profitability, earnings contribution, and growth through internal development rather than acquisitions. While Cisco experienced a net loss of $1.0 billion in 2001, down from a $2.7 billion profit in 2000, Chambers' optimism seems well founded. Cisco reported a net profit in 2002 of almost $1.9 billion, representing a significant turnaround. Additionally, its cash reserves were higher in 2002 than they were in 2000, the previous high, and profits continued to increase in 2003. Thus, Cisco appears to be in good financial condition.

Chambers predicted that brand would become especially important and promised to protect the good brand of Cisco. Recent actions show that Chambers was serious. Cisco filed suit against Huawei Technologies, a Chinese company, for infringement of its patents. In June 2003, a U.S. federal judge issued an injunction against Huawei preventing it from selling, importing, exporting, or using the software questioned by Cisco. Huawei withdrew the products in question from the U.S. market.

SOURCES: 2003, Judge issues injunction against Chinese company in suit by Cisco, *New York Times*, http://www.nytimes.com, June 9; 2003, Cisco Annual Report 2002, http://www.cisco.com, March; B. Elgin, 2001, A do-it-yourself plan at Cisco, *Business Week*, September 10, 52; G. Anders, 2001, John Chambers after the deluge, *Fast Company*, July, 100–111; S. N. Mehta, 2001, Cisco fractures its own tale, *Fortune*, May 14, 105–112; P. Abrahams, 2001, Cisco chief must sink or swim, *Financial Times*, http://www.ft.com, April 19.

good net profit in 2002 (especially in poor economic times) and a strong cash position. Cisco is a survivor, and its stakeholders should be relieved, if not highly pleased to see the performance turnaround.

Classification of Stakeholders

The parties involved with a firm's operations can be separated into at least three groups.[103] As shown in Figure 1.4, these groups are the capital market stakeholders (shareholders and the major suppliers of a firm's capital), the product market stakeholders (the firm's primary customers, suppliers, host communities, and unions representing the workforce), and the organizational stakeholders (all of a firm's employees, including both nonmanagerial and managerial personnel).

Figure 1.4 — The Three Stakeholder Groups

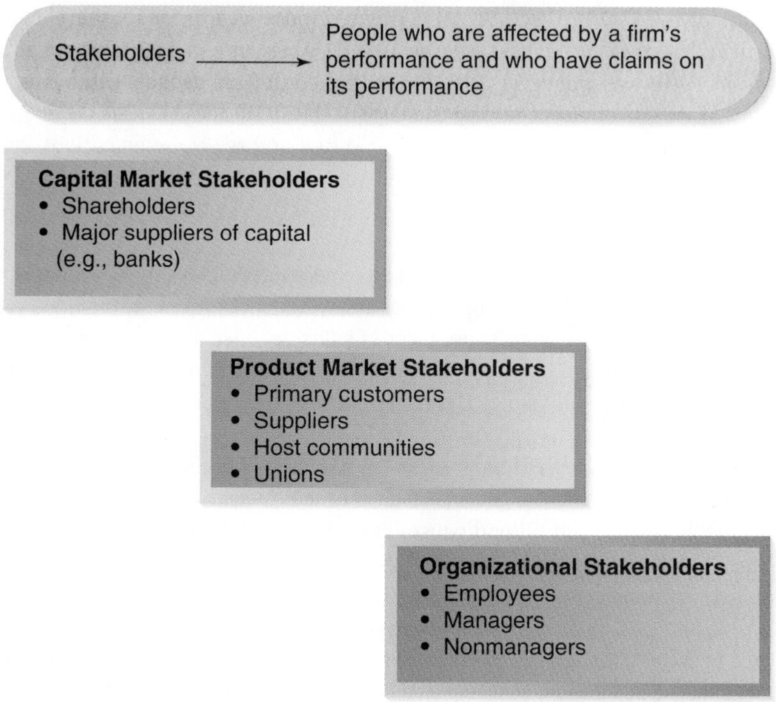

Stakeholders $\longrightarrow$	People who are affected by a firm's performance and who have claims on its performance

Capital Market Stakeholders
- Shareholders
- Major suppliers of capital (e.g., banks)

Product Market Stakeholders
- Primary customers
- Suppliers
- Host communities
- Unions

Organizational Stakeholders
- Employees
- Managers
- Nonmanagers

Each stakeholder group expects those making strategic decisions in a firm to provide the leadership through which its valued objectives will be accomplished.[104] The objectives of the various stakeholder groups often differ from one another, sometimes placing managers in situations where trade-offs have to be made. The most obvious stakeholders, at least in U.S. organizations, are shareholders—those who have invested capital in a firm in the expectation of earning a positive return on their investments. These stakeholders' rights are grounded in laws governing private property and private enterprise.

Shareholders want the return on their investment (and, hence, their wealth) to be maximized. Maximization of returns sometimes is accomplished at the expense of investing in a firm's future. Gains achieved by reducing investment in research and development, for example, could be returned to shareholders, thereby increasing the short-term return on their investments. However, this short-term enhancement of shareholders' wealth can negatively affect the firm's future competitive ability, and sophisticated shareholders with diversified portfolios may sell their interests if a firm fails to invest in its future. Those making strategic decisions are responsible for a firm's survival in both the short and the long term. Accordingly, it is not in the interests of any stakeholders for investments in the company to be unduly minimized.

In contrast to shareholders, another group of stakeholders—the firm's customers—prefers that investors receive a minimum return on their investments. Customers could have their interests maximized when the quality and reliability of a firm's products are improved, but without a price increase. High returns to customers might come at the expense of lower returns negotiated with capital market shareholders.

Because of potential conflicts, each firm is challenged to manage its stakeholders. First, a firm must carefully identify all important stakeholders. Second, it must prioritize them, in case it cannot satisfy all of them. Power is the most critical criterion in prioritizing stakeholders. Other criteria might include the urgency of satisfying each particular stakeholder group and the degree of importance of each to the firm.[105]

When the firm earns above-average returns, the challenge of effectively managing stakeholder relationships is lessened substantially. With the capability and flexibility provided by above-average returns, a firm can more easily satisfy multiple stakeholders simultaneously. When the firm is earning only average returns, it is unable to maximize the interests of all stakeholders. The objective then becomes one of at least minimally satisfying each stakeholder. Trade-off decisions are made in light of how important the support of each stakeholder group is to the firm. For example, environmental groups may be very important to firms in the energy industry but less important to professional service firms.[106] A firm earning below-average returns does not have the capacity to minimally satisfy all stakeholders. The managerial challenge in this case is to make trade-offs that minimize the amount of support lost from stakeholders. Societal values also influence the general weightings allocated among the three stakeholder groups shown in Figure 1.4. Although all three groups are served by firms in the major industrialized nations, the priorities in their service vary because of cultural differences.

CAPITAL MARKET STAKEHOLDERS

Shareholders and lenders both expect a firm to preserve and enhance the wealth they have entrusted to it. The returns they expect are commensurate with the degree of risk accepted with those investments (that is, lower returns are expected with low-risk investments, and higher returns are expected with high-risk investments). Dissatisfied lenders may impose stricter covenants on subsequent borrowing of capital. Dissatisfied shareholders may reflect their concerns through several means, including selling their stock.

When a firm is aware of potential or actual dissatisfactions among capital market stakeholders, it may respond to their concerns. The firm's response to dissatisfied stakeholders is affected by the nature of its dependency relationship with them (which, as noted earlier, is also influenced by a society's values). The greater and more significant the dependency relationship is, the more direct and significant the firm's response becomes.

As discussed in a previous Strategic Focus, United Airlines and US Airways have both filed for bankruptcy and their stock has very little value. The capital market stakeholders in this case (i.e., stockholders and lenders) lost a large amount of money on their investments or loans. There is little that they can do to recoup their monies. In another Strategic Focus, it was noted that Cisco's stock price remains low, but the future of the firm is looking brighter. Thus, this firm's stockholders likely will want to hold on to their shares of stock in the hopes that the firm's profits will drive up the stock price. Lenders may also be feeling relief after news of Cisco's recent profits and positive future projections.

PRODUCT MARKET STAKEHOLDERS

Some might think that there is little commonality among the interests of customers, suppliers, host communities, and unions (product market stakeholders). However, all four groups can benefit as firms engage in competitive battles. For example, depending on product and industry characteristics, marketplace competition may result in lower product prices being charged to a firm's customers and higher prices being paid to its suppliers (the firm might be willing to pay higher supplier prices to ensure delivery of the types of goods and services that are linked with its competitive success).

As is noted in Chapter 4, customers, as stakeholders, demand reliable products at the lowest possible prices. Suppliers seek loyal customers who are willing to pay the highest sustainable prices for the goods and services they receive. Host communities want companies willing to be long-term employers and providers of tax revenues without placing excessive demands on public support services. Union officials are interested in secure jobs, under highly desirable working conditions, for employees they represent. Thus, product market stakeholders are generally satisfied when a firm's profit margin reflects at least a balance between the returns to capital market stakeholders (i.e., the returns lenders and shareholders will accept and still retain their interests in the firm) and the returns in which they share.

All product market stakeholders are important in a competitive business environment, but many firms emphasize the importance of the customer. As the preceding Strategic Focus suggests, Cisco experienced problems with consumer demand even before the poor economic conditions at the end of the decade. Some of Cisco's shareholders and employees (organizational stakeholders) were displeased with the firm's establishment of long-term contracts with suppliers that produced large investments in inventories when the economy slowed. These extra costs required Cisco to cut costs in other areas (e.g., by laying off employees) and contributed to a lower stock price. Cisco seems to have weathered the storm and is returning to profitability, as shown by its 2002 results and its continuing positive performance in 2003.

ORGANIZATIONAL STAKEHOLDERS

Employees—the firm's organizational stakeholders—expect the firm to provide a dynamic, stimulating, and rewarding work environment. They are usually satisfied working for a company that is growing and actively developing their skills, especially those skills required to be effective team members and to meet or exceed global work standards. Workers who learn how to use new knowledge productively are critical to organizational success. In a collective sense, the education and skills of a firm's workforce are competitive weapons affecting strategy implementation and firm performance.[107]

Strategic Leaders

Strategic leaders are the people responsible for the design and execution of strategic management processes. These individuals may also be called top-level managers, executives, the top management team, and general managers. Throughout this book, these names are used interchangeably. As discussed in Chapter 12, top-level managers can be a source of competitive advantage as a result of the value created by their strategic decisions.

Small organizations may have a single strategic leader; in many cases, this person owns the firm and is deeply involved with its daily operations. At the other extreme, large, diversified firms often have multiple top-level managers. In addition to the CEO and other top-level officials (e.g., the chief operating officer and chief financial officer), other managers of these companies are responsible for the performance of individual business units.

Top-level managers play critical roles in a firm's efforts to achieve desired strategic outcomes. In fact, some believe that every organizational failure is actually a failure of those who hold the final responsibility for the quality and effectiveness of a firm's decisions and actions. Failure can stem from changing strategic assumptions, which can cause the strategic mission to become a strategic blunder. This appears to have been a problem at United Airlines and US Airways described earlier in a Strategic Focus. While they all exist in a highly changing environment, several other airlines are not in danger of bankruptcy, and a few, especially Southwest, are profitable. This suggests that the decisions made by strategic leaders at United Airlines and US Airways were not as effective as those made by the strategic leaders at other airlines. Recent research suggests that many smart executives make major mistakes and fail. For example, these otherwise intelligent executives remove all people on the staff who disagree with them. As a result, no dissenting opinions are offered and major mistakes are inevitable.[108]

Decisions that strategic leaders make include how resources will be developed or acquired, at what price they will be obtained, and how they will be used. Managerial decisions also influence how information flows in a company, the strategies a firm chooses to implement, and the scope of its operations. In making these decisions, managers must assess the risk involved in taking the actions being considered. The level of risk is then factored into the decision.[109] The firm's strategic intent and managers' strategic orientations both affect their decisions. The decisions made by a firm's strategic leaders affect its ability to develop a competitive advantage.

Critical to strategic leadership practices and the implementation of strategies, **organizational culture** refers to the complex set of ideologies, symbols, and core values that are shared throughout the firm and that influence how the firm conducts business. Thus, culture is the social energy that drives—or fails to drive—the organization. For example, Southwest Airlines, one of the successful firms discussed in an earlier Strategic Focus, is known for having a unique and valuable culture. Its culture encourages employees to work hard but also to have fun while doing so. Moreover, its culture entails respect for others—employees and customers alike. The firm also places a premium on service, as suggested by its commitment to provide POS (Positively Outrageous Service) to each customer. These core values at Southwest Airlines provide a particular type of social energy that drives the firm's efforts. Organizational culture thus becomes a potential source of competitive advantage.

Given the importance of strategic leaders to a firm's success, the selection of those to fill these positions is critical. Planning for the succession of key leaders is important. Most planned successions of CEOs, for example, have been found to have positive effects on a firm's stock price regardless of whether the successor comes from the inside or outside.[110] When strategic change is needed, however, an outside successor is often selected for a key strategic leadership position. This is done because he or she can bring new ideas to the firm and is not tied to past decisions or to internal political processes. But, outside successors are disadvantaged early because of their lack of firm-specific knowledge. Thus, early performance after such a change may not be positive. Outside successors, however, are likely to make changes that have long-term positive consequences for the firm.[111] Careful decisions regarding leadership succession are important because of the potential for mistakes made by executives, as noted above. When executives are powerful, they are more likely to display hubris and make mistakes. When "heirs apparent" are selected from inside the firm relatively early, they are more likely to have greater power when they move into the strategic leadership position.[112] After the new strategic leader is chosen, his or her focus is on making effective strategic decisions.

The Work of Effective Strategic Leaders

Perhaps not surprisingly, hard work, thorough analyses, a willingness to be brutally honest, a penchant for wanting the firm and its people to accomplish more, and common sense are prerequisites to an individual's success as a strategic leader.[113] In addition to possessing these characteristics, effective

AP Photo/Paul Sakuma

strategic leaders must be able to think clearly and ask many questions. In particular, top-level managers are challenged to "think seriously and deeply . . . about the purposes of the organizations they head or functions they perform, about the strategies, tactics, technologies, systems, and people necessary to attain these purposes and about the important questions that always need to be asked."[114]

As the Internet has changed the nature of competition, it is also changing strategic decision making. Speed has become a much more prominent competitive factor, and it makes strategic thinking even more critical. Most high-tech firms operate in hypercompetitive industry environments. As a result of the intense competition in these industries, some product life cycles have decreased from a period of one to two years to a period of six to nine months, leaving less time for a company's products to generate revenue. Speed and flexibility have become key sources of competitive advantage for companies competing in these industries. Thinking strategically, in concert with others, increases the probability of identifying bold, innovative ideas.[115] When these ideas lead to the development of core competencies, they become the foundation for taking advantage of environmental opportunities.

Our discussion highlights the nature of a strategic leader's work. Strategic leaders often work long hours, and the work is filled with ambiguous decision situations for which effective solutions are not easily determined.[116] However, the opportunities afforded by this work are appealing and offer exciting chances to dream and to act. The following words, given as advice to the late Time Warner chairman and co-CEO Steven J. Ross by his father, describe the opportunities in a strategic leader's work:

> There are three categories of people—the person who goes into the office, puts his feet up on his desk, and dreams for 12 hours; the person who arrives at 5 A.M. and works for 16 hours, never once stopping to dream; and the person who puts his feet up, dreams for one hour, then does something about those dreams.[117]

The organizational term used for a dream that challenges and energizes a company is strategic intent (discussed earlier in this chapter). Strategic leaders have opportunities to dream and to act, and the most effective ones provide a vision (the strategic intent) to effectively elicit the help of others in creating a firm's competitive advantage.

Predicting Outcomes of Strategic Decisions: Profit Pools

Strategic leaders attempt to predict the outcomes of strategic decisions they make before they are implemented. In most cases, outcomes are determined only after the decisions have been implemented. For example, executives at Montana Power decided to change the firm from a utility company to a high-tech company focusing on broadband services. The firm announced in March 2000 that it would invest $1.6 billion to build a coast-to-coast fiber optic network. Unfortunately for Montana Power, the utility industry began to grow and the broadband industry declined substantially in 2001. As a result, the firm's stock price declined from $65 per share in 2000 to less than $1 per share in 2001. In fact, the new firm in which the assets were invested, Touch America, was on the verge of bankruptcy in 2003. While it may have been difficult for Montana Power to predict the rapid decline in the high-tech businesses, it should have been much easier to predict the growth in the utility business.[118] One means of helping managers understand the potential outcomes of their strategic decisions is to map their industry's profit pools. There are four steps to doing this: (1) define the pool's boundaries, (2) estimate the pool's overall size, (3) estimate the size of the value-chain activity in the pool, and (4) reconcile the calculations.[119]

A **profit pool** entails the total profits earned in an industry at all points along the value chain.[120] Analyzing the profit pool in the industry may help a firm see something others are unable to see by helping it understand the primary sources of profits in an industry. After these sources have been identified, managers must link the profit poten-

A **profit pool** entails the total profits earned in an industry at all points along the value chain.

tial identified to specific strategies. In a sense, they map the profit potential of their departmental units by linking to the firm's overall profits. They can then better link the strategic actions considered to potential profits.[121]

Mapping profit pools and linking potential profits to strategic actions before they are implemented should be a regular part of the strategic management process. General Motors' strategic leaders would have done well to take these actions when they decided to continue investing resources in the Oldsmobile brand instead of investing them in their Saturn brand. The firm's investments in Oldsmobile in essence starved Saturn for resources, even though Oldsmobile was no longer a successful product in the market. Finally, after making a decision to stop marketing Oldsmobile, GM decided to invest $1.5 billion in developing a full line of Saturn products.[122]

The Strategic Management Process

As suggested by Figure 1.1, the strategic management process is intended to be a rational approach to help a firm effectively respond to the challenges of the 21st-century competitive landscape. Figure 1.1 also outlines the topics examined in this book to study the strategic management process. Part 1 of this book shows how this process requires a firm to study its external environment (Chapter 2) and internal environment (Chapter 3) to identify marketplace opportunities and threats and determine how to use its resources, capabilities, and core competencies to pursue desired strategic outcomes. With this knowledge, the firm forms its strategic intent to leverage its resources, capabilities, and core competencies and to win competitive battles. Flowing from its strategic intent, the firm's strategic mission specifies, in writing, the products the firm intends to produce and the markets it will serve when leveraging those resources, capabilities, and core competencies.

The firm's strategic inputs provide the foundation for its strategic actions to formulate and implement strategies. Both formulating and implementing strategies are critical to achieving strategic competitiveness and earning above-average returns. As suggested in Figure 1.1 by the horizontal arrow linking the two types of strategic actions, formulation and implementation must be simultaneously integrated. In formulating strategies, thought should be given to implementing them. During implementation, effective strategic leaders also seek feedback to improve selected strategies. Only when these two sets of actions are carefully integrated can the firm achieve its desired strategic outcomes.

In Part 2 of this book, the formulation of strategies is explained. First, we examine the formulation of strategies at the business-unit level (Chapter 4). A diversified firm competing in multiple product markets and businesses has a business-level strategy for each distinct product market area. A company competing in a single product market has but one business-level strategy. In all instances, a business-level strategy describes a firm's actions designed to exploit its competitive advantage over rivals. On the other hand, business-level strategies are not formulated and implemented in isolation (Chapter 5). Competitors respond to and try to anticipate each other's actions. Thus, the dynamics of competition are an important input when selecting and implementing strategies.

For the diversified firm, corporate-level strategy (Chapter 6) is concerned with determining the businesses in which the company intends to compete as well as how resources are to be allocated among those businesses. Other topics vital to strategy formulation, particularly in the diversified firm, include the acquisition of other companies and, as appropriate, the restructuring of the firm's portfolio of businesses (Chapter 7) and the selection of an international strategy (Chapter 8). Increasingly important in a global economy, cooperative strategies are used by a firm to gain competitive advantage by forming advantageous relationships with other firms (Chapter 9).

To examine actions taken to implement strategies, we consider several topics in Part 3 of the book. First, the different mechanisms used to govern firms are explained (Chapter 10). With demands for improved corporate governance voiced by various stakeholders, organizations are challenged to satisfy stakeholders' interests and the attainment of desired strategic outcomes. Finally, the organizational structure and actions needed to control a firm's operations (Chapter 11), the patterns of strategic leadership appropriate for today's firms and competitive environments (Chapter 12), and strategic entrepreneurship (Chapter 13) are addressed.

As noted earlier, competition requires firms to make choices to survive and succeed. Some of these choices are strategic in nature, including those of selecting a strategic intent and strategic mission, determining which strategies to implement, choosing an appropriate level of corporate scope, designing governance and organization structures to properly coordinate a firm's work, and, through strategic leadership, encouraging and nurturing organizational innovation.[123] The goal is to achieve and maintain a competitive advantage over rivals.

Primarily because they are related to how a firm interacts with its stakeholders, almost all strategic decisions have ethical dimensions.[124] Organizational ethics are revealed by an organization's culture; that is to say, a firm's strategic decisions are a product of the core values that are shared by most or all of a company's managers and employees. Especially in the turbulent and often ambiguous 21st-century competitive landscape, those making strategic decisions are challenged to recognize that their decisions affect capital market, product market, and organizational stakeholders differently and to evaluate the ethical implications of their decisions.

As you will discover, the strategic management process examined in this book calls for disciplined approaches to the development of competitive advantage. These approaches provide the pathway through which firms will be able to achieve strategic competitiveness and earn above-average returns in the 21st century. Mastery of this strategic management process will effectively serve readers and the organizations for which they choose to work.

Summary

- Through their actions, firms seek strategic competitiveness and above-average returns. Strategic competitiveness is achieved when a firm has developed and learned how to implement a value-creating strategy. Above-average returns (in excess of what investors expect to earn from other investments with similar levels of risk) allow a firm to simultaneously satisfy all of its stakeholders.

- In the 21st-century competitive landscape, the fundamental nature of competition has changed. As a result, those making strategic decisions must adopt a new mind-set that is global in nature. Firms must learn how to compete in highly turbulent and chaotic environments that produce disorder and a great deal of uncertainty. The globalization of industries and their markets and rapid and significant technological changes are the two primary factors contributing to the 21st-century competitive landscape.

- There are two major models of what a firm should do to earn above-average returns. The I/O model suggests that the external environment is the primary determinant of

the firm's strategies. Above-average returns are earned when the firm locates an attractive industry and successfully implements the strategy dictated by that industry's characteristics.

- The resource-based model assumes that each firm is a collection of unique resources and capabilities that determine its strategy. Above-average returns are earned when the firm uses its valuable, rare, costly-to-imitate, and nonsubstitutable resources and capabilities (i.e., core competencies) as the source of its competitive advantage(s).

- Strategic intent and strategic mission are formed in light of the information and insights gained from studying a firm's internal and external environments. Strategic intent suggests how resources, capabilities, and core competencies will be leveraged to achieve desired outcomes. The strategic mission is an application of strategic intent. The mission is used to specify the product markets and customers a firm intends to serve through the leveraging of its resources, capabilities, and core competencies.

- Stakeholders are those who can affect, and are affected by, a firm's strategic outcomes. Because a firm is dependent on the continuing support of stakeholders (shareholders, customers, suppliers, employees, host communities, etc.), they have enforceable claims on the company's performance. When earning above-average returns, a firm can adequately satisfy all stakeholders' interests. However, when earning only average returns, a firm's strategic leaders must carefully manage all stakeholder groups in order to retain their support. A firm earning below-average returns must minimize the amount of support it loses from dissatisfied stakeholders.

- Strategic leaders are responsible for the design and execution of an effective strategic management process.

Today, the most effective of these processes are grounded in ethical intentions and conduct. Strategic leaders can be a source of competitive advantage. The strategic leader's work demands decision trade-offs, often among attractive alternatives. Successful top-level managers work hard, conduct thorough analyses of situations, are brutally and consistently honest, and ask the right questions of the right people at the right time.

- Managers must predict the potential outcomes of their strategic decisions. To do so, they must first calculate profit pools in their industry that are linked to the value chain activities. In so doing, they are less likely to formulate and implement an ineffective strategy.

Review Questions

Review Questions Review Questions

1. What are strategic competitiveness, competitive advantage, and above-average returns?

2. What are the characteristics of the 21st-century landscape? What two factors are the primary drivers of this landscape?

3. According to the I/O model, what should a firm do to earn above-average returns?

4. What does the resource-based model suggest a firm should do to earn above-average returns?

5. What are strategic intent and strategic mission? What is their value for the strategic management process?

6. What are stakeholders? How do the three primary stakeholder groups influence organizations?

7. How would you describe the work of strategic leaders?

8. What are the elements of the strategic management process? How are they interrelated?

Experiential Exercises

Experiential Exercise

For the experiential exercises in Part 1, choose a company or an industry in which you would like to work. You can gain valuable insight about your future employment while learning about the strategic management process. You will find it helpful to peruse the business press (e.g., *Wall Street Journal*, *Business Week*, *Fortune*, and so forth) for information about the firm or industry of interest to you.

Effective Stakeholder Management

Effective stakeholder management is an important part of successful strategic management processes. Stakeholders are the individuals or groups with objectives or interests that can be affected by the firm's strategic outcomes. Each stakeholder group also has the ability to affect the outcomes achieved by the firm.

Prepare a report for the top management team at the firm of interest to you. The purpose of your report is to provide advice about how to effectively manage the firm's stakeholders. Your report should include the following:

a. Identify all important stakeholders for your company (or industry).

b. Determine the primary objectives of each stakeholder group.

c. Assess the power of each group to affect the firm's strategic outcomes and the ways in which this power may be exercised.

d. Explain how the firm may satisfy the interests or objectives of each group.

e. Recommend trade-offs that managers may make in satisfying stakeholder groups that will improve firm performance.

Strategic Mission Statements

A strategic mission describes a firm's unique purpose and the scope of its operations in terms of the products it intends to produce and the markets it will serve using its core competencies. An effective strategic mission establishes a firm's individuality and is inspiring and relevant to all stakeholders.

On the basis of this description of a strategic mission, evaluate the following mission statements of several competitors in the pharmaceutical industry. Each statement was clearly identified on the company's website as the company's mission. Examine the similarities and differences. In your opinion, which firm has the most effective mission statement? Why? Discuss ways in which the statements could be changed to provide a more effective basis for strategy formulation or implementation.

GlaxoSmithKline: GSK's mission is to improve the quality of human life by enabling people to do more, feel better and live longer.

AstraZeneca: The people of AstraZeneca are dedicated to discovering, developing and delivering innovative pharmaceutical solutions; enriching the lives of patients, families, communities and other stakeholders; and creating a challenging and rewarding work environment for everyone.

Bristol-Myers Squibb: At Bristol-Myers Squibb, our mission is to extend and enhance human life by providing the highest-quality pharmaceuticals and health care products. Our medicines are making a difference in the lives of millions of customers across the globe. And by living our mission and growing our company for well over a century, we are making a difference in the lives of our shareholders, employees and neighbors as well.

Merck & Co., Inc.: The mission of Merck is to provide society with superior products and services by developing innovations and solutions that improve the quality of life and satisfy customer needs, and to provide employees with meaningful work and advancement opportunities, and investors with a superior rate of return.

Novartis: We want to discover, develop, and successfully market innovative products to cure diseases, to ease suffering and to enhance the quality of life. We also want to provide a shareholder return that reflects outstanding performance and to adequately reward those who invest ideas and work in our company.

Pfizer: We will become the world's most valued company to patients, customers, colleagues, investors, business partners, and the communities where we work and live.

Notes

1. D. G. Sirmon & M. A. Hitt, 2003, Managing resources: Linking unique resources, management and wealth creation in family firms, *Entrepreneurship Theory and Practice*, 27(4): 339–358; D. G. Sirmon, M. A. Hitt, & R. D. Ireland, 2003, Managing the firm's resources in order to achieve and maintain a competitive advantage, presented at the Academy of Management, Seattle; C. E. Helfat, 2000, The evolution of firm capabilities, *Strategic Management Journal*, 21(Special Issue): 955–959; J. B. Barney, 1999, How firms' capabilities affect boundary decisions, *Sloan Management Review*, 40(3): 137–145.

2. T. J. Douglas & J. A. Ryman, 2003, Understanding competitive advantage in the general hospital industry: Evaluating strategic competencies, *Strategic Management Journal*, 24: 333–347; W. Mitchell, 2000, Path-dependent and path-breaking change: Reconfiguring business resources following acquisitions in the U.S. medical sector, 1978–1995, *Strategic Management Journal*, 21(Special Issue): 1061–1081.

3. E. Bonabeau & C. Meyer, 2001, Swarm intelligence, *Harvard Business Review*, 79(5): 107–114; D. J. Teece, G. Pisano, & A. Shuen, 1997, Dynamic capabilities and strategic management, *Strategic Management Journal*, 18: 509–533.

4. A. M. McGahan & M. E. Porter, 2003, The emergence and sustainability of abnormal profits, *Strategic Organization*, 1: 79–108; T. C. Powell, 2001, Competitive advantage: Logical and philosophical considerations, *Strategic Management Journal*, 22: 875–888.

5. P. Shrivastava, 1995, Ecocentric management for a risk society, *Academy of Management Review*, 20: 119.

6. F. Delmar, P. Davidsson, & W. B. Gartner, 2003, Arriving at a high-growth firm, *Journal of Business Venturing*, 18: 189–216.

7. R. P. Rumelt, D. E. Schendel, & D. J. Teece (eds.), 1994, *Fundamental Issues in Strategy*, Boston: Harvard Business School Press, 527–530.

8. M. J. Epstein & R. A. Westbrook, 2001, Linking actions to profits in strategic decision making, *Sloan Management Review*, 42(3): 39–49.

9. S. Dutta, M. J. Zbaracki, & M. Bergen, 2003, Pricing process as a capability: A resource-based perspective, *Strategic Management Journal*, 24: 615–630; Rumelt, Schendel, & Teece, *Fundamental Issues in Strategy*, 543–547.

10. S. Tallman & K. Fladmoe-Lindquist, 2002, Internationalization, globalization, and capability-based strategy, *California Management Review*, 45(1): 116–135; M. A. Hitt, R. D. Ireland, S. M. Camp, & D. L. Sexton, 2001, Strategic entrepreneurship: Entrepreneurial strategies for wealth creation, *Strategic Management Journal* 22(Special Issue): 479–491; S. A. Zahra, R. D. Ireland, & M. A. Hitt, 2000, International expansion by new venture firms: International diversity, mode of market entry, technological learning and performance, *Academy of Management Journal*, 43: 925–950.

11. P. Davidsson & B. Honig, 2003, The role of social and human capital among nascent entrepreneurs, *Journal of Business Venturing*, 18: 301–333; M. A. Hitt, L. Bierman, K. Shimizu, & R. Kochhar, 2001, Direct and moderating effects of human capital on strategy and performance in professional service firms, *Academy of Management Journal*, 44: 13–28.

12. A. Nair & S. Kotha, 2001, Does group membership matter? Evidence from the Japanese steel industry, *Strategic Management Journal*, 22: 221–235; A. M. McGahan & M. E. Porter, 1997, How much does industry matter, really? *Strategic Management Journal*, 18 (Special Issue): 15–30.

13. Sirmon & Hitt, Managing resources; J. B. Barney, 2001, Is the resource-based "view" a useful perspective for strategic management research? Yes, *Academy of Management Review*, 26: 41–56.

14. S. N. Mehta, 2001, Cisco fractures its own fairy tale, *Fortune*, 105–112.

15. S. Day, 2001, Shares surge after Cisco says its business has stabilized, *New York Times*, http://www.nytimes.com, August 25.

16. 2003, Cisco Systems 2002 Annual Report, http://www.cisco.com; K. Talley, 2003, Cisco, Apple and Dell advance, riding gains of tech shares, *Wall Street Journal Online*, http://www.wsj.com, May 6.

17. 2003, Bankruptcies, 2003, *Timesizing*, http://www.timesizing.com, February 15; M. Krantz, 2002, U.S. bankruptcies set record in 2002, *Honolulu Advertiser*, http://www.honoluluadvertiser.com, December 22.

18. Rumelt, Schendel, & Teece, *Fundamental Issues in Strategy*, 530.

19. C. J. Loomis, 1993, Dinosaurs, *Fortune*, May 3, 36–46.

20. V. Marsh, 1998, Attributes: Strong strategy tops the list, *Financial Times*, http://www.ft.com, November 30.

21. A. Barrett & D. Foust, 2003, Hot growth companies, *Business Week*, June 9, 74–77.

22. M. Farjoun, 2002, Towards an organic perspective on strategy, *Strategic Management Journal*, 23: 561–594.

23. A. Reinhardt, 1997, Paranoia, aggression, and other strengths, *Business Week*, October 13, 14; A. S. Grove, 1995, A high-tech CEO updates his views on managing and careers, *Fortune*, September 18, 229–230.

24. M. A. Hitt, B. W. Keats, & S. M. DeMarie, 1998, Navigating in the new competitive landscape: Building competitive advantage and strategic flexibility in the 21st century, *Academy of Management Executive*, 12(4): 22–42; R. A. Bettis & M. A. Hitt, 1995, The new competitive landscape, *Strategic Management Journal*, 16 (Special Issue): 7–19.

25. M. H. Zack, 2003, Rethinking the knowledge-based organization, *MIT Sloan Management Review*, 44(4): 67–71.

26. M. A. Hitt & V. Pisano, 2003, The cross-border merger and acquisition strategy, *Management Research*, 1: 133–144.

27. R. M. Grant, 2003, Strategic planning in a turbulent environment: Evidence from the oil majors, *Strategic Management Journal*, 24: 491–517.

28. R. A. D'Aveni, 1995, Coping with hypercompetition: Utilizing the new 7S's framework, *Academy of Management Executive*, 9(3): 46.

29. W. J. Ferrier, 2001, Navigating the competitive landscape: The drivers and consequences of competitive aggressiveness, *Academy of Management Journal*, 44: 858–877.

30. D. G. McKendrick, 2001, Global strategy and population level learning: The case of hard disk drives, *Strategic Management Journal*, 22: 307–334; T. P. Murtha, S. A. Lenway, & R. Bagozzi, 1998, Global mind-sets and cognitive shifts in a complex multinational corporation, *Strategic Management Journal*, 19: 97–114.

31. 2003, Economic Research Service, U.S. Department of Agriculture Long-term Macroeconomic Data, http://www.ers.usda.gov/data/macroeconomic/historicalrealGDPvalue.xls; S. Koudsi & L. A. Costa, 1998, America vs. the new Europe: By the numbers, *Fortune*, December 21, 149–156.

32. T. A. Stewart, 1993, The new face of American power, *Fortune*, July 26, 70–86.

33. S. Clegg & T. Kono, 2002, Trends in Japanese management: An overview of embedded continuities and disembedded discontinuities, *Asia Pacific Journal of Management*, 19: 269–285.

34. S. Garelli, 2001, Executive summary, *The World Competitiveness Yearbook*, http://www.imd.ch.wcy.esummary.

35. K. Kling & I. Goteman, 2003, IKEA CEO Anders Dahlvig on international growth and IKEA's unique corporate culture and brand identity, *Academy of Management Executive*, 17(1): 31–37.

36. Tallman & Fladmoe-Lindquist, Internationalization, globalization, and capability-based strategy; V. Govindarajan & A. K. Gupta, 2001, *The Quest for Global Dominance*, San Francisco: Jossey-Bass.

37. 2003, Wal-Mart website, http://www.walmartstores.com, May; D. Luhnow, 2001, Lower tariffs, retail muscle translate into big sales for Wal-Mart in Mexico, *Wall Street Journal Online*, http://www.wsj.com/articles, September 1.

38. 1999, Business: Ford swallows Volvo, *The Economist*, January 30, 58.

39. J. Porretto, 2002, Automakers face uncertain economy, growing foreign competition, union contract talks in 2003, *Dallas Morning News*, http://www.dallasnews.com, December.

40. Govindarajan & Gupta, *The Quest for Global Dominance*; R. Ruggiero, 1997, The high stakes of world trade, *Wall Street Journal*, April 28, A18.

41. M. Subramaniam & N. Venkataraman, 2001, Determinants of transnational new product development capability: Testing the influence of transferring and deploying tacit overseas knowledge, *Strategic Management Journal*, 22: 359–378; S. A. Zahra, 1999, The changing rules of global competitiveness in the 21st century, *Academy of Management Executive*, 13(1): 36–47; R. M. Kanter, 1995, Thriving locally in the global economy, *Harvard Business Review*, 73(5): 151–160.

42. D. E. Thomas, L. Eden, & M. A. Hitt, 2002, Who goes abroad? The role of knowledge and relation-based resources in emerging market firms' entry into developed markets, Paper presented at the Academy of Management, August; S. A. Zahra, R. D. Ireland, I. Gutierrez, & M. A. Hitt, 2000, Privatization and entrepreneurial transformation: Emerging issues and a future research agenda, *Academy of Management Review*, 25: 509–524.

43. L. Nachum, 2003, Does nationality of ownership make any difference and if so, under what circumstances? Professional service MNEs in global competition, *Journal of International Management*, 9: 1–32.

44. M. A. Hitt, D. Ahlstrom, M. T. Dacin, E. Levitas, & L. Svobodina, 2004, The institutional effects on strategic alliance partner selection in transition economies: China versus Russia, *Organization Science* (in press); M. W. Peng, 2002, Towards an institution-based view of business strategy, *Asia Pacific Journal of Management*, 19: 251–267.

45. S. Zaheer & E. Mosakowski, 1997, The dynamics of the liability of foreignness: A global study of survival in financial services, *Strategic Management Journal*, 18: 439–464.

46. D. Arnold, 2000, Seven rules of international distribution, *Harvard Business Review*, 78(6): 131–137; J. S. Black & H. B. Gregersen, 1999, The right way to manage expats, *Harvard Business Review*, 77(2): 52–63.

47. M. A. Hitt, R. E. Hoskisson, & H. Kim, 1997, International diversification: Effects on innovation and firm performance in product-diversified firms, *Academy of Management Journal*, 40: 767–798.

48. D'Aveni, Coping with hypercompetition, 46.

49. G. Hamel, 2001, Revolution vs. evolution: You need both, *Harvard Business Review*, 79(5): 150–156; T. Nakahara, 1997, Innovation in a borderless world economy, *Research-Technology Management*, May/June, 7–9.

50. G. Apfelthaler, H. J. Muller, & R. R. Rehder, 2002, Corporate global culture as competitive advantage: Learning from Germany and Japan in Alabama and Austria, *Journal of World Business*, 37: 108–118; J. Birkinshaw & N. Hood, 2001, Unleash innovation in foreign subsidiaries, *Harvard Business Review*, 79(3): 131–137.

51. J.-R. Lee & J-S. Chen, 2003, Internationalization, local adaptation and subsidiary's entrepreneurship: An exploratory study on Taiwanese manufacturing firms in Indonesia and Malaysia, *Asia Pacific Journal of Management*, 20: 51–72.

52. K. H. Hammonds, 2001, What is the state of the new economy? *Fast Company*, September, 101–104.

53. K. H. Hammonds, 2001, How do fast companies work now? *Fast Company*, September, 134–142; K. M. Eisenhardt, 1999, Strategy as strategic decision making, *Sloan Management Review*, 40(3): 65–72.

54. S. Lohr, 2003, Technology hits a midlife bump, *New York Times*, http://www.nytimes.com, May 4.

55. C. W. L. Hill, 1997, Establishing a standard: Competitive strategy and technological standards in winner-take-all industries, *Academy of Management Executive*, 11(2): 7–25.

56. C. Gilbert, 2003, The disruptive opportunity, *MIT Sloan Management Review*, 44(4): 27–32; C. M. Christiansen, 1997, *The Innovator's Dilemma*, Boston: Harvard Business School Press.

57. R. Adner, 2002, When are technologies disruptive? A demand-based view of the emergence of competition, *Strategic Management Journal*, 23: 667–688; G. Ahuja & C. M. Lampert, 2001, Entrepreneurship in the large corporation: A longitudinal study of how established firms create breakthrough inventions, *Strategic Management Journal*, 22(Special Issue): 521–543.

58. C. L. Nichols-Nixon & C. Y. Woo, 2003, Technology sourcing and output of established firms in a regime of encompassing technological change, *Strategic Management Journal*, 24: 651–666; C. W. L. Hill & F. T. Rothaermel, 2003, The performance of incumbent firms in the face of radical technological innovation, *Academy of Management Review*, 28: 257–274.

59. R. Amit & C. Zott, 2001, Value creation in e-business, *Strategic Management Journal*, 22(Special Issue): 493–520.

60. T. J. Mullaney, H. Green, M. Arndt, R. D. Hof, & L. Himmelstein, 2003, The e-biz surprise, *Business Week*, May 12, 60–68.

61. R. M. Kanter, 2001, *e-volve: Succeeding in the Digital Culture of Tomorrow*, Boston: Harvard Business School Press.

62. A. S. DeNisi, M. A. Hitt, & S. E. Jackson, 2003, The knowledge-based approach to sustainable competitive advantage, in S. E. Jackson, M. A. Hitt, & A. S. DeNisi (eds.), *Managing Knowledge for Sustained Competitive Advantage*, San Franciso: Jossey-Bass, 3–33.

63. S. K. McEvily & B. Chakravarthy, 2002, The persistence of knowledge-based advantage: An empirical test for product performance and technological knowledge, *Strategic Management Journal*, 23: 285–305; F. Warner, 2001, The drills for knowledge, *Fast Company*, September, 186–191; B. L. Simonin, 1999, Ambiguity and the process of knowledge transfer in strategic alliances, *Strategic Management Journal*, 20: 595–624.

64. A. W. King & C. P. Zeithaml, 2003, Measuring organizational knowledge: A conceptual and methodological framework, *Strategic Management Journal*, 24: 763–772; L. Rosenkopf & A. Nerkar, 2001, Beyond local search: Boundary-spanning, exploration, and impact on the optical disk industry, *Strategic Management Journal*, 22: 287–306.

65. Sirmon, Hitt, & Ireland, Managing the firm's resources.

66. K. Asakawa & M. Lehrer, 2003, Managing local knowledge assets globally: The role of regional innovation relays, *Journal of World Business*, 38: 31–42.

67. N. Worren, K. Moore, & P. Cardona, 2002, Modularity, strategic flexibility and firm performance: A study of the home appliance industry, *Strategic Management Journal*, 23: 1123–1140; K. R. Harrigan, 2001, Strategic flexibility in old and new economies, in M. A. Hitt, R. E. Freeman, & J. S. Harrison (eds.), *Handbook of Strategic Management*, Oxford, UK: Blackwell Publishers, 97–123.

68. H. Lee, M. A. Hitt, & E. Jeong, 2003, The impact of CEO and TMT characteristics on strategic flexibility and firm performance, Working paper, University of Connecticut; J. L. C. Cheng & I. F. Kesner, 1997, Organizational slack and response to environmental shifts: The impact of resource allocation patterns, *Journal of Management*, 23: 1–18.

69. M. A. Hitt, R. D. Ireland, & J. S. Harrison, 2001, Mergers and acquisitions: A value creating or value destroying strategy? in M. A. Hitt, R. E. Freeman, & J. S. Harrison (eds.), *Handbook of Strategic Management*, Oxford, UK: Blackwell Publishers, 384–408; W. Boeker, 1997, Strategic change: The influence of managerial characteristics and organizational growth, *Academy of Management Journal*, 40: 152–170.

70. K. Uhlenbruck, K. E. Meyer, & M. A. Hitt, 2003, Organizational transformation in transition economies: Resource-based and organizational learning perspectives, *Journal of Management Studies*, 40: 257–282; R. T. Pascale, 1999, Surviving the edge of chaos, *Sloan Management Review*, 40(3): 83–94.

71. R. E. Hoskisson, M. A. Hitt, W. P. Wan, & D. Yiu, 1999, Swings of a pendulum: Theory and research in strategic management, *Journal of Management*, 25: 417–456.

72. E. H. Bowman & C. E. Helfat, 2001, Does corporate strategy matter? *Strategic Management Journal*, 22: 1–23.

73. J. Shamsie, 2003, The context of dominance: An industry-driven framework for exploiting reputation, *Strategic Management Journal*, 24: 199–215; A. Seth & H. Thomas, 1994, Theories of the firm: Implications for strategy research, *Journal of Management Studies*, 31: 165–191.

74. Seth & Thomas, 169–173.

75. M. E. Porter, 1985, *Competitive Advantage*, New York: Free Press; M. E. Porter, 1980, *Competitive Strategy*, New York: Free Press.

76. A. M. McGahan, 1999, Competition, strategy and business performance, *California Management Review*, 41(3): 74–101; McGahan & Porter, How much does industry matter, really?

77. R. Henderson & W. Mitchell, 1997, The interactions of organizational and competitive influences on strategy and performance, *Strategic Management Journal* 18(Special Issue), 5–14; C. Oliver, 1997, Sustainable competitive advantage: Combining institutional and resource-based views, *Strategic Management Journal*, 18: 697–713; J. L. Stimpert & I. M. Duhaime, 1997, Seeing the big picture: The influence of industry, diversification, and business strategy on performance, *Academy of Management Journal*, 40: 560–583.

78. M. Blyler & R. W. Coff, 2003, Dynamic capabilities, social capital, and rent appropriation: Ties that split pies, *Strategic Management Journal*, 24: 677–686; C. Lee, K. Lee, & J. M. Pennings, 2001, Internal capabilities, external networks, and performance: A study on technology-based ventures, *Strategic Management Journal*, 22 (Special Issue): 615–640.

79. B.-S. Teng & J. L. Cummings, 2002, Trade-offs in managing resources and capabilities, *Academy of Management Executive*, 16(2): 81–91; R. L. Priem & J. E. Butler, 2001, Is the resource-based "view" a useful perspective for strategic management research? *Academy of Management Review*, 26: 22–40.

80. P. J. H. Schoemaker & R. Amit, 1994, Investment in strategic assets: Industry and firm-level perspectives, in P. Shrivastava, A. Huff, & J. Dutton (eds.), *Advances in Strategic Management*, Greenwich, CT: JAI Press, 9.

81. D. M. DeCarolis, 2003, Competencies and imitability in the pharmaceutical industry: An analysis of their relationship with firm performance, *Journal of Management*, 29: 27–50; Barney, Is the resource-based "view" a useful perspective for strategic management research? Yes; J. B. Barney, 1995, Looking inside for competitive advantage, *Academy of Management Executive*, 9(4): 56.

82. C. Zott, 2003, Dynamic capabilities and the emergence of intraindustry differential firm performance: Insights from a simulation study, *Strategic Management Journal*, 24: 97–125.

83. Davidsson & Honig, The role of social and human capital among nascent entrepreneurs.

84. R. D. Ireland, J. G. Covin, & D. F. Kuratko, 2003, Antecedents, elements, and consequences of corporate entrepreneurship as strategy, Working paper, University of Richmond.

85. G. Hawawini, V. Subramanian, & P. Verdin, 2003, Is performance driven by industry- or firm-specific factors? A new look at the evidence, *Strategic Management Journal*, 24: 1–16.

86. M. Makhija, 2003, Comparing the resource-based and market-based views of the firm: Empirical evidence from Czech privatization, *Strategic Management Journal*, 24: 433–451; T. J. Douglas & J. A. Ryman, 2003, Understanding competitive advantage in the general hospital industry: Evaluating strategic competencies, *Strategic Management Journal*, 24: 333–347.

87. G. Hamel & C. K. Prahalad, 1989, Strategic intent, *Harvard Business Review*, 67(3): 63–76.

88. Hamel & Prahalad, Strategic intent, 66.

89. P.-W. Tam, B. Orwall, & A. W. Mathews, 2003, As Apple stalls, Steve Jobs looks to digital entertainment, *Wall Street Journal*, April 25, A1, A5.

90. Hamel & Prahalad, Strategic intent, 64.

91. M. A. Hitt, D. Park, C. Hardee, & B. B. Tyler, 1995, Understanding strategic intent in the global marketplace, *Academy of Management Executive*, 9(2): 12–19.

92. R. D. Ireland & M. A. Hitt, 1992, Mission statements: Importance, challenge, and recommendations for development, *Business Horizons*, 35(3): 34–42.

93. W. J. Duncan, 1999, *Management: Ideas and Actions*, New York: Oxford University Press, 122–125.

94. R. M. Fulmer, 2001, Johnson & Johnson: Frameworks for leadership, *Organizational Dynamics*, 29(3): 211–220.

95. P. Martin, 1999, Lessons in humility, *Financial Times*, June 22, 18.

96. I. M. Levin, 2000, Vision revisited, *Journal of Applied Behavioral Science*, 36: 91–107.

97. I. R. Baum, E. A. Locke, & S. A. Kirkpatrick, 1998, A longitudinal study of the relation of vision and vision communication to venture growth in entrepreneurial firms, *Journal of Applied Psychology*, 83: 43–54.

98. J. Frooman, 1999, Stakeholder influence strategies, *Academy of Management Review*, 24: 191–205.

99. T. M. Jones & A. C. Wicks, 1999, Convergent stakeholder theory, *Academy of Management Review*, 24: 206–221; R. E. Freeman, 1984, *Strategic Management: A Stakeholder Approach*, Boston: Pitman, 53–54.

100. G. Donaldson & J. W. Lorsch, 1983, *Decision Making at the Top: The Shaping of Strategic Direction*, New York: Basic Books, 37–40.

101. A. J. Hillman & G. D. Keim, 2001, Shareholder value, stakeholder management, and social issues: What's the bottom line? *Strategic Management Journal*, 22: 125–139.

102. R. E. Freeman & J. McVea, 2001, A stakeholder approach to strategic management, in M. A. Hitt, R. E. Freeman, & J. S. Harrison (eds.), *Handbook of Strategic Management*, Oxford, UK: Blackwell Publishers, 189–207.

103. Ibid.

104. P. Brandes, R. Dharwadkar, & G. V. Lemesis, 2003, Effective employee stock option design: Reconciling stakeholder, strategic and motivational factors, *Academy of Management Executive*, 17(1): 77–93; A. McWilliams & D. Siegel, 2001, Corporate social responsibility: A theory of the firm perspective, *Academy of Management Review*, 26: 117–127.

105. Freeman & McVea, A stakeholder approach to strategic management; R. K. Mitchell, B. R. Agle, & D. J. Wood, 1997, Toward a theory of stakeholder identification and salience: Defining the principle of who and what really count, *Academy of Management Review*, 22: 853–886.

106. A. L. Hart & M. B. Milstein, 2003, Creating sustainable value, *Academy of Management Executive*, 17(2): 56–67.

107. Hitt, Bierman, Shimizu, & Kochhar, Direct and moderating effects of human capital.

108. S. Finkelstein, 2003, *Why Smart Executives Fail: And What You Can Learn from Their Mistakes*, New York: Portfolio-Penguin Putnam Publishers.

109. P. Bromiley, K. D. Miller, & D. Rau, 2001, Risk in strategic management research, in M. A. Hitt, R. E. Freeman, & J. S. Harrison (eds.), *Handbook of Strategic Management*, Oxford, UK: Blackwell Publishers, 259–288.

110. W. Shen & A. A. Cannella, 2003, Will succession planning increase shareholder wealth? Evidence from investor reactions to relay CEO successions, *Strategic Management Journal*, 24: 191–198.

111. W. Shen & A. A. Cannella, 2002, Revisiting the performance consequences of CEO succession: The impacts of successor type, postsuccession senior executive turnover and departing CEO tenure, *Academy of Management Journal*, 45: 717–733.

112. G. A. Bigley & M. F. Wiersema, 2002, New CEOs and corporate strategic focusing: How experience as heir apparent influences the use of power, *Administrative Science Quarterly*, 47: 707–727.

113. W. C. Taylor, 1999, Whatever happened to globalization? *Fast Company*, September, 288–294.

114. T. Leavitt, 1991, *Thinking about Management*, New York: Free Press, 9.

115. K. Lovelace, D. L. Shapiro, & L. R. Weingart, 2001, Maximizing cross-functional new product teams' innovativeness and constraint adherence: A conflict communications perspective, *Academy of Management Journal*, 44: 779–793.

116. J. Brett & L. K. Stroh, 2003, Working 61 plus hours a week: Why do managers do it? *Journal of Applied Psychology*, 88: 67–78.

117. M. Loeb, 1993, Steven J. Ross, 1927–1992, *Fortune*, January 25, 4.

118. 2003, Who killed Montana Power? *CBSNews*, http://www.cbsnews.com, February 10; B. Richards, 2001, For Montana Power, a broadband dream may turn out to be more of a nightmare, *Wall Street Journal Online*, http://www.wsj.com/articles, August 22.

119. O. Gadiesh & J. L. Gilbert, 1998, How to map your industry's profit pool, *Harvard Business Review*, 76(3): 149–162.

120. O. Gadiesh & J. L. Gilbert, 1998, Profit pools: A fresh look at strategy, *Harvard Business Review*, 76(3): 139–147.

121. M. J. Epstein & R. A. Westbrook, 2001, Linking actions to profits in strategic decision making, *Sloan Management Review*, 42(3): 39–49.

122. 2001, Trading places, *Forbes*, http://www.forbes.com, June 14.

123. R. D. Ireland, M. A. Hitt, S. M. Camp, & D. L. Sexton, 2001, Integrating entrepreneurship and strategic management actions to create firm wealth, *Academy of Management Executive*, 15(1): 49–63; Rumelt, Schendel, & Teece, *Fundamental Issues in Strategy*, 9–10.

124. L. K. Trevino & G. R. Weaver, 2003, *Managing Ethics in Business Organizations*, Stanford, CA: Stanford University Press; D. R. Gilbert, 2001, Corporate strategy and ethics as corporate strategy comes of age, in M. A. Hitt, R. E. Freeman, & J. S. Harrison (eds.), *Handbook of Strategic Management*, Oxford, UK: Blackwell Publishers, 564–582.

The External Environment: Opportunities, Threats, Industry Competition, and Competitor Analysis

Chapter Two

Knowledge Objectives

Studying this chapter should provide you with the strategic management knowledge needed to:

1. Explain the importance of analyzing and understanding the firm's external environment.

2. Define and describe the general environment and the industry environment.

3. Discuss the four activities of the external environmental analysis process.

4. Name and describe the general environment's six segments.

5. Identify the five competitive forces and explain how they determine an industry's profit potential.

6. Define strategic groups and describe their influence on the firm.

7. Describe what firms need to know about their competitors and different methods used to collect intelligence about them.

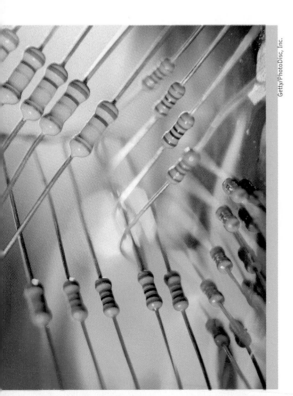

Getty/PhotoDisc, Inc.

High-technology products and services have languished in the recent poor economic climate. One example of a company that has struggled to regain its former profitability is Sun Microsystems. As we saw in Chapter 1, one of the keys to turning around this company—and the industry in general—is continuous innovation.

The Economic Aftermath in High Technology: Will We Ever See the Sun Set?

The economic malaise experienced in the early part of the 21st century hit the high-technology firms especially hard. Analysts argue that it is more than a reaction to the "bubble years" in the 1990s. They suggest that the industry (actually several overlapping industries such as hardware, software, and Internet commerce) has entered a post-technology era. Many hardware products are almost becoming commodities where costs, along with quality and service, are important competitive characteristics. Additionally, the power has shifted from the supplier to the customer. Yet, many expect that the industry will continue to deliver innovation, and it has become a highly important economic engine in the United States. The high-technology industry accounts for approximately 10 percent of the U.S. economy and 60 percent of the capital spending by U.S. businesses.

There are many facets of the high-technology industry, but one of its former stars is struggling, perhaps for its very survival. Sun Microsystems once enjoyed $64 a share for its stock, but the share price fell to below $3. Scott McNealy, the founder and CEO, remains in firm control and is convinced that he has the company headed toward success. While critics believe that Sun needs to control its costs more effectively, McNealy is spending heavily on R&D to enhance innovation that will serve as a catalyst for revenue growth. His goal is to introduce sophisticated new computer hardware and cutting-edge software. In fact, in 2003, Sun introduced several new hardware and software products to increase its competitiveness in the market. These new products are directly competitive with IBM and Hewlett-Packard (HP) and target product areas in which both firms currently have products, especially network technology.

Sun faces a weak economic climate and especially strong competition from several quarters. None of its competitors is remaining static. For example, IBM's new CEO is developing a strategy of offering computing power on demand (similar to water or electricity). In this way, customers do not have to invest substantial capital in equipment and software or in knowledgeable human resources and worry about underutilizing the assets. Rather, they pay only for what they need, and they always receive high-quality service. Additionally, Sun cannot overlook Dell Inc. Dell is expanding its product lines and services and has dropped the word "computer" from its name to better represent the product lines it is planning. And, Dell was recently ranked among the top ten best-managed companies and was ranked as the second best technology firm. Sun was not ranked among the top 100. Most of Sun's competitors were among the top 100 technology companies, however.

Sun has survived and overcome major obstacles in the past. Additionally, it is investing in innovation, noted in Chapter 1 to be critical to success in most industries. There is little doubt as to the importance of innovation in the high-technology industry. Sun must even watch out for a non-firm, Linux, the open source operating system, pushed by a group of technology specialists to compete with Microsoft. Linux is backed by Intel, HP, IBM, and Dell Inc. and is being used in a number of technology-based products. Thus, Sun exists in a critical industry where innovation is required for survival. It is also an industry populated by a formidable group of competitors. Sun faces a difficult economic climate and a world of uncertainties, all of which heightens the uncertainty of its future.

SOURCES: S. Hamm, S. Rosenbush, & C. Edwards, 2003, Tech comes out swinging, *Business Week*, June 23, 62–66; S. Lohr, 2003, Technology hits a midlife bump, *New York Times*, http://www.nytimes.com, May 4; G. McWilliams, 2003, Dell pushes PC strategy into corporate products, *Wall Street Journal Online*, http://www.wsj.com, April 3; 2003, The ranking, *Business Week*, Spring (Special Annual Issue), 44–56; G. McWilliams, 2003, Pay as you go, *Wall Street Journal*, March 31, R8; 2003, Dell enters printer market, stepping up rivalry with H-P, *Wall Street Journal Online*, http://www.wsj.com, March 26; S. E. Ante, 2003, The new blue, *Business Week*, March 17, 80–88; J. Greens, 2003, The Linux uprising, *Business Week*, March 3, 78–86; S. Lohr, 2003, Sun rolls out its new effort to gain edge over 2 rivals, *New York Times*, http://www.nytimes.com, February 10; 2003, The best and worst managers of the year, *Business Week*, January 13, 58–92; J. Kerstetter & J. Greens, 2002, Will Sun rise again? *Business Week*, November 25, 120–130.

Companies' experiences and research suggest that the external environment affects firm growth and profitability.[1] Major political events such as the war in Iraq, the strength of separate nations' economies at different times, and the emergence of new technologies are a few examples of conditions in the external environment that affect firms in the United States and throughout the world. External environmental conditions such as these create threats to and opportunities for firms that, in turn, have major effects on their strategic actions.[2]

The economic problems in the early 21st century affected all industries, most negatively, but one of the industries hurt the most was high technology. Many firms in the industry were hurt, and some ceased to exist. Some firms, such as IBM, are beginning to turn around their performance, and others, such as Dell Inc., seem to continue to do well. However, one formerly successful firm, Sun Microsystems, continues to perform poorly. Its founder and CEO, Scott McNealy, claims that because of its innovation in hardware and software products, Sun will again thrive in the industry. Based on what we learned in Chapter 1, innovation is a key to success, particularly in the high-technology industry. Thus, it appears that Sun is taking the correct actions, despite analysts' criticisms. However, Sun also faces significant competition, continuing economic conditions that are challenging, and a highly uncertain environment. Regardless of the industry, the external environment is critical to a firm's survival and success. This chapter focuses on what firms do to analyze and understand the external environment. As the discussion of the high-technology industry shows, the external environment influences the firm's strategic options as well as the decisions made in light of them. The firm's understanding of the external environment is matched with knowledge about its internal environment (discussed in the next chapter) to form its strategic intent, to develop its strategic mission, and to take actions that result in strategic competitiveness and above-average returns (see Figure 1.1).

As noted in Chapter 1, the environmental conditions in the current global economy differ from those previously faced by firms. Technological changes and the continuing growth of information gathering and processing capabilities demand more timely and effective competitive actions and responses.[3] The rapid sociological changes occurring in many countries affect labor practices and the nature of products demanded by increasingly diverse consumers. Governmental policies and laws also affect where and how firms may choose to compete.[4] Deregulation and local government changes, such as those in the global electric utilities industry, affect not only the general competitive environment, but also the strategic decisions made by companies competing globally. To achieve strategic competitiveness, firms must be aware of and understand the different dimensions of the external environment.

Firms understand the external environment by acquiring information about competitors, customers, and other stakeholders to build their own base of knowledge and capabilities.[5] Firms may use this base to imitate the capabilities of their able competitors (and even may imitate successful firms in other industries), and they may use it to build new knowledge and capabilities to achieve a competitive advantage. On the basis of the new information, knowledge, and capabilities, firms may take actions to buffer themselves against environmental effects or to build relationships with stakeholders in their environment.[6] To strengthen their knowledge and capabilities and to take actions that buffer or build bridges to external stakeholders, organizations must effectively analyze the external environment.

The General, Industry, and Competitor Environments

An integrated understanding of the external and internal environments is essential for firms to understand the present and predict the future.[7] As shown in Figure 2.1, a firm's external environment is divided into three major areas: the general, industry, and competitor environments.

The **general environment** is composed of dimensions in the broader society that influence an industry and the firms within it.[8] We group these dimensions into six

*The **general environment** is composed of dimensions in the broader society that influence an industry and the firms within it.*

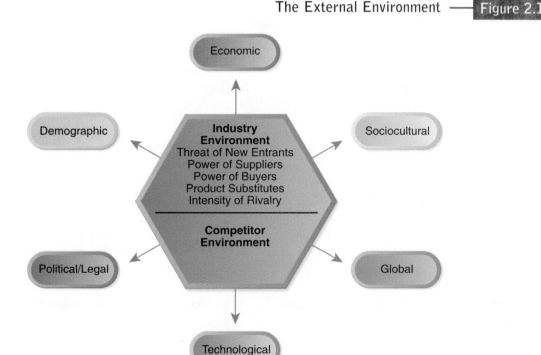

The External Environment — Figure 2.1

environmental *segments:* demographic, economic, political/legal, sociocultural, technological, and global. Examples of *elements* analyzed in each of these segments are shown in Table 2.1.

Firms cannot directly control the general environment's segments and elements. Accordingly, successful companies gather the information required to understand each segment and its implications for the selection and implementation of the appropriate strategies. For example, most firms have little individual effect on the U.S. economy, although that economy has a major effect on their ability to operate and even survive. Thus, companies around the globe were challenged to understand the effects of this economy's decline on their current and future strategies. Certainly, this is the case for Sun Microsystems as explained in the Opening Case. And there are legitimate differences of opinion regarding the particular strategies that should be followed in reaction to the economic changes. Analysts argue that Sun should be controlling costs while Sun's CEO believes that he must invest heavily in R&D if Sun is to succeed over time. We soon may learn whose evaluation of the environment and strategies was the most appropriate in Sun's case.

The **industry environment** *is the set of factors that directly influences a firm and its competitive actions and competitive responses: the threat of new entrants, the power of suppliers, the power of buyers, the threat of product substitutes, and the intensity of rivalry among competitors.*

The **industry environment** is the set of factors that directly influences a firm and its competitive actions and competitive responses: the threat of new entrants, the power of suppliers, the power of buyers, the threat of product substitutes, and the intensity of rivalry among competitors. In total, the interactions among these five factors determine an industry's profit potential. The challenge is to locate a position within an industry where a firm can favorably influence those factors or where it can successfully defend against their influence. In fact, positioning is a major issue for Sun Microsystems, discussed in the Opening Case. It faces substantial competitive rivalry. The greater a firm's capacity to favorably influence its industry environment, the greater is the likelihood that the firm will earn above-average returns.

Table 2.1	The General Environment: Segments and Elements	
Demographic Segment	• Population size • Age structure • Geographic distribution	• Ethnic mix • Income distribution
Economic Segment	• Inflation rates • Interest rates • Trade deficits or surpluses • Budget deficits or surpluses	• Personal savings rate • Business savings rates • Gross domestic product
Political/Legal Segment	• Antitrust laws • Taxation laws • Deregulation philosophies	• Labor training laws • Educational philosophies and policies
Sociocultural Segment	• Women in the workforce • Workforce diversity • Attitudes about the quality of work life	• Concerns about the environment • Shifts in work and career preferences • Shifts in preferences regarding product and service characteristics
Technological Segment	• Product innovations • Applications of knowledge	• Focus of private and government-supported R&D expenditures • New communication technologies
Global Segment	• Important political events • Critical global markets	• Newly industrialized countries • Different cultural and institutional attributes

How companies gather and interpret information about their competitors is called *competitor analysis.* Understanding the firm's competitor environment complements the insights provided by studying the general and industry environments. Understanding its competitor environment may be critical to Sun Microsystems' survival.

Analysis of the general environment is focused on the future; analysis of the industry environment is focused on the factors and conditions influencing a firm's profitability within its industry; and analysis of competitors is focused on predicting the dynamics of competitors' actions, responses, and intentions. In combination, the results of the three analyses the firm uses to understand its external environment influence its strategic intent, strategic mission, and strategic actions. Although we discuss each analysis separately, performance improves when the firm integrates the insights provided by analyses of the general environment, the industry environment, and the competitor environment.

External Environmental Analysis

Most firms face external environments that are highly turbulent, complex, and global—conditions that make interpreting them increasingly difficult.[9] To cope with what are often ambiguous and incomplete environmental data and to increase their understanding of the general environment, firms engage in a process called external environmental analysis. The continuous process includes four activities: scanning, monitoring, forecasting, and assessing (see Table 2.2). Those analyzing the external environment should understand that completing this analysis is a difficult, yet significant, activity.[10]

An important objective of studying the general environment is identifying opportunities and threats. An **opportunity** is a condition in the general environment that, if exploited, helps a company achieve strategic competitiveness. For example, the fact that 1 billion of the world's total population of 6.1 billion has cheap access to a telephone is a huge opportunity for global telecommunications companies.[11] And, global telephone use is growing at a rate of more than 300 billion minutes annually.[12] A **threat** is a condition in the general environment that may hinder a company's efforts to achieve strategic competitiveness.[13] The once revered firm Polaroid can attest to the seriousness of external threats. Polaroid was a leader in its industry and considered one of the top 50 firms in the United States, but it filed for bankruptcy in 2001. When its competitors developed photographic equipment using digital technology, Polaroid was unprepared and never responded effectively. Mired in substantial debt, Polaroid was unable to reduce its costs to acceptable levels (and unable to repay its debt) and eventually had to declare bankruptcy. In 2002, the former Polaroid Corp. was sold to Bank One's OEP Imaging unit, which promptly changed its name to Polaroid Corp. The old

An opportunity is a condition in the general environment that, if exploited, helps a company achieve strategic competitiveness.

A threat is a condition in the general environment that may hinder a company's efforts to achieve strategic competitiveness.

Components of the External Environmental Analysis — Table 2.2

Scanning	• Identifying early signals of environmental changes and trends
Monitoring	• Detecting meaning through ongoing observations of environmental changes and trends
Forecasting	• Developing projections of anticipated outcomes based on monitored changes and trends
Assessing	• Determining the timing and importance of environmental changes and trends for firms' strategies and their management

©Royalty-Free/CORBIS

Polaroid was renamed Primary PDC, Inc., but is barely in existence.[14] As these examples indicate, opportunities suggest competitive *possibilities*, while threats are potential *constraints*.

Several sources can be used to analyze the general environment, including a wide variety of printed materials (such as trade publications, newspapers, business publications, and the results of academic research and public polls), trade shows and suppliers, customers, and employees of public-sector organizations.[15] External network contacts can be particularly rich sources of information on the environment.[16] People in "boundary-spanning" positions can obtain much information. Salespersons, purchasing managers, public relations directors, and customer service representatives, each of whom interacts with external constituents, are examples of individuals in boundary-spanning positions.[17]

An old Polaroid camera now looks like an artifact that represents an earlier stage of technological development in photography. Since the time when Polaroid was a leader in the industry, other companies have long surpassed its success through the innovation of digital photography. The bankruptcy of Polaroid bears testimony to the importance of responding effectively to external threats.

Scanning

Scanning entails the study of all segments in the general environment. Through scanning, firms identify early signals of potential changes in the general environment and detect changes that are already under way.[18] When scanning, the firm often deals with ambiguous, incomplete, or unconnected data and information. Environmental scanning is critically important for firms competing in highly volatile environments.[19] In addition, scanning activities must be aligned with the organizational context; a scanning system designed for a volatile environment is inappropriate for a firm in a stable environment.[20]

Some analysts expect the pressure brought to bear by the early retirement trend on countries such as the United States, France, Germany, and Japan to be quite significant and challenging. Governments in these countries appear to be offering state-funded pensions to their future elderly populations—but the costs of those pensions cannot be met with the present taxes and social security contribution rates.[21] Firms selling financial planning services and options should analyze this trend to determine if it represents an opportunity for them to help governments find ways to meet their responsibilities.

The Internet provides multiple opportunities for scanning. For example, Amazon.com, similar to many Internet companies, records significant information about individuals visiting its website, particularly if a purchase is made. Amazon then welcomes these customers by name when they visit the website again. The firm even sends messages to them about specials and new products similar to those purchased in previous visits. Additionally, many websites and advertisers on the Internet obtain information from those who visit their sites using files called "cookies." These files are saved to the visitors' hard drives, allowing customers to connect more quickly to a firm's website, but also allowing the firm to solicit a variety of information about them. Because cookies are often placed without customers' knowledge, their use can be a questionable practice. Recently, a privacy standard, Platform for Privacy Preferences, was developed that provides more control over these "digital messengers" and allows users to block the cookies from their hard drives.[22]

PART 1 / Strategic Management Inputs

Monitoring

When *monitoring,* analysts observe environmental changes to see if an important trend is emerging from among those spotted by scanning.[23] Critical to successful monitoring is the firm's ability to detect meaning in different environmental events and trends. For example, the size of the middle class of African Americans continues to grow in the United States. With increasing wealth, this group of citizens is beginning to more aggressively pursue investment options.[24] Companies in the financial planning sector could monitor this change in the economic segment to determine the degree to which a competitively important trend and a business opportunity are emerging. By monitoring trends, firms can be prepared to introduce new goods and services at the appropriate time to take advantage of the opportunities these trends provide.[25]

Effective monitoring requires the firm to identify important stakeholders. Because the importance of different stakeholders can vary over a firm's life cycle, careful attention must be given to the firm's needs and its stakeholder groups across time.[26] Scanning and monitoring are particularly important when a firm competes in an industry with high technological uncertainty.[27] Scanning and monitoring not only can provide the firm with information, they also serve as a means of importing new knowledge about markets and how to successfully commercialize new technologies that the firm has developed.[28]

Forecasting

Scanning and monitoring are concerned with events and trends in the general environment at a point in time. When *forecasting,* analysts develop feasible projections of what might happen, and how quickly, as a result of the changes and trends detected through scanning and monitoring.[29] For example, analysts might forecast the time that will be required for a new technology to reach the marketplace, the length of time before different corporate training procedures are required to deal with anticipated changes in the composition of the workforce, or how much time will elapse before changes in governmental taxation policies affect consumers' purchasing patterns.

Forecasting events and outcomes accurately is challenging. For example, in 2001, few would have forecasted that the U.S. Federal Reserve Board would lower the federal funds rate, which affects the short-term interest that banks charge customers, to 1 percent. Others might not have forecasted a war in Iraq in 2003. Thus, uncertainty makes forecasting a difficult task.

Assessing

The objective of *assessing* is to determine the timing and significance of the effects of environmental changes and trends on the strategic management of the firm.[30] Through scanning, monitoring, and forecasting, analysts are able to understand the general environment. Going a step farther, the intent of assessment is to specify the implications of that understanding for the organization. Without assessment, the firm is left with data that may be interesting but are of unknown competitive relevance.

Cosi, Inc., a relatively small fast-food chain with 90 stores, announced it lost $114 million in 2002. Cosi provides a good product. The food is tasty, and the stores have a lively décor. It also has some unique but flavorful sandwiches. However, while it has many positive qualities, Cosi expanded without adequate assessment of its external environment. Its all-day service throws it into competition not only with McDonald's, but also Starbucks, especially in the mornings. Recently, the firm announced that it would eliminate its all company-owned stores strategy and move to franchises. Analysts worry, however, that the firm's management has not fully assessed the challenges and requirements of successful franchising. Thus, there is much more to success than providing a good product to customers.[31]

The general environment is composed of segments (and their individual elements) that are external to the firm (see Table 2.1). Although the degree of impact varies, these environmental segments affect each industry and its firms. The challenge to the firm is to scan, monitor, forecast, and assess those elements in each segment that are of the greatest importance. Resulting from these efforts should be recognition of environmental changes, trends, opportunities, and threats. Opportunities are then matched with a firm's core competencies (the matching process is discussed further in Chapter 3).

The Demographic Segment

The **demographic segment** is concerned with a population's size, age structure, geographic distribution, ethnic mix, and income distribution.[32] Demographic segments are analyzed on a global basis because of their potential effects across countries' borders and because many firms compete in global markets.

POPULATION SIZE

Before the end of 2005, the world's population is expected to be slightly less than 6.5 billion, up from 6.1 billion in 2000. Combined, China and India accounted for one-third of the 6.1 billion. Experts speculate that the population might stabilize at 10 billion after 2200 if the deceleration in the rate of increase in the world's head count continues. By 2050, India (with over 1.5 billion people projected) and China (with just under 1.5 billion people projected) are expected to be the most populous countries.[33]

Observing demographic changes in populations highlights the importance of this environmental segment. For example, some advanced nations have a negative population growth, after discounting the effects of immigration. In 2002, Bulgaria had the lowest birthrate, with slightly over 8 births per 1,000 citizens, while Niger had the highest birthrate, with almost 50 per 1,000 citizens. The birthrate in the United States is slightly above 14 for every 1,000 people.[34] However, some believe that a baby boom will occur in the United States during the first 12 years of the 21st century and that by 2012, the annual number of births could exceed 4.3 million. Such a birthrate in the United States would equal the all-time high that was set in 1957.[35] These projections suggest major 21st-century challenges and business opportunities.

AGE STRUCTURE

In some countries, the population's average age is increasing. For example, worldwide, the number of people aged 65 and older is projected to grow by 88 percent, or almost one million people per month, by 2025.[36] Contributing to this growth are increasing life expectancies. This trend may suggest numerous opportunities for firms to develop goods and services to meet the needs of an increasingly older population. For example, GlaxoSmithKline has created a program for low-income elderly people without prescription drug coverage. The program provides drugs to these individuals at a 25 percent reduction in price. The firm's intent is to increase its sales and provide an important service to a population who might not be able to afford the drugs otherwise.[37]

It has been projected that up to one-half of the females and one-third of the males born at the end of the 1990s in

The demographic segment is concerned with a population's size, age structure, geographic distribution, ethnic mix, and income distribution.

An analysis of the external environment would include population size, which is one of the components of the *demographic segment.* China is expected to have approximately 1.5 billion people by the year 2050. How will this affect how firms make decisions in their strategy for global business? What future challenges might arise from the expected population growth in Asia?

AP Photo/Str

developed countries could live to be 100 years old, with some of them possibly living to be 200 or more.[38] Also, the odds that a U.S. baby boomer (a person born between the years 1946 and 1964) will reach age 90 are now one in nine.[39] If these life spans become a reality, a host of interesting business opportunities and societal issues will emerge. For example, the effect on individuals' pension plans will be significant and will create potential opportunities for financial institutions, as well as possible threats to government-sponsored retirement and health plans.[40]

GEOGRAPHIC DISTRIBUTION

For decades, the U.S. population has been shifting from the north and east to the west and south. Similarly, the trend of relocating from metropolitan to non-metropolitan areas continues and may well accelerate with the terrorist attacks in New York City and Washington, D.C. These trends are changing local and state governments' tax bases. In turn, business firms' decisions regarding location are influenced by the degree of support different taxing agencies offer as well as the rates at which these agencies tax businesses.

The geographic distribution of populations throughout the world is also affected by the capabilities resulting from advances in communications technology. Through computer technologies, for example, people can remain in their homes, communicating with others in remote locations to complete their work.

ETHNIC MIX

The ethnic mix of countries' populations continues to change. Within the United States, the ethnicity of states and their cities varies significantly. For firms, the challenge is to be sensitive to these changes. Through careful study, companies can develop and market products that satisfy the unique needs of different ethnic groups.

Changes in the ethnic mix also affect a workforce's composition. In the United States, for example, the population and labor force will continue to diversify, as immigration accounts for a sizable part of growth. Projections are that the Latino and Asian population shares will increase to 34 percent of the total U.S. population by 2050. By 2006, it is expected that (1) 72.7 percent of the U.S. labor force will be white non-Latino (down from 75.3 percent in 1996), (2) 11.7 percent will be Latino (compared with 9.5 percent in 1996), (3) 11.6 percent will be African American (up from 11.3 percent in 1996), and (4) 5.4 percent will be Asian (up from 4.3 percent in 1996). By 2020, white non-Latino workers will make up only 68 percent of the workforce.[41]

As with the U.S. labor force, other countries also are witnessing a trend toward an older workforce. By 2030, the proportion of the total labor force of 45- to 59-year-olds of countries in the Organisation for Economic Co-operation and Development (industrialized countries) is projected to increase from 25.6 to 31.8 percent; the share of workers aged 60 and over is expected to increase from 4.7 to 7.8 percent. Because a labor force can be critical to competitive success, firms across the globe, including those competing in OECD countries, must learn to work effectively with labor forces that are becoming more diverse and older.[42]

Workforce diversity is also a sociocultural issue. Effective management of a culturally diverse workforce can produce a competitive advantage. For example, heterogeneous work teams have been shown to produce more effective strategic analyses, more creativity and innovation, and higher-quality decisions than homogeneous work teams.[43] However, evidence also suggests that diverse work teams are difficult to manage to achieve these outcomes.[44]

INCOME DISTRIBUTION

Understanding how income is distributed within and across populations informs firms of different groups' purchasing power and discretionary income. Studies of income distributions suggest that although living standards have improved over time, variations exist within and between nations.[45] Of interest to firms are the average incomes of households and individuals. For instance, the increase in dual-career couples has had a notable effect on average incomes. Although real income has been declining in general, the income of dual-career couples has increased. These figures yield strategically relevant information for firms.

The Economic Segment

The health of a nation's economy affects individual firms and industries. Because of this, companies study the economic environment to identify changes, trends, and their strategic implications.

The economic environment refers to the nature and direction of the economy in which a firm competes or may compete.

The **economic environment** refers to the nature and direction of the economy in which a firm competes or may compete.[46] Because nations are interconnected as a result of the global economy, firms must scan, monitor, forecast, and assess the health of economies outside their host nation. For example, many nations throughout the world are affected by the U.S. economy.

The U.S. economy declined into a recession in 2001 that extended into 2002. However, the economy remained weak in 2003 despite efforts to revive it by the U.S. government. Interest rates in the United States reached almost record lows in 2003, equaling the rates in 1958.[47] Additionally, global trade grew in the last two decades of the 20th century. For example, equity market capitalization grew by 1,300 percent during this period to $36 trillion. The U.S. capital markets grew by 3,500 percent to $2.6 trillion.[48] Globalization and opening of new markets such as China contributed to this phenomenal growth. While bilateral trade can enrich the economies of the countries involved, it also makes each country more vulnerable to negative events. For example, the September 11, 2001, terrorist attacks in the United States have had more than a $100 billion negative effect on the U.S. economy. As a result, the European Union (E.U.) also suffered negative economic effects because of the reduction in bilateral trade between the United States and the E.U.[49]

As our discussion of the economic segment suggests, economic issues are intertwined closely with the realities of the external environment's political/legal segment.

The Political/Legal Segment

The political/legal segment is the arena in which organizations and interest groups compete for attention, resources, and a voice in overseeing the body of laws and regulations guiding the interactions among nations.

The **political/legal segment** is the arena in which organizations and interest groups compete for attention, resources, and a voice in overseeing the body of laws and regulations guiding the interactions among nations.[50] Essentially, this segment represents how organizations try to influence government and how governments influence them. Constantly changing, the segment influences the nature of competition (see Table 2.1). For example, there has been a significant global trend toward privatization of government-owned or -regulated firms. The transformation from state-owned to private firms has substantial implications for the competitive landscapes in countries and industries.[51]

Firms must carefully analyze a new political administration's business-related policies and philosophies. Antitrust laws, taxation laws, industries chosen for deregulation, labor training laws, and the degree of commitment to educational institutions are areas in which an administration's policies can affect the operations and profitability of industries and individual firms. Often, firms develop a political strategy to influence governmental policies and actions that might affect them. The effects of global governmental policies on a firm's competitive position increase the importance of forming an effective political strategy.[52]

Business firms across the globe today confront an interesting array of political/legal questions and issues. For example, the debate continues over trade policies. Some believe that a nation should erect trade barriers to protect products produced by its companies. Others argue that free trade across nations serves the best interests of individual countries and their citizens. The International Monetary Fund (IMF) classifies trade barriers as restrictive when tariffs total at least 25 percent of a product's price. At the other extreme, the IMF stipulates that a nation has open trade when its tariffs are below 9 percent. To foster trade, New Zealand initially cut its tariffs from 16 to 8.5 percent and then to 3 percent in 2000. Colombia reduced its tariffs to less than 12 percent. The IMF classifies this percentage as "relatively open."[53] Additionally, extensive trade networks are developing among the United States, Europe, Latin America, and Asia. For example, European firms acquired over 800 U.S. companies in 2000 alone.[54]

The regulations related to pharmaceuticals and telecommunications, along with the approval or disapproval of major acquisitions, shows the power of government entities. This power also suggests how important it is for firms to have a political strategy. Alternatively, the Food and Drug Administration (FDA) was criticized in 2003 for being too slow to act. A letter to TAP Pharmaceutical Products to stop misleading advertising for its drug Prevacid was held up 78 days for review by the office of the FDA's chief council. External critics with knowledge of agency operations expressed concerns that the FDA was limiting enforcement actions to avoid potential litigation. Thus, the regulations are too few for some and too many for others. Regardless, regulations tend to vary with different presidential administrations, and firms must cope with these variances.[55]

The Sociocultural Segment

The **sociocultural segment** is concerned with a society's attitudes and cultural values. Because attitudes and values form the cornerstone of a society, they often drive demographic, economic, political/legal, and technological conditions and changes.

Sociocultural segments differ across countries. For example, in the United States, 13.1 percent of the nation's GDP is spent on health care. This is the highest percentage of any country in the world. Germany allocates 10.4 percent of GDP to health care, while in Switzerland the percentage is 10.2. Interestingly, the U.S. rate of citizens' access to health care is below that of these and other countries.[56] Countries' citizens have different attitudes about retirement savings as well. In Italy, just 9 percent of citizens say that they are saving primarily for retirement, while the percentages are 18 in Germany and 48 in the United States.[57] Attitudes regarding saving for retirement affect a nation's economic and political/legal segments.

In the United States, boundaries between work and home are becoming blurred, as employees' workweeks continue to be stretched, perhaps because a strong Protestant work ethic is a part of the U.S. culture. Describing a culture's effect on a society, columnist George Will suggested that it is vital for people to understand that a nation's culture has a primary effect on its social character and health.[58] Thus, companies must understand the implications of a society's attitudes and its cultural values to offer products that meet consumers' needs.

A significant trend in many countries is increased workforce diversity. As noted earlier, the composition of the U.S. workforce is changing such that Caucasians will be in the minority

The sociocultural segment is concerned with a society's attitudes and cultural values.

As the U.S. population becomes more diverse and the number of businesses owned by women continues to increase, we can expect more service businesses like this one to appear. Currently over half of the businesses owned by women are in services such as restaurants. Whereas this restaurant would currently be considered a minority-run business, that will soon no longer be the case as Caucasians become the next minority.

©Ariel Skelley/CORBIS

in a few years. Thus, firms are trying to diversify their employee bases, but also must contend with a complex set of laws and regulations. For example, in a recent ruling, the U.S. Supreme Court declared the use of race in college and university admissions decisions to be legal if it was for the purposes of creating useful diversity among the student population and providing access to economic success for all regardless of race.[59]

As diversity increases, so does the size of the labor force in the United States. In 1993, the total workforce was slightly below 130 million, but in 2003, it was slightly over 146 million.[60] An increasing number of women are also starting and managing their own businesses. For example, the U.S. Census Bureau reports that women own approximately 5.4 million businesses that generate $819 billion in annual sales. The Center for Women's Business Research suggests that these figures substantially understate the number of women-owned businesses. The center claims that women started over 9 million businesses in 2000. Approximately 55 percent of women-owned businesses are in services, with the second largest group (about 18 percent) in some form of retailing. The number of new businesses started by women continues to increase, and thus women own a larger percentage of the total number of businesses.[61]

The growing gender, ethnic, and cultural diversity in the workforce creates challenges and opportunities,[62] including those related to combining the best of both men's and women's traditional leadership styles for a firm's benefit and identifying ways to facilitate all employees' contributions to forming and using their firm's strategies. Some companies provide training to nurture women's and ethnic minorities' leadership potential. Changes in organizational structure and management practices often are required to eliminate subtle barriers that may exist. Learning to manage diversity in the domestic workforce can increase a firm's effectiveness in managing a globally diverse workforce, as the firm acquires more international operations.

Another manifestation of changing attitudes toward work is the continuing growth of contingency workers (part-time, temporary, and contract employees) throughout the global economy. This trend is significant in several parts of the world, including Canada, Japan, Latin America, Western Europe, and the United States. The fastest growing group of contingency workers is in the technical and professional area. Contributing to this growth are corporate restructurings and downsizings in poor economic conditions along with a breakdown of lifetime employment practices (e.g., in Japan).

The continued growth of suburban communities in the United States and abroad is another major sociocultural trend. The increasing number of people living in the suburbs has a number of effects. For example, because of the resulting often-longer commute times to urban businesses, there is pressure for better transportation systems and superhighway systems (e.g., outer beltways to serve the suburban communities). On the other hand, some businesses are locating in the suburbs closer to their employees. Suburban growth also has an effect on the number of electronic telecommuters, which is expected to increase rapidly in the 21st century. This work-style option is feasible because of changes in the technological segment, including the Internet's rapid growth and evolution.[63]

The Technological Segment

Pervasive and diversified in scope, technological changes affect many parts of societies. These effects occur primarily through new products, processes, and materials. The **technological segment** includes the institutions and activities involved with creating new knowledge and translating that knowledge into new outputs, products, processes, and materials.

Given the rapid pace of technological change, it is vital for firms to thoroughly study the technological segment. The importance of these efforts is suggested by the finding that early adopters of new technology often achieve higher market shares and

The technological segment includes the institutions and activities involved with creating new knowledge and translating that knowledge into new outputs, products, processes, and materials.

earn higher returns. Thus, executives must verify that their firm is continuously scanning the external environment to identify potential substitutes for technologies that are in current use, as well as to spot newly emerging technologies from which their firm could derive competitive advantage.[64]

The importance of technology in business and our daily lives has never been greater. A fully automated plant that operates 24 hours a day exemplifies this fact. In fact, when employees arrive in the morning, they find boxes filled with gears made overnight while they slept. The employees prepare the boxes for delivery but do not participate in the manufacturing process (except in maintaining the machinery).[65]

Internet technology is playing an increasingly important role in global commerce. For example, Internet pharmacies have facilitated senior U.S. citizens' access to cheaper drugs in Canada. U.S. citizens can save as much as 80 percent on drug costs through the Internet pharmacies in Canada. Legislation was passed in the United States in 2003 to ensure that U.S. citizens could continue to access drugs from Canada. As a result, the number of Canadian Internet pharmacies grew sharply in 2003.[66]

Among its other valuable uses, the Internet is an excellent source of data and information for a firm to use to understand its external environment. Access to experts on topics from chemical engineering to semiconductor manufacturing, to the Library of Congress, and even to satellite photographs is available through the Internet. Other information available through this technology includes Securities and Exchange Commission (SEC) filings, Department of Commerce data, information from the Census Bureau, new patent filings, and stock market updates.

While the Internet was a significant technological advance providing substantial power to companies utilizing its potential, wireless communication technology is predicted to be the next critical technological opportunity. By 2003, handheld devices and other wireless communications equipment were being used to access a variety of network-based services. The use of handheld computers with wireless network connectivity, web-enabled mobile phone handsets, and other emerging platforms (i.e., consumer Internet access devices) is expected to increase substantially, soon becoming the dominant form of communication and commerce.[67]

Clearly, the Internet and wireless forms of communications are important technological developments for many reasons. One reason for their importance, however, is that they facilitate the diffusion of other technology and knowledge critical for achieving and maintaining a competitive advantage.[68] Technologies evolve over time, and new technologies are developed. Disruptive technologies, such as the Internet, are developed and implemented and, in turn, often make current technologies obsolete.[69] Companies must stay current with technologies as they evolve, but also must be prepared to act quickly to embrace important new disruptive technologies shortly after they are introduced.[70] Certainly on a global scale, the technological opportunities and threats in the general environment have an effect on whether firms obtain new technology from external sources (such as by licensing and acquisition) or develop it internally.

The Global Segment

The **global segment** includes relevant new global markets, existing markets that are changing, important international political events, and critical cultural and institutional characteristics of global markets.[71] Globalization of business markets creates both opportunities and challenges for firms.[72] For example, firms can identify and enter valuable new global markets.[73] Many global markets (such as those in some South American nations and in South Korea and Taiwan) are becoming borderless and integrated.[74] In addition to contemplating opportunities, firms should recognize potential competitive threats in these markets. China presents many opportunities and some threats for international firms.[75] Creating additional opportunities is China's

The global segment includes relevant new global markets, existing markets that are changing, important international political events, and critical cultural and institutional characteristics of global markets.

recent admission to the World Trade Organization (WTO). A Geneva-based organization, the WTO establishes rules for global trade. China's membership in this organization suggests the possibility of increasing and less-restricted participation by the country in the global economy.[76] In return for gaining entry to the WTO, China agreed to reduce trade barriers in multiple industries, including telecommunications, banking, automobiles, movies, and professional services (for example, the services of lawyers, physicians, and accountants).

Exemplifying the globalization trend is the increasing amount of global outsourcing. For example, Bank of America began major reductions of its back office operations staff (approximately 3,700), outsourcing many of the jobs to Indian businesses. In particular, Wipro Spectramind has been a major beneficiary of technology outsourcing by U.S. firms. It provides IT services, chip design, call centers, and back office functions for a number of firms. Accenture outsourced the jobs of 5,000 accounting, software, and back office employees to the Philippines. Conseco outsourced insurance claim processing to India involving 1,700 jobs, and more such actions are planned. Fluor outsourced to the Philippines 700 jobs that involved preparing architectural blueprints. And, General Electric has outsourced 20,000 jobs to companies in India for a variety of technical tasks. Over 8,000 foreign companies have outsourced IT work to the Philippines.[77]

Moving into international markets extends a firm's reach and potential. Toyota receives almost 50 percent of its total sales revenue from outside Japan, its home country. Over 60 percent of McDonald's sales revenues and almost 98 percent of Nokia's sales revenues are from outside their home countries.[78] Because the opportunity is coupled with uncertainty, some view entering new international markets to be entrepreneurial.[79] Firms can increase the opportunity to sell innovations by entering international markets. The larger total market increases the probability that the firm will earn a return on its innovations. Certainly, firms entering new markets can diffuse new knowledge they have created and learn from the new markets as well.[80]

Firms should recognize the different sociocultural and institutional attributes of global markets. Companies competing in South Korea, for example, must understand the value placed on hierarchical order, formality, and self-control, as well as on duty rather than rights. Furthermore, Korean ideology emphasizes communitarianism, a characteristic of many Asian countries. Korea's approach differs from those of Japan and China, however, in that it focuses on *Inhwa,* or harmony. Inhwa is based on a respect of hierarchical relationships and obedience to authority. Alternatively, the approach in China stresses *Guanxi*—personal relationships or good connections— while in Japan, the focus is on *Wa,* or group harmony and social cohesion.[81] The institutional context of China suggests a major emphasis on centralized planning by the government. The Chinese government provides incentives to firms to develop alliances with foreign firms having sophisticated technology in hopes of building knowledge and introducing new technologies to the Chinese markets over time.[82]

Firms based in other countries that compete in these markets can learn from them. For example, the cultural characteristics above suggest the value of relationships. In particular, Guanxi emphasizes social capital's importance when doing business in China.[83] But, social capital is important for success in most markets around the world.[84]

Global markets offer firms more opportunities to obtain the resources needed for success. For example, the Kuwait Investment Authority is the second largest shareholder of DaimlerChrysler. Additionally, Global Crossing sought financial assistance from potential investors in Europe and Asia. But, it was to no avail as Global Crossing, citing overcapacity in the telecommunications network market as the primary cause of its problems, filed for bankruptcy in 2001. Global Crossing filed a reorganization plan in 2002 and continued the struggle to turn its fortunes around in 2003.[85] Alternatively, globalization can be threatening. In particular, companies in emerging

War, Rivalry, and General Pestilence: The Airline Industry Is Experiencing Trauma

No industry has probably experienced more traumas in recent years than the airline industry. Like most industries, it suffered reduced demand because of the economic downturn in the early part of the 21st century. However, the industry was crippled by the terrorist attacks on September 11, 2001. Then foreign travel was curtailed due to the SARS crisis that occurred in 2003. The SARS epidemic in Asia was expected to reduce travel revenues by 5 percent in 2003. Two of the major firms, United Airlines and US Airways, filed for bankruptcy, as we learned in Chapter 1. And, American Airlines narrowly avoided bankruptcy because of a last minute agreement with its unions. As evidenced by these problems, the general environment in which the airline companies must operate, especially the economic, political/legal, and sociocultural dimensions, has significantly affected them.

The airlines are also greatly affected by their industry environment. In fact, the major negative effects of dimensions of the general environment have made the airlines' industry environment more salient. For example, the rivalry in the industry is severe as airlines compete for fewer air travelers. In turn, airlines have delayed or cancelled orders for new aircraft, negatively affecting major aircraft manufacturers, especially Boeing. Interestingly, even though most analysts evaluate the airline industry as being highly unattractive, it continues to have new entrants. Probably the most important of the new entrants in recent years is JetBlue, an airline that has largely imitated Southwest Airlines' strategy. In Chapter 5, we learn more about how JetBlue and Song, mentioned below, are competing in the airline industry.

Due to the success of Southwest Airlines and others such as JetBlue, and because of the general environment described earlier, the airline industry is in the process of restructuring. First, the major airlines are trying desperately to reduce their cost structures. To do this requires the approval of their unions. Unions at United Airlines and US Airways made major concessions to allow these firms to continue operations. American Airlines' CEO had to resign to achieve the wage concessions from the unions that allowed the firm to avoid bankruptcy. But, the reduction of costs is only the first step in the restructuring likely to occur.

Delta Airlines, for example, has announced the development of a low-cost airline, named Song, to compete in the low-price market niche. Other major airlines are likely to follow. British Airways has announced major changes that include a reduction of 13,000 employees, cuts in the variety of aircraft used, reductions in the number of suppliers, limitations on the amount of ticket pricing options, and an increase in the number of short-haul flights. These changes are expected to decrease the firm's costs by approximately $1.8 billion annually (almost 13 percent of total costs) and to increase its flexibility and competitiveness. Some analysts also predict consolidation in the industry as airlines are likely to merge. The

AP Photo/Michael Dwyer

John Selvaggio, president of Song airlines, plays his trumpet on the tarmac in front of one of the company's planes at an event to inaugurate its service to Boston. Song is a low-cost carrier that represents Delta's effort to increase profit in a troubled industry environment.

only thing that may prevent consolidation could be government regulations disallowing anticompetitive moves. Certainly, the future of the airline industry will be interesting to observe.

SOURCES: R. Neidl, 2003, Winners and losers as airlines restructure, *Barron's Online*, http://www.wsj.com/barrons, May 29; D. Michaels, 2003, As airlines suffer, British Air tries takeoff strategy, *Wall Street Journal*, May 22, A1, A5; S. Carey, 2003, Encountering turbulence, *Wall Street Journal*, May 1, B1, B4; M. Chung & D. Shellock, 2003, Transatlantic markets: Risky times for airlines, *Financial Times*, http://www.ft.com, May 9; N. Harris, 2003, Can Delta's song attract "discount divas"? *Wall Street Journal*, April 11, B1, B6; 2003, Death, war and pestilence. What next for corporate travel? *The Economist*, http://www.economist.com, April 3.

market countries may be vulnerable to larger, more resource-rich, and more effective competitors from developed markets.

Additionally, there are risks in global markets. A few years ago, Argentina's market was full of promise, but in 2001, Argentina experienced a financial crisis that placed it on the brink of bankruptcy. Fortunately, Argentina's economy survived, but the country continues to struggle economically.[86] Thus, the global segment of the general environment is quite important for most firms. As a result, it is necessary to have a top management team with the experience, knowledge, and sensitivity required to effectively analyze this segment of the environment.[87]

A key objective of analyzing the general environment is identifying anticipated changes and trends among external elements. With a focus on the future, the analysis of the general environment allows firms to identify opportunities and threats. As noted in the Strategic Focus, there have been and continue to be a number of threats to airlines from the general environment. Perhaps the biggest threat comes from the economy; the industry badly needs an economic recovery to increase the demand for air travel. Also critical to a firm's future operations is an understanding of its industry environment and its competitors; these issues are considered next.

Industry Environment Analysis

An industry is a group of firms producing products that are close substitutes.

An **industry** is a group of firms producing products that are close substitutes. In the course of competition, these firms influence one another. Typically, industries include a rich mix of competitive strategies that companies use in pursuing strategic competitiveness and above-average returns. In part, these strategies are chosen because of the influence of an industry's characteristics.[88] The economic malaise suffered in the early part of the 21st century showed the vulnerability of the information technology industry, as discussed in this chapter's Opening Case. Because of these problems, the industry has undergone a number of changes in recent years, including major changes in the competitive landscape (loss of firms) and major changes in the strategies employed, exemplified by IBM's new strategy of computing on demand.

Compared to the general environment, the industry environment often has a more direct effect on the firm's strategic competitiveness and above-average returns.[89] The intensity of industry competition and an industry's profit potential (as measured by the long-run return on invested capital) are functions of five forces of competition: the threats posed by new entrants, the power of suppliers, the power of buyers, product substitutes, and the intensity of rivalry among competitors (see Figure 2.2).

The five forces model of competition expands the arena for competitive analysis. Historically, when studying the competitive environment, firms concentrated on companies with which they competed directly. However, firms must search more broadly to

identify current and potential competitors by identifying potential customers as well as the firms serving them. Competing for the same customers and thus being influenced by how customers value location and firm capabilities in their decisions is referred to as the market microstructure.[90] Understanding this area is particularly important, because in recent years industry boundaries have become blurred. For example, in the electrical utilities industry, cogenerators (firms that also produce power) are competing with regional utility companies. Moreover, telecommunications companies now compete with broadcasters, software manufacturers provide personal financial services, airlines sell mutual funds, and automakers sell insurance and provide financing.[91] In addition to focusing on customers rather than on specific industry boundaries to define markets, geographic boundaries are also relevant. Research suggests that different geographic markets for the same product can have considerably different competitive conditions.[92]

The five forces model recognizes that suppliers can become a firm's competitors (by integrating forward), as can buyers (by integrating backward). Several firms have integrated forward in the pharmaceutical industry by acquiring distributors or wholesalers. In addition, firms choosing to enter a new market and those producing products that are adequate substitutes for existing products can become a company's competitors.

Threat of New Entrants

Evidence suggests that companies often find it difficult to identify new competitors.[93] Identifying new entrants is important because they can threaten the market share of existing competitors. One reason new entrants pose such a threat is that they bring additional production capacity. Unless the demand for a good or service is increasing, additional capacity holds consumers' costs down, resulting in less revenue and lower returns for competing firms. Often, new entrants have a keen interest in gaining a large market share. As a result, new competitors may force existing firms to be more effective and efficient and to learn how to compete on new dimensions (for example, using an Internet-based distribution channel).

The likelihood that firms will enter an industry is a function of two factors: barriers to entry and the retaliation expected from current industry participants. Entry barriers make it difficult for new firms to enter an industry and often place them at a competitive disadvantage even when they are able to enter. As such, high entry barriers increase the returns for existing firms in the industry and may allow some firms to dominate the industry.[94] Interestingly, there are high entry barriers in the airline industry (e.g., substantial capital costs), but new firms have entered in recent years, among them AirTran Airways and JetBlue. Both entrants are creating competitive challenges for the major airlines, especially with the economic problems in the early 21st century. Both firms compete in the low-cost segments, and the demand for low-cost air travel has increased, making the major high-cost airlines less competitive and vulnerable to these newer airlines' competitive actions.

BARRIERS TO ENTRY

Existing competitors try to develop barriers to entry. In contrast, potential entrants seek markets in which the entry barriers are relatively insignificant. The absence of entry barriers increases the probability that a new entrant can operate profitably. There are several kinds of potentially significant entry barriers.

Economies of Scale. *Economies of scale* are "the marginal improvements in efficiency that a firm experiences as it incrementally increases its size."[95] Therefore, as the quantity of a product produced during a given period increases, the cost of manufacturing each unit declines. Economies of scale can be developed in most business functions, such as marketing, manufacturing, research and development, and purchasing. Increasing economies of scale enhances a firm's flexibility. For example, a firm may choose to reduce its price and capture a greater share of the market. Alternatively, it may keep its price constant to increase profits. In so doing, it likely will increase its free cash flow, which is helpful in times of recession.

New entrants face a dilemma when confronting current competitors' scale economies. Small-scale entry places them at a cost disadvantage. Alternatively, large-scale entry, in which the new entrant manufactures large volumes of a product to gain economies of scale, risks strong competitive retaliation.

Also important for the firm to understand are competitive conditions that reduce the ability of economies of scale to create an entry barrier. Many companies now customize their products for large numbers of small customer groups. Customized products are not manufactured in the volumes necessary to achieve economies of scale. Customization is made possible by new flexible manufacturing systems (this point is discussed further in Chapter 4). In fact, the new manufacturing technology facilitated by advanced information systems has allowed the development of mass customization in an increasing number of industries. While customization is not appropriate for all products, mass customization is becoming increasingly common in manufacturing products. In fact, online ordering has enhanced the ability of customers to obtain customized products. They are often referred to as "markets of one."[96] Companies manufacturing customized products learn how to respond quickly to customers' desires rather than develop scale economies.

Product Differentiation. Over time, customers may come to believe that a firm's product is unique. This belief can result from the firm's service to the customer, effective advertising campaigns, or being the first to market a good or service. Companies such as Coca-Cola, PepsiCo, and the world's automobile manufacturers spend a great deal of money on advertising to convince potential customers of their products' distinctiveness. Customers valuing a product's uniqueness tend to become loyal to both the product and the company producing it. Typically, new entrants must allocate many resources over time to overcome existing customer loyalties. To combat the perception of uniqueness, new entrants frequently offer products at lower prices. This decision, however, may result in lower profits or even losses.

Capital Requirements. Competing in a new industry requires a firm to have resources to invest. In addition to physical facilities, capital is needed for inventories, marketing activities, and other critical business functions. Even when competing in a new industry is attractive, the capital required for successful market entry may not be available to pursue an apparent market opportunity. For example, entering the steel and defense industries would be very difficult because of the substantial resource investments required to be competitive. One way a firm could enter the steel industry, however, is with a highly efficient mini-mill. Alternatively, because of the high knowledge requirements, a firm might enter the defense industry through the acquisition of an existing firm.

Switching Costs. Switching costs are the one-time costs customers incur when they buy from a different supplier. The costs of buying new ancillary equipment and of retraining employees, and even the psychic costs of ending a relationship, may be incurred in switching to a new supplier. In some cases, switching costs are low, such as when the consumer switches to a different soft drink. Switching costs can vary as a function of time. For example, in terms of credit hours toward graduation, the cost to a student to transfer from one university to another as a freshman is much lower than it is when the student is entering the senior year. Occasionally, a decision made by manufacturers to produce a new, innovative product creates high switching costs for the final consumer. Customer loyalty programs, such as airlines' frequent flier miles, are intended to increase the customer's switching costs.

If switching costs are high, a new entrant must offer either a substantially lower price or a much better product to attract buyers. Usually, the more established the relationship between parties, the greater is the cost incurred to switch to an alternative offering.

Access to Distribution Channels. Over time, industry participants typically develop effective means of distributing products. Once a relationship with its distributors has been developed, a firm will nurture it to create switching costs for the distributors.

Access to distribution channels can be a strong entry barrier for new entrants, particularly in consumer nondurable goods industries (for example, in grocery stores where shelf space is limited) and in international markets. Thus, new entrants have to persuade distributors to carry their products, either in addition to or in place of those currently distributed. Price breaks and cooperative advertising allowances may be used for this purpose; however, those practices reduce the new entrant's profit potential.

Cost Disadvantages Independent of Scale. Sometimes, established competitors have cost advantages that new entrants cannot duplicate. Proprietary product technology, favorable access to raw materials, desirable locations, and government subsidies are examples. Successful competition requires new entrants to reduce the strategic relevance of these factors. Delivering purchases directly to the buyer can counter the advantage of a desirable location; new food establishments in an undesirable location often follow this practice. Similarly, automobile dealerships located in unattractive areas (perhaps in a city's downtown area) can provide superior service (such as picking up the car to be serviced and then delivering it to the customer) to overcome a competitor's location advantage.

Government Policy. Through licensing and permit requirements, governments can also control entry into an industry. Liquor retailing, banking, and trucking are examples of industries in which government decisions and actions affect entry possibilities. Also, governments often restrict entry into some industries because of the need to provide quality service or the need to protect jobs. Alternatively, deregulation of industries, exemplified by the airline industry (see earlier Strategic Focus) and utilities in the United States, allows more firms to enter.[97] Some of the most publicized government actions are those involving antitrust. For example, the U.S. government dropped its antitrust case against IBM in 1982 after 13 years of highly publicized litigation. More recently, the U.S. government pursued an antitrust case against Microsoft. The final settlement involved a relatively small penalty for the company.[98] In recent years, the government has reduced many regulations, such as those involving ownership of radio stations. The loosening of these restrictions allowed Clear Channel Communications to increase its market share considerably; it now owns over 1,200 radio stations as described in the Strategic Focus later in this chapter.

EXPECTED RETALIATION

Firms seeking to enter an industry also anticipate the reactions of firms in the industry. An expectation of swift and vigorous competitive responses reduces the likelihood of entry. Vigorous retaliation can be expected when the existing firm has a major stake in the industry (for example, it has fixed assets with few, if any, alternative uses), when it has substantial resources, and when industry growth is slow or constrained. For example, any firm attempting to enter the steel or IT industries at the current time can expect significant retaliation from existing competitors.

Locating market niches not being served by incumbents allows the new entrant to avoid entry barriers. Small entrepreneurial firms are generally best suited for identifying and serving neglected market segments. When Honda first entered the U.S. market, it concentrated on small-engine motorcycles, a market that firms such as Harley-Davidson ignored. By targeting this neglected niche, Honda avoided competition. After consolidating its position, Honda used its strength to attack rivals by introducing larger motorcycles and competing in the broader market. Competitive actions and competitive responses between firms such as Honda and Harley-Davidson are discussed fully in Chapter 5.

Bargaining Power of Suppliers

Increasing prices and reducing the quality of their products are potential means used by suppliers to exert power over firms competing within an industry. If a firm is unable to recover cost increases by its suppliers through its pricing structure, its profitability is reduced by its suppliers' actions. A supplier group is powerful when

- It is dominated by a few large companies and is more concentrated than the industry to which it sells.
- Satisfactory substitute products are not available to industry firms.
- Industry firms are not a significant customer for the supplier group.
- Suppliers' goods are critical to buyers' marketplace success.
- The effectiveness of suppliers' products has created high switching costs for industry firms.
- It poses a credible threat to integrate forward into the buyers' industry. Credibility is enhanced when suppliers have substantial resources and provide a highly differentiated product.

The airline industry is an example of an industry in which suppliers' bargaining power is relatively low. While the number of suppliers is low, the demand for the major aircraft is also relatively low. Boeing and Airbus compete strongly for most orders of major aircraft.[99] Also, the shift in airline strategy to short-haul flights and low costs has enhanced the fortunes of other aircraft manufacturers who make smaller and more efficient aircraft.

Bargaining Power of Buyers

Firms seek to maximize the return on their invested capital. Alternatively, buyers (customers of an industry or a firm) want to buy products at the lowest possible price—the point at which the industry earns the lowest acceptable rate of return on its invested capital. To reduce their costs, buyers bargain for higher quality, greater levels of service, and lower prices. These outcomes are achieved by encouraging competitive battles among the industry's firms. Customers (buyer groups) are powerful when

- They purchase a large portion of an industry's total output.
- The sales of the product being purchased account for a significant portion of the seller's annual revenues.
- They could switch to another product at little, if any, cost.
- The industry's products are undifferentiated or standardized, and the buyers pose a credible threat if they were to integrate backward into the sellers' industry.

Armed with greater amounts of information about the manufacturer's costs and the power of the Internet as a shopping and distribution alternative, consumers appear to be increasing their bargaining power in many industries. One reason for this shift is that individual buyers incur virtually zero switching costs when they decide to purchase from one manufacturer rather than another or from one dealer as opposed to a second or third one. These realities are also forcing airlines to change their strategies. There is very little differentiation in air travel, and the switching costs are very low.

Threat of Substitute Products

Substitute products are goods or services from outside a given industry that perform similar or the same functions as a product that the industry produces. For example, as a sugar substitute, NutraSweet places an upper limit on sugar manufacturers' prices—NutraSweet and sugar perform the same function, but with different characteristics. Other product substitutes include fax machines instead of overnight deliveries, plastic containers rather than glass jars, and tea instead of coffee. Recently, firms have introduced to the market several low-alcohol, fruit-flavored drinks that many customers substitute for beer. For example, Smirnoff's Ice was introduced with substantial advertising of the type often used for beer. Other firms have introduced lemonade with 5 percent alcohol (e.g., "Doc's" Hard Lemon) and tea and lemon combinations with alcohol (e.g., Boston Beer Company's Twisted Tea). These products are increasingly popular, especially among younger people, and as product substitutes, they have the potential to reduce overall sales of beer.[100]

In general, product substitutes present a strong threat to a firm when customers face few, if any, switching costs and when the substitute product's price is lower or its quality and performance capabilities are equal to or greater than those of the competing product. Differentiating a product along dimensions that customers value (such as price, quality, service after the sale, and location) reduces a substitute's attractiveness.

Intensity of Rivalry among Competitors

Because an industry's firms are mutually dependent, actions taken by one company usually invite competitive responses. Thus, in many industries, firms actively compete against one another. Competitive rivalry intensifies when a firm is challenged by a competitor's actions or when a company recognizes an opportunity to improve its market position.

Firms within industries are rarely homogeneous; they differ in resources and capabilities and seek to differentiate themselves from competitors.[101] Typically, firms seek to differentiate their products from competitors' offerings in ways that customers value and in which the firms have a competitive advantage. Visible dimensions on which rivalry is based include price, quality, and innovation.

As explained in the Strategic Focus, the rivalry between competitors, such as United, US Airways, American, and other major airlines, is intense. The competitive rivalry is also intense in the computer hardware and software markets, as described in the Opening Case. In fact, the rivalry is so intense, a formerly highly successful firm, Sun Microsystems, may have trouble surviving over the next several years.

As suggested by the Opening Case and Strategic Focus, various factors influence the intensity of rivalry between or among competitors. Next, we discuss the most prominent factors that experience shows to affect the intensity of firms' rivalries.

NUMEROUS OR EQUALLY BALANCED COMPETITORS

Intense rivalries are common in industries with many companies. With multiple competitors, it is common for a few firms to believe that they can act without eliciting a response. However, evidence suggests that other firms generally are aware of competitors' actions, often choosing to respond to them. At the other extreme, industries with only a few firms of equivalent size and power also tend to have strong rivalries. The large and often similar-sized resource bases of these firms permit vigorous actions and responses. The Airbus and Boeing competitive battles exemplify intense rivalry between relatively equivalent competitors.[102]

SLOW INDUSTRY GROWTH

When a market is growing, firms try to effectively use resources to serve an expanding customer base. Growing markets reduce the pressure to take customers from competitors. However, rivalry in no-growth or slow-growth markets becomes more intense as firms battle to increase their market shares by attracting competitors' customers.

Typically, battles to protect market shares are fierce. Certainly, this has been the case in the airline industry. The instability in the market that results from these competitive engagements reduces profitability for all airlines throughout the industry. Reduced profitability is one of the reasons that two major U.S.-based airlines have declared bankruptcy and others on a global basis have experienced major net losses since 2000.

HIGH FIXED COSTS OR HIGH STORAGE COSTS

When fixed costs account for a large part of total costs, companies try to maximize the use of their productive capacity. Doing so allows the firm to spread costs across a larger volume of output. However, when many firms attempt to maximize their productive capacity, excess capacity is created on an industry-wide basis. To then reduce inventories, individual companies typically cut the price of their product and offer rebates and other special discounts to customers. However, these practices, common in the automobile manufacturing industry, often intensify competition. The pattern of excess capacity at the industry level followed by intense rivalry at the firm level is observed frequently in industries with high storage costs. Perishable products, for example, lose their value rapidly with the passage of time. As their inventories grow, producers of perishable goods often use pricing strategies to sell products quickly.

LACK OF DIFFERENTIATION OR LOW SWITCHING COSTS

When buyers find a differentiated product that satisfies their needs, they frequently purchase the product loyally over time. Industries with many companies that have successfully differentiated their products have less rivalry, resulting in lower competition for individual firms. Firms that develop and sustain a differentiated product that cannot be easily imitated by competitors often earn higher returns.[103] However, when buyers view products as commodities (as products with few differentiated features or capabilities), rivalry intensifies. In these instances, buyers' purchasing decisions are based primarily on price and, to a lesser degree, service. Personal computers are becoming a commodity. Thus, the competition among Dell, HP, and other computer manufacturers is expected to be strong.

The effect of switching costs is identical to that described for differentiated products. The lower the buyers' switching costs, the easier it is for competitors to attract buyers through pricing and service offerings. High switching costs, however, at least partially insulate the firm from rivals' efforts to attract customers. Interestingly, the switching costs—such as pilot and mechanic training—are high in aircraft purchases, yet the rivalry between Boeing and Airbus remains intense because the stakes for both are extremely high.

HIGH STRATEGIC STAKES

Competitive rivalry is likely to be high when it is important for several of the competitors to perform well in the market. For example, although it is diversified and is a market leader in other businesses, Samsung has targeted market leadership in the consumer electronics market and is doing quite well. This market is quite important to Sony and other major competitors, such as Hitachi, Matsushita, NEC, and Mitsubishi. Thus, there is substantial rivalry in this market, and it is likely to continue over the next few years.

High strategic stakes can also exist in terms of geographic locations. For example, Japanese automobile manufacturers are committed to a significant presence in the U.S. marketplace. A key reason for this is that the United States is the world's largest single market for auto manufacturers' products. Because of the stakes involved in this country for Japanese and U.S. manufacturers, rivalry among firms in the U.S. and the global automobile industry is highly intense. It should be noted that while proximity tends to promote greater rivalry, physically proximate competition has potentially positive benefits as well. For example, when competitors are located near each other, it is easier for suppliers to serve them, and they can develop economies of scale that lead to lower production costs. Additionally, communications with key industry stakeholders such as suppliers are facilitated and more efficient when they are close to the firm.[104]

HIGH EXIT BARRIERS

Sometimes companies continue competing in an industry even though the returns on their invested capital are low or negative. Firms making this choice likely face high exit barriers, which include economic, strategic, and emotional factors causing companies to remain in an industry when the profitability of doing so is questionable. Exit barriers are especially high in the airline industry. Common exit barriers are

- Specialized assets (assets with values linked to a particular business or location).
- Fixed costs of exit (such as labor agreements).
- Strategic interrelationships (relationships of mutual dependence, such as those between one business and other parts of a company's operations, including shared facilities and access to financial markets).
- Emotional barriers (aversion to economically justified business decisions because of fear for one's own career, loyalty to employees, and so forth).
- Government and social restrictions (more common outside the United States, these restrictions often are based on government concerns for job losses and regional economic effects).

Will the Real Media Industry Please Stand Up?

Only a few years ago it seemed that everyone wanted to get into the media industry and to expand it farther. Although there were differences of opinion, many analysts expressed positive evaluations of such firms as AOL Time Warner, Vivendi, Bertelsmann, Sony Entertainment, and related companies (e.g., in the cable business). Yet, since the AOL Time Warner merger in 2000, the situations have soured for many of these companies. AOL Time Warner CEO Gerald Levine retired, and Steve Case stepped down as chairman. Jean-Marie Messier, CEO of Vivendi, was asked to resign, and Bertelsmann CEO Thomas Middlehof was forced to resign. All of these firms were formed into large conglomerates with the purpose of obtaining synergies and becoming the leaders across several industries.

AOL Time Warner was formed to provide content to AOL and to provide new outlets for the content beyond magazines and movies. AOL Time Warner provides Internet access (the major business of AOL), cable services, filmed entertainment, networks (e.g., CNN for news), music, and publishing. As a result, the company competes in several markets and against different firms in each one. For example, it competes against Disney in filmed entertainment and, to some degree, in networks. It competes against Comcast in cable and Sony and Apple in music. The number of and diversity among its competitors create challenges for managing this large, monolithic firm. And, unfortunately, the AOL business has been a drain on the company almost since the time of the merger. The major problem was the bursting of the Internet bubble. Beyond that, actions to create synergy by using content in AOL have not yet produced dividends. For example, the music service offered by AOL has been usurped by Apple's recent entry into providing entertainment services, especially music.

AOL has also been crippled by competition in its basic Internet access business. It has been hit from two sides—cut-rate Internet services and the new broadband services from cable providers. As a result of the two-sided competitive attack, AOL's subscriber base has declined from its high in 2002. And, although AOL has offered a new broadband service, it has largely managed only to change some of its dial-up service customers to the broadband service. It has not yet attracted much appeal beyond its current customers. Comcast, which acquired AT&T's broadband service in late 2002, has become a formidable competitor.

Essentially, AOL Time Warner must decide which problems to solve. It has so many competitors in different markets, and its inability to find synergies has caused significant problems for the firm. Some analysts have argued that the firm should spin off AOL so it does not drain the basic media business. However, Jonathon Miller, CEO of AOL, a division of AOL Time Warner, is developing a plan to revive the firm to sell subscriptions to online customers for high-demand entertainment such as *The Sopranos*. Thus, he continues to search for the elusive synergy across the businesses in the company.

SOURCES: D. D. Kirkpatrick, 2003, In HBO, AOL sees a sibling and, crucially, a role model, *New York Times,* http://www.nytimes.com, May 5; J. Angwin, 2003, America Online faces new threat from cut-rate Internet services, *Wall Street Journal,* February 3, A1, A11; J. Angwin, 2003, America Online's fate grows more uncertain, *Wall Street Journal,* January 14, B1, B4; B. Orwall & M. Peers, 2003, Facing crisis, media giants scrounge for fresh strategies, *Wall Street Journal,* January 14, A1, A6; G. Anders, 2002, AOL's true believers, *Fast Company,* July, 96–104; T. Lowry, A. Barrett, & R. Grover, 2002, A new cable giant, *Business Week,* November 18, 108–118.

Interpreting Industry Analyses

Effective industry analyses are products of careful study and interpretation of data and information from multiple sources. A wealth of industry-specific data is available to be analyzed. Because of globalization, international markets and rivalries must be included in the firm's analyses. In fact, research shows that in some industries, international variables are more important than domestic ones as determinants of strategic competitiveness. Furthermore, because of the development of global markets, a country's borders no longer restrict industry structures. In fact, movement into international markets enhances the chances of success for new ventures as well as more established firms.[105]

Following study of the five forces of competition, the firm can develop the insights required to determine an industry's attractiveness in terms of the firm's potential to earn adequate or superior returns on its invested capital. In general, the stronger competitive forces are, the lower is the profit potential for an industry's firms. An unattractive industry has low entry barriers, suppliers and buyers with strong bargaining positions, strong competitive threats from product substitutes, and intense rivalry among competitors. These industry characteristics make it very difficult for firms to achieve strategic competitiveness and earn above-average returns. Alternatively, an attractive industry has high entry barriers, suppliers and buyers with little bargaining power, few competitive threats from product substitutes, and relatively moderate rivalry.[106]

As noted in the Strategic Focus, AOL Time Warner operates in multiple industries. As such, it must analyze several industries to better know the opportunities and threats that each poses. In fact, a thorough industry analysis might have prevented Time Warner's merger with AOL, as it should have identified a number of threats faced in that industry. Interestingly, each of the media conglomerates developed in the late 1990s has suffered substantial problems since the birth of the 21st century. Next, we turn to strategic groups operating within industries.

Strategic Groups

A set of firms emphasizing similar strategic dimensions to use a similar strategy is called a **strategic group**.[107] The competition between firms within a strategic group is greater than the competition between a member of a strategic group and companies outside that strategic group. Another way of saying this is that intra-strategic group competition is more intense than is inter-strategic group competition. In fact, there is more heterogeneity in the performance of firms within strategic groups than across the groups. The performance leaders within groups are able to follow strategies similar to those of other firms in the group and yet maintain strategic distinctiveness to gain and sustain a competitive advantage.[108]

The extent of technological leadership, product quality, pricing policies, distribution channels, and customer service are examples of strategic dimensions that firms in a strategic group may treat similarly. Patterns of competition within strategic groups may be described this way: "Organizations in a strategic group occupy similar positions in the market, offer similar goods to similar customers, and may also make similar choices about production technology and other organizational features."[109] Thus, membership in a particular strategic group defines the essential characteristics of the firm's strategy.[110]

The notion of strategic groups can be useful for analyzing an industry's competitive structure. Such analyses can be helpful in diagnosing competition, positioning, and the profitability of firms within an industry.[111] High mobility barriers, high rivalry, and low resources among the firms within an industry will limit the formation of strategic groups.[112] However, research suggests that after strategic groups are formed, their membership remains relatively stable over time, making analysis easier and more useful.[113]

A **strategic group** *is a set of firms emphasizing similar strategic dimensions to use a similar strategy.*

There are approximately 30 different formats in the radio industry. These formats represent different preferences in music, scheduling, and announcer style as well as nonmusic broadcasting (news, talk radio). Resulting listening formats are specifically suited for various audiences to gain competitive advantage for each market.

©Spencer Grant/PhotoEdit

It's a Competitive World: Some Succeed and Some Fail

Home Depot is the number one home improvement company, and only a few years ago, it seemed to be unbeatable. However, its stock price reached a five-year low in 2003. Its new CEO, Bob Nardelli, has cut costs and centralized operations in the face of a bad economy. He forced the hiring of more part-time workers and increased discipline by cutting inventories. While these actions reduced costs, some customers complained that the firm reduced service. Also, the centralization allows fewer creative approaches to be used by the store managers, one of the factors often credited for Home Depot's success. As a result, Lowe's Companies, which is number two in the market, has been increasing its market share relative to Home Depot's share. Lowe's has been successful in attracting women customers, not the target for Home Depot.

Radio for many years was a highly fragmented industry. However, after the industry was deregulated through legislation, consolidation began, especially by Clear Channel Communications. In 1995, Clear Channel controlled approximately 1.3 percent of the market. By 2001, however, it had a 20.2 percent market share. It grew largely by acquisitions and now owns over 1,200 radio stations. But, Clear Channel's success comes from the synergies it has created with other businesses such as billboards. It owns more than 770,000 billboards and advertising displays. As such, it can offer advertisers "more bang for their bucks" by advertising on the radio and on billboards that people will see as they drive by listening to their radio. Clear Channel has also become the largest concert promoter (through acquisitions) and promotes those concerts on the radio. It has been accused of "strong-arm tactics" and has the economic power to do so. But, while Clear Channel is large and has built several competitive advantages through the synergies among its businesses, it still controls only about 10 percent of the radio stations in the United States.

GlaxoSmithKline is the second largest pharmaceutical firm in the world. But, it has a problem. Its pipeline of new products makes analysts and investors wary about its future. The firm has experienced strong earnings but has grown largely through acquisitions in recent years. By doing so, it has bought new products rather than developed them internally. Competition in this industry is based on the new "blockbuster" drugs developed and brought to the market. Glaxo may start paying the price for not emphasizing R&D by losing its competitive advantage as other pharmaceutical firms introduce new products and take Glaxo's market away. This concern was exacerbated when the firm failed to schedule an expected meeting with analysts to discuss its research and development program.

Paradoxically, one firm has gotten into trouble by investing heavily in R&D. Volkswagen invested billions of dollars to develop and introduce several new luxury automobiles, only to find that they were not in demand in the marketplace. One of these new cars, the Phaeton, is priced at $70,000. Sales of the Phaeton reached only 25 percent of the expected number in 2002, its year of introduction. The competition is fierce in the premium auto market. The wasted R&D investments and a lack of attention to Volkswagen's primary mid-priced auto market have allowed competitors to gain market share there as well. Thus, Volkswagen's financial results have suffered, and unless it regains a competitive advantage, its performance will continue to suffer.

SOURCES: N. E. Boudette, 2003, Volkswagen stalls on several fronts after luxury drive, *Wall Street Journal*, May 8, A1, A17; R. Abelson, 2003, For Glaxo, the answers are in the pipeline, *New York Times*, http://www.nytimes.com, May 4; C. Y. Chen, 2003, The bad boys of radio, *Fortune*, March 3, 119–122; D. Morse, 2003, A hardware chain struggles to adjust to a new blueprint, *Wall Street Journal*, January 17, A1, A6; 2003, A do-it-yourself disaster, *The Economist*, January 11, 54–55.

Using strategic groups to understand an industry's competitive structure requires the firm to plot companies' competitive actions and competitive responses along strategic dimensions such as pricing decisions, product quality, distribution channels, and so forth. Doing this shows the firm how certain companies are competing similarly in terms of how they use similar strategic dimensions. For example, there are unique radio markets because consumers prefer different music formats and programming (news radio, talk radio, and so forth). Typically, a radio format is created through choices made regarding music or nonmusic style, scheduling, and announcer style.[114] It is estimated that approximately 30 different radio formats exist, suggesting that there are many strategic groups in this industry. The strategies within each of the 30 groups are similar, while the strategies across the total set of strategic groups are dissimilar. As a result, Clear Channel Communications (described in the Strategic Focus) often owns several stations in a large city, but each uses a different format. Therefore, Clear Channel likely has stations operating in most or all of the 30 strategic groups in this industry. Thus, firms could increase their understanding of competition in the commercial radio industry by plotting companies' actions and responses in terms of important strategic dimensions, such as those we have mentioned.

Strategic groups have several implications. First, because firms within a group offer similar products to the same customers, the competitive rivalry among them can be intense. The more intense the rivalry, the greater is the threat to each firm's profitability. Second, the strengths of the five industry forces (the threats posed by new entrants, the power of suppliers, the power of buyers, product substitutes, and the intensity of rivalry among competitors) differ across strategic groups. Third, the closer the strategic groups are in terms of their strategies, the greater is the likelihood of rivalry between the groups.

Having a thorough understanding of primary competitors helps a firm formulate and implement an appropriate strategy. Clearly Home Depot and Lowe's are in a strategic group and compete directly against each other. Lowe's has been successful in selling products to women. Observing this, Home Depot has recently added new product lines to attract women to its stores. Volkswagen tried to break out of its strategic group selling mid-priced autos. But, it was unsuccessful in entering the strategic group of firms using similar strategies selling premium autos (e.g., Mercedes-Benz, BMW). Additionally, because of these efforts, VW is losing market share in its primary markets. Glaxo has used a strategy different from that of several of its primary competitors and now is in danger of losing an advantage over them. It can no longer sustain new product lines by acquisition. Research has shown that this outcome is to be expected when a firm continuously emphasizes obtaining new products through acquisitions rather than internal development.[115]

Competitor Analysis

The competitor environment is the final part of the external environment requiring study. Competitor analysis focuses on each company against which a firm directly competes. For example, Home Depot and Lowe's and GlaxoSmithKline and Merck should be keenly interested in understanding each other's objectives, strategies, assumptions, and capabilities. Furthermore, intense rivalry creates a strong need to understand competitors. In a competitor analysis, the firm seeks to understand

- What drives the competitor, as shown by its *future objectives*.
- What the competitor is doing and can do, as revealed by its *current strategy*.
- What the competitor believes about the industry, as shown by its *assumptions*.
- What the competitor's capabilities are, as shown by its *strengths* and *weaknesses*.[116]

Information about these four dimensions helps the firm prepare an anticipated response profile for each competitor (see Figure 2.3). Thus, the results of an effective competitor analysis help a firm understand, interpret, and predict its competitors' actions and responses. Understanding the actions of competitors clearly contributes to the firm's ability to compete successfully within the industry.[117]

Critical to an effective competitor analysis is gathering data and information that can help the firm understand its competitors' intentions and the strategic implications resulting from them.[118] Useful data and information combine to form **competitor intelligence:** the set of data and information the firm gathers to better understand and better anticipate competitors' objectives, strategies, assumptions, and capabilities. In competitor analysis, the firm should gather intelligence not only about its competitors, but also regarding public policies in countries across the world. Intelligence about public policies "provides an early warning of threats and opportunities emerging from the global public policy environment, and analyzes how they will affect the achievement of the company's strategy."[119]

Through effective competitive and public policy intelligence, the firm gains the insights needed to create a competitive advantage and to increase the quality of the strategic decisions it makes when deciding how to compete against its rivals. Factiva, a news and information service, has used competitor intelligence to improve its competitive position and to build an excellent service. The firm was named among the top 100 Companies in Knowledge Management by KMWorld magazine and received the 2003 Codie Award for the Best Online Business News or Information Service and the Best Online Professional Financial Information Service. Additionally, the CEO, Clare Hart,

Competitor intelligence is the set of data and information the firm gathers to better understand and better anticipate competitors' objectives, strategies, assumptions, and capabilities.

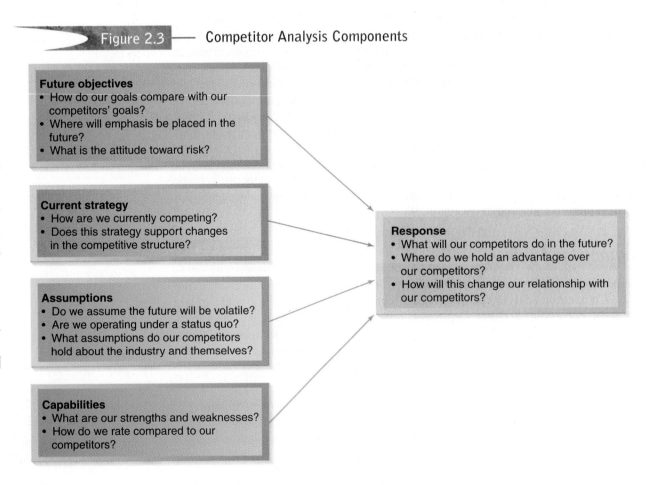

Figure 2.3 — Competitor Analysis Components

Future objectives
• How do our goals compare with our competitors' goals?
• Where will emphasis be placed in the future?
• What is the attitude toward risk?

Current strategy
• How are we currently competing?
• Does this strategy support changes in the competitive structure?

Assumptions
• Do we assume the future will be volatile?
• Are we operating under a status quo?
• What assumptions do our competitors hold about the industry and themselves?

Capabilities
• What are our strengths and weaknesses?
• How do we rate compared to our competitors?

Response
• What will our competitors do in the future?
• Where do we hold an advantage over our competitors?
• How will this change our relationship with our competitors?

states that competitor intelligence will play an important role in her firm's efforts to reach its objective of becoming the top firm in the industry.[120]

Firms should follow generally accepted ethical practices in gathering competitor intelligence. Industry associations often develop lists of these practices that firms can adopt. Practices considered both legal and ethical include (1) obtaining publicly available information (such as court records, competitors' help-wanted advertisements, annual reports, financial reports of publicly held corporations, and Uniform Commercial Code filings), and (2) attending trade fairs and shows to obtain competitors' brochures, view their exhibits, and listen to discussions about their products.

In contrast, certain practices (including blackmail; trespassing; eavesdropping; and stealing drawings, samples, or documents) are widely viewed as unethical and often are illegal. To protect themselves from digital fraud or theft by competitors that break into their employees' PCs, some companies buy insurance to protect against PC hacking.[121]

Some competitor intelligence practices may be legal, but a firm must decide whether they are also ethical, given the image it desires as a corporate citizen. Especially with electronic transmissions, the line between legal and ethical practices can be difficult to determine. For example, a firm may develop website addresses that are very similar to those of its competitors and thus occasionally receive e-mail transmissions that were intended for those competitors. According to legal experts, the legality of this "e-mail snagging" remains unclear.[122] Nonetheless, the practice is an example of the challenges companies face when deciding how to gather intelligence about competitors while simultaneously determining what to do to prevent competitors from learning too much about them.

In 2001, Procter & Gamble (P&G) notified Unilever that its own rules regarding gathering intelligence on competitors were violated when obtaining information on Unilever practices. P&G returned over 80 documents that were taken from Unilever's trash bins. The two firms then negotiated a potential settlement. Unilever wanted P&G to delay several of its planned new product launches, but P&G resisted. Moreover, both firms had to take special care in the negotiations not to violate antitrust laws, thereby spurring regulators to take action. Therefore, for several reasons, competitive intelligence must be handled with sensitivity.[123]

Open discussions of intelligence-gathering techniques can help a firm to ensure that people understand its convictions to follow ethical practices for gathering competitor intelligence. An appropriate guideline for competitor intelligence practices is to respect the principles of common morality and the right of competitors not to reveal certain information about their products, operations, and strategic intentions.[124]

Despite the importance of studying competitors, evidence suggests that only a relatively small percentage of firms use formal processes to collect and disseminate competitive intelligence. Beyond this, some firms forget to analyze competitors' future objectives as they try to understand their current strategies, assumptions, and capabilities, which will yield incomplete insights about those competitors.[125]

Summary

- The firm's external environment is challenging and complex. Because of the external environment's effect on performance, the firm must develop the skills required to identify opportunities and threats existing in that environment.

- The external environment has three major parts: (1) the general environment (elements in the broader society that affect industries and their firms), (2) the industry environment (factors that influence a firm, its competitive actions and responses, and the industry's profit potential), and (3) the competitor environment (in which the firm analyzes each major competitor's future objectives, current strategies, assumptions, and capabilities).

- The external environmental analysis process has four steps: scanning, monitoring, forecasting, and assessing. Through environmental analyses, the firm identifies opportunities and threats.

- The general environment has six segments: demographic, economic, political/legal, sociocultural, technological, and global. For each segment, the firm wants to determine the strategic relevance of environmental changes and trends.

- Compared to the general environment, the industry environment has a more direct effect on the firm's strategic actions. The five forces model of competition includes the threat of entry, the power of suppliers, the power of buyers, product substitutes, and the intensity of rivalry among competitors. By studying these forces, the firm finds a position in an industry where it can influence the forces in its favor or where it can buffer itself from the power of the forces in order to increase its ability to earn above-average returns.

- Industries are populated with different strategic groups. A strategic group is a collection of firms that follow similar strategies along similar dimensions. Competitive rivalry is greater within a strategic group than it is between strategic groups.

- Competitor analysis informs the firm about the future objectives, current strategies, assumptions, and capabilities of the companies with whom it competes directly.

- Different techniques are used to create competitor intelligence: the set of data, information, and knowledge that allows the firm to better understand its competitors and thereby predict their likely strategic and tactical actions. Firms should use only legal and ethical practices to gather intelligence. The Internet enhances firms' capabilities to gather insights about competitors and their strategic intentions.

Review Questions

Review Question Review Questions

1. Why is it important for a firm to study and understand the external environment?

2. What are the differences between the general environment and the industry environment? Why are these differences important?

3. What is the external environmental analysis process? What does the firm want to learn when using this process?

4. What are the six segments of the general environment? Explain the differences among them.

5. How do the five forces of competition in an industry affect its profit potential? Explain.

6. What is a strategic group? Of what value is knowledge of the firm's strategic group in formulating that firm's strategy?

7. What is the importance of collecting and interpreting data and information about competitors? What practices should a firm use to gather competitor intelligence and why?

Experiential Exercises

Experiential Exercise

Scanning the External Environment

For the company or industry of primary interest to you, scan the key segments of the external environment and identify two key trends in each segment that may present challenges to your firm in the future. Indicate whether each trend is an opportunity or a threat for your company, and briefly explain your reasoning. Which of the segments do you anticipate will have the most significant effect on your company of interest over the next five years, and why?

Five Forces Model

In order to develop your understanding of the structure of your industry of interest, conduct a brief analysis of the five forces of competition.

Rivalry of competing firms: Identify the key competitors in the industry and assess the intensity of rivalry. Briefly explain the basis of competition in the industry.

Threat of new entrants: Assess the threat of new entrants to the industry. Briefly explain the barriers to entry.

Bargaining power of suppliers: Identify key supplier groups and assess the strength of their relative bargaining power. Briefly explain the characteristics determining their power.

Bargaining power of buyers: Identify key buyer groups (from the channel of distribution to the end user) and assess the strength of their relative bargaining power. Briefly explain the characteristics determining their power.

Threat of substitute products: Identify goods or services that may serve as close substitutes for the output of the industry. Briefly explain the relative value (cost of inputs and product performance) a substitute may deliver to a buyer.

Notes

1. J. Song, 2002, Firm capabilities and technology ladders: Sequential foreign direct investments of Japanese electronics firms in East Asia, *Strategic Management Journal*, 23: 191–210; D. J. Ketchen, Jr., & T. B. Palmer, 1999, Strategic responses to poor organizational performance: A test of competing perspectives, *Journal of Management*, 25: 683–706; V. P. Rindova & C. J. Fombrun, 1999, Constructing competitive advantage: The role of firm-constituent interactions, *Strategic Management Journal*, 20: 691–710.

2. J. T. Eckhardt & S. A. Shane, 2003, Opportunities and entrepreneurship, *Journal of Management*, 29: 333–349; A. Ardichvili, R. Cardozo, & S. Ray, 2003, A theory of entrepreneurial opportunity identification and development, *Journal of Business Venturing*, 18: 105–123; P. Chattopadhyay, W. H. Glick, & G. P. Huber, 2001, Organizational actions in response to threats and opportunities, *Academy of Management Journal*, 44: 937–955.

3. J. R. Hough & M. A. White, 2003, Environmental dynamism and strategic decision-making rationality: An examination at the decision level, *Strategic Management Journal*, 24: 481–489; R. J. Herbold, 2002, Inside Microsoft: Balancing creativity and discipline, *Harvard Business Review*, 80(1): 73–79; C. M. Grimm & K. G. Smith, 1997, *Strategy as Action: Industry Rivalry and Coordination*, Cincinnati: South-Western; C. J. Fombrun, 1992, *Turning Point: Creating Strategic Change in Organizations*, New York: McGraw-Hill, 13.

4. J. M. Mezias, 2002, Identifying liabilities of foreignness and strategies to minimize their effects: The case of labor lawsuit judgments in the United States, *Strategic Management Journal*, 23: 229–244.

5. R. M. Kanter, 2002, Strategy as improvisational theater, *Sloan Management Review*, 43(2): 76–81; S. A. Zahra, A. P. Nielsen, & W. C. Bogner, 1999, Corporate entrepreneurship, knowledge, and competence development, *Entrepreneurship: Theory and Practice*, 23(3): 169–189.

6. R. M. Grant, 2003, Strategic planning in a turbulent environment: Evidence from the oil majors, *Strategic Management Journal*, 24: 491–517; M. A. Hitt, J. E. Ricart, I. Costa, & R. D. Nixon, 1998, The new frontier, in M. A. Hitt, J. E. Ricart, I. Costa, & R. D. Nixon (eds.), *Managing Strategically in an Interconnected World*, Chichester: John Wiley & Sons, 1–12.

7. S. A. Zahra & G. George, 2002, International entrepreneurship: The current status of the field and future research agenda, in M. A. Hitt, R. D. Ireland, S. M. Camp, & D. L. Sexton (eds.), *Strategic Entrepreneurship: Creating a New Mindset*, Oxford, UK: Blackwell Publishers, 255–288; W. C. Bogner & P. Bansal, 1998, Controlling unique knowledge development as the basis for sustained high performance, in M. A. Hitt, J. E. Ricart, I. Costa, & R. D. Nixon (eds.), *Managing Strategically in an Interconnected World*, Chichester: John Wiley & Sons, 167–184.

8. L. Fahey, 1999, *Competitors*, New York: John Wiley & Sons; B. A. Walters & R. L. Priem, 1999, Business strategy and CEO intelligence acquisition, *Competitive Intelligence Review*, 10(2): 15–22.

9. R. D. Ireland & M. A. Hitt, 1999, Achieving and maintaining strategic competitiveness in the 21st century: The role of strategic leadership, *Academy of Management Executive*, 13(1): 43–57; M. A. Hitt, B. W. Keats, & S. M. DeMarie, 1998, Navigating in the new competitive landscape: Building strategic flexibility and competitive advantage in the 21st century, *Academy of Management Executive*, 12(4): 22–42.

10. Q. Nguyen & H. Mintzberg, 2003, The rhythm of change, *MIT Sloan Management Review*, 44(4): 79–84; J. K. Sebenius, 2002, The hidden challenge of cross-border negotiations, *Harvard Business Review*, 80(3): 76–85.

11. R. Karlgaard, 1999, Digital rules: Technology and the new economy, *Forbes*, May 17, 43.

12. P. Uppaluru, 2001, The rebirth of telecommunications, *Web Voice Today*, http://www.telera.com, Winter.

13. V. Prior, 1999, The language of competitive intelligence: Part four, *Competitive Intelligence Review*, 10(1): 84–87.

14. T. Becker, 2003, Former Polaroid gets two-month extension of exclusivity, *Wall Street Journal Online*, http://www.wsj.com, March 5.

15. G. Young, 1999, "Strategic value analysis" for competitive advantage, *Competitive Intelligence Review*, 10(2): 52–64.

16. M. A. Hitt, R. D. Ireland, S. M. Camp, & D. L. Sexton, 2001, Strategic entrepreneurship: Entrepreneurial strategies for wealth creation, *Strategic Management Journal*, 22(Special Issue): 479–491.

17. L. Rosenkopf & A. Nerkar, 2001, Beyond local search: Boundary-spanning exploration, and impact in the optical disk industry, *Strategic Management Journal*, 22: 287–306.

18. D. F. Kuratko, R. D. Ireland, & J. S. Hornsby, 2001, Improving firm performance through entrepreneurial actions: Acordia's corporate entrepreneurship strategy, *Academy of Management Executive*, 15(4): 60–71; D. S. Elenkov, 1997, Strategic uncertainty and environmental scanning: The case for institutional influences on scanning behavior, *Strategic Management Journal*, 18: 287–302.

19. K. M. Eisenhardt, 2002, Has strategy changed? *Sloan Management Review*, 43(2): 88–91; I. Goll & A. M. A. Rasheed, 1997, Rational decision-making and firm performance: The moderating role of environment, *Strategic Management Journal*, 18: 583–591.

20. V. K. Garg, B. A. Walters, & R. L. Priem, 2003, Chief executive scanning emphases, environmental dynamism, and manufacturing firm performance, *Strategic Management Journal*, 24: 725–744; R. Aggarwal, 1999, Technology and globalization as mutual reinforcers in business: Reorienting strategic thinking for the new millennium, *Management International Review*, 39(2): 83–104.

21. R. Donkin, 1999, Too young to retire, *Financial Times*, July 2, 9.

22. B. Richards, 2001, Following the crumbs, *Wall Street Journal Online*, http://www.wsj.com, October 29.

23. Fahey, *Competitors*, 71–73.

24. P. Yip, 1999, The road to wealth, *Dallas Morning News*, August 2, D1, D3.

25. F. Dahlsten, 2003, Avoiding the customer satisfaction rut, *MIT Sloan Management Review*, 44(4): 73–77; Y. Luo & S. H. Park, 2001, Strategic alignment and performance of market-seeking MNCs in China, *Strategic Management Journal*, 22: 141–155.

26. K. Buysse & A. Verbke, 2003, Proactive strategies: A stakeholder management perspective, *Strategic Management Journal*, 24: 453–470; I. M. Jawahar & G. L. McLaughlin, 2001, Toward a prescriptive stakeholder theory: An organizational life cycle approach, *Academy of Management Review*, 26: 397–414.

27. M. Song & M. M. Montoya-Weiss, 2001, The effect of perceived technological uncertainty on Japanese new product development, *Academy of Management Journal*, 44: 61–80.

28. M. H. Zack, 2003, Rethinking the knowledge-based organization, *MIT Sloan Management Review*, 44(4): 67–71; H. Yli-Renko, E. Autio, & H. J. Sapienza, 2001, Social capital, knowledge acquisition, and knowledge exploitation in young technologically based firms, *Strategic Management Journal*, 22 (Special Issue): 587–613.

29. Fahey, *Competitors*.

30. Fahey, *Competitors*, 75–77.

31. J. Baily, 2003, In fast food, being bigger doesn't ensure your success, *Wall Street Journal Online*, http://www.wsj.com, March 18.

32. L. Fahey & V. K. Narayanan, 1986, *Macroenvironmental Analysis for Strategic Management*, St. Paul, MN: West Publishing Company, 58.

33. 2003, United Nations Populations Division, World Population Prospects, http://www.esa.un.org; D. Fishburn, 1999, *The World in 1999*, The Economist Publications, 9; 1999, Six billion . . . and counting, *Time*, October 4, 16.

34. 2002, *The World Factbook*, http://www.bartleby.com.

35. R. Poe & C. L. Courter, 1999, The next baby boom, *Across the Board*, May, 1; 1999, Trends and forecasts for the next 25 years, Bethesda, Maryland: World Future Society, 3.

36. 2001, Millennium in motion: Global trends shaping the health sciences industry, Ernst & Young, http://www.ey.com/industry/health, June.

37. M. Peterson & M. Freudenheim, 2001, Drug giant to introduce discount drug plan for the elderly, *New York Times*, http://www.nytimes.com, October 3.

38. D. Stipp, 1999, Hell no, we won't go! *Fortune*, July 19, 102–108; G. Colvin, 1997, How to beat the boomer rush, *Fortune*, August 18, 59–63.

39. J. MacIntyre, 1999, Figuratively speaking, *Across the Board*, November/December, 15.

40. Colvin, How to beat the boomer rush, 60.

41. 2001, Millennium in motion; 1999, U.S. Department of Labor, Demographic change and the future workforce, *Futurework*, http://www.dol.gov, November 8.

42. P. R. Drucker, 2002, They're not employees, they're people, *Harvard Business Review*, 80(2): 70–77.

43. D. M. Schweiger, T. Atamer, & R. Calori, 2003, Transnational project teams and networks: Making the multinational organization more effective, *Journal of World Business*, 38: 127–140; G. Dessler, 1999, How to earn your employees' commitment, *Academy of Management Executive*, 13(2): 58–67; S. Finkelstein & D. C. Hambrick, 1996, *Strategic Leadership: Top Executives and Their Effect on Organizations*, Minneapolis, MN: West Publishing Company.

44. L. H. Pelled, K. M. Eisenhardt, & K. R. Xin, 1999, Exploring the black box: An analysis of work group diversity, conflict, and performance, *Administrative Science Quarterly*, 44: 1–28.

45. 2001, Millennium in motion; E. S. Rubenstein, 1999, Inequality, *Forbes*, November 1, 158–160.

46. Fahey & Narayanan, *Macroenvironmental Analysis*, 105.

47. G. Ip, 2003, Federal Reserve maintains interest-rate target at 1%, *Wall Street Journal Online*, http://www.wsj.com, August 13.

48. 2001, Millennium in motion.

49. J. L. Hilsenrath, 2001, Shock waves keep spreading, changing the outlook for cars, hotels—even for cola, *Wall Street Journal Online*, http://www.wsj.com, October 9.

50. G. Keim, 2001, Business and public policy: Competing in the political marketplace, in M. A. Hitt, R. E. Freeman, and J. S. Harrison (eds.), *Handbook of Strategic Management*, Oxford, UK: Blackwell Publishers, 583–601.

51. J. O. De Castro & K. Uhlenbruck, 2003, The transformation into entrepreneurial firms, *Management Research*, 1: 171–184.

52. M. D. Lord, 2003, Constituency building as the foundation for corporate political strategy, *Academy of Management Executive*, 17(1): 112–124; D. A. Schuler, K. Rehbein, & R. D. Cramer, 2003, Pursuing strategic advantage through political means: A multivariate approach, *Academy of Management Journal*, 45: 659–672; A. J. Hillman & M. A. Hitt, 1999, Corporate political strategy formulation: A model of approach, participation, and strategy decisions, *Academy of Management Review*, 24: 825–842.

53. M. Carson, 1998, *Global Competitiveness Quarterly*, March 9, 1.

54. 2001, Millennium in motion.

55. M. Peterson, 2003, Who's minding the drugstore? *New York Times*, http://www.nytimes.com, June 29.

56. 2003, U.S. spends the most on healthcare but dollars do not equal health, MEDICA Portal, http://www4.medica.de; J. MacIntyre, 1999, Figuratively speaking, *Across the Board*, May 11.

57. A. R. Varey & G. Lynn, 1999, Americans save for retirement, *USA Today*, November 16, B1.

58. G. F. Will, 1999, The primacy of culture, *Newsweek*, January 18, 64.

59. J. Kronholz, R. Tomsho, D. Golden, & R. S. Greenberger, 2003, Court upholds affirmative action, *Wall Street Journal Online*, http://www.wsj.com, June 24.

60. 2003, U.S. Department of Labor, Bureau of Labor Statistics data, http://www.bls.gov, June.

61. J. Raymond, 2001, Defining women: Does the Census Bureau undercount female entrepreneurs? *Business Week Small Biz*, May 21, 12.

62. C. A. Bartlett & S. Ghoshal, 2002, Building competitive advantage through people, *MIT Sloan Management Review*, 43(2): 33–41.

63. T. Fleming, 2003, Benefits of taking the superhighway to work, *Canadian HR Reporter*, 16(11): G7.

64. C. W. L. Hill & F. T. Rothaermel, 2003, The performance of incumbent firms in the face of radical technological innovation, *Academy of Management Review*, 28: 257–274; A. Afuah, 2002, Mapping technological capabilities into product markets and competitive advantage: The case of cholesterol drugs, *Strategic Management Journal*, 23: 171–179.

65. T. Aeppel, 2002, In lights-out factories machines still make things even when no one is there, *Wall Street Journal Online*, http://www.wsj.com, November 19.

66. J. Baglole, 2003, Canada's southern drug drain, *Wall Street Journal Online*, http://www.wsj.com, March 31.

67. N. Wingfield, 2003, Anytime, anywhere: The number of Wi-Fi spots is set to explode, bringing the wireless technology to the rest of us, *Wall Street Journal*, March 31, R6, R12.

68. A. Andal-Ancion, P. A. Cartwright, & G. S. Yip, 2003, The digital transformation of traditional businesses, *MIT Sloan Management Review* 44(4): 34–41; M. A. Hitt, R. D. Ireland, & H. Lee, 2000, Technological learning, knowledge management, firm growth and performance, *Journal of Technology and Engineering Management*, 17: 231–246.

69. R. Adner, 2002, When are technologies disruptive? A demand-based view of the emergence of competition, *Strategic Management Journal*, 23: 667–688; R. Adner & D. A. Levinthal, 2002, The emergence of emerging technologies, *California Management Review*, 45(1): 50–66.

70. C. Nichols-Nixon & C. Y. Woo, 2003, Technology sourcing and output of established firms in a regime of encompassing technological change, *Strategic Management Journal*, 24: 651–666.

71. W. P. Wan & R. E. Hoskisson, 2003, Home country environments, corporate diversification strategies and firm performance, *Academy of Management Journal*, 46: 27–45; S. Zahra, R. D. Ireland, I. Gutierrez, & M. A. Hitt, 2000, Privatization and entrepreneurial transformation: Emerging issues and a future research agenda, *Academy of Management Review*, 25: 509–524.

72. F. Vermeulen & H. Barkema, 2002, Pace, rhythm, and scope: Process dependence in building a multinational corporation, *Strategic Management Journal*, 23: 637–653.

73. L. Tihanyi, R. A. Johnson, R. E. Hoskisson, & M. A. Hitt, 2003, Institutional ownership differences, and international diversification: The effects of boards of directors and technological opportunity, *Academy of Management Journal*, 46: 195–211.

74. S. M. Lee, 2003, South Korea: From the land of morning calm to ICT hotbed, *Academy of Management Executive*, 17(2): 7–18; A. K. Gupta, V. Govindarajan, & A. Malhotra, 1999, Feedback-seeking behavior within multinational corporations, *Strategic Management Journal*, 20: 205–222.

75. G. D. Bruton & D. Ahlstrom, 2002, An institutional view of China's venture capital industry: Explaining the differences between China and the West, *Journal of Business Venturing*, 18: 233–259.

76. 2003, Sales of office and commercial buildings soaring in Shenzhen, *SinoCast China Business Daily News*, August 7, D1.

77. P. Engardio, A. Bernstein, & M. Kripalani, 2003, Is your job next? *Business Week*, February 3, 50–60.

78. R. D. Ireland, M. A. Hitt, S. M. Camp, & D. L. Sexton, 2001, Integrating entrepreneurship and strategic management actions to create firm wealth, *Academy of Management Executive*, 15(1): 49–63.

79. J. W. Lu & P. W. Beamish, 2001, The internationalization and performance of SMEs, *Strategic Management Journal*, 22(Special Issue): 565–586.

80. M. Subramaniam & N. Venkataraman, 2001, Determinants of transnational new product development capability: Testing the influence of transferring and deploying tacit overseas knowledge, *Strategic Management Journal*, 22: 359–378; P. J. Lane, J. E. Salk, & M. A. Lyles, 2001, Absorptive capacity, learning and performance in international joint ventures, *Strategic Management Journal*, 22: 1139–1161.

81. G. D. Bruton, D. Ahlstrom, & J. C. Wan, 2003, Turnaround in East Asian firms: Evidence from ethnic overseas Chinese communities, *Strategic Management Journal*, 24: 519–540; S. H. Park & Y. Luo, 2001, Guanxi and organizational

dynamics: Organizational networking in Chinese firms, *Strategic Management Journal*, 22: 455–477; M. A. Hitt M. T. Dacin, B. B. Tyler, & D. Park, 1997, Understanding the differences in Korean and U.S. executives' strategic orientations, *Strategic Management Journal*, 18: 159–167.

82. M. A. Hitt, D. Ahlstrom, M. T. Dacin, E. Levitas, and L. Svobodina, 2004, The institutional effects on strategic alliance partner selection: China versus Russia, *Organization Science*, in press.

83. Park & Luo, Guanxi and organizational dynamics.

84. M. A. Hitt, H. Lee, & E. Yucel, 2002, The importance of social capital to the management of multinational enterprises: Relational capital among Asian and Western firms, *Asia Pacific Journal of Management*, 19: 353–372.

85. 2003, Global Crossing's restructuring process, http://www.globalcrossing.com, June; 2002, Global Crossing denies resemblance to Enron, *Richmond Times Dispatch*, March 22, B15; S. Romero, 2001, Global Crossing looks overseas for financing, *New York Times*, http://www.nytimes.com, December 20; T. Burt, 2001, DaimlerChrysler in talks with Kuwaiti investors, *Financial Times*, http://www.ft.com, February 11.

86. 2002, Devaluation's downbeat start, *The Economist*, http://www.economist.com, January 10; J. Fuerbringer & R. W. Stevenson, 2001, No bailout is planned for Argentina, *New York Times*, http://www.nytimes.com, July 14; K. L. Newman, 2000, Organizational transformation during institutional upheaval, *Academy of Management Review*, 25: 602–619.

87. C. A. Bartlett & S. Ghoshal, 2003, What is a global manager? *Harvard Business Review*, 81(8): 101–108; M. A. Carpenter & J. W. Fredrickson, 2001, Top management teams, global strategic posture and the moderating role of uncertainty, *Academy of Management Journal*, 44: 533–545.

88. N. Argyres & A. M. McGahan, 2002, An interview with Michael Porter, *Academy of Management Executive*, 16(2): 43–52; Y. E. Spanos & S. Lioukas, 2001, An examination into the causal logic of rent generation: Contrasting Porter's competitive strategy framework and the resource-based perspective, *Strategic Management Journal*, 22: 907–934.

89. G. Hawawini, V. Subramanian, & P. Verdin, 2003, Is performance driven by industry or firm-specific factors? A new look at the evidence, *Strategic Management Journal*, 24: 1–16.

90. S. Zaheer & A. Zaheer, 2001, Market microstructure in a global b2b network, *Strategic Management Journal*, 22: 859–873.

91. Hitt, Ricart, Costa, & Nixon, The new frontier.

92. C. Garcia-Pont & N. Nohria, 2002, Local versus global mimetism: The dynamics of alliance formation in the automobile industry, *Strategic Management Journal*, 23: 307–321; Y. Pan & P. S. K. Chi, 1999, Financial performance and survival of multinational corporations in China, *Strategic Management Journal*, 20: 359–374.

93. P. A. Geroski, 1999, Early warning of new rivals, *Sloan Management Review*, 40(3): 107–116.

94. J. Shamsie, 2003, The context of dominance: An industry-driven framework for exploiting reputation, *Strategic Management Journal*, 24: 199–215; K. C. Robinson & P. P. McDougall, 2001, Entry barriers and new venture performance: A comparison of universal and contingency approaches, *Strategic Management Journal*, 22(Special Issue): 659–685.

95. R. Makadok, 1999, Interfirm differences in scale economies and the evolution of market shares, *Strategic Management Journal*, 20: 935–952.

96. F. Keenan, S. Holmes, J. Greene, & R. O. Crockett, 2002, A mass market of one, *Business Week*, December 2, 68–72; R. Wise & P. Baumgartner, 1999, Go downstream: The new profit imperative in manufacturing, *Harvard Business Review*, 77(5): 133–141.

97. G. Walker, T. L. Madsen, & G. Carini, 2002, How does institutional change affect heterogeneity among firms? *Strategic Management Journal*, 23: 89–104.

98. 2002, The long shadow of big blue, *The Economist*, November 9, 63–64.

99. D. Michaels & J. L. Lunsford, 2003, Airbus clings to output gains, *Wall Street Journal*, January 14, B4.

100. G. Khermouch, 2001, Grown-up drinks for tender taste buds, *Business Week*, March 5, 96.

101. A. M. Knott, 2003, Persistent heterogeneity and sustainable innovation, *Strategic Management Journal*, 24: 687–705; T. Noda & D. J. Collies, 2001, The evolution of intraindustry firm heterogeneity: Insights from a process study, *Academy of Management Journal*, 44: 897–925.

102. C. Matlack & S. Holmes, 2002, Look out, Boeing: Airbus is grabbing market share, but can it make money this way? *Business Week*, October 28, 50–51.

103. D. M. De Carolis, 2003, Competencies and imitability in the pharmaceutical industry: An analysis of their relationship with firm performance, *Journal of Management*, 29: 27–50; D. L. Deephouse, 1999, To be different, or to be the same? It's a question (and theory) of strategic balance, *Strategic Management Journal*, 20: 147–166.

104. W. Chung & A. Kalnins, 2001, Agglomeration effects and performance: Test of the Texas lodging industry, *Strategic Management Journal*, 22: 969–988.

105. W. Kuemmerle, 2001, Home base and knowledge management in international ventures, *Journal of Business Venturing*, 17: 99–122; G. Lorenzoni & A. Lipparini, 1999, The leveraging of interfirm relationships as a distinctive organizational capability: A longitudinal study, *Strategic Management Journal*, 20: 317–338.

106. M. E. Porter, 1980, *Competitive Strategy*, New York: Free Press.

107. M. S. Hunt, 1972, Competition in the major home appliance industry, 1960–1970 (doctoral dissertation, Harvard University); Porter, *Competitive Strategy*, 129.

108. G. McNamara, D. L. Deephouse, & R. A. Luce, 2003, Competitive positioning within and across a strategic group structure: The performance of core, secondary, and solitary firms, *Strategic Management Journal*, 24: 161–181.

109. H. R. Greve, 1999, Managerial cognition and the mimetic adoption of market positions: What you see is what you do, *Strategic Management Journal*, 19: 967–988.

110. R. K. Reger & A. S. Huff, 1993, Strategic groups: A cognitive perspective, *Strategic Management Journal*, 14: 103–123.

111. M. Peteraf & M. Shanley, 1997, Getting to know you: A theory of strategic group identity, *Strategic Management Journal*, 18 (Special Issue): 165–186.

112. J. Lee, K. Lee, & S. Rho, 2002, An evolutionary perspective on strategic group emergence: A genetic algorithm-based model, *Strategic Management Journal*, 23: 727–746.

113. J. D. Osborne, C. I. Stubbart, & A. Ramaprasad, 2001, Strategic groups and competitive enactment: A study of dynamic relationships between mental models and performance, *Strategic Management Journal*, 22: 435–454.

114. Greve, Managerial cognition, 972–973.

115. M. A. Hitt, R. E. Hoskisson, R. A. Johnson, & D. D. Moesel, 1996, The market for corporate control and firm innovation, *Academy of Management Journal*, 39: 1084–1119.

116. Porter, *Competitive Strategy*, 49.

117. G. McNamara, R. A. Luce, & G. H. Tompson, 2002, Examining the effect of complexity in strategic group knowledge structures on firm performance, *Strategic Management Journal*, 23: 153–170.

118. P. M. Norman, R. D. Ireland, K. W. Artz, & M. A. Hitt, 2000, Acquiring and using competitive intelligence in entrepreneurial teams. Paper presented at the Academy of Management, Toronto, Canada.

119. C. S. Fleisher, 1999, Public policy competitive intelligence, *Competitive Intelligence Review*, 10(2): 24.

120. 2003, Factiva: Strategic steps to web content and solutions, http://www.factiva.com, June 20; 2001, Fuld & Co., CEO interview: Clare Hart, president and CEO, Factiva, http://www.dowjones.com, April 4.

121. V. Drucker, 1999, Is your computer a sitting duck during a deal? *Mergers & Acquisitions*, July/August, 25–28.

122. M. Moss, 1999, Inside the game of e-mail hijacking, *Wall Street Journal*, November 9, B1, B4.

123. A. Jones, 2001, P&G to seek new resolution of spy dispute, *Financial Times*, http://www.ft.com, September 4.

124. J. H. Hallaq & K. Steinhorst, 1994, Business intelligence methods: How ethical? *Journal of Business Ethics*, 13: 787–794.

125. L. Fahey, 1999, Competitor scenarios: Projecting a rival's marketplace strategy, *Competitive Intelligence Review*, 10(2): 65–85.

The Internal Environment: Resources, Capabilities, and Core Competencies

Chapter Three

3

Knowledge Objectives

Studying this chapter should provide you with the strategic management knowledge needed to:

1. Explain the need for firms to study and understand their internal environment.

2. Define value and discuss its importance.

3. Describe the differences between tangible and intangible resources.

4. Define capabilities and discuss how they are developed.

5. Describe four criteria used to determine whether resources and capabilities are core competencies.

6. Explain how value chain analysis is used to identify and evaluate resources and capabilities.

7. Define outsourcing and discuss the reasons for its use.

8. Discuss the importance of preventing core competencies from becoming core rigidities.

Caterpillar carefully assesses its internal environment and supports its strengths by continuously investing in its resources. The company spends $4 million per day to maintain its competitive advantage through technology. It is also quick to help its worldwide dealers with whatever they need to run their businesses efficiently. Finally, Caterpillar is service oriented, utilizing 6 Sigma to change its distribution as new customer needs emerge.

Technology and Dealer Service: Caterpillar's Sources of Competitive Advantage

A *Fortune* 500 company, Caterpillar (Cat) is a manufacturer of construction and mining equipment, diesel and natural gas engines, and industrial gas turbines, and is a provider of an array of financial products. It is a technology leader in most of its manufacturing areas. The firm wants to increase its total revenue to $30 billion by 2010 while increasing its return to shareholders. A substantial commitment to participating in the development of emerging economies such as China is expected to contribute to achievement of these goals. In recent times, Cat was recognized by *Fortune* as the most admired company in the industrial and farm equipment industry, while *Forbes* named the firm to its Platinum 400 list of the best big U.S. companies.

Cat's strategic intent is to be the global leader in creating customer value. More diversified than it was ten years ago, Cat is no longer just a "tractor" company. Deriving approximately 49 percent of its sales revenue from outside the United States, Cat's distinctive yellow machines are in service in almost every country in the world. The firm's products and services are grouped into three primary business units—machinery (59 percent of revenues), engines (33 percent of revenues), and financial products (8 percent of revenues). The engines business unit derives 90 percent of its revenue from third-party customers such as Paccar Inc., manufacturer of the well-known Kenworth and Peterbilt brand tractors and trailers. As a primary area of growth, Cat expects the engines unit to account for as much as 45 percent of total revenue by 2007. According to company documents, Cat's machines are used to build the world's infrastructure, its reciprocating engines and engine systems provide power to the world, and its financial products make it possible for Cat customers around the world to buy new and used Cat machines and engines and related equipment.

Technology is one of Cat's primary competitive advantages. Cat invests approximately $4 million daily in technology. These investments are part of the firm's total allocation of over $700 million annually to research and development. Several achievements, including the fact that its employees earned over 2,800 patents in a recent six-year period, indicate that technology is a competitive advantage for Cat. Approval from the U.S. Environmental Protection Agency for its heavy-duty truck diesel engine using the firm's advanced combustion emission reduction technology, or Acert, also denotes Cat's technology competitive advantage. Cat officials indicate that Acert, developed in 2003, is a stepping-stone for the firm to meet particulate-matter standards that go into effect in 2007. In concert with a partner, Cat also recently developed a new type of stainless steel. To be used in diesel engines, this raw material permits greater engine efficiencies and fewer emissions.

A global network of independent dealers is Cat's second primary competitive advantage. In speaking to its service competence, Cat claims that its "global dealer network provides a key competitive edge—customers deal with people they know and trust." A large number of Cat's dealers have been associated with the company for decades, and many of them have relationships with their customers that span at least two generations. Regardless of customers' locations across the globe, Cat dealers support them with the machines, parts, and expertise that are required to effectively and efficiently operate their businesses.

Because service is a competitive advantage, Cat is committed to continuous improvements in order to meet the ever-changing needs of its customers. The firm is using 6 Sigma (a fact-based, data-driven discipline that focuses on maximizing customer value) to reengineer its distribution channels. This is being accomplished by focusing on processes that are common between the firm and its dealers, including e-business capabilities, customer relationship management, market segment focus, and parts and products sales opportunities.

SOURCES: 2003, Caterpillar Home Page, http://www.cat.com, July 6; 2003, Caterpillar Inc., *Standard & Poor's Stock Reports*, http://www.standardandpoors.com, July 3; J. B. Arndorfer, 2003, Cat is set to dig deeper in China, *Crain's Chicago Business*, 26(26): 4–5; J. Eig, 2003, Caterpillar's net nearly doubles amid signs of rebound in sales, *Wall Street Journal Online*, http://www.wsj.com, July 18; D. Jones, 2003, Oak Ridge, Caterpillar fashion new type of stainless steel for advanced engines, *Inside Energy*, July 7, 14–16; J. Wislocki, 2003, Caterpillar wins EPA approval for Acert heavy-duty engines, *Transport Topics*, June 16, 5.

As discussed in the first two chapters, several factors in the global economy, including the rapid development of the Internet's capabilities,[1] have made it increasingly difficult for firms to develop a competitive advantage that can be sustained for any period of time.[2] In these instances, firms try to create advantages that can be sustained longer than can others. The probability of developing a sustainable competitive advantage increases when firms use their own unique resources, capabilities, and core competencies to implement their strategies.[3] As described in the Opening Case, Caterpillar has been able to establish sustainable competitive advantages in terms of technology and dealer service. Because of their importance, Cat devotes substantial resources to support, nurture, and continuously develop these advantages.

The fact that competitive advantages and the differences in performances among firms they create continue to provide the central agenda in strategy research highlights the importance of studying competitive advantage and firm performance.[4] Research about competitive advantage is critical because "resources are the foundation for strategy and unique bundles of resources generate competitive advantages leading to wealth creation."[5] To identify and successfully use their competitive advantages over time, firms think constantly about their strategic management process and how to increase the value it creates.[6] As this chapter's discussion indicates, firms achieve strategic competitiveness and earn above-average returns when their unique core competencies are effectively acquired, bundled, and leveraged to take advantage of opportunities in the external environment.[7]

Increasingly, people are a key source of competitive advantage as organizations compete in the global economy.[8] This is true at Enterprise Rent-A-Car. Established in 1957, the firm has over 50,000 employees with 5,000-plus offices in the United States, Germany, the United Kingdom, Canada, and Ireland. When asked about his firm's ability to continue expanding, CEO Andy Taylor said that if he "had to choose one critical success factor in [the firm's] move into new markets, [he] would point to motivated, pioneering employees who have been excited about taking on a new challenge and making the business work." Taylor believes his firm succeeds because of the intellectual capital and efforts of individuals who thrive on being in charge and dream of becoming effective entrepreneurs.[9]

CEO Andy Taylor attributes Enterprise Rent-A-Car's success to employees' efforts and the intellectual capital they represent.

Over time, the benefits of any firm's value-creating strategy can be duplicated by its competitors. In other words, all competitive advantages have a limited life.[10] The question of duplication is not *if* it will happen, but *when*. In general, the sustainability of a competitive advantage is a function of three factors: (1) the rate of core competence obsolescence because of environmental changes, (2) the availability of substitutes for the core competence, and (3) the imitability of the core competence.[11]

The challenge in all firms is to effectively manage current core competencies while simultaneously developing new ones.[12] In the words of Michael Dell, CEO of Dell Inc., "No [competitive] advantage and no success is ever permanent. The winners are those who keep moving. The only constant in our business is that everything is changing. We have to be ahead of the game."[13] Only when firms develop a continuous stream of competitive advantages do they achieve strategic competitiveness, earn above-average returns, and remain ahead of competitors (see Chapter 5).

In Chapter 2, we examined general, industry, and competitor environments. Armed with this knowledge about the realities and conditions of their environments, firms have a better understanding of marketplace opportunities and the characteristics of the competitive environment in which they exist. In this chapter, we focus on the firm itself. By analyzing its internal environment, a firm determines what it *can do*—that is, the actions permitted by its unique resources, capabilities, and core competencies. As discussed in Chapter 1, core competencies are a firm's source of competitive advantage. The magnitude of that competitive advantage is a function primarily of the uniqueness of the firm's core competencies compared to those of its competitors.[14] Matching what a firm *can do* with what it *might do* (a function of opportunities and threats in the external environment) allows the firm to develop strategic intent, pursue its strategic mission, and select and implement its strategies. Outcomes resulting from internal and external environmental analyses are shown in Figure 3.1.

We begin this chapter with a discussion of the nature of an analysis of the firm's internal environment. We then discuss the roles of resources and capabilities in developing core competencies, which are the firm's competitive advantages. Included in this discussion are the techniques firms can use to identify and evaluate resources and capabilities and the criteria for selecting core competencies from among them. Resources and capabilities are not inherently valuable, but they create value when the firm can use them to perform certain activities that result in a competitive advantage. Accordingly, we also discuss in this chapter the value chain concept and examine four criteria to evaluate core competencies that establish competitive advantage.[15] The chapter closes with cautionary comments about the need for firms to prevent their core competencies from becoming core rigidities. The existence of core rigidities indicates that the firm is too anchored to its past, which prevents it from continuously developing new competitive advantages.

Figure 3.1 — Outcomes from External and Internal Environmental Analyses

By studying the external environment, firms determine • what they *might* choose to *do*	By studying the internal environment, firms determine • what they *can do*

The Nature of Internal Environmental Analysis

The Context of Internal Analysis

In the global economy, traditional factors—such as labor costs, access to financial resources and raw materials, and protected or regulated markets—continue to be sources of competitive advantage, but to a lesser degree.[16] One important reason for this decline is that the advantages created by these more traditional sources can be overcome through an international strategy (discussed in Chapter 8) and by the relatively free flow of resources throughout the global economy. The need to identify additional and perhaps new sources of competitive advantage highlights the importance of looking inside the firm to carefully study its resources and capabilities.

Few firms can consistently make effective strategic decisions about how to use their resources and capabilities unless they can change. A key challenge to developing the ability to change is fostering an organizational setting in which experimentation and learning are expected and promoted in order to determine what the firm *can do* (see Figure 3.1).[17] For example, Levi Strauss previously refused to sell its jeans through Wal-Mart, believing that doing so would tarnish the value of its brand. However, "desperate" to reverse declines in the sales of its jeans, the firm began selling a new line (Levi Strauss Signature) through Wal-Mart's stores in mid-2003. The 43 percent decline in sales revenue Levi Strauss experienced between 1996 and 2002 influenced the firm's willingness to reevaluate how it was using its resources and capabilities to compete in what had become a vastly changed competitive environment for the firm.[18]

In addition to an ability to change how a firm competes, exemplified by the decision made by Levi Strauss to sell jeans through Wal-Mart, a different managerial mind-set is required for firms to effectively analyze their internal environment. Increasingly, those analyzing their firm's internal environment should use a global mind-set. A global mind-set is the ability to study an internal environment in ways that are not dependent on the assumptions of a single country, culture, or context.[19] Those with a global mind-set recognize that their firms must possess resources and capabilities that allow them to understand and appropriately respond to competitive situations that are influenced by country-specific factors as well as by unique societal cultures.

Finally, analysis of the firm's internal environment finds evaluators thinking of their firm as a *bundle* of heterogeneous resources and capabilities that can be used to create

Levi Strauss created a new product line, Levi Strauss' Signature Jeans, that is sold through a new distribution channel, Wal-Mart stores.

©David Young-Wolff/PhotoEdit

an exclusive market position.[20] This perspective suggests that individual firms possess at least some resources and capabilities that other companies do not—at least not in the same combination. Resources are the source of capabilities, some of which lead to the development of a firm's core competencies or its competitive advantages.[21] Understanding how to *leverage* the firm's unique bundle of resources and capabilities is a key outcome decision makers seek when analyzing the internal environment. Figure 3.2 illustrates the relationships among resources, capabilities, and core competencies and shows how firms use them to create strategic competitiveness. Before examining these topics in depth, we describe value and how firms use their resources, capabilities, and core competencies to create it.

Creating Value

By exploiting their core competencies or competitive advantages to at least meet if not exceed the demanding standards of global competition, firms create value for customers.[22] **Value** is measured by a product's performance characteristics and by its attributes for which customers are willing to pay.[23] Evidence suggests that increasingly, customers perceive higher value in global rather than domestic-only brands.[24] Firms create value by innovatively bundling and leveraging their resources and capabilities.[25] Firms unable to creatively bundle and leverage their resources and capabilities in ways that create value for customers suffer performance declines. In the Strategic Focus, we examine venerable Sears, Roebuck and Co. For some years now, the giant retailer has struggled in its efforts to use its resources and capabilities to create customer value. As we explain, Sears is taking multiple actions to correct this situation and to offer more value to a larger number of customers.

Value is measured by a product's performance characteristics and by its attributes for which customers are willing to pay.

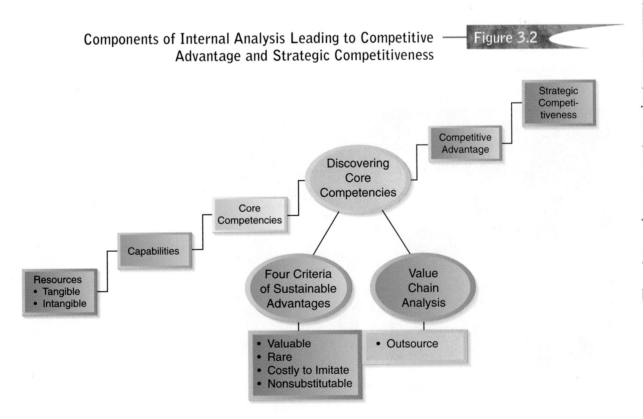

Components of Internal Analysis Leading to Competitive Advantage and Strategic Competitiveness — Figure 3.2

Sears, Roebuck and Co.: Still Where America Shops?

Sears, Roebuck and Co. is a leading retailer of appliances and home and automotive products as well as related services, such as product repairs through maintenance contracts and the installation and repair of all major brands of home products. But for some time, the firm hasn't been consistent in how it seeks to create value for customers. Over the last two decades, Sears has vacillated from soft goods to hard goods while entering and exiting a number of different businesses. Even today, some believe that "Sears is still trying to figure out what it wants to be." Others believe that "the long-term outlook for Sears as a merchandising company is very difficult" and that Sears is "still trying to figure out what its customers . . . want." Given these conditions, what is Sears trying to do to create value for customers, and how is it positioning itself to improve its ability to compete against firms such as Wal-Mart and Target?

Critical to Sears' efforts to create more customer value is the decision to refocus its operations. In mid-2003, Sears sold its credit card operation to Citigroup for approximately $3 billion. This was the last major divestiture of Sears' assets that were unrelated to its core retailing and service operations. As Sears' CEO said, selling its credit card operations was a "logical progression in [the firm's] ongoing strategy of focusing on growing [its] core retail and related-services businesses."

Appliances are a core retail and service area for Sears. To increase customer value in this product category, the firm is offering a larger number of items in the lowest-price-level categories. Sears is doing this to match competitors' (such as Lowe's and Home Depot) prices for lower-priced appliances. Sears is also increasing the size of its appliance departments and is emphasizing that it sells the top five appliance brands in addition to its own Kenmore line. To assist in improving its clothing merchandise, Sears acquired specialty-retailer Lands' End. It also jettisoned underperforming clothing lines, launching its own private labels such as Covington and introducing women's clothing by Lucy Pereda, who has been dubbed "the Hispanic Martha Stewart." Pereda hosts a popular show on Galavisión as well as a radio program on Radio Unica that concentrates on decorating and cooking. According to company officials, the relationship with Pereda was established because "Hispanics are a very fast-growing segment of the population and a very strong asset with Sears." To offer more convenience to customers, Sears is establishing stand-alone concept stores called Sears Grand. Located outside large regional malls, long the traditional location for Sears' stores, these new units are intended to help the firm sell a wider selection of merchandise and allow customers to quickly enter the store, buy merchandise, and be on their way in less time than is required to shop in Sears' mall locations.

Sears is attempting to increase its profitability by creating value for its customers. One means of doing this is marketing to the growing Hispanic community through products such as Lucy Pereda's women's clothing.

©Myrleen Ferguson Cate/PhotoEdit

SOURCES: D. Alexander, 2003, Online retailers discover value in reaching Hispanic audience, *Knight Ridder Tribune Business News,* http://www.knightridder.com, June 18; J. Bailey, 2003, For a big score, think small towns, *Wall Street Journal Online,* http://www.wsj.com, July 15; R. Crain, 2003, Recalling 25 years of "CCB" turns up reminder for Sears, *Advertising Age,* 74(24): 16; T. Kern, 2003, Sears under siege, *Home Channel News,* 29(12): 1, 56–57; M. Pacelle, R. Sidel, & A. Merrick, 2003, Citigroup agrees to buy Sears's credit-card unit, *Wall Street Journal Online,* http://www.wsj.com, July 16; L. Yue, 2003, Sears reshapes apparel division, makes stronger play for minority shoppers, *Knight Ridder Tribune Business News,* http://www.knightridder.com, June 19.

Ultimately, value creating is the source of a firm's potential to earn above-average returns. What the firm intends regarding value creation affects its choice of business-level strategy (see Chapter 4) and its organizational structure (see Chapter 11).[26] In Chapter 4's discussion of business-level strategies, we note that value is created by a product's low cost, by its highly differentiated features, or by a combination of low cost and high differentiation, compared to competitors' offerings. A business-level strategy is effective only when its use is grounded in exploiting the firm's current core competencies while actions are being taken to develop the core competencies that will be needed to effectively use "tomorrow's" business-level strategy. Thus, successful firms continuously examine the effectiveness of current and future core competencies.[27]

During the last several decades, the strategic management process was concerned largely with understanding the characteristics of the industry in which the firm competed and, in light of those characteristics, determining how the firm should position itself relative to competitors. This emphasis on industry characteristics and competitive strategy may have underestimated the role of the firm's resources and capabilities in developing competitive advantage. In fact, core competencies, in combination with product-market positions, are the firm's most important sources of competitive advantage.[28] The core competencies of a firm, in addition to its analysis of its general, industry, and competitor environments, should drive its selection of strategies. As Clayton Christensen noted, "Successful strategists need to cultivate a deep understanding of the processes of competition and progress and of the factors that undergird each advantage. Only thus will they be able to see when old advantages are poised to disappear and how new advantages can be built in their stead."[29] By emphasizing core competencies when formulating strategies, companies learn to compete primarily on the basis of firm-specific differences, but they must be very aware of how things are changing in the external environment as well.

The Challenge of Internal Analysis

The strategic decisions managers make in terms of the firm's resources, capabilities, and core competencies are nonroutine,[30] have ethical implications,[31] and significantly influence the firm's ability to earn above-average returns.[32] Making these decisions—identifying, developing, deploying, and protecting resources, capabilities, and core competencies—may appear to be relatively easy. In fact, however, this task is as challenging and difficult as any other with which managers are involved; moreover, it is increasingly internationalized.[33] Some believe that the pressure on managers to pursue only those decisions that help the firm meet the quarterly earning numbers expected by market analysts makes it harder to carefully analyze the firm's internal resources, the most valuable of which are developed across time and events.[34] Recognizing the firm's core competencies is essential before the firm can make important strategic decisions, including those related to entering or exiting markets, investing in new technologies, building new or additional manufacturing capacity, or forming strategic partnerships.[35] Patterns of interactions between individuals and groups that occur as strategic decisions affect decision quality as well as how effectively and quickly these decisions are implemented.[36]

The challenge and difficulty of making effective decisions are implied by preliminary evidence suggesting that one-half of organizational decisions fail.[37] Sometimes, mistakes are made as the firm analyzes its internal environment. Managers might, for example, select resources and capabilities as the firm's core competencies that do not create a competitive advantage. When a mistake occurs, decision makers must have the confidence to admit it and take corrective actions.[38] A firm can still grow through well-intended errors—the learning generated by making and correcting mistakes can be important to the creation of new competitive advantages.[39] Moreover, firms can learn from the failure resulting from a mistake—that is, what *not* to do when seeking competitive advantage.[40]

To facilitate developing and using core competencies, managers must have courage, self-confidence, integrity, the capacity to deal with uncertainty and complexity, and a willingness to hold people accountable for their work and to be held accountable themselves. Thus, difficult managerial decisions concerning resources, capabilities, and core competencies are characterized by three conditions: uncertainty, complexity, and intraorganizational conflicts (see Figure 3.3).[41]

Managers face *uncertainty* in terms of new proprietary technologies, rapidly changing economic and political trends, transformations in societal values, and shifts in customer demands.[42] Environmental uncertainty increases the *complexity* and range of issues to examine when studying the internal environment.[43] Biases about how to cope with uncertainty affect decisions about the resources and capabilities that will become the foundation of the firm's competitive advantage. Finally, *intraorganizational conflict* surfaces when decisions are made about the core competencies to nurture as well as how to nurture them.

In making decisions affected by these three conditions, judgment should be used. *Judgment* is the capability of making successful decisions when no obviously correct model or rule is available or when relevant data are unreliable or incomplete. In this type of situation, decision makers must be aware of possible cognitive biases. Overconfidence, for example, can often lower value when a correct decision is not obvious, such as making a judgment as to whether an internal resource is a strength or a weakness.[44]

When exercising judgment, decision makers demonstrate a willingness to take intelligent risks in a timely manner. In the current competitive landscape, executive judgment can be a particularly important source of competitive advantage. One reason for this is that, over time, effective judgment allows a firm to build a strong reputation and retain the loyalty of stakeholders whose support is linked to above-average returns.[45]

Significant changes in the value-creating potential of a firm's resources and capabilities can occur in a rapidly changing global economy. Because these changes affect a company's power and social structure, inertia or resistance to change may surface. Even though these reactions may happen, decision makers should not deny the changes needed to assure the firm's strategic competitiveness. By denying the need for change, difficult experiences can be avoided in the short run.[46] However, in the long

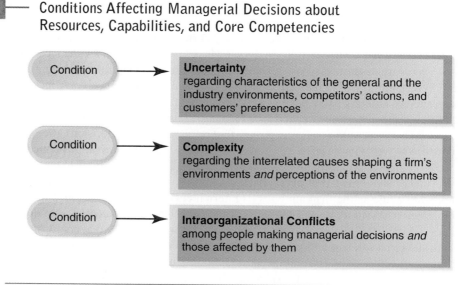

Figure 3.3 — Conditions Affecting Managerial Decisions about Resources, Capabilities, and Core Competencies

Condition → **Uncertainty**
regarding characteristics of the general and the industry environments, competitors' actions, and customers' preferences

Condition → **Complexity**
regarding the interrelated causes shaping a firm's environments *and* perceptions of the environments

Condition → **Intraorganizational Conflicts**
among people making managerial decisions *and* those affected by them

SOURCE: Adapted from R. Amit & P. J. H. Schoemaker, 1993, Strategic assets and organizational rent, *Strategic Management Journal*, 14: 33.

run, the failure to change when needed leads to performance declines and, in the worst-case scenario, to failure. Thus, Levi Strauss' decision to begin selling its jeans in Wal-Mart stores may prevent further reductions in the firm's sales volume.

Resources, Capabilities, and Core Competencies

Resources, capabilities, and core competencies are the characteristics that make up the foundation of competitive advantage. Resources are the source of a firm's capabilities. Capabilities in turn are the source of a firm's core competencies, which are the basis of competitive advantages.[47] As shown in Figure 3.2, combinations of resources and capabilities are managed to create core competencies. In this section, we define and provide examples of these building blocks of competitive advantage.

Resources

Broad in scope, resources cover a spectrum of individual, social, and organizational phenomena.[48] Typically, resources alone do not yield a competitive advantage.[49] In fact, a competitive advantage is created through the *unique bundling of several resources.*[50] For example, Amazon.com has combined service and distribution resources to develop its competitive advantages. The firm started as an online bookseller, directly shipping orders to customers. It quickly grew large and established a distribution network through which it could ship "millions of different items to millions of different customers." Compared to Amazon's use of combined resources, traditional bricks-and-mortar companies, such as Toys 'R' Us and Borders, found it hard to establish an effective online presence. These difficulties led them to develop partnerships with Amazon. Through these arrangements, Amazon now handles the online presence and the shipping of goods for several firms, including Toys 'R' Us and Borders—which now can focus on sales in their stores. Arrangements such as these are useful to the bricks-and-mortar companies because they are not accustomed to shipping so much diverse merchandise directly to individuals.[51]

Some of a firm's resources (defined in Chapter 1 as inputs to the firm's production process) are tangible while others are intangible. **Tangible resources** are assets that can be seen and quantified. Production equipment, manufacturing plants, and formal reporting structures are examples of tangible resources. **Intangible resources** include assets that typically are rooted deeply in the firm's history and have accumulated over time. Because they are embedded in unique patterns of routines, intangible resources are relatively difficult for competitors to analyze and imitate. Knowledge, trust between managers and employees, ideas, the capacity for innovation, managerial capabilities, organizational routines (the unique ways people work together), scientific capabilities, and the firm's reputation for its goods or services and how it interacts with people (such as employees, customers, and suppliers) are all examples of intangible resources.[52]

The four types of tangible resources are financial, organizational, physical, and technological (see Table 3.1). The three types of intangible resources are human, innovation, and reputational (see Table 3.2).

TANGIBLE RESOURCES

As tangible resources, a firm's borrowing capacity and the status of its plant and equipment are visible. The value of many tangible resources can be established through financial statements, but these statements do not account for the value of all of a firm's assets, because they disregard some intangible resources.[53] As such, each of the firm's sources of competitive advantage typically is not fully reflected on corporate financial statements. The value of tangible resources is also constrained because they are difficult to leverage—it is hard to derive additional business or value from a tangible resource.

Tangible resources *are assets that can be seen and quantified.*

Intangible resources *include assets that typically are rooted deeply in the firm's history and have accumulated over time.*

Table 3.1

Tangible Resources

Financial Resources	• The firm's borrowing capacity
	• The firm's ability to generate internal funds
Organizational Resources	• The firm's formal reporting structure and its formal planning, controlling, and coordinating systems
Physical Resources	• Sophistication and location of a firm's plant and equipment
	• Access to raw materials
Technological Resources	• Stock of technology, such as patents, trademarks, copyrights, and trade secrets

SOURCES: Adapted from J. B. Barney, 1991, Firm resources and sustained competitive advantage, *Journal of Management,* 17: 101; R. M. Grant, 1991, *Contemporary Strategy Analysis,* Cambridge, U.K.: Blackwell Business, 100–102.

For example, an airplane is a tangible resource or asset, but: "You can't use the same airplane on five different routes at the same time. You can't put the same crew on five different routes at the same time. And the same goes for the financial investment you've made in the airplane."[54]

Although production assets are tangible, many of the processes to use these assets are intangible. Thus, the learning and potential proprietary processes associated with a tangible resource, such as manufacturing equipment, can have unique intangible attributes, such as quality, just-in-time management practices, and unique manufacturing processes that develop over time and create competitive advantage.[55]

Table 3.2

Intangible Resources

Human Resources	• Knowledge
	• Trust
	• Managerial capabilities
	• Organizational routines
Innovation Resources	• Ideas
	• Scientific capabilities
	• Capacity to innovate
Reputational Resources	• Reputation with customers
	• Brand name
	• Perceptions of product quality, durability, and reliability
	• Reputation with suppliers
	• For efficient, effective, supportive, and mutually beneficial interactions and relationships

SOURCES: Adapted from R. Hall, 1992, The strategic analysis of intangible resources, *Strategic Management Journal,* 13: 136–139; R. M. Grant, 1991, *Contemporary Strategy Analysis,* Cambridge, U.K.: Blackwell Business, 101–104.

INTANGIBLE RESOURCES

As suggested above, compared to tangible resources, intangible resources are a superior and more potent source of core competencies.[56] In fact, in the global economy, "the success of a corporation lies more in its intellectual and systems capabilities than in its physical assets. [Moreover], the capacity to manage human intellect—and to convert it into useful products and services—is fast becoming the critical executive skill of the age."[57]

Even though it is hard to measure the value of intangible assets such as knowledge,[58] there is some evidence that the value of intangible assets is growing relative to that of tangible assets.[59] John Kendrick, a well-known economist studying the main drivers of economic growth, found a general increase in the contribution of intangible assets to U.S. economic growth since the early 1900s: "In 1929, the ratio of intangible business capital to tangible business capital was 30 percent to 70 percent. In 1990, that ratio was 63 percent to 37 percent."[60]

Because intangible resources are less visible and more difficult for competitors to understand, purchase, imitate, or substitute for, firms prefer to rely on them rather than on tangible resources as the foundation for their capabilities and core competencies. In fact, the more unobservable (that is, intangible) a resource is, the more sustainable will be the competitive advantage that is based on it.[61] Another benefit of intangible resources is that, unlike most tangible resources, their use can be leveraged. With intangible resources, the larger the network of users, the greater is the benefit to each party.[62] For instance, sharing knowledge among employees does not diminish its value for any one person. To the contrary, two people sharing their individualized knowledge sets often can be leveraged to create additional knowledge that, although new to each of them, contributes to performance improvements for the firm.[63]

As shown in Table 3.2, the intangible resource of reputation is an important source of competitive advantage. Earned through the firm's actions as well as its words, a value-creating reputation is a product of years of superior marketplace competence as perceived by stakeholders.[64] A reputation indicates the level of awareness a firm has been able to develop among stakeholders[65] and the degree to which they hold the firm in high esteem.[66] A well-known and highly valued brand name is an application of reputation as a source of competitive advantage.[67] A continuing commitment to innovation and aggressive advertising facilitates firms' efforts to take advantage of the reputation associated with their brands.[68] Because of the desirability of its reputation, the Harley-Davidson brand name, for example, has such status that it adorns a limited edition Barbie doll, a popular restaurant in New York City, and a line of L'Oréal cologne. Moreover, Harley-Davidson MotorClothes annually generates well in excess of $100 million in revenue for the firm and offers a broad range of clothing items, from black leather jackets to fashions for tots.[69]

The Harley-Davidson name has such status that it reaches even "unlicensed" motorcycle aficionados.

©Lon C. Diehl/PhotoEdit

Capabilities

Capabilities are the firm's capacity to deploy resources that have been purposely integrated to achieve a desired end state.[70] The glue binding an organization together, capabilities emerge over time through complex interactions among tangible and intangible resources. Critical to the forming of competitive advantages, capabilities are often based on developing, carrying, and exchanging information and knowledge through the firm's human capital.[71] Because a knowledge base is grounded in organizational actions that may not be explicitly understood by all employees, repetition and practice increase the value of a firm's capabilities.[72]

The foundation of many capabilities lies in the unique skills and knowledge of a firm's employees[73] and, often, their functional expertise. Hence, the value of human capital in developing and using capabilities and, ultimately, core competencies cannot be overstated. Firms committed to continuously developing their people's capabilities seem to accept the adage that "the person who knows how will always have a job. The person who knows why will always be his boss."[74]

Global business leaders increasingly support the view that the knowledge possessed by human capital is among the most significant of an organization's capabilities and may ultimately be at the root of all competitive advantages.[75] But firms must also be able to utilize the knowledge that they have and transfer it among their operating businesses.[76] For example, researchers have suggested that "in the information age, things are ancillary, knowledge is central. A company's value derives not from things, but from knowledge, know-how, intellectual assets, competencies—all of it embedded in people."[77] Given this reality, the firm's challenge is to create an environment that allows people to fit their individual pieces of knowledge together so that, collectively, employees possess as much organizational knowledge as possible.[78]

To help them develop an environment in which knowledge is widely spread across all employees, some organizations have created the new upper-level managerial position of chief learning officer (CLO). Establishing a CLO position highlights a firm's belief that "future success will depend on competencies that traditionally have not been actively managed or measured—including creativity and the speed with which new ideas are learned and shared."[79] In general, the firm should manage knowledge in ways that will support its efforts to create value for customers.[80]

As illustrated in Table 3.3, capabilities are often developed in specific functional areas (such as manufacturing, R&D, and marketing) or in a part of a functional area (for example, advertising). Research indicates a relationship between capabilities developed in particular functional areas and the firm's financial performance at both the corporate and business-unit levels,[81] suggesting the need to develop capabilities at both levels. Table 3.3 shows a grouping of organizational functions and the capabilities that some companies are thought to possess in terms of all or parts of those functions.

Core Competencies

Defined in Chapter 1, *core competencies* are resources and capabilities that serve as a source of a firm's competitive advantage over rivals. Core competencies distinguish a company competitively and reflect its personality. Core competencies emerge over time through an organizational process of accumulating and learning how to deploy different resources and capabilities.[82] As the capacity to take action, core competencies are "crown jewels of a company," the activities the company performs especially well compared to competitors and through which the firm adds unique value to its goods or services over a long period of time.[83]

Not all of a firm's resources and capabilities are *strategic assets*—that is, assets that have competitive value and the potential to serve as a source of competitive advantage.[84] Some resources and capabilities may result in incompetence, because they represent competitive areas in which the firm is weak compared to competitors. Thus, some resources or capabilities may stifle or prevent the development of a core competence. Firms with the tangible resource of financial capital, such as Microsoft, which has a large amount of cash on hand, may be able to purchase facilities or hire the skilled workers required to manufacture products that yield customer value. However, firms without financial capital would have a weakness in regard to being able to buy

Functional Areas	Capabilities	Examples of Firms
Distribution	Effective use of logistics management techniques	Wal-Mart
Human resources	Motivating, empowering, and retaining employees	Microsoft Corp.
Management information systems	Effective and efficient control of inventories through point-of-purchase data collection methods	Wal-Mart
Marketing	Effective promotion of brand-name products	Gillette Co.
		Polo Ralph Lauren Corp.
		McKinsey & Co.
	Effective customer service	Nordstrom Inc.
		Solectron Corporation
		Norrell Corporation
	Innovative merchandising	Crate & Barrel
Management	Ability to envision the future of clothing	Gap Inc.
	Effective organizational structure	PepsiCo
Manufacturing	Design and production skills yielding reliable products	Komatsu
	Product and design quality	Gap Inc.
	Miniaturization of components and products	Sony
Research & development	Innovative technology	Caterpillar
	Development of sophisticated elevator control solutions	Otis Elevator Co.
	Rapid transformation of technology into new products and processes	Chaparral Steel
	Digital technology	Thomson Consumer Electronics

or build new capabilities. To be successful, firms must locate external environmental opportunities that can be exploited through their capabilities, while avoiding competition in areas of weakness.[85]

An important question is, "How many core competencies are required for the firm to have a sustained competitive advantage?" Responses to this question vary. McKinsey & Co. recommends that its clients identify three or four competencies around which their strategic actions can be framed.[86] Supporting and nurturing more than four core competencies may prevent a firm from developing the focus it needs to fully exploit its competencies in the marketplace.

Firms should take actions that are based on their core competencies. Recent actions by Starbucks demonstrate this point. Growing rapidly, Starbucks decided that it could use the Internet as a distribution channel to bring about additional growth. The firm quickly realized that it lacks the capabilities required to successfully distribute its products through this channel and that its unique coffee, not the delivery of that product, is its competitive advantage. In part, this recognition caused Starbucks to renew its emphasis on existing capabilities to create more value through its supply chain. Trimming the number of its milk suppliers from 65 to fewer than 25 and negotiating long-term contracts with coffee-bean growers are actions Starbucks has taken to do this. The firm also decided to place automated espresso machines in its busy units. These machines reduce Starbucks' cost while providing improved service to its customers, who can now move through the line much faster. Using its supply chain and service capabilities in these manners allows Starbucks to strengthen its competitive advantages of coffee and the unique venue in which on-site customers experience it. These efforts contributed to what analysts called Starbucks' "outstanding" performance in mid-2003.[87]

Of course, not all resources and capabilities are core competencies. The next section discusses two approaches for identifying core competencies.

Building Core Competencies

Two tools help the firm identify and build its core competencies.[88] The first consists of four specific criteria of sustainable competitive advantage that firms can use to determine those resources and capabilities that are core competencies. Because the capabilities shown in Table 3.3 have satisfied these four criteria, they are core competencies. The second tool is the value chain analysis. Firms use this tool to select the value-creating competencies that should be maintained, upgraded, or developed and those that should be outsourced.

Four Criteria of Sustainable Competitive Advantage

As shown in Table 3.4, capabilities that are valuable, rare, costly to imitate, and non-substitutable are core competencies. In turn, core competencies are sources of competitive advantage for the firm over its rivals. Capabilities failing to satisfy the four criteria of sustainable competitive advantage are not core competencies, meaning that although every core competence is a capability, not every capability is a core competence. In slightly different words, for a capability to be a core competence, it must be "valuable and nonsubstitutable, from a customer's point of view, and unique and inimitable, from a competitor's point of view."[89]

Starbucks' analysis of its core competencies has led it to deemphasize Internet distribution and place greater emphasis on its supply chain and service capabilities. Examples include its renegotiated contracts with milk and coffee bean suppliers and its installation of automated espresso machines in busy stores.

A sustained competitive advantage is achieved only when competitors have failed in efforts to duplicate the benefits of a firm's strategy or when they lack the confidence to attempt imitation. For some period of time, the firm may earn a competitive advantage by using capabilities that are, for example, valuable and rare, but that are imitable.[90] In this instance, the length of time a firm can expect to retain its competitive advantage is a function of how quickly competitors can successfully imitate a good, service, or process. Sustainable competitive advantage results only when all four criteria are satisfied.

VALUABLE

Valuable capabilities allow the firm to exploit opportunities or neutralize threats in its external environment. By effectively using capabilities to exploit opportunities, a firm creates value for customers.

Bricks-and-mortar grocers such as Safeway Inc. and Albertson's Inc. are using their existing capabilities to create value for online grocery shoppers. Unlike failed Internet ventures Webvan, HomeRuns.com, Streamline.com, and others of the same ilk, these established companies "stick to what they know best" to serve the needs of those wanting to buy groceries online. Rather than using expensive marketing ploys, for example, these new players advertise to those filling the online grocery market niche (no chain expects online rev-

©Michael Newman/PhotoEdit

Valuable Capabilities	• Help a firm neutralize threats or exploit opportunities
Rare Capabilities	• Are not possessed by many others
Costly-to-Imitate Capabilities	• Historical: A unique and a valuable organizational culture or brand name
	• Ambiguous cause: The causes and uses of a competence are unclear
	• Social complexity: Interpersonal relationships, trust, and friendship among managers, suppliers, and customers
Nonsubstitutable Capabilities	• No strategic equivalent

enue to account for more than 5 percent of total sales volume) with the same weekly flyers and local TV ads used to promote their storefront operations. Commonly serving their affluent customers, established grocers are finding that online orders exceed average in-store ticket prices. "At Safeway, the average online order size is $120, twice that of the average in-store ticket."[91]

RARE

Rare capabilities are capabilities that few, if any, competitors possess. A key question to be answered when evaluating this criterion is, "How many rival firms possess these valuable capabilities?" Capabilities possessed by many rivals are unlikely to be sources of competitive advantage for any one of them. Instead, valuable but common (i.e., not rare) resources and capabilities are sources of competitive parity.[92] Competitive advantage results only when firms develop and exploit capabilities that differ from those shared with competitors.

Rare capabilities are capabilities that few, if any, competitors possess.

COSTLY TO IMITATE

Costly-to-imitate capabilities are capabilities that other firms cannot easily develop. Capabilities that are costly to imitate are created because of one reason or a combination of three reasons (see Table 3.4). First, a firm sometimes is able to develop capabilities because of *unique historical conditions*. "As firms evolve, they pick up skills, abilities and resources that are unique to them, reflecting their particular path through history."[93] Another way of saying this is that firms sometimes are able to develop capabilities because they were in the right place at the right time.[94]

Costly-to-imitate capabilities are capabilities that other firms cannot easily develop.

A firm with a unique and valuable *organizational culture* that emerged in the early stages of the company's history "may have an imperfectly imitable advantage over firms founded in another historical period"[95]—one in which less valuable or less competitively useful values and beliefs strongly influenced the development of the firm's culture. This may be the case for the consulting firm McKinsey & Co. "It is that culture, unique to McKinsey and eccentric, which sets the firm apart from virtually any other business organization and which often mystifies even those who engage [its] services."[96] Briefly discussed in Chapter 1, organizational culture is "something that people connect with, feel inspired by, think of as a normal way of operating. It's in their hearts and minds, and its core is voluntary behavior."[97] An organizational culture is a source of advantage when employees are held together tightly by their belief in it.[98]

UPS has been the prototype in many areas of the parcel delivery business because of its excellence in products, systems, marketing, and other operational business capabilities. "Its fundamental competitive strength, however, derives from the

Competitive Parity in the Airline Industry: The Best That Can Be Done?

Airline service has become a commodity-like good, meaning that the price variable is a primary source of competition among industry participants. Through various marketing campaigns, consumers are well aware of "discount" and "low-cost" fares that airline firms offer to induce ticket purchases. As we discuss in Chapter 5, pricing decisions are tactical rather than strategic actions. In essence, this means that although pricing decisions are easy to implement and reverse, competitors can easily imitate them, allowing the possibility of only a temporary competitive advantage at best. As discussed in Chapter 2, competing principally on the basis of price has the potential to substantially reduce firms' ability to operate profitably within an industry and virtually precludes the possibility of generating customer loyalty. However, Southwest Airlines and JetBlue Airways (discussed further in Chapters 4 and 5, respectively) operate with cost structures that allow their prices to consumers to be a competitive advantage. Even in these instances, though, the firms have other sources of differentiation that are competitive advantages. "Despite its low costs, Southwest delivers consistently high levels of service," while JetBlue "differentiates itself by flying new aircraft and offering leather seats and free direct satellite TV at every seat."

Companies prefer to be as different from competitors on as many competitive dimensions as possible. Because of this, the history of the airline industry since it was deregulated is filled with companies' efforts to distinguish themselves from competitors in ways that create value for customers. Stated more directly, each airline wants to use its resources and capabilities to establish a sustainable competitive advantage over its rivals. American Airlines, for example, launched the frequent flyer program to offer consumers a reason to frequently, if not exclusively, use its services. Although this innovation created value for customers and was rare when started, it is easily imitated. Today, virtually all carriers offer consumers a frequent flyer program, meaning that American's innovation is no longer rare nor is it a source of competitive advantage.

The third largest U.S. airline, and committed to achieving its strategic intent of providing distinctive customer service and hospitality from the heart, Delta is using its technological resources and capabilities to create what the firm believes will be a sustainable competitive advantage. At the core of this effort is a three-year commitment of $200 million to bring about a technology makeover in the firm. With a goal that no e-ticketed, self-service customer should wait more than two minutes to check in at an airport, even during peak times, Delta is rapidly installing kiosks in its airport locations. New employee roles, such as Lobby Assist Agents and Service Excellence Coordinators, and the availability of Delta Direct phones, which provide customers having complex ticket transactions with quick access to dedicated reservations agents, are other aspects of what Delta champions as a "comprehensive, hassle-free customer service system." Company officials believe that Delta is "pioneering significant changes in the way passengers will move through airports" and that how Delta customers will move through airports creates value (in the form of convenience and saved time) and is rare and imperfectly imitable. But is this the case? Delta purchases its kiosks from Kinetics Inc., a Florida-based firm that has already sold more than 3,000 of its automated check-in kiosks. Thus, any competitor with capital can purchase the same kiosk that Delta is using. Moreover, competitors can study how Delta's employees are interacting differently with technology (e.g., agents assisting customers in their use of an automated kiosk) and may be able to imitate those practices. Indeed, most other U.S. airlines are already using kiosks in manners that are similar to Delta's practices. Thus, although Delta's integrated use of technology to create customer value in the form of convenience and saved time is valuable, it may also be imitable. Once capabilities have been imitated, the competitive advantage gained by using resources and capabilities in a certain combination still creates value, but is no longer rare because competitors also possess the capabilities. Time will tell, of course. However, it seems that Delta's technological innovations may result in a temporary rather than a sustainable competitive advantage. If this proves to be the case, virtually all airline companies will develop technological deliverables similar to those available from Delta, creating a situation of competitive parity between Delta and its rivals in terms of certain technological innovations.

SOURCES: 2003, AMR Corp., *Standard & Poor's Stock Reports*, http://www.standardandpoors.com, July 16; 2003, Delta Airlines, *Standard & Poor's Stock Reports*, http://www.standardandpoors.com, July 12; 2003, Delta Airlines Home Page, Corporate information, http://www.deltaairlines.com, July 25; 2003, Southwest Airlines, *Standard & Poor's Stock Reports*, http://www.standardandpoors.com, July 19; K. Fieweger, 2003, JetBlue posts profit, like other low-cost carriers, *Reuters*, http://www.reuters.com, July 24; C. Haddad, 2003, Delta's flight to self-service, *Wall Street Journal Online*, http://www.wsj.com, July 7.

organization's unique culture, which has spanned almost a century, growing deeper all along. This culture provides solid, consistent roots for everything the company does, from skills training to technological innovation."[99]

A second condition of being costly to imitate occurs when the link between the firm's capabilities and its competitive advantage is *causally ambiguous*.[100] In these instances, competitors can't clearly understand how a firm uses its capabilities as the foundation for competitive advantage. As a result, firms are uncertain about the capabilities they should develop to duplicate the benefits of a competitor's value-creating strategy. Chaparral Steel, for example, allows competitors to tour its facilities. In the CEO's words, competitors can be shown almost "everything and we will be giving away nothing because they can't take it home with them."[101] Contributing to Chaparral Steel's causally ambiguous operations is the fact that workers use the concept of *mentefacturing,* by which they manufacture steel by using their minds instead of their hands: "In mentefacturing, workers use computers to monitor operations and don't need to be on the shop floor during production."[102]

Social complexity is the third reason that capabilities can be costly to imitate. Social complexity means that at least some, and frequently many, of the firm's capabilities are the product of complex social phenomena. Interpersonal relationships, trust, friendships among managers and between managers and employees, and a firm's reputation with suppliers and customers are examples of socially complex capabilities. Nucor Steel has been able to create "a hunger for new knowledge through a high-powered incentive system for every employee." This socially complex process has allowed Nucor "to push the boundaries of manufacturing process know-how."[103]

Nonsubstitutable

Nonsubstitutable capabilities are capabilities that do not have strategic equivalents. This final criterion for a capability to be a source of competitive advantage "is that there must be no strategically equivalent valuable resources that are themselves either not rare or imitable. Two valuable firm resources (or two bundles of firm resources) are strategically equivalent when they each can be separately exploited to implement the same strategies."[104] In general, the strategic value of capabilities increases as they become more difficult to substitute.[105] The more invisible capabilities are, the more difficult it is for firms to find substitutes and the greater the challenge is to competitors trying to imitate a firm's value-creating strategy. Firm-specific knowledge and trust-based working relationships between managers and nonmanagerial personnel are examples of capabilities that are difficult to identify and for which finding a substitute is challenging. However, causal ambiguity may make it difficult for the firm to learn as

Nonsubstitutable capabilities *are capabilities that do not have strategic equivalents.*

well and may stifle progress, because the firm may not know how to improve processes that are not easily codified and thus are ambiguous.[106]

For example, competitors are deeply familiar with Dell Inc.'s successful direct sales model. However, to date, no competitor has been able to imitate Dell's capabilities, as suggested by the following comment: "There's no better way to make, sell, and deliver PCs than the way Dell does it, and nobody executes that model better than Dell."[107] Moreover, no competitor has been able to develop and use substitute capabilities that can duplicate the value Dell creates by using its capabilities. Thus, experience suggests that Dell's direct sales model capabilities are nonsubstitutable.

In summary, only using valuable, rare, costly-to-imitate, and nonsubstitutable capabilities creates sustainable competitive advantage. Table 3.5 shows the competitive consequences and performance implications resulting from combinations of the four criteria of sustainability. The analysis suggested by the table helps managers determine the strategic value of a firm's capabilities. The firm should not emphasize resources and capabilities falling into the first row in the table (that is, resources and capabilities that are neither valuable nor rare and that are imitable and for which strategic substitutes exist). Capabilities yielding competitive parity and either temporary or sustainable competitive advantage, however, will be supported. Some competitors such as Coca-Cola and PepsiCo may have capabilities that result in competitive parity. In such cases, the firms will nurture these capabilities while simultaneously trying to develop capabilities that can yield either a temporary or sustainable competitive advantage.

As discussed in the Strategic Focus, it is hard for airline companies to develop sustainable competitive advantages. As mentioned earlier in the chapter, an airplane is a tangible resource. As noted in Table 3.5, competitive parity results when a resource is valuable and may or may not be substitutable, but isn't rare or costly to imitate. At best, airplanes are a source of competitive parity. Because airplanes aren't a source of competitive advantage, airline companies rely on some of their other resources and capabilities to try to create competitive advantages. While reading the Strategic Focus, try to determine if Delta Airlines' use of its technological resources and capabilities can create the competitive advantage hoped for by the company.

Table 3.5 — Outcomes from Combinations of the Criteria for Sustainable Competitive Advantage

Is the Resource or Capability Valuable?	Is the Resource or Capability Rare?	Is the Resource or Capability Costly to Imitate?	Is the Resource or Capability Nonsubstitutable?	Competitive Consequences	Performance Implications
No	No	No	No	Competitive disadvantage	Below-average returns
Yes	No	No	Yes/no	Competitive parity	Average returns
Yes	Yes	No	Yes/no	Temporary competitive advantage	Average returns to above-average returns
Yes	Yes	Yes	Yes	Sustainable competitive advantage	Above-average returns

Value Chain Analysis

Value chain analysis allows the firm to understand the parts of its operations that create value and those that do not. Understanding these issues is important because the firm earns above-average returns only when the value it creates is greater than the costs incurred to create that value.[108]

The value chain is a template that firms use to understand their cost position and to identify the multiple means that might be used to facilitate implementation of a chosen business-level strategy.[109] As shown in Figure 3.4, a firm's value chain is segmented into primary and support activities. **Primary activities** are involved with a product's physical creation, its sale and distribution to buyers, and its service after the sale. **Support activities** provide the assistance necessary for the primary activities to take place.

The value chain shows how a product moves from the raw-material stage to the final customer. For individual firms, the essential idea of the value chain is to create additional value without incurring significant costs while doing so and to capture the value that has been created. In a globally competitive economy, the most valuable links on the chain tend to belong to people who have knowledge about customers.[110] This locus of value-creating possibilities applies just as strongly to retail and service firms as to manufacturers. Moreover, for organizations in all sectors, the effects of e-commerce make it increasingly necessary for companies to develop value-adding knowledge processes to compensate for the value and margin that the Internet strips from physical processes.[111]

Primary activities are involved with a product's physical creation, its sale and distribution to buyers, and its service after the sale.

Support activities provide the assistance necessary for the primary activities to take place.

The Basic Value Chain —— Figure 3.4

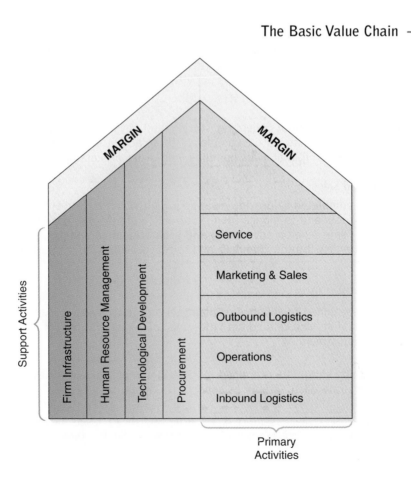

Table 3.6 lists the items to be studied to assess the value-creating potential of primary activities. In Table 3.7, the items to consider when studying support activities are shown. As with the analysis of primary activities, the intent in examining these items is to determine areas where the firm has the potential to create and capture value. All items in both tables should be evaluated relative to competitors' capabilities. To be a source of competitive advantage, a resource or capability must allow the firm (1) to perform an activity in a manner that is superior to the way competitors perform it, or (2) to perform a value-creating activity that competitors cannot complete. Only under these conditions does a firm create value for customers and have opportunities to capture that value.

Sometimes start-up firms create value by uniquely reconfiguring or recombining parts of the value chain. Federal Express (FedEx) changed the nature of the delivery business by reconfiguring outbound logistics (a primary activity) and human resource management (a support activity) to provide overnight deliveries, creating value in the process. As shown in Figure 3.5, the Internet is changing many aspects of the value chain for a broad range of firms. A key reason for this is that the Internet affects how people communicate, locate information, and buy goods and services. For example, some believe that travel products are quite suitable for selling online. Indeed, the signif-

Table 3.6

Examining the Value-Creating Potential of Primary Activities

Inbound Logistics

Activities, such as materials handling, warehousing, and inventory control, used to receive, store, and disseminate inputs to a product.

Operations

Activities necessary to convert the inputs provided by inbound logistics into final product form. Machining, packaging, assembly, and equipment maintenance are examples of operations activities.

Outbound Logistics

Activities involved with collecting, storing, and physically distributing the final product to customers. Examples of these activities include finished-goods warehousing, materials handling, and order processing.

Marketing and Sales

Activities completed to provide means through which customers can purchase products and to induce them to do so. To effectively market and sell products, firms develop advertising and promotional campaigns, select appropriate distribution channels, and select, develop, and support their sales force.

Service

Activities designed to enhance or maintain a product's value. Firms engage in a range of service-related activities, including installation, repair, training, and adjustment.

Each activity should be examined relative to competitors' abilities. Accordingly, firms rate each activity as *superior, equivalent,* or *inferior.*

SOURCE: Adapted with the permission of The Free Press, an imprint of Simon & Schuster Adult Publishing Group, from *Competitive Advantage: Creating and Sustaining Superior Performance,* by Michael E. Porter, pp. 39–40, Copyright © 1985, 1998 by Michael E. Porter.

Procurement

Activities completed to purchase the inputs needed to produce a firm's products. Purchased inputs include items fully consumed during the manufacture of products (e.g., raw materials and supplies, as well as fixed assets—machinery, laboratory equipment, office equipment, and buildings).

Technological Development

Activities completed to improve a firm's product and the processes used to manufacture it. Technological development takes many forms, such as process equipment, basic research and product design, and servicing procedures.

Human Resource Management

Activities involved with recruiting, hiring, training, developing, and compensating all personnel.

Firm Infrastructure

Firm infrastructure includes activities such as general management, planning, finance, accounting, legal support, and governmental relations that are required to support the work of the entire value chain. Through its infrastructure, the firm strives to effectively and consistently identify external opportunities and threats, identify resources and capabilities, and support core competencies.

Each activity should be examined relative to competitors' abilities. Accordingly, firms rate each activity as *superior, equivalent,* or *inferior.*

SOURCE: Adapted with the permission of The Free Press, an imprint of Simon & Schuster Adult Publishing Group, from *Competitive Advantage: Creating and Sustaining Superior Performance,* by Michael E. Porter, pp. 40–43, Copyright © 1985, 1998 by Michael E. Porter.

icance of Internet-based hotel distribution routes has greatly increased over the last few years. According to industry trade data, direct hotel reservations fell from roughly 39 percent of business in 1995 to 33 percent in 1999. The shift in sales between these years went almost exclusively to electronic channels.[112] This change obviously affects the marketing and sales support activity, especially in terms of pricing, for hotels and motels.

Rating a firm's capability to execute its primary and support activities is challenging. Earlier in the chapter, we noted that identifying and assessing the value of a firm's resources and capabilities requires judgment. Judgment is equally necessary when using value chain analysis. The reason is that there is no obviously correct model or rule available to help in the process.

What should a firm do about primary and support activities in which its resources and capabilities are not a source of core competence and, hence, of competitive advantage? Outsourcing is one solution to consider.

Outsourcing

Concerned with how components, finished goods, or services will be obtained, **outsourcing** is the purchase of a value-creating activity from an external supplier.[113] Not-for-profit agencies as well as for-profit organizations are actively engaging in outsourcing.[114] During the 1990s, outsourcing became a prominent strategic action among many

Outsourcing is the purchase of a value-creating activity from an external supplier.

Figure 3.5 ——— Prominent Applications of the Internet in the Value Chain

Firm Infrastructure
- Web-based, distributed financial and ERP systems
- Online investor relations (e.g., information dissemination, broadcast conference calls)

Human Resource Management
- Self-service personnel and benefits administration
- Web-based training
- Internet-based sharing and dissemination of company information
- Electronic time and expense reporting

Technology Development
- Collaborative product design across locations and among multiple value-system participants
- Knowledge directories accessible from all parts of the organization
- Real-time access by R&D to online sales and service information

Procurement
- Internet-enabled demand planning; real-time available-to-promise/capable-to-promise and fulfillment
- Other linkage of purchase, inventory, and forecasting systems with suppliers
- Automated "requisition to pay"
- Direct and indirect procurement via marketplaces, exchanges, auctions, and buyer-seller matching

Inbound Logistics	Operations	Outbound Logistics	Marketing and Sales	After-Sales Service
• Real-time integrated scheduling, shipping, warehouse management, demand management, and planning, and advanced planning and scheduling across the company and its suppliers • Dissemination throughout the company of real-time inbound and in-progress inventory data	• Integrated information exchange, scheduling and decision making in in-house plants, contract assemblers, and components suppliers • Real-time available-to-promise and capable-to-promise information available to the sales force and channels	• Real-time transaction of orders whether initiated by an end consumer, a salesperson, or a channel partner • Automated customer-specific agreements and contract terms • Customer and channel access to product development and delivery status • Collaborative integration with customer forecasting systems • Integrated channel management including information exchange, warranty claims, and contract management (process control)	• Online sales channels including websites and marketplaces • Real-time inside and outside access to customer information, product catalogs, dynamic pricing, inventory availability, online submission of quotes, and order entry • Online product configurators • Customer-tailored marketing via customer profiling • Push advertising • Tailored online access • Real-time customer feedback through Web surveys, opt-in/opt-out marketing, and promotion response tracking	• Online support of customer service representatives through e-mail response management, billing integration, co-browse, chat, "call me now," voice-over-IP, and other uses of video streaming • Customer self-service via websites and intelligent service request processing including updates to billing and shipping profiles • Real-time field service access to customer account review, schematic review, parts availability and ordering, work-order update, and service parts management

←———————— • Web-distributed supply chain management ————————→

SOURCE: Reprinted by permission of *Harvard Business Review* from "Strategy and the Internet" by Michael E. Porter, March 2001, p. 75. Copyright © 2001 by the Harvard Business School Publishing Corporation; all rights reserved.

types of companies.[115] Firms engaging in effective outsourcing increase their flexibility, mitigate risks, and reduce their capital investments.[116] In multiple global industries, the trend toward outsourcing continues at a rapid pace.[117] Moreover, in some industries virtually all firms seek the value that can be captured through effective outsourcing. The auto manufacturing industry and, more recently, the electronics industry are examples of this situation.[118] As with other strategic management process decisions, careful study is required before the firm decides to engage in outsourcing.[119]

Outsourcing can be effective because few, if any, organizations possess the resources and capabilities required to achieve competitive superiority in all primary and support activities. With respect to technologies, for example, research suggests that few

The Use of Outsourcing: Nothing but Positive Outcomes?

Firms engage in outsourcing, now a global phenomenon, to complete activities in which they do not possess a competitive advantage or in which they prefer not to develop an advantage. Information technology (IT) and research and development (R&D) are two organizational functions that are commonly outsourced. In IT, offshore outsourcing is the world's fastest growing segment of the industry. A set of "global players," including companies in India, is emerging to satisfy the growing demand for IT services to be performed by outside vendors. In R&D, General Motors, IBM, Motorola, Monsanto, Siemens, Microsoft, and Nokia are just a few of the companies that have established centers in India. These corporate giants aren't alone in their decision to outsource some of their R&D activities to other nations. In fact, between 2001 and 2003, 77 global firms established R&D centers in India alone. On a more comprehensive basis, Forester Research Inc. estimates that by 2020, roughly 3.3 million U.S. services jobs and $136 billion in wages will move offshore to countries such as India, China, Russia, and the Philippines. Other analysts believe that as much as 10 percent of the existing stock of U.S. jobs could be lost due to outsourcing by the end of 2004. The results of Forester's analysis showing that outsourcing can reduce firms' costs by as much as one-half may influence the growing use of this particular strategic action.

The fact that some nations, such as the Philippines, are gearing parts of their economy toward developing competitive advantages in certain areas stimulates the use of outsourcing. In response to aggressive advertising of such advantages and to more efficiently complete certain tasks, a growing number of U.S. companies is more actively considering either using companies in the Philippines or establishing units there using local labor. JPMorgan, for example, is evaluating the possibility of forming a unit in the Philippines to handle its backroom and customer services.

The benefits of outsourcing, such as lower costs and the ability to more readily allocate resources to core competencies that create competitive advantages, are understandable. However, issues about outsourcing's consequences have been sounded. In the United States, for example, concerns have been raised about the contraction of domestic innovation. The fact that the "rate of increase for new patent applications in the IT area is down by nearly 90 percent" is one example of this concern. Workers at Boeing believe that it will be increasingly difficult for the firm to maintain its technological expertise if jobs continue to be outsourced.

Increasingly formal responses to the growing use of outsourcing are surfacing. Members of at least one of the unions representing Boeing's workers are seeking to track "where Boeing jobs are going and why." Some displaced U.S. workers are forming support groups to mount a collective challenge to the use of outsourcing. A displaced Microsoft employee, for instance, has established a website (http://www.goodetech.com) to provide a forum and to post materials about the movement of U.S. jobs to offshore locations.

SOURCES: 2003, Outsourcing ventures, *BusinessWorld*, July 15, 1; S. Aggarwal, 2003, Tech outsourcing: Two scenarios, *Business Week*, July 14, 8; C. Ansberry, 2003, The economy—the outlook: Outsourcing abroad draws debate at home, *Wall Street Journal Online*, http://www.wsj.com, July 14; A. Goldstein, 2003, Outsourcing breeds backlash at home, *Dallas Morning News*, July 9, D1, D4; M. McMillin, 2003, Union for Boeing launches effort to keep track of outsourcing, *Knight Ridder Tribune Business News*, July 10, 23; P. Fox, 2002, Avoid the decline of IT innovation, *Computerworld*, October 14, 20–21.

companies can afford to develop internally all the technologies that might lead to competitive advantage.[120] By nurturing a smaller number of capabilities, a firm increases the probability of developing a competitive advantage because it does not become overextended. In addition, by outsourcing activities in which it lacks competence, the firm can fully concentrate on those areas in which it can create value.[121]

Other research suggests that outsourcing does not work effectively without extensive internal capabilities to coordinate external sourcing as well as core competencies.[122] Dell Inc., for example, outsources most of its manufacturing and customer service activities, allowing the firm to concentrate on creating value through its service and online distribution capabilities. In addition, the value generated by outsourcing must be sufficient to cover a firm's costs. For example, research indicates that for European banks outsourcing various information technology activities, "a provider must beat a bank's internal costs by about 40 percent."[123]

To verify that the appropriate primary and support activities are outsourced, four skills are essential for managers involved in outsourcing programs: strategic thinking, deal making, partnership governance, and change management.[124] Managers should understand whether and how outsourcing creates competitive advantage within their company—they need to be able to think strategically.[125] To complete effective outsourcing transactions, these managers must also be deal makers to be able to secure rights from external providers that can be fully used by internal managers. They must be able to oversee and govern appropriately the relationship with the company to which the services were outsourced. Because outsourcing can significantly change how an organization operates, managers administering these programs must also be able to manage that change, including resolving employee resistance that accompanies any significant change effort.[126]

As explained in the Strategic Focus, some have concerns about the consequences of outsourcing. For the most part, these concerns revolve around the potential loss in firms' innovative ability and the loss of jobs within companies that decide to outsource some of their work activities to others. Companies should be aware of these issues and be prepared to fully consider the concerns about outsourcing when different stakeholders (e.g., employees) express them.

Core Competencies: Cautions and Reminders

Tools such as outsourcing help the firm focus on its core competencies as the source of its competitive advantages. However, evidence shows that the value-creating ability of core competencies should never be taken for granted. Moreover, the ability of a core competence to be a permanent competitive advantage can't be assumed. The reason for these cautions is that all core competencies have the potential to become *core rigidities*. As Leslie Wexner, CEO of Limited Brands, says: "Success doesn't beget success. Success begets failure because the more that you know a thing works, the less likely you are to think that it won't work. When you've had a long string of victories, it's harder to foresee your own vulnerabilities."[127] Thus, each core competence is a strength and a weakness—a strength because it is the source of competitive advantage and, hence, strategic competitiveness, and a weakness because, if emphasized when it is no longer competitively relevant, it can be a seed of organizational inertia.[128]

Events occurring in the firm's external environment create conditions through which core competencies can become core rigidities, generate inertia, and stifle innovation. "Often the flip side, the dark side, of core capabilities is revealed due to external events when new competitors figure out a better way to serve the firm's customers, when new technologies emerge, or when political or social events shift the ground underneath."[129] However, in the final analysis, changes in the external environment do not cause core competencies to become core rigidities; rather, strategic myopia and inflexibility on the part of managers are the cause.[130] Determining what the firm *can do* through continuous and effective analyses of its internal environment increases the likelihood of long-term competitive success.

Summary

- In the global landscape, traditional factors (e.g., labor costs and superior access to financial resources and raw materials) can still create a competitive advantage. However, this happens in a declining number of instances. In the new landscape, the resources, capabilities, and core competencies in the firm's internal environment may have a relatively stronger influence on its performance than do conditions in the external environment. The most effective firms recognize that strategic competitiveness and above-average returns result only when core competencies (identified through the study of the firm's internal environment) are matched with opportunities (determined through the study of the firm's external environment).

- No competitive advantage lasts forever. Over time, rivals use their own unique resources, capabilities, and core competencies to form different value-creating propositions that duplicate the value-creating ability of the firm's competitive advantages. In general, the Internet's capabilities are reducing the sustainability of many competitive advantages. Thus, because competitive advantages are not sustainable on a permanent basis, firms must exploit their current advantages while simultaneously using their resources and capabilities to form new advantages that can lead to competitive success in the future.

- Effective management of core competencies requires careful analysis of the firm's resources (inputs to the production process) and capabilities (capacities for teams of resources to perform a task or activity in an integrative manner). To successfully manage core competencies, decision makers must be self-confident, courageous, and willing both to hold others accountable for their work and to be held accountable for the outcomes of their own efforts.

- Individual resources are usually not a source of competitive advantage. Capabilities, which are groupings of tangible and intangible resources, are a more likely source of competitive advantages, especially relatively sustainable

ones. A key reason for this is that the firm's nurturing and support of core competencies that are based on capabilities is less visible to rivals and, as such, is harder to understand and imitate.

- Increasingly, employees' knowledge is viewed as perhaps the most relevant source of competitive advantage. To gain maximum benefit from knowledge, efforts are taken to find ways for individuals' unique knowledge sets to be shared throughout the firm. The Internet's capabilities affect both the development and the sharing of knowledge.

- Only when a capability is valuable, rare, costly to imitate, and nonsubstitutable is it a core competence and a source of competitive advantage. Over time, core competencies must be supported, but they cannot be allowed to become core rigidities. Core competencies are a source of competitive advantage only when they allow the firm to create value by exploiting opportunities in the external environment. When this is no longer the case, attention shifts to selecting or forming other capabilities that do satisfy the four criteria of sustainable competitive advantage.

- Value chain analysis is used to identify and evaluate the competitive potential of resources and capabilities. By studying their skills relative to those associated with primary and support activities, firms can understand their cost structure and identify the activities through which they can create value.

- When the firm cannot create value in either a primary or support activity, outsourcing is considered. Used commonly in the global economy, outsourcing is the purchase of a value-creating activity from an external supplier. The firm must outsource only to companies possessing a competitive advantage in terms of the particular primary or support activity under consideration. In addition, the firm must continuously verify that it is not outsourcing activities from which it could create value.

Review Questions

1. Why is it important for a firm to study and understand its internal environment?

2. What is value? Why is it critical for the firm to create value? How does it do so?

3. What are the differences between tangible and intangible resources? Why is it important for decision makers to understand these differences? Are tangible resources linked more closely to the creation of competitive advantages than are intangible resources, or is the reverse true? Why?

4. What are capabilities? What must firms do to create capabilities?

5. What are the four criteria used to determine which of a firm's capabilities are core competencies? Why is it important for these criteria to be used?

6. What is value chain analysis? What does the firm gain when it successfully uses this tool?

7. What is outsourcing? Why do firms outsource? Will outsourcing's importance grow in the 21st century? If so, why?

8. What are core rigidities? Why is it vital that firms prevent core competencies from becoming core rigidities?

Scanning the Internal Environment

The resources, capabilities, and core competencies in a firm's internal environment play a critical role in determining strategic performance. A firm must have core competencies that provide the basis for responding to environmental opportunities in order to earn above-average returns.

For a company that is of interest to you, identify the four or five strongest capabilities. You may find it helpful to think in terms of functional areas or value activities to identify the strongest capabilities.

a. Evaluate each capability using the four criteria established in the chapter (see Table 3.4).

b. Which capabilities appear to provide a basis for competitive parity? Temporary competitive advantage? Sustainable competitive advantage?

c. Generate some ideas about developments in the external environment (i.e., the general, industry, and competitor environments) that may dilute or destroy the value of the existing core competencies and, thereby, erode the basis of competitive advantage.

d. Discuss the implications of these trends for the firm's strategic performance

Organizational Resources

The organizations listed in the table below have different capabilities and core competencies.

Part One. In small groups, consider each firm and use logic and consensus to complete the table. Alternatively, complete the table on an individual basis.

Organization	Capabilities	Core Competencies
Wal-Mart		
Starbucks		
U.S. Post Office		
Southwest Airlines		

Part Two. Based on your responses to the table, now compare each type of firm in terms of its resources and suggest some reasons for the differences.

	Is the Resource or Capability				Competitive consequences: • Competitive disadvantage • Competitive parity • Temporary competitive advantage • Sustainable competitive advantage	Performance implications: • Below-average returns • Average returns • Above-average returns
	Valuable?	Rare?	Costly to Imitate?	Nonsubstitutable?		
Wal-Mart						
Starbucks						
U.S. Post Office						
Southwest Airlines						

Part Three. In order to protect their competitive advantage, firms must continuously watch for developments that might dilute or destroy the value of their core competencies. For each firm, generate ideas about developments that may erode the basis of their competitive advantage.

Notes

1. A. Andal-Ancion, P. A. Cartwright, & G. S. Yip, 2003, The digital transformation of traditional businesses, *MIT Sloan Management Review*, 44(4): 34–41.

2. R. R. Wiggins & T. W. Ruefli, 2002, Sustained competitive advantage: Temporal dynamics and the incidence of persistence of superior economic performance, *Organization Science*, 13: 82–105.

3. M. Iansiti, F. W. McFarlan, & G. Westerman, 2003, Leveraging the incumbent's advantage, *MIT Sloan Management Review*, 44(4): 58–64; P. W. Roberts & G. R. Dowling, 2002, Corporate reputation and sustained superior financial performance, *Strategic Management Journal*, 23: 1077–1093.

4. S. Dutta, M. J. Zbaracki, & M. Bergen, 2003, Pricing process as a capability: A resource-based perspective, *Strategic Management Journal*, 24: 615–630; A. M. Knott, 2003, Persistent heterogeneity and sustainable innovation, *Strategic Management Journal*, 24: 687–705.

5. C. G. Brush, P. G. Greene, & M. M. Hart, 2001, From initial idea to unique advantage: The entrepreneurial challenge of constructing a resource base, *Academy of Management Executive*, 15(1): 64–78.

6. T. J. Douglas & J. A. Ryman, 2003, Understanding competitive advantage in the general hospital industry: Evaluating strategic competencies, *Strategic Management Journal*, 24: 333–347; R. Makadok, 2001, Toward a synthesis of the resource-based and dynamic-capability views of rent creation, *Strategic Management Journal*, 22: 387–401; K. M. Eisenhardt & J. A. Martin, 2000, Dynamic capabilities: What are they? *Strategic Management Journal*, 21: 1105–1121.

7. D. G. Sirmon, M. A. Hitt, & R. D. Ireland, 2003, Dynamically managing firm resources for competitive advantage: Creating value for stakeholders, Paper presented at Academy of Management, Seattle.

8. G. Hamel & L. Valikangas, 2003, The quest for resilience, *Harvard Business Review*, 81(9): 52–63; S. A. Way, 2002, High-performance work systems and intermediate indicators of firm performance within the U.S. small-business sector, *Journal of Management*, 28: 765–785; M. A. Hitt, L. Bierman, K. Shimizu, & R. Kochhar, 2001, Direct and moderating effects of human capital on strategy and performance in professional service firms: A resource-based perspective, *Academy of Management Journal*, 44: 13–28.

9. J. Schlereth, 2003, Putting people first, *BizEd*, July/August, 16–20.

10. J. Shamsie, 2003, The context of dominance: An industry-driven framework for exploiting reputation, *Strategic Management Journal*, 24: 199–215; E. Autio, H. J. Sapienza, & J. G. Almeida, 2000, Effects of age at entry, knowledge intensity, and imitability on international growth, *Academy of Management Journal*, 43: 909–924.

11. M. Makhija, 2003, Comparing the resource-based and market-based view of the firm: Empirical evidence from Czech privatization, *Strategic Management Journal*, 24: 433–451; P. L. Yeoh & K. Roth, 1999, An empirical analysis of sustained advantage in the U.S. pharmaceutical industry: Impact of firm resources and capabilities, *Strategic Management Journal*, 20: 637–653.

12. D. F. Abell, 1999, Competing today while preparing for tomorrow, *Sloan Management Review*, 40(3): 73–81; D. Leonard-Barton, 1995, *Wellsprings of Knowledge: Building and Sustaining the Sources of Innovation*, Boston: Harvard Business School Press; R. A. McGrath, J. C. MacMillan, & S. Venkataraman, 1995, Defining and developing competence: A strategic process paradigm, *Strategic Management Journal*, 16: 251–275.

13. K. M. Eisenhardt, 1999, Strategy as strategic decision making, *Sloan Management Review*, 40(3): 65–72.

14. H. K. Steensma & K. G. Corley, 2000, On the performance of technology-sourcing partnerships: The interaction between partner interdependence and technology attributes, *Academy of Management Journal*, 43: 1045–1067.

15. J. B. Barney, 2001, Is the resource-based "view" a useful perspective for strategic management research? Yes, *Academy of Management Review*, 26: 41–56.

16. M. Subramani & N. Venkataraman, 2003, Safeguarding investments in asymmetric interorganizational relationships: Theory and evidence, *Academy of Management Journal*, 46: 46–62; J. K. Sebenius, 2002, The hidden challenge of cross-border negotiations, *Harvard Business Review*, 80(3): 76–85.

17. R. Cross, W. Baker, & A. Parker, 2003, What creates energy in organizations? *MIT Sloan Management Review*, 44(4): 51–56; P. F. Drucker, 2002, They're not employees, they're people, *Harvard Business Review*, 80(2): 70–77; G. Verona, 1999, A resource-based view of product development, *Academy of Management Review*, 24: 132–142.

18. B. Grow & R. Berner, 2003, More rough-and-tumble for Lee and Wrangler, *Business Week*, June 2, 84.

19. T. M. Begley & D. P. Boyd, 2003, The need for a corporate global mind-set, *MIT Sloan Management Review*, 44(2): 25–32.

20. M. C. Bolino, W. H. Turnley, & J. M. Bloodgood, 2002, Citizenship behavior and the creation of social capital in organizations, *Academy of Management Review*, 27: 505–522; V. P. Rindova & C. J. Fombrun, 1999, Constructing competitive advantage: The role of firm-constituent interactions, *Strategic Management Journal*, 20: 691–710; M. A. Peteraf, 1993, The cornerstones of competitive strategy: A resource-based view, *Strategic Management Journal*, 14: 179–191.

21. Barney, Is the resource-based "view" a useful perspective for strategic management research? Yes; T. H. Brush & K. W. Artz, 1999, Toward a contingent resource-based theory: The impact of information asymmetry on the value of capabilities in veterinary medicine, *Strategic Management Journal*, 20: 223–250.

22. S. K. McEvily & B. Chakravarthy, 2002, The persistence of knowledge-based advantage: An empirical test for product performance and technological knowledge, *Strategic Management Journal*, 23: 285–305.

23. 1998, Pocket Strategy, *Value*, The Economist Books, 165.

24. J. Benedict, E. M. Steenkamp, R. Batra, & D. L. Alden, 2003, How perceived brand globalness creates brand value, *Journal of International Business Studies*, 34: 53–65.

25. S. Nambisan, 2002, Designing virtual customer environments for new product development: Toward a theory, *Academy of Management Review*, 27: 392–413.

26. J. Wolf & W. G. Egelhoff, 2002, A reexamination and extension of international strategy-structure theory, *Strategic Management Journal*, 23: 181–189; R. Ramirez, 1999, Value co-production: Intellectual origins and implications for practice and research, *Strategic Management Journal*, 20: 49–65.

27. V. Shankar & B. L. Bayus, 2003, Network effects and competition: An empirical analysis of the home video game industry, *Strategic Management Journal*, 24: 375–384; S. W. Floyd & B. Wooldridge, 1999, Knowledge creation and social networks in corporate entrepreneurship: The renewal of organizational capability, *Entrepreneurship: Theory and Practice*, 23(3): 123–143.

28. G. Hawawini, V. Subramanian, & P. Verdin, 2003, Is performance driven by industry- or firm-specific factors? A new look at the evidence, *Strategic Management Journal*, 24: 1–16; M. A. Hitt, R. D. Nixon, P. G. Clifford, & K. P. Coyne, 1999, The development and use of strategic resources, in M. A. Hitt, P. G. Clifford, R. D. Nixon, & K. P. Coyne (eds.), *Dynamic Strategic Resources*, Chichester: John Wiley & Sons, 1–14.

29. C. M. Christensen, 2001, The past and future of competitive advantage, *Sloan Management Review*, 42(2): 105–109.

30. J. R. Hough & M. A. White, 2003, Environmental dynamism and strategic decision-making rationality: An examination at the decision level, *Strategic Management Journal*, 24: 481–489.

31. C. J. Robertson & W. F. Crittenden, 2003, Mapping moral philosophies: Strategic implications for multinational firms, *Strategic Management Journal*, 24: 385–392.

32. C. M. Christensen & M. E. Raynor, 2003, Why hard-nosed executives should care about management theory, *Harvard Business Review*, 81(9): 66–74; T. H. Davenport, 2001, Data to knowledge to results: Building an analytic capability, *California Management Review*, 43(2): 117–138.

33. N. Checa, J. Maguire, & J. Barney, 2003, The new world disorder, *Harvard Business Review*, 81(8): 70–79; P. Westhead, M. Wright, & D. Ucbasaran, 2001, The internationalization of new and small firms: A resource-based view, *Journal of Business Venturing* 16(4): 333–358; A. McWilliams, D. D. Van Fleet, & P. M. Wright, 2001, Strategic management of human resources for global competitive advantage, *Journal of Business Strategies* 18(1): 1–24.

34. H. J. Smith, 2003, The shareholders vs. stakeholders debate, *MIT Sloan Management Review*, 44(4): 85–90; H. Collingwood, 2001, The earnings game: Everyone plays, nobody wins, *Harvard Business Review*, 79(6): 65–74.

35. Eisenhardt, Strategy as strategic decision making.

36. R. S. Dooley & G. E. Fryxell, 1999, Attaining decision quality and commitment from dissent: The moderating effects of loyalty and competence in strategic decision-making teams, *Academy of Management Journal*, 42: 389–402.

37. P. C. Nutt, 1999, Surprising but true: Half the decisions in organizations fail, *Academy of Management Executive*, 13(4): 75–90.

38. J. M. Mezias & W. H. Starbuck, 2003, What do managers know, anyway? *Harvard Business Review*, 81(5): 16–17; M. Keil, 2000, Cutting your losses: Extricating your organization when a big project goes awry, *Sloan Management Review*, 41(3): 55–68.

39. P. G. Audia, E. Locke, & K. G. Smith, 2000, The paradox of success: An archival and a laboratory study of strategic persistence following radical environmental change, *Academy of Management Journal*, 43: 837–853; R. G. McGrath, 1999, Falling forward: Real options reasoning and entrepreneurial failure, *Academy of Management Review*, 24: 13–30.

40. G. P. West III & J. DeCastro, 2001, The Achilles heel of firm strategy: Resource weaknesses and distinctive inadequacies, *Journal of Management Studies*, 38: 417–442; G. Gavetti & D. Levinthal, 2000, Looking forward and looking backward: Cognitive and experimental search, *Administrative Science Quarterly*, 45: 113–137.

41. R. Amit & P. J. H. Schoemaker, 1993, Strategic assets and organizational rent, *Strategic Management Journal*, 14: 33–46.

42. R. E. Hoskisson & L. W. Busenitz, 2001, Market uncertainty and learning distance in corporate entrepreneurship entry mode choice, in, M. A. Hitt, R. D. Ireland, S. M. Camp, & D. L. Sexton (eds.), *Strategic Entrepreneurship: Creating a New Integrated Mindset*, Oxford, UK: Blackwell Publishers, 151–172.

43. C. M. Fiol & E. J. O'Connor, 2003, Waking up! Mindfulness in the face of bandwagons, *Academy of Management Review*, 28: 54–70.

44. C. Roxburgh, 2003, Hidden flaws in strategy, *The McKinsey Quarterly*, Number 2, 26–39; A. L. Zacharakis & D. L. Shepherd, 2001, The nature of information and overconfidence on venture capitalists' decision making, *Journal of Business Venturing*, 16: 311–332.

45. P. Burrows & A. Park, 2002, What price victory at Hewlett-Packard? *Business Week*, April 1, 36–37.

46. J. M. Mezias, P. Grinyer, & W. D. Guth, 2001, Changing collective cognition: A process model for strategic change, *Long Range Planning*, 34(1): 71–95.

47. D. M. De Carolis, 2003, Competencies and imitability in the pharmaceutical industry: An analysis of their relationship with firm performance, *Journal of Management*, 29: 27–50.

48. Eisenhardt & Martin, Dynamic capabilities: What are they?; M. D. Michalisin, D. M. Kline, & R. D. Smith, 2000, Intangible strategic assets and firm performance: A multi-industry study of the resource-based view, *Journal of Business Strategies*, 17(2): 91–117.

49. D. L. Deeds, D. De Carolis, & J. Coombs, 2000, Dynamic capabilities and new product development in high-technology ventures: An empirical analysis of new biotechnology firms, *Journal of Business Venturing*, 15: 211–229; T. Chi, 1994, Trading in strategic resources: Necessary conditions, transaction cost problems, and choice of exchange structure, *Strategic Management Journal*, 15: 271–290.

50. Sirmon, Hitt, & Ireland, Dynamically managing firm resources; S. Berman, J. Down, & C. Hill, 2002, Tacit knowledge as a source of competitive advantage in the National Basketball Association, *Academy of Management Journal*, 45: 13–31.

51. 2003, About Borders Group, http://www.borders.com, July 18; S. Shepard, 2001, Interview: "The company is not in the stock," *Business Week*, April 30, 94–96.

52. M. S. Feldman, 2000, Organizational routines as a source of continuous change, *Organization Science*, 11: 611–629; A. M. Knott & B. McKelvey, 1999, Nirvana efficiency: A comparative test of residual claims and routines, *Journal of Economic Behavior & Organization*, 38: 365–383.

53. Subramani & Venkataraman, Safeguarding investments; R. Lubit, 2001, Tacit knowledge and knowledge management: The keys to sustainable competitive advantage, *Organizational Dynamics*, 29(3): 164–178.

54. A. M. Webber, 2000, New math for a new economy, *Fast Company*, January/February, 214–224.

55. R. G. Schroeder, K. A. Bates, & M. A. Junttila, 2002, A resource-based view of manufacturing strategy and the relationship to manufacturing performance, *Strategic Management Journal*, 23: 105–117.

56. M. A. Hitt & R. D. Ireland, 2002, The essence of strategic leadership: Managing human and social capital, *Journal of Leadership and Organization Studies*, 9(1): 3–14.

57. J. B. Quinn, P. Anderson, & S. Finkelstein, 1996, Making the most of the best, *Harvard Business Review*, 74(2): 71–80.

58. A. W. King & C. P. Zeithaml, 2003, Measuring organizational knowledge: A conceptual and methodological framework, *Strategic Management Journal*, 24: 763–772.

59. 2003, Intellectual property, Special Advertising Section, *Business Week*, July 28.

60. Webber, New math, 217.

61. K. Funk, 2003, Sustainability and performance, *MIT Sloan Management Review*, 44(2): 65–70.

62. Bolino, Turnley, & Bloodgood, Citizenship behavior.

63. R. D. Ireland, M. A. Hitt, & D. Vaidyanath, 2002, Managing strategic alliances to achieve a competitive advantage, *Journal of Management*, 28: 416–446.

64. D. L. Deephouse, 2000, Media reputation as a strategic resource: An integration of mass communication and resource-based theories, *Journal of Management*, 26: 1091–1112.

65. Shamsie, The context of dominance.

66. Roberts & Dowling, Corporate reputation, 1078.

67. P. Berthon, M. B. Holbrook, & J. M. Hulbert, 2003, Understanding and managing the brand space, *MIT Sloan Management Review*, 44(2): 49–54; D. B. Holt, 2003, What becomes an icon most? *Harvard Business Review*, 81(3): 43–49.

68. J. Blasberg & V. Vishwanath, 2003, Making cool brands hot, *Harvard Business Review*, 81(6): 20–22.

69. 2003, Harley-Davidson MotorClothes Merchandise, http://www.harleydavidson.com, July 20; M. Kleinman, 2001, Harley pushes brand prestige, *Marketing*, May 17, 16.

70. M. Blyler & R. W. Coff, 2003, Dynamic capabilities, social capital, and rent appropriation: Ties that split pies, *Strategic Management Journal*, 24: 677–686; C. E. Helfat & R. S. Raubitschek, 2000, Product sequencing: Co-evolution of knowledge, capabilities and products, *Strategic Management Journal*, 21: 961–979; Eisenhardt & Martin, Dynamic capabilities.

71. Hitt, Bierman, Shimizu, & Kochhar, Direct and moderating effects of human capital on strategy and performance in professional service firms: A resource-based perspective; M. A. Hitt, R. D. Ireland, & H. Lee, 2000, Technological learning, knowledge management, firm growth and performance: An introductory essay, *Journal of Engineering and Technology Management*, 17: 231–246; D. G. Hoopes & S. Postrel, 1999, Shared knowledge: "Glitches," and product development performance, *Strategic Management Journal*, 20: 837–865.

72. M. Burket, 2003, Funny business, *Forbes*, June 9, 173.

73. R. W. Coff & P. M. Lee, 2003, Insider trading as a vehicle to appropriate rent from R&D, *Strategic Management Journal*, 24: 183–190.

74. 1999, Thoughts on the business of life, *Forbes*, May 17, 352.

75. D. L. Deeds, 2003, Alternative strategies for acquiring knowledge, in S. E. Jackson, M. A. Hitt, & A. S. DeNisi (eds.), *Managing Knowledge for Sustained Competitive Advantage*, San Francisco: Jossey-Bass, 37–63.

76. R. A. Noe, J. A. Colquitt, M. J. Simmering, & S. A. Alvarez, 2003, Knowledge management: Developing intellectual and social capital, in S. E. Jackson, M. A. Hitt, & A. S. DeNisi (eds.), *Managing Knowledge for Sustained Competitive Advantage*, San Francisco: Jossey-Bass, 209–242; L. Argote & P. Ingram, 2000, Knowledge transfer: A basis for competitive advantage in firms, *Organizational Behavior and Human Decision Processes*, 82: 150–169.

77. G. G. Dess & J. C. Picken, 1999, *Beyond Productivity*, New York: AMACOM.

78. M. J. Tippins & R. S. Sohi, 2003, IT competency and firm performance: Is organizational learning a missing link? *Strategic Management Journal*, 24: 745–761.

79. T. T. Baldwin & C. C. Danielson, 2000, Building a learning strategy at the top: Interviews with ten of America's CLOs, *Business Horizons*, 43(6): 5–14.

80. D. F. Kuratko, R. D. Ireland, & J. S. Hornsby, 2001, Improving firm performance through entrepreneurial actions: Acordia's corporate entrepreneurship strategy, *Academy of Management Executive*, 15(4): 60–71; M. T. Hansen, N. Nhoria, & T. Tierney, 1999, What's your strategy for managing knowledge? *Harvard Business Review*, 77(2): 106–116.

81. M. A. Hitt & R. D. Ireland, 1986, Relationships among corporate level distinctive competencies, diversification strategy, corporate structure, and

performance, *Journal of Management Studies*, 23: 401–416; M. A. Hitt & R. D. Ireland, 1985, Corporate distinctive competence, strategy, industry, and performance, *Strategic Management Journal*, 6: 273–293; M. A. Hitt, R. D. Ireland, & K. A. Palia, 1982, Industrial firms' grand strategy and functional importance, *Academy of Management Journal*, 25: 265–298; M. A. Hitt, R. D. Ireland, & G. Stadter, 1982, Functional importance and company performance: Moderating effects of grand strategy and industry type, *Strategic Management Journal*, 3: 315–330; C. C. Snow & E. G. Hrebiniak, 1980, Strategy, distinctive competence, and organizational performance, *Administrative Science Quarterly*, 25: 317–336.

82. C. Zott, 2003, Dynamic capabilities and the emergence of intraindustry differential firm performance: Insights from a simulation study, *Strategic Management Journal*, 24: 97–125.

83. K. Hafeez, Y. B. Zhang, & N. Malak, 2002, Core competence for sustainable competitive advantage: A structured methodology for identifying core competence, *IEEE Transactions on Engineering Management*, 49(1): 28–35; C. K. Prahalad & G. Hamel, 1990, The core competence of the corporation, *Harvard Business Review*, 68(3): 79–93.

84. C. Bowman & V. Ambrosini, 2000, Value creation versus value capture: Towards a coherent definition of value in strategy, *British Journal of Management*, 11: 1–15; T. Chi, 1994, Trading in strategic resources: Necessary conditions, transaction cost problems, and choice of exchange structure, *Strategic Management Journal*, 15: 271–290.

85. C. Bowman, 2001, "Value" in the resource-based view of the firm: A contribution to the debate, *Academy of Management Review*, 26: 501–502.

86. C. Ames, 1995, Sales soft? Profits flat? It's time to rethink your business, *Fortune*, June 25, 142–146.

87. S. Lee, 2003, Starbucks reports outstanding August revenues, *Wall Street Journal Online*, http://www.wsj.com, August 28; N. D. Schwartz, 2001, Remedies for an economic hangover, *Fortune*, June 25, 130–138.

88. J. B. Barney, 1999, How a firm's capabilities affect boundary decisions, *Sloan Management Review*, 40(3): 137–145; J. B. Barney, 1995, Looking inside for competitive advantage, *Academy of Management Executive*, 9(4): 59–60; J. B. Barney, 1991, Firm resources and sustained competitive advantage, *Journal of Management*, 17: 99–120.

89. C. H. St. John & J. S. Harrison, 1999, Manufacturing-based relatedness, synergy, and coordination, *Strategic Management Journal*, 20: 129–145.

90. Barney, Looking inside for competitive advantage.

91. L. Lee, 2003, Online grocers: Finally delivering the lettuce, *Business Week Online*, http://www.businessweek.com, April 28.

92. Barney, Looking inside for competitive advantage, 52.

93. Ibid., 53.

94. Barney, How a firm's capabilities, 141.

95. Barney, Firm resources, 108.

96. J. Huey, 1993, How McKinsey does it, *Fortune*, November 1, 56–81.

97. J. Kurtzman, 1997, An interview with Rosabeth Moss Kanter, *Strategy & Business*, 16: 85–94.

98. L. E. Tetrick & N. Da Silva, 2003, Assessing the culture and climate for organizational learning, in S. E. Jackson, M. A. Hitt, & A. S. DeNisi (eds.), *Managing Knowledge for Sustained Competitive Advantage*, San Francisco: Jossey-Bass, 333–359; R. Burt, 1999, When is corporate culture a competitive asset? "Mastering Strategy" (Part Six), *Financial Times*, November 1, 14–15.

99. L. Soupata, 2001, Managing culture for competitive advantage at United Parcel Service, *Journal of Organizational Excellence*, 20(3): 19–26.

100. A. W. King & C. P. Zeithaml, 2001, Competencies and firm performance: Examining the causal ambiguity paradox, *Strategic Management Journal*, 22: 75–99; R. Reed & R. DeFillippi, 1990, Causal ambiguity, barriers to imitation, and sustainable competitive advantage, *Academy of Management Review*, 15: 88–102.

101. Leonard-Barton, *Wellsprings of Knowledge*, 7.

102. A. Ritt, 2000, Reaching for maximum flexibility, *Iron Age New Steel*, January, 20–26.

103. A. K. Gupta & V. Govindarajan, 2000, Knowledge management's social dimension: Lessons from Nucor Steel, *Sloan Management Review*, 42(1): 71–80.

104. Barney, Firm resources, 111.

105. Amit & Schoemaker, Strategic assets, 39.

106. M. J. Benner & M. L. Tushman, 2003, Exploitation, exploration, and process management: The productivity dilemma revisited, *Academy of Management Review*, 28: 238–256; S. K. McEvily, S. Das, & K. McCabe, 2000, Avoiding competence substitution through knowledge sharing, *Academy of Management Review*, 25: 294–311.

107. A. Serwer, 2002, Dell does domination, *Fortune*, January 21, 70–75.

108. M. E. Porter, 1985, *Competitive Advantage*, New York: Free Press, 33–61.

109. G. G. Dess, A. Gupta, J.-F. Hennart, & C. W. L. Hill, 1995, Conducting and integrating strategy research at the international corporate and business levels: Issues and directions, *Journal of Management*, 21: 376.

110. J. W. Boudreau, 2003, Strategic knowledge measurement and management, in S. E. Jackson, M. A. Hitt, & A. S. DeNisi (eds.), *Managing Knowledge for Sustained Competitive Advantage*, San Francisco: Jossey-Bass: 330–359; J. Webb & C. Gile, 2001, Reversing the value chain, *Journal of Business Strategy*, 22(2): 13–17.

111. R. Amit & C. Zott, 2001, Value creation in e-business, *Strategic Management Journal*, 22(Special Issue): 493–520; M. E. Porter, 2001, Strategy and the Internet, *Harvard Business Review*, 79(3): 62–78.

112. P. O'Connor, 2003, On-line pricing: An analysis of hotel-company practices, *Cornell Hotel and Restaurant Administration Quarterly*, 44: 88–96.

113. T. W. Gainey & B. S. Klaas, 2003, The outsourcing of training and development: Factors impacting client satisfaction, *Journal of Management*, 29: 207–229; J. Y. Murray & M. Kotabe, 1999, Sourcing strategies of U.S. service companies: A modified transaction-cost analysis, *Strategic Management Journal*, 20: 791–809.

114. M. Rola, 2002, Secrets to successful outsourcing management, *Computing Canada*, 28(23): 11.

115. C. Ansberry, 2003, The economy—the outlook: Outsourcing abroad draws debate at home, *Wall Street Journal Online*, http://www.wsj.com, July 14.

116. P. Bendor-Samuel, 2003, Outsourcing: Transforming the corporation, *Forbes*, Special Advertising Section, May 26.

117. K. Madigan & M. J. Mandel, 2003, Commentary: Outsourcing Jobs: Is it bad? *Business Week Online*, http://www.businessweek.com, August 25.

118. J. Palmer, 2003, Auto supplier stands out by focusing on the inside, *Wall Street Journal Online*, http://www.wsj.com, August 17; A. Takeishi, 2001, Bridging inter- and intra-firm boundaries: Management of supplier involvement in automobile product development, *Strategic Management Journal*, 22: 403–433; H. Y. Park, C. S. Reddy, & S. Sarkar, 2000, Make or buy strategy of firms in the U.S., *Multinational Business Review*, 8(2): 89–97.

119. M. J. Leiblein, J. J. Reuer, & F. Dalsace, 2002, Do make or buy decisions matter? The influence of organizational governance on technological performance, *Strategic Management Journal*, 23: 817–833.

120. J. C. Linder, S. Jarvenpaa, & T. H. Davenport, 2003, Toward an innovation sourcing strategy, *MIT Sloan Management Review*, 44(4): 43–49.

121. Hafeez, Zhang, & Malak, Core competence for sustainable competitive advantage; B. H. Jevnaker & M. Bruce, 1999, Design as a strategic alliance: Expanding the creative capability of the firm, in M. A. Hitt, P. G. Clifford, R. D. Nixon, & K. P. Coyne (eds.), *Dynamic Strategic Resources*, Chichester: John Wiley & Sons, 266–298.

122. Takeishi, Bridging inter- and intra-firm boundaries.

123. R. Lancellotti, O. Schein, & V. Stadler, 2003, When outsourcing pays off, *The McKinsey Quarterly*, Number 1, 10.

124. M. Useem & J. Harder, 2000, Leading laterally in company outsourcing, *Sloan Management Review*, 41(2): 25–36.

125. R. C. Insinga & M. J. Werle, 2000, Linking outsourcing to business strategy, *Academy of Management Executive*, 14(4): 58–70.

126. M. Katz, 2001, Planning ahead for manufacturing facility changes: A case study in outsourcing, *Pharmaceutical Technology*, March: 160–164.

127. G. G. Dess & J. C. Picken, 1999, Creating competitive (dis)advantage: Learning from Food Lion's freefall, *Academy of Management Executive*, 13(3): 97–111.

128. De Carolis, Competencies and imitability, 28; M. Hannan & J. Freeman, 1977, The population ecology of organizations, *American Journal of Sociology*, 82: 929–964.

129. Leonard-Barton, *Wellsprings of Knowledge*, 30–31.

130. West & DeCastro, The Achilles heel of firm strategy; Keil, Cutting your losses.

2

Part Two

Strategic Actions: Strategy Formulation

Business-Level Strategy

Chapter Four

4

Knowledge Objectives

Studying this chapter should provide you with the strategic management knowledge needed to:

1. Define business-level strategy.

2. Discuss the relationship between customers and business-level strategies in terms of *who*, *what*, and *how*.

3. Explain the differences among business-level strategies.

4. Use the five forces of competition model to explain how above-average returns can be earned through each business-level strategy.

5. Describe the risks of using each of the business-level strategies.

Corel Corporation

Krispy Kreme doughnuts utilizes a *differentiation business-level strategy* in that its products' perceived uniqueness is critical to the company's success. The uniqueness of Krispy Kreme and its products derives in part from making customers feel connected with the doughnut-making process. As one example, customers delight in anticipating the taste of the doughnuts by watching them bake in the "Doughnut Theatre."

Krispy Kreme is a leading specialty retailer of premium-quality doughnuts. The firm makes close to 3 billion doughnuts annually in approximately 280 stores in the United States and Canada. Krispy Kreme is expanding internationally into markets such as Australia, Spain, New Zealand, and the United Kingdom. As with its recently completed transaction with Grupo AXO in Mexico, much of the international expansion is taking place by forming joint venture agreements with local companies. The fact that there is a Krispy Kreme exhibit at the Smithsonian Institution's National Museum of American History is evidence that the firm is a cultural icon in the United States.

The differences in opinion about Krispy Kreme doughnuts are dramatic. Some believe that the high quality of the firm's offerings indicate that it is indeed the Michelangelo of doughnut makers and that there is "an art to making the doughnut." Others comment that Krispy Kreme doughnuts are "heavenly inspired." At the other extreme, passersby sometimes shout, "They're just doughnuts!" at loyalists waiting in line to be the first to purchase some of the products from a new Krispy Kreme store. Traffic jams and waits of two hours or more are common on the first day of a new unit. To be the first to buy doughnuts at a new location, some people begin camping out as much as 24 hours in advance of the store opening.

Krispy Kreme is implementing a differentiation business-level strategy. Discussed further in this chapter, the differentiation strategy is one in which the firm produces a good or service that customers perceive as being unique in ways that are important to them. The perception of uniqueness is critical in that it is what causes customers to buy a product that is more expensive than are offerings from competitors. The importance of uniqueness applies to Krispy Kreme as well, as suggested by an analyst who proposed, "It isn't what's inside a Krispy Kreme doughnut that creates the demand. It's what's inside the customer's head that makes a Krispy Kreme Krispy Kreme." The Doughnut Theatre—in which customers watch doughnuts being made in the store, wait for the "Hot Now" sign to illuminate, and look forward to trying the "doughnut of the month" to taste a new entry—and the firm's efforts to make customers feel that they are a part of the company and what it does are widely perceived as unique attributes of the Krispy Kreme experience and, as such, are competitive advantages for the firm. As part of the marketing effort, customers are encouraged to use the company's website to become a "Friend of Krispy Kreme." As a friend, customers receive information about product updates, warm requests for honest feedback about the firm's doughnuts and the experience surrounding their purchase and consumption, and news about Krispy Kreme's future plans. Through its marketing campaigns, Krispy Kreme attempts to find ways to create excitement that builds customer pride. Purchasing collectibles (e.g., shirts, sweatshirts, boxer shorts, mugs, hats, and toys) is thought to make customers feel as though they are a part of the company. Krispy Kreme uses its information technology capabilities (the firm's information technology department has won multiple industry awards) and its vertically integrated manufacturing process capability (the firm develops proprietary mixes which are made into doughnuts by its proprietary manufacturing equipment) to develop and support the Doughnut Theatre and marketing campaigns as competitive advantages.

Krispy Kreme also sells its doughnuts in other outlets such as grocery stores. This worries analysts who fear that the difference in quality between buying a hot doughnut in a Krispy Kreme store and buying one as a prepackaged item will dilute the value of the brand name and the bond between the firm and its on-site customers. A second major concern is the high fat content in Krispy Kreme's products. As discussed in a Strategic Focus in this chapter, McDonald's was alleged in a class-action lawsuit to be responsible for obesity in children. Might Krispy Kreme face such allegations in the future? Krispy Kreme must find ways to overcome potential problems while determining additional sources of differentiation that its customers will perceive as important to them.

SOURCES: 2003, Food brief—Krispy Kreme Doughnuts Inc.: Four inside directors resign, *Wall Street Journal Online*, http://www.wsj.com, April 10; T. Derpinghaus, 2003, Krispy Kreme restructures board, *Wall Street Journal Online*, http://www.wsj.com, April 9; C. Dyrness, 2003, Krispy Kreme adds new technologies to its arsenal, *News & Observer*, April 23; J. R. Graham, 2003, It's a Krispy Kreme world, *American Salesman*, April, 8–10; J. Harrison, 2003, Krispy Kreme chooses a bread maker as a platform for its café concept, *Mergers and Acquisitions*, 38(3): 12–13; J. Peters, 2003, Niche players seek to perk up sales with variety, *Nation's Restaurant News*, February 10, 1, 77; C. Skipp, 2003, Hot bytes, by the dozen, *Newsweek*, April 28, 42.

Increasingly important to firm success,[1] strategy is concerned with making choices among two or more alternatives. When choosing a strategy, the firm decides to pursue one course of action instead of others. Indeed, the main point of strategy is to help decision makers choose among competing priorities and alternatives.[2] Sound strategic decisions are the foundation on which successful strategies are built.[3] Business-level strategy, this chapter's focus, is the choice a firm makes when deciding how to compete in individual product markets. The choices are important, as there is an established link between a firm's strategies and its long-term performance.[4] Given the complexity of successfully competing in the global economy, these choices are difficult, often even gutwrenching.[5] Thus, Krispy Kreme's choices about how to make and distribute its products as well as how to interact with its customers will affect the firm's ability to earn above-average returns across time.

Determining the businesses in which the firm will compete is a question of corporate-level strategy and is discussed in Chapter 6. Competition in individual product markets is a question of business-level strategy. For all types of strategies, companies acquire the information and knowledge needed to make choices as they study external environmental opportunities and threats as well as identify and evaluate their internal resources, capabilities, and core competencies.

In Chapter 1, we defined a *strategy* as an integrated and coordinated set of commitments and actions designed to exploit core competencies and gain a competitive advantage. The different strategies that firms use to gain competitive advantages are shown in Figure 1.1 in Chapter 1. As described in the individual chapters outlined in the figure, the firm tries to establish and exploit a competitive advantage when using each type of strategy.[6] As explained in the Opening Case, Krispy Kreme is using a differentiation strategy to develop competitive advantages and exploit them for marketplace success.

Every firm needs a business-level strategy.[7] However, every firm may not use all the strategies—corporate-level, acquisition and restructuring, international, and cooperative—that are examined in Chapters 6 through 9. For example, the firm competing in a single-product market area in a single geographic location does not need a corporate-level strategy to deal with product diversity or an international strategy to deal with geographic diversity. Think of a local dry cleaner with only one location offering a single service (the cleaning and laundering of clothes) in a single storefront. In contrast, a diversified firm will use one of the corporate-level strategies as well as choose a separate business-level strategy for each product market area in which the company competes (the relationship between corporate-level and business-level strategies is further examined in Chapter 6). Thus, every firm—from the local dry cleaner to the multinational corporation—chooses at least one business-level strategy. Business-level strategy can be thought of as the firm's *core* strategy—the strategy that must be formed to describe how the firm will compete.[8]

Each strategy the firm uses specifies desired outcomes and how they are to be achieved.[9] Integrating external and internal foci, strategies reflect the firm's theory about how it intends to compete.[10] The fundamental objective of using each strategy is to create value for stakeholders. Strategies are purposeful, precede the taking of actions to which they apply, and demonstrate a shared understanding of the firm's strategic intent and strategic mission.[11] An effectively formulated strategy marshals, integrates, and allocates the firm's resources, capabilities, and competencies so that it will be properly aligned with its external environment.[12] A properly developed strategy also rationalizes the firm's strategic intent and strategic mission along with the actions taken to achieve them.[13] Information about a host of variables, including markets, customers, technology, worldwide finance, and the changing world economy, must be collected and analyzed to properly form and use strategies.[14] Increasingly, Internet technology affects how organizations gather and study data and information that are related to decisions about the choice and use of strategy.[15]

Business-level strategy, this chapter's focus, is an integrated and coordinated set of commitments and actions the firm uses to gain a competitive advantage by exploiting core competencies in specific product markets.[16] Only firms that continuously upgrade their competitive advantages over time are able to achieve long-term success with their business-level strategy.[17] Key issues the firm must address when choosing a business-level strategy are what good or service to offer customers, how to manufacture or create it, and how to distribute it to the marketplace. Once formed, the business-level strategy reflects where and how the firm has an advantage over its rivals.[18] The essence of a firm's business-level strategy is "choosing to perform activities differently or to perform different activities than rivals."[19]

Customers are the foundation of successful business-level strategies and should never be taken for granted.[20] In fact, some believe that an effective business-level strategy demonstrates the firm's ability to "build and maintain relationships to the best people for maximum value creation, both 'internally' (to firm members) and 'externally' (to customers)."[21] Thus, successful organizations think of their employees as internal customers who produce value-creating products for which customers are willing to pay; such organizations also understand that the quality of their interactions with customers has a direct effect on firm performance.[22]

Because of their strategic importance, customers are the focus of discussion at the beginning of this chapter. Three issues are considered in this analysis. In selecting

A **business-level strategy** *is an integrated and coordinated set of commitments and actions the firm uses to gain a competitive advantage by exploiting core competencies in specific product markets.*

a business-level strategy, the firm determines (1) *who* will be served, (2) *what* needs those target customers have that it will satisfy, and (3) *how* those needs will be satisfied. Selecting customers and deciding which of their needs the firm will try to satisfy, as well as how it will do so, are challenging choices for today's organizations. Global competition, which has created many attractive options for customers, is one reason for this. In the current competitive environment, effective global competitors have become adept at identifying the needs of customers in different cultures and geographic regions as well as learning how to quickly and successfully adapt the functionality of the firms' good or service to meet those needs.

Descriptions of five business-level strategies follow the discussion of customers. These five strategies are sometimes called *generic* because they can be used in any business and in any industry.[23] Our analysis of these strategies describes how effective use of each strategy allows the firm to favorably position itself relative to the five competitive forces in the industry (see Chapter 2). In addition, we use the value chain (see Chapter 3) to show examples of the primary and support activities that are necessary to implement each business-level strategy. We also describe the different risks the firm may encounter when using one of these strategies.

Organizational structures and controls that are linked with successful use of each business-level strategy are explained in Chapter 11.

Customers: Who, What, and How

Strategic competitiveness results only when the firm is able to satisfy a group of customers by using its competitive advantages as the basis for competing in individual product markets. A key reason firms must satisfy customers with their business-level strategy is that returns earned from relationships with customers are the lifeblood of all organizations.[24] Executives at Motley Fool capture this reality crisply by noting that "the customer is the person who pays us."[25]

The most successful companies such as Dell Inc. constantly seek to chart new competitive space in order to serve new customers as they simultaneously find ways to better serve existing customers. The former Dell Computer Corp. recently dropped the word *computer* from its name and became Dell Inc. This action was partly taken to signal to the market that while continuing to find ways to better serve its PC users, the company is also entering new markets and serving new customers with its network switches, handheld devices, projectors, printers, and server computers for large corporations.[26]

One of the key issues that firms must address in their business-level strategy is how to distribute their products to the marketplace. Amazon.com manages its relationships with its customers well by anticipating their needs. In this case, distribution of its products plays a key role as staff at online bookseller Amazon.com U.K. prepare to ship out 65,000 copies of the latest *Harry Potter* book.

©Reuters NewMedia Inc./CORBIS

The Importance of Effectively Managing Relationships with Customers

The firm's relationships with its customers are strengthened when it delivers superior value to them. Superior value at Harrah's Entertainment is largely defined as providing outstanding service to customers.[27] Importantly, delivering superior value often results in increased loyalty from customers to the firm providing it. In turn, customer loyalty has a positive relationship with profitability. Ford Motor Company, for example, estimates that each percentage-point increase in customer loyalty—defined as how many Ford owners purchase a Ford product the next time—creates at least $100 million in additional profits annually. MBNA, a credit card issuer, determined that reducing customer defection rates by 5 percent increases the lifetime profitability of the average customer by 125 percent.[28] However, increased choice and easily accessible information about the functionality of firms' products are creating increasingly sophisticated and knowledgeable customers, making it difficult to earn their loyalty.[29]

A number of companies have become skilled at the art of *managing* all aspects of their relationship with their customers.[30] For example, Amazon.com is an Internet-based venture widely recognized for the quality of information it maintains about its customers, the services it renders, and its ability to anticipate customers' needs.[31] Based in Mexico, Cemex SA is the world's third largest cement maker. Cemex uses the Internet to link its customers, cement plants, and main control room, allowing the firm to automate orders and optimize truck deliveries in highly congested Mexico City. Analysts believe that Cemex's integration of Web technology with its cost leadership strategy is helping to differentiate it from competitors.[32] GE is using Internet technology to save money and to enhance relationships with its customers by reaching them faster with products of ever-increasing quality.[33]

As we discuss next, there are three dimensions of firms' relationships with customers. Companies such as Amazon.com, Cemex, and GE understand these dimensions and manage their relationships with customers in light of them.

Reach, Richness, and Affiliation

The *reach* dimension of relationships with customers is concerned with the firm's access and connection to customers. For instance, the largest physical retailer in bookstores, Barnes & Noble, carries approximately 200,000 titles in over 900 stores. By contrast, Amazon.com offers more than 4.5 million titles and is located on tens of millions of computer screens with additional customer connections being established. Thus, Amazon. com's reach is significantly magnified relative to that associated with Barnes & Noble's physical bookstores.[34] In general, firms seek to extend their reach, adding customers in the process of doing so.

Richness, the second dimension, is concerned with the depth and detail of the two-way flow of information between the firm and the customer. The potential of the richness dimension to help the firm establish a competitive advantage in its relationship with customers led traditional financial services brokers, such as Merrill Lynch, Lehman Brothers, and others, to offer online services in order to better manage information exchanges with their customers. Broader and deeper information-based exchanges allow firms to better understand their customers and their needs. Such exchanges also enable customers to become more knowledgeable about how the firm can satisfy them. Internet technology and e-commerce transactions have substantially reduced the costs of meaningful information exchanges with current and possible future customers.

Affiliation, the third dimension, is concerned with facilitating useful interactions with customers. Internet navigators such as Microsoft CarPoint help online clients find and sort information. CarPoint provides data and software to prospective car buyers that enable them to compare car models along multiple objective specifications. The program can supply this information because Internet technology allows a great deal of information to be collected from a variety of sources at a low cost. A prospective buyer who has selected a specific car based on comparisons of different models can then be linked to dealers that meet the customer's needs and purchasing requirements. An auto manufacturing company represents its own products, creating a situation in which its financial interests differ substantially from those of consumers. Because its revenues come from sources other than the final customer or end user (such as advertisements on its website, hyperlinks, and associated products and services), CarPoint represents the customer's interests, a service that fosters affiliation.[35] Viewing the world through the customer's eyes and constantly seeking ways to create more value for the customer have positive effects in terms of affiliation.

As we discuss next, effective management of customer relationships helps the firm answer questions related to the issues of *who, what,* and *how.*

Who: Determining the Customers to Serve

Market segmentation *is a process used to cluster people with similar needs into individual and identifiable groups.*

The Y (top left), Baby Boomer (lower left), and World War II (lower right) generations each have unique needs and interests that affect the implementation of targeted marketing strategies.

A crucial business-level strategy decision is the one made about the target customers for the firm's goods or services (*who*).[36] To make this decision, companies divide customers into groups based on differences in the customers' needs (needs are defined and further discussed in the next section). Called **market segmentation,** this process clusters people with similar needs into individual and identifiable groups.[37] In the animal health business, for example, the needs for food products of owners of companion pets (e.g., dogs and cats) differ from the needs for food products of those owning production animals (e.g., livestock).[38] As part of its business-level strategy, the firm develops a marketing program to effectively sell products to its particular target customer group.

Almost any identifiable human or organizational characteristic can be used to subdivide a market into segments that differ from one another on a given characteristic. Common characteristics on which customers' needs vary are illustrated in Table 4.1. Based on their internal core competencies and opportunities in the external environment, companies choose a business-level strategy to deliver value to target customers and satisfy their specific needs.

Customer characteristics are often combined to segment a large market into specific groups that have unique needs. For example, McDonald's dominates the fast-food market. However, for college students interested in healthy eating, surveys suggest that Subway is the dominant fast-food choice.[39] This more specific breakdown of the fast-food market for college students is a product of jointly studying demographic, psychological, and consumption-pattern characteristics (see Table 4.1). This knowledge suggests that on a relative basis, Subway's business-level strategy should target college students with a desire for healthier foods more aggressively than should McDonald's.

Demographic characteristics (see the discussion in Chapter 2 and Table 4.1) can also be used to segment markets into generations with unique interests and needs. Evidence suggests, for example, that direct mail is an effective communication medium for the World War II generation (those born before 1932). The Swing generation (those born between 1933 and 1945) values taking cruises and purchasing second homes. Once financially conservative but now willing to spend money, members of this generation seek product information from knowledgeable sources. The Baby Boom generation (born between 1946 and 1964) desires products that reduce the stress generated by juggling career demands and the needs of older parents with those of their own children. Ellen Tracy

Consumer Markets

1. Demographic factors (age, income, sex, etc.)
2. Socioeconomic factors (social class, stage in the family life cycle)
3. Geographic factors (cultural, regional, and national differences)
4. Psychological factors (lifestyle, personality traits)
5. Consumption patterns (heavy, moderate, and light users)
6. Perceptual factors (benefit segmentation, perceptual mapping)

Industrial Markets

1. End-use segments (identified by SIC code)
2. Product segments (based on technological differences or production economics)
3. Geographic segments (defined by boundaries between countries or by regional differences within them)
4. Common buying factor segments (cut across product market and geographic segments)
5. Customer size segments

SOURCE: Adapted from S. C. Jain, 2000, *Marketing Planning and Strategy,* Cincinnati: South-Western College Publishing, 120.

clothes, known for their consistency of fit and color, are targeted to Baby Boomer women. More conscious of hype, the 60-million-plus people in Generation X (born between 1965 and 1976) want products that deliver as promised. The Xers use the Internet as a primary shopping tool and expect visually compelling marketing. Members of this group are the fastest growing segment of mutual-fund shareholders, with their holdings overwhelmingly invested in stock funds. As employees, the top priorities of Xers are to work in a creative learning environment, to receive constant feedback from managers, and to be rewarded for using their technical skills.[40] Different marketing campaigns and distribution channels (e.g., the Internet for Generation X customers as compared to direct mail for the World War II generation) affect the implementation of strategies for those companies interested in serving the needs of different generations.

As this discussion suggests, markets are being segmented into increasingly specialized niches of customers with unique needs and interests. Generation Y (born between 1977 and 1984) is yet another market segment with specific characteristics that affect how firms use business-level strategies to serve customers' needs. Analysis of purchasing patterns shows that this segment prefers to buy in stores rather than online, but that these customers may use the Internet to study products online prior to visiting a store to make a purchase. This preference suggests that companies targeting this segment might want to combine their storefront operations with a robust and active website.[41] Other examples of targeting specific market segments include New Balance's marketing of its shoes to members of the Baby Boom generation (see the Strategic Focus in this chapter), Christopher & Banks' focusing on working women over the age of 40, and Abercrombie & Fitch's targeting of the subgroup of teenagers who demand fashion-oriented casual apparel.[42]

What: Determining Which Customer Needs to Satisfy

After the firm decides *who* it will serve, it must identify the targeted customer group's needs that its goods or services can satisfy. *Needs (what)* are related to a product's benefits and features.[43] Having close and frequent interactions with both current and potential customers helps the firm identify those individuals' and groups' current and future needs.[44] From a strategic perspective, a basic need of all customers is to buy products that create value for them. The generalized forms of value goods or services provide are either low cost with acceptable features or highly differentiated features with acceptable cost. The most effective firms continuously strive to anticipate changes in customers' needs. Failure to do this results in the loss of customers to competitors who are offering greater value in terms of product features and functionalities.[45]

In any given industry, there is great variety among consumers in terms of their needs.[46] The need some consumers have for high-quality, fresh sandwiches is what Pret A Manger seeks to satisfy with its menu items. In contrast, many large fast-food companies satisfy customer needs for lower-cost food items with acceptable quality that are delivered quickly.[47] Diversified food and soft-drink producer PepsiCo believes that "any one consumer has different needs at different times of the day." Through its soft drinks (Pepsi products), snacks (Frito-Lay), juices (Tropicana), and cereals (Quaker), PepsiCo is working on developing new products from breakfast bars to healthier potato chips "to make certain sure that it covers all those needs."[48] In the information technology area, a growing number of customers seem to want firms to help them learn how to use currently owned technologies to improve productivity.[49] Thus, instead of trying to sell increasingly sophisticated technology products, some technology companies are focusing on helping such customers improve their ability to fully use the products they've already bought. In contrast, some information technology consumers are more interested in "being on the cutting edge of the technological age," as shown by their desire to continuously buy products with the most sophisticated technological capabilities. In general, and across multiple product groups (e.g., automobiles, clothing, food), evidence suggests that middle-market consumers in the United States want to trade up to higher levels of quality and taste. These customers "are willing to pay premiums of 20% to 200% for the kinds of well-designed, well-engineered, and well-crafted goods—often possessing the artisanal touches of traditional luxury goods—not before found in the mass middle market."[50] These needs represent opportunities for some firms to pursue through their business-level strategies.

To ensure success, a firm must be able to fully understand the needs of the customers in the target group it has selected to serve. In this sense, customer needs are neither right nor wrong, good nor bad. Instead, customer needs simply represent the desires in terms of features and performance capabilities of those customers the firm has targeted to serve with its goods or services. The most effective firms are filled with people committed to understanding the customers' current as well as future needs.

How: Determining Core Competencies Necessary to Satisfy Customer Needs

As explained in Chapters 1 and 3, *core competencies* are resources and capabilities that serve as a source of competitive advantage for the firm over its rivals. Firms use core competencies (*how*) to implement value-creating strategies and thereby satisfy customers' needs. Only those firms with the capacity to continuously improve, innovate, and upgrade their competencies can expect to meet and hopefully exceed customers' expectations across time.[51]

Companies draw from a wide range of core competencies to produce goods or services that can satisfy customers' needs. IBM, for example, emphasizes its core competence in technology to rapidly develop new service-related products. Beginning in

1993, then newly appointed CEO Lou Gerstner changed IBM by leveraging its "strength in network integration and consulting to transform [the firm] from a moribund maker of mainframe computers to a sexy services company that can basically design, build, and manage a corporation's entire data system."[52] SAS Institute is the world's largest privately owned software company and is the leader in business intelligence and analytics. Customers use SAS' programs for data warehousing, data mining, and decision support purposes. Allocating over 30 percent of revenues to research and development (R&D), SAS relies on its core competence in R&D to satisfy the data-related needs of such customers as the U.S. Census Bureau and a host of consumer goods firms (e.g., hotels, banks, and catalog companies).[53] Vans Inc. relies on its core competencies in innovation and marketing to design and sell such products as skateboards. The firm also pioneered thick-soled, slip-on sneakers that can absorb the shock of 5-foot leaps on wheels. Vans uses what is recognized as an offbeat marketing mix to capitalize on its pioneering products. In lieu of mass media ads, the firm sponsors skateboarding events, supported the making of a documentary film that celebrates the "outlaw nature" of the skateboarding culture, and is building skateboard parks at malls around the country.[54]

All organizations, including IBM, SAS, and Vans Inc., must be able to use their core competencies (the *how*) to satisfy the needs (the *what*) of the target group of customers (the *who*) the firm has chosen to serve by using its business-level strategy.

Next, we discuss the business-level strategies firms use when pursuing strategic competitiveness and above-average returns.

Types of Business-Level Strategy

Business-level strategies are intended to create differences between the firm's position and those of its rivals.[55] To position itself, the firm must decide whether it intends to *perform activities differently* or to *perform different activities* as compared to its rivals.[56] Thus, the firm's business-level strategy is a deliberate choice about how it will perform the value chain's primary and support activities in ways that create unique value.

Successful use of a chosen strategy results only when the firm integrates its primary and support activities to provide the unique value it intends to deliver. Value is delivered to customers when the firm is able to use competitive advantages resulting from the integration of activities. Superior fit among primary and support activities forms an activity system. In turn, an effective activity system helps the firm establish and exploit its strategic position. We describe Southwest Airlines' activity system in the Strategic Focus. The firm's integrated cost leadership/differentiation strategy has created great wealth for shareholders in that an initial $1,000 investment in 1972 grew to $102 million by the end of 2002.[57]

The importance of fit between primary and support activities isn't unique to Southwest, in that fit among activities is a key to the sustainability of competitive advantage for all firms. As Michael Porter comments, "Strategic fit among many activities is fundamental not only to competitive advantage but also to the sustainability of that advantage. It is harder for a rival to match an array of interlocked activities than it is merely to imitate a particular sales-force approach, match a process technology, or replicate a set of product features. Positions built on systems of activities are far more sustainable than those built on individual activities."[58]

Favorably positioned firms such as Southwest Airlines have a competitive advantage over their industry rivals and are better able to cope with the five forces of competition (see Chapter 2). Favorable positioning is important in that the universal objective of all companies is to develop and sustain competitive advantages.[59] Improperly positioned firms encounter competitive difficulties and likely will fail to sustain competitive advantages. For example, its ineffective responses to competitors such as Wal-Mart left

Southwest Airlines' Activity System: Is It Imitable?

Launched in 1971 with service among three Texas cities—Dallas, Houston, and San Antonio—Southwest Airlines offers short-haul, low-cost, point-to-point service between midsized cities and secondary airports in large cities. It performs its activities in ways that drive the firm's costs lower and lower. According to company officials, Southwest is "always looking for an opportunity to make the lowest even lower" as it simultaneously provides customers with some unique, value-creating sources of differentiation (such as an "entertaining experience" while in the air).

Relying on customer service and organizational culture as its two major competitive advantages, the firm is successfully using its integrated cost leadership/differentiation strategy. As of the end of the second quarter of 2003, for example, Southwest was the only major airline to post a profit in every quarter since the September 11, 2001, terrorist attacks on the United States. Moreover, the firm hadn't canceled any flights or furloughed any employees during that time period. The posting of a 14 percent profit gain on a 7 percent rise in sales in 2003's second quarter is strong evidence of Southwest's ability to continuously drive its costs lower.

Because Southwest's fares are as much as 20 percent below those charged by mainstream carriers, the firm's effect on pricing in the markets it serves can be dramatic. Average fares in Raleigh-Durham, N.C., for example, are roughly half those in Charlotte, N.C. Southwest serves the Raleigh-Durham airport, but not the Charlotte airport. Dallas, Texas' Love Field has the lowest average fares in the country. This is important because only Southwest serves Love Field. As former CEO and cofounder Herb Kelleher said, "If you're going to be a low-fare airline, you have to charge low fares even when you don't have competition."

An activity system can be mapped to show how individual activities are integrated to achieve fit, as the map for Southwest's activities on the next page shows. Higher-order strategic themes are critical to successful use of the firm's strategy. For Southwest Airlines, these strategic themes are limited passenger service; frequent, reliable departures; lean, highly productive ground and gate crews; high aircraft utilization; very low ticket prices; and short-haul, point-to-point routes between midsized cities and secondary airports. Individual clusters of tightly linked activities make it possible for the outcome of a strategic theme to be achieved. For example, no meals, no seat assignments, and no baggage transfers form a cluster of individual activities that support the strategic theme of limited passenger service.

Southwest's tightly integrated primary and support activities make it difficult for competitors to imitate the firm's strategy. The firm's culture influences these activities and their integration and contributes to the firm's ability to continuously identify additional ways to differentiate Southwest's service from its competitors' as well as to lower its costs. In fact, the firm's unique culture and customer service, both of which are sources of differentiated customer features, are competitive advantages rivals have not been able to imitate, although some have tried. US Airways' MetroJet subsidiary, United Airlines' United Shuttle, and Continental Airlines' Continental Lite all failed in attempts to imitate Southwest's strategy. Hindsight shows that these competitors offered low prices to customers, but weren't able to operate at costs close to those of Southwest or to provide customers with any notable sources of differentiation, such as a unique experience while in the air.

(continued on next page)

SOURCES: 2003, Southwest Airlines, *Standard & Poor's Stock Reports,* http://www.standardandpoors.com, May 3; E. Torbenson, 2003, Southwest cheers its growth at annual meeting, *Dallas Morning News,* May 15, D1, D3; A. Tsao, 2003, Getting the carriers back in the air, *BusinessWeek Online,* http://www.businessweek.com, April 2; M. Arndt, 2001, A simple and elegant flight pattern, *Business Week,* June 11, 118; J. H. Gittell, 2001, Investing in relationships, *Harvard Business Review,* 79(6): 28–30; M. E. Porter, 1996, What is strategy? *Harvard Business Review,* 74(6): 61–78.

Southwest Airlines' Activity System

Sears, Roebuck and Co. in a weak competitive position for years. These ineffective responses resulted from the inability of Sears to properly implement strategies that were appropriate in light of its external opportunities and threats and its internal competencies. Two researchers describe this situation: "Once a towering force in retailing, Sears spent 10 years vacillating between an emphasis on hard goods and soft goods, venturing in and out of ill-chosen arenas, failing to differentiate itself in any of them, and never building a compelling economic logic."[60] As we described in Chapter 3, Sears is now taking actions to effectively position itself and to develop and effectively exploit competitive advantages.

Firms choose from among five business-level strategies to establish and defend their desired strategic position against rivals: *cost leadership, differentiation, focused cost leadership, focused differentiation,* and *integrated cost leadership/differentiation* (see Figure 4.1). Each business-level strategy helps the firm to establish and exploit a competitive advantage within a particular competitive scope. Once chosen, a firm's business-level strategy and its use demonstrate how the firm differs from competitors.[61]

When selecting a business-level strategy, firms evaluate two types of potential competitive advantage: "lower cost than rivals, or the ability to differentiate and command a premium price that exceeds the extra cost of doing so."[62] Having lower cost derives from the firm's ability to perform activities differently than rivals; being able to differentiate indicates the firm's capacity to perform different (and valuable) activities.[63] Competitive advantage is thus achieved within some scope and is the cause of superior firm performance.[64]

Scope has several dimensions, including the group of product and customer segments served and the array of geographic markets in which the firm competes. Competitive advantage is sought by competing in many customer segments when implementing either the cost leadership or the differentiation strategy. In contrast, when using focus strategies, firms seek a cost competitive advantage or a differentiation competitive

Figure 4.1 —— Five Business-Level Strategies

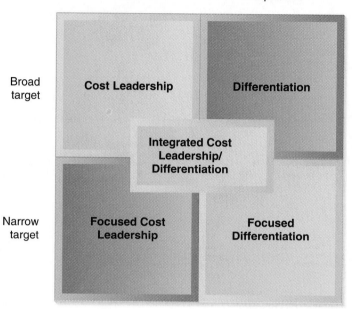

SOURCE: Adapted with the permission of The Free Press, an imprint of Simon & Schuster Adult Publishing Group, from *Competitive Advantage: Creating and Sustaining Superior Performance,* by Michael E. Porter, 12. Copyright © 1985, 1998 by Michael E. Porter.

advantage in a *narrow competitive scope, segment,* or *niche.* With focus strategies, the firm "selects a segment or group of segments in the industry and tailors its strategy to serving them to the exclusion of others."[65]

None of the five business-level strategies is inherently or universally superior to the others.[66] The effectiveness of each strategy is contingent both on the opportunities and threats in a firm's external environment and on the possibilities provided by the firm's unique resources, capabilities, and core competencies. It is critical, therefore, for the firm to select a strategy that is based on a match between the opportunities and threats in its external environment and the strengths of its internal environment as shown by its core competencies.

Cost Leadership Strategy

The **cost leadership strategy** is an integrated set of actions taken to produce goods or services with features that are acceptable to customers at the lowest cost, relative to that of competitors.[67] Cost leaders' goods and services must have competitive levels of differentiation in terms of features that create value for customers. Indeed, emphasizing cost reductions while ignoring competitive levels of differentiation is ineffective. At the extreme, concentrating only on reducing costs could find the firm very efficiently producing products that no customer wants to purchase. When the firm designs, produces, and markets a comparable product more efficiently than its rivals, there is evidence that it is successfully using the cost leadership strategy.[68] Firms using the cost leadership strategy sell no-frills, standardized goods or services (but with competitive levels of differentiation) to the industry's most typical customers. Cost leaders concentrate on finding ways to lower their costs relative to those of their competitors by constantly rethink-

The cost leadership strategy is an integrated set of actions taken to produce goods or services with features that are acceptable to customers at the lowest cost, relative to that of competitors.

ing how to complete their primary and support activities (see Chapter 2) to reduce costs still further while maintaining competitive levels of differentiation.[69]

As primary activities, inbound logistics (e.g., materials handling, warehousing, and inventory control) and outbound logistics (e.g., collecting, storing, and distributing products to customers) often account for significant portions of the total cost to produce some goods and services. Research suggests that having a competitive advantage in terms of logistics creates more value when using the cost leadership strategy than when using the differentiation strategy.[70] Thus, cost leaders seeking competitively valuable ways to reduce costs may want to concentrate on the primary activities of inbound logistics and outbound logistics.

Cost leaders also carefully examine all support activities to find additional sources of potential cost reductions. Developing new systems for finding the optimal combination of low cost and acceptable quality in the raw materials required to produce the firm's goods or services is an example of how the procurement support activity can facilitate successful use of the cost leadership strategy.

Big Lots uses the cost leadership strategy. Committed to the strategic intent of being "The World's Best Bargain Place," Big Lots is the largest broadline closeout discount chain in the United States. Operating under the format names of Big Lots, Big Lots Furniture, Wisconsin Toy, Consolidated International, and Big Lots Wholesale, the firm strives constantly to drive its costs lower relative to its competitors' by relying on what some analysts see as a highly disciplined merchandise cost and inventory management system.[71] The firm's stores sell name-brand products at prices that are 15 to 35 percent below those of discount retailers and roughly 80 percent below those of traditional retailers.[72] Big Lots' buyers travel the country looking through manufacturer overruns and discontinued styles, finding goods priced at well below wholesale prices. In addition, the firm buys from overseas suppliers. Big Lots thinks of itself as the undertaker of the retailing business, purchasing merchandise that others can't sell or don't want. The target customer is one seeking what Big Lots calls the "closeout moment," which is the feeling customers have after they recognize their significant savings from buying a brand name item at a steeply discounted price.[73] The customer need Big Lots satisfies is to access the differentiated features and capabilities of brand-name products, but at a fraction of their initial cost. The tight integration of purchasing and inventory management activities across its full set of stores is the main core competence Big Lots uses to satisfy its customers' needs.

As described in Chapter 3, firms use value-chain analysis to determine the parts of the company's operations that create value and those that do not. Figure 4.2 demonstrates the primary and support activities that allow a firm to create value through the cost leadership strategy. Companies unable to link the activities shown in this figure typically lack the core competencies needed to successfully use the cost leadership strategy.

Effective use of the cost leadership strategy allows a firm to earn above-average returns in spite of the presence of strong competitive forces (see Chapter 2). The next sections (one for each of the five forces) explain how firms are able to do this.

RIVALRY WITH EXISTING COMPETITORS

Having the low-cost position is a valuable defense against rivals. Because of the cost leader's advantageous position, rivals hesitate to compete on the basis of price, especially before evaluating the potential outcomes of such competition.[74] Wal-Mart is known for its ability to both control and reduce costs, making it difficult for firms to compete against it on the basis of costs. The discount retailer achieves strict cost control in several ways: "Wal-Mart's 660,000-square-foot main headquarters, with its drab gray interiors and frayed carpets, looks more like a government building than the home of one of the world's largest corporations. Business often is done in the no-frills cafeteria, and suppliers meet with managers in stark, cramped rooms. Employees have to throw out their own garbage at the end of the day and double up in hotel rooms on business

Figure 4.2 — Examples of Value-Creating Activities Associated with the Cost Leadership Strategy

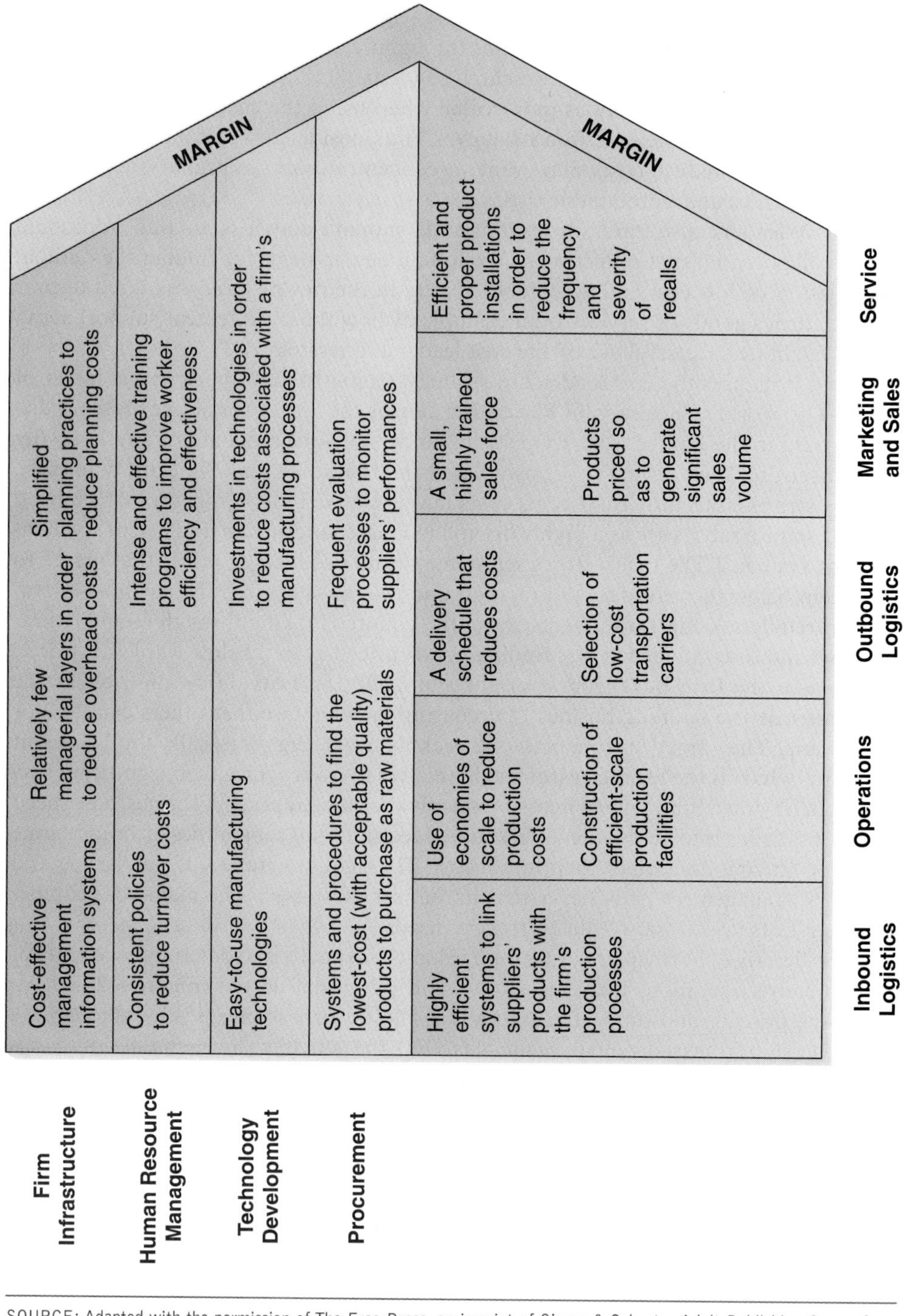

Firm Infrastructure
- Cost-effective management information systems
- Relatively few managerial layers in order to reduce overhead costs
- Simplified planning practices to reduce planning costs

Human Resource Management
- Consistent policies to reduce turnover costs
- Intense and effective training programs to improve worker efficiency and effectiveness

Technology Development
- Easy-to-use manufacturing technologies
- Investments in technologies in order to reduce costs associated with a firm's manufacturing processes

Procurement
- Systems and procedures to find the lowest-cost (with acceptable quality) products to purchase as raw materials
- Frequent evaluation processes to monitor suppliers' performances

Inbound Logistics
- Highly efficient systems to link suppliers' products with the firm's production processes

Operations
- Use of economies of scale to reduce production costs
- Construction of efficient-scale production facilities

Outbound Logistics
- A delivery schedule that reduces costs
- Selection of low-cost transportation carriers

Marketing and Sales
- A small, highly trained sales force
- Products priced so as to generate significant sales volume

Service
- Efficient and proper product installations in order to reduce the frequency and severity of recalls

MARGIN

SOURCE: Adapted with the permission of The Free Press, an imprint of Simon & Schuster Adult Publishing Group, from *Competitive Advantage: Creating and Sustaining Superior Performance*, by Michael E. Porter, 47. Copyright © 1985, 1998 by Michael E. Porter.

trips."[75] Kmart's decision to compete against Wal-Mart on the basis of cost contributed to the firm's failure and subsequent bankruptcy filing. Its competitively inferior distribution system—an inefficient and high-cost system compared to Wal-Mart's—is one of the factors that prevented Kmart from having a competitive cost structure relative to Wal-Mart.

As noted earlier, research suggests that having a competitive advantage in terms of logistics significantly contributes to the cost leader's ability to earn above-average returns.[76] Because Wal-Mart developed a logistics competitive advantage that has become the world standard, the probability that Kmart could successfully engage in price competition with the retailing giant was very low. Also contending with strong pricing pressure from Wal-Mart,[77] Target Corp. relies on means other than specific price competition, including its Target credit card. With almost $6 billion in credit card receivables at the end of fiscal year 2002, Target earned $150 million in that year's fourth quarter alone from its credit card operations. Target continues to try to find ways to increase the value its customers can derive by using the Target credit card, hoping that being able to do so will create a competitive advantage for the firm.[78]

BARGAINING POWER OF BUYERS (CUSTOMERS)

Powerful customers can force a cost leader to reduce its prices, but not below the level at which the cost leader's next-most-efficient industry competitor can earn average returns. Although powerful customers might be able to force the cost leader to reduce prices even below this level, they probably would not choose to do so. Prices that are low enough to prevent the next-most-efficient competitor from earning average returns would force that firm to exit the market, leaving the cost leader with less competition and in an even stronger position. Customers would thus lose their power and pay higher prices if they were forced to purchase from a single firm operating in an industry without rivals.

BARGAINING POWER OF SUPPLIERS

The cost leader operates with margins greater than those of competitors. Among other benefits, higher margins relative to those of competitors make it possible for the cost leader to absorb its suppliers' price increases. When an industry faces substantial increases in the cost of its supplies, only the cost leader may be able to pay the higher prices and continue to earn either average or above-average returns. Alternatively, a powerful cost leader may be able to force its suppliers to hold down their prices, which would reduce the suppliers' margins in the process. Wal-Mart uses its power with suppliers (gained because it buys such large quantities from many suppliers) to extract lower prices from them. These savings are then passed on to customers in the form of lower prices, which further strengthens Wal-Mart's position relative to competitors lacking the power to extract lower prices from suppliers.[79]

POTENTIAL ENTRANTS

Through continuous efforts to reduce costs to levels that are lower than competitors', a cost leader becomes highly efficient. Because ever-improving levels of efficiency enhance profit margins, they serve as a significant entry barrier to potential competitors. New entrants must be willing and able to accept no-better-than-average returns until they gain the experience required to approach the cost leader's efficiency. To earn even average returns, new entrants must have the competencies required to match the cost levels of competitors other than the cost leader. The low profit margins (relative to margins earned by firms implementing the differentiation strategy) make it necessary for the cost leader to sell large volumes of its product to earn above-average returns. However, firms striving to be the cost leader must avoid pricing their products so low that their ability to operate profitably is reduced, even though volume increases.

PRODUCT SUBSTITUTES

Compared to its industry rivals, the cost leader also holds an attractive position in terms of product substitutes. A product substitute becomes an issue for the cost leader when its features and characteristics, in terms of cost and differentiated features, are potentially attractive to the firm's customers. When faced with possible substitutes, the cost leader has more flexibility than its competitors. To retain customers, it can reduce the price of its good or service. With still lower prices and competitive levels of differentiation, the cost leader increases the probability that customers will prefer its product rather than a substitute.

COMPETITIVE RISKS OF THE COST LEADERSHIP STRATEGY

The cost leadership strategy is not risk free. One risk is that the processes used by the cost leader to produce and distribute its good or service could become obsolete because of competitors' innovations. These innovations may allow rivals to produce at costs lower than those of the original cost leader, or to provide additional differentiated features without increasing the product's price to customers.

A second risk is that too much focus by the cost leader on cost reductions may occur at the expense of trying to understand customers' perceptions of "competitive levels of differentiation." As noted earlier, Wal-Mart is well known for constantly and aggressively reducing its costs. At the same time, however, the firm must understand when a cost-reducing decision to eliminate differentiated features (e.g., extended shopping hours, a large number of checkout counters to reduce waits) would create a loss of value for customers.

A final risk of the cost leadership strategy concerns imitation. Using their own core competencies, competitors sometimes learn how to successfully imitate the cost leader's strategy. When this occurs, the cost leader must increase the value that its good or service provides to customers. Commonly, value is increased by selling the current product at an even lower price or by adding differentiated features that customers value while maintaining price.

Differentiation Strategy

The **differentiation strategy** is an integrated set of actions taken to produce goods or services (at an acceptable cost) that customers perceive as being different in ways that are important to them.[80] While cost leaders serve an industry's typical customer, differentiators target customers who perceive that value is added by the manner in which the firm's products differ from those produced and marketed by competitors.

Firms must be able to produce differentiated products at competitive costs to reduce upward pressure on the price customers pay for them. When a product's differentiated features are produced with noncompetitive costs, the price for the product can exceed what the firm's target customers are willing to pay. When the firm has a thorough understanding of what its target customers value, the relative importance they attach to the satisfaction of different needs, and for what they are willing to pay a premium, the differentiation strategy can be successfully used.[81]

Through the differentiation strategy, the firm produces nonstandardized products for customers who value differentiated features more than they value low cost. For example, superior product reliability and durability and high-performance sound systems are among the differentiated features of Toyota Motor Corporation's Lexus products. The often-used Lexus promotional statement—"The Passionate Pursuit of Perfection"—suggests a strong commitment to overall product quality as a source of differentiation. However, Lexus offers its vehicles to customers at a competitive purchase

*The **differentiation strategy** is an integrated set of actions taken to produce goods or services (at an acceptable cost) that customers perceive as being different in ways that are important to them.*

Heinz's EZ Squirt Blastin' Green ketchup, which tastes like Heinz's traditional ketchup, illustrates the company's effort to be innovative by offering a differentiated product when the firm's research found that kids would like to see ketchup in a color other than red. "We wanted to create something where that bottle is pulled out of the fridge more often," a Heinz spokesperson said.

©TRAMONTINA GARY/CORBIS SYGMA

price. As with Lexus products, a good's or service's unique attributes, rather than its purchase price, provide the value for which customers are willing to pay. As described in the Opening Case, Krispy Kreme uses what the firm believes is a truly unique recipe to make its doughnuts. The Doughnut Theatre and interactions with its customers are other sources of differentiation for this firm.

Continuous success with the differentiation strategy results when the firm consistently upgrades differentiated features that customers value, without significant cost increases. Because a differentiated product satisfies customers' unique needs, firms following the differentiation strategy are able to charge premium prices. For customers to be willing to pay a premium price, a "firm must truly be unique at something or be perceived as unique."[82] The ability to sell a good or service at a price that substantially exceeds the cost of creating its differentiated features allows the firm to outperform rivals and earn above-average returns. For example, shirt and neckwear manufacturer Robert Talbott follows stringent standards of craftsmanship and pays meticulous attention to every detail of production. The firm imports exclusive fabrics from the world's finest mills to make men's dress shirts and neckwear. Single-needle tailoring is used, and precise collar cuts are made to produce shirts. According to the company, customers purchasing one of its products can be assured that they are being provided with the finest quality available.[83] Thus, Robert Talbott's success rests on the firm's ability to produce and sell its differentiated products at a price significantly higher than the costs of imported fabrics and its unique manufacturing processes.

Rather than costs, a firm using the differentiation strategy always concentrates on investing in and developing features that differentiate a good or service in ways that customers value. Robert Talbott, for example, uses the finest silks from Europe and Asia to produce its "Best of Class" collection of ties. Overall, a firm using the differentiation strategy seeks to be different from its competitors on as many dimensions as possible. The less similarity between a firm's goods or services and those of competitors, the more buffered it is from rivals' actions. Commonly recognized differentiated goods include Toyota's Lexus, Ralph Lauren's clothing lines, and Caterpillar's heavy-duty earth-moving equipment. Thought by some to be the world's most expensive and prestigious consulting firm, McKinsey & Co. is a well-known example of a firm that offers differentiated services.

A product can be differentiated in many ways. Unusual features, responsive customer service, rapid product innovations and technological leadership, perceived prestige and status, different tastes, and engineering design and performance are examples of approaches to differentiation. There may be a limited number of ways to reduce costs (as demanded by successful use of the cost leadership strategy). In contrast, virtually anything a firm can do to create real or perceived value is a basis for differentiation. For example, trying to differentiate its luxury products from those of global competitors, Detroit's automakers are turning to design and styling to create what the industry is calling "gotta have" products. Hard to precisely define, "gotta have" cars and trucks look different, look good, and make customers turn their heads.[84] For Detroit automakers as well as all firms using the differentiation strategy for one or more of their product lines, the challenge is to identify features that create value for the customers the firm has chosen to serve.

Firms sometimes introduce a new source of differentiation to test consumer reaction before extending it. H. J. Heinz, for example, recently added color as a source of differentiation for its highly successful ketchup. Called Blastin' Green, the first color Heinz introduced proved very popular with customers, causing the firm to experiment further by introducing Funky Purple and Wicked Orange colors as well (with additional colors being considered). Positive reactions to these product introductions suggest that color does create perceived value for at least some of Heinz's target customers.[85]

A firm's value chain can be analyzed to determine whether the firm is able to link the activities required to create value by using the differentiation strategy. Examples of primary and support activities that are commonly used to differentiate a good or service are shown in Figure 4.3. Companies without the skills needed to link these activities cannot expect to successfully use the differentiation strategy. Next, we explain how firms using the differentiation strategy can successfully position themselves in terms of the five forces of competition (see Chapter 2) to earn above-average returns.

Figure 4.3 — Examples of Value-Creating Activities Associated with the Differentiation Strategy

	Inbound Logistics	Operations	Outbound Logistics	Marketing and Sales	Service
Firm Infrastructure	Highly developed information systems to better understand customers' purchasing preferences				
Human Resource Management	Compensation programs intended to encourage worker creativity and productivity				Somewhat extensive use of subjective rather than objective performance measures	Superior personnel training
Technology Development	Strong capability in basic research				Investments in technologies that will allow the firm to produce highly differentiated products
Procurement	Systems and procedures used to find the highest-quality raw materials				Purchase of highest-quality replacement parts
	Superior handling of incoming raw materials so as to minimize damage and to improve the quality of the final product	Consistent manufacturing of attractive products; Rapid responses to customers' unique manufacturing specifications	Accurate and responsive order-processing procedures; Rapid and timely product deliveries to customers	Extensive granting of credit buying arrangements for customers; Extensive personal relationships with buyers and suppliers	Extensive buyer training to assure high-quality product installations; Complete field stocking of replacement parts

A company-wide emphasis on the importance of producing high-quality products

MARGIN

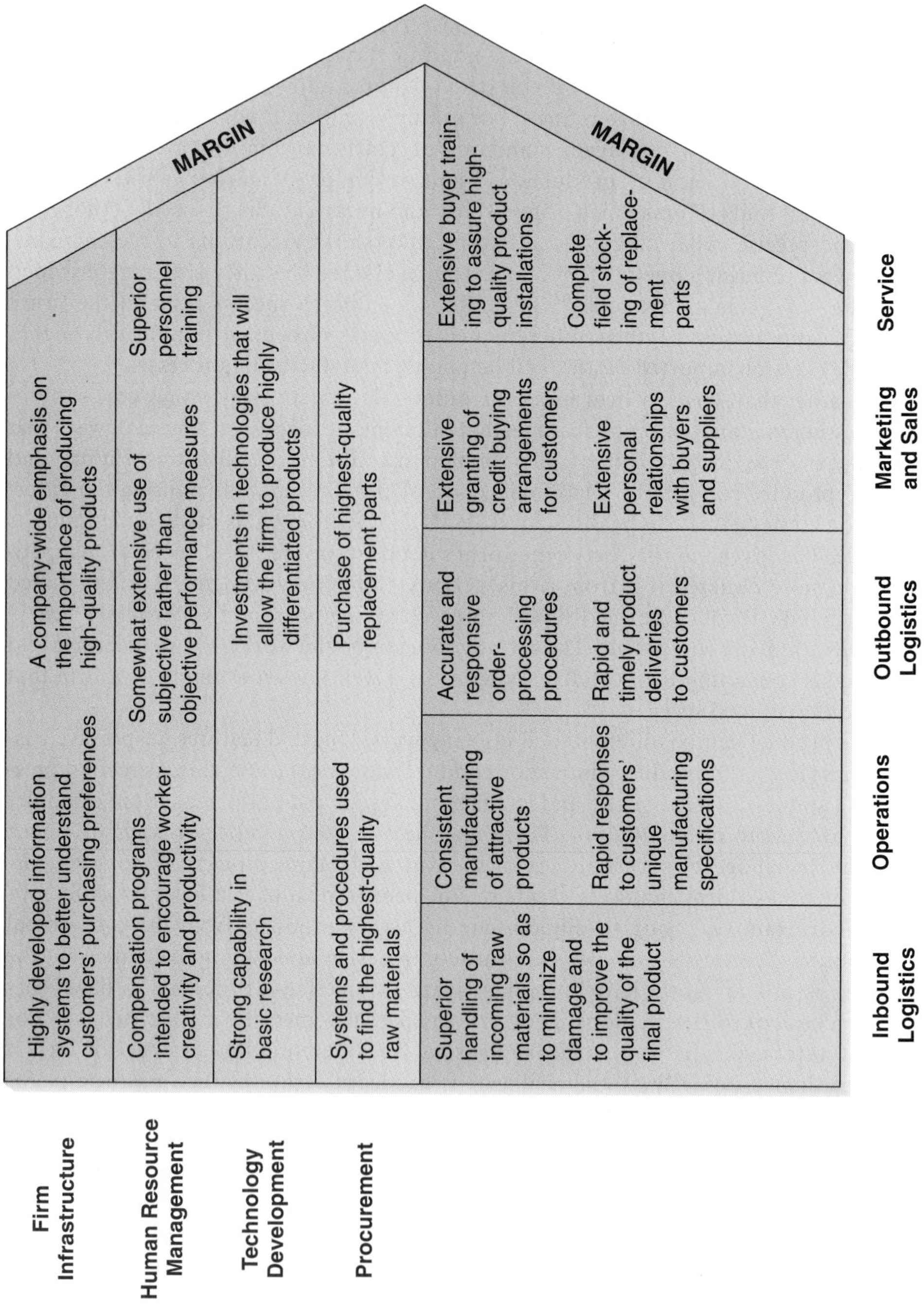

SOURCE: Adapted with the permission of The Free Press, an imprint of Simon & Schuster Adult Publishing Group, from *Competitive Advantage: Creating and Sustaining Superior Performance*, by Michael E. Porter, 47. Copyright © 1985, 1998 by Michael E. Porter.

RIVALRY WITH EXISTING COMPETITORS

Customers tend to be loyal purchasers of products that are differentiated in ways that are meaningful to them. As their loyalty to a brand increases, customers' sensitivity to price increases is reduced. The relationship between brand loyalty and price sensitivity insulates a firm from competitive rivalry. Thus, McKinsey & Co. is insulated from its competitors, even on the basis of price, as long as it continues to satisfy the differentiated needs of its customer group. Likewise, Bose is insulated from intense rivalry as long as customers continue to perceive that its stereo equipment offers superior sound quality at a competitive cost.

BARGAINING POWER OF BUYERS (CUSTOMERS)

The uniqueness of differentiated goods or services reduces customers' sensitivity to price increases. On the basis of a combination of unique materials and brand image, "L'Oréal has developed a winning formula: a growing portfolio of international brands that has transformed the French company into the United Nations of beauty. Blink an eye, and L'Oréal has just sold 85 products around the world, from Maybelline eye makeup, Redken hair care, and Ralph Lauren perfumes to Helena Rubinstein cosmetics and Vichy skin care." L'Oréal is finding success in markets stretching from China to Mexico as some other consumer product companies falter. L'Oréal's differentiation strategy seeks to convey the allure of different cultures through its many products: "Whether it's selling Italian elegance, New York street smarts, or French beauty through its brands, L'Oréal is reaching out to more people across a bigger range of incomes and cultures than just about any other beauty-products company in the world."[86]

L'Oréal seeks to satisfy customers' unique needs better than its competitors can. Some buyers are willing to pay a premium price for the firm's cosmetic items because, for these buyers, other products do not offer a comparable combination of features and cost. The lack of perceived acceptable alternatives increases the firm's power relative to that of its customers.

BARGAINING POWER OF SUPPLIERS

Because the firm using the differentiation strategy charges a premium price for its products, suppliers must provide high-quality components, driving up the firm's costs. However, the high margins the firm earns in these cases partially insulate it from the influence of suppliers in that higher supplier costs can be paid through these margins. Alternatively, because of buyers' relative insensitivity to price increases, the differentiated firm might choose to pass the additional cost of supplies on to the customer by increasing the price of its unique product.

POTENTIAL ENTRANTS

Customer loyalty and the need to overcome the uniqueness of a differentiated product present substantial entry barriers to potential entrants. Entering an industry under these conditions typically demands significant investments of resources and patience while seeking customers' loyalty.

PRODUCT SUBSTITUTES

Firms selling brand-name goods and services to loyal customers are positioned effectively against product substitutes. In contrast, companies without brand loyalty face a higher probability of their customers switching either to products that offer differentiated features that serve the same function (particularly if the substitute has a lower price) or to products that offer more features and perform more attractive functions.

COMPETITIVE RISKS OF THE DIFFERENTIATION STRATEGY

As with the other business-level strategies, the differentiation strategy is not risk free. One risk is that customers might decide that the price differential between the differentiator's product and the cost leader's product is too large. In this instance, a firm may be offering differentiated features that exceed target customers' needs. The firm then becomes vulnerable to competitors that are able to offer customers a combination of features and price that is more consistent with their needs.

Another risk of the differentiation strategy is that a firm's means of differentiation may cease to provide value for which customers are willing to pay. A differentiated product becomes less valuable if imitation by rivals causes customers to perceive that competitors offer essentially the same good or service, but at a lower price. For example, Walt Disney Company operates different theme parks, including The Magic Kingdom, Epcot Center, and the newly developed Animal Kingdom. Each park offers entertainment and educational opportunities. However, Disney's competitors, such as Six Flags Corporation, also offer entertainment and educational experiences similar to those available at Disney's locations. To ensure that its facilities create value for which customers will be willing to pay, Disney continuously reinvests in its operations to more crisply differentiate them from those of its rivals.[87]

A third risk of the differentiation strategy is that experience can narrow customers' perceptions of the value of a product's differentiated features. For example, the value of the IBM name provided a differentiated feature for the firm's personal computers for which some users were willing to pay a premium price in the early life cycle of the product. However, as customers familiarized themselves with the product's standard features, and as a host of other firms' personal computers entered the market, IBM brand loyalty ceased to create value for which some customers were willing to pay. The substitutes offered features similar to those found in the IBM product at a substantially lower price, reducing the attractiveness of IBM's product.

Counterfeiting is the differentiation strategy's fourth risk. Makers of counterfeit goods—products that attempt to convey a firm's differentiated features to customers at significantly reduced prices—are a concern for many firms using the differentiation strategy. For example, Callaway Golf Company's success at producing differentiated products that create value, coupled with golf's increasing global popularity, has created great demand for counterfeited Callaway equipment. Through the U.S. Customs Service's "Project Teed Off" program, agents seized over 110 shipments with a total of more than 100,000 counterfeit Callaway golf club components over a three-year period.[88] Altria Group's domestic tobacco division, Philip Morris USA, files lawsuits against retailers selling counterfeit versions of its cigarettes, such as Marlboro. Judgments Philip Morris has won in these suits include immediate discontinuance of selling the counterfeit products as well as significant financial penalties for any future violations.[89]

Focus Strategies

Firms choose a focus strategy when they intend to use their core competencies to serve the needs of a particular industry segment or niche to the exclusion of others. Examples of specific market segments that can be targeted by a focus strategy include (1) a particular buyer group (e.g., youths or senior citizens), (2) a different segment of a product line (e.g., products for professional painters or those for "do-it-yourselfers"), or (3) a different geographic market (e.g., the East or the West in the United States).[90] Thus, the **focus strategy** is an integrated set of actions taken to produce goods or services that serve the needs of a particular competitive segment.

Although the breadth of a target is clearly a matter of degree, the essence of the focus strategy "is the exploitation of a narrow target's differences from the balance of the industry."[91] Firms using the focus strategy intend to serve a particular segment of an industry more effectively than can industry-wide competitors. They succeed when they effectively serve a segment whose unique needs are so specialized that broad-based competitors choose not to serve that segment or when they satisfy the needs of a segment being served poorly by industry-wide competitors.[92]

To satisfy the needs of a certain size of company competing in a particular geographic market, Los Angeles–based investment banking firm Greif & Company posi-

The focus strategy is an integrated set of actions taken to produce goods or services that serve the needs of a particular competitive segment.

tions itself as "The Entrepreneur's Investment Bank." Greif & Company is a "leading purveyor of merger and acquisition advisory services to medium-sized businesses based in the Western United States."[93] Partly because of costs and liability, governments are outsourcing health care to private companies. Nicknamed the "HMO behind bars," American Services Group Inc. (ASG) specializes in providing contract health care for prisons and jails such as New York's Rikers Island facility.[94] Through successful use of the focus strategy, firms such as Greif & Company and ASG gain a competitive advantage in specific market niches or segments, even though they do not possess an industry-wide competitive advantage.[95]

Firms can create value for customers in specific and unique market segments by using the focused cost leadership strategy or the focused differentiation strategy.

FOCUSED COST LEADERSHIP STRATEGY

Based in Sweden, Ikea, a global furniture retailer with locations in over 30 countries, follows the focused cost leadership strategy.[96] Young buyers desiring style at a low cost are Ikea's market segment.[97] For these customers, the firm offers home furnishings that combine good design, function, and acceptable quality with low prices. According to the firm, "low cost is always in focus. This applies to every phase of our activities."[98] The firm continues its global expansion, recently opening stores in Russia and China.[99]

Ikea emphasizes several activities to keep its costs low. For example, instead of relying primarily on third-party manufacturers, the firm's engineers design low-cost, modular furniture ready for assembly by customers. Ikea also positions its products in roomlike settings. Typically, competitors' furniture stores display multiple varieties of a single item in separate rooms, and their customers examine living room sofas in one room, tables in another room, chairs in yet another location, and accessories in still another area. In contrast, Ikea's customers can view different living combinations (complete with sofas, chairs, tables, and so forth) in a single setting, which eliminates the need for sales associates or decorators to help the customer imagine how a batch of furniture will look when placed in the customer's home. This approach requires fewer sales personnel, allowing Ikea to keep its costs low. A third practice that helps keep Ikea's costs low is expecting customers to transport their own purchases rather than providing delivery service.

Although a cost leader, Ikea also offers some differentiated features that appeal to its target customers, including in-store playrooms for children, wheelchairs for customer use, and extended hours. Stores outside those in the home country have "Sweden Shops" that sell Swedish specialties, such as herring, crisp bread, Swedish caviar, and gingerbread biscuits. Ikea believes that these services and products "are uniquely aligned with the needs of [its] customers, who are young, are not wealthy, are likely to have children (but no nanny), and, because they work for a living, have a need to shop at odd hours."[100] Thus, Ikea's focused cost leadership strategy finds the firm offering some differentiated features with its low-cost products.

Ikea is an example of a company successfully using the focused cost leadership strategy. Stores display their furniture in what look like completely furnished rooms to increase the appeal of their products as well as reduce costs by employing fewer sales personnel.

FOCUSED DIFFERENTIATION STRATEGY

Other firms implement the focused differentiation strategy. As noted earlier, firms can differentiate their products in many ways. The Internet furniture venture Casketfurniture.com, for example, targets Generation X people

©Spencer Grant/PhotoEdit

Satisfying Unique Needs: Of Shoes and Cars

Privately held New Balance Athletic Shoe Inc. concentrates on the athletic shoe needs of the Baby Boom generation (born between 1946 and 1964). Indicating the firm's focus on a particular customer segment is the perspective that "we don't want New Balance to be all things to all people." The high-quality "fit" that its shoes provide is the primary source of differentiation, for which the firm's target customer group is willing to pay a premium price.

Early research by New Balance suggested that active Baby Boomers want shoes that fit extremely well rather than shoes that are recognized for their style. A key indicator of the company's commitment to fit is that it is the only shoe manufacturer producing a complete line in a variety of widths—from AA to EEEE. New Balance's philosophy about fit is straightforward: "The better your shoes fit, the more comfortable you will be, the better you will enjoy yourself."

To support the design and manufacture of products with the "best possible fit," New Balance invests significantly in technological research and development (R&D) activities. Several patented technologies resulting from the firm's R&D efforts have been instrumental in developing suspension systems for the firm's shoes. Well-trained workers use highly sophisticated manufacturing equipment to produce the firm's differentiated products. The successful differentiation of New Balance's shoes in terms of fit is suggested by the fact that several models have received special recognition by the American Podiatric Medical Association. To further support these efforts, the firm recently installed a product-life-cycle management (PLM) software system. Linking all people involved with product development, distribution, and service after the sale, this new system facilitates New Balance's commitment to appropriately modify its products to satisfy consumer preferences in different regions of the world while continuously improving product quality.

Committed to innovation and serving an array of product niches by using its focused differentiation strategy, New Balance launched a new brand in spring 2004. Called Aravon, this line seeks to satisfy physicians' needs to prescribe running shoes for patients with unique foot characteristics.

Fiat Group, the Italian manufacturer of mass-market cars, owns 90 percent of Ferrari SpA, the famous sports car company with the well-recognized Prancing Horse emblem on its products. In the late 1990s, Ferrari bought Maserati. After a ten-year absence from the U.S. market, a Maserati product was reintroduced in early 2002 after being successfully relaunched earlier in France, Italy, Switzerland, and Germany. Demonstrating precise segmentation of the market for expensive sports cars, Ferrari determined that the Maserati would appeal to wealthy sports car enthusiasts lacking either the resources or the desire to purchase a Ferrari. The target customer is the person with "good taste who is looking for a unique emotion from driving." With a base price of approximately $80,000, the two-seater Maserati Spider (the product offered in the United States) competes against the Porsche 911 and the Jaguar XKR. Like its rivals, the Spider travels from zero to 60 miles per hour in roughly 5.3 seconds.

Early evidence suggests that the focused differentiation strategy is allowing Ferrari to use the Maserati to expand into different segments without diluting Ferrari's own brand. In late 2003, Maserati unveiled a new four-door luxury sedan as its entry into that particular segment. The firm hoped this sedan would account for half of all Maserati sales by 2006. Along with Porsche and BMW, Maserati also established an outlet in Beijing to satisfy the growing demand in China for luxury automobiles.

SOURCES: M. Davis, 2003, Frank Stephenson talks about his new life at Ferrari-Maserati, *Autoweek*, 53(4): 20–21; S. Hill, Jr., 2003, A new vision, *MSI*, 21(2): 30–32; J. Lerner, 2003, New Balance takes strides to comfort-casual market, *Boston Business Journal*, February 14, D6; C. Reidy, 2003, New Balance hopes casual-footwear line attracts younger customers, *Boston Globe*, March 14, C1; D. Roberts, 2003, Bentley Beijing: Chariots on fire, *Business Week*, March 24, 66–67; A. Bernstein, 2001, Low-skilled jobs: Do they have to move? *Business Week*, February 26, 94–95; A. Kirkman, 2001, Zoom! Zoom! *Forbes*, May 14, 208.

who are interested in using the Internet as a shopping vehicle and who want to buy items with multiple purposes. The firm offers a collection of products, including display cabinets, coffee tables, and entertainment centers, that can be easily converted into coffins if desired. The $1,975 display cabinet is the company's best-selling item. With 16 units on the East Coast, hair salon Cartoon Cuts serves children between the ages of 8 and 14. This age group is a profitable and growing niche in the $50 billion U.S. hair salon industry. Upscale bed and breakfast facilities, such as Harbor Light Inn in Boston, Mass., provide an extensive array of services for business travelers desiring the finest in amenities.[101]

In the Strategic Focus, we discuss individual sources of differentiation that two firms—New Balance and Maserati (part of Fiat Group)—have created to use the focused differentiation strategy. Technology, R&D capability, managerial creativity, and an empowered and talented workforce are the competitive advantages New Balance uses to offer customers a shoe with an ideal "fit." Relying on its advantages of reputation, design skills, and manufacturing expertise, Maserati has produced the Maserati Spider to appeal to the *emotions* of its target customer group. In both instances, perceived value is created for a narrow segment of broader markets (for athletic shoes and automobiles, respectively).

Firms must be able to complete various primary and support activities in a competitively superior manner to develop and sustain a competitive advantage and earn above-average returns with a focus strategy. The activities required to use the focused cost leadership strategy are virtually identical to the activities shown in Figure 4.2, and activities required to use the focused differentiation strategy are virtually identical to those shown in Figure 4.3. Similarly, the manner in which each of the two focus strategies allows a firm to deal successfully with the five competitive forces parallels those described with respect to the cost leadership strategy and the differentiation strategy. The only difference is that the competitive scope changes from an industry-wide market to a narrow industry segment. Thus, a review of Figures 4.2 and 4.3 and the text regarding the five competitive forces yields a description of the relationship between each of the two focus strategies and competitive advantage.

COMPETITIVE RISKS OF FOCUS STRATEGIES

With either focus strategy, the firm faces the same general risks as does the company using the cost leadership or the differentiation strategy, respectively, on an industry-wide basis. However, focus strategies have three additional risks.

First, a competitor may be able to focus on a more narrowly defined competitive segment and "outfocus" the focuser. For example, Big Dog Motorcycles is trying to outfocus Harley-Davidson, which is pursuing a broader-focus differentiation strategy. While Harley focuses solely on producing heavyweight motorcycles, Big Dog Motorcycles builds motorcycles that target only the very high end of the heavyweight market—the high-end premium cruiser market—with such names as Pitbull, Wolf, Mastiff, and Bulldog. Big Dog Motorcycles

Big Dog Motorcycles offers several models, including Pitbull, Wolf, Mastiff, and Bulldog. Big Dog Motorcycles has arguably outfocused its major competitor, Harley-Davidson, by producing high-end heavyweight motorcycles.

©Lon C. Diehl/PhotoEdit.

is careful to differentiate its products from those of Harley-Davidson, citing its larger motors, fat rear tires, unique state-of-the-art electronics, and four-piston caliper brakes as examples of value-creating features. The estimate that eight out of ten of its customers either own or have owned a Harley-Davidson product suggests the apparent success of Big Dog Motorcycles' efforts to outfocus its major competitor.[102]

Second, a company competing on an industry-wide basis may decide that the market segment served by the focus strategy firm is attractive and worthy of competitive pursuit. For example, Building Materials Holding Company (BMHC) is a profitable regional retailer of building materials and construction services with operations in 12 western and southern states. Targeting professional contractors, BMHC provides customers with "a number of specialized services not offered by home center retailers" such as Home Depot and Lowe's.[103] Continuing growth in the size of the professional contractor market as well as the population of western and southern states might induce more concentrated efforts by Home Depot and Lowe's to learn how to serve the specialized needs of BMHC's core customer.

The third risk involved with a focus strategy is that the needs of customers within a narrow competitive segment may become more similar to those of industry-wide customers as a whole. As a result, the advantages of a focus strategy are either reduced or eliminated. At some point, for example, the needs of Ikea's customers for stylish furniture may dissipate, although their desire to buy relatively inexpensive furnishings may not. If this change in needs were to happen, Ikea's customers might buy from large chain stores that sell somewhat standardized furniture at low costs.

Integrated Cost Leadership/Differentiation Strategy

Particularly in global markets, the firm's ability to integrate the means of competition necessary to implement the cost leadership and differentiation strategies may be critical to developing competitive advantages. Compared to firms implementing one dominant business-level strategy, the company that successfully uses an integrated cost leadership/differentiation strategy should be in a better position to (1) adapt quickly to environmental changes, (2) learn new skills and technologies more quickly, and (3) effectively leverage its core competencies while competing against its rivals.

Concentrating on the needs of its core customer group (higher-income, fashion-conscious discount shoppers), Target Stores uses an integrated strategy. One reason for the use of this strategy is that, as we discussed earlier, trying to imitate major competitor Wal-Mart's cost leadership strategy is virtually impossible (because of how successfully Wal-Mart is positioned relative to the five forces of competition). Thus, Target has chosen to use its core competencies to serve the needs of a target customer group that differs from Wal-Mart's. Target relies on its relationships with Michael Graves in home, garden, and electronics products, Sonia Kashuk in cosmetics, Mossimo in apparel, and Eddie Bauer in camping and outdoor gear, among others, to offer differentiated products at discounted prices to its core customers. Committed to presenting a consistent upscale image, the firm carefully studies trends to find new branded items that it believes can satisfy its customers' needs.[104]

Evidence suggests a relationship between successful use of the integrated strategy and above-average returns.[105] Thus, firms able to produce relatively differentiated products at relatively low costs can expect to perform well.[106] Indeed, a researcher found that the most successful firms competing in low-profit-potential industries were integrating the attributes of the cost leadership and differentiation strategies.[107] Other researchers have discovered that "businesses which combined multiple forms of competitive advantage outperformed businesses that only were identified with a single form."[108] The results of another study showed that the highest-performing companies in the Korean electronics industry combined the value-creating aspects of the cost leadership and differentiation strategies.[109] This finding suggests the usefulness of the integrated strategy in settings outside the United States.

McDonald's is a corporation with a strong global brand, offering products at a relatively low cost but with some differentiated features. Historically, its global scale, relationships with franchisees, and rigorous standardization of processes have allowed McDonald's to lower its costs, while its brand recognition and product consistency have been sources of differentiation allowing the restaurant chain to charge slightly higher prices.[110] Thus, the firm uses the integrated cost leadership/differentiation strategy.[111]

The future success of McDonald's is being questioned, however. One analyst, for example, suggests, "Already in the U.S., competition is eroding its dominance; its great days are probably over. It must now manage a decline which will be bumpy, even violent."[112] Does this comment accurately describe McDonald's future as it uses the integrated strategy? Are the firm's glory days "over" as the analyst foresees? We consider these matters in the Strategic Focus.

Will McDonald's efforts to reduce costs through a more simplified menu while offering some additional differentiated features in new storefront formats be sufficient to assure success in the years to come? Only time will tell. However, information in the Strategic Focus suggests that the firm needs either to more effectively implement the integrated cost leadership/differentiation strategy or to change its strategy to one that is a better match between opportunities and threats in the firm's external environment and the core competencies of its internal environment.

Unlike McDonald's, which uses the integrated cost leadership/differentiation strategy on an industry-wide basis, air-conditioning and heating-systems maker Aaon concentrates on a particular competitive scope. Thus, Aaon is implementing a focused integrated strategy. Aaon manufactures semicustomized rooftop air conditioning systems for large retailers, including Wal-Mart, Target, and Home Depot. Aaon positions its rooftop systems between low-priced commodity equipment and high-end customized systems. The firm's innovative manufacturing capabilities allow it to tailor a production line for units with special heat-recovery options unavailable on low-end systems. Combining custom features with assembly-line production methods results in significant cost savings. Aaon's prices are approximately 5 percent higher than low-end products but are only one-third the price of comparable customized systems.[113] Thus, the firm's narrowly defined target customers receive some differentiated features (e.g., special heat-recovery options) at a low, but not the lowest, cost.

A commitment to strategic flexibility (see Chapter 1) is necessary for firms to effectively use the integrated cost leadership/differentiation strategy. Strategic flexibility results from developing systems, procedures, and methods that enable a firm to quickly and effectively respond to opportunities that reduce costs or increase differentiation. Flexible manufacturing systems, information networks, and total quality management systems are three sources of strategic flexibility that facilitate use of the integrated strategy and make firms more globally competitive as a result.[114] Valuable to the successful use of each business-level strategy, the strategic flexibility provided by these three tools is especially important to firms trying to balance the objectives of continuous cost reductions and continuous enhancements to sources of differentiation.

FLEXIBLE MANUFACTURING SYSTEMS

Flexible manufacturing systems (FMS) increase the "flexibilities of human, physical, and information resources"[115] that the firm integrates to create relatively differentiated products at relatively low costs. A *flexible manufacturing system* is a computer-controlled process used to produce a variety of products in moderate, flexible quantities with a minimum of manual intervention.[116] Particularly in situations where parts are too heavy for people to handle or when other methods are less effective in creating manufacturing and assembly flexibility, robots are integral to use of an FMS.[117] In spite of their promise, only one in five *Fortune* 1000 companies are using the productive capabilities of an FMS.[118]

Global Burgers: Are McDonald's Glory Days a Thing of the Past?

McDonald's is the world's leading global food service retailer. The firm serves approximately 46 million people daily in its 31,000 units that are located in 120 countries. System-wide sales were $41.5 billion in fiscal year 2002. However, all is not well in Ronald McDonald land. Sales grew only 2 percent in 2002 with same-store sales down in all regions except Europe and Latin America. McDonald's faces fierce competition from traditional competitors as well as from the rapidly growing fast-casual format (a segment where customers "get a meal that tastes home-cooked in a short amount of time, then sit down and eat it at their leisure"). Although the case was dismissed, McDonald's has been sued on the allegation that its fatty foods made the company responsible for the rise in childhood obesity. Even more discouraging for McDonald's stakeholders, especially shareholders, was the posting of the firm's first quarterly loss in its history during the October–December 2002 quarter.

What are the root causes of McDonald's problems? Historically, McDonald's has used value pricing (the source of relatively low costs to customers) while offering menu and storefront variety and relying on the power of its brand name (sources of differentiation). Globally, the company has tried to provide its combination of relatively low costs and some levels of differentiation in a culturally sensitive manner. In India, for example, the Maharaja Mac, which is made from lamb, substitutes for the beef-based Big Mac. Popular corn soup is offered on the chain's menu in its Japanese units while the locally oriented McNifica is popular in Argentina.

McDonald's is taking actions to improve the implementation of its integrated cost leadership/product differentiation strategy. In 1999, the firm launched its "Made for You" system. Replacing the firm's historic practice of producing food and storing it in a large tray until purchased, the new system was designed to increase product quality, variety, and delivery speed (sources of differentiation). To do this, new computer equipment and cooking and food preparation machinery were installed in each unit. Crew members and managers received extensive training to learn how to maximize efficiency by using the new system. However, after two years and a $1 billion investment, McDonald's moved from "Made for You" to a more simplified system. A primary reason for this change was that the cost of using the "Made for You" system to increase sources of differentiation exceeded acceptable levels for successful use of the integrated cost leadership/differentiation strategy.

More recently, McDonald's has tried to control costs through simplification. A decision made in this respect was to trim the standard 36-item core menu, jettisoning such items as the McFlurry. Menu simplification is appealing to a large segment of McDonald's franchisees, one of whom observed, "You can't be everything to everybody. If you do, you fracture your clientele and your business. Then you're nothing to everyone. You have to hang onto your niche and try to do that well." Other decisions have been made to improve the firm's performance, including "fixing operating inadequacies in existing restaurants; taking a more integrated and focused approach to growth, with an emphasis on increasing sales, margins and returns in existing restaurants; and ensuring the correct operating structure and resources, aligned behind focusing priorities that create benefits for its customers and restaurants." In addition, McDonald's is evaluating several sources of differentiation, such as coin changers, self-order kiosks, and cashless drive-throughs, for possible introduction by mid-2005.

SOURCES: 2003, McDonald's Corp., *Standard & Poor's Stock Reports*, http://www.standardandpoors.com, May 17; 2003, McDonald's Japan to keep low-price burgers, *Jiji Press English News Service*, May 12; B. Herzog, 2003, *Oregonian*, May 1; J. R. McPherson, A. V. Mitchell, & M. R. Mitten, 2003, Fast-food fight, *The McKinsey Quarterly*, no. 2, 11–14; R. Sims, 2003, Tallahassee, Fla., hosts McDonald's new version of its Boston Market chain, *Tallahassee Democrat*, May 7; R. Dzinkowski, 2001, McDonald's Europe, *Strategic Finance*, May, 24–27; K. MacArthur, 2001, McDonald's sees 100%, *Advertising Age*, May/June, 12–14.

The goal of an FMS is to eliminate the "low-cost-versus-product-variety" trade-off that is inherent in traditional manufacturing technologies. Firms use an FMS to change quickly and easily from making one product to making another.[119] Used properly, an FMS allows the firm to respond more effectively to changes in its customers' needs, while retaining low-cost advantages and consistent product quality.[120] Because an FMS also enables the firm to reduce the lot size needed to manufacture a product efficiently, the firm increases its capacity to serve the unique needs of a narrow competitive scope.

Thus, FMS technology is a significant technological advance that allows firms to produce a large variety of products at relatively low costs. The effective use of an FMS is linked with a firm's ability to understand the constraints these systems may create (in terms of materials handling and the flow of supporting resources in scheduling, for example) and to design an effective mix of machines, computer systems, and people.[121] In industries of all types, effective mixes of the firm's tangible assets (e.g., machines) and intangible assets (e.g., people's skills) facilitate implementation of complex competitive strategies, especially the integrated cost leadership/differentiation strategy.[122]

An FMS is a complex engineering project. UNOVA Inc. uses a differentiation strategy to develop and implement flexible manufacturing systems for end users. An industrial technologies company, UNOVA provides global customers in the automotive, aerospace, and heavy equipment industries with flexible manufacturing solutions to the need to improve their efficiency and productivity. In markets throughout the world, the firm provides customers with the most technologically advanced, high-quality systems. To increase the functionality of its FMS systems to satisfy unique customer needs, especially the need to produce a wide variety of unique products at a relatively low cost for each item, the firm forms strategic alliances with companies located in many different countries (e.g., Korea, China, and Japan). To enhance the flexibility its systems provide to end users, UNOVA continuously evaluates its own manufacturing processes to find ways to enhance the sources of value its differentiated product features create for customers.[123]

INFORMATION NETWORKS

By linking companies with their suppliers, distributors, and customers, information networks provide another source of strategic flexibility. Among other outcomes, these networks, when used effectively,[124] facilitate the firm's efforts to satisfy customer expectations in terms of product quality and delivery speed.[125] In addition, effective information networks improve the flow of work among employees in the focal firm as well as between those employees and their counterparts, such as suppliers and distributors, with whom they interact.[126]

Customer relationship management (CRM) is one form of an information-based network process that firms use to better understand customers and their needs.[127] An effective CRM system provides a 360-degree view of the company's relationship with customers, encompassing all contact points, involving all business processes, and incorporating all communication media and sales channels.[128] The firm can then use this information to determine the trade-offs its customers are willing to make between differentiated features and low cost, which is vital for companies using the integrated cost leadership/differentiation strategy.

Information networks are also critical to the establishment and successful use of an enterprise resource planning (ERP) system. ERP is an information system used to identify and plan the resources required across the firm to receive, record, produce, and ship customer orders.[129] For example, salespeople for aircraft parts distributor Aviall use handheld equipment to scan bar-code labels on bins in customers' facilities to determine when parts need to be restocked. Data gathered through this procedure are uploaded via the Web to the Aviall back-end replenishment and ERP system, allowing the order fulfillment process to begin within minutes of scanning.[130] Growth in ERP applications such as the one used at Aviall has been significant.[131] Full installations of an ERP system are expensive, running into the tens of millions of dollars for large-scale applications.

Improving efficiency on a company-wide basis is a primary objective of using an ERP system. Efficiency improvements result from the use of systems through which financial and operational data are moved rapidly from one department to another. The transfer of sales data from Aviall salespeople to the order entry point at the firm's manufacturing facility demonstrates the rapid movement of information from one function to another. Integrating data across parties that are involved with detailing product specifications and then manufacturing those products and distributing them in ways that are consistent with customers' unique needs enable the firm to respond with flexibility to customer preferences relative to cost and differentiation.

TOTAL QUALITY MANAGEMENT SYSTEMS

Total quality management (TQM) is a "managerial innovation that emphasizes an organization's total commitment to the customer and to continuous improvement of every process through the use of data-driven, problem-solving approaches based on empowerment of employee groups and teams."[132] Firms develop and use TQM systems in order to (1) increase customer satisfaction, (2) cut costs, and (3) reduce the amount of time required to introduce innovative products to the marketplace.[133] Ford Motor Company is relying on TQM to help "root out" its quality flaws,[134] while General Motors is "scrambling to narrow the quality gap that its executives say is the main reason consumers shy away from GM."[135] The focus by these firms on TQM to improve product and service quality is appropriate,[136] in that while U.S. auto manufacturers have made progress, "the Big Three still lag behind some foreign competitors, primarily the Japanese, by most quality measures."[137]

Firms able to simultaneously cut costs while enhancing their ability to develop innovative products increase their strategic flexibility. The increased flexibility associated with the ability to jointly reduce costs and become more innovative is particularly helpful to firms implementing the integrated cost leadership/differentiation strategy. At least meeting (and perhaps exceeding) customers' expectations regarding quality is a differentiating feature, and eliminating process inefficiencies to cut costs allows the firm to offer that quality to customers at a relatively low price. Thus, an effective TQM system helps the firm develop the flexibility needed to spot opportunities to simultaneously increase differentiation and reduce costs.

COMPETITIVE RISKS OF THE INTEGRATED COST LEADERSHIP/DIFFERENTIATION STRATEGY

The potential to earn above-average returns by successfully using the integrated cost leadership/differentiation strategy is appealing. However, experience shows that substantial risk accompanies this potential. As noted at the beginning of the chapter, selecting a business-level strategy requires the firm to make choices about how it intends to compete. Achieving the low-cost position in an industry or a segment of an industry by using a cost leadership strategy or a focused cost leadership strategy demands that the firm consistently reduce its costs relative to competitors' costs. The use of the differentiation strategy, with either an industry-wide or a focused competitive scope (see Figure 4.1), requires the firm to provide its customers with differentiated goods or services they value and for which they are willing to pay a premium price.

The firm that uses the integrated strategy yet fails to establish a leadership position risks becoming "stuck in the middle."[138] Being in this position prevents the firm from dealing successfully with the competitive forces in its industry and from having a distinguishable competitive advantage. Not only will the firm not be able to earn above-average returns, but earning even average returns will be possible only when the structure of the industry in which it competes is highly favorable or if its competitors are also in the same position.[139] Without these conditions, the firm will earn below-average returns. Thus, companies implementing the integrated cost leadership/differentiation strategy must be certain that their competitive actions allow them both to offer some differentiated features that their customers value and to provide those products at a relatively low cost. The discussion of McDonald's in the Strategic Focus suggests that the firm may be "stuck in the middle" as a result of ineffective use of the integrated cost leadership/product differentiation strategy. In contrast, the earlier description of Southwest Airlines' performance over its 30-plus years of life indicates that it continues to be extremely successful as it uses the integrated cost leadership/differentiation strategy.

In spite of McDonald's performance problems, there is very little if any research evidence showing that the attributes of the cost leadership and differentiation strategies *cannot* be effectively integrated.[140] The integrated strategy, therefore, is an appropriate strategic choice for firms with the core competencies required to produce somewhat differentiated products at relatively low costs.

Summary

- A business-level strategy is an integrated and coordinated set of commitments and actions the firm uses to gain a competitive advantage by exploiting core competencies in specific product markets. Five business-level strategies (cost leadership, differentiation, focused cost leadership, focused differentiation, and integrated cost leadership/ differentiation) are examined in the chapter.

- Customers are the foundation of successful business-level strategies. When considering customers, a firm simultaneously examines three issues: *who*, *what*, and *how*. These issues, respectively, refer to the customer groups to be served, the needs those customers have that the firm seeks to satisfy, and the core competencies the firm will use to satisfy customers' needs. Increasing segmentation of markets throughout the global economy creates opportunities for firms to identify increasingly unique customer needs.

- Firms seeking competitive advantage through the cost leadership strategy produce no-frills, standardized products for an industry's typical customer. However, these low-cost products must be offered with competitive levels of differentiation. Above-average returns are earned when firms continuously drive their costs lower than those of their competitors, while providing customers with products that have low prices and acceptable levels of differentiated features.

- Competitive risks associated with the cost leadership strategy include (1) a loss of competitive advantage to newer technologies, (2) a failure to detect changes in customers' needs, and (3) the ability of competitors to imitate the cost leader's competitive advantage through their own unique strategic actions.

- Through the differentiation strategy, firms provide customers with products that have different (and valued) features. Differentiated products must be sold at a cost that customers believe is competitive given the product's features as compared to the cost/feature combination available through competitors' offerings. Because of their uniqueness, differentiated goods or services are sold at a premium price. Products can be differentiated along any dimension that some customer group values. Firms using this strategy seek to differentiate their products from competitors' goods or services along as many dimensions as possible. The less similarity with competitors' products, the more buffered a firm is from competition with its rivals.

- Risks associated with the differentiation strategy include (1) a customer group's decision that the differences between the differentiated product and the cost leader's good or service are no longer worth a premium price, (2) the inability of a differentiated product to create the type of value for which customers are willing to pay a premium price, (3) the ability of competitors to provide customers with products that have features similar to those associated with the differentiated product, but at a lower cost, and (4) the threat of counterfeiting, whereby firms produce a cheap "knock-off" of a differentiated good or service.

- Through the cost leadership and the differentiated focus strategies, firms serve the needs of a narrow competitive segment (e.g., a buyer group, product segment, or geographic area). This strategy is successful when firms have the core competencies required to provide value to a narrow competitive segment that exceeds the value available from firms serving customers on an industry-wide basis.

- The competitive risks of focus strategies include (1) a competitor's ability to use its core competencies to "out-focus" the focuser by serving an even more narrowly defined competitive segment, (2) decisions by industry-wide competitors to serve a customer group's specialized needs that the focuser has been serving, and (3) a reduction in differences of the needs between customers in a narrow competitive segment and the industry-wide market.

- Firms using the integrated cost leadership/differentiation strategy strive to provide customers with relatively low-cost products that have some valued differentiated features. The primary risk of this strategy is that a firm might produce products that do not offer sufficient value in terms of either low cost or differentiation. When this occurs, the company is "stuck in the middle." Firms stuck in the middle compete at a disadvantage and are unable to earn more than average returns.

Review Questions

Review Questions Review Questions

1. What is a business-level strategy?

2. What is the relationship between a firm's customers and its business-level strategy in terms of who, what, and how? Why is this relationship important?

3. What are the differences among the cost leadership, differentiation, focused cost leadership, focused differentiation, and integrated cost leadership/differentiation business-level strategies?

4. How can each one of the business-level strategies be used to position the firm relative to the five forces of competition in a way that permits the earning of above-average returns?

5. What are the specific risks associated with using each business-level strategy?

Experiential Exercises

Experiential Exercise

Warehouse Clubs' Strategies

Although warehouse clubs have traditionally offered low-priced merchandise to small-business owners, they are increasingly servicing the end-use consumer in this $70 billion industry. Two giants in the field are Sam's Club and Costco. Costco has surpassed Sam's in sales, nearly doubling Sam's sales on a per-store basis by some estimates. Sam's tends to offer average-quality goods in bulk at low margins. Costco increasingly offers special selections of high-quality, even designer, goods, attracting customers whose incomes are approximately twice the national average. Although each competitor regularly stocks certain products, other offerings may be one time only with limited stock. Costco uses this scenario to entice customers into the store to see what is there today, perhaps gone tomorrow. This type of shopping experience has reportedly grown into a cultural fad for some Costco shoppers, who often look for a value on high-end goods and compare bargain finds with their friends. Sam's Clubs are often located near major interstates to capitalize on their quick, efficient distribution system. Costcos are increasingly located in affluent suburbs, near their customer bases.

Use the Internet to research the home pages and annual statements of both Sam's Club and Costco. Using your knowledge of these businesses and any relevant researched information, label each strategy. (See Figure 4.1.) Based on each of their identified business strategies, how are each of these firms positioned relative to the five forces of competition? To better understand each of their competitive positions, compare total sales and sales per store; number of memberships and sales per membership; and operating income and sales growth for 2001 to 2003. Finally, how does each of these two firms appear to be positioned relative to the who, what, and how of customer elements of strategic competitiveness? (See Table 4.1.)

Business-Level Strategy

Natural and organic foods are the fastest growing segment of food retailing, and almost every supermarket in America has begun offering at least a limited selection of these products. According to chairman and CEO John Mackey, "Whole Foods is the 'category killer' for natural and organic products, offering the largest selection at competitive prices and the most informed customer service."

The first Whole Foods Markets opened in 1980, in Austin, Texas, and realized $4 million in sales. By 2001, the firm had become the world's largest retailer of natural and organic foods, with 126 stores across the country and the District of Columbia. A strong performer for several years with consistently high same-store sales, cash flow, gross margins, and controlled expansion, the firm's sales grew to $2.27 billion and earnings per share to $1.03 for fiscal 2001. Shares were up more than 50 percent over the previous year, and analysts expected the performance to continue, anticipating 18 percent earnings growth in fiscal 2002 and 20 percent growth in 2003.

Whole Foods purchases its products both locally and from all over the world, supporting organic farming on a global level, and prides itself on providing its customers with the highest-quality, least-processed, most flavorful and naturally preserved foods. Although the firm concedes that organic foods generally cost more than conventional foods, it notes that organic farming is not government subsidized and that organic products must meet stricter regulations governing growing, harvesting, transportation, and storage. All of these steps make the process more labor and management intensive.

Whole Foods staff members are encouraged to make their own decisions and play a critical role in helping build the store into a profitable and beneficial part of its community.

Answer the following questions and be prepared to make a short presentation or to discuss your findings with the rest of the class.

1. What type of business-level strategy does Whole Foods appear to follow, based on the above information?

2. What are some of the risks Whole Foods faces with this strategy?

3. Use the following table and show how Whole Foods might apply each strategy to its business activities, based on the information given above (also see Figures 4.2 and 4.3).

Activities	Cost Leadership Strategy	Differentiation Strategy
Inbound Logistics		
Operations		
Outbound Logistics		
Marketing and Sales		
Service		

SOURCES: L. DiCarlo, 2001, The overachievers, *Forbes.com*, http://www.forbes.com, December 5; 2000, Whole Foods Annual Report, Chairman's Letter, http://www.wholefoods.com/investor/ar00_letter.html.

Notes

1. L. L. Bryan, 2003, Strategic minds at work, *The McKinsey Quarterly*, Number 2, 6–7.
2. C. Roxburgh, 2003, Hidden flaws in strategy, *The McKinsey Quarterly*, Number 2, 27–39; J. Stopford, 2001, Should strategy makers become dream weavers? *Harvard Business Review*, 79(1): 165–169.
3. S. Kaplan & E. D. Beinhocker, 2003, The real value of strategic planning, *MIT Sloan Management Review*, 44(2): 71–76.
4. T. J. Douglas & J. A. Ryman, 2003, Understanding competitive advantage in the general hospital industry: Evaluating strategic competencies, *Strategic Management Journal*, 24: 333–347.
5. B. Pittman, 2003, Leading for value, *Harvard Business Review*, 81(4): 41–46.
6. D. A. Schuler, K. Rehbein, & R. D. Cramer, 2002, Pursuing strategic advantage through political means: A multivariate approach, *Academy of Management Journal*, 45: 659–672.
7. H. Bowman & C. E. Helfat, 2001, Does corporate strategy matter? *Strategic Management Journal*, 22: 1–23.
8. C. B. Dobni & G. Luffman, 2003, Determining the scope and impact of market orientation profiles on strategy implementation and performance, *Strategic Management Journal*, 24: 577–585; G. Hamel, 2000, *Leading the Revolution*, Boston: Harvard Business School Press, 71.
9. L. G. Love, R. L. Priem, & G. T. Lumpkin, 2002, Explicitly articulated strategy and firm performance under alternative levels of centralization, *Journal of Management*, 28: 611–627; R. S. Kaplan & D. P. Norton, 2001, *The Strategy-Focused Organization*, Boston: Harvard Business School Press, 90.
10. J. B. Barney, 2002, *Gaining and Sustaining Competitive Advantage*, 2nd ed., Upper Saddle River, NJ: Prentice-Hall, 6; D. C. Hambrick & J. W. Fredrickson, 2001, Are you sure you have a strategy? *Academy of Management Executive*, 15(4): 48–59.
11. R. D. Ireland, M. A. Hitt, S. M. Camp, & D. L. Sexton, 2001, Integrating entrepreneurship and strategic management actions to create firm wealth, *Academy of Management Executive*, 15(1): 49–63.
12. I. C. MacMillan, A. B. van Putten, & R. M. McGrath, 2003, Global gamesmanship, *Harvard Business Review*, 81(5): 62–71; M. A. Geletkanycz & S. S. Black, 2001, Bound by the past? Experience-based effects on commitment to the strategic status quo, *Journal of Management*, 27: 3–21.
13. D. F. Kuratko, R. D. Ireland, & J. S. Hornsby, 2001, The power of entrepreneurial actions: Insights from Acordia, Inc., *Academy of Management Executive*, 15(4): 60–71; T. J. Dean, R. L. Brown, & C. E. Bamford, 1998, Differences in large and small firm responses to environmental context: Strategic implications from a comparative analysis of business formations, *Strategic Management Journal*, 19: 709–728.
14. D. Farrell, T. Terwilliger, & A. P. Webb, 2002, Getting IT spending right this time, *The McKinsey Quarterly*, Number 2, 118–129; L. Tihanyi, A. E. Ellstrand, C. M. Daily, & D. R. Dalton, 2000, Composition of top management team and firm international diversification, *Journal of Management*, 26: 1157–1177.
15. A. M. Appel, A. Dhadwal, & W. E. Pietraszek, 2003, More bang for the IT buck, *The McKinsey Quarterly*, Number 2, 130–141; S. Nambisan, 2002, Designing virtual customer environments for new product development: Toward a theory, *Academy of Management Review*, 27: 392–413.
16. P. Rindova & C. J. Fombrun, 1999, Constructing competitive advantage: The role of firm-constituent interactions, *Strategic Management Journal*, 20: 691–710; G. G. Dess, A. Gupta, J. F. Hennart, & C. W. L. Hill, 1995, Conducting and integrating strategy research at the international, corporate, and business levels: Issues and directions, *Journal of Management*, 21: 357–393.
17. R. D. Ireland, M. A. Hitt, & D. G. Sirmon, 2003, A model of strategic entrepreneurship: The construct and its dimensions, *Journal of Management*, in press.
18. T. L. Pett & J. A. Wolff, 2003, Firm characteristics and managerial perceptions of NAFTA: An assessment of export implications for U.S. SMEs, *Journal of Small Business Management*, 41(2): 117–132; S. F. Slater & E. M. Olsen, 2000, Strategy type and performance: The influence of sales force management, *Strategic Management Journal*, 21: 813–829; M. E. Porter, 1998, *On Competition*, Boston: Harvard Business School Press.
19. M. E. Porter, 1996, What is strategy? *Harvard Business Review*, 74(6): 61–78.
20. T. A. Stewart, 2003, Dear shareholders, *Harvard Business Review*, 81(5): 10.
21. B. Lowendahl & O. Revang, 1998, Challenges to existing strategy theory in a postindustrial society, *Strategic Management Journal*, 19: 755–773.

22. D. M. De Carolis, 2003, Competencies and imitability in the pharmaceutical industry: An analysis of their relationship with firm performance, *Journal of Management*, 29: 27–50.

23. M. E. Porter, 1980, *Competitive Strategy*, New York: Free Press.

24. G. S. Day, 2003, Creating a superior customer-relating capability, *The McKinsey Quarterly*, 44(3): 77–82; L. L. Berry, 2001, The old pillars of new retailing, *Harvard Business Review*, 79(4): 131–137; A. Afuah, 1999, Technology approaches for the information age, in "Mastering Strategy" (Part One), *Financial Times*, September 27, 8.

25. N. Irwin, 2001, Motley Fool branches out, *Washington Post*, May 22, B5.

26. C. Harrison, 2003, Hoping a new name still computes, *Dallas Morning News*, May 6, D1.

27. D. O. Becker, 2003, Gambling on customers, *The McKinsey Quarterly*, Number 2, 46–59.

28. T. A. Stewart, 1999, *Intellectual Capital*, New York: Currency Doubleday, 144.

29. B. Magura, 2003, What hooks M-commerce customers? *The McKinsey Quarterly*, 44(3): 9; S. Winer, 2001, A framework for customer relationship management, *California Management Review*, 43(4): 89–105.

30. R. Dhar & R. Glazer, 2003, Hedging customers, *Harvard Business Review*, 81(5): 86–92.

31. L. K. Geller, 2002, CRM: What does it mean? *Target Marketing*, 25(8): 23–24.

32. 2003, Fitch Mexico assigns AA qualifications to certificates of Cemex, *Emerging Markets Economy*, April 8, 3; L. Walker, 2001, Plugged in for maximum efficiency, *Washington Post*, June 20, G1, G4.

33. P. Panepento, 2003, Erie, Pa., plant leads GE profits, *Erie Times-News*, April 12, B4; 2001, While Welch waited, *The Economist*, May 19, 75–76.

34. 2003, Amazon.com, *Standard & Poor's Stock Reports*, http://www.standardandpoors.com, May 3; 2003, Barnes & Noble, *Standard & Poor's Stock Reports*, http://www.standardandpoors.com, May 3.

35. 2003, http://www.carpoint.com, May 17; P. Evans & T. S. Wurster, 1999, Getting real about virtual commerce, *Harvard Business Review*, 77(6): 84–94; S. F. Slater & J. C. Narver, 1999, Market-oriented is more than being customer-led, *Strategic Management Journal*, 20: 1165–1168.

36. D. Rosenblum, D. Tomlinson, & L. Scott, 2003, Bottom-feeding for blockbuster businesses, *Harvard Business Review*, 81(3): 52–59.

37. W. D. Neal & J. Wurst, 2001, Advances in market segmentation, *Marketing Research*, 13(1): 14–18.

38. A. Baur, S. P. Hehner, & G. Nederegger, 2003, Pharma for Fido, *The McKinsey Quarterly*, Number 2, 7–10.

39. B. J. Knutson, 2000, College students and fast food—how students perceive restaurant brands, *Cornell Hotel and Restaurant Administration Quarterly*, 41(3): 68–74.

40. 2003, Unions and Gen-X: What does the future hold? *HR Focus*, March, 3; F. Marshall, 2003, Storehouse wakes up to Gen-X employees, *Furniture Today*, February 10, 2–3; J. Pereira, 2003, Best on the street, *Wall Street Journal*, May 12, R7; C. Burritt, 2001, Aging boomers reshape resort segment, *Lodging Hospitality*, 57(3): 31–32; J. D. Zbar, 2001, On a segmented dial, digital cuts wire finer, *Advertising Age*, 72(16): S12.

41. F. Warner, 2003, Learning how to speak to Gen Y, *Fast Company*, July, 36–37; T. Elkin, 2003, Study: GenY is key to convergence, *Advertising Age*, 74(17): 61; 2001, Is Gen Y shopping online? *Business Week*, June 11, 16.

42. 2003, Abercrombie & Fitch, *Standard & Poor's Stock Reports*, http://www.standardandpoors.com, May 3; D. Little, 2001, Hot growth companies, *Business Week*, June 11, 107–110.

43. D. A. Aaker, 1998, *Strategic Marketing Management*, 5th ed., New York: John Wiley & Sons, 20.

44. E. Danneels, 2003, Tight-loose coupling with customers: The enactment of customer orientation, *Strategic Management Journal*, 24: 559–576.

45. 2003, Giving people what they want, *The Economist*, May 10, 58.

46. J. P. O'Brien, 2003, The capital structure implications of pursuing a strategy of innovation, *Strategic Management Journal*, 24: 415–431.

47. L. Mazur, 2003, Forget risk-free rules to tap into customer needs, *Marketing*, April 10, 16.

48. D. Foust, F. F. Jespersen, F. Katzenberg, A. Barrett, & R. O. Crockett, 2003, The best performers, *BusinessWeek Online*, http://www.businessweek.com, March 24.

49. 2003, Less is Moore, *The Economist*, May 10, 10.

50. M. J. Silverstein & N. Fiske, 2003, Luxury for the masses, *Harvard Business Review*, 81(4): 48–57.

51. C. W. L. Hill & F. T. Rothaermel, 2003, The performance of incumbent firms in the face of radical technological innovation, *Academy of Management Review*, 28: 257–274; A. W. King, S. W. Fowler, & C. P. Zeithaml, 2001, Managing organizational competencies for competitive advantage: The middle-management edge, *Academy of Management Executive*, 15(2): 95–106.

52. S. N. Mehta, 2001, What Lucent can learn from IBM, *Fortune*, June 25, 40–44.

53. 2003, http://www.sas.com, May 15; C. A. O'Reilly III & J. Pfeffer, 2000, *Hidden Value: How Great Companies Achieve Extraordinary Results with Ordinary People*, Boston: Harvard Business School Press, 102.

54. 2003, http://www.vans.com; A. Weintraub & G. Khermouch, 2001, Chairman of the board, *Business Week*, May 28, 94.

55. M. E. Porter, 1985, *Competitive Advantage*, New York: Free Press, 26.

56. Porter, What is strategy?

57. 2003, What makes Southwest Airlines fly? *Knowledge at Wharton*, http://knowledge.wharton.upenn.edu, April 24.

58. Porter, What is strategy?

59. G. Hawawini, V. Subramanian, & P. Verdin, 2003, Is performance driven by industry- or firm-specific factors? A new look at the evidence, *Strategic Management Journal*, 24: 1–16; B. McEvily & A. Zaheer, 1999, Bridging ties: A source of firm heterogeneity in competitive capabilities, *Strategic Management Journal*, 20: 133–156.

60. Hambrick & Fredrickson, Are you sure you have a strategy?

61. C. Zott, 2003, Dynamic capabilities and the emergence of intraindustry differential firm performance: Insights from a simulation study, *Strategic Management Journal*, 24: 97–125.

62. M. E. Porter, 1994, Toward a dynamic theory of strategy, in R. P. Rumelt, D. E. Schendel, & D. J. Teece (eds.), *Fundamental Issues in Strategy*, Boston: Harvard Business School Press, 423–461.

63. Porter, What is strategy?, 62.

64. R. J. Arend, 2003, Revisiting the logical and research considerations of competitive advantage, *Strategic Management Journal*, 24: 279–284.

65. Porter, *Competitive Advantage*, 15.

66. G. G. Dess, G. T. Lumpkin, & J. E. McGee, 1999, Linking corporate entrepreneurship to strategy, structure, and process: Suggested research directions, *Entrepreneurship: Theory & Practice*, 23(3): 85–102; P. M. Wright, D. L. Smart, & G. C. McMahan, 1995, Matches between human resources and strategy among NCAA basketball teams, *Academy of Management Journal*, 38: 1052–1074.

67. Porter, *Competitive Strategy*, 35–40.

68. S. D. Dobrev & G. R. Carroll, 2003, Size (and competition) among organizations: Modeling scale-based selection among automobile producers in four major countries, 1885–1981, *Strategic Management Journal*, 24: 541–558; J. A. Parnell, 2000, Reframing the combination strategy debate: Defining forms of combination, *Journal of Management Studies*, 9(1): 33–54.

69. D. F. Spulber, 2004, *Management Strategy*, New York: McGrawHill/Irwin, 175.

70. D. F. Lynch, S. B. Keller, & J. Ozment, 2000, The effects of logistics capabilities and strategy on firm performance, *Journal of Business Logistics*, 21(2): 47–68.

71. 2003, Big Lots, *Standard & Poor's Stock Reports*, http://www.standardandpoors.com, May 3.

72. F. Green, 2003, Bargain retailers get pick of top-notch holiday goods, *San Diego Union-Tribune*, January 25, D4.

73. D. Howell, 2003, "National" Big Lots aims to expand, *DSN Retailing*, 42(8): 2.

74. L. K. Johnson, 2003, Dueling pricing strategies, *The McKinsey Quarterly*, 44(3): 10–11.

75. A. D'Innocenzio, 2001, We are paranoid, *Richmond Times-Dispatch*, June 10, E1, E2.

76. Lynch, Keller, & Ozment, The effects of logistics capabilities.

77. 2003, Target Corp., *Standard & Poor's Stock Reports*, http://www.standardandpoors.com, May 3.

78. S. Carlson, 2003, Target sees 4.4 percent earnings rise in fourth quarter, *Saint Paul Pioneer News*, February 21, B2.

79. J. Collins, 2003, Bigger, better, faster, *Fast Company*, June, 74–78.

80. Porter, *Competitive Strategy*, 35–40.

81. Ibid., 65.

82. Porter, *Competitive Advantage*, 14.

83. 2003, http://www.roberttalbott.com.

84. J. Flint, 2003, Gotta have, *Forbes*, May 26, 97.

85. M. Carmichael, 2002, It's wicked—Heinz ketchup now goes an orange colour, *Grocer*, February 16, 54; 2001, Business in Brief, *Washington Post*, June 20, E2.

86. G. Edmondson, E. Neuborne, A. L. Kazmin, E. Thornton, & K. N. Anhalt, 1999, L'Oréal: The beauty of global branding, *Business Week e-biz*, June 28.

87. Barney, *Gaining and Sustaining Competitive Advantage*, 268.

88. 2003, Callaway Golf Company, *Standard & Poor's Stock Reports*, http://www.standardandpoors.com, May 3; H. R. Goldstein, A. E. Roth, T. Young, & J. D. Lawrence, 2001, US manufacturers take a swing at counterfeit golf clubs, *Intellectual Property & Technology Law Journal*, May, 23.

89. 2003, Philip Morris files to stop counterfeit cigarette sales, *Wall Street Journal Online*, http://www.wsj.com, March 3.

90. Porter, *Competitive Strategy*, 98.

91. Porter, *Competitive Advantage*, 15.

92. Ibid., 15–16.

93. D. Kasler, 2003, Sacramento, Calif., family look for buyer for records retailer, *Sacramento Bee*, May 12, B3; 1999, Lloyd Greif Center for Entrepreneurial Studies, Discussion of the Greif Center's founder, http://www.marshall.usc.edu.

94. D. Raiford, 2002, Prison health ends contract with Philly, *Nashville Business Journal*, July 12; D. Foust & B. Grow, 2001, This company likes it in jail, *Business Week*, June 11, 112.

95. Porter, *Competitive Advantage*, 15.

96. Porter, What is strategy?, 67.

97. K. Kling & I. Goteman, 2003, Ikea CEO Andres Dahlvig on international growth and Ikea's unique corporate culture and brand identity, *Academy of Management Executive*, 17(1): 31–37.

98. 2003, http://www.ikea.com.

99. W. Stewart, 2003, Ikea's flat-pack revolution changing rooms in Russia, *Knight Ridder Tribune Business News*, http://www.knightridder.com, April 24; 2003, Ikea's RMB 500-million outlet opens in Shanghai, *SinoCast China Business Daily News*, April 18.

100. G. Evans, 2003, Why some stores strike me as special, *Furniture Today*, 27(24): 91; Porter, What is strategy?, 65.

101. 2003, http://casketfurniture.com, May 20; F. Keenan, 2003, Execs cozy up to B&Bs, *Business Week*, May 19, 132; S. Jones, 2001, Cutting a swath in hair care, *Washington Post*, May 5, E1, E8.

102. D. Voorhis, 2003, Wichita, Kan., motorcycle manufacturer kicks into high gear, *Wichita Eagle*, May 9, A1; 2003, http://www.bigdogmotorcycles.com, May 20.

103. 2003, Building Materials Holding Company, *Standard & Poor's Stock Reports*, http://www.standardandpoors.com, May 3.

104. 2001, The engine that drives differentiation, *DSN Retailing Today*, April 2, 52.

105. Dess, Lumpkin, & McGee, Linking corporate entrepreneurship to strategy, 89.

106. P. Ghemawat, 2001, *Strategy and the Business Landscape*, Upper Saddle River, NJ: Prentice-Hall, 56.

107. W. K. Hall, 1980, Survival strategies in a hostile environment, *Harvard Business Review* 58(5): 75–87.

108. Dess, Gupta, Hennart, & Hill, Conducting and integrating strategy research, 377.

109. L. Kim & Y. Lim, 1988, Environment, generic strategies, and performance in a rapidly developing country: A taxonomic approach, *Academy of Management Journal*, 31: 802–827.

110. Ghemawat, *Strategy and the Business Landscape*, 56.

111. Ibid.

112. M. Naim, 2001, McAtlas shrugged, *Foreign Policy*, May/June, 26–37.

113. S. A. Forest, 2001, When cool heads prevail, *Business Week*, June 11, 114.

114. A. Aston & M. Arndt, 2003, The flexible factory: Leaning heavily on technology, some U.S. plants stay competitive with offshore rivals, *Business Week*, May 5, 90–91; J. Markoff, 2003, Computing's big shift: Flexibility in the chips, *New York Times*, http://www.nytimes.com, June 16.

115. R. Sanchez, 1995, Strategic flexibility in product competition, *Strategic Management Journal*, 16(Special Issue): 140.

116. Ibid., 105.

117. J. Portelli, 2003, Agile assembly with robots, *Manufacturing Engineering*, 130(3): 83–87; R. Olexa, 2001, Flexible parts feeding boosts productivity, *Manufacturing Engineering*, 126(4): 106–114.

118. I. Mount & B. Caulfield, 2001, The missing link, *Ecompany* Now, May, 82–88.

119. J. Baljko, 2003, Built for speed—When putting the reams of supply chain data they've amassed to use, companies are discovering that agility counts, *EBN*, 1352: 25–28.

120. 2001, ABB: Integrated drives and process control, *Textile World*, April, 60–61.

121. R. S. Russell & B. W. Taylor III, 2000, *Operations Management*, 3rd ed., Upper Saddle River, NJ: Prentice-Hall, 262–264.

122. J. B. Dilworth, 2000, *Operations Management: Providing Value in Goods and Services*, 3rd ed., Fort Worth, TX: The Dryden Press, 286–289; D. Lei, M. A. Hitt, & J. D. Goldhar, 1996, Advanced manufacturing technology, organization design and strategic flexibility, *Organization Studies*, 17: 501–523.

123. 2003, UNOVA Industrial Automotive Systems—Using strategic business alliances to tap global markets, http://activequote.fidelity.com, April 29; 2003, Fix machine tools with less fuss, *American Machinist*, 147(1): 30; R. E. Chalmers, 2001, Assembly systems maximize efficiency, *Manufacturing Engineering*, May, 130–138.

124. A. McAfee, 2003, When too much IT knowledge is a dangerous thing, *The McKinsey Quarterly*, 44(2): 83–89.

125. F. Mattern, S. Schonwalder, & W. Stein, 2003, Fighting complexity in IT, *The McKinsey Quarterly*, Number 1, 57–65.

126. K. H. Doerr, T. R. Mitchell, C. A. Schriesheim, T. Freed, & X. Zhou, 2002, Heterogeneity and variability in the context of work flows, *Academy of Management Review*, 27: 594–607.

127. S. W. Brown, 2003, The employee experience, *Marketing Management*, 12(2): 12–13.

128. S. Isaac & R. N. Tooker, 2001, The many faces of CRM, *LIMRA's MarketFacts Quarterly*, 20(1): 84–89.

129. P. J. Rondeau & L. A. Litteral, 2001, The evolution of manufacturing planning and control systems: From reorder point to enterprise resource planning, *Production and Inventory Management*, 42(2): 1–7.

130. A. L. Velocci, Jr., 2003, Near-term market offers little growth, *Aviation Week & Space Technology*, 158(1): 41–42; M. L. Songini, 2001, Companies test their wireless supply chain wings, *Computerworld*, May 21, 35.

131. V. A. Mabert, A. Soni, & M. A. Venkataramanan, 2003, Enterprise resource planning: Managing the implementation process, *European Journal of Operational Research*, 146(2): 302–314.

132. J. D. Westphal, R. Gulati, & S. M. Shortell, 1997, Customization or conformity: An institutional and network perspective on the content and consequences of TQM adoption, *Administrative Science Quarterly*, 42: 366–394.

133. V. W. S. Yeung & R. W. Armstrong, 2003, A key to TQM benefits: Manager involvement in customer processes, *International Journal of Services Technology and Management*, 4(1): 14–29; S. Sanghera, 1999, Making continuous improvement better, *Financial Times*, April 21, 28.

134. J. Muller, 2001, Ford: Why it's worse than you think, *Business Week*, June 25, 80–89.

135. J. White, G. L. White, & N. Shirouzu, 2001, Soon, the big three won't be, as foreigners make inroads, *Wall Street Journal*, August 13, A1, A12.

136. D. Welch, K. Kerwin, & C. Tierney, 2003, Way to go, Detroit—Now go a lot farther, *Business Week*, May 26, 44.

137. N. Ganguli, T. V. Kumaresh, & A. Satpathy, 2003, Detroit's new quality gap, *The McKinsey Quarterly*, Number 1, 148–151.

138. Porter, *Competitive Advantage*, 16.

139. Ibid., 17.

140. Parnell, Reframing the combination strategy debate, 33.

Competitive Rivalry and Competitive Dynamics

Chapter Five **5**

Knowledge Objectives

Studying this chapter should provide you with the strategic management knowledge needed to:

1. Define competitors, competitive rivalry, competitive behavior, and competitive dynamics.

2. Describe market commonality and resource similarity as the building blocks of a competitor analysis.

3. Explain awareness, motivation, and ability as drivers of competitive behavior.

4. Discuss factors affecting the likelihood a competitor will take competitive actions.

5. Discuss factors affecting the likelihood a competitor will respond to actions taken against it.

6. Explain competitive dynamics in slow-cycle, fast-cycle, and standard-cycle markets.

BrandX Pictures

JetBlue and Song are direct competitors on the east coast. Song represents Delta's strategic response to the founding of JetBlue, which could be considered JetBlue's first strategic action.

JetBlue and Song: Competitive Rivalry between Low-Cost Carriers

JetBlue was launched on February 11, 2000, with a maiden flight between John F. Kennedy (JFK) International Airport and Fort Lauderdale, Florida. Using its fleet of new Airbus A320 planes, this start-up venture serves over 20 cities with plans to serve many more over the next few years. Founder and CEO David Neeleman has extensive experience in the airline industry having started and sold Salt-Lake City Air and Morris Air as well as establishing and selling Open Skies, an e-ticketing system he developed at Morris Air. Neeleman believed that his formula of low cost and great service could be successfully used out of New York City, which is the world's largest aviation market. With much fanfare, his JetBlue Airways was founded as a new airline that "would bring humanity back to air travel." Price-conscious leisure travelers were JetBlue's target customer—a group whose needs Neeleman felt weren't being well served by existing competitors. Thus, JetBlue is the product of an entrepreneur's identification of an entrepreneurial opportunity (entrepreneurs and entrepreneurial opportunities are further discussed in Chapter 13). The decision to launch JetBlue demonstrates what is called a strategic action, a term that is defined and discussed in this chapter.

Song, a wholly owned subsidiary of Delta Air Lines, launched its maiden voyage from JFK to West Palm Beach on April 15, 2003. The primary routes initially served by Song with its fleet of Boeing 757 aircraft were between the Northeast and Florida. Company officials noted that Song was a "new airline service developed to revolutionize customer expectations for high-quality, low-fare air travel." In more specific terms, Song was established to "make flying the way it used to be—fun, exciting, interesting or simply relaxing—what the customer is looking for that day." Delta's decision to establish Song as a replacement for Delta Express, its previously established but unsuccessful low-fare venture, demonstrates a strategic response (another term defined and discussed in this chapter).

Song is competing directly with JetBlue for the leisure travel market on the east coast. As competitors, Song and JetBlue have a high degree of market commonality, another term that is discussed and defined in this chapter. Some analysts claim that one reason for the direct competition between these two companies is that Delta had to do something to "recapture customers taken by highly profitable low-fare carrier JetBlue Airways." Thus, Song represents Delta's strategic response to the founding of JetBlue, which was a strategic action. For several reasons, Delta decided to establish a new venture to compete against JetBlue instead of continuing to use low-fare carrier Delta Express or to rely on its own Delta Air Line flights to do so. The problem with Delta Express (which Song replaced) is that while the carrier matched and sometimes beat the discount airlines' (such as JetBlue and

Southwest Airlines) fares, inefficient spending increased costs to the point where it couldn't earn a profit. Full-size operators such as Delta Air Lines aren't profitable (Delta, United, and American lost a combined $9 billion in 2002) and, according to industry analysts, simply can't compete against low-cost carriers in terms of CASM (cost per available seat mile) and RASM (revenue per available seat mile).

As competitors engaged in competitive rivalry, JetBlue and Song are trying to "outcompete" each other in terms of providing value-creating services along with the lowest fare to the same customer. JetBlue, for example, is the only carrier offering passengers live satellite television with up to 24 channels of DirecTV programming free of charge at each seat. As a competitive response, Song partnered with several firms to offer customers personal video monitors at each seat with touchscreen technology and credit card "swipe" capability. In addition, Song passengers have all-digital satellite television programming from DISH Network available to them. Each JetBlue seat is leather while Song emphasizes the 33 inches of legroom between rows on its 757 jets. As competitors, JetBlue and Song can be expected to closely monitor each other's competitive actions and competitive responses as each firm seeks to outcompete the other one.

SOURCES: 2003, Delta Airlines 2002 Annual Report, http://www.delta.com, May 25; 2003, Delta Airlines Home Page, Introducing the world's most innovative low-fare airline service, http://www.delta.com, May 25; 2003, Delta's Song to offer satellite TV, *Satellite News*, 26(17): B2; 2003, JetBlue Home Page, Welcome from our CEO, http://www.jetblue.com, May 25; S. Kirsner, 2003, Song's flight plan, *Fast Company*, June, 98–107; J. Naudi, 2003, Airlines aim to recapture business with low-fare tickets, *Indianapolis Star*, February 23, D3; R. Thomaselli, 2003, Delta takes low-key approach to low-cost carrier, *Advertising Age*, 74(18): 4, 36.

Firms operating in the same market, offering similar products, and targeting similar cutomers are competitors.

Competitive rivalry *is the ongoing set of competitive actions and competitive responses occurring between competitors as they compete against each other for an advantageous market position.*

Competitive behavior *is the set of competitive actions and competitive responses the firm takes to build or defend its competitive advantages and to improve its market position.*

Firms operating in the same market, offering similar products, and targeting similar customers are **competitors.**[1] JetBlue and Song are competitors as are Teradyne and Applied Materials and PepsiCo and Coca-Cola Company. Firms interact with their competitors that are part of the broad context within which they operate while attempting to earn above-average returns.[2] The decisions firms make about who their competitors will be and especially about how they will compete against their rivals have an important effect on their ability to earn above-average returns.[3]

Competitive rivalry is the ongoing set of competitive actions and competitive responses occurring between competitors as they compete against each other for an advantageous market position. Especially in highly competitive industries, firms constantly jockey for advantage as they launch strategic actions and respond or react to rivals' moves.[4] It is important for those leading organizations to understand competitive rivalry, in that "the central, brute empirical fact in strategy is that some firms outperform others,"[5] meaning that competitive rivalry influences an individual firm's ability to gain and sustain competitive advantages.[6]

A sequence of firm-level moves, rivalry results from firms initiating their own competitive actions and then responding to actions taken by competitors.[7] **Competitive behavior** is the set of competitive actions and competitive responses the firm takes to build or defend its competitive advantages and to improve its market position.[8] Through competitive behavior, the firm tries to successfully position itself relative to the five forces of competition (see Chapter 2) and to defend and use current competitive advantages while building advantages for the future (see Chapter 3). Increasingly, competitors engage in competitive actions and responses in more than one market.[9] Firms competing against each other in several product or geographic markets are engaged in **multimarket competition.**[10] All competitive behavior—that is, the total set of actions and responses taken by all firms competing within a market—is called **competitive dynamics.** The relationships among these key concepts are shown in Figure 5.1.

This chapter focuses on competitive rivalry and competitive dynamics. The essence of these important topics is that a firm's strategies are dynamic in nature. Actions taken by one firm elicit responses from competitors that, in turn, typically result in responses from the firm that took the initial action.[11] This chain of events is illustrated in the Opening Case that describes the competitive actions and competitive responses occurring between JetBlue and Song.

Another way of highlighting competitive rivalry's effect on the firm's strategies is to say that a strategy's success is determined not only by the firm's initial competitive actions but also by how well it anticipates competitors' responses to them *and* by how well the firm anticipates and responds to its competitors' initial actions (also called attacks).[12] Although competitive rivalry affects all types of strategies (for example, corporate-level, acquisition, and international), its most dominant influence is on the firm's business-level strategy or strategies. Indeed, firms' actions and responses to those of their rivals are the basic building block of business-level strategies.[13] Recall from Chapter 4 that business-level strategy is concerned with what the firm does to successfully use its competitive advantages in specific product markets. In the global economy, competitive rivalry is intensifying,[14] meaning that the significance of its effect on firms' business-level strategies is increasing. However, firms that develop and use effective business-level strategies tend to outperform competitors in individual product markets, even when experiencing intense competitive rivalry.[15]

An expanding geographic scope contributes to the increasing intensity in the competitive rivalry between firms. Some believe, for example, that an aptitude for cross-border management practices and a facility with cultural diversity find European

Firms competing against each other in several product or geographic markets are engaged in multimarket competition.

All competitive behavior— that is, the total set of actions and responses taken by all firms competing within a market—is called competitive dynamics.

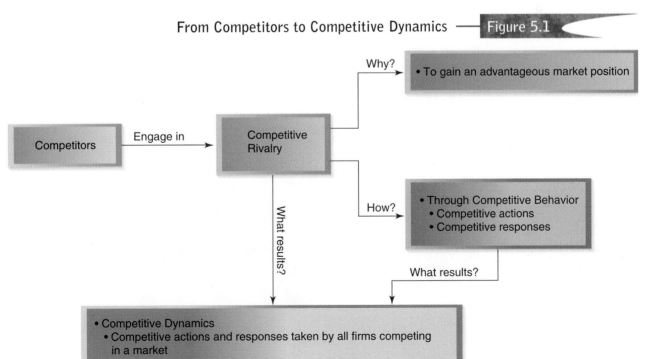

From Competitors to Competitive Dynamics ——— Figure 5.1

- Competitors — Engage in → Competitive Rivalry
  - Why? → • To gain an advantageous market position
  - How? → • Through Competitive Behavior
    - • Competitive actions
    - • Competitive responses
  - What results? → • Competitive Dynamics
    - • Competitive actions and responses taken by all firms competing in a market
  - What results? → • Competitive Dynamics

SOURCE: Adapted from M.-J. Chen, 1996, Competitor analysis and interfirm rivalry: Toward a theoretical integration, *Academy of Management Review,* 21: 100–134.

Union firms emerging as formidable global competitors.[16] In the global brewing industry, for example, Belgian brewer Interbrew bought 70 percent of K.K. Brewery, the leading beer maker in Zhejiang Province, in the Yangtze delta in China. Interbrew is bringing its brewing skills to this facility to establish a strong competitive position in a highly fragmented, rapidly growing market that it believes is very attractive.[17] Similarly, Diageo PLC, the giant U.K.-based spirits and beer group, is expanding aggressively on a global scale.[18] Viewing the expansion's outcomes favorably, some analysts think that "Diageo could easily mop up 10 points of market share over the next five years in the U.S."[19] Diageo's bold entry into U.S. markets could engender strong competitive responses from Anheuser Busch and SABMiller.

A Model of Competitive Rivalry

Over time, firms take many competitive actions and responses.[20] As noted earlier, competitive rivalry evolves from this pattern of actions and responses as one firm's competitive actions have noticeable effects on competitors, eliciting competitive responses from them.[21] This pattern shows that firms are mutually interdependent, that they feel each other's actions and responses, and that marketplace success is a function of both individual strategies and the consequences of their use.[22] Increasingly, too, executives recognize that competitive rivalry can have a major and direct effect on the firm's financial performance.[23] Research findings showing that intensified rivalry within an industry results in decreased average profitability for firms competing in it support the importance of understanding these effects.[24]

We offer a model (see Figure 5.2) to show what is involved with competitive rivalry at the firm level.[25] We study rivalry at the firm level because the competitive actions and responses the firm takes are the foundation for successfully building and using its competitive advantages to gain an advantageous market position.[26] Thus, we use the model in Figure 5.2 to help us explain competition between a particular firm and each of its competitors. Successful use of the model finds companies able to predict competitors' behavior (actions and responses) and reduce the unpredictable variation or the uncertainty associated with competitors' actions.[27] Being able to predict competitors' competitive actions and responses has a positive effect on the firm's market position and its subsequent financial performance.[28] The sum of all the individual rivalries modeled in Figure 5.2 that are occurring in a particular market reflects the competitive dynamics in that market.

Figure 5.2 —— A Model of Competitive Rivalry

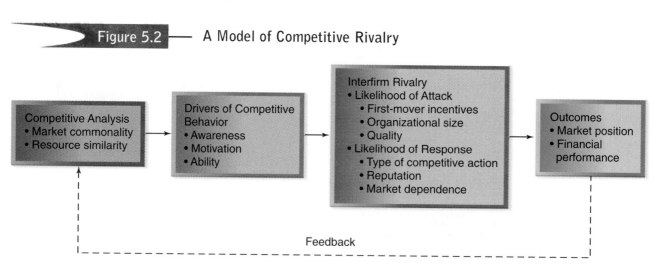

SOURCE: Adapted from M.-J. Chen, 1996, Competitor analysis and interfirm rivalry: Toward a theoretical integration, *Academy of Management Review*, 21: 100–134.

The remainder of the chapter discusses the model shown in Figure 5.2. We first describe market commonality and resource similarity as the building blocks of a competitor analysis. Next, we discuss the effects of three organizational characteristics—awareness, motivation, and ability—on the firm's competitive behavior. We then examine competitive rivalry between firms, or interfirm rivalry, in detail by describing the factors that affect the likelihood a firm will take a competitive action and the factors that affect the likelihood a firm will respond to a competitor's action. In the chapter's final section, we turn our attention to competitive dynamics to describe how market characteristics affect competitive rivalry in slow-cycle, fast-cycle, and standard-cycle markets.

Competitor Analysis

As previously noted, a competitor analysis is the first step the firm takes to be able to predict the extent and nature of its rivalry with each competitor. Recall that a competitor is a firm operating in the same market, offering similar products, and targeting similar customers. The number of markets in which firms compete against each other (called market commonality, defined below) and the similarity in their resources (called resource similarity, also defined below) determine the extent to which the firms are competitors. Firms with high market commonality and highly similar resources are "clearly direct and mutually acknowledged competitors."[29] However, being direct competitors does not necessarily mean that the rivalry between the firms will be intense. The drivers of competitive behavior—as well as factors influencing the likelihood that a competitor will initiate competitive actions and will respond to its competitor's competitive actions—influence the intensity of rivalry, even for direct competitors.[30]

In Chapter 2, we discussed competitor analysis as a technique firms use to understand their competitive environment. Together, the general, industry, and competitive environments comprise the firm's external environment. In the earlier chapter we described how competitor analysis is used to help the firm *understand* its competitors. This understanding results from studying competitors' future objectives, current strategies, assumptions, and capabilities (see Figure 2.3). In this chapter, the discussion of competitor analysis is extended to describe what firms study to be able to *predict* competitors' behavior in the form of their competitive actions and responses. The discussions of competitor analysis in Chapter 2 and Chapter 5 are complementary in that firms must first *understand* competitors (Chapter 2) before their competitive actions and competitive responses can be *predicted* (Chapter 5).

Market Commonality

Each industry is composed of various markets. The financial services industry has markets for insurance, brokerage services, banks, and so forth. Denoting an interest to concentrate on the needs of different, unique customer groups, markets can be further subdivided. The insurance market, for example, could be broken into market segments (such as commercial and consumer), product segments (such as health insurance and life insurance), and geographic markets (such as Western Europe and Southeast Asia). In general, the Internet's capabilities are shaping the nature of industry markets as well as competition within them.[31] For example, widely available electronic news sources affect how traditional print news distributors such as newspapers conduct their business.

In general, competitors agree about the different characteristics of individual markets that form an industry.[32] For example, in the transportation industry, there is an understanding that the commercial air travel market differs from the ground transportation market that is served by such firms as Yellow Freight System and J.B. Hunt Transport Services Inc. Although differences exist, most industries' markets are somewhat related in terms of technologies used or core competencies needed to develop a competitive advantage.[33] For example, different types of transportation companies need to provide reliable and timely service. Commercial air carriers such as Song and JetBlue (see the Opening Case) must therefore develop service competencies to satisfy their passengers, while Yellow Freight System and J.B. Hunt Transport Services Inc. must develop such competencies to serve the needs of those using their fleets to ship goods.

Firms competing in several or even many markets, some of which may be in different industries, are likely to come into contact with a particular competitor several times,[34] a situation that involves the concept of market commonality. **Market commonality** is concerned with the number of markets with which the firm and a competitor are jointly involved and the degree of importance of the individual markets to each.[35] Firms competing against one another in several or many markets engage in multimarket competition.[36] As noted in the Opening Case, JetBlue and Song were initially competing against each other to serve customers traveling between a number of northeast locations and Florida. McDonald's and Burger King compete against each other in multiple geographic markets across the world,[37] while Prudential and Cigna compete against each other in several market segments (institutional and retail) as well as product markets (such as life insurance and health insurance).[38] Airlines, chemicals, pharmaceuticals, and consumer foods are other industries in which firms often simultaneously engage each other in competition in multiple markets.

Firms competing in several markets have the potential to respond to a competitor's actions not only within the market in which the actions are taken, but also in other markets where they compete with the rival. This potential creates a complicated competitive mosaic in which "the moves an organization makes in one market are designed to achieve goals in another market in ways that aren't immediately apparent to its rivals."[39] This potential complicates the rivalry between competitors. In fact, research suggests that "a firm with greater multimarket contact is less likely to initiate an attack, but more likely to move (respond) aggressively when attacked."[40] Thus, in general, multimarket competition reduces competitive rivalry.[41] However, other research suggests that market commonality and multimarket competition sometimes occur almost by chance.[42] But, once it begins, the rivalry between the unexpected competitors becomes intentional and often intense.

Resource Similarity

Resource similarity is the extent to which the firm's tangible and intangible resources are comparable to a competitor's in terms of both type and amount.[43] Firms with similar types and amounts of resources are likely to have similar strengths and weaknesses and use similar strategies.[44] The competition between competitors CVS Corp. and Walgreens to be the largest drugstore chain in the United States demonstrates these expectations. These firms are using the integrated cost leadership/differentiation strategy to offer relatively low-cost goods with some differentiated features, such as services.

When performing a competitor analysis, firms analyze each of their competitors in terms of market commonality and resource similarity. With respect to market commonality, CVS and Walgreens, for example, are quite aware of the total number of markets in which they compete against each other as well as the number of storefronts each operates.[45] Recent statistics show that there are over 4,000 CVS stores in 32 states and the District of Columbia while Walgreens has over 4,000 stores in 43 states and Puerto Rico. CVS is the largest U.S. retail drugstore chain in terms of store count while Walgreens is the largest U.S. retail drug chain in terms of revenues. Thus, these firms compete against each other in many markets, indicating that there is a high degree of market commonality between them.[46]

In contrast to market commonality, assessing resource similarity can be difficult, particularly when critical resources are intangible (such as brand name, knowledge, trust, and the capacity to innovate) rather than tangible (for example, access to raw materials and a competitor's ability to borrow capital). As discussed in Chapter 3, a competitor's intangible resources are difficult to identify and understand, making an assessment of their value challenging. CVS and Walgreens know the amount of each other's annual net income (a tangible resource). However, it is difficult for CVS and Walgreens to determine if any intangible resources (such as knowledge and trust among employees) its competitor possesses can lead to a competitive advantage.

©Tom Prettyman/PhotoEdit

The results of the firm's competitor analyses can be mapped for visual comparisons. In Figure 5.3, we show different hypothetical intersections between the firm and individual competitors in terms of market commonality and resource similarity. These intersections indicate the extent to which the firm and those to which it has compared itself are competitors.[47] For example, the firm and its competitor displayed in quadrant I of Figure 5.3 have similar types and amounts of resources and use them to compete against each other in many markets that are important to each. These conditions lead to the conclusion that the firms modeled in quadrant I are direct and mutually acknowledged competitors. In contrast, the firm and its competitor shown in quadrant III share few markets and have little similarity in

their resources, indicating that they aren't direct and mutually acknowledged competitors. The firm's mapping of its competitive relationship with rivals is fluid as firms enter and exit markets and as companies' resources change in type and amount. Thus, the companies with which the firm is a direct competitor change across time.

CVS and Walgreens are direct competitors with a high degree of market commonality. Their sales volume, total number of stores, and strategies are all similar.

Toyota Motor Corp. and Volkswagen AG have high market commonality as they compete in many of the same global markets. In years past, the companies also had similar types and quantities of resources. This is changing, though, in that the companies' resources are becoming dissimilar, especially in terms of profitability and sales revenue. In fact, the companies are moving in opposite directions—Toyota's sales and profits are increasing while Volkswagen's sales and profits are decreasing. Thus, quadrant II in Figure 5.3 captures the degree to which Toyota and Volkswagen are direct competitors. In the Strategic Focus, we discuss the possibility that some of Toyota's recent competitive actions may create a situation in which Volkswagen will encounter more competition from Toyota.

How will Volkswagen respond to the possibility of increased competition from Toyota in Europe and China? The challenge is daunting, in that it is difficult if not impossible to "out-Toyota Toyota."[48] Volkswagen's CEO believes that his firm is on the right course, however. Among other actions, the CEO is concentrating on reducing the

Figure 5.3 — A Framework of Competitor Analysis

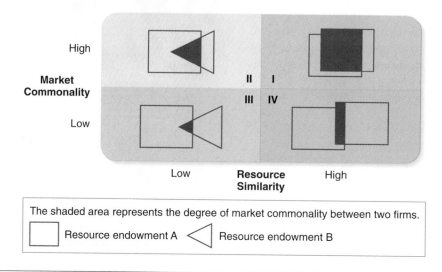

The shaded area represents the degree of market commonality between two firms.

☐ Resource endowment A   ◁ Resource endowment B

SOURCE: Adapted from M.-J. Chen, 1996, Competitor analysis and interfirm rivalry: Toward a theoretical integration, *Academy of Management Review*, 21: 100–134.

firm's costs and changing the culture to facilitate productive interactions among those designing, manufacturing, and selling the products. Reduced costs and a changed culture will help Volkswagen produce innovative vehicles to fill in gaps in its product line (such as sport-utility vehicles and minivans), the CEO believes.[49]

Drivers of Competitive Actions and Responses

As shown in Figure 5.2, market commonality and resource similarity influence the drivers (awareness, motivation, and ability) of competitive behavior. In turn, the drivers influence the firm's competitive behavior, as shown by the actions and responses it takes while engaged in competitive rivalry.[50]

Awareness, which is a prerequisite to any competitive action or response being taken by the firm or its competitor, refers to the extent to which competitors recognize the degree of their mutual interdependence that results from market commonality and resource similarity.[51] Awareness tends to be greatest when firms have highly similar resources (in terms of types and amounts) to use while competing against each other in multiple markets. CVS and Walgreens are fully aware of each other, as are JetBlue and Song and Wal-Mart and France's Carrefour, the two largest supermarket groups in the world. The last two firms' joint awareness has increased as they use similar resources to compete against each other for dominant positions in multiple European and South American markets.[52] Awareness affects the extent to which the firm understands the consequences of its competitive actions and responses. A lack of awareness can lead to excessive competition, resulting in a negative effect on all competitors' performance.[53]

Motivation, which concerns the firm's incentive to take action or to respond to a competitor's attack, relates to perceived gains and losses. Thus, a firm may be aware of competitors but may not be motivated to engage in rivalry with them if it perceives that its position will not improve as a result of doing so or that its market position won't be damaged if it doesn't respond.[54]

Market commonality affects the firm's perceptions and resulting motivation. For example, all else being equal, the firm is more likely to attack the rival with whom it

Toyota and Volkswagen: Direct Competitors or Not?

The world's third largest auto manufacturer (behind General Motors and Ford Motor Company), Toyota Motor Corporation manufactures and sells cars, trucks, recreational vehicles, minivans, trucks, buses, and related parts on a global basis under the Toyota, Lexus, and Daihatsu brand names. The firm's intention is to "build cars that people want to buy" and to participate in every market segment "wherever there's money to be made and market share to be gained." Toyota's market share is increasing in both the United States and Europe.

Evidence suggests that Toyota has competitive advantages in terms of efficiency and quality. In a recent year, for example, Toyota's profit margin per vehicle was 9.3 percent— more than a threefold increase over General Motors' at 3 percent. This efficiency advantage allows Toyota to increase product quality and/or add value-creating features with its new vehicles while simultaneously reducing the price to customers. Toyota's minivan, the Sienna, is a case in point. Compared to previous models, the all-new 2004 Sienna minivan had greater power and fuel efficiency as well as new seat configurations creating more passenger room, among other new features. However, the base price was 6 percent lower than the previous year's version of the Sienna. The 2003 results from J.D. Power's initial quality survey found Lexus again at the top of the list with only 76 problems per 100 vehicles. Products under the Toyota nameplate had 121 problems per 100 vehicles. With 143 problems per 100 vehicles, Volkswagen fell below the industry average. (The Hummer was at the other end of the initial quality scale with 225 problems per 100 vehicles.)

Volkswagen AG (VW) makes and sells cars and other vehicles on a global basis under the brand names of Volkswagen, Audi, Seat, Skoda, Lamborghini, Bugatti, Rolls Royce, and Bentley. Thus, compared to Toyota, Volkswagen's product lines are more diverse, especially at the upper end with entries from Lamborghini, Bugatti, Rolls Royce, and Bentley.

Volkswagen's current fortunes differ from those of Toyota: "Once Europe's dominant car seller by a wide margin, VW this year (2003) is only slightly ahead of No. 2 PSA Peugeot Citroen." Moreover, VW's share of the all-important U.S. market continues to decline as well.

What has caused these problems for Volkswagen? Some believe that the firm is simply "trying to compete on too many battlefields," including the luxury car market. "But, the drive for luxury diverted VW from its bread-and-butter business—making fun cars for average folks." Another problem was the decision to use the same platform for products in the different lines. This caused confusion among consumers, some of whom felt, for example, that they shouldn't pay an Audi price for a vehicle with the same platform as a VW. Compounding these problems, the firm lost its focus on quality while trying to develop new products for all of its brands.

As it looks to its future, Volkswagen faces the prospect of increasing competition from Toyota, a firm with advantages in terms of manufacturing efficiency, product quality, and available resources. Toyota is concentrating more on European markets, challenging Volkswagen as a result of doing so. Of equal concern to Volkswagen should be Toyota's decision to invest heavily in its Chinese operations. China is Volkswagen's second largest market, indicating that the firm must defend its share against the likes of Toyota as well as other competitors.

SOURCES: N. E. Boudette, 2003, Drivers wanted: Volkswagen stalls on several fronts after luxury drive, *Wall Street Journal*, Eastern edition, May 8, A1; G. Edmondson, 2003, Volkswagen needs a jump, *Business Week*, May 12, 48–49; D. Kiley, 2003, Toyota, Volkswagen take different journeys, *USA Today*, May 9, B5; D. Murphy, 2003, Volkswagen races to keep up in China, *Wall Street Journal*, Eastern edition, March 5, B.11E; L. Ulrich, 2003, Outside the box, *Money*, 32(6): 137–138; G. C. Williams III, 2003, Toyota strategy includes San Antonio expansion, *San Antonio Express-News*, February 7, C3; C. Condon, 2002, Companies head to Eastern Europe to partake in land of low costs, *Sunday Business*, November 17, D1; T. Zaun, 2002, The economy—A global journal report, *Wall Street Journal*, Eastern edition, October 31, A2.

has low market commonality than the one with whom it competes in multiple markets. The primary reason is that there are high stakes involved in trying to gain a more advantageous position over a rival with whom the firm shares many markets. As we mentioned earlier, multimarket competition can find a competitor responding to the firm's action in a market different from the one in which the initial action was taken. Actions and responses of this type can cause both firms to lose focus on core markets and to battle each other with resources that had been allocated for other purposes. Because of the high stakes of competition under the condition of market commonality, there is a high probability that the attacked firm will respond to its competitor's action in an effort to protect its position in one or more markets.[55]

In some instances, the firm may be aware of the large number of markets it shares with a competitor and may be motivated to respond to an attack by that competitor, but it lacks the ability to do so. *Ability* relates to each firm's resources and the flexibility they provide. Without available resources (such as financial capital and people), the firm lacks the ability to attack a competitor or respond to its actions. However, similar resources suggest similar abilities to attack and respond. When a firm faces a competitor with similar resources, careful study of a possible attack before initiating it is essential because the similarly resourced competitor is likely to respond to that action.

Resource *dissimilarity* also influences competitive actions and responses between firms, in that "the greater is the resource imbalance between the acting firm and competitors or potential responders, the greater will be the delay in response"[56] by the firm with a resource disadvantage. For example, Wal-Mart initially used a focused cost leadership strategy to compete only in small communities (those with a population of 25,000 or less). Using sophisticated logistics systems and extremely efficient purchasing practices as advantages, among others, Wal-Mart created what was at that time a new type of value (primarily in the form of wide selections of products at the lowest competitive prices) for customers in small retail markets. Local stores, facing resource deficiencies relative to Wal-Mart, lacked the ability to marshal resources at the pace required to respond quickly and effectively. However, even when facing competitors with greater resources (greater ability) or more attractive market positions, firms should eventually respond, no matter how daunting doing so seems.[57] Choosing not to respond can ultimately result in failure, as happened with at least some local retailers who didn't respond to Wal-Mart's competitive actions.

Competitive Rivalry

As defined earlier in the chapter, *competitive rivalry* is the ongoing set of competitive actions and competitive responses occurring between competing firms for an advantageous market position. Because the ongoing competitive action/response sequence between a firm and a competitor affects the performance of both firms,[58] it is important for companies to carefully study competitive rivalry to successfully use their strategies. Understanding a competitor's awareness, motivation, and ability helps the firm to predict the likelihood of an attack by that competitor and how likely it is that a competitor will respond to the actions taken against it.

As we described earlier, the predictions drawn from study of competitors in terms of awareness, motivation, and ability are grounded in market commonality and resource similarity. These predictions are fairly general. The value of the final set of predictions the firm develops about each of its competitors' competitive actions and responses is enhanced by studying the "Likelihood of Attack" factors (such as first-mover incentives and organizational size) and the "Likelihood of Response" factors (such as the actor's reputation) that are shown in Figure 5.2. Studying these factors allows the firm to develop a deeper understanding in order to refine the predictions it makes about its competitors' actions and responses.

Strategic and Tactical Actions

Firms use both strategic and tactical actions when forming their competitive actions and competitive responses in the course of engaging in competitive rivalry.[59] A **competitive action** is a strategic or tactical action the firm takes to build or defend its competitive advantages or improve its market position. A **competitive response** is a strategic or tactical action the firm takes to counter the effects of a competitor's competitive action. A **strategic action or a strategic response** is a market-based move that involves a significant commitment of organizational resources and is difficult to implement and reverse. A **tactical action or a tactical response** is a market-based move that is taken to fine-tune a strategy; it involves fewer resources and is relatively easy to implement and reverse. Hyundai Motor Co.'s expenditures on research and development and plant expansion to support the firm's desire to be one of the world's largest carmakers by 2010 and to sell at least one million units annually in the United States by 2010[60] are strategic actions. Likewise, Boeing Corp.'s decision to commit the resources required to build the superefficient 7E7 midsized jetliner for delivery in 2008[61] demonstrates a strategic action. Changes in airfares are somewhat frequently announced by airlines. As tactical actions that are easily reversed, pricing decisions are often taken by these firms to increase demand in certain markets during certain periods.

As explained in the Strategic Focus, Coca-Cola Company, PepsiCo Inc., and Nestlé SA are aware of one another as they compete in the bottled water market. Moreover, this awareness influences the competitive actions and responses these firms initiate as they engage in competitive rivalry.

Of course, bottled water isn't the only product category (outside of soft drinks) in which multimarket competitors Coca-Cola and PepsiCo compete against each other. Consider the emerging competition between these firms in the milk-based products area as a case in point. Partly because of the potential damage of the price wars in the bottled water market that we describe in the Strategic Focus and in order to expand beyond soda into healthier beverages, Coca-Cola introduced Swerve in July 2003. Containing 52 percent milk and initially offered in three flavors (chocolate, blueberry, and vanilla/banana), Swerve was sold in 12-ounce cans labeled with a grinning cow in dark glasses.[62] The target market for such products was parents seeking a substitute for sugary or caffeinated drinks for their children.[63] At the time of Swerve's introduction, PepsiCo was already offering a chocolate dairy drink called Love Bus Brew, which is made with milk, vitamins, ginseng, and Dutch chocolate.[64] Swerve and Love Bus Brew were two entries in the small but growing beverage category of milk-based drinks. Because of the degree of their market commonality and resource similarity and the fact that they engage in multimarket competition, Coca-Cola and PepsiCo will continue to carefully monitor each other's competitive actions and responses in multiple product areas as part of their competitive rivalry.

A **competitive action** is a strategic or tactical action the firm takes to build or defend its competitive advantages or improve its market position.

A **competitive response** is a strategic or tactical action the firm takes to counter the effects of a competitor's competitive action.

A **strategic action or a strategic response** is a market-based move that involves a significant commitment of organizational resources and is difficult to implement and reverse.

A **tactical action or a tactical response** is a market-based move that is taken to fine-tune a strategy; it involves fewer resources and is relatively easy to implement and reverse.

Vice-president Robert Pollack presents the new 7E7 CDream Liner at an air show. Committing the resources to build this type of aircraft represents a strategic action on Boeing's part.

©Reuters NewMedia Inc./CORBIS

Water, Water Everywhere: Which to Drink?

There are simple facts about bottled water that explain why some of the world's largest companies are interested in expanding their share of the market for this product. First, bottled water in the United States alone is almost an $8 billion market on an annual basis. Moreover, demand for water is growing roughly 10 percent per year, which is faster than the growth rate for other drinks. American consumers drink an average of 21.2 gallons of bottled water per year, making it the second most popular drink (behind soft drinks at a huge 54 gallons per person, per year). Speaking to these issues, an analyst observed that competition among beverage companies in the bottled water segment is "becoming more intense as growth in the [soft drink] industry slows and consumers show a willingness to purchase less expensive private-label brands." Also making bottled water sales attractive is the 22 percent-plus margin they generate when sold in multi-packs in such outlets as discount club chains, grocery stores, and discount stores, such as Wal-Mart.

Because of market-based realities such as these, as well as the high degree of market commonality experienced by the three companies (Coca-Cola Company, Nestlé SA, and PepsiCo) dominating the U.S. bottled water market, these firms are clearly aware of one another's competitive actions and responses as they engage in intense rivalry to expand their shares of the bottled water market. Currently, the U.S. bottled water market is significantly influenced by these firms' competitive actions, largely because their combined share is close to 70 percent, with Nestlé having the largest share among the three firms. Also increasing the rivalry among these firms to sell their bottled waters is that while the brands vary by price, pedigree, and process—purified versus spring water, for example—many of them are essentially the same thing. Indeed, according to the editor of the *Beverage Digest*, all of these waters "hydrate equally well." In the United States, Nestlé offers nine domestic brands (e.g., Arrowhead and Deer Park) and five imports, including Perrier. PepsiCo makes Aquafina, which is the leading brand of water, while Coca-Cola produces Dasani, the second largest single brand, and distributes Group Danone's Evian and Dannon waters through a joint venture.

To gain market share, Coca-Cola lowered the prices of Dannon waters by 25 percent in grocery stores and mass retailers such as Wal-Mart late in the spring of 2003. Dannon waters are lower-tier bottled waters that tend to sell well in mass retail outlets. A tactical rather than a strategic action, the price reductions resulted in increased market share for Coca-Cola in these outlets. The double-digit growth of the lower-priced waters in mass retailers may have influenced Coca-Cola's decision to lower the prices on its offerings in this category in order to gain greater share in a fast-growth segment of the bottled water market. Certainly aware of Coca-Cola's tactical action, Nestlé and PepsiCo didn't respond immediately with price cuts, but vowed to defend their market positions as necessary. According to industry analysts, the initial price cut could stimulate a price war that would reduce the substantial profit margins the three competitors earn from these products in the mass retailer distribution channel. Indeed, there was concern in the industry that if one were to last for an extended period of time, a price war would result in material harm to the profitability of all three companies. As is common when companies engage in intense rivalry and are aware of each other while doing so, Nestlé and PepsiCo immediately started studying the effects of Coca-Cola's price reductions before choosing their competitive responses to Coca-Cola's competitive action.

SOURCES: 2003, Bottled water to be no. 2 U.S. drink, *Chicago Tribune*, April 6, C8; S. Day, 2003, Summer may bring a bottled water price war, *New York Times*, http://www.nytimes.com, May 10; R. Frank & B. McKay, 2002, Leading the news: Danone nears pact for purchase of Canada's Sparkling Spring, *Wall Street Journal*, Eastern edition, November 12, A3.

In addition to market commonality, resource similarity, and the drivers of awareness, motivation, and ability, other factors affect the likelihood a competitor will use strategic actions and tactical actions to attack its competitors. Three of these factors—first-mover incentives, organizational size, and quality—are discussed next.

First-Mover Incentives

A **first mover** is a firm that takes an initial competitive action in order to build or defend its competitive advantages or to improve its market position. The first-mover concept has been influenced by the work of the famous economist Joseph Schumpeter, who argued that firms achieve competitive advantage by taking innovative actions[65] (innovation is defined and described in detail in Chapter 13). In general, first movers "allocate funds for product innovation and development, aggressive advertising, and advanced research and development."[66]

The benefits of being a successful first mover can be substantial. Especially in fast-cycle markets (discussed later in the chapter) where changes occur rapidly and where it is virtually impossible to sustain a competitive advantage for any length of time, "a first mover may experience five to ten times the valuation and revenue of a second mover."[67] This evidence suggests that although first-mover benefits are never absolute, they are often critical to firm success in industries experiencing rapid technological developments and relatively short product life cycles.[68] In addition to earning above-average returns until its competitors respond to its successful competitive action, the first mover can gain (1) the loyalty of customers who may become committed to the goods or services of the firm that first made them available and (2) market share that can be difficult for competitors to take during future competitive rivalry.[69] The general evidence that first movers have greater survival rates compared to later market entrants[70] is perhaps the culmination of first-mover benefits.

The firm trying to predict its competitors' competitive actions might rightly conclude that the benefits of being a first mover are incentives for many of them to act as first movers. However, while a firm's competitors might be motivated to be first movers, they may lack the ability to do so. First movers tend to be aggressive and willing to experiment with innovation and take higher, yet reasonable levels of risk.[71] To be a first mover, the firm must have readily available the amount of resources that is required to significantly invest in R&D as well as to rapidly and successfully produce and market a stream of innovative products.

Organizational slack makes it possible for firms to have the ability (as measured by available resources) to be first movers. *Slack* is the buffer or cushion provided by actual or obtainable resources that aren't currently in use[72] and as such, are in excess of the minimum resources needed to produce a given level of organizational output.[73] In 2003, Cisco Systems Inc. had substantial financial slack as suggested by the firm's more than $21 billion in cash and liquid investments.[74]

As a liquid resource, slack can quickly be allocated to support the competitive actions, such as R&D investments and aggressive marketing campaigns, that lead to first-mover benefits. This relationship between slack and the ability to be a first mover allows the firm to predict that a competitor who is a first mover likely has available slack and will probably take aggressive competitive actions to continuously introduce innovative products. Furthermore, the firm can predict that as a first mover, a competitor will try to rapidly gain market share and customer loyalty in order to earn above-average returns until its competitors are able to effectively respond to its first move.

Firms studying competitors should realize that being a first mover carries risk. For example, it is difficult to accurately estimate the returns that will be earned from

*A **first mover** is a firm that takes an initial competitive action in order to build or defend its competitive advantages or to improve its market position.*

introducing product innovations to the marketplace.[75] Additionally, the first mover's cost to develop a product innovation can be substantial, reducing the slack available to it to support further innovation. Thus, the firm should carefully study the results a competitor achieves as a first mover. Continuous success by the competitor suggests additional product innovations, while lack of product acceptance over the course of the competitor's innovations may indicate less willingness in the future to accept the risks of being a first mover.

A **second mover** is a firm that responds to the first mover's competitive action, typically through imitation. More cautious than the first mover, the second mover studies customers' reactions to product innovations. In the course of doing so, the second mover also tries to find any mistakes the first mover made so that it can avoid them and the problems they created. Often, successful imitation of the first mover's innovations allows the second mover "to avoid both the mistakes and the huge spending of the pioneers [first movers]."[76]

Second movers also have the time to develop processes and technologies that are more efficient than those used by the first mover.[77] Greater efficiencies could result in lower costs for the second mover. American Home Mortgage Holdings Inc. (AHMH) is a second mover with its Internet-based offering, MortgageSelect.com. In the words of the firm's CEO, being the second mover allowed it "to see where other firms had failed." Based on its observations of earlier Internet mortgage market entrants, AHMH doesn't brand its own services (instead providing mortgages for other companies) and has fine-tuned the offering of a "high-touch" call center to support its website.[78] Overall, the outcomes of the first mover's competitive actions may provide an effective blueprint for second and even late movers as they determine the nature and timing of their competitive responses.[79]

Determining that a competitor thinks of itself as an effective second mover allows the firm to predict that that competitor will tend to respond quickly to first movers' successful, innovation-based market entries. If the firm itself is a first mover, then it can expect a successful second mover competitor to study its market entries and to respond to them quickly. As a second mover, the competitor will try to respond with a product that creates customer value exceeding the value provided by the product initially introduced by the first mover. The most successful second movers are able to rapidly and meaningfully interpret market feedback to respond quickly, yet successfully, to the first mover's successful innovations.[80]

A **late mover** is a firm that responds to a competitive action, but only after considerable time has elapsed after the first mover's action and the second mover's response. Typically, a late response is better than no response at all, although any success achieved from the late competitive response tends to be slow in coming and considerably less than that achieved by first and second movers. Thus, the firm competing against a late mover can predict that that competitor will likely enter a particular market only after both the first and second movers have achieved success by doing so. Moreover, on a relative basis, the firm can predict that the late mover's competitive action will allow it to earn even average returns only when enough time has elapsed for it to understand how to create value that is more attractive to customers than is the value offered by the first and second movers' products. Although exceptions do exist, the firm can predict that as a competitor, the late mover's competitive actions will be relatively ineffective, certainly as compared to those initiated by first movers and second movers.

Organizational Size

An organization's size affects the likelihood that it will take competitive actions as well as the types of actions it will take and their timing.[81] In general, compared to large companies, small firms are more likely to launch competitive actions and tend to be quicker in doing so. Smaller firms are thus perceived as nimble and flexible competitors who rely on speed and surprise to defend their competitive advantages or develop new ones while engaged in competitive rivalry, especially with large companies, to gain an advantageous market position.[82] Small firms' flexibility and nimbleness allow them to develop greater variety in their competitive actions as compared to large firms, which tend to limit the types of competitive actions used when competing with rivals.[83]

Compared to small firms, large ones are likely to initiate more competitive actions as well as strategic actions during a given period.[84] Thus, when studying its competitors in terms of organizational size, the firm should use a measurement such as total sales revenue or total number of employees to compare itself with each competitor. The competitive actions the firm likely will encounter from competitors larger than it is will be different than the competitive actions it will encounter from competitors that are smaller.

The organizational size factor has an additional layer of complexity associated with it. When engaging in competitive rivalry, the firm usually wants to take a large number of competitive actions against its competitors. As we have described, large organizations commonly have the slack resources required to launch a larger number of total competitive actions. On the other hand, smaller firms have the flexibility needed to launch a greater variety of competitive actions. Ideally, the firm would like to have the ability to launch a large number of unique competitive actions. Herb Kelleher, cofounder and former CEO of Southwest Airlines, addressed this matter, "Think and act big and we'll get smaller. Think and act small and we'll get bigger."[85]

In the context of competitive rivalry, Kelleher's statement can be interpreted to mean that relying on a limited number or types of competitive actions (which is the large firm's tendency) can lead to reduced competitive success across time, partly because competitors learn how to effectively respond to what is a limited set of competitive actions taken by a given firm. In contrast, remaining flexible and nimble (which is the small firm's tendency) in order to develop and use a wide variety of competitive actions contributes to success against rivals.

Wal-Mart appears to be an example of a large firm that has the flexibility required to take many types of competitive actions. With $254 billion in sales expected in 2004 and market capitalization over $252 billion,[86] Wal-Mart is one of the world's two largest companies in terms of sales revenue (the other is ExxonMobil). In less than a decade, Wal-Mart has become one of the largest grocery retailers in the United States. This accomplishment demonstrates Wal-Mart's ability to successfully compete against its various rivals, even long-established grocers.

In spite of its size, the firm remains highly flexible as it takes both strategic actions (such as rapid global expansion) and tactical actions. A recent strategic action is the opening of more Neighborhood Markets. The company is careful to note that its freestanding grocery units won't compete against its other concepts. In the words of a company spokesperson, "Neighborhood Markets are close to residential areas in more convenient locations. They're big enough to fulfill all of shoppers' grocery needs, but small enough that you can stop in for last-minute items as well."[87] Wal-Mart is opening these stores to take more market share from its competitors in the grocery market.

Analysts believe that Wal-Mart's tactical actions are as critical to its success as are its strategic actions and that its tactical actions demonstrate a great deal of flexibility. For example, "every humble store worker has the power to lower the price on any Wal-Mart product if he spots it cheaper elsewhere."[88] Decision-making responsibility and authority have been delegated to the level of the individual worker to make certain that the firm's cost leadership business-level strategy always results in the lowest prices for customers. Managers and employees both spend a good deal of time thinking about additional strategic and tactical actions, respectively, that might enhance the firm's performance. Thus, it is possible that Wal-Mart has met the expectation suggested by

Kelleher's statement, in that it is a large firm that "remains stuck to its small-town roots" in order to think and act like the small firm capable of using a wide variety of competitive actions.[89] Wal-Mart's competitors might feel confident in predicting that the firm's competitive actions will be a combination of the tendencies shown by small and large companies.

Quality

Quality has many definitions, including well-established ones relating it to the production of goods or services with zero defects[90] and seeing it as a never-ending cycle of continuous improvement.[91] From a strategic perspective, we consider quality to be an outcome of how the firm completes primary and support activities (see Chapter 3). Thus, **quality** exists when the firm's goods or services meet or exceed customers' expectations. Some evidence suggests that quality may be the most critical component in satisfying the firm's customers.[92]

Customers may be interested in measuring the quality of a firm's products against a broad range of dimensions. Sample quality dimensions for goods and services in which customers commonly express an interest are shown in Table 5.1. Thus, in the eyes of customers, quality is about doing the right things relative to performance measures that are important to them.[93] Quality is possible only when top-level managers support it and when its importance is institutionalized throughout the entire organization.[94] When quality is institutionalized and valued by all, employees and managers alike become vigilant about continuously finding ways to improve quality.[95]

Quality is a universal theme in the global economy and is a necessary but not sufficient condition for competitive success. In other words, "Quality used to be a compet-

Table 5.1

Quality Dimensions of Goods and Services

Product Quality Dimensions
1. *Performance*—Operating characteristics
2. *Features*—Important special characteristics
3. *Flexibility*—Meeting operating specifications over some period of time
4. *Durability*—Amount of use before performance deteriorates
5. *Conformance*—Match with preestablished standards
6. *Serviceability*—Ease and speed of repair
7. *Aesthetics*—How a product looks and feels
8. *Perceived quality*—Subjective assessment of characteristics (product image)

Service Quality Dimensions
1. *Timeliness*—Performed in the promised period of time
2. *Courtesy*—Performed cheerfully
3. *Consistency*—Giving all customers similar experiences each time
4. *Convenience*—Accessibility to customers
5. *Completeness*—Fully serviced, as required
6. *Accuracy*—Performed correctly each time

SOURCES: Adapted from J. W. Dean, Jr., & J. R. Evans, 1994, *Total Quality: Management, Organization and Society*, St. Paul, MN: West Publishing Company; H. V. Roberts & B. F. Sergesketter, 1993, *Quality Is Personal*, New York: The Free Press; D. Garvin, 1988, *Managed Quality: The Strategic and Competitive Edge*, New York: The Free Press.

itive issue out there, but now it's just the basic denominator to being in the market."[96] Without quality, a firm's products lack credibility, meaning that customers don't think of them as viable options. Indeed, customers won't consider buying a product until they believe that it can satisfy at least their base-level expectations in terms of quality dimensions that are important to them. For years, quality was an issue for Jaguar automobiles as the carmaker endured frequent complaints from drivers about poor quality. As a result of recent actions addressing this issue, quality has improved to the point where customers now view the cars as credible products.[97]

Getty Images

Hyundai cars await shipment from Korea. An emphasis on quality at Hyundai Motors has turned the company around from a low point in 1999. Hyundai is now competing successfully with Honda and Toyota.

Quality affects competitive rivalry. The firm studying a competitor whose products suffer from poor quality can predict that the competitor's costs are high and that its sales revenue will likely decline until the quality issues are resolved. In addition, the firm can predict that the competitor likely won't be aggressive in terms of taking competitive actions, given that its quality problems must be corrected in order to gain credibility with customers. However, after the problems are corrected, that competitor is likely to take competitive actions emphasizing additional dimensions of competition. Hyundai Motor Co.'s experiences illustrate these expectations.

Immediately upon becoming CEO of Hyundai Motor Co. in March 1999, Mong Koo Chung started touring the firm's manufacturing facilities. Appalled at what he saw, he told workers and managers alike, "The only way we can survive is to raise our quality to Toyota's level."[98] To dramatically improve quality, a quality-control unit was established, and significant resources (over $1 billion annually) were allocated to research and development (R&D) in order to build cars that could compete on price and deliver on quality. Today, quality is still viewed as the firm's number one priority.[99]

Outcomes from Hyundai's focus on quality improvements are impressive. The 2002 *Consumer Reports* survey observed that Hyundai's ratings were among the worst of the products the magazine tested a decade ago. However, the firm's 2002 model-year vehicles were tied with those of Honda for second place in reliability.[100] In 2003, the director of automotive quality research at J.D. Power observed, "Since 1998, Hyundai is the most improved car in the initial quality survey. They have dropped their number of quality problems by 50 percent."[101] Signaling a strong belief in its products' quality, Hyundai offers a ten-year drive-train warranty in the United States, which the firm has selected as a key market.

While concentrating on quality improvements, Hyundai didn't launch aggressive competitive actions, as competitors could predict would likely be the case. However, as could also be predicted by firms studying Hyundai as a competitor, improvements to the quality of Hyundai's products helped the firm to become a more aggressive competitor.

The introduction of the Santa Fe in 2000 is one indication of Hyundai's more aggressive orientation to competition. A well-conceived sport-utility vehicle (SUV), the Santa Fe was designed and built to outperform Toyota's RAV4 and Honda's CR-V. Considered a successful market entry, partly because of its quality, the second-generation Santa Fe is to be built in Hyundai's plant in Alabama beginning in March 2005. With its quality issues perhaps behind it, Hyundai is challenging competitors on other competitive dimensions, including design and styling.[102]

The success of a firm's competitive action is affected by the likelihood that a competitor will respond to it as well as by the type (strategic or tactical) and effectiveness of that response. As noted earlier, a competitive response is a strategic or tactical action the firm takes to counter the effects of a competitor's competitive action. In general, a firm is likely to respond to a competitor's action when (1) the consequences of that action are better use of the competitor's competitive advantages or improvement in its market position, (2) the action damages the firm's ability to use its advantages, or (3) the firm's market position becomes less defensible.[103]

In addition to market commonality and resource similarity and awareness, motivation, and ability, firms study three other factors—type of competitive action, reputation, and market dependence—to predict how a competitor is likely to respond to competitive actions (see Figure 5.2).

Type of Competitive Action

Competitive responses to strategic actions differ from responses to tactical actions. These differences allow the firm to predict a competitor's likely response to a competitive action that has been launched against it. Of course, a general prediction is that strategic actions receive strategic responses while tactical responses are taken to counter the effects of tactical actions.

In general, strategic actions elicit fewer total competitive responses because strategic responses, such as market-based moves, involve a significant commitment of resources and are difficult to implement and reverse.[104] Moreover, the time needed for a strategic action to be implemented and its effectiveness assessed delays the competitor's response to that action.[105] In contrast, a competitor likely will respond quickly to a tactical action, such as when an airline company almost immediately matches a competitor's tactical action of reducing prices in certain markets. And, either strategic actions or tactical actions that target a large number of a rival's customers are likely to be targeted with strong responses.[106]

Actor's Reputation

In the context of competitive rivalry, an *actor* is the firm taking an action or a response while *reputation* is "the positive or negative attribute ascribed by one rival to another based on past competitive behavior."[107] A positive reputation may be a source of above-average returns, especially for consumer goods producers.[108] Thus, a positive corporate reputation is of strategic value[109] and affects competitive rivalry. To predict the likelihood of a competitor's response to a current or planned action, the firm studies the responses that the competitor has taken previously when attacked—past behavior is assumed to be a reasonable predictor of future behavior.

Competitors are more likely to respond to either strategic or tactical actions that are taken by a market leader.[110] For example, Home Depot is the world's largest home improvement

Home Depot is the innovator in home improvement retailing. Its EXPO Design Center, a new store format, has led to Lowe's transformation into "home improvement warehouses."

©Michael Newman/PhotoEdit

retailer and the second largest U.S. retailer (behind Wal-Mart). Known for being an innovator in its core home improvement market as well as for having an ability to develop successful new store formats (such as its EXPO Design Centers and Villager's Hardware Stores), Home Depot can predict that its competitors carefully study its actions, especially the strategic ones, and that they are likely to respond to them. Lowe's Companies, the second largest U.S. home improvement retailer and Home Depot's major competitor, is aware of Home Depot's actions. Lowe's also has both the motivation and ability to respond to actions by Home Depot. For example, partly in response to Home Depot's consistent focus on updating the retail concept of its core home improvement stores, Lowe's continues to transform "its store base from a chain of small stores into a chain of destination home improvement warehouses,"[111] increasing the similarity of its store design to Home Depot's.

Other evidence suggests that commonly successful actions, especially strategic actions, will be quickly imitated, almost regardless of the actor's reputation. For example, although a second mover, IBM committed significant resources to enter the PC market. When IBM was immediately successful in this endeavor, competitors such as Dell, Compaq, and Gateway responded with strategic actions to enter the market. IBM's reputation as well as its successful strategic action strongly influenced entry by these competitors. Thus, in terms of competitive rivalry, IBM could predict that responses would follow its entry to the PC market if that entry proved successful. In addition, IBM could predict that those competitors would try to create value in slightly different ways, such as Dell's legendary decision to sell directly to consumers rather than to use storefronts as a distribution channel.

In contrast to a firm with a strong reputation, such as IBM, competitors are less likely to take responses against companies with reputations for competitive behavior that is risky, complex, and unpredictable. The firm with a reputation as a price predator (an actor that frequently reduces prices to gain or maintain market share) generates few responses to its pricing tactical actions because price predators, which typically increase prices once their market share objective is reached, lack credibility with their competitors.[112] The opposite of a price predator in terms of reputation, Wal-Mart is widely recognized for its pricing integrity, giving the firm a great deal of credibility when it launches a tactical action or response around the prices of its goods.

Dependence on the Market

Market dependence denotes the extent to which a firm's revenues or profits are derived from a particular market.[113] In general, firms can predict that competitors with high market dependence are likely to respond strongly to attacks threatening their market position.[114] Interestingly, the threatened firm in these instances tends not to respond quickly, suggesting the importance of an effective response to an attack on the firm's position in a critical market.

A firm such as Wm. Wrigley Company would be expected to respond aggressively, but not necessarily quickly, to an attack. With such well-known brands as Spearmint, Doublemint, Juicy Fruit, Big Red, Extra, and Hubba Bubba bubble gum, Wrigley is the world's largest producer of chewing gum, accounting for roughly 50 percent of total chewing gum sales volume worldwide and over 90 percent of the U.K. market.[115] Through its Amurol Confections subsidiary (which produces several products such as liquid gel candy, suckers, and hard roll candies) and Healthcare Division (which develops and markets products using chewing gum to deliver active ingredients that provide health benefits), Wrigley has a minor amount of diversification. However, chewing gum accounts for more than 90 percent of the firm's total revenue as well as earnings.[116] Wrigley's dominant market position provides the flexibility needed to respond aggressively but carefully to actions that a competitor such as Adams might take. But, if Adams were to attack Wrigley's sugarless Extra gum through actions related to Adams' Trident, for example, it should understand that Wrigley's dependence on the chewing gum market will induce it to respond aggressively to protect its position in the sugarless gum market.

Competitive Dynamics

Whereas competitive rivalry concerns the ongoing actions and responses between a firm and its competitors for an advantageous market position, competitive dynamics concerns the ongoing actions and responses taking place among *all* firms competing within a market for advantageous positions.

To explain competitive rivalry, we described (1) factors that determine the degree to which firms are competitors (market commonality and resource similarity), (2) the drivers of competitive behavior for individual firms (awareness, motivation, and ability) and (3) factors affecting the likelihood a competitor will act or attack (first-mover incentives, organizational size, and quality) and respond (type of competitive action, reputation, and market dependence). Building and sustaining competitive advantages are at the core of competitive rivalry, in that advantages are the link to an advantageous market position.[117]

To explain competitive dynamics, we discuss the effects of varying rates of competitive speed in different markets (called slow-cycle, fast-cycle, and standard-cycle markets, defined below) on the behavior (actions and responses) of all competitors within a given market. Competitive behaviors as well as the reasons or logic for taking them are similar within each market type, but differ across market type.[118] Thus, competitive dynamics differ in slow-cycle, fast-cycle, and standard-cycle markets. The sustainability of the firm's competitive advantages is an important difference among the three market types.

As noted in Chapter 1, firms want to sustain their competitive advantages for as long as possible, although no advantage is permanently sustainable. The degree of sustainability is affected by how quickly competitive advantages can be imitated and how costly it is to do so.

Slow-Cycle Markets

Slow-cycle markets are markets in which the firm's competitive advantages are shielded from imitation for what are commonly long periods of time and where imitation is costly.[119] Competitive advantages are sustainable in slow-cycle markets.

Building a one-of-a-kind competitive advantage that is proprietary leads to competitive success in a slow-cycle market. This type of advantage is difficult for competitors to understand. As discussed in Chapter 3, a difficult-to-understand and costly-to-imitate advantage results from unique historical conditions, causal ambiguity, and/or social complexity. Copyrights, geography, patents, and ownership of an information resource are examples of what leads to one-of-a-kind advantages.[120] Once a proprietary advantage is developed, the firm's competitive behavior in a slow-cycle market is oriented to protecting, maintaining, and extending that advantage. Thus, the competitive dynamics in slow-cycle markets involve all firms concentrating on competitive actions and responses that enable them to protect, maintain, and extend their proprietary competitive advantage.

Walt Disney Co. continues to extend its proprietary characters, such as Mickey Mouse, Minnie Mouse, and Goofy. These characters have a unique historical development as a result of Walt and Roy Disney's creativity and vision for entertaining people. Products based on the characters seen in Disney's animated films are sold through Disney's theme park shops as well as freestanding retail outlets called Disney Stores. The list of character-based products is extensive, including everything from the char-

Slow-cycle markets are markets in which the firm's competitive advantages are shielded from imitation for what are commonly long periods of time and where imitation is costly.

acters to clothing with the characters' images. Because patents shield it, the proprietary nature of Disney's advantage in terms of animated characters protects the firm from imitation by competitors.

Consistent with another attribute of competition in a slow-cycle market, Disney remains committed to protecting its exclusive rights to its characters and their use as shown by the fact that "the company once sued a day-care center, forcing it to remove the likeness of Mickey Mouse from a wall of the facility."[121] As with all firms competing in slow-cycle markets, Disney's competitive actions (such as building theme parks in France and Japan and other potential locations such as China) and responses (such as lawsuits to protect its right to fully control use of its animated characters) maintain and extend its proprietary competitive advantage while protecting it. Disney has been able to establish through actions and defend through responses an advantageous market position as a result of its competitive behavior.

Patent laws and regulatory requirements such as those in the United States requiring FDA (Food and Drug Administration) approval to launch new products shield pharmaceutical companies' positions. Competitors in this market try to extend patents on their drugs to maintain advantageous positions that they (patents) provide. However, once a patent expires, the firm is no longer shielded from competition, a situation that has financial implications.

As is true with Walt Disney Co., pharmaceutical companies aggressively pursue legal courses of action to protect their patents. This is demonstrated by recent actions taken by Pfizer Inc., the maker and seller of Lipitor, the world's most prescribed cholesterol-lowering drug. In 2003, Ranbaxy applied to the U.S. Food and Drug Administration to begin immediately marketing its generic version of Lipitor. Pfizer filed a suit asking a judge to prohibit Ranbaxy from making and marketing Lipitor before its 1987 U.S. patent expires in 2010. The stakes were high, in that Pfizer generated over $8 billion in revenue from sales of Lipitor in 2002.[122] As with its competitors, Pfizer is also vigilant in working with the FDA's Criminal Investigations office to control counterfeiting. Fake versions of Lipitor are common as are counterfeit Viagra pills (Viagra is Pfizer's treatment for impotence in men). In addition to damage to its sales, Pfizer is concerned about possible serious health risks for customers who consume counterfeit versions of its products.[123]

The competitive dynamics generated by firms competing in slow-cycle markets are shown in Figure 5.4. In slow-cycle markets, firms launch a product (e.g., a new drug) that has been developed through a proprietary advantage (e.g., R&D) and then exploit it for as long as possible while the product is shielded from competition. Eventually, competitors respond to the action with a counterattack. In markets for drugs, this counterattack commonly occurs as patents expire or are broken through legal means, creating the need for another product launch by the firm seeking a shielded market position.

Fast-Cycle Markets

Fast-cycle markets are markets in which the firm's competitive advantages aren't shielded from imitation and where imitation happens quickly and perhaps somewhat inexpensively. Competitive advantages aren't sustainable in fast-cycle markets. Thus, firms competing in fast-cycle markets recognize the importance of speed, meaning that these companies appreciate that "time is as precious a business resource as money or head count—and that the costs of hesitation and delay are just as steep as going over budget or missing a financial forecast."[124]

Reverse engineering and the rate of technology diffusion in fast-cycle markets facilitate rapid imitation. A competitor uses reverse engineering to quickly gain the knowledge required to imitate or improve the firm's products, usually in only a few months. Technology is diffused rapidly in fast-cycle markets, making it available to competitors in a short period. The technology often used by fast-cycle competitors

Fast-cycle markets are markets in which the firm's competitive advantages aren't shielded from imitation and where imitation happens quickly and perhaps somewhat inexpensively.

Figure 5.4 — Gradual Erosion of a Sustained Competitive Advantage

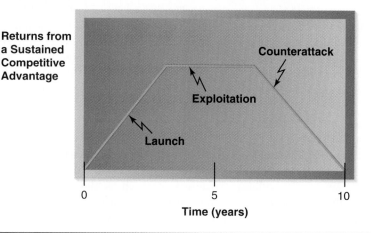

SOURCE: Adapted from I. C. MacMillan, 1988, Controlling competitive dynamics by taking strategic initiative, *Academy of Management Executive*, II(2): 111–118.

isn't proprietary, nor is it protected by patents as is the technology used by firms competing in slow-cycle markets. For example, only a few hundred parts, which are readily available on the open market, are required to build a PC. Patents protect only a few of these parts, such as microprocessor chips.[125]

Fast-cycle markets are more volatile than slow-cycle and standard-cycle markets. Indeed, the pace of competition in fast-cycle markets is almost frenzied, as companies rely on ideas and the innovations resulting from them as the engines of their growth. Because prices fall quickly in these markets, companies need to profit quickly from their product innovations. For example, rapid declines in the prices of microprocessor chips produced by Intel and Advanced Micro Devices, among others, make it possible for personal computer manufacturers to continuously reduce their prices to end users. Imitation of many fast-cycle products is relatively easy, as demonstrated by such firms as Dell Inc. and Hewlett-Packard, along with a host of local PC vendors. All of these firms have partly or largely imitated IBM's PC design to create their products. Continuous declines in the costs of parts, as well as the fact that the information required to assemble a PC isn't especially complicated and is readily available, make it possible for additional competitors to enter this market without significant difficulty.[126]

The fast-cycle market characteristics described above make it virtually impossible for companies in this type of market to develop sustainable competitive advantages. Recognizing this, firms avoid "loyalty" to any of their products, preferring to cannibalize their own before competitors learn how to do so through successful imitation. This emphasis creates competitive dynamics that differ substantially from those found in slow-cycle markets. Instead of concentrating on protecting, maintaining, and extending competitive advantages, as is the case for firms in slow-cycle markets, companies competing in fast-cycle markets focus on learning how to rapidly and continuously develop new competitive advantages that are superior to those they replace. In fast-cycle markets, firms don't concentrate on trying to protect a given competitive advantage because they understand that the advantage won't exist long enough to extend it.

The competitive behavior of firms competing in fast-cycle markets is shown in Figure 5.5. As suggested by the figure, competitive dynamics in this market type find firms taking actions and responses in the course of competitive rivalry that are oriented to rapid and continuous product introductions and the use of a stream of ever-changing competitive advantages. The firm launches a product as a competitive action and then exploits the advantage associated with it for as long as possible. However, the firm also tries to move to another temporary competitive advantage before competitors can respond to the first one (see Figure 5.5). Thus, competitive dynamics in fast-cycle markets, in which all firms seek to achieve new competitive advantages before competitors learn how to effectively respond to current ones, often result in rapid product upgrades as well as quick product innovations.[127]

As our discussion suggests, innovation has a dominant effect on competitive dynamics in fast-cycle markets. For individual firms, this means that innovation is a key source of competitive advantage. Through innovation, the firm can cannibalize its own products before competitors successfully imitate them.

In the Strategic Focus, we describe the experiences of Teradyne Inc., a company competing in a fast-cycle market. Teradyne allocates over 13 percent of sales revenue to R&D, suggesting the importance of innovation to this firm.

As noted earlier, it is difficult for firms competing in fast-cycle markets to maintain a competitive advantage in terms of their products. Partly because of this, Teradyne has chosen to emphasize its ability to design and manufacture assembly equipment and the skills it uses to serve customers as possible sources of competitive advantage. It may be difficult for competitors to fully understand and imitate these core competencies, meaning that they may be sustainable competitive advantages for a firm competing in fast-cycle markets.

Standard-Cycle Markets

Standard-cycle markets are markets in which the firm's competitive advantages are moderately shielded from imitation and where imitation is moderately costly. Competitive advantages are partially sustainable in standard-cycle markets, but only when the firm is able to continuously upgrade the quality of its competitive advantages. The competitive actions and responses that form a standard-cycle market's competitive dynamics find firms seeking large market shares, trying to gain customer loyalty through brand names, and carefully controlling their operations to consistently provide the same usage experience for customers without surprises.[128]

Standard-cycle markets are markets in which the firm's competitive advantages are moderately shielded from imitation and where imitation is moderately costly.

Developing Temporary Advantages to Create Sustained Advantage — Figure 5.5

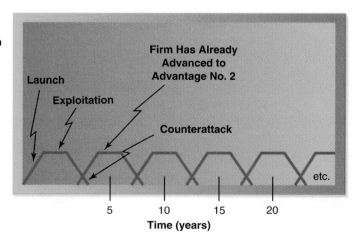

SOURCE: Adapted from I. C. MacMillan, 1988, Controlling competitive dynamics by taking strategic initiative, *Academy of Management Executive*, II(2): 111–118.

Teradyne Inc.: Life in the Fast Lane

The CEO's opening words in his letter to shareholders from Teradyne Inc.'s 2002 Annual Report capture the rollercoaster experience firms competing in fast-cycle markets may encounter: "Two years ago in this space, I was telling you about the best year in Teradyne's history. Now I am here to report our worst."

Teradyne designs and manufactures automatic test equipment and interconnection systems that are sold primarily to semiconductor, electronics, network systems, and automotive companies. Teradyne's products are used to test the performance and functionality of semiconductors, circuit boards and modules, automotive electronics, and voice and broadband networks. Teradyne products are intended to help customers more quickly introduce innovative goods to the marketplace with greater reliability and at a lower cost.

Teradyne's business is directly tied to the semiconductor industry. Beginning in 2000 and running through mid-2003, chip demand declined from the highs of the 1990s. Lower consumer demand for personal computers, cellular telephones, and other technology-related products made with semiconductors accounted for the decline in the demand for chips. Derivatively, lower demand for chips results in lower demand for equipment to test their performance and functionality, a reality that affects Teradyne's sales. In fast-cycle markets, firms must react quickly to market demand. Because of market growth in the mid- to late 1990s, Teradyne expanded to ship what it expected would be $3 billion worth of product sales in 2000. However, sales revenue of less than half of the expectation in 2002 caused Teradyne to restructure. In the company's words: "A lot of good employees had to be released and a lot of plants had to be closed. We dropped marginal product lines, and we borrowed and mortgaged to prepare for the worst. We squeezed costs wherever we could, while protecting the engineering programs vital to our future and making sure that our customers were well supported."

Teradyne is organized into four strategic business units—interconnection systems, circuit board test and inspection, automotive test and diagnosis, and broadband test. As is true for its competitors—firms such as Applied Materials Inc., KLA-Tencor Corp., and Lam Research Corp.—Teradyne's products typically have relatively short shelf lives. While engaged in competitive rivalry, these companies strive diligently to develop and introduce products that are superior to their own before competitors do so.

Proprietary assembly equipment (equipment that is designed and made in-house) and customer service are core competencies Teradyne believes are competitive advantages for the firm. One of the "latest of these innovative machines," according to the company, "is BRIM (for Backplane Rotary Insertion Machine), which automatically inserts tiny gold-plated pins into backplane modules." Allocating 13 percent or more of sales revenue to R&D, some of which supports analysis of how to develop ever more sophisticated, value-creating assembly equipment, demonstrates Teradyne's effort to sustain proprietary assembly equipment as a competitive advantage. Moreover, even when experiencing negative growth, Teradyne remains committed to providing the high level of support it believes customers expect from it. Continuous training and reliance on a total quality management system facilitate the firm's efforts to provide superior service to customers. When describing why it chose a Teradyne product to test its experimental Smart Card, users at Samsung Electronics noted that excellent local support was a key factor in their decision.

SOURCES: 2003, Teradyne and Boeing offer new avionics testing system, *Aviation Daily*, 352(68): 6; 2003, Teradyne posts narrower loss, *Wall Street Journal Online*, http://www.wsj.com, April 15; 2003, NetVendor acquires Teradyne's manufacturing group, *Wall Street Journal Online*, http://www.wsj.com, February 26; 2003, Teradyne Inc. Home Page, http://www.teradyne.com, May 28; 2002, Teradyne Inc. Annual Report, Because technology never stops, 1–9; T. Witkowsi, 2002, Weathering the storm: Teradyne Inc., *Boston Business Journal*, December 27, 22(47): 11.

Standard-cycle companies serve many customers in competitive markets. Because the capabilities and core competencies on which their competitive advantages are based are less specialized, imitation is faster and less costly for standard-cycle firms than for those competing in slow-cycle markets. However, imitation is slower and more expensive in these markets than in fast-cycle markets. Thus, competitive dynamics in standard-cycle markets rest midway between the characteristics of dynamics in slow-cycle and fast-cycle markets. The quickness of imitation is reduced and becomes more expensive for standard-cycle competitors when a firm is able to develop economies of scale by com-

AP Photo/Procter & Gamble, Bob Riha Jr.

bining coordinated and integrated design and manufacturing processes with a large sales volume for its products.

A Crest spokesperson (right) explains to a customer how to apply the new Crest Whitestrips to her teeth during a nationwide unveiling in Santa Monica, California. This has been a very successful product for P&G in a standard-cycle market.

Because of large volumes, the size of mass markets, and the need to develop scale economies, the competition for market share is intense in standard-cycle markets. Procter & Gamble (P&G) and Unilever compete in standard-cycle markets. A competitor analysis reveals that P&G and Unilever are direct competitors in that they share multiple markets as they engage each other in competition in over 140 countries, and they have similar types and amounts of resources and follow similar strategies. One of the product lines in which these two firms aggressively compete for market share is laundry detergents. The market for these products is large, with an annual sales volume of over $6 billion in the United States alone. The sheer size of this market highlights the importance of market share, as a mere percentage point gain in share translates into at least a $60 million increase in revenues. As analysts have noted, in a standard-cycle market, "It's a death struggle to incrementally gain share." For P&G and Unilever, this means that the firms must "slog it out for every fraction of every share in every category in every market where they compete."[129]

Innovation can also drive competitive actions and responses in standard-cycle markets, especially when rivalry is intense. Some innovations in standard-cycle markets are incremental rather than radical in nature (incremental and radical innovations are discussed in Chapter 13). Recently, Procter & Gamble introduced high-margin incremental variations of some of its mainstay brands, such as Tide, Pampers, and Crest. Almost overnight, the introductions of Crest Whitestrips and the Crest SpinBrush, both of which are product extensions of the Crest brand, made Crest P&G's 12th brand to exceed $1 billion in annual sales revenue.[130] Because Unilever and P&G battle for every share of each market in which they compete, P&G can expect a competitive reaction from Unilever in the form of possible changes to its toothpaste products, such as Close-Up.

In the final analysis, innovation has a substantial influence on competitive dynamics as it affects the actions and responses of all companies competing within a slow-cycle, fast-cycle, or standard-cycle market. We have emphasized the importance of innovation to the firm's strategic competitiveness in earlier chapters and will do so again in Chapter 13. Our discussion of innovation in terms of competitive dynamics extends the earlier discussions by showing its importance in all types of markets in which firms compete.

- Competitors are firms competing in the same market, offering similar products, and targeting similar customers. Competitive rivalry is the ongoing set of competitive actions and competitive responses occurring between competitors as they compete against each other for an advantageous market position. The outcomes of competitive rivalry influence the firm's ability to sustain its competitive advantages as well as the level (average, below-average, or above-average) of its financial returns.

- For the individual firm, the set of competitive actions and responses it takes while engaged in competitive rivalry is called competitive behavior. Competitive dynamics is the set of actions and responses taken by all firms that are competitors within a particular market.

- Firms study competitive rivalry in order to be able to predict the competitive actions and responses that each of their competitors likely will take. Competitive actions are either strategic or tactical in nature. The firm takes competitive actions to defend or build its competitive advantages or to improve its market position. Competitive responses are taken to counter the effects of a competitor's competitive action. A strategic action or a strategic response requires a significant commitment of organizational resources, is difficult to successfully implement, and is difficult to reverse. In contrast, a tactical action or a tactical response requires fewer organizational resources and is easier to implement and reverse. For an airline company, for example, entering major new markets is an example of a strategic action or a strategic response while changing its prices in a particular market is an example of a tactical action or a tactical response.

- A competitor analysis is the first step the firm takes to be able to predict its competitors' actions and responses. In Chapter 2, we discussed what firms do to *understand* competitors. This discussion is extended in this chapter as we described what the firm does to *predict* competitors' market-based actions. Thus, understanding precedes prediction. Market commonality (the number of markets with which competitors are jointly involved and their importance to each) and resource similarity (how comparable competitors' resources are in terms of type and amount) are studied to complete a competitor analysis. In general, the greater are market commonality and resource similarity, the more firms acknowledge that they are direct competitors.

- Market commonality and resource similarity shape the firm's awareness (the degree to which it and its competitor understand their mutual interdependence), motivation (the firm's incentive to attack or respond), and ability (the quality of the resources available to the firm to attack and respond). Having knowledge of a competitor in terms of these characteristics increases the quality of the firm's predictions about that competitor's actions and responses.

- In addition to market commonality and resource similarity and awareness, motivation and ability, three more specific factors affect the likelihood a competitor will take competitive actions. The first of these concerns first-mover incentives. First movers, those taking an initial competitive action, often earn above-average returns until competitors can successfully respond to their action and gain loyal customers. Not all firms can be first movers in that they may lack the awareness, motivation, or ability required to engage in this type of competitive behavior. Moreover, some firms prefer to be a second mover (the firm responding to the first mover's action). One reason for this is that second movers, especially those acting quickly, can successfully compete against the first mover. By studying the first mover's product, customers' reactions to it, and the responses of other competitors to the first mover, the second mover can avoid the early entrant's mistakes and find ways to improve upon the value created for customers by the first mover's good or service. Late movers (those that respond a long time after the original action was taken) commonly are lower performers and are much less competitive.

    Organizational size, the second factor, tends to reduce the number of different types of competitive actions that large firms launch while it increases the variety of actions undertaken by smaller competitors. Ideally, the firm would like to initiate a large number of diverse actions when engaged in competitive rivalry.

    The third factor, quality, dampens firms' abilities to take competitive actions, in that product quality is a base denominator to successful competition in the global economy.

- The type of action (strategic or tactical) the firm took, the competitor's reputation for the nature of its competitor behavior, and that competitor's dependence on the market in which the action was taken are studied to predict a competitor's response to the firm's action. In general, the number of tactical responses taken exceeds the number of strategic responses. Competitors respond more frequently to the actions taken by the firm with a reputation for predictable and understandable competitive behavior, especially if that firm is a market leader. In general, the firm can predict that when its competitor is highly dependent for its revenue and profitability in the market in which the firm took a competitive action, that competitor is likely to launch a strong response. However, firms that are more diversified across markets are less likely to respond to a particular action that affects only one of the markets in which they compete.

- Competitive dynamics concerns the ongoing competitive behavior occurring among all firms competing in a market for advantageous positions. Market characteristics affect the set of actions and responses firms take while competing in a given market as well as the sustainability of firms' competitive advantages. In slow-cycle markets, where competitive advantages can be maintained, competitive dynamics finds firms taking actions and responses that are intended to protect, maintain, and extend their proprietary advantages. In fast-cycle markets, competition is almost frenzied as firms concentrate on developing a series of temporary competitive advantages. This emphasis is necessary because firms' advantages in fast-cycle markets aren't proprietary and, as such, are subject to rapid and relatively inexpensive imitation. Standard-cycle markets are between slow-cycle and fast-cycle markets, in that firms are moderately shielded from competition in these markets as they use competitive advantages that are moderately sustainable. Competitors in standard-cycle markets serve mass markets and try to develop economies of scale to enhance their profitability. Innovation is vital to competitive success in each of the three types of markets. Companies should recognize that the set of competitive actions and responses taken by all firms differs by type of market.

Review Questions

1. Who are competitors? How are competitive rivalry, competitive behavior, and competitive dynamics defined in the chapter?

2. What is market commonality? What is resource similarity? What does it mean to say that these concepts are the building blocks for a competitor analysis?

3. How do awareness, motivation, and ability affect the firm's competitive behavior?

4. What factors affect the likelihood a firm will take a competitive action?

5. What factors affect the likelihood a firm will initiate a competitive response to the action taken by a competitor?

6. How are competitive dynamics in slow-cycle markets described in the chapter? In fast-cycle markets? In standard-cycle markets?

Experiential Exercises

Competitive Rivalry

Part One. Define first mover and second mover, and provide examples of firms for each category.

First mover:

Second mover:

Part Two. In the following table, list the advantages and disadvantages of being the first mover and of being the second mover for the firms you identified.

First Mover		Second Mover	
Advantages	**Disadvantages**	**Advantages**	**Disadvantages**

Part Three. Based on the above information, what are the most important issues that you feel first and second movers must consider before initiating a competitive move?

Intra-Industry Competitive Rivalry

Choose an industry for which you would like to more fully understand the competitive environment, or base your work on an industry assigned by your professor. Both the popular business press and the Internet are potential information sources for this exercise, as is the InfoTrac College Edition online database that can be accessed using information on your subscription card. (See http://www.infotrac-college.com.) Additionally, efforts should be made to find industry-level information through trade councils and trade publications.

1. Analyze the general state of competitive dynamics within the industry of study. What evidence or indicators do you have that the industry operates in a slow-, fast-, or standard-cycle market? How might this influence the overall competitive environment in the industry?

2. Analyze the position of several major competitors within the industry. That is, pick a firm active in the industry, along with two or three principal competitors, and, at a minimum, analyze:

   a. Market commonality (e.g., products and customers) and resource similarities across competitors.

   b. Three major competitive actions that occurred in the industry within the past two years. Identify whether these were strategic or tactical actions, who took the actions, as well as whether and how competitors responded. How do these actions and reactions fit into the Model of Competitive Rivalry presented in Figure 5.2?

   c. Competitors in terms of market position. Will the competitive positioning and importance of major industry competitors significantly change in the next five years? Why or why not? Overall, what are the drivers of change within the industry?

Notes

1. D. F. Spulber, 2004, *Management Strategy*, Boston: McGraw-Hill/Irwin, 87–88; M.-J. Chen, 1996, Competitor analysis and interfirm rivalry: Toward a theoretical integration, *Academy of Management Review*, 21: 100–134.

2. T. Galvin, 2002, Examining institutional change: Evidence from the founding dynamics of U.S. health care interest associations, *Academy of Management Journal*, 45: 673–696.

3. B. Pittman, 2003, Leading for value, *Harvard Business Review*, 81(4): 41–46.

4. A. Nair & L. Filer, 2003, Cointegration of firm strategies within groups: A long-run analysis of firm behavior in the Japanese steel industry, *Strategic Management Journal*, 24: 145–159.

5. T. C. Powell, 2003, Varieties of competitive parity, *Strategic Management Journal*, 24: 61–86.

6. S. Jayachandran, J. Gimeno, & P. R. Varadarajan, 1999, Theory of multimarket competition: A synthesis and implications for marketing strategy, *Journal of Marketing*, 63(3): 49–66.

7. R. E. Caves, 1984, Economic analysis and the quest for competitive advantage, in *Papers and Proceedings of the 96th Annual Meeting of the American Economic Association*, 127–132.

8. G. Young, K. G. Smith, C. M. Grimm, & D. Simon, 2000, Multimarket contact and resource dissimilarity: A competitive dynamics perspective, *Journal of Management*, 26: 1217–1236; C. M. Grimm & K. G. Smith, 1997, *Strategy as Action: Industry Rivalry and Coordination*, Cincinnati: South-Western College Publishing, 53–74.

9. H. A. Haveman & L. Nonnemaker, 2000, Competition in multiple geographic markets: The impact on growth and market entry, *Administrative Science Quarterly*, 45: 232–267.

10. K. G. Smith, W. J. Ferrier, & H. Ndofor, 2001, Competitive dynamics research: Critique and future directions, in M. A. Hitt, R. E. Freeman, & J. S. Harrison (eds.), *Handbook of Strategic Management*, Oxford, UK: Blackwell Publishers, 326.

11. G. Young, K. G. Smith, & C. M. Grimm, 1996, "Austrian" and industrial organization perspectives on firm-level competitive activity and performance, *Organization Science*, 73: 243–254.

12. H. D. Hopkins, 2003, The response strategies of dominant U.S. firms to Japanese challengers, *Journal of Management*, 29: 5–25; G. S. Day & D. J.

Reibstein, 1997, The dynamic challenges for theory and practice, in G. S. Day & D. J. Reibstein (eds.), *Wharton on Competitive Strategy*, New York: John Wiley & Sons, 2.

13. M.-J. Chen & D. C. Hambrick, 1995, Speed, stealth, and selective attack: How small firms differ from large firms in competitive behavior, *Academy of Management Journal*, 38: 453–482.

14. D. Foust, F. F. Jespersen, & F. Katzenberg, 2003, The best performers, *BusinessWeek Online*, http://www.businessweek.com, March 24; D. L. Deeds, D. De Carolis, & J. Coombs, 2000, Dynamic capabilities and new product development in high technology ventures: An empirical analysis of new biotechnology firms, *Journal of Business Venturing*, 15: 211–299.

15. T. J. Douglas & J. A. Ryman, 2003, Understanding competitive advantage in the general hospital industry: Evaluating strategic competencies, *Strategic Management Journal*, 24: 333–347; W. P. Putsis, Jr., 1999, Empirical analysis of competitive interaction in food product categories, *Agribusiness*, 15(3): 295–311.

16. S. Crainer, 2001, And the new economy winner is . . . Europe, *Strategy & Business*, Second Quarter, 40–47.

17. 2003, Masks off, down the hatch, *The Economist*, May 17, 57.

18. G. Khermouch & K. Capell, 2003, Spiking the booze business, *Business Week*, May 19, 77–78.

19. C. Lawton & D. Ball, 2003, Diageo mixes it up—liquor giant targets system dating to end of prohibition, *Wall Street Journal Online*, http://www.wsj.com, May 8.

20. S. J. Marsh, 1998, Creating barriers for foreign competitors: A study of the impact of anti-dumping actions on the performance of U.S. firms, *Strategic Management Journal*, 19: 25–37; K. G. Smith, C. M. Grimm, G. Young, & S. Wally, 1997, Strategic groups and rivalrous firm behavior: Toward a reconciliation, *Strategic Management Journal*, 18: 149–157.

21. W. J. Ferrier, 2001, Navigating the competitive landscape: The drivers and consequences of competitive aggressiveness, *Academy of Management Journal*, 44: 858–877; M. E. Porter, 1980, *Competitive Strategy*, New York: Free Press.

22. Smith, Ferrier, & Ndofor, Competitive dynamics research, 319.

23. J. Shamsie, 2003, The context of dominance: An industry-driven framework for exploiting reputation, *Strategic Management Journal*, 24: 199–215;

K. Ramaswamy, 2001, Organizational ownership, competitive intensity, and firm performance: An empirical study of the Indian manufacturing sector, *Strategic Management Journal*, 22: 989–998.

24. K. Cool, L. H. Roller, & B. Leleux, 1999, The relative impact of actual and potential rivalry on firm profitability in the pharmaceutical industry, *Strategic Management Journal*, 20: 1–14.

25. D. R. Gnyawali & R. Madhavan, 2001, Cooperative networks and competitive dynamics: A structural embeddedness perspective, *Academy of Management Review*, 26: 431–445.

26. Young, Smith, Grimm, & Simon, Multimarket contact and resource dissimilarity, 1217; M. E. Porter, 1991, Towards a dynamic theory of strategy, *Strategic Management Journal*, 12: 95–117.

27. R. L. Priem, L. G. Love, & M. A. Shaffer, 2002, Executives' perceptions of uncertainty scores: A numerical taxonomy and underlying dimensions, *Journal of Management*, 28: 725–746.

28. I. C. MacMillan, A. B. van Putten, & R. S. McGrath, 2003, Global gamesmanship, *Harvard Business Review*, 81(5): 62–71; S. Godin, 2002, Survival is not enough, *Fast Company*, January, 90–94.

29. Chen, Competitor analysis, 108.

30. Ibid., 109.

31. A. Afuah, 2003, Redefining firm boundaries in the face of the Internet: Are firms really shrinking? *Academy of Management Review*, 28: 34–53.

32. G. K. Deans, F. Kroeger, & S. Zeisel, 2002, The consolidation curve, *Harvard Business Review*, 80(12): 20–21; E. Abrahamson & C. J. Fombrun, 1994, Macrocultures: Determinants and consequences, *Academy of Management Review*, 19: 728–755.

33. C. Salter, 2002, On the road again, *Fast Company*, January, 50–58.

34. Young, Smith, Grimm, & Simon, Multimarket contact, 1219.

35. Chen, Competitor analysis, 106.

36. J. Gimeno & C. Y. Woo, 1999, Multimarket contact, economies of scope, and firm performance, *Academy of Management Journal*, 42: 239–259.

37. K. MacArthur, 2001, McDonald's flips business strategy, *Advertising Age*, April 2, 1, 36.

38. 2003, Prudential Financial Inc., *Standard & Poor's Stock Reports*, http://www.standardandpoors.com, May 17.

39. MacMillan, van Putten, & McGrath, Global gamesmanship, 63.

40. Young, Smith, Grimm, & Simon, Multimarket contact, 1230.

41. J. Gimeno, 1999, Reciprocal threats in multimarket rivalry: Staking out "spheres of influence" in the U.S. airline industry, *Strategic Management Journal*, 20: 101–128; N. Fernandez & P. L. Marin, 1998, Market power and multimarket contact: Some evidence from the Spanish hotel industry, *Journal of Industrial Economics*, 46: 301–315.

42. H. J. Korn & J. A. C. Baum, 1999, Chance, imitative, and strategic antecedents to multimarket contact, *Academy of Management Journal*, 42: 171–193.

43. Jayachandran, Gimeno, & Varadarajan, Theory of multimarket competition, 59; Chen, Competitor analysis, 107.

44. J. Gimeno & C. Y. Woo, 1996, Hypercompetition in a multimarket environment: The role of strategic similarity and multimarket contact on competitive de-escalation, *Organization Science*, 7: 322–341.

45. M. Halkias, 2003, Three drugstores stake claims on same intersection in Collin County, Texas, *Dallas Morning News*, May 8, D1, D3.

46. 2003, CVS Corp., *Standard & Poor's Stock Reports*, http://www.standardandpoors.com, May 17; 2003, Walgreen Co., *Standard & Poor's Stock Reports*, http://www.standardandpoors.com, May 17.

47. Chen, Competitor analysis, 107–108.

48. L. Ulrich, 2003, Outside the box, *Money*, 32(6): 137–138.

49. N. E. Boudette, 2003, Drivers wanted: Volkswagen stalls on several fronts after luxury drive, *Wall Street Journal*, Eastern edition, May 8, A1.

50. Chen, Competitor analysis, 110.

51. Ibid.; W. Ocasio, 1997, Towards an attention-based view of the firm, *Strategic Management Journal*, 18 (Special Issue): 187–206; Smith, Ferrier, & Ndofor, Competitive dynamics research, 320.

52. M. Selva, 2003, Wal-Mart, France's Carrefour set sights on Ahold businesses, *Sunday Business*, April 6, B3; 2001, Wal around the world, *The Economist*, December 8, 55–56.

53. G. P. Hodgkinson & G. Johnson, 1994, Exploring the mental models of competitive strategists: The case for a processual approach, *Journal of Management Studies*, 31: 525–551; J. F. Porac & H. Thomas, 1994, Cognitive categorization and subjective rivalry among retailers in a small city, *Journal of Applied Psychology*, 79: 54–66.

54. Smith, Ferrier, & Ndofor, Competitive dynamics research, 320.

55. Chen, Competitor analysis, 113.

56. Grimm & Smith, *Strategy as Action*, 125.

57. 2002, Blue light blues, *The Economist*, January 29, 54; D. B. Yoffie & M. Kwak, 2001, Mastering strategic movement at Palm, *MIT Sloan Management Review*, 43(1): 55–63.

58. K. G. Smith, W. J. Ferrier, & C. M. Grimm, 2001, King of the hill: Dethroning the industry leader, *Academy of Management Executive*, 15(2): 59–70.

59. W. J. Ferrier & H. Lee, 2003, Strategic aggressiveness, variation, and surprise: How the sequential pattern of competitive rivalry influences stock market returns, *Journal of Managerial Issues*, 14: 162–180; G. S. Day, 1997, Assessing competitive arenas: Who are your competitors? in G. S. Day & D. J. Reibstein (eds.), *Wharton on Competitive Strategy*, New York: John Wiley & Sons, 25–26.

60. R. Truett, 2003, A chance to shape design destiny, *Automotive News*, April 7, D2; M. Ihlwan, L. Armstrong, & K. Kerwin, 2001, Hyundai gets hot, *Business Week*, December 17, 84–86.

61. 2003, Boeing says to build new 7E7 in United States, *Reuters*, http://www.reuters.com, May 16.

62. B. McKay, 2003, Coke plans to launch milk-based beverage, *Wall Street Journal Online*, http://www.wsj.com, May 23.

63. S. Day, 2003, Summer may bring a bottled water price war, *New York Times*, http://www.nytimes.com, May 12.

64. 2003, Coke aims milk-based drink at kids, teens, *Richmond Times-Dispatch*, May 27, B5.

65. J. Schumpeter, 1934, *The Theory of Economic Development*, Cambridge, MA: Harvard University Press.

66. J. L. C. Cheng & I. F. Kesner, 1997, Organizational slack and response to environmental shifts: The impact of resource allocation patterns, *Journal of Management*, 23: 1–18.

67. F. Wang, 2000, Too appealing to overlook, *America's Network*, December, 10–12.

68. G. Hamel, 2000, *Leading the Revolution*, Boston: Harvard Business School Press, 103.

69. W. T. Robinson & S. Min, 2002, Is the first to market the first to fail? Empirical evidence for industrial goods businesses, *Journal of Marketing Research*, 39: 120–128.

70. R. Agarwal, M. B. Sarkar, & R. Echambadi, 2002, The conditioning effect of time on firm survival: An industry life cycle approach, *Academy of Management Journal*, 45: 971–994.

71. Smith, Ferrier, & Ndofor, Competitive dynamics research, 331.

72. L. J. Bourgeois, 1981, On the measurement of organizational slack, *Academy of Management Review*, 6: 29–39.

73. S. W. Geiger & L. H. Cashen, 2002, A multidimensional examination of slack and its impact on innovation, *Journal of Managerial Issues*, 14: 68–84.

74. S. Thurm, 2003, Leading the news: Cisco net income rises 50% despite decline in revenue, *Wall Street Journal*, February 3, A3.

75. M. B. Lieberman & D. B. Montgomery, 1988, First-mover advantages, *Strategic Management Journal*, 9: 41–58.

76. 2001, Older, wiser, webbier, *The Economist*, June 30, 10.

77. M. Shank, 2002, Executive strategy report, IBM business strategy consulting, http://www.ibm.com, March 14; W. Boulding & M. Christen, 2001, First-mover disadvantage, *Harvard Business Review*, 79(9): 20–21.

78. B. Finkelstein, 2003, AHMH took two-pronged approach to building volume, *Origination News*, 11(4): 19.

79. K. G. Smith, C. M. Grimm, & M. J. Gannon, 1992, *Dynamics of Competitive Strategy*, Newberry Park, CA.: Sage Publications.

80. H. R. Greve, 1998, Managerial cognition and the mimetic adoption of market positions: What you see is what you do, *Strategic Management Journal*, 19: 967–988.

81. S. D. Dobrev & G. R. Carroll, 2003, Size (and competition) among organizations: Modeling scale-based selection among automobile producers in four major countries, 1885–1981, *Strategic Management Journal*, 24: 541–558; Smith, Ferrier, & Ndofor, Competitive dynamics research, 327.

82. F. K. Pil & M. Hoiweg, 2003, Exploring scale: The advantage of thinking small, *The McKinsey Quarterly*, 44(2): 33–39; Chen & Hambrick, Speed, stealth, and selective attack.

83. D. Miller & M.-J. Chen, 1996, The simplicity of competitive repertoires: An empirical analysis, *Strategic Management Journal*, 17: 419–440.

84. Young, Smith, & Grimm, "Austrian" and industrial organization perspectives.

85. B. A. Melcher, 1993, How Goliaths can act like Davids, *Business Week*, Special Issue, 193.

86. 2003, Wal-Mart Stores, *Standard & Poor's Stock Reports*, http://www.standardandpoors.com, May 17.

87. J. DeMoss, 2003, Wal-Mart grocery store concept to debut in Utah at South Ogden site, *Standard-Examiner*, March 25, B6.

88. 2001, Wal around the world, 55.

89. Ibid.

90. P. B. Crosby, 1980, *Quality Is Free*, New York: Penguin.

91. W. E. Deming, 1986, *Out of the Crisis*, Cambridge, MA: MIT Press.

92. L. B. Crosby, R. DeVito, & J. M. Pearson, 2003, Manage your customers' perception of quality, *Review of Business*, 24(1): 18–24.

93. R. S. Kaplan & D. P. Norton, 2001, *The Strategy-Focused Organization*, Boston: Harvard Business School Press.

94. R. Cullen, S. Nicholls, & A. Halligan, 2001, Measurement to demonstrate success, *British Journal of Clinical Governance*, 6(4): 273–278.

95. K. E. Weick & K. M. Sutcliffe, 2001, *Managing the Unexpected*, San Francisco: Jossey-Bass, 81–82.

96. J. Aley, 1994, Manufacturers grade themselves, *Fortune*, March 21, 26.

97. J. Green & D. Welch, 2001, Jaguar may find it's a jungle out there, *Business Week*, March 26, 62.

98. Ihlwan, Armstrong, & Kerwin, Hyundai gets hot, 84.

99. J. C. Armstrong, 2003, Hyundai Motor begins sourcing 2006 Santa Fe, *Automotive News*, April 28, 21.

100. K. Lundegaard, 2003, GM, Hyundai excel in consumer reports survey—Ford, Mercedes do poorly, *Wall Street Journal*, March 11, D3.

101. T. Box, 2003, Accelerating quality, *Dallas Morning News*, May 17, D1, D3.

102. R. Truett, 2003, A chance to shape design destiny, *Automotive News*, April 7, 2D.

103. J. Schumpeter, 1950, *Capitalism, Socialism and Democracy*, New York: Harper; Smith, Ferrier, & Ndofor, Competitive dynamics research, 323.

104. M.-J. Chen & I. C. MacMillan, 1992, Nonresponse and delayed response to competitive moves, *Academy of Management Journal*, 35: 539–570; Smith, Ferrier, & Ndofor, Competitive dynamics research, 335.

105. M.-J. Chen, K. G. Smith, & C. M. Grimm, 1992, Action characteristics as predictors of competitive responses, *Management Science*, 38: 439–455.

106. M.-J. Chen & D. Miller, 1994, Competitive attack, retaliation and performance: An expectancy-valence framework, *Strategic Management Journal*, 15: 85–102.

107. Smith, Ferrier, & Ndofor, Competitive dynamics research, 333.

108. J. Shamsie, 2003, The context of dominance: An industry-driven framework for exploiting reputation, *Strategic Management Journal*, 24: 199–215.

109. P. W. Roberts & G. R. Dowling, 2003, Corporate reputation and sustained superior financial performance, *Strategic Management Journal*, 24: 1077–1093.

110. W. J. Ferrier, K. G. Smith, & C. M. Grimm, 1999, The role of competitive actions in market share erosion and industry dethronement: A study of industry leaders and challengers, *Academy of Management Journal*, 42: 372–388.

111. 2001, Lowe's Companies, *Standard & Poor's Stock Reports*, http://www.standardandpoors.com, December 26.

112. Smith, Grimm, & Gannon, *Dynamics of Competitive Strategy*.

113. A. Karnani & B. Wernerfelt, 1985, Research note and communication: Multiple point competition, *Strategic Management Journal*, 6: 87–97.

114. Smith, Ferrier, & Ndofor, Competitive dynamics research, 330.

115. M. J. McCarthy, 2002, Wrigley must chew on its next move, *Wall Street Journal*, September 19, B1.

116. 2003, Wm. Wrigley Company, About Us, *http://www.wrigley.com*, May 26.

117. G. McNamara, P. M. Vaaler, & C. Devers, 2003, Same as it ever was: The search for evidence of increasing hypercompetition, *Strategic Management Journal*, 24: 261–278.

118. J. R. Williams, 1999, *Renewable Advantage: Crafting Strategy through Economic Time*, New York: Free Press.

119. J. R. Williams, 1992, How sustainable is your competitive advantage? *California Management Review* 34(3): 29–51.

120. Ibid., 6.

121. Ibid., 57.

122. 2003, Pfizer suit is for a blockbuster drug, *Businessline*, February 26, 13.

123. 2003, U.S. FDA says counterfeit Lipitor recalled by distributor, *Reuters*, http://www.reuters.com, May 23.

124. 2003, How fast is your company? *Fast Company*, June, 18.

125. Williams, *Renewable Advantage*, 8.

126. Ibid.

127. R. Sanchez, 1995, Strategic flexibility in production competition, *Strategic Management Journal*, 16 (Special Issue): 9–26.

128. Williams, *Renewable Advantage*, 7.

129. K. Brooker, 2001, A game of inches, *Fortune*, February 5, 98–100.

130. D. Foust, F. F. Jespersen, & F. Katzenberg, 2003, The best performers, *BusinessWeek Online*, http://www.businessweek.com, March 24.

Corporate-Level Strategy

Chapter Six

Knowledge Objectives

Studying this chapter should provide you with the strategic management knowledge needed to:

1. Define corporate-level strategy and discuss its importance to the diversified firm.

2. Describe the advantages and disadvantages of single- and dominant-business strategies.

3. Explain three primary reasons why firms move from single- and dominant-business strategies to more diversified strategies.

4. Describe how related diversified firms create value by sharing or transferring core competencies.

5. Explain the two ways value can be created with an unrelated diversification strategy.

6. Discuss the incentives and resources that encourage diversification.

7. Describe motives that can encourage managers to overdiversify a firm.

Getty/PhotoDisc, Inc.

Sony has been successful in adding technology to content in a way that has been innovative and profitable.

Sony's Chairman Idei Seeks to Foster Related Diversification

The development of technology is revolutionizing the media industry. Media content producers have sought, so far unsuccessfully, to merge their companies with content distribution firms, hoping to maximize returns by controlling outlets for their content. Bertelsmann AG, Vivendi Universal, and AOL Time Warner, for example, have multiple media and content outlet business units in publishing, movies, cable TV, and Internet websites. Despite the failure of executives Thomas Middelhoff at Bertelsmann, Jean-Marie Messier at Vivendi Universal, and Gerald M. Levin at AOL Time Warner to achieve similar goals, Nobuyuki Idei, the chairman of Sony, is undauntedly pursuing convergence in music, movies, games, and communications in all forms.

Mr. Idei argued that Sony's unique advantage over other media behemoths was that it makes the actual electronic devices (TVs, personal computers, game consoles, and mobile phones) that deliver the content Sony controls. Across its personal device divisions, Sony has achieved operational relatedness (defined later in the chapter) in its consumer electronics businesses. Now, Sony is seeking corporate relatedness (defined later in the chapter) across its electronic devices, software, and content divisions. As Sony's chairman, Idei has made significant strides in building a company where content meshes with the electronics. Many Walkmans are no longer stand-alone tape players, but can also download music from the Internet; Clié personal digital assistants (PDAs) come with cameras; CoCoonhome video recorders can be programmed from a mobile phone. "In terms of building networked products," said Lee Kun Soo, an analyst at West LB Securities in Tokyo, "no company has come so far."

But inside Sony, there remains the major challenge of balancing the divergent aims of the content divisions, which are fighting to protect their song and movie copyrights, and the gadget makers in the consumer electronics divisions, who are creating products that will allow consumers to swap content. Sony's acquisition of Columbia Pictures in the late 1980s brought the struggle between hardware and software in-house, and new technological advances are likely to make that struggle even more intense in coming years.

Chairman Idei maintains that by 2005 the telecommunications infrastructure (broadband) meshed with content products (music, video, and games software) will be in place, allowing the company to reap the benefits of the convergence of media and technology. The number of high-speed Internet and mobile phone connections is exploding. Sony's Memory Stick is now embedded in most of its new products, making it possible for users to easily swap data between cameras, computers, and PDAs. One-third, or nearly 1,200, of Sony's movies through Columbia Pictures have been digitized, which will allow them to be used on many hardware devices.

In this era of increasingly indistinguishable electronics, preserving Sony's corporate brand is paramount. "People don't just buy for economic reasons," Mr. Idei says. "When you touch a product, you should feel something." However, to accomplish this diversification strategy, the integration necessary between divisions has led to some changes in leadership. "The necessity for such bridge building led to the recent ouster of Sony Music's longtime leader, Tommy Mottola, whose unwillingness to confer with the rest of Sony on a new business model forced the change to an outsider, NBC television executive Andrew Lack." Thus, implementing the related diversification strategy and vision of Mr. Idei has not been without difficulties. Furthermore, any diversification strategy has to create value over and above the value created by the businesses involved. To this point, although the operational relatedness strategy has been fairly successful, the strategy to foster both operational and corporate relatedness has yet to achieve the desired success.

SOURCES: K. Belson, 2003, 65 and just itching for a little convergence, *New York Times*, http://www.nytimes.com, April 3; 2003, Special Report: The complete home entertainer? Sony, *The Economist*, March 1, 62–64; R. A. Guth, 2003, Sony's board will divide up responsibilities, *Wall Street Journal*, January 29, B6; S. Levy, 2003, Sony's new day, *Newsweek*, January 27, 50–53; J. Ordonez & J. Lippman, 2003, Sony taps NBC's Lack in hope success will rub off—high costs, piracy, other woes plague its sickly music unit, *Wall Street Journal*, January 13, B1.

Our discussions of business-level strategies (Chapter 4) and the competitive rivalry and competitive dynamics associated with them (Chapter 5) concentrate on firms competing in a single industry or product market.[1] When a firm chooses to diversify beyond a single industry and to operate businesses in several industries, it uses a corporate-level strategy of diversification. As explained in the Opening Case, Sony is best known for its consumer electronics business where it seeks to create synergy between businesses (operational relatedness). Now it seeks to have integration across its electronic and media businesses through corporate relatedness. A corporate-level strategy of diversification such as Sony's allows the firm to use its core competencies to pursue opportunities in the external environment.[2] In particular, the convergence among these industries is creating an opportunity that requires a diversification strategy such as Sony's. As the Opening Case illustrates, diversification strategies play a major role in the behavior of large firms.[3] Strategic choices regarding diversification are, however, fraught with uncertainty, as in the Sony illustration.[4]

A diversified company has two levels of strategy: business (or competitive) and corporate (or company-wide).[5] Each business unit in the diversified firm chooses a business-level strategy as its means of competing in individual product markets. The firm's corporate-level strategy is concerned with two key questions: what businesses the firm should be in and how the corporate office should manage the group of businesses.[6] Defined formally, **corporate-level strategy** specifies actions the firm takes to gain a competitive advantage by selecting and managing a group of different businesses competing in several industries and product markets. In the current global environment, top executives should view their firm's businesses as a portfolio of core competencies when they select new businesses and decide how to manage them.

A corporate-level strategy is expected to help the firm earn above-average returns by creating value, just as with the diversified firm's business-level strategies.[7] Some suggest that few corporate-level strategies actually create value.[8] A corporate-level strat-

Corporate-level strategy specifies actions the firm takes to gain a competitive advantage by selecting and managing a group of different businesses competing in several industries and product markets.

egy's value is ultimately determined by the degree to which "the businesses in the portfolio are worth more under the management of the company than they would be under any other ownership."[9] Thus, the effective corporate-level strategy creates, across all business units, aggregate returns that exceed what those returns would be without the strategy[10] and contributes to the firm's strategic competitiveness and its ability to earn above-average returns.[11]

Product diversification, a primary corporate-level strategy, concerns the scope of the industries and markets in which the firm competes as well as "how managers buy, create and sell different businesses to match skills and strengths with opportunities presented to the firm."[12] Successful diversification is expected to reduce variability in the firm's profitability in that earnings are generated from several different business units.[13] Because firms incur development and monitoring costs when diversifying, the ideal business portfolio balances diversification's costs and benefits.[14] Increasingly, for example, a number of "traditional economy" firms are diversifying into Internet and e-commerce businesses in attempts to develop a properly balanced portfolio.[15]

Diversification requires the crafting of a multibusiness or corporate-level strategy. Multibusiness strategies often involve the firm with many different industry environments and product markets and, as explained in Chapter 11, require unique organizational structures. In the Opening Case, we describe Sony's use of a multibusiness diversification strategy to compete in the consumer electronics, media content, and games businesses. The prevailing logic of diversification suggests that the firm should diversify into additional markets when it has excess resources, capabilities, and core competencies with multiple value-creating uses.[16] The probability of success increases when top-level managers verify that the firm has excess, value-creating resources, capabilities, and core competencies before choosing and trying to implement a corporate-level strategy.[17]

We begin the chapter by examining different levels (from low to high) of diversification. Value-creating reasons for firms to use a corporate-level strategy are explored next. When diversification results in companies simultaneously competing against one another in multiple markets, they are engaging in multipoint competition.[18] The chapter also describes the use of the vertical integration strategy as a means to gain power over competitors. Two types of diversification strategies denoting moderate to very high levels of diversification—related and unrelated—are then examined. The chapter also explores value-neutral incentives to diversify as well as managerial motives for diversification, which can be value destructive.

Levels of Diversification

Diversified firms vary according to their level of diversification and the connections between and among their businesses. Figure 6.1 lists and defines five categories of businesses according to increasing levels of diversification. In addition to the single- and dominant-business categories, which denote relatively low levels of diversification, more fully diversified firms are classified into related and unrelated categories. A firm is related through its diversification when there are several links between its business units; for example, units may share products or services, technologies, or distribution channels. The more links among businesses, the more "constrained" is the relatedness of diversification. Unrelatedness refers to the absence of direct links between businesses.

Low Levels of Diversification

A firm pursing a *low level of diversification* uses either a single or a dominant corporate-level diversification strategy. A single-business diversification strategy is a corporate-level strategy wherein the firm generates 95 percent or more of its sales revenue from

Figure 6.1 ——— Levels and Types of Diversification

Low Levels of Diversification

Single business: More than 95% of revenue comes from a single business.

Dominant business: Between 70% and 95% of revenue comes from a single business.

Moderate to High Levels of Diversification

Related constrained: Less than 70% of revenue comes from the dominant business, and all businesses share product, technological, and distribution linkages.

Related linked (mixed related and unrelated):   Less than 70% of revenue comes from the dominant business, and there are only limited links between businesses.

Very High Levels of Diversification

Unrelated: Less than 70% of revenue comes from the dominant business, and there are no common links between businesses.

SOURCE: Adapted from R. P. Rumelt, 1974, *Strategy, Structure and Economic Performance*, Boston: Harvard Business School.

its core business area.[19] For example, focusing on the chewing-gum market, Wm. Wrigley Jr. Company historically used a single-business strategy while operating in relatively few product markets.[20] Wrigley's trademark chewing-gum brands include Spearmint, Doublemint, and Juicy Fruit. Sugarfree gums Hubba Bubba, Orbit, and Ice White were added in the 1990s. Its collaboration with Procter & Gamble (P&G) to produce a dental chewing gum caused Wrigley to become more diversified than it had been, moving it toward the dominant business strategy. The dental chewing gum is being marketed under P&G's Crest brand.[21] Furthermore, William Wrigley, Jr., the current chairman, has suggested that he would like "to double the size of the company over a number of years."[22] In fact, he sought but failed to buy out chocolate maker Hershey Foods to partially accomplish this goal.

With the dominant-business corporate-level diversification strategy, the firm generates between 70 and 95 percent of its total revenue within a single business area. Smithfield Foods uses the dominant-business diversification strategy in that the majority of its sales are generated from raising and butchering hogs. Recently, however, Smithfield diversified into beef packing by acquiring Moyer Packing Co., a smaller beef processor. Smithfield also attempted to acquire IBP, the largest beef packer, but was outbid by Tyson Foods.[23] Also, it lost a bid to the bankruptcy court for Farmland, a large beef processing cooperative.[24] Smithfield often seeks to buy troubled companies such as Farmland and then restructure the business operations to make them more profitable. Although it is still using the dominant-business diversification strategy, the firm's addition of beef packing operations suggests that its portfolio of businesses is becoming more diversified. If Smithfield were to become even more diversified, its corporate-level strategy could be more accurately described as moderately diversified.

Moderate and High Levels of Diversification

A firm generating more than 30 percent of its sales revenue outside a dominant business and whose businesses are related to each other in some manner uses a *related diversification corporate-level strategy*. When the links between the diversified firm's businesses are rather direct, a *related constrained diversification strategy* is being used. Campbell Soup, Procter & Gamble, Kodak, and Merck & Company all use a related constrained strategy. A related constrained firm shares a number of resources and activities between its businesses.

The diversified company with a portfolio of businesses with only a few links between them is called a mixed related and unrelated firm and is using the *related linked diversification corporate-level strategy* (see Figure 6.1). Johnson & Johnson, General Electric, and Cendant follow this corporate-level diversification strategy. Compared to related constrained firms, related linked firms share fewer resources and assets between their businesses, concentrating on transferring knowledge and competencies between the businesses instead.

A highly diversified firm, which has no relationships between its businesses, follows an *unrelated diversification corporate-level strategy*. United Technologies, Textron, and Samsung are examples of firms using this type of corporate-level strategy.[25] Although many U.S. firms using the unrelated diversification strategy have refocused to become less diversified, a number continue to have high levels of diversification. In Latin America and other emerging economies such as China, Korea, and India, conglomerates (firms following the unrelated diversification strategy) continue to dominate the private sector.[26] For instance, in Taiwan, "the largest 100 groups produced one third of the GNP in the past 20 years."[27] Typically family controlled, these corporations account for the greatest percentage of private firms in India.[28] Similarly, the largest business groups in Brazil, Mexico, Argentina, and Colombia are family-owned, diversified enterprises.[29] Questions are being raised as to the viability of these large diversified business groups,[30] especially in developed economies such as Japan.[31] However, evidence suggests that where capital markets and the legal system are underdeveloped, diversification produces better performance.[32]

Reasons for Diversification

There are many reasons firms use a corporate-level diversification strategy (see Table 6.1). Typically, a diversification strategy is used to increase the firm's value by improving its overall performance. Value is created either through related diversification or through unrelated diversification when the strategy allows a company's business units to increase revenues or reduce costs while implementing their business-level strategies. Another reason for diversification is to gain market power relative to competitors. Often, this is achieved through vertical integration (see the discussion later in the chapter).

Other reasons for using a diversification strategy may not increase the firm's value; in fact, diversification could have neutral effects, increase costs, or reduce a firm's revenues and its value. These reasons include diversification to match and thereby neutralize a competitor's market power (such as to neutralize another firm's advantage by acquiring a similar distribution outlet) and diversification to expand a firm's portfolio of businesses to reduce managerial employment risk (if one of the businesses in a diversified firm fails, the top executive of the firm remains employed). Because diversification can increase a firm's size and thus managerial compensation, managers have motives to diversify a firm to a level that reduces its value.[33] Diversification rationales that may have a neutral or negative effect on the firm's value are discussed in a later section.

To provide an overview of value-creating diversification strategies, Figure 6.2 illustrates operational relatedness and corporate relatedness. Study of these independent

Table 6.1 — Motives, Incentives, and Resources for Diversification

Motives to Enhance Strategic Competitiveness
- Economies of scope (related diversification)
  - Sharing activities
  - Transferring core competencies
- Market power (related diversification)
  - Blocking competitors through multipoint competition
  - Vertical integration
- Financial economies (unrelated diversification)
  - Efficient internal capital allocation
  - Business restructuring

Incentives and Resources with Neutral Effects on Strategic Competitiveness
- Antitrust regulation
- Tax laws
- Low performance
- Uncertain future cash flows
- Risk reduction for firm
- Tangible resources
- Intangible resources

Managerial Motives (Value Reduction)
- Diversifying managerial employment risk
- Increasing managerial compensation

relatedness dimensions shows the importance of resources and key competencies.[34] The figure's vertical dimension points to opportunities for sharing operational activities between businesses (operational relatedness) while its horizontal dimension depicts corporate capabilities for transferring knowledge (corporate relatedness). The firm with a strong capability in managing operational synergy, especially in sharing assets between its businesses, falls in the upper left quadrant, which also represents vertical sharing of assets through vertical integration. The lower right quadrant represents a highly developed corporate capability for transferring a skill across businesses. This capability is located primarily in the corporate office. The use of either operational or corporate relatedness is based on a knowledge asset that the firm can either share or transfer.[35] Unrelated diversification is also illustrated in Figure 6.2 in the lower left quadrant. As shown, the unrelated diversification strategy creates value through financial economies rather than through either operational or corporate relatedness among business units.

Related Diversification

With the related diversification corporate-level strategy, the firm builds upon or extends its resources, capabilities, and core competencies to create value.[36] The company using the related diversification strategy wants to develop and exploit economies of scope between its business units. Available to companies operating in multiple industries or product markets,[37] **economies of scope** are cost savings that the firm creates by successfully transferring some of its capabilities and competencies that were developed in one of its businesses to another of its businesses.

Economies of scope are cost savings that the firm creates by successfully transferring some of its capabilities and competencies that were developed in one of its businesses to another of its businesses.

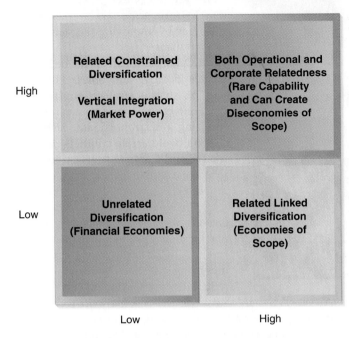

Sharing: Operational Relatedness between Businesses

High —
- Related Constrained Diversification / Vertical Integration (Market Power)
- Both Operational and Corporate Relatedness (Rare Capability and Can Create Diseconomies of Scope)

Low —
- Unrelated Diversification (Financial Economies)
- Related Linked Diversification (Economies of Scope)

Low   High

Corporate Relatedness: Transferring Skills into Businesses through Corporate Headquarters

As illustrated in Figure 6.2, firms seek to create value from economies of scope through two basic kinds of operational economies: sharing activities (operational relatedness) and transferring skills or corporate core competencies (corporate relatedness). The difference between sharing activities and transferring competencies is based on how separate resources are jointly used to create economies of scope. Tangible resources, such as plant and equipment or other business-unit physical assets, often must be shared to create economies of scope. Less tangible resources, such as manufacturing know-how, also can be shared.[38] However, when know-how is transferred between separate activities and there is no physical or tangible resource involved, a corporate core competence has been transferred as opposed to operational sharing of activities having taken place.

Operational Relatedness: Sharing Activities

Firms can create operational relatedness by sharing either a primary activity (such as inventory delivery systems) or a support activity (for example, purchasing practices)—see Chapter 3's discussion of the value chain. Sharing activities is quite common, especially among related constrained firms. Procter & Gamble's paper towel business and baby diaper business both use paper products as a primary input to the manufacturing process. The firm's paper production plant produces inputs for both divisions and is an example of a shared activity. In addition, these two businesses are likely to share distribution channels and sales networks, because they both produce consumer products.

Firms expect activity sharing among units to result in increased strategic competitiveness and improved financial returns.[39] For example, Hewlett-Packard's (HP) acquisition of Compaq is significantly improving the cost structure of the merged firm. One analyst observed that the team in charge of "untangling 163 overlapping product

lines—from Intel-based home computers to Unix workstations to handhelds—[has met] the $2.5 billion in cost reductions that Carly Fiorina [CEO of HP] was promising investors."[40] In mid-2003, the team was on track to save another $500 million that year by improving the sharing of resources between the merged firms.

Other issues affect the degree to which activity sharing creates positive outcomes. For example, activity sharing requires sharing strategic control over business units. Moreover, one business unit manager may feel that another unit is receiving a disproportionate share of the gains. Such a perception could create conflicts between division managers. In the HP and Compaq transaction, 15,000 employees lost their jobs because the sharing of resources between the two firms reduced the need for these employees.[41]

Activity sharing also is risky because business-unit ties create links between outcomes. For instance, if demand for one business's product is reduced, there may not be sufficient revenues to cover the fixed costs required to operate the facilities being shared. Organizational difficulties such as these can reduce activity sharing success.[42]

Hewlett-Packard's acquisition of Compaq is an example of activity sharing across companies that can be complex and difficult to manage. Because of CEO Carly Fiorina's strength in the facilitation of the acquisition, the firm has experienced more positive than negative outcomes.

Although activity sharing across business units isn't risk free, research shows that it can create value. For example, studies that examined acquisitions of firms in the same industry (called horizontal acquisitions), such as the banking industry, have found that sharing resources and activities and thereby creating economies of scope contributed to postacquisition increases in performance and higher returns to shareholders.[43] Additionally, firms that sold off related units in which resource sharing was a possible source of economies of scope have been found to produce lower returns than those that sold off businesses unrelated to the firm's core business.[44] Still other research discovered that firms with more related units had lower risk.[45] These results suggest that gaining economies of scope by sharing activities across a firm's businesses may be important in reducing risk and in creating value. Further, more attractive results are obtained through activity sharing when a strong corporate office facilitates it.[46]

Corporate Relatedness: Transferring of Core Competencies

Over time, the firm's intangible resources, such as its know-how, become the foundation of core competencies. As suggested by Figure 6.2, corporate core competencies are complex sets of resources and capabilities that link different businesses, primarily through managerial and technological knowledge, experience, and expertise.[47] One corporate capability that has been suggested by research is the ability to appropriately price new products, no matter the business line of origin.[48]

Related linked firms often transfer competencies across businesses, thereby creating value in at least two ways.[49] First, the expense of developing a competence has been incurred in one unit. Transferring it to a second business unit eliminates the need for the second unit to allocate resources to develop the competence. Resource intangibility is a second source of value creation through corporate relatedness. Intangible resources are difficult for competitors to understand and imitate. Because of this difficulty, the unit receiving a transferred competence often gains an immediate competitive advantage over its rivals.[50]

As an example of corporate relatedness, Pininfarina is famous for cars it has designed in the past, namely the Ferrari Testarossa and the Alfa Romeo Spider. But its CEO, Andrea Pininfarina, is seeking to move it into higher-margin service businesses, such as engineering new models and testing prototypes. In the CEO's words, "The

Cendant: A Diversified Service Conglomerate

Cendant Corporation was created in December 1997 by a merger between HFS, Inc., and CUC International. The merger combined a marketing company (CUC) with HFS, a diversified firm with franchising operations in several industries, including real estate, hospitality, and vehicle services. Henry Silverman, CEO of the former HFS, was appointed chairman of the merged company. Massive accounting irregularities in CUC's businesses caused Cendant's shares to lose nearly half their market value four months after the merger and resulted in criminal charges against some of CUC's former executives.

Cendant Corporation owns a diversified set of service businesses, including its fee-for-service businesses—hotels, real estate, tax preparation, rental cars, fleet and fuel cards, mortgage origination, employee relocation, and vacation exchange and rental services. Cendant grows through acquisitions as well as through internal means, such as development of new product lines, to implement its related linked corporate-level diversification strategy. Discussed in detail in the chapter, this strategy mixes related and unrelated diversification. Cendant also uses joint ventures and franchising (types of cooperative strategies that we discuss further in Chapter 9) to reach its growth objectives.

The focus of Cendant's corporate-level strategy is rapid growth through buying strong brands that are effectively positioned in the fee-for-service business area. Its businesses usually have low to moderate capital requirements but generate high margins and provide growing returns on capital and strong cash flows. Furthermore, Cendant seeks productivity improvements to lower costs by employing newer technologies.

Cendant's real estate franchises include Century 21, Coldwell Banker Commercial, and ERA—some of the most well-known franchises in the commercial and residential real estate brokerage market. Furthermore, it is one of the largest real estate retail mortgage originators in the United States. It also has a relocation service called Cendant Mobility. Real estate services generate approximately 40 percent of revenues for this diversified company.

In travel services, Cendant has a vast array of lodging franchises, including Days Inn, Howard Johnson, Ramada, Super 8, and Travelodge, among others. In fact, one in four customers in the budget segment stay in a Cendant franchised property. Because its customer base is budget conscious, the September 11, 2001, strikes on the United States had less effect on Cendant's revenues than on those of highly differentiated and more expensive lodging facilities. Cendant also owns Fairfield Resorts, Inc., through which vacation ownership interests are sold. To complement its travel business, Cendant acquired Galileo International, a distributor of electronic global reservation services for the travel industry. Customers in 115 countries use Galileo's services to access schedule and fare information, make reservations, and obtain tickets. Another recent Cendant acquisition, CheapTickets, provides additional opportunity in the online travel reservation segment. With the capability formed through its acquisitions, Cendant feels that it can effectively compete with such online travel companies as Travelocity and Priceline.com. Travel services generate approximately 28 percent of Cendant's revenues.

Cendant has a vehicle service division and is the leader in providing fleet and fuel management service cards. Avis Rent A Car System and Budget Car and Truck Rental, as well as PHH Arval and Wright Express form the core of this division. In total, this group of businesses accounts for roughly 17 percent of Cendant's sales revenue.

In regard to financial services, Cendant owns Jackson Hewitt Tax Service, the second largest U.S. tax preparation company, as well as Benefit Consultants, FISI-Madison Financial, and Long Term Preferred Care in the insurance and loyalty marketing area. On a combined basis, Cendant's financial services business unit contributes approximately 15 percent to the firm's total revenues.

Part of Cendant's related linked diversification strategy is to acquire companies that complement its prestigious branded businesses. For instance, Galileo International, originally United Airlines' Apollo reservation system, has the second largest share of the electronic travel reservation business. Sabre Holdings Corporation, a competitor that operates the Sabre computer reservation system and also controls Travelocity, holds the largest share of this market. The Galileo network connects 43,000 travel agency sites to 550 airlines, 37 car rental companies, 47,000 hotel properties, 368 tour operators, and three major cruise lines. Thus, this acquisition creates a stronger link among Cendant's travel businesses.

A key objective of Cendant's acquisition strategy is to add companies that augment growth, strengthening the various businesses or segments where the firm has competitive advantages. Its best success with cross market knowledge sharing has been in its array of real estate franchises. Although Cendant's businesses within each service type demonstrate some degree of relatedness and knowledge sharing across service businesses, it has yet to realize the potential synergy between service categories. As is the case for all diversified businesses, Cendant must provide clear and transparent reports of its operational successes so investors and other stakeholders can fairly judge the value being created by exploiting interrelationships among the firm's business units.

SOURCES: G. G. Marcial, 2003, Cendant comes back, *Business Week*, May 12, 110; A. Tsao, 2003, Just the ticket for travel stocks, *BusinessWeek Online*, http://www.businessweek.com, March 19; A. Barrett, 2002, Keep it simple, Cendant, Wall Street is slamming the company for complex financials, *Business Week*, October 14, 54; A. Serwer, 2002, Dirty rotten numbers, *Fortune*, February 18, 74–84; A. Barrett & D. Brady, 2001, Just when it seems on the mend, *Business Week*, October 15, 75–76; D. Colarusso, 2001, Wall Street is pondering Cendant's fresh start, *New York Times*, http://www.nytimes.com, April 22; M. Rich, 2001, Cendant agrees to buy CheapTickets, *Wall Street Journal*, August 14, B6; C. Rosen, 2001, Cendant ventures into travel, *Information Week*, June 25, 24; R. Sorkin & B. J. Feder, 2001, Owner of Avis and Day's Inn seen buying travel service, *New York Times*, http://www.nytimes.com, June 18; A. Barrett, S. A. Forest, & T. Lowry, 2000, Henry Silverman's long road back, *Business Week*, February 28, 126–136.

unique asset of Pininfarina is creativity." Ford has transferred the responsibility for the design, engineering, and assembly of its newest European convertible to the Italian automotive design firm. By calling on Pininfarina's talent to create and engineer the new convertible, Ford is availing itself of Pininfarina's core competence, namely, managing the creative process beyond mere design.[51]

The Strategic Focus on Cendant illustrates how this diversified services firm shares knowledge between its groups of businesses. For instance, in April 2002, Cendant unveiled the website CheapTickets.com, which allows the user to plan an entire trip, including plane tickets, hotel rooms, and car rentals. Although not devoted exclusively to Cendant brands, this website could help correlate the company's holdings in these markets. The September 11, 2001, terrorist attacks and the wars in Afghanistan and Iraq have had negative effects on the global travel market. However, the expectation of an improved travel market in the future bodes well for Cendant's businesses. The knowledge gained through the new website might also help Cendant's other businesses because online travel booking is one of the few areas of growth among Internet businesses.[52]

A number of firms have successfully transferred some of their resources and capabilities across businesses. Virgin Industries transferred its marketing skills across travel, cosmetics, music, drinks, mobile phones, and a number of other businesses. Thermo Electron uses its entrepreneurial skills to start new ventures and maintain a new-venture network. Coopers Industries manages a number of manufacturing-related businesses. Honda has developed and transferred its expertise in small and now larger engines for different types of vehicles, from motorcycles and lawnmowers to its range of automotive products.[53]

As the Strategic Focus suggests, the decision to merge CUC International with HFS seemed to have potential for improving the marketing capabilities of the merged firm, Cendant. However, because of accounting irregularities in some CUC businesses, the merger created significant difficulties, resulting in an initial precipitous decline in Cendant's market value. Also, because of the complexities in its financial statements, Cendant's market value declined subsequent to the Enron debacle.[54] Thus, there are significant risks to this strategy. Sony's chairman, Nobuyuki Idei, is finding how difficult pursuing corporate relatedness can be, as illustrated in this chapter's Opening Case.

One way managers facilitate the transfer of competencies is to move key people into new management positions.[55] However, a business-unit manager of an older division may be reluctant to transfer key people who have accumulated knowledge and experience critical to the business unit's success. Thus, managers with the ability to facilitate the transfer of a core competence may come at a premium, or the key people involved may not want to transfer. Additionally, the top-level managers from the transferring division may not want the competencies transferred to a new division to fulfill the firm's diversification objectives. As the Opening Case illustrates, because the former music businesss manager was unwilling to integrate the music content with other divisions, Idei, Sony's chairman, replaced him with Andrew Lack. However, research suggests that transferring expertise in manufacturing-based businesses often does not result in improved performance.[56] Businesses in which performance does improve often demonstrate a corporate passion for pursuing skill transfer and appropriate coordination mechanisms for realizing economies of scope.

Market Power

Related diversification can also be used to gain market power. Market power exists when a firm is able to sell its products above the existing competitive level or to reduce the costs of its primary and support activities below the competitive level, or both.[57]

One approach to gaining market power through diversification is *multipoint competition*. Multipoint competition exists when two or more diversified firms simultaneously compete in the same product areas or geographic markets.[58] The actions taken by United Parcel Service (UPS) and FedEx in two markets, overnight delivery and ground shipping, illustrate the concept of multipoint competition. UPS has moved into the stronghold of FedEx, overnight delivery, and FedEx has been buying trucking and ground shipping assets to move into the stronghold of UPS. Additionally, there is geographic competition for markets as DHL, the strongest shipping company in Europe, tries to move into the U.S. market.[59] Additionally, all three competitors are seeking to move into large foreign markets to establish market shares. For instance, because China was allowed into the World Trade Organization (WTO) and government officials have declared the market more open to foreign competition, the battle for global market share among these three top shippers is raging in China and other countries throughout the world.[60]

Some firms choose to create value by using vertical integration to gain market power (see Figure 6.2). **Vertical integration** exists when a company produces its own inputs (backward integration) or owns its own source of output distribution (forward integration). In some instances, firms

Vertical integration *exists when a company produces its own inputs (backward integration) or owns its own source of distribution of outputs (forward integration).*

DHL, UPS, and FedEx are vying for market share in large foreign markets. Here, a Chinese airport official stands near the Panda Express, a FedEx plane painted with a giant panda's face that carries live giant pandas in Beijing, China.

AP Photo/Ng Han Guan

partially integrate their operations, producing and selling their products by using company units as well as outside sources.

Vertical integration is commonly used in the firm's core business to gain market power over rivals. Market power is gained as the firm develops the ability to save on its operations, avoid market costs, improve product quality, and, possibly, protect its technology from imitation by rivals.[61] Market power also is created when firms have strong ties between their assets for which no market prices exist. Establishing a market price would result in high search and transaction costs, so firms seek to vertically integrate rather than remain separate businesses.[62]

Apple has recently forward integrated into the music business. Steven Jobs, Apple's CEO, saw people copying songs off CDs to use on their computers. Accordingly, Apple created iTunes jukebox computer software, which allows users to create their own list of songs or have the computer select songs randomly. Then, Apple developed the iPod, which is a portable device with a very large hard drive and which works seamlessly with iTunes so that music put on a personal computer becomes portable. Recently, Jobs has gone a step farther by vertically integrating forward into music purchases on the Internet, allowing iTune and iPod users as well as others to buy music directly from the Apple Store, an online store already selling more than $1 billion in hardware and software. Customers can now buy a specific song or a set of songs rather than pay a monthly subscription fee to such firms as Time Warner's music division, Pressplay, or MusicNet. One observer noted, "It's a lot easier to get people to migrate from physical CDs to buying individual songs online than it is to jump-start a subscription service."[63]

There are limits to vertical integration. For example, an outside supplier may produce the product at a lower cost. As a result, internal transactions from vertical integration may be expensive and reduce profitability relative to competitors. Also, bureaucratic costs may occur with vertical integration. And, because vertical integration can require substantial investments in specific technologies, it may reduce the firm's flexibility, especially when technology changes quickly. Finally, changes in demand create capacity balance and coordination problems. If one division is building a part for another internal division, but achieving economies of scale requires the first division to manufacture quantities that are beyond the capacity of the internal buyer to absorb, it would be necessary to sell the parts outside the firm as well as to the internal division. Thus, although vertical integration can create value, especially through market power over competitors, it is not without risks and costs.

For example, Merck, the pharmaceutical company, previously owned a pharmacy-benefits management company called Medco Health. Medco acts as a middleman between patients, insurers, and drugmakers, which led to conflicts of interest with its parent company. By revenue, Medco was 50 percent larger than Merck, but had a much smaller profit margin. Because of the legal headaches caused by the conflicts of interest, as well as the small profit margin and a desire to focus more attention on its own underlying profitability, Merck spun off Medco in mid-2003. This decision indicates that the benefits Merck expected from vertical integration did not fully materialize.[64]

Many manufacturing firms no longer pursue vertical integration.[65] In fact, deintegration is the focus of most manufacturing firms, such as Intel and Dell, and even some large auto companies, such as Ford and General Motors, as they develop independent supplier networks.[66] Solectron Corp., a contract manufacturer, represents a new breed of large contract manufacturers that is helping to foster this revolution in supply-chain management.[67] Such firms often manage their customers' entire product lines and offer services ranging from inventory management to delivery and after-sales service. Conducting business through e-commerce also allows vertical integration to be changed into "virtual integration."[68] Thus, closer relationships are possible with suppliers and customers through virtual integration or electronic means of integration, allowing firms to reduce the costs of processing transactions while improving their supply-chain management skills and tightening the control of their inventories.

Johnson & Johnson Seeks to Combine Diagnostic Devices and Drugs

Johnson & Johnson (J&J) is a 117-year-old company with 204 different and complex enterprises. It is organized into three major strategic groups: drugs, medical devices and diagnostics, and consumer products. Significantly, 61 percent of its operating profits came from the drugs group in 2002. With $36 billion in revenue, J&J is one of the largest health-care companies in the United States. In consumer products, it has prestigious brands, such as Band-Aid® and its famous Johnson & Johnson baby powder. It has a strong research and development capability as well as an effective program to acquire new products. Once it has a new product revenue stream, developed internally or acquired, the firm seeks to sell it aggressively around the world. Because of the company's size, it can offer favorable prices, for instance, to hospitals, which are likely to buy a "whole package" from J&J because of this competitiveness.

Over the last decade, Johnson & Johnson has spent $30 billion to acquire 52 businesses. However, because of the company's size, making a contribution to income through an acquisition program is very difficult, and, thus, the sustainability of an acquisition strategy is questionable. Primarily because of the acquisition strategy, as well as internal development and diversification, J&J's set of businesses is quite decentralized. The near total autonomy and independence that have been maintained in the corporation have fostered an entrepreneurial attitude that has kept J&J quite competitive in world markets.

However, William C. Weldon, J&J's current CEO, sees an opportunity for top-line growth in the scientific convergence of drugs, devices, and diagnostics. The convergence in science has allowed contributions from one discipline to another, leading to significantly greater sophistication in disease treatments. "Sutures are coated with drugs to prevent infections; tests based on genomic research could determine who would respond to a certain cancer drug; defibrillators may be linked to computers that alert doctors when patients have abnormal heart rhythms." J&J will soon release a drug-emitting stent. A stent is a tubelike device that holds arteries open in heart patients. The drug-emitting stent will release a drug that helps keep the artery from narrowing again. These stents are expected to be enormously popular with doctors and heart patients, resulting in a significant commercial success for J&J. Weldon suggests that this convergence will allow J&J to do many things it has not done before. However, convergence also requires operating relatedness between the company's various business units in a specific product area as well as corporate relatedness, which enables transfer of knowledge between different businesses.

To achieve this opportunity, however, the systems necessary to manage J&J's diversified set of businesses must change. J&J's famed autonomy (which accompanies its highly decentralized operations) must evolve to a new system that fosters better communication and much more frequent collaboration among the company's decentralized operations and between the head office and formerly independent businesses. The challenge will be to foster cooperation and collaboration among businesses without undermining the entrepreneurial

Johnson & Johnson is improving its top-line growth through the convergence of drugs, devices, and diagnostics. This image shows its CYPHER™ Sirolimus-eluting Coronary Stent (a drug-emitting stent) inside an artery.

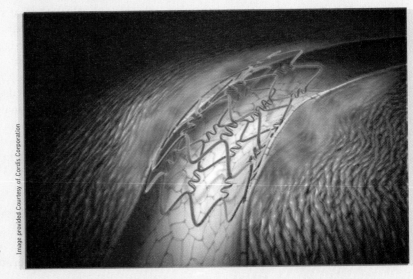

Image provided Courtesy of Cordis Corporation

spirit that has created J&J's success. This collaboration will require more centralization than heretofore has been the norm at J&J.

In summary, capitalizing on product convergence will require that J&J move toward both operational and corporate relatedness simultaneously. This seems risky for a company that has been totally decentralized. However, Weldon is very competitive and will seek to accomplish this desirable outcome as he has in the past, by pursuing "near impossible goals for his people and holding them to it." It will be interesting to see whether J&J can effectively pursue operational and corporate relatedness simultaneously.

SOURCES: A. Barrett, 2003, Staying on top: Can he keep up the growth? *Business Week*, May 5, 60–68; J. Carey & M. Arndt, 2003, Combo medicine: The union of drugs and devices offers major breakthroughs in health care—but can regulators keep up? *Business Week*, March 25, 156–158; M. E. Egan, 2003, Patchwork, *Forbes*, http://www.forbes.com, June 9; M. Herper, 2003, For drug deals, think small, *Forbes*, http://www.forbes.com, February 10; M. Herper, 2003, J&J earnings soar, but competition looms, *Forbes*, http://www.forbes.com, January 21.

Simultaneous Operational Relatedness and Corporate Relatedness

As Figure 6.2 suggests, some firms simultaneously seek operational and corporate forms of economies of scope.[69] Because simultaneously managing two sources of knowledge is very difficult, such efforts often fail, creating diseconomies of scope.[70] Although this strategy is difficult to implement, if the firm is successful, it could create value that is hard for competitors to imitate.

Johnson & Johnson is trying to achieve both operational relatedness and corporate relatedness in a decentralized set of businesses. Johnson & Johnson's strategy, as illustrated in the Strategic Focus, may be difficult to achieve because of a corporate culture focused on decentralization.

Although it may be difficult for J&J to pursue both operational and corporate synergy, Disney's strategy has been effective compared to others when measured by revenues generated from successful movies. By using operational relatedness and corporate relatedness, Disney made $3 billion on the 150 products that were marketed with its movie *The Lion King*. Sony's *Men in Black* was a super hit at the box office and earned $600 million, but box-office and video revenues were practically the entire story. Disney was able to accomplish its great success by sharing activities around the *Lion King* theme within its movie, theme park, music, and retail products divisions, while at the same time transferring knowledge into these same divisions, creating a music CD, *Rhythm of the Pride Lands*, and producing a video, *Simba's Pride*. In addition, there were *Lion King* themes at Disney resorts and Animal Kingdom parks.[71] However, it is difficult for analysts from outside the firm to fully assess the value-creating potential of pursuing both operational relatedness and corporate relatedness. Disney's assets as well as those of other media firms such as AOL Time Warner have been discounted somewhat because "the biggest lingering question is whether multiple revenue streams will outpace multiple-platform overhead."[72]

Unrelated Diversification

Firms do not seek either operational relatedness or corporate relatedness when using the unrelated diversification corporate-level strategy. An unrelated diversification strategy (see Figure 6.2) can create value through two types of financial economies.

Financial economies are cost savings realized through improved allocations of financial resources based on investments inside or outside the firm.[73]

The first type of financial economy results from efficient internal capital allocations. This approach seeks to reduce risk among the firm's business units—for example, through the development of a portfolio of businesses with different risk profiles. The approach thereby reduces business risk for the total corporation. The second type of financial economy is concerned with purchasing other corporations and restructuring their assets. This approach finds the diversified firm buying another company, restructuring that company's assets in ways that allow it to operate more profitably, and then selling the company for a profit in the external market.[74]

Efficient Internal Capital Market Allocation

In a market economy, capital markets are thought to efficiently allocate capital. Efficiency results from investors' purchasing of firm equity shares (ownership) that have high future cash-flow values. Capital is also allocated through debt as shareholders and debtholders try to improve the value of their investments by taking stakes in businesses with high growth prospects.

In large diversified firms, the corporate office distributes capital to business divisions to create value for the overall company. Such an approach may provide gains from internal capital market allocation relative to the external capital market.[75] This happens because while managing the firm's portfolio of businesses, the corporate office may gain access to detailed and accurate information regarding those businesses' actual and prospective performance.

The corporate office needs to convey its ability to create value in this manner to the market. One way firms can do this is through tracking stocks, as General Motors (GM) has done for its Hughes Electronics division.[76] GM created a new stock listing for Hughes that conveyed better information to the market about this additional asset. This approach allows more scrutiny by the market and thus more transparency of increasingly complex and diversified internal operations. It also increases the ability to move the assets to another company through a sell-off if this becomes necessary. In fact, in 2003, News Corp. made a $6 billion offer for the Hughes assets that operate DirecTV, a satellite TV system.[77]

Compared with corporate office personnel, investors have relatively limited access to internal information and can only estimate divisional performance and future business prospects. Although businesses seeking capital must provide information to potential suppliers (such as banks or insurance companies), firms with internal capital markets may have at least two informational advantages. First, information provided to capital markets through annual reports and other sources may not include negative information, instead emphasizing positive prospects and outcomes. External sources of capital have limited ability to understand the operational dynamics of large organizations. Even external shareholders who have access to information have no guarantee of full and complete disclosure.[78] Second, although a firm must disseminate information, that information also becomes simultaneously available to the firm's current and potential competitors. With insights gained by studying such information, competitors might attempt to duplicate a firm's competitive advantage. Thus, an ability to efficiently allocate capital through an internal market may help the firm protect its competitive advantages.

If intervention from outside the firm is required to make corrections to capital allocations, only significant changes are possible, such as forcing the firm into bankruptcy or changing the top management team. Alternatively, in an internal capital market, the corporate office can fine-tune its corrections, such as choosing to adjust managerial incentives or suggesting strategic changes in a division. Thus, capital can be allocated according to more specific criteria than is possible with external market

Financial economies are cost savings realized through improved allocations of financial resources based on investments inside or outside the firm.

allocations. Because it has less accurate information, the external capital market may fail to allocate resources adequately to high-potential investments compared with corporate office investments. The corporate office of a diversified company can more effectively perform such tasks as disciplining underperforming management teams through resource allocations.[79]

Research suggests, however, that in efficient capital markets, the unrelated diversification strategy may be discounted.[80] "For years, stock markets have applied a 'conglomerate discount': they value diversified manufacturing conglomerates at 20 percent less, on average, than the value of the sum of their parts. The discount still applies, in good economic times and bad. Extraordinary manufacturers (like GE) can defy it for a while, but more ordinary ones (like Philips and Siemens) cannot."[81]

Some firms still use the unrelated diversification strategy.[82] These large, diversified business groups are found in many European countries (for example, Spain's Grupo Ferrovial, an industrial, engineering, and financial conglomerate) and throughout emerging economies (for example, Hong Kong's Shanghai Industrial Holdings Ltd. and Malaysia's Sime Darby Berhad). Research indicates that the conglomerate or unrelated diversification strategy has not disappeared in Europe, where the number of firms using it has actually increased.[83] Although many conglomerates, such as ITT and Hansen Trust, have refocused, other unrelated diversified firms have replaced them.

The Achilles' heel of the unrelated diversification strategy is that conglomerates in developed economies have a fairly short life cycle because financial economies are more easily duplicated than are the gains derived from operational relatedness and corporate relatedness. This is less of a problem in emerging economies, where the absence of a "soft infrastructure" (including effective financial intermediaries, sound regulations, and contract laws) supports and encourages use of the unrelated diversification strategy.[84] In fact, in emerging economies such as those in India and Chile, diversification increases performance of firms affiliated with large diversified business groups.[85]

Restructuring

Financial economies can also be created when firms learn how to create value by buying and selling other companies' assets in the external market.[86] As in the real estate business, buying assets at low prices, restructuring them, and selling them at a price exceeding their cost generates a positive return on the firm's invested capital.[87]

Sara Lee Corporation is a prime example of a diversified company that seeks to acquire and then restructure the operations acquired. It owns over 200 brands, including Jimmy Dean sausages, its namesake baked goods, Hanes underwear, and Earthgrains bread. Managing so many different brands has proven a challenge: growth has been flat for the past several years. Thus, the company has not excelled at restructuring the businesses that it has acquired. Unlike Procter & Gamble, Sara Lee hasn't discovered how to focus on key brands to drive growth. L'eggs pantyhose has had years of double-digit volume declines. Folgers has outperformed Chock full o'Nuts coffee. The current CEO, Steven McMillan, is busy sorting out which businesses and brands to keep and which to sell in an attempt to reduce the firm's diversification. One proposal suggests that the best option would be to split the firm into its three main businesses—food (52 percent of sales), apparel (37 percent), and household goods (11 percent).[88]

Under former CEO Dennis L. Kozlowski, Tyco International, Ltd., excelled at financial economies through restructuring. Tyco focused on two types of acquisitions: platform, which represent new bases for future acquisitions, and add-on, in markets in which Tyco currently has a major presence. As with many unrelated diversified firms, Tyco acquires mature product lines. However, completing large numbers of complex transactions has resulted in accounting practices that aren't as transparent as stakeholders now demand. In fact, many of Tyco's top executives, including Kozlowski, were arrested for fraud, and the new CEO, Edward Breen, has been restructuring the firm's businesses to overcome "the flagrant accounting, ethical, and governance abuses of his predecessor." Actions being taken in firms such as Tyco suggest that firms creating value through financial economies are responding to the demand for greater transparency in their practices, thus providing the information the market requires to more accurately estimate the value the diversified firm is creating when using the unrelated diversification strategy.[89]

Creating financial economies by acquiring and restructuring other companies' assets requires an understanding of significant trade-offs. Success usually calls for a focus on mature, low-technology businesses because of the uncertainty of demand for high-technology products. Otherwise, resource allocation decisions become too complex, creating information-processing overload on the small corporate staffs of unrelated diversified firms. High-technology businesses are often human resource dependent; these people can leave or demand higher pay and thus appropriate or deplete the value of an acquired firm.[90] Service businesses with a client orientation are also difficult to buy and sell because of their client-based sales orientation. Sales staffs of service businesses are more mobile than those of manufacturing-oriented businesses and may seek jobs with a competitor, taking clients with them.[91] David Bell, CEO of Interpublic Group (IPG), has found it very difficult to manage the advertising agency conglomerate. IPG bought more than 300 advertising agencies and consulting firms in five years. Saddled with significant debt because it paid high prices for some of its acquisitions, IPG has not been able to gain economies of scope between the units; very few large firms have sought to take advantage of its global scale. The separate IPG agencies seem to be fiercely independent, and clients are mainly relationship based, because advertising is sold more through personal flare than firm reputation.[92] Thus, restructuring a service business can be a difficult strategy to effectively implement.

Diversification: Incentives and Resources

The economic reasons given in the preceding section summarize conditions under which diversification strategies can increase a firm's value. Diversification, however, is also often undertaken with the expectation that it will prevent reductions in firm value. Thus, there are reasons to diversify that are value neutral. In fact, some research suggests that all diversification leads to trade-offs and some suboptimization.[93] Nonetheless, as we explain next, several incentives may lead a firm to pursue further diversification.

Incentives to Diversify

Incentives to diversify come from both the external environment and a firm's internal environment. The term *incentive* implies that managers have choices. External incentives include antitrust regulations and tax laws. Internal incentives include low performance, uncertain future cash flows, and pursuit of synergy and reduction of risk for the firm. Several of these incentives are illustrated in the Strategic Focus on Yahoo!.

ANTITRUST REGULATION AND TAX LAWS

Government antitrust policies and tax laws provided incentives for U.S. firms to diversify in the 1960s and 1970s.[94] Antitrust laws prohibiting mergers that created increased market power (via either vertical or horizontal integration) were stringently enforced during that period.[95] As a result, many of the mergers during the 1960s and 1970s were "conglomerate" in character, involving companies pursuing different lines of business. Merger activity that produced conglomerate diversification was encouraged primarily by the Celler-Kefauver Antimerger Act (1950), which discouraged horizontal and vertical mergers. For example, between 1973 and 1977, 79.1 percent of all mergers were conglomerate.[96]

Yahoo!'s Low Performance and Uncertain Future Have Led to Strategic Diversification

After a brush with bankruptcy when the Internet bubble burst in 1999, Yahoo! has managed to improve performance under the management of new CEO Terry Semel. By changing the culture at Yahoo! from that of the quintessential "go-go" Internet start-up to a more conservative and principled style, Semel has made significant progress. Yahoo! realized poor performance along with many other Internet companies when its sky-high market capitalization evaporated in 1999. In addition, Yahoo! experienced continued uncertainty due to competition. Low performance and uncertainty created an incentive to change the firm's speculative approach. Accordingly, Semel guided Yahoo! in pursuing a diversification strategy that included acquiring HotJobs.com (a job search website) and Inktomi (focused on search engine technology), and forming partnerships with Overture Services, Inc. (a web advertising specialist) and SBC Communications (to extend Yahoo!'s services on SBC's broadband network). As a result of these diversification moves, revenues have grown significantly, and Yahoo! is profitable again. However, the market is competitive, and Yahoo! must continue to make appropriate investments to diversify its offerings.

Because Yahoo! began as a free service, its biggest obstacle has been finding a way to turn all of its viewers into paying customers. Looking to the future, Semel envisions Yahoo! as a "digital theme park" where customers can access a set of appealing offerings: digital music, online games, job listings, and premium e-mail. However, other firms, including media giant AOL Time Warner and software powerhouse Microsoft, have the same strategy, each with competitive advantages. AOL, for example, has access to a huge library of popular content from Time Warner while MSN benefits from Microsoft's software muscle and significant cash reserves as well as its broadband partnerships (like Yahoo!'s partnership with SBC Communications) that get it into 27 percent more homes than Yahoo!. Thus, although Yahoo!'s diversification strategy has helped it survive, the winner of this battle for domination is unknown. In addition to competing with AOL and MSN, Yahoo! competes in its original arena—search engines. The popular search engine Google is Yahoo!'s main rival in this arena, especially since Google won 4 percent more viewers in the last quarter of 2002 than did Yahoo!. Web surfers favor Google's uncluttered searches over Internet portals such as Yahoo! and MSN. This is important because advertisers are starting to shift advertising dollars from portals like Yahoo! to search engines like Google. This trend is occurring because "people are tuned out on banner ads and tuned in to search results." Banner ads are generally ignored, but when advertised products appear when a user instigates a search through a search engine, more exposure and sales success result. Yahoo! currently uses Google's search technology, but recently purchased Inktomi, another search technology firm, and may seek to move away from Google in order to gain additional revenue from advertisers.

Yahoo! competes in two different markets—web portals and search engines—with different competitors in each market. The firm has diversified the paid product offerings on its portal, including job opportunities through HotJobs.com, and is looking into deals

Terry Semel, chairman and CEO of Yahoo!, talks with Jean-Marie Messier (left), former chairman and CEO of Vivendi Universal, before a session of the World Economic Forum in New York.

AP Photo/Henny Abrams, Pool

to add online travel and classified ads for cars. Yahoo! is now more profitable, but the competition is stiff as the Internet moves to broadband offerings. Yahoo!'s continued profitability and survival depend on the quality of its diversification strategy.

SOURCES: 2003, A dotcom revival? *The Economist*, http//:www.economist.com, May 7; B. Elgin, 2003, Yahoo! Act two, *Business Week*, June 2, 70–76; B. Elgin, 2003, Can Yahoo! make the bounce last? Maybe, if new broadband and Net search efforts succeed, *Business Week*, February 17, 41; M. Mangalindan, 2003, Leading the news: Yahoo tops profit forecasts on 47% revenue jump, *Wall Street Journal*, April 10, A3.

During the 1980s, antitrust enforcement lessened, resulting in more and larger horizontal mergers (acquisitions of target firms in the same line of business, such as a merger between two oil companies).[97] In addition, investment bankers became more open to the kinds of mergers facilitated by the change in the regulation; as a consequence, takeovers increased to unprecedented numbers.[98] The conglomerates, or highly diversified firms, of the 1960s and 1970s became more "focused" in the 1980s and early 1990s as merger constraints were relaxed and restructuring was implemented.[99]

In the late 1990s and early 2000s, antitrust concerns emerged again with the large volume of mergers and acquisitions (see Chapter 7).[100] Thus, mergers are now receiving more scrutiny than they did in the 1980s and through the early 1990s.[101]

The tax effects of diversification stem not only from individual tax rates, but also from corporate tax changes. Some companies (especially mature ones) generate more cash from their operations than they can reinvest profitably. Some argue that *free cash flows* (liquid financial assets for which investments in current businesses are no longer economically viable) should be redistributed to shareholders as dividends.[102] However, in the 1960s and 1970s, dividends were taxed more heavily than ordinary personal income. As a result, before 1980, shareholders preferred that firms use free cash flows to buy and build companies in high-performance industries. If the firm's stock value appreciated over the long term, shareholders might receive a better return on those funds than if the funds had been redistributed as dividends, because returns from stock sales would be taxed more lightly under capital gains rules than would dividends.

Under the 1986 Tax Reform Act, however, the top individual ordinary income tax rate was reduced from 50 to 28 percent, and the special capital gains tax was also changed, treating capital gains as ordinary income. These changes created an incentive for shareholders to stop encouraging firms to retain funds for purposes of diversification. These tax law changes also influenced an increase in divestitures of unrelated business units after 1984. Thus, while individual tax rates for capital gains and dividends created a shareholder incentive to increase diversification before 1986, they encouraged less diversification after 1986, unless it was funded by tax-deductible debt. The elimination of personal interest deductions, as well as the lower attractiveness of retained earnings to shareholders, might prompt the use of more leverage by firms, for which interest expense is tax deductible.

Corporate tax laws also affect diversification. Acquisitions typically increase a firm's depreciable asset allowances. Increased depreciation (a non-cash-flow expense) produces lower taxable income, thereby providing an additional incentive for acquisitions. Before 1986, acquisitions may have been the most attractive means for securing tax benefits,[103] but the 1986 Tax Reform Act diminished some of the corporate tax advantages of diversification.[104] The recent changes recommended by the Financial Accounting Standards Board (FASB) regarding the elimination of the "pooling of interests" method for accounting for the acquired firm's assets and the elimination of the write-off for research and development in process reduce some of the incentives to make acquisitions, especially related acquisitions in high-technology industries (these changes are discussed further in Chapter 7).[105]

Although there was a loosening of federal regulations in the 1980s and a retightening in the late 1990s, a number of industries have experienced increased merger activity due to industry-specific deregulation activity, including banking, telecommunications, oil and gas, and electric utilities. Regulations changes have also affected convergence between media and telecommunications industries, which has allowed a number of mergers, such as the successive Time Warner and AOL Time Warner mergers. The Federal Communications Commission (FCC) has made a highly contested ruling "allowing broadcasters to own TV stations that reach 45 percent of U.S. households, up from 35 percent, own three stations in the largest markets (up from two) and own a TV station and newspaper in the same town."[106] Critics argued that the change in regulations would allow "an orgy of mergers and acquisitions" and that "it is a victory for free enterprise, but it is not a victory for free speech."[107] Because of the impending regulatory change, a number of firms have been eyeing potential acquisitions. For example, the FCC has allowed cable companies to get into local phone service. In Orange County, California, cable TV companies now provide 25 percent of local phone service. Phone companies have also been moving into selling TV service, although technology has been hindered until recently because high frequencies, which TV signals use, fade out on thin copper wires. At one point, to overcome this problem, SBC, a large local telephone operator, considered acquiring DirecTV, a satellite TV market leader.[108] Thus, regulatory changes create incentives for diversification.

LOW PERFORMANCE

Some research shows that low returns are related to greater levels of diversification.[109] If "high performance eliminates the need for greater diversification,"[110] then low performance may provide an incentive for diversification. As the Strategic Focus on Yahoo! illustrates, firms plagued by poor performance often take higher risks.[111] Poor performance may lead to increased diversification, as it did with Sears, Roebuck and Co., especially if resources exist to do so.[112] Sears has struggled on the edge of bankruptcy the past few years. Its high-margin appliance business is under attack from Home Depot and Lowe's. Sears has strong internal reasons to diversify, and it did so by purchasing clothes maker Lands' End in 2002. Sears expects that the company's high-quality image will improve its own apparel's reputation, although some question whether this will be at the cost of Lands' End's own reputation.[113] Continued poor returns following additional diversification, however, may slow the pace of diversification and even lead to divestitures.

This has happened to Sears previously. In 1981, Sears diversified into financial services by acquiring Coldwell Banker and Dean Witter Reynolds, Inc. The anticipated synergies in financial services did not materialize, and Sears' retail performance deteriorated. In 1992, Sears announced the divestiture of financial services and a refocusing on retail operations.[114] At least, the Lands' End acquisition is closely related to Sears' core business of retail sales.

A firm can overdiversify as Sears did earlier in its history. Thus, an overall curvilinear relationship, as illustrated in Figure 6.3, may exist between diversification and performance.[115] The German media company Bertelsmann was led by its former CEO Thomas Middelhoff into a variety of new ventures, especially Internet ones, that have proved to be a drag on the company's resources and have provided very little

Sears hopes that diversification through Lands' End apparel will increase the reputation of its own apparel and help push it out of the near-bankruptcy conditions it has experienced in the last few years.

© Susan Van Etten/PhotoEdit

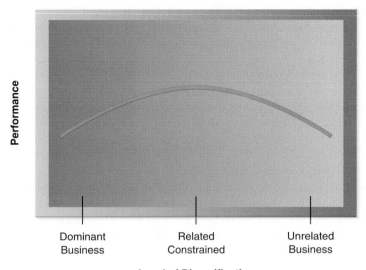

Level of Diversification

return on investment. The new CEO, Gunter Thielen, is emphasizing a return to basics by getting rid of non-core businesses, such as the Internet ventures. "The course has been pretty clear since Middelhoff left," says a German consultant: "Focus on the businesses that they understand and dominate." These businesses include producing books, magazines, music, and TV shows. Under Thielen's leadership, Bertelsmann has regrouped and refocused on what it does best.[116]

UNCERTAIN FUTURE CASH FLOWS

As a firm's product line matures or is threatened, diversification may be taken as an important defensive strategy.[117] Small firms and companies in mature or maturing industries sometimes find it necessary to diversify for long-term survival.[118] Yahoo!'s strategy has been built on diversification in order to survive competition from other portals such as AOL and MSN and search engine Google (see the Strategic Focus). Certainly, uncertainty was one of the dominant reasons for diversification among railroad firms during the 1960s and 1970s. Railroads diversified primarily because the trucking industry was perceived to have significant negative effects for rail transportation and thus created demand uncertainty. Uncertainty, however, can be derived from supply and distribution sources as well as from demand sources.

Intel is turning its core competence of technical development toward developing chips for cell phones. As the functions of PCs and phones continue to merge, Intel must learn to master wireless technology or begin to lose its core microprocessor market. With a goal to provide the "brains" of cellular phones, Intel is moving from just providing memory chips to providing the microprocessors for high-end cell phones. In the next iteration of its Manitoba chip, it will combine memory, processor, and voice transmission ability on a single chip. As Intel learns to bring its technological and financial resources (the company has $11 billion in cash) to bear on the market, it could change the handset market to a commodities market, threatening the profits and business models of handset makers.[119] But the move to diversify is driven by the uncertainty in the memory chip area for cell phones.

Diversified firms pursuing economies of scope often have investments that are too inflexible to realize synergy between business units. As a result, a number of problems may arise. **Synergy** exists when the value created by business units working together exceeds the value those same units create working independently. But, as a firm increases its relatedness between business units, it also increases its risk of corporate failure, because synergy produces joint interdependence between business units and the firm's flexibility to respond is constrained. This threat may force two basic decisions.

First, the firm may reduce its level of technological change by operating in more certain environments. This behavior may make the firm risk averse and thus uninterested in pursuing new product lines that have potential, but are not proven. Alternatively, the firm may constrain its level of activity sharing and forgo synergy's benefits. Either or both decisions may lead to further diversification. The former would lead to related diversification into industries in which more certainty exists. The latter may produce additional, but unrelated, diversification.[120] Research suggests that a firm using a related diversification strategy is more careful in bidding for new businesses, whereas a firm pursuing an unrelated diversification strategy may be more likely to overprice its bid, because an unrelated bidder may not have full information about the acquired firm.[121]

For example, Volkswagen's U.S. sales slipped almost 11 percent in the first quarter of 2003, and in Europe its Golf model was dethroned by Peugeot as the best-selling car. Net profit dropped 11.2 percent from the previous year. While there is tough competition in the auto industry, VW's conservative relatedness strategy is also partly to blame for the firm's foundering. All of its cars (from Audis to VWs to Skodas) are built on just a few platforms, which blurs brand image and cannibalizes sales within the group. Volkswagen has pursued related diversification in an effort to make operations more efficient, but in doing so, it has been too conservative in design and seems to have dimmed the distinctions between its auto brands.[122] The Crossfire, branded as a Chrysler product, is a bolder move because it is the first "synergistic" model offered to the market by Chrysler and Mercedes-Benz. Nearly 40 percent of the upscale car is based on Mercedes' content, "including its 3.2 liter engine, transmission and axles." However, the risk is that consumers will perceive it as a "Mercedes that is somewhat cheaper" and devalue the Mercedes brand.[123] Thus, although synergy is a strong incentive to diversify, it may compromise the pursuit of appropriate levels of diversification and risk.

Resources and Diversification

Although a firm may have incentives to diversify, it must also possess the resources required to create value through diversification.[124] As mentioned earlier, tangible, intangible, and financial resources all facilitate diversification. Resources vary in their utility for value creation, however, because of differences in rarity and mobility—that is, some resources are easier for competitors to duplicate because they are not rare, valuable, costly to imitate, and nonsubstitutable (see Chapter 3). For instance, free cash flows are a financial resource that may be used to diversify the firm. Because financial resources are more flexible and common, they are less likely to create value compared with other types of resources and less likely to be a source of competitive advantage.[125]

However, as a financial resource, cash can be used to invest in other resources that can lead to more valuable and less imitable advantages. For example, "Microsoft's net cash stash of $43 billion would, by itself, make it the 35th-largest company in the S&P 500 and exceeds the combined market values of Ford and General Motors."[126] With this much cash in reserve (more, by far, than any other company), Microsoft is able to invest heavily in R&D, to gradually build a market presence with products such as Xbox, Microsoft's video game machine, and to make diversifying acquisitions of other companies and new business ventures. "Microsoft is able to spend more than $4.3 billion a year on R&D."[127] This level of cash creates significant flexibility, allowing Microsoft to invest in new product ideas and provide the support required for an idea to evolve into a possible competitive advantage. Hence, as this example suggests, excess cash can be the conduit the firm needs to create more sustainable advantages.[128]

Tangible resources usually include the plant and equipment necessary to produce a product and tend to be less-flexible assets. Any excess capacity often can be used only for closely related products, especially those requiring highly similar manufacturing technologies. Excess capacity of other tangible resources, such as a sales force, can be used to diversify more easily. Again, excess capacity in a sales force is more effective with related diversification, because it may be utilized to sell similar products. The sales force would be more knowledgeable about related-product characteristics, customers, and distribution channels.[129] Tangible resources may create resource interrelationships in production, marketing, procurement, and technology, defined earlier as activity sharing. Intangible resources are more flexible than tangible physical assets in facilitating diversification. Although the sharing of tangible resources may induce diversification, intangible resources such as tacit knowledge could encourage even more diversification.[130]

Sometimes, however, the perceived resources advantages to diversification do not work out as expected. Media companies that invested in sports teams are realizing that they don't have the resources for this type of diversification and that their resources might be better spent elsewhere. News Corp., AOL Time Warner, and Disney are trying to sell the L.A. Dodgers, the Atlanta Braves, and the Anaheim Angels, respectively. Both Disney and News Corp. overvalued the teams they purchased as programming assets and undervalued their liabilities. Additionally, the traditional use of sports teams' losses as a tax write-off is less acceptable in the current rigorous corporate governance environment. Finally, cable TV economies have changed, and companies are unable to recoup astronomical player salaries through increased charges to cable operators. Unwilling to take additional losses, the media companies are seeking to sell the teams and divert their resources elsewhere.[131]

Managerial Motives to Diversify

Managerial motives for diversification may exist independently of incentives and resources and include managerial risk reduction and a desire for increased compensation.[132] For instance, diversification may reduce top-level managers' employment risk (the risk of job loss or income reduction). That is, corporate executives may diversify a firm in order to diversify their own employment risk, as long as profitability does not suffer excessively.[133]

Diversification provides an additional benefit to managers that shareholders do not enjoy. Diversification and firm size are highly correlated, and as size increases, so does executive compensation.[134] Large firms are more complex and difficult to manage; thus, managers of larger firms usually receive more compensation.[135] Higher compensation may serve as a motive for managers to engage in greater diversification. Governance mechanisms, such as the board of directors, monitoring by owners, executive compensation ceilings, and the market for corporate control, may limit managerial tendencies to overdiversify. These mechanisms are discussed in more detail in Chapter 10.

On the other hand, governance mechanisms may not be strong, and, in some instances, managers may diversify the firm to the point that it fails to earn even average returns.[136] The loss of adequate internal governance may result in poor relative performance, thereby triggering a threat of takeover. Although takeovers may improve efficiency by replacing ineffective managerial teams, managers may avoid takeovers through defensive tactics, such as "poison pills," or may reduce their own exposure with "golden parachute" agreements.[137] Therefore, an external governance threat, although restraining managers, does not flawlessly control managerial motives for diversification.[138]

Most large publicly held firms are profitable because managers are positive stewards of firm resources, and many of their strategic actions (e.g., diversification strategies) contribute to the firm's success.[139] As mentioned, governance devices should be designed to deal with exceptions to the norms of achieving strategic competitiveness and increasing shareholder wealth through the firm's earning of above-average returns. Thus, it is overly pessimistic to assume that managers usually act in their own self-interest as opposed to their firm's interest.[140]

Managers may also be held in check by concerns for their reputation. If a positive reputation facilitates power, a poor reputation may reduce it. Likewise, a strong external market for managerial talent may deter managers from pursuing inappropriate diversification.[141] In addition, a diversified firm may police other firms by acquiring those that are poorly managed in order to restructure its own asset base. Knowing that their firms could be acquired if they are not managed successfully encourages managers to use value-creating strategies.

Even when governance mechanisms cause managers to correct a problem of poorly implemented diversification or overdiversification, these moves are not without trade-offs. For instance, firms that are spun off may not realize productivity gains, even though spinning them off is in the best interest of the divesting firm.[142] Accordingly, the assumption that managers need disciplining may not be entirely correct, and sometimes governance may create consequences that are worse than those resulting from overdiversification. Governance that is excessive may cause a firm's managers to be overly cautious and risk averse.[143]

As shown in Figure 6.4, the level of diversification that can be expected to have the greatest positive effect on performance is based partly on how the interaction of resources, managerial motives, and incentives affects the adoption of particular diversification strategies. As indicated earlier, the greater the incentives and the more flexible the resources, the higher is the level of expected diversification. Financial resources (the most flexible) should have a stronger relationship to the extent of diversification than either tangible or intangible resources. Tangible resources (the most inflexible) are useful primarily for related diversification.

As discussed in this chapter, firms can create more value by effectively using diversification strategies. However, diversification must be kept in check by corporate governance (see Chapter 10). Appropriate strategy implementation tools, such as organizational structures, are also important (see Chapter 11).

We have described corporate-level strategies in this chapter. In the next one, we discuss mergers and acquisitions as prominent means for firms to diversify. These trends toward more diversification through acquisitions, which have been partially reversed due to restructuring (see Chapter 7), indicate that learning has taken place regarding corporate-level diversification strategies.[144] Accordingly, firms that diversify should do so cautiously, choosing to focus on relatively few, rather than many, businesses.[145] In fact, research suggests that although unrelated diversification has decreased, related diversification has increased, possibly due to the restructuring that continued into the 1990s and early 21st century.[146] This sequence of diversification followed by restructuring is now taking place in Europe and other places such as Korea, mirroring actions of firms in the United States and the United Kingdom.[147] Firms can improve their strategic competitiveness when they pursue a level of diversification that is appropriate for their resources (especially financial resources) and core competencies and the opportunities and threats in their country's institutional and competitive environments.[148]

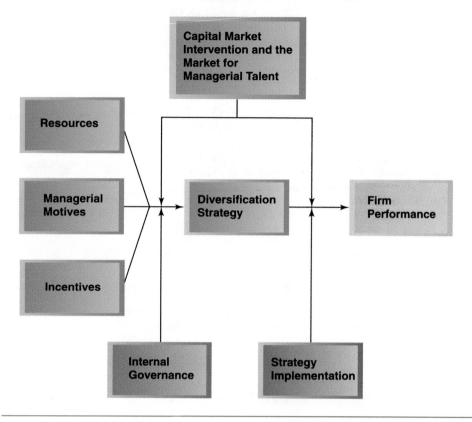

SOURCE: R. E. Hoskisson & M. A. Hitt, 1990, Antecedents and performance outcomes of diversification: A review and critique of theoretical perspectives, *Journal of Management,* 16: 498.

Summary

- Using a single- or dominant-business corporate-level strategy may be preferable to seeking a more diversified strategy, unless a corporation can develop economies of scope or financial economies between businesses, or unless it can obtain market power through additional levels of diversification. These economies and market power are the main sources of value creation when the firm diversifies.

- Related diversification creates value through the sharing of activities or the transfer of core competencies.

- Sharing activities usually involves sharing tangible resources between businesses. Transferring core competencies involves transferring core competencies developed in one business to another one. It also may involve transferring competencies between the corporate office and a business unit.

- Sharing activities is usually associated with the related constrained diversification corporate-level strategy. Activity sharing is costly to implement and coordinate, may create unequal benefits for the divisions involved in the sharing, and may lead to fewer managerial risk-taking behaviors.

- Transferring core competencies is often associated with related linked (or mixed related and unrelated) diversification, although firms pursuing both sharing activities and transferring core competencies can use it.

- Efficiently allocating resources or restructuring a target firm's assets and placing them under rigorous financial controls are two ways to accomplish successful unrelated diversification. These methods focus on obtaining financial economies.

- The primary reason a firm diversifies is to create more value. However, diversification is sometimes pursued because of incentives from tax and antitrust government policies, performance disappointments, or uncertainties about future cash flow, or to reduce risk.

- Managerial motives to diversify (including to increase compensation) can lead to overdiversification and a reduction in the firm's value-creating ability. On the other hand, managers can also be good stewards of the firm's assets.

- Managers need to pay attention to their firm's internal environment and its external environment when making decisions about the optimum level of diversification for their company. Of course, internal resources are important determinants of the direction that diversification should take. However, conditions in the firm's external environment may facilitate additional levels of diversification as might unexpected threats from competitors.

Review Questions

1. What is corporate-level strategy? Why is it important to the diversified firm?

2. What are the advantages and disadvantages of single- and dominant-business strategies, compared with those of firms with higher levels of diversification?

3. What are three reasons that firms choose to become more diversified by moving away from either a single- or a dominant-business corporate-level strategy?

4. How do firms share activities or transfer core competencies to obtain economies of scope when using a related diversification strategy?

5. What are the two ways to obtain financial economies when using an unrelated diversification strategy?

6. What incentives and resources encourage diversification?

7. What motives might encourage managers to diversify the firm beyond an appropriate level?

Experiential Exercises

Diversification: The Good and the Not So Good

As a member of the strategic management team for a very successful sporting goods firm that specializes in the manufacturing and marketing of soccer equipment, you have been asked to provide your thoughts as to whether the firm should diversify and to what extent.

Part One. List the advantages and disadvantages of diversification in the following table.

Part Two. Provide examples of related and unrelated diversification areas that you feel might be appropriate for the firm, including some specific advantages and disadvantages that the firm might find for each.

Advantages	Disadvantages

Diversification at Citibank

Organizations often anticipate that following a diversification strategy can create value on many fronts, including economies of scale and scope, along with increased market power. However, not all diversification efforts prove to be as successful as originally planned. Firms sometimes must reconsider their initial diversification strategy and frequently reverse or drastically alter their strategic decisions, often within a very short time frame. For instance, Citibank and Travelers Insurance Group merged in the late 1990s to form Citigroup, a huge financial supermarket of sorts that offered a plethora of products, including investment banking, credit cards, mortgages, insurance, and more. By 2002, Travelers Property Casualty Corporation had been spun out of Citigroup. Explore the circumstances and expected outcome of the original Travelers–Citibank merger. What went wrong? Could such problems have been avoided?

1. M. E. Porter, 1980, *Competitive Strategy*, New York: The Free Press, xvi.

2. W. P. Wan & R. E. Hoskisson, 2003, Home country environments, corporate diversification strategies and firm performance, *Academy of Management Journal*, 46: 27–45; D. D. Bergh, 2001, Diversification strategy research at a crossroads: Established, emerging and anticipated paths, in M. A. Hitt, R. E. Freeman, & J. S. Harrison (eds.), *Handbook of Strategic Management*, Oxford, UK: Blackwell Publishers, 363–383; E. Hoskisson, R. A. Johnson, D. Yiu, & W. P. Wan, 2001, Restructuring strategies of diversified business groups: Differences associated with country institutional environments, in M. A. Hitt, R. E. Freeman, & J. S. Harrison (eds.), *Handbook of Strategic Management*, Oxford, UK: Blackwell Publishers, 433–463.

3. E. H. Bowman & C. E. Helfat, 2001, Does corporate strategy matter? *Strategic Management Journal*, 22: 1–23; M. A. Hitt, R. E. Hoskisson, & H. Kim, 1997, International diversification: Effects on innovation and firm performance in product-diversified firms, *Academy of Management Journal*, 40: 767–798.

4. M. Mayer & R. Whittington, 2003, Diversification in context: A cross-national and cross-temporal extension, *Strategic Management Journal*, 24: 773–781; R. L. Simerly & M. Li, 2000, Environmental dynamism, capital structure and performance: A theoretical integration and an empirical test, *Strategic Management Journal*, 21: 31–49; D. D. Bergh & M. W. Lawless, 1998, Portfolio restructuring and limits to hierarchical governance: The effects of environmental uncertainty and diversification strategy, *Organization Science*, 9: 87–102.

5. M. E. Porter, 1987, From competitive advantage to corporate strategy, *Harvard Business Review*, 65(3): 43–59.

6. Porter, From competitive advantage to corporate strategy; C. A. Montgomery, 1994, Corporate diversification, *Journal of Economic Perspectives*, 8: 163–178.

7. M. Kwak, 2002, Maximizing value through diversification, *MIT Sloan Management Review*, 43(2): 10; R. A. Burgelman & Y. L. Doz, 2001, The power of strategic integration, *MIT Sloan Management Review*, 42(3): 28–38; C. C. Markides, 1997, To diversify or not to diversify, *Harvard Business Review*, 75(6): 93–99.

8. S. A. Mansi & D. M. Reeb, 2002, Corporate diversification: What gets discounted? *Journal of Finance*, 57: 2167–2183; P. Wright, M. Kroll, A. Lado, & B. Van Ness, 2002, The structure of ownership and corporate acquisition strategies, *Strategic Management Journal*, 23: 41–53; C. C. Markides & P. J. Williamson, 1996, Corporate diversification and organizational structure: A resource-based view, *Academy of Management Journal*, 39: 340–367.

9. A. Campbell, M. Goold, & M. Alexander, 1995, Corporate strategy: The question for parenting advantage, *Harvard Business Review*, 73(2): 120–132.

10. M. Goold & A. Campbell, 2002, Parenting in complex structures, *Long Range Planning*, 35(3): 219–243; T. H. Brush, P. Bromiley, & M. Hendrickx, 1999, The relative influence of industry and corporation on business segment performance: An alternative estimate, *Strategic Management Journal*, 20: 519–547; T. H. Brush & P. Bromiley, 1997, What does a small corporate effect mean? A variance components simulation of corporate and business effects, *Strategic Management Journal*, 18: 825–835.

11. J. B. Barney, 2002, *Gaining and Sustaining Competitive Advantage*, 2nd ed., Upper Saddle River, NJ: Prentice-Hall.

12. Bergh, Diversification strategy research at a crossroads, 363.

13. C. Kim, S. Kim, & C. Pantzalis, 2001, Firm diversification and earnings volatility: An empirical analysis of U.S.-based MNCs, *American Business Review*, 19(1): 26–38; W. Lewellen, 1971, A pure financial rationale for the conglomerate merger, *Journal of Finance*, 26: 521–537.

14. D. E. M. Sappington, 2003, Regulating horizontal diversification, *International Journal of Industrial Organization*, 21: 291–315.

15. H. von Kranenburg, M. Cloodt, & J. Hagedoorn, 2001, An exploratory story of recent trends in the diversification of Dutch publishing companies in the multimedia and information industries, *International Studies of Management & Organization*, 31(10): 64–86.

16. T. J. Douglas & J. A. Ryman, 2003, Understanding competitive advantage in the general hospital industry: Evaluating strategic competencies, *Strategic Management Journal*, 24: 333–347; B. S. Silverman, 1999, Technological resources and the direction of corporate diversification: Toward an integration of the resource-based view and transaction cost economics, *Management Science*, 45: 1109–1124; D. Collis & C. A. Montgomery, 1995, Competing on resources: Strategy in the 1990s, *Harvard Business Review*, 73(4): 118–128; M. A. Peteraf, 1993, The cornerstones of competitive advantage: A resource-based view, *Strategic Management Journal*, 14: 179–191.

17. T. J. Waite, 2002, Stick to the core—or go for more? *Harvard Business Review*, 80(2): 31–41.

18. Bergh, Diversification strategy research at a crossroads, 369.

19. R. P. Rumelt, *Strategy, Structure, and Economic Performance*, Boston: Harvard Business School, 1974; L. Wrigley, 1970, *Divisional Autonomy and Diversification* (Ph.D. dissertation), Harvard Business School.

20. J. Boorstin, 2003, Why is Wrigley so wrapper up? *Fortune*, March 3, 133–134.

21. T. Mason, 2001, Can gum and dental care mix? *Marketing*, August 23, 21.

22. Boorstin, Why is Wrigley so wrapper up?

23. S. Killman, 2001, Smithfield Foods CEO welcomes backlash over its hog farms, *Wall Street Journal*, August 21, B4; J. Forster, 2001, Who's afraid of a little mud? *Business Week*, May 21, 112–113.

24. S. Kilman, 2002, Farmland rebuffs Smithfield offer—Farm cooperative files for Chapter 11 protection, leaves door open to talks, *Wall Street Journal*, June 3, A6.

25. H. W. Choi, 2003, Korean leader poses challenge to conglomerates, *Wall Street Journal*, February 24, A13.

26. L. Fauver, J. Houston, & A. Naranjo, 2003, Capital market development, international integration, legal systems, and the value of corporate diversification: A cross-country analysis, *Journal of Financial and Quantitative Analysis*, 38: 135–157; Wan & Hoskisson, Home country environments, corporate diversification strategies and firm performance; T. Khanna & J. W. Rivkin, 2001, Estimating the performance effects of business groups in emerging markets, *Strategic Management Journal*, 22: 45–74; L. A. Keister, 2000, *Chinese Business Groups: The Structure and Impact of Inter-Firm Relations During Economic Development*, New York: Oxford University Press; T. Khanna & K. Palepu, 1997, Why focused strategies may be wrong for emerging markets, *Harvard Business Review*, 75(4): 41–50.

27. C. Chung, 2001, Markets, culture and institutions: The emergence of large business groups in Taiwan, 1950s–1970s, *Journal of Management Studies*, 38: 719–745.

28. S. Manikutty, 2000, Family business groups in India: A resource-based view of the emerging trends, *Family Business Review*, 13: 279–292.

29. 1997, Inside story, *The Economist*, December 6, 7–9.

30. S. P. Ferris, K. A. Kim, & P. Kitsabunnarat, 2003, The costs (and benefits?) of diversified business groups: The case of Korean chaebols, *Journal of Banking & Finance*, 27: 251–273; S. J. Chang & J. Hong, 2002, How much does the business group matter in Korea? *Strategic Management Journal*, 23: 265–274; K. V. Lins & H. Servaes, 2002, Is corporate diversification beneficial in emerging markets? *Financial Management*, 31(2): 5–31.

31. K. Dewenter, W. Novaes, & R. H. Pettway, 2001, Visibility versus complexity in business groups: Evidence from Japanese keiretsus, *Journal of Business*, 74: 79–100.

32. Fauver, Houston, & Naranjo, Capital market development, international integration, legal systems, and the value of corporate diversification; Wan & Hoskisson, Home country environments, corporate diversification strategies and firm performance.

33. R. K. Aggarwal & A. A. Samwick, 2003, Why do managers diversify their firms? Agency reconsidered, *Journal of Finance*, 58: 71–118; P. Wright, M. Kroll, & D. Elenkov, 2002, Acquisition returns, increase in firm size, and chief executive officer compensation: The moderating role of monitoring, *Academy of Management Journal*, 45: 599–608.

34. J. Song, 2002, Firm capabilities and technology ladders, *Strategic Management Journal*, 23: 191–210; J. Lampel & J. Shamsie, 2000, Probing the unobtrusive link: Dominant logic and the design of joint ventures at General Electric, *Strategic Management Journal*, 21: 593–602; M. Farjoun, 1998, The independent and joint effects of the skill and physical bases of relatedness in diversification, *Strategic Management Journal*, 19: 611–630.

35. R. E. Hoskisson & L.W. Busenitz, 2002, Market uncertainty and learning distance in corporate entrepreneurship entry mode choice, in M. A. Hitt, R. D. Ireland, S. M. Camp, & D. L. Sexton (eds.), *Strategic Entrepreneurship: Creating a New Mindset*, Oxford, UK: Blackwell Publishers, 150–172;

A. Seth, K. P. Song, & R. R. Pettit, 2002, Value creation and destruction in cross-border acquisitions: An empirical analysis of foreign acquisitions of U.S. firms, *Strategic Management Journal*, 23: 921–940.

36. J. A. Doukas & L. H. P. Lang, 2003, Foreign direct investment, diversification and firm performance, *Journal of International Business Studies*, 34: 153–172; L. Capron, 1999, The long term performance of horizontal acquisitions, *Strategic Management Journal*, 20: 987–1018.

37. M. E. Porter, 1985, *Competitive Advantage*, New York: The Free Press, 328.

38. R. G. Schroeder, K. A. Bates, & M.A. Junttila, 2002, A resource-based view of manufacturing strategy and the relationship to manufacturing performance, *Strategic Management Journal*, 23: 105–117.

39. D. Gupta & Y. Gerchak, 2002, Quantifying operational synergies in a merger/acquisition, *Management Science*, 48: 517–533.

40. B. Caulfield, 2003, Saving $3 billion the HP way, *Business 2.0*, May, 52–54.

41. Ibid.

42. M. L. Marks & P. H. Mirvis, 2000, Managing mergers, acquisitions, and alliances: Creating an effective transition structure, *Organizational Dynamics*, 28(3): 35–47.

43. C. Park, 2003, Prior performance characteristics of related and unrelated acquirers, *Strategic Management Journal*, 24: 471–480; G. Delong, 2001, Stockholder gains from focusing versus diversifying bank mergers, *Journal of Financial Economics*, 2: 221–252; T. H. Brush, 1996, Predicted change in operational synergy and post-acquisition performance of acquired businesses, *Strategic Management Journal*, 17: 1–24; H. Zhang, 1995, Wealth effects of U.S. bank takeovers, *Applied Financial Economics*, 5: 329–336.

44. D. D. Bergh, 1995, Size and relatedness of units sold: An agency theory and resource-based perspective, *Strategic Management Journal*, 16: 221–239.

45. M. Lubatkin & S. Chatterjee, 1994, Extending modern portfolio theory into the domain of corporate diversification: Does it apply? *Academy of Management Journal*, 37: 109–136.

46. A. Van Oijen, 2001, Product diversification, corporate management instruments, resource sharing, and performance, *Academy of Management Best Paper Proceedings* (on CD-ROM, Business Policy and Strategy Division); T. Kono, 1999, A strong head office makes a strong company, *Long Range Planning*, 32(2): 225.

47. M. Kotabe, X. Martin, & H. Domoto, 2003, Gaining from vertical partnerships: Knowledge transfer, relationship duration, and supplier performance improvement in the U.S. and Japanese automotive industries, *Strategic Management Journal*, 24: 293–316; M. Y. Brannen, J. K. Liker, & W. M. Fruin, 1999, Recontextualization and factory-to-factory knowledge transfer from Japan to the U.S.: The case of NSK, in J. K. Liker, W. M. Fruin, & P. Adler (eds.), *Remade in America: Transplanting and Transforming Japanese Systems*, New York: Oxford University Press, 117–153; L. Capron, P. Dussauge, & W. Mitchell, 1998, Resource redeployment following horizontal acquisitions in Europe and the United States, 1988–1992, *Strategic Management Journal*, 19: 631–661; A. Mehra, 1996, Resource and market based determinants of performance in the U.S. banking industry, *Strategic Management Journal*, 17: 307–322; S. Chatterjee & B. Wernerfelt, 1991, The link between resources and type of diversification: Theory and evidence, *Strategic Management Journal*, 12: 33–48.

48. S. Dutta, M. J. Zbaracki, & M. Bergen, 2003, Pricing process as a capability: A resource-based perspective, *Strategic Management Journal*, 24: 615–630.

49. L. Capron & N. Pistre, 2002, When do acquirers earn abnormal returns? *Strategic Management Journal*, 23: 781–794.

50. J. W. Spencer, 2003, Firms' knowledge-sharing strategies in the global innovation system: Empirical evidence from the flat panel display industry, *Strategic Management Journal*, 24: 217–233.

51. G. Edmondson, 2003, Pininfarina's snazzy new design—for itself, *Business Week*, March 3, 56.

52. G. Marcial, 2003, Cendant comes back, *BusinessWeek Online*, http://www.businessweek.com, May 12; A. Tsao, 2003, Just the ticket for travel stocks, *BusinessWeek Online*, http://www.businessweek.com, March 19.

53. B. Einhorn, F. Balfour, & K. Capell, 2002, More Virgin territory, *Business Week*, April 8, 25; R. Whittington, 1999, In praise of the evergreen conglomerate, "Mastering Strategy" (Part 6), *Financial Times*, November 1, 4–6; W. Ruigrok, A. Pettigrew, S. Peck, & R. Whittington, 1999, Corporate restructuring and new forms of organizing: Evidence from Europe, *Management International Review*, 39 (Special Issue): 41–64.

54. A. Barrett, 2002, Keep it simple, Cendant, Wall Street is slamming the company for complex financials, *Business Week*, October 14, 54.

55. C. Zellner & D. Fornahl, 2002, Scientific knowledge and implications for its diffusion, *Journal of Knowledge Management*, 6(2): 190–198.

56. C. St. John & J. S. Harrison, 1999, Manufacturing-based relatedness, synergy, and coordination, *Strategic Management Journal*, 20: 129–145.

57. S. Chatterjee & J. Singh, 1999, Are tradeoffs inherent in diversification moves? A simultaneous model for type of diversification and mode of expansion decisions, *Management Science*, 45: 25–41.

58. G. Symeonidis, 2002, Cartel stability with multiproduct firms, *International Journal of Industrial Organization*, 20: 339–352; J. Gimeno & C. Y. Woo, 1999, Multimarket contact, economies of scope, and firm performance, *Academy of Management Journal*, 42: 239–259.

59. R. Brooks, 2003, DHL Airways' CEO-led buyout moves forward, *Wall Street Journal* (Eastern Edition), May 22, B4.

60. L. Wozniak, 2003, DHL and FedEx race to integrate China, *Far Eastern Economic Review*, February 27, 42–44.

61. A. Darr & I. Talmud, 2003, The structure of knowledge and seller-buyer networks in markets for emergent technologies, *Organization Studies*, 24: 443–461.

62. O. E. Williamson, 1996, Economics and organization: A primer, *California Management Review*, 38(2): 131–146.

63. D. Leonard, 2003, Songs in the key of Steve, *Fortune*, May 12, 52–62.

64. R. Barker, 2003, How high will Medco fly on its own? *Business Week*, May 26, 118.

65. L. R. Kopczak & M. E. Johnson, 2003, The supply-chain management effect, *MIT Sloan Management Review*, 3: 27–34; K. R. Harrigan, 2001, Strategic flexibility in the old and new economies, in M. A. Hitt, R. E. Freeman, & J. S. Harrison (eds.), *Handbook of Strategic Management*, Oxford, UK: Blackwell Publishers, 97–123.

66. M. R. Subramani & N. Venkatraman, 2003, Safeguarding investments in asymmetric interorganizational relationships: Theory and evidence, *Academy of Management Journal*, 46: 46–62; R. E. Kranton & D. F. Minehart, 2001, Networks versus vertical integration, *Rand Journal of Economics*, 3: 570–601.

67. C. Serant, 2003, Mexico spins a new orbit—The country's venerable contract manufacturing complex is assuming a dramatic new form as China asserts its position as the EMS industry's cost leader, *EBN*, January 20, 27.

68. P. Kothandaraman & D. T. Wilson, 2001, The future of competition: Value-creating networks, *Industrial Marketing Management*, 30: 379–389.

69. K. M. Eisenhardt & D. C. Galunic, 2000, Coevolving: At last, a way to make synergies work, *Harvard Business Review*, 78(1): 91–111.

70. R. Schoenberg, 2001, Knowledge transfer and resource sharing as value creation mechanisms in inbound continental European acquisitions, *Journal of Euro-Marketing*, 10: 99–114.

71. Eisenhardt & Galunic, Coevolving, 94.

72. M. Freeman, 2002, Forging a model for profitability, *Electronic Media*, January 28, 1, 13.

73. D. D. Bergh, 1997, Predicting divestiture of unrelated acquisitions: An integrative model of ex ante conditions, *Strategic Management Journal*, 18: 715–731; C. W. L. Hill, 1994, Diversification and economic performance: Bringing structure and corporate management back into the picture, in R. P. Rumelt, D. E. Schendel, & D. J. Teece (eds.), *Fundamental Issues in Strategy*, Boston: Harvard Business School Press, 297–321.

74. Porter, *Competitive Advantage*.

75. O. E. Williamson, 1975, *Markets and Hierarchies: Analysis and Antitrust Implications*, New York: Macmillan Free Press.

76. J. T. Harper & J. Madura, 2002, Sources of hidden value and risk within tracking stock, *Financial Management*, 31(3): 91–109; M. T. Billet & D. Mauer, 2001, Diversification and the value of internal capital markets: The case of tracking stock, *Journal of Banking & Finance*, 9: 1457–1490.

77. A. Pasztor, 2003, Hughes Electronics has sharply narrower loss, *Wall Street Journal*, April 15, B3.

78. J. McTague, 2002, Security in numbers, *Barron's*, December 30, 26; C. Botosan & M. Harris, 2000, Motivations for changes in disclosure frequency and its consequences: An examination of voluntary quarterly segment disclosure, *Journal of Accounting Research*, 38: 329–353; R. Kochhar & M. A. Hitt, 1998, Linking corporate strategy to capital structure: Diversification strategy, type, and source of financing, *Strategic Management Journal*, 19: 601–610.

79. D. Miller, R. Eisenstat, & N. Foote, 2002, Strategy from the inside out: Building capability-creating organizations, *California Management Review*, 44(3): 37–54; M. E. Raynor & J. L. Bower, 2001, Lead from the center:

How to manage divisions dynamically, *Harvard Business Review*, 79(5): 92–100; P. Taylor & J. Lowe, 1995, A note on corporate strategy and capital structure, *Strategic Management Journal*, 16: 411–414.

80. J. M. Campa & S. Kedia, 2002, Explaining the diversification discount, *Journal of Finance*, 57: 1731–1762; M. Kwak, 2001, Spinoffs lead to better financing decisions, *MIT Sloan Management Review*, 42(4): 10; O. A. Lamont & C. Polk, 2001, The diversification discount: Cash flows versus returns, *Journal of Finance*, 56: 1693–1721; R. Rajan, H. Servaes, & L. Zingales, 2001, The cost of diversity: The diversification discount and inefficient investment, *Journal of Finance*, 55: 35–79.

81. 2001, Spoilt for choice, *The Economist*, http://www.economist.com, July 5.

82. D. J. Denis, D. K. Denis, & A. Sarin, 1999, Agency theory and the reference of equity ownership structure on corporate diversification strategies, *Strategic Management Journal*, 20: 1071–1076; R. Amit & J. Livnat, 1988, A concept of conglomerate diversification, *Journal of Management*, 14: 593–604.

83. Whittington, In praise of the evergreen conglomerate, 4.

84. Khanna & Rivkin, Estimating the performance effects of business groups in emerging markets.

85. T. Khanna & K. Palepu, 2000, Is group affiliation profitable in emerging markets? An analysis of diversified Indian business groups, *Journal of Finance*, 55: 867–892; T. Khanna & K. Palepu, 2000, The future of business groups in emerging markets: Long-run evidence from Chile, *Academy of Management Journal*, 43: 268–285.

86. R. E. Hoskisson, R. A. Johnson, D. Yiu, & W. P. Wan, 2001. Restructuring strategies and diversified business groups: Differences associated with country institutional environments, in M. A. Hitt, R. E. Freeman, & J. S. Harrison (eds.), *Handbook of Strategic Management*, Oxford, UK: Blackwell Publishers, 433–463; S. J. Chang & H. Singh, 1999, The impact of entry and resource fit on modes of exit by multibusiness firms, *Strategic Management Journal*, 20: 1019–1035.

87. W. Ng & C. de Cock, 2002, Battle in the boardroom: A discursive perspective, *Journal of Management Studies*, 39: 23–49.

88. P. Gogoi, 2003, Sara Lee: No piece of cake, *Business Week*, May 26, 66–68.

89. M. Warner, 2003, Exorcism at Tyco: CEO Ed Breen & Co. aim to run a big, solid, and, yes, boring company, *Fortune*, April 28, 106.

90. R. Coff, 2003, Bidding wars over R&D-intensive firms: Knowledge, opportunism, and the market for corporate control, *Academy of Management Journal*, 46: 74–85.

91. S. Nambisan, 2001, Why service businesses are not product businesses, *MIT Sloan Management Review*, 42(4): 72–80.

92. G. Khermouch, 2003, Interpublic Group: Synergy—or sinkhole? *Business Week*, April 21, 76–77.

93. E. Stickel, 2001, Uncertainty reduction in a competitive environment, *Journal of Business Research*, 51: 169–177; Chatterjee & Singh, Are tradeoffs inherent in diversification moves?

94. M. Lubatkin, H. Merchant, & M. Srinivasan, 1997, Merger strategies and shareholder value during times of relaxed antitrust enforcement: The case of large mergers during the 1980s, *Journal of Management*, 23: 61–81.

95. D. P. Champlin & J. T. Knoedler, 1999, Restructuring by design? Government's complicity in corporate restructuring, *Journal of Economic Issues*, 33(1): 41–57.

96. R. M. Scherer & D. Ross, 1990, *Industrial Market Structure and Economic Performance*, Boston: Houghton Mifflin.

97. A. Shleifer & R. W. Vishny, 1994, Takeovers in the 1960s and 1980s: Evidence and implications, in R. P. Rumelt, D. E. Schendel, & D. J. Teece (eds.), *Fundamental Issues in Strategy*, Boston: Harvard Business School Press, 403–422.

98. S. Chatterjee, J. S. Harrison, & D. D. Bergh, 2003, Failed takeover attempts, corporate governance and refocusing, *Strategic Management Journal*, 24: 87–96; Lubatkin, Merchant, & Srinivasan, Merger strategies and shareholder value; D. J. Ravenscraft & R. M. Scherer, 1987, *Mergers, Sell-Offs and Economic Efficiency*, Washington, DC: Brookings Institution, 22.

99. D. A. Zalewski, 2001, Corporate takeovers, fairness, and public policy, *Journal of Economic Issues*, 35: 431–437; P. L. Zweig, J. P. Kline, S. A. Forest, & K. Gudridge, 1995, The case against mergers, *Business Week*, October 30, 122–130; J. R. Williams, B. L. Paez, & L. Sanders, 1988, Conglomerates revisited, *Strategic Management Journal*, 9: 403–414.

100. E. J. Lopez, 2001, New anti-merger theories: A critique, *Cato Journal*, 20: 359–378; 1998, The trustbusters' new tools, *The Economist*, May 2, 62–64.

101. R. Croyle & P. Kager, 2002, Giving mergers a head start, *Harvard Business Review*, 80(10): 20–21.

102. M. C. Jensen, 1986, Agency costs of free cash flow, corporate finance, and takeovers, *American Economic Review*, 76: 323–329.

103. R. Gilson, M. Scholes, & M. Wolfson, 1988, Taxation and the dynamics of corporate control: The uncertain case for tax motivated acquisitions, in J. C. Coffee, L. Lowenstein, & S. Rose-Ackerman (eds.), *Knights, Raiders, and Targets: The Impact of the Hostile Takeover*, New York: Oxford University Press, 271–299.

104. C. Steindel, 1986, Tax reform and the merger and acquisition market: The repeal of the general utilities, *Federal Reserve Bank of New York Quarterly Review*, 11(3): 31–35.

105. M. A. Hitt, J. S. Harrison, & R. D. Ireland, 2001, *Mergers and Acquisitions: A Guide to Creating Value for Stakeholders*, New York: Oxford University Press.

106. D. B. Wilkerson & Russ Britt, 2003, It's showtime for media deals: Radio lessons fuel debate over control of TV, newspapers, CBS MarketWatch, http://cbs.marketwatch.com, May 30.

107. S. Labaton, 2003, Senators move to restore F.C.C. limits on the media, *New York Times*, http//:www.nytimes.com, June 5.

108. S. Wooley, 2003, Telco TV (take 2), *Forbes*, May 12, 68.

109. C. Park, 2002, The effects of prior performance on the choice between related and unrelated acquisitions: Implications for the performance consequences of diversification strategy, *Journal of Management Studies*, 39: 1003–1019.

110. Rumelt, *Strategy, Structure and Economic Performance*, 125.

111. M. N. Nickel & M. C. Rodriguez, 2002, A review of research on the negative accounting relationship between risk and return: Bowman's paradox, *Omega*, 30(1): 1–18; R. M. Wiseman & L. R. Gomez-Mejia, 1998, A behavioral agency model of managerial risk taking, *Academy of Management Review*, 23: 133–153; E. H. Bowman, 1982, Risk seeking by troubled firms, *Sloan Management Review*, 23: 33–42.

112. J. G. Matsusaka, 2001, Corporate diversification, value maximization, and organizational capabilities, *Journal of Business*, 74: 409–432.

113. R. Berner, 2003, Dark days in white goods for Sears, *Business Week*, March 10, 78–79.

114. S. L. Gillan, J. W. Kensinger, & J. D. Martin, 2000, Value creation and corporate diversification: The case of Sears, Roebuck & Co., *Journal of Financial Economics*, 55: 103–137.

115. L. E. Palich, L. B. Cardinal, & C. C. Miller, 2000, Curvilinearity in the diversification-performance linkage: An examination of over three decades of research, *Strategic Management Journal*, 21: 155–174.

116. J. Ewing, 2003, Back to basics, *Business Week*, March 10, 46–47.

117. A. E. Bernardo & B. Chowdhry, 2002, Resources, real options, and corporate strategy, *Journal of Financial Economics*, 63: 211–234; Simerly & Li, Environmental dynamism, capital structure and performance; Bergh & Lawless, Portfolio restructuring and limits to hierarchical governance.

118. N. W. C. Harper & S. P. Viguerie, 2002, Are you too focused? *The McKinsey Quarterly*, Mid-Summer, 29–38; J. C. Sandvig & L. Coakley, 1998, Best practices in small firm diversification, *Business Horizons*, 41(3): 33–40; C. G. Smith & A. C. Cooper, 1988, Established companies diversifying into young industries: A comparison of firms with different levels of performance, *Strategic Management Journal*, 9: 111–121.

119. C. Edwards, A. Reinhardt, & R. O. Crockett, 2003, The hulk haunting cell phones, *Business Week*, March 3, 44.

120. N. M. Kay & A. Diamantopoulos, 1987, Uncertainty and synergy: Towards a formal model of corporate strategy, *Managerial and Decision Economics*, 8: 121–130.

121. M. E. Raynor, 2002, Diversification as real options and the implications of firm-specific risk and performance, *Engineering Economist*, 47(4): 371–389; R. W. Coff, 1999, How buyers cope with uncertainty when acquiring firms in knowledge-intensive industries: Caveat emptor, *Organization Science*, 10: 144–161.

122. G. Edmondson, 2003, Volkswagen needs a jump, *Business Week*, May 12, 48–49.

123. J. Muller, 2003, Crossbreed: Is it a Chrysler or a Mercedes? Only your engineer knows for sure, *Forbes*, March 17, 54.

124. Chatterjee & Singh, Are tradeoffs inherent in diversification moves?; S. J. Chatterjee & B. Wernerfelt, 1991, The link between resources and type of diversification: Theory and evidence, *Strategic Management Journal*, 12: 33–48.

125. W. Keuslein, 2003, The Ebitda folly, *Forbes*, March 17, 165–167; Kochhar & Hitt, Linking corporate strategy to capital structure.

126. 2003, Microsoft's cash stash, *Kiplinger's Personal Finance*, May, 37; J. Greene, 2001, Microsoft: How it became stronger than ever, *Business Week*, June 4, 75–85.

127. M. Sivy, 2003, The big payoff from R&D, *Money*, June, 63–64.

128. K. Haanes & O. Fjeldstad, 2000, Linking intangible resources and competition, *European Management Journal*, 18(1): 52–62.

129. L. Capron & J. Hulland, 1999, Redeployment of brands, sales forces, and general marketing management expertise following horizontal acquisitions: A resource-based view, *Journal of Marketing*, 63(2): 41–54.

130. A. M. Knott, D. J. Bryce, & H. E. Pose, 2003, On the strategic accumulation of intangible assets, *Organization Science*, 14: 192–207; J. Castillo, 2002, A note on the concept of tacit knowledge, *Journal of Management Inquiry*, 11(1): 46–57; R. D. Smith, 2000, Intangible strategic assets and firm performance: A multi-industry study of the resource-based view, *Journal of Business Strategies*, 17(2): 91–117.

131. J. Helyar, 2003, Media strike out, *Fortune*, March 17, 42.

132. J. G. Combs & M. S. Skill, 2003, Managerialist and human capital explanation for key executive pay premiums: A contingency perspective, *Academy of Management Journal*, 46: 63–73; M. A. Geletkanycz, B. K. Boyd, & S. Finkelstein, 2001, The strategic value of CEO external directorate networks: Implications for CEO compensation, *Strategic Management Journal*, 9: 889–898; W. Grossman & R. E. Hoskisson, 1998, CEO pay at the crossroads of Wall Street and Main: Toward the strategic design of executive compensation, *Academy of Management Executive*, 12(1): 43–57; S. Finkelstein & D. C. Hambrick, 1996, *Strategic Leadership: Top Executives and Their Effects on Organizations*, St. Paul, MN: West Publishing Company.

133. Aggarwal & Samwick, Why do managers diversify their firms?; W. Shen & A. A. Cannella, Jr., 2002, Power dynamics within top management and their impacts on CEO dismissal followed by inside succession, *Academy of Management Journal*, 45: 1195–1206; W. Shen & A. A. Cannella, Jr., 2002, Revisiting the performance consequences of CEO succession: The impacts of successor type, postsuccession senior executive turnover, and departing CEO tenure, *Academy of Management Journal*, 45: 717–733; P. J. Lane, A. A. Cannella, Jr., & M. H. Lubatkin, 1998, Agency problems as antecedents to unrelated mergers and diversification: Amihud and Lev reconsidered, *Strategic Management Journal*, 19: 555–578; D. L. May, 1995, Do managerial motives influence firm risk reduction strategies? *Journal of Finance*, 50: 1291–1308; Y. Amihud and B. Lev, 1981, Risk reduction as a managerial motive for conglomerate mergers, *Bell Journal of Economics*, 12: 605–617.

134. J. J. Cordeiro & R. Veliyath, 2003, Beyond pay for performance: A panel study of the determinants of CEO compensation, *American Business Review*, 21(1): 56–66; Wright, Kroll, & Elenkov, Acquisition returns, increase in firm size, and chief executive officer compensation; S. R. Gray & A. A. Cannella, Jr., 1997, The role of risk in executive compensation, *Journal of Management*, 23: 517–540.

135. Combs & Skill, Managerialist and human capital explanation for key executive pay premiums; R. Bliss & R. Rosen, 2001, CEO compensation and bank mergers, *Journal of Financial Economics*, 1:107–138; W. G. Sanders & M. A. Carpenter, 1998, Internationalization and firm governance: The roles of CEO compensation, top team composition, and board structure, *Academy of Management Journal*, 41: 158–178.

136. J. J. Janney, 2002, Eat or get eaten? How equity ownership and diversification shape CEO risk-taking, *Academy of Management Executive*, 14(4): 157–158; J. W. Lorsch, A. S. Zelleke, & K. Pick, 2001, Unbalanced boards, *Harvard Business Review*, 79(2): 28–30; R. E. Hoskisson & T. Turk, 1990, Corporate restructuring: Governance and control limits of the internal market, *Academy of Management Review*, 15: 459–477.

137. M. Kahan & E. B. Rock, 2002, How I learned to stop worrying and love the pill: Adaptive responses to takeover law, *University of Chicago Law Review*, 69(3): 871–915.

138. R. C. Anderson, T. W. Bates, J. M. Bizjak, & M. L. Lemmon, 2000, Corporate governance and firm diversification, *Financial Management*, 29(1): 5–22; J. D. Westphal, 1998, Board games: How CEOs adapt to increases in structural board independence from management, *Administrative Science Quarterly*, 43: 511–537; J. K. Seward & J. P. Walsh, 1996, The governance and control of voluntary corporate spin offs, *Strategic Management Journal*, 17: 25–39; J. P. Walsh & J. K. Seward, 1990, On the efficiency of internal and external corporate control mechanisms, *Academy of Management Review*, 15: 421–458.

139. M. Wiersema, 2002, Holes at the top: Why CEO firings backfire, *Harvard Business Review*, 80(12): 70–77.

140. V. Kisfalvi & P. Pitcher, 2003, Doing what feels right: The influence of CEO character and emotions on top management team dynamics, *Journal of Management Inquiry*, 12(10): 42–66; R. Larsson, K. R. Brousseau, M. J. Driver, & M. Homqvist, 2003, International growth through cooperation: Brand-driven strategies, leadership, and career development in Sweden, *Academy of Management Executive*, 17(1): 7–21; W. G. Bennis & R. J. Thomas, 2002, Crucibles of leadership, *Harvard Business Review*, 80(9): 39–45; W. G. Rowe, 2001, Creating wealth in organizations: The role of strategic leadership, *Academy of Management Executive*, 15(1): 81–94.

141. E. F. Fama, 1980, Agency problems and the theory of the firm, *Journal of Political Economy*, 88: 288–307.

142. H. Chesbrough, 2003, The governance and performance of Xerox's technology spin-off companies, *Research Policy*, 32(3): 403–421; R. A. Johnson, 1996, Antecedents and outcomes of corporate refocusing, *Journal of Management*, 22: 439–483; C. Y. Woo, G. E. Willard, & U. S. Dallenbach, 1992, Spin-off performance: A case of overstated expectations, *Strategic Management Journal*, 13: 433–448.

143. M. Wright, R. E. Hoskisson, & L. W. Busenitz, 2001, Firm rebirth: Buyouts as facilitators of strategic growth and entrepreneurship, *Academy of Management Executive*, 15(1): 111–125; H. Kim & R. E. Hoskisson, 1996, Japanese governance systems: A critical review, in S. B. Prasad (ed.), *Advances in International Comparative Management*, Greenwich, CT: JAI Press, 165–189.

144. M. L. A. Hayward, 2002, When do firms learn from their acquisition experience? Evidence from 1990–1995, *Strategic Management Journal*, 23: 21–39; L. Capron, W. Mitchell, & A. Swaminathan, 2001, Asset divestiture following horizontal acquisitions: A dynamic view, *Strategic Management Journal*, 22: 817–844.

145. Bergh, Diversification strategy research at a crossroads, 370–371; W. M. Bulkeley, 1994, Conglomerates make a surprising come-back—with a '90s twist, *Wall Street Journal*, March 1, A1, A6.

146. J. P. H. Fan & L. H. P. Lang, 2000, The measurement of relatedness: An application to corporate diversification, *Journal of Business*, 73: 629–660.

147. Khanna & Palepu, The future of business groups in emerging markets; P. Ghemawat & T. Khanna, 1998, The nature of diversified business groups: A research design and two case studies, *Journal of Industrial Economics*, 46: 35–61.

148. Wan & Hoskisson, Home country environments, corporate diversification strategies, and firm performance.

Acquisition and Restructuring Strategies

Chapter Seven 7

Knowledge Objectives

Studying this chapter should provide you with the strategic management knowledge needed to:

1. Explain the popularity of acquisition strategies in firms competing in the global economy.

2. Discuss reasons firms use an acquisition strategy to achieve strategic competitiveness.

3. Describe seven problems that work against developing a competitive advantage using an acquisition strategy.

4. Name and describe attributes of effective acquisitions.

5. Define the restructuring strategy and distinguish among its common forms.

6. Explain the short- and long-term outcomes of the different types of restructuring strategies.

Getty/PhotoDisc, Inc.

News Corporation has an opportunity for complementarity through the vertical acquisition of a satellite television producer, DirecTV, to distribute the content it already produces.

Comparing the Acquisition Strategies of News Corp. and AOL Time Warner

Beginning with an Australian newspaper inherited from his father, Rupert Murdoch built News Corporation and continues to manage it today. He has a large ownership position in the company and includes family members in its management structure. He began acquiring British newspapers in the 1970s, and then began an acquisition program in the United States in 1976 when he acquired the *New York Post*. Books (Harper-Collins), magazines (*TV Guide*), television networks (Fox), and movies (Twentieth Century Fox) have been added to make News Corp. the most profitable media company in the world in 2002. Murdoch recently acquired a controlling interest in DirecTV by offering $6.6 billion to buy General Motors' 20 percent stake in Hughes Electronics. The deal for DirecTV, a satellite television producer, is a vertical acquisition (defined later in the chapter), which gives Murdoch's firm another media distribution outlet for the content that it produces. Through both vertical and horizontal acquisitions (defined later in the chapter) as well as starting businesses internally, Murdoch has made his company influential and powerful in the media industry.

Rupert Murdoch is sworn in during a hearing before the House Committee on the Judiciary, Capitol Hill, Washington, D.C., May 8, 2003. The hearing examined the state of competition in direct broadcast satellite service in the multichannel video programming distribution market, particularly in light of the recent News Corporation/DirecTV merger announcement. Murdoch manages one of the most profitable media companies in the world.

Getty Images

Another media company, AOL Time Warner, is the product of an unsuccessful merger between an Internet portal and a broadscale media company. Time Warner was created by a merger of Time Inc. and Warner Communications in 1989 while the combination of Time Warner and America Online occurred in 2001. In the two years following the merger, the company's market capitalization declined in value by $223 billion. To AOL, Time Warner's content was a vertical acquisition to fill AOL's growing Internet pipeline, but to Time Warner, AOL was just another new distribution outlet to accelerate the growth of established media content businesses. The two worldviews were incompatible culturally, and the supposed complementarity from either point of view never fully materialized. There is pressure on CEO Richard Parsons to spin off AOL and return Time Warner to its premerger state. While the Time Warner part of the company is still profitable and growing, AOL is struggling, and the combined company is seeking ways to pay down the debt incurred as a result of the merger.

A well-managed acquisition strategy can add much value to a company. However, when it is ill-considered and poorly implemented, it can be the downfall of a previously successful company. News Corporation and AOL Time Warner are two such polar examples. While News Corp. continues to grow and expand though its track record is far from perfect, AOL Time Warner is managing for damage control in order to establish a firmer foundation from which its strategies can be successfully implemented. News Corp. has also made poor acquisitions; its acquisition of Gemstar–TV Guide, for example, has created a significant drag on earnings and lost market capitalization. However, examining the acquisitions strategies of these two firms can be instructive. Murdoch has been careful to stay away from music and Internet acquisitions. This decision has benefited his firm compared to the other media conglomerates Bertelsmann, Vivendi, and, especially, AOL Time Warner. Like Viacom, which owns CBS and MTV, News Corp. has focused primarily on producing good content; as a result, these firms have fared better than the more diversified media firms. Choosing appropriate acquisition targets and remaining focused on their own expertise has contributed to both Viacom and News Corp.'s success.

SOURCES: 2003, News Corporation home page, http://www.newscorp.com, June 6; J. Friedman, 2003, An aging News Corp. contrasts with paralyzed AOL, http://CBS.marketwatch.com, June 2; A. Bianco & T. Lowry, 2003, Can Dick Parsons rescue AOL Time Warner? *Business Week*, May 19, 87–96; M. Gunther & D. Leonard, 2003, Murdoch's prime time, *Fortune*, February 17, 52–62; 2002, Business: Still rocking; Viacom and News Corporation, *The Economist*, November 23, 55–56.

In Chapter 6, we studied corporate-level strategies, focusing on types and levels of product diversification strategies that can build core competencies and create competitive advantage. As noted in that chapter, diversification allows a firm to create value by productively using excess resources.[1] In this chapter, we explore mergers and acquisitions, often combined with a diversification strategy, as a prominent strategy employed by firms throughout the world. The acquisition of DirecTV by News Corporation is a vertical acquisition, as DirecTV is a satellite TV company through which News Corp. can distribute more of its media content: news, movies, and television shows. As such, combining the two firms creates an opportunity for complementarity as described in the Opening Case.

In the latter half of the 20th century, acquisition became a prominent strategy used by major corporations. Even smaller and more focused firms began employing acquisition strategies to grow and to enter new markets. However, acquisition strategies are not without problems; a number of acquisitions fail. Thus, we focus on how acquisitions can be used to produce value for the firm's stakeholders.[2] Before describing attributes associated with effective acquisitions, we examine the most prominent problems companies experience with an acquisition strategy. For example, when acquisitions contribute to poor performance, a firm may deem it necessary to restructure its operations. Closing the chapter are descriptions of three restructuring strategies, as well as the short- and long-term outcomes resulting from their use. Setting the stage for these topics is an examination of the popularity of mergers and acquisitions and a discussion of the differences among mergers, acquisitions, and takeovers.

The Popularity of Merger and Acquisition Strategies

The acquisition strategy has been a popular strategy among U.S. firms for many years. Some believe that this strategy played a central role in an effective restructuring of U.S. businesses during the 1980s and 1990s and into the 21st century.[3] Increasingly, acquisition strategies are becoming more popular with firms in other nations and economic regions, including Europe. In fact, about 40 to 45 percent of the acquisitions in recent years have been made across country borders (i.e., a firm headquartered in one country acquiring a firm headquartered in another country).[4]

Five waves of mergers and acquisitions took place in the 20th century with the last two occurring in the 1980s and 1990s.[5] There were 55,000 acquisitions valued at $1.3 trillion in the 1980s, but acquisitions in the 1990s exceeded $11 trillion in value.[6] World economies, particularly the U.S. economy, slowed in the new millennium, reducing the number of mergers and acquisitions completed.[7] The annual value of mergers and acquisitions peaked in 2000 at about $3.4 trillion and fell to about $1.75 trillion in 2001.[8] Slightly more than 15,000 acquisitions were announced in 2001 compared to over 33,000 in 2000.[9] In 2002, the total value for U.S. deals was $447.8 billion, the lowest level since 1994.[10] However, the number of firms anticipating making acquisitions increased significantly from 2002 to 2003.[11]

Although acquisitions have slowed, their number remains high. In fact, an acquisition strategy is sometimes used because of the uncertainty in the competitive landscape. A firm may make an acquisition to increase its market power because of a competitive threat, to enter a new market because of the opportunity available in that market, or to spread the risk due to the uncertain environment.[12] In addition, a firm may acquire other companies as options that allow the firm to shift its core business into different markets as volatility brings undesirable changes to its primary markets.[13] Such options may arise because of industry or regulatory changes. For instance, Clear Channel Communications built its business by buying radio stations in many geographic markets when the Telecommunications Act of 1996 changed the regulations regarding such acquisitions.[14]

The strategic management process (see Figure 1.1) calls for an acquisition strategy to increase a firm's strategic competitiveness as well as its returns to shareholders. Thus, an acquisition strategy should be used only when the acquiring firm will be able to increase its economic value through ownership and the use of an acquired firm's assets.[15]

Evidence suggests, however, that at least for acquiring firms, acquisition strategies may not always result in these desirable outcomes.[16] Studies by academic researchers have found that shareholders of acquired firms often earn above-average returns from an acquisition, while shareholders of acquiring firms are less likely to do so, typically earning returns from the transaction that are close to zero.[17] In approximately two-thirds of all acquisitions, the acquiring firm's stock price falls immediately after the intended transaction is announced. This negative response is an indication of investors' skepticism about the likelihood that the acquirer will be able to achieve the synergies required to justify the premium.[18] For example, as the Opening Case illustrates, the value of AOL Time Warner, now the world's largest media company, has continued to decline since the merger.

Mergers, Acquisitions, and Takeovers: What Are the Differences?

A **merger** is a strategy through which two firms agree to integrate their operations on a relatively coequal basis. There are few true mergers, because one party is usually dominant. DaimlerChrysler AG was termed a "merger of equals" and, although Daimler-Benz was the dominant party in the automakers' transaction, Chrysler managers would not allow the business deal to be consummated unless it was termed a merger.[19]

An **acquisition** is a strategy through which one firm buys a controlling, or 100 percent, interest in another firm with the intent of making the acquired firm a subsidiary business within its portfolio. In this case, the management of the acquired firm reports to the management of the acquiring firm. While most mergers are friendly transactions, acquisitions include unfriendly takeovers.

A **takeover** is a special type of an acquisition strategy wherein the target firm does not solicit the acquiring firm's bid. For example, the Strategic Focus on Oracle's unsolicited bid for PeopleSoft illustrates a takeover attempt. Often, takeover bids spawn bidding wars. Safeway, a U.K. grocery (unrelated to its U.S. namesake), received six bids when there was a signal that its assets were for sale. Following an agreed-upon offer from Morrison J. Sainsbury PLC, Wal-Mart Stores, Inc.'s U.K. arm Asda, Tesco PLC, and Arcadia showed interest. Also, Kohlberg Kravis Roberts & Co. (KKR), a buyout specialist, considered making a leveraged buyout offer (defined later in the chapter).[20] The number of unsolicited takeover bids increased in the economic downturn of 2001–2002, a common occurrence in economic recessions, because the poorly managed firms that are undervalued relative to their assets are more easily identified.[21]

Many takeover attempts are not desired by the target firm's managers and are referred to as hostile. In a few cases, unsolicited offers may come from parties familiar to the target firm. For example, financier Kirk Kerkorian, who specializes in takeovers, has acquired Metro-Goldwyn-Mayer (MGM) five separate times. The value of his investment in MGM has grown considerably, outperforming the Standard and Poor's 500. Still, MGM has struggled against fierce competition in recent years, and Kerkorian is trying to sell it (again).[22]

On a comparative basis, acquisitions are more common than mergers and takeovers. Accordingly, this chapter focuses on acquisitions.

Reasons for Acquisitions

In this section, we discuss reasons that support the use of an acquisition strategy. Although each reason can provide a legitimate rationale for an acquisition, the acquisition may not necessarily lead to a competitive advantage.

Increased Market Power

A primary reason for acquisitions is to achieve greater market power.[23] Defined in Chapter 6, *market power* exists when a firm is able to sell its goods or services above competitive levels or when the costs of its primary or support activities are below those of its competitors. Market power usually is derived from the size of the firm and its resources and capabilities to compete in the marketplace.[24] It is also affected by the firm's share of the market. Therefore, most acquisitions designed to achieve greater market power entail buying a competitor, a supplier, a distributor, or a business in a highly related industry to allow exercise of a core competence and to gain competitive advantage in the acquiring firm's primary market. One goal in achieving market power is to become a market leader.[25] For example, two Russian oil companies, Yukos and Sibneft, recently merged to become the fourth largest oil producer in the world. The merger increases the companies' market power to the extent that the merged firm can now compete with ExxonMobil, BP, Shell, and the other "supermajors."[26] Also, as

Oracle Tries to Build Market Power through Acquisition of PeopleSoft

Oracle, a corporate database software company, made a $5.1 billion initial hostile takeover bid for PeopleSoft, an applications company, in June 2003. These companies produce software used by corporations to manage such business functions as "human resources, inventory management, and customer relations." Hostile takeovers are rare in the software business, but Larry Ellison, Oracle's CEO, initiated it as part of a strategy to increase Oracle's market power. Having seen how Microsoft became a more potent player when it released applications bundled with its operating system, Ellison is seeking applications to bundle with Oracle's database software, which is perceived as an operating system equivalent for corporate computing comparable to Microsoft Windows XP on a PC. Ellison has said that he is most interested in PeopleSoft's customers and in switching them over to Oracle applications.

In its own effort to build more market power in a consolidating industry, People-Soft had attempted to purchase J.D. Edwards. PeopleSoft objected to Oracle's bid on the grounds that it would not pass Department of Justice antitrust scrutiny. It countered Oracle's effort by revising its all-stock offer for J.D. Edwards to one that included a large amount of cash, making it more difficult for Oracle to appeal to shareholders. "Making the deal half cash and issuing half as much stock means they are below the NASDAQ threshold and don't have to go to the PeopleSoft shareholders" to complete the transaction. Oracle also made itself less attractive as a takeover target by reducing its cash on hand. In addition, PeopleSoft mounted an ad campaign that promised refunds to PeopleSoft subscribers if Oracle won the takeover battle. Oracle executives said that this move was like "a poison pill" that would make PeopleSoft more costly to acquire.

Many analysts agreed that the software business was ripe for consolidation, especially at that time, when the economy was down and managers, trying to cut costs, were cutting software spending. Ellison's announcement would put the number two, three, and four enterprise computing companies together into one (PeopleSoft is number three and J.D. Edwards is number four). However, even with the addition of PeopleSoft, Oracle would still come in a distant second to SAP, the major enterprise computing company, potentially holding 23 percent of the market while SAP had 35 percent.

SAP could benefit from Oracle's takeover bid, whether or not it were to be completed. At that moment of turmoil, SAP looked like a reliable provider that would be around for years supporting its software, an image that appealed to corporate customers. Additionally, if the takeover were to be completed, SAP would have an even chance to convince PeopleSoft customers to switch to SAP instead of to Oracle. The company launched an ad campaign to woo discontented PeopleSoft customers and authorized financial incentives to lure them over to SAP.

On the other hand, even if the takeover bid were to fail, Oracle could gain. The chances of a successful bid were viewed as remote because of antitrust objections. However, the bid caused enough uncertainty that PeopleSoft's sales declined, and the company was expected to report lower-than-expected earnings during the second quarter of 2003 as a direct result. Whether Oracle or SAP would gain the most is undetermined. Either way, Oracle managed to paralyze its rival and gain an opportunity for growing its market share.

SOURCES: L. J. Flynn & A. R. Sorkin, 2003, PeopleSoft revises a bid in its battle with Oracle, *New York Times,* http://www.nytimes.com, June 17; S. Hamm, 2003, Why SAP is sitting pretty, *BusinessWeek Online,* http://www.businessweek.com, June 12; S. Lohr, 2003, PeopleSoft bid mirrors lofty goals of Oracle chief executive, *New York Times,* http://www.nytimes.com, June 11; M. Prince, 2003, PeopleSoft board rejects revised offer from Oracle, *Wall Street Journal Online,* http://www.wsj.com, June 20; A. R. Sorkin, 2003, Has Oracle's chief disarmed a rival? *New York Times,* http://www.nytimes.com, June 16; F. Vogelstein, 2003, Oracle's Ellison turns hostile, *Fortune,* June 23, 28.

illustrated in the Strategic Focus, Oracle's hostile bid to acquire PeopleSoft in the corporate database software business (which facilitates management of functions such as human resources, inventory management, and customer relations) may create more market power for Oracle. The PeopleSoft acquisition would allow Oracle to remain the number two software leader in its segment behind SAP. To increase their market power, firms often use horizontal, vertical, and related acquisitions.

HORIZONTAL ACQUISITIONS

The acquisition of a company competing in the same industry in which the acquiring firm competes is referred to as a *horizontal acquisition.* Horizontal acquisitions increase a firm's market power by exploiting cost-based and revenue-based synergies.[27] Research suggests that horizontal acquisitions of firms with similar characteristics result in higher performance than when firms with dissimilar characteristics combine their operations. Examples of important similar characteristics include strategy, managerial styles, and resource allocation patterns. Similarities in these characteristics make the integration of the two firms proceed more smoothly.[28] Horizontal acquisitions are often most effective when the acquiring firm integrates the acquired firm's assets with its assets, but only after evaluating and divesting excess capacity and assets that do not complement the newly combined firm's core competencies.[29]

After a strategy dispute with Palm's chairman, Palm founders Jeff Hawkins and Donna Dubinsky split off and founded another company, Handspring, modeled on Palm. Handspring has done well, and Palm recently announced that it is acquiring Handspring, bringing the founders' talent and technology back into Palm. It hopes that Handspring's Treo device, a combination phone-PDA, will help Palm's performance, as PDA sales have declined in favor of combined devices. Palm's horizontal acquisition of Handspring will likely save about $25 million a year by eliminating overlapping programs and taking advantage of more volume in the combined firm's manufacturing operations.[30]

Handspring's Treo, a combination phone/PDA, is a product that occasioned a horizontal acquisition of Handspring by Palm.

Getty Images

PART 2 / Strategic Actions: Strategy Formulation

VERTICAL ACQUISITIONS

A *vertical acquisition* refers to a firm acquiring a supplier or distributor of one or more of its goods or services.[31] A firm becomes vertically integrated through this type of acquisition, in that it controls additional parts of the value chain (see Chapters 3 and 6). Sony's acquisition of Columbia Pictures in the late 1980s was a vertical acquisition in which movie content could be used by Sony's hardware devices. Sony's additional acquisition of CBS Records, a music producer, and development of the PlayStation hardware have formed the bases for more vertical integration. The spread of broadband and the technological shift from analog to digital hardware require media firms to find new ways to sell their content to consumers. Sony's CEO, Nobuyuki Idei, believes that this shift has created a new opportunity to sell hardware that integrates this change by selling "televisions, personal computers, game consoles and handheld devices through which all of that wonderful content will one day be streaming."[32]

RELATED ACQUISITIONS

The acquisition of a firm in a highly related industry is referred to as a *related acquisition.* Tyson Foods, which has almost a quarter of the market for chicken, acquired IBP, the leader in beef and number two in pork. Most of Tyson's sales come from value-added products, such as breaded, marinated, or ready-to-microwave items, and it is hoping to apply this same recipe to its new beef and pork business, achieving economies of scope.[33] However, because of the difficulty in achieving synergy, related acquisitions are often difficult to value.[34]

Acquisitions intended to increase market power are subject to regulatory review as well as to analysis by financial markets.[35] For example, as noted in the Strategic Focus, the takeover attempt of PeopleSoft by Oracle received a significant amount of government scrutiny as well as close examination by financial analysts. European regulators did not approve the GE acquisition of Honeywell, dooming this strategic action and leaving Honeywell as a possible takeover target.[36] Thus, firms seeking growth and market power through acquisitions must understand the political/legal segment of the general environment (see Chapter 2) in order to successfully use an acquisition strategy.

Overcoming Entry Barriers

Barriers to entry (introduced in Chapter 2) are factors associated with the market or with the firms currently operating in it that increase the expense and difficulty faced by new ventures trying to enter that particular market. For example, well-established competitors may have substantial economies of scale in the manufacture or service of their products. In addition, enduring relationships with customers often create product loyalties that are difficult for new entrants to overcome. When facing differentiated products, new entrants typically must spend considerable resources to advertise their goods or services and may find it necessary to sell at prices below competitors' to entice customers.

Facing the entry barriers created by economies of scale and differentiated products, a new entrant may find the acquisition of an established company to be more effective than entering the market as a competitor offering a good or service that is unfamiliar to current buyers. In fact, the higher the barriers to market entry, the greater the probability that a firm will acquire an existing firm to overcome them. Although an acquisition can be expensive, it does provide the new entrant with immediate market access.

As it struggles to compete with UPS and FedEx in the air cargo industry, DHL Airways is finding many barriers to entry it must overcome, including a court case and a hearing before the U.S. Department of Transportation. UPS and FedEx have dominated this market for years in the United States. However, these arch rivals have banded together in an effort to exclude DHL Airways, alleging that the carrier is controlled by Deutsche Post World Net, a German firm, whose ownership may be illegal under American law. DHL Airways was formed by a takeover of Seattle-based Airborne Inc. DHL was surprised by how high the barriers to entry have become. "We had anticipated that there would be a tremendous effort to keep us from getting a toehold," said one DHL executive. "The surprise has been that it has taken on a life of its own."[37]

As in the DHL example above, firms trying to enter international markets often face quite steep entry barriers.[38] However, acquisitions are commonly used to overcome those barriers.[39] At least for large multinational corporations, another indicator of the importance of entering and then competing successfully in international markets is the fact that five emerging markets (China, India, Brazil, Mexico, and Indonesia) are among the 12 largest economies in the world, with a combined purchasing power that is already one-half that of the Group of Seven industrial nations (United States, Japan, Britain, France, Germany, Canada, and Italy).[40]

CROSS-BORDER ACQUISITIONS

Acquisitions made between companies with headquarters in different countries are called *cross-border acquisitions*. These acquisitions are often made to overcome entry barriers. In Chapter 9, we examine cross-border alliances and the reason for their use.

Compared to a cross-border alliance, a cross-border acquisition gives a firm more control over its international operations.[41]

Historically, U.S. firms have been the most active acquirers of companies outside their domestic market.[42] However, in the global economy, companies throughout the world are choosing this strategic option with increasing frequency. In recent years, cross-border acquisitions have represented as much as 45 percent of the total number of annual acquisitions.[43] The Daimler-Benz acquisition of Chrysler Corporation provides an example of this activity. Because of relaxed regulations, the amount of cross-border activity among nations within the European community also continues to increase. Accounting for this growth in the range of cross-border acquisitions, some analysts believe, is the fact that many large European corporations have approached the limits of growth within their domestic markets and thus seek growth in other markets. Research has indicated that many European and U.S. firms participated in cross-border acquisitions across Asian countries that experienced a financial crisis due to significant currency devaluations in 1997. These acquisitions, it is argued, facilitated the survival and restructuring of many large Asian companies such that these economies recovered more quickly than they would have without the cross-border acquisitions.[44]

Firms in all types of industries are completing cross-border acquisitions. For example, in 2002, the largest cross-border deal in the United States was the acquisition of Beneficial and Household Finance brands ("the largest independent consumer finance company in the United States and the country's second-largest third-party issuer of private label credit cards") by London-headquartered HSBC, now the largest foreign-owned bank in the United States.[45] In the second largest transaction, Miller Brewing was purchased from Philip Morris (now Altria Group Inc.) by South African Breweries (SAB). Although South African Breweries' acquisition (now SABMiller) "doubled its global market share and gave it a foothold in the lucrative U.S. market, . . . the beer brand's sales have fallen nearly 5 percent in the U.S."[46] As the South African Breweries experience indicates, such cross-border acquisitions can be difficult to negotiate and operate because of the differences in foreign cultures.[47]

Cost of New Product Development and Increased Speed to Market

Developing new products internally and successfully introducing them into the marketplace often require significant investments of a firm's resources, including time, making it difficult to quickly earn a profitable return.[48] Also of concern to firms' managers is achieving adequate returns from the capital invested to develop and commercialize new products—an estimated 88 percent of innovations fail to achieve adequate returns. Perhaps contributing to these less-than-desirable rates of return is the successful imitation of approximately 60 percent of innovations within four years after the patents are obtained. Because of outcomes such as these, managers often perceive internal product development as a high-risk activity.[49]

Acquisitions are another means a firm can use to gain access to new products and to current products that are new to the firm. Compared to internal product development processes, acquisitions provide more predictable returns as well as faster market entry. Returns are more predictable because the performance of the acquired firm's products can be assessed prior to completing the acquisition.[50] For these reasons, extensive bidding wars and acquisitions are more frequent in high-technology industries.[51]

Acquisition activity is also extensive throughout the pharmaceutical industry, where firms frequently use acquisitions to enter markets quickly, to overcome the high costs of developing products internally, and to increase the predictability of returns on their investments. Interestingly, although the value of the deals decreased 22 percent to $26.4 billion, the number of deals increased significantly, from 21 in 2001 to 45 in 2003. The increase in the number of smaller deals is probably "driven by the trend among pharma firms to buy biotechnology companies to bolster late-stage R&D pipelines." Although one large deal, the $60 billion acquisition of Pharmacia by Pfizer, was completed in April 2003, most firms are targeting small acquisitions to supplement market power and reinvigorate or create innovative drug pipelines.[52]

As indicated previously, compared to internal product development, acquisitions result in more rapid market entries.[53] Acquisitions often represent the fastest means to enter international markets and help firms overcome the liabilities associated with such strategic moves.[54] Acquisitions provide rapid access both to new markets and to new capabilities. Using new capabilities to pioneer new products and to enter markets quickly can create advantageous market positions.[55] Pharmaceutical firms, for example, access new products through acquisitions of other drug manufacturers. They also acquire biotechnology firms both for new products and for new technological capabilities. Pharmaceutical firms often provide the manufacturing and marketing capabilities to take the new products developed by biotechnology firms to the market.[56] Novartis, for example, has a significant ownership position in Roche, another Swiss-headquartered pharmaceutical firm, which has helped to develop the biotech powerhouse, Genentech. Through this relationship and other acquisitions over the years, Novartis' "pipeline is full." However, it would like to purchase the remaining shares of Roche to improve its position even more.[57]

Lower Risk Compared to Developing New Products

Because an acquisition's outcomes can be estimated more easily and accurately compared to the outcomes of an internal product development process, managers may view acquisitions as lowering risk.[58] The difference in risk between an internal product development process and an acquisition can be seen in the results of Novartis' strategy and that of its competitors described above.

As with other strategic actions discussed in this book, the firm must exercise caution when using a strategy of acquiring new products rather than developing them internally. While research suggests that acquisitions have become a common means of avoiding risky internal ventures (and therefore risky R&D investments), they may also become a substitute for innovation.[59] Thus, acquisitions are not a risk-free alternative to entering new markets through internally developed products.

Increased Diversification

Acquisitions are also used to diversify firms. Based on experience and the insights resulting from it, firms typically find it easier to develop and introduce new products in markets currently served by the firm. In contrast, it is difficult for companies to develop products that differ from their current lines for markets in which they lack experience.[60] Thus, it is uncommon for a firm to develop new products internally to diversify its product lines.[61] Using acquisitions to diversify a firm is the quickest and, typically, the easiest way to change its portfolio of businesses.[62] For example, Goodrich Corp. has evolved from a tire maker to a top-tier aerospace supplier through over 40 acquisitions that began in the mid-1980s. The firm has indicated that it will reduce the number of acquisitions over the next several years as it seeks to integrate its sizable acquisition of the former TRW Aeronautical Systems.[63]

Both related diversification and unrelated diversification strategies can be implemented through acquisitions.[64] For example, United Technologies has used acquisitions to

Acquisitions are a quick way for a firm to diversify. Using acquisitions, Goodrich Corp., for example, has evolved from being a tire maker to a top-tier aerospace supplier.

©Russ Schleipman

build a conglomerate—a highly unrelated diversified firm.[65] It has been building a portfolio of stable and noncyclical businesses, including Otis Elevator Co. and Carrier Corporation (air conditioners), since the mid-1970s in order to reduce its dependence on the volatile aerospace industry. Its main businesses have been Pratt & Whitney (jet engines), Sikorsky (helicopters), and Hamilton Sundstrand (aerospace parts). It has also acquired a hydrogen-fuel-cell business. However, perceiving an opportunity in security caused by problems at airports and because security has become a top concern both for governments and for corporations, United Technologies has agreed to acquire Chubb PLC, a British electronic-security company, for $1 billion. This is the largest deal United Technologies has attempted since its 2001 bid for Honeywell Inc., which failed due to an offer from General Electric (GE). However, as mentioned earlier, the GE offer did not materialize because it was not approved by European regulators.[66]

Research has shown that the more related the acquired firm is to the acquiring firm, the greater is the probability the acquisition will be successful.[67] Thus, horizontal acquisitions (through which a firm acquires a competitor) and related acquisitions tend to contribute more to the firm's strategic competitiveness than acquiring a company that operates in product markets quite different from those in which the firm competes.[68]

Reshaping the Firm's Competitive Scope

As discussed in Chapter 2, the intensity of competitive rivalry is an industry characteristic that affects the firm's profitability.[69] To reduce the negative effect of an intense rivalry on their financial performance, firms may use acquisitions to lessen their dependence on one or more products or markets. Reducing a company's dependence on specific markets alters the firm's competitive scope.

One of the arguments used in the Strategic Focus on Oracle's acquisition of PeopleSoft is that the acquisition would strengthen Oracle's competitive scope relative to its competitors. In an effort to copy Microsoft's successful strategy of bundling applications with an operating system, Oracle made a bid for PeopleSoft, a maker of human resource management software. Oracle's database in corporate computing is comparable to Microsoft's operating system on desktops, and Oracle was attempting to reduce its reliance on its database software by adding more applications to its bundle.[70] Similarly, GE reduced its emphasis in the electronics market many years ago by making acquisitions in the financial services industry. Today, GE is considered a service firm because a majority of its revenue now comes from services instead of industrial products.[71]

Learning and Developing New Capabilities

Some acquisitions are made to gain capabilities that the firm does not possess. For example, acquisitions may be used to acquire a special technological capability. Research has shown that firms can broaden their knowledge base and reduce inertia through acquisitions.[72] Therefore, acquiring firms with skills and capabilities that differ from its own helps the acquiring firm to learn new knowledge and remain agile.[73] Of course, firms are better able to learn these capabilities if they share some similar properties with the firm's current capabilities. Thus, firms should seek to acquire companies with different but related and complementary capabilities in order to build their own knowledge base.[74]

One of Cisco Systems' primary goals in its early acquisitions was to gain access to capabilities that it needed to compete in the fast-changing networking equipment industry that connects the Internet. Cisco developed an intricate process to quickly integrate the acquired firms and their capabilities (knowledge). Cisco's processes accounted for its phenomenal success in the latter half of the 1990s. However, "Cisco today is evolving from a loose federation of start-ups that rewarded 'speed at the expense of teamwork' and last-minute scrambling to grab opportunities." The goal is now more internal cooperation to "avoid the diving catch." Although Cisco continues to pursue acquisitions that build new capabilities, it completed only 10 acquisitions from January 2001 through July 2003, including four companies that Cisco cultivated, versus 23 acquisitions in 2000 alone.[75]

Problems in Achieving Acquisition Success

Acquisition strategies based on legitimate reasons described in this chapter can increase strategic competitiveness and help firms earn above-average returns. However, acquisition strategies are not risk-free. Reasons for the use of acquisition strategies and potential problems with such strategies are shown in Figure 7.1.

Reasons for Acquisitions and Problems in Achieving Success — Figure 7.1

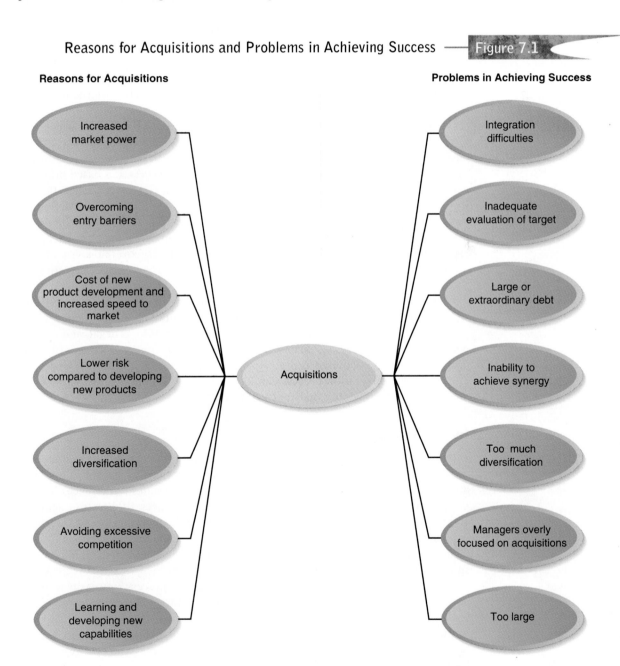

Reasons for Acquisitions

- Increased market power
- Overcoming entry barriers
- Cost of new product development and increased speed to market
- Lower risk compared to developing new products
- Increased diversification
- Avoiding excessive competition
- Learning and developing new capabilities

Acquisitions

Problems in Achieving Success

- Integration difficulties
- Inadequate evaluation of target
- Large or extraordinary debt
- Inability to achieve synergy
- Too much diversification
- Managers overly focused on acquisitions
- Too large

Research suggests that perhaps 20 percent of all mergers and acquisitions are successful, approximately 60 percent produce disappointing results, and the last 20 percent are clear failures.[76] Successful acquisitions generally involve a well-conceived strategy in selecting the target, avoiding paying too high a premium, and employing an effective integration process.[77] As shown in Figure 7.1, several problems may prevent successful acquisitions.

Integration Difficulties

Integrating two companies following an acquisition can be quite difficult. Integration challenges include melding two disparate corporate cultures, linking different financial and control systems, building effective working relationships (particularly when management styles differ), and resolving problems regarding the status of the newly acquired firm's executives.[78]

The importance of a successful integration should not be underestimated.[79] Without it, an acquisition is unlikely to produce positive returns. Thus, as suggested by a researcher studying the process, "managerial practice and academic writings show that the post-acquisition integration phase is probably the single most important determinant of shareholder value creation (and equally of value destruction) in mergers and acquisitions."[80]

Integration is complex and involves a large number of activities, which if overlooked can lead to significant difficulties. For instance, HealthSouth Corporation developed into a major power in the hospital and health-care industries through an aggressive acquisition strategy. However, the strategy's success was based primarily on generous government Medicare reimbursements. When Congress slashed the budget for such reimbursements, HealthSouth was not in a position to take advantage of its scale because the managers had not sought possible improved cost savings through integration. In fact, the CEO was accused of fraudulent reporting to make up for the significant losses, which went unreported. "Acquisitions covered a lot of sins. It allowed the company to layer on a lot of growth without necessarily digesting any of its purchases."[81]

It is important to maintain the human capital of the target firm after the acquisition. Much of an organization's knowledge is contained in its human capital.[82] Turnover of key personnel from the acquired firm can have a negative effect on the performance of the merged firm.[83] The loss of key personnel, such as critical managers, weakens the acquired firm's capabilities and reduces its value. If implemented effectively, the integration process can have a positive effect on target firm managers and reduce the probability that they will leave.[84]

Inadequate Evaluation of Target

Due diligence is a process through which a potential acquirer evaluates a target firm for acquisition. In an effective due-diligence process hundreds of items are examined in areas as diverse as the financing for the intended transaction, differences in cultures between the acquiring and target firm, tax consequences of the transaction, and actions that would be necessary to successfully meld the two workforces. Due diligence is commonly performed by investment bankers, accountants, lawyers, and management consultants specializing in that activity, although firms actively pursuing acquisitions may form their own internal due-diligence team.[85]

The failure to complete an effective due-diligence process may easily result in the acquiring firm paying an excessive premium for the target company. In fact, research shows that without due diligence, "the purchase price is driven by the pricing of other 'comparable' acquisitions rather than by a rigorous assessment of where, when, and how management can drive real performance gains. [In these cases], the price paid may have little to do with achievable value."[86]

Because many firms previously used investment banks to perform their due diligence, in the post-Enron era many firms are bringing their due diligence in-house. While investment bankers such as Credit Suisse First Boston and Citibank still play a large role in due diligence for big mergers and acquisitions, their role in smaller mergers and acquisitions seems to be decreasing. Deals completed through May 21, 2003, without any investment banking assistance for either buyer or seller, comprised 83 percent of the total number of deals, up from 73 percent during the same period ending in 2002. A growing number of companies are building their own internal operations to advise and finance mergers. First, companies are less inclined toward the sort of complex megadeals that took place regularly in the 1990s, and they don't feel that they need the investment banks' expensive counsel for small purchases. Second, some companies feel that no one should be more aware of their industry than they are; in other words, individual firms are just as capable, if not more capable, of finding appropriate partnerships for mergers or acquisitions. Third, it's much cheaper for companies to do without the expensive advice of investment bankers. However, although they are playing a lesser role, there will always be the need for an outside opinion for a company's board of directors—to reassure them about a planned merger and reduce their liability.[87]

As the Strategic Focus indicates, larger brewers have been paying too much for their latest acquisitions. Thus, better due diligence may be appropriate, even if the acquired firms increase the acquiring firm's market share.

Large or Extraordinary Debt

To finance a number of acquisitions completed during the 1980s and 1990s, some companies significantly increased their levels of debt. A financial innovation called junk bonds helped make this increase possible. *Junk bonds* are a financing option through which risky acquisitions are financed with money (debt) that provides a large potential return to lenders (bondholders). Because junk bonds are unsecured obligations that are not tied to specific assets for collateral, interest rates for these high-risk debt instruments sometimes reached between 18 and 20 percent during the 1980s.[88] Some prominent financial economists viewed debt as a means to discipline managers, causing them to act in shareholders' best interests.[89]

Junk bonds are now used less frequently to finance acquisitions, and the conviction that debt disciplines managers is less strong. Nonetheless, some firms still take on significant debt to acquire companies. For example, AOL Time Warner increased its total debt to $26 billion after its acquisition of AOL. Now it is straining to pay the debt and may need to break up the firm and sell off some of its myriad businesses (including its Internet assets [AOL], cable TV, filmed entertainment, network TV, music, and publishing) to do so.[90]

High debt can have several negative effects on the firm. For example, because high debt increases the likelihood of bankruptcy, it can lead to a downgrade in the firm's credit rating by agencies such as Moody's and Standard and Poor's.[91] In addition, high debt may preclude needed investment in activities that contribute to the firm's long-term success, such as R&D, human resource training, and marketing.[92] Still, use of leverage can be a positive force in a firm's development, allowing it to take advantage of attractive expansion opportunities. However, too much leverage (such as extraordinary debt) can lead to negative outcomes, including postponing or eliminating investments, such as R&D expenditures, that are necessary to maintain strategic competitiveness over the long term.

Inability to Achieve Synergy

Derived from *synergos*, a Greek word that means "working together," *synergy* exists when the value created by units working together exceeds the value those units could create working independently (see Chapter 6). That is, synergy exists when assets are

Consolidation in the Global Beer Industry and Firms Overpaying for Acquisitions

Large global brewers are faced with prospects for slow volume growth in their traditional developed markets. Although the world's ten largest brewers have grown more than four times relative to the total industry since the mid-1990s, combined volume of all brewers actually decreased during the same period. Consequently, this lack of growth has fueled the consolidation and acquisition process. Accordingly, this has led brewers either to make acquisitions of other brewers in already developed markets or to seek to develop strategic alliances or pursue acquisitions in developing markets. For instance, as noted earlier in the chapter, Miller Brewing was purchased by South African Breweries (SAB) from Philip Morris (now Altria Group Inc.) and the combined firm was named SAB-Miller. At the same time, this consolidation process has led to the rapid disappearance of many local brewers.

Anheuser-Busch has been very active as exemplified by its acquiring 27 percent (over time) of Tsingtao Brewery, the top brewer in China by volume sold. Coors has also joined the process by purchasing Carling Brewery in the United Kingdom, and each of Europe's leading brewers—Heineken, Interbrew, Carlsberg, and Scottish & Newcastle—has made significant acquisitions in the recent past.

AmBev, a Brazilian brewer, has made acquisitions in Latin America and aims to become a pan-American brewer, while Canada's Molson bought Kaiser, Brazil's largest competitor to AmBev. Although there is still no sign of a top global brewer, there are dominant players in each region. For instance, Heineken is big in Western Europe and the United States, but not large elsewhere.

In a recent acquisition, Heineken won the bidding for Austrian brewer BBAG, while SABMiller won the bidding for privately held Peroni, Italy's second largest brewer. However, analysts are arguing that the big five in Europe (Carlsberg, Heineken, Interbrew, SABMiller, and Scottish & Newcastle) have destroyed shareholder value and economic profit since 2001 through their acquisitions. These analysts were dumping shares of Heineken, for instance, because the acquisition of BBAG looked overpriced and would dilute Heineken's shareholder value. Heineken paid Euro 124 per share for BBAG, which was 30 percent higher than the price at which BBAG's shares had been trading.

It has been a year since SABMiller has released results, and analysts have downgraded the stock because the Miller acquisition further devalued it. The consensus was that Miller had not realized the synergies or benefits from the combination and, although Miller's performance could still turn around, the stock price has remained lower since the acquisition.

In the long run, the large brewers making these acquisitions may win out through market share dominance. In the short run, however, it might behoove some of the less nimble players to prepare for being purchased, because target firm shareholders are receiving more value from the acquisition process. Thus, for those firms willing to sell, value can be collected from selling to a bidder willing to overpay.

SOURCES: 2003, Food brief—Heineken NV: Dutch brewer set to acquire BBAG in $2.13 million deal, *Wall Street Journal*, May 5, A12; D. Bilefsky, 2003, Miller Beer aims to be icon in Europe, *Wall Street Journal*, June 13, B7; A. Caplan, 2003, Global beer: Tapping into growth, *Beverage World*, February 15, 24–29; J. Cioletti, 2003, Top 10 beers scoring 100, *Beverage World*, April 15, 29–31; B. Truscott, 2003, European trader: Is the beer stein half-full or half-empty? *Barron's*, June 2, MW6–MW7.

worth more when used in conjunction with each other than when they are used separately.[93] For shareholders, synergy generates gains in their wealth that they could not duplicate or exceed through their own portfolio diversification decisions.[94] Synergy is created by the efficiencies derived from economies of scale and economies of scope and by sharing resources (e.g., human capital and knowledge) across the businesses in the merged firm.[95]

A firm develops a competitive advantage through an acquisition strategy only when a transaction generates private synergy. *Private synergy* is created when the combination and integration of the acquiring and acquired firms' assets yield capabilities and core competencies that could not be developed by combining and integrating either firm's assets with another company. Private synergy is possible when firms' assets are complementary in unique ways; that is, the unique type of asset complementarity is not possible by combining either company's assets with another firm's assets.[96] Because of its uniqueness, private synergy is difficult for competitors to understand and imitate. However, private synergy is difficult to create.

A firm's ability to account for costs that are necessary to create anticipated revenue- and cost-based synergies affects the acquisition's success. Firms experience several expenses when trying to create private synergy through acquisitions. Called transaction costs, these expenses are incurred when firms use acquisition strategies to create synergy.[97] Transaction costs may be direct or indirect. Direct costs include legal fees and charges from investment bankers who complete due diligence for the acquiring firm. Indirect costs include managerial time to evaluate target firms and then to complete negotiations, as well as the loss of key managers and employees following an acquisition.[98] Firms tend to underestimate the sum of indirect costs when the value of the synergy that may be created by combining and integrating the acquired firm's assets with the acquiring firm's assets is calculated.

Interpublic Group is an example of a company that has failed to achieve synergy with its acquisitions. Interpublic Group (IPG) is an ad agency holding company that has bought more than 300 companies in the past five years. IPG is loaded with debt, and the promised synergies between advertising and marketing properties have failed to appear. Non-advertising businesses were supposed to hedge the notorious cycles of the ad business, but that also has not been the case in the recent downturn. CEO David Bell envisioned "one-stop shopping" for advertising, packaging, and promotions, but the subsidiary companies fought the idea. The cultural differences between advertisers and non-advertisers were wide, and clients themselves overwhelmingly believed that they should choose the best talent in each discipline, regardless of which company owned it. While CEO Bell hasn't given up yet on making the one-stop shopping concept work, many customers and investors have.[99] Similarly, as the Strategic Focus on the global brewing industry indicates, the synergies expected from many of the acquisitions between beer producers have not materialized as expected.

Too Much Diversification

As explained in Chapter 6, diversification strategies can lead to strategic competitiveness and above-average returns. In general, firms using related diversification strategies outperform those employing unrelated diversification strategies. However, conglomerates, formed by using an unrelated diversification strategy, also can be successful. For example, Virgin Group, the U.K. firm with interests ranging from cosmetics to trains, is successful.[100]

At some point, firms can become overdiversified. The level at which overdiversification occurs varies across companies because each firm has different capabilities to manage diversification. Recall from Chapter 6 that related diversification requires more information processing than does unrelated diversification. The need for related diversified firms to process more information of greater diversity is such that they become overdiversified with a smaller number of business units, compared to firms using an unrelated diversification strategy.[101] Regardless of the type of diversification strategy implemented, however, declines in performance result from overdiversification, after which business units are often divested.[102] The pattern of excessive diversification followed by divestments of underperforming business units acquired earlier is currently taking place in the media industry, as the Opening Case illustrates. Many firms in the media industry have been seeking to divest businesses bought in the boom era of the late 1990s through 2001 when the Internet economy collapsed.[103] These cycles were also frequently observed among U.S. firms during the 1960s through the 1980s.[104]

Even when a firm is not overdiversified, a high level of diversification can have a negative effect on the firm's long-term performance. For example, the scope created by additional amounts of diversification often causes managers to rely on financial rather than strategic controls to evaluate business units' performances (financial and strategic controls are defined and explained in Chapters 11 and 12). Top-level executives often rely on financial controls to assess the performance of business units when they do not have a rich understanding of business units' objectives and strategies. Use of financial controls, such as return on investment (ROI), causes individual business-unit managers to focus on short-term outcomes at the expense of long-term investments. When long-term investments are reduced to increase short-term profits, a firm's overall strategic competitiveness may be harmed.[105]

Another problem resulting from too much diversification is the tendency for acquisitions to become substitutes for innovation. Typically, managers do not intend acquisitions to be used in that way. However, a reinforcing cycle evolves. Costs associated with acquisitions may result in fewer allocations to activities, such as R&D, that are linked to innovation. Without adequate support, a firm's innovation skills begin to atrophy. Without internal innovation skills, the only option available to a firm is to complete still additional acquisitions to gain access to innovation. Evidence suggests that a firm using acquisitions as a substitute for internal innovations eventually encounters performance problems.[106]

Managers Overly Focused on Acquisitions

Typically, a fairly substantial amount of managerial time and energy is required for acquisition strategies to contribute to the firm's strategic competitiveness. Activities with which managers become involved include (1) searching for viable acquisition candidates, (2) completing effective due-diligence processes, (3) preparing for negotiations, and (4) managing the integration process after the acquisition is completed.

Top-level managers do not personally gather all data and information required to make acquisitions. However, these executives do make critical decisions on the firms to be targeted, the nature of the negotiations, and so forth. Company experiences show that participating in and overseeing the activities required for making acquisitions can divert managerial attention from other matters that are necessary for long-term competitive success, such as identifying and taking advantage of other opportunities and interacting with important external stakeholders.[107]

Both theory and research suggest that managers can get overly involved in the process of making acquisitions.[108] "The urge to merge is still like an addiction in many companies: Doing deals is much more fun and interesting than fixing fundamental problems. So, as in dealing with any other addiction or temptation maybe it is best to just say no."[109] The overinvolvement can be surmounted by learning from mistakes and by not having too much agreement in the board room. Encouraging dissent is helpful to make sure that all sides of a question are considered (see Chapter 10).[110] When failure does occur, leaders may be tempted to blame the failure on others and on unforeseen circumstances rather than on their excessive involvement in the acquisition process.[111]

Corus was created in 1999 when British and Dutch steel firms combined to become the world's third largest steel company through $6 billion of market capitalization. However, in 2003, it was worth $200 million and was threatened with bankruptcy or possible breakup. Although the merger looked good and steel prices have recently risen, problems arose because of differing management practices of the British and Dutch systems and because the managers involved became focused on protecting their countries' interests.[112] Acquisitions can consume significant amounts of managerial time and energy in both the acquiring and target firms. In particular, managers in target firms may operate in a state of virtual suspended animation during an acquisition.[113] Although the target firm's day-to-day operations continue, most of the company's executives are hesitant to make decisions with long-term consequences until negotiations have been completed. Evidence suggests that the acquisition process can create a short-term perspective and a greater aversion to risk among top-level executives in a target firm.[114]

Too Large

Most acquisitions create a larger firm that should help increase its economies of scale. These economies can then lead to more efficient operations—for example, the two sales organizations can be integrated using fewer sales reps because a sales rep can sell the products of both firms (particularly if the products of the acquiring and target firms are highly related).

Many firms seek increases in size because of the potential economies of scale and enhanced market power (discussed earlier). For example, funeral home operators Service Corporation International (SCI), Stewart Enterprises, and Loewen Group each made numerous acquisitions of funeral home operations and sought to consolidate them to increase size and achieve better economies of scale. However, all three ultimately lost significant market share because they grew too fast and in a downturn lost most of their market capitalization. Through excessive debt and a slowdown in takeovers, for example, SCI and Stewart "fell more than 90 percent to lows of less than 2 dollars," although they have improved more recently. Loewen Group ultimately filed for bankruptcy and reorganized into the Alderwoods Group.[115]

At some level, the additional costs required to manage the larger firm will exceed the benefits of the economies of scale and additional market power, as in the funeral home operators example above. Additionally, there is an incentive to grow larger because size serves as a takeover defense.[116] Research in the United Kingdom indicates that firms that acquire other firms and grow larger are less likely to be taken over.[117] However, the complexities generated by the larger size often lead managers to implement more bureaucratic controls to manage the combined firm's operations. Bureaucratic controls are formalized supervisory and behavioral rules and policies designed to ensure consistency of decisions and actions across different units of a firm. However, through time, formalized controls often lead to relatively rigid and standardized managerial behavior. Certainly, in the long run, the diminished flexibility that accompanies rigid and standardized managerial behavior may produce less innovation. Because of innovation's importance to competitive success, the bureaucratic controls resulting from a large organization (that is, built by acquisitions) can have a detrimental effect on performance.[118]

Effective Acquisitions

Earlier in the chapter, we noted that acquisition strategies do not consistently produce above-average returns for the acquiring firm's shareholders.[119] Nonetheless, some companies are able to create value when using an acquisition strategy.[120] For example, few companies have grown so successfully by acquisition as Computer Associates (CA). Charles Wang, the founder, watched and waited for software companies to show signs of weakness and then purchased them. By staying ultra-lean, CA kept many programs running and supported that otherwise would have been untenable. Although customers with existing software complained about increased fees and shoddy service after CA moved in, new customers delighted in the innovative pricing. Through its expansion, CA could serve a valuable function, especially for mainframe owners, as an alternative to IBM with its more rigid pricing and contracts, thus keeping IBM more nimble.[121]

Results from a research study shed light on the differences between unsuccessful and successful acquisition strategies and suggest that there is a pattern of actions that can improve the probability of acquisition success.[122] The study shows that when the target firm's assets are complementary to the acquired firm's assets, an acquisition is more successful. With complementary assets, integrating two firms' operations has a higher probability of creating synergy. In fact, integrating two firms with complementary assets frequently produces unique capabilities and core competencies.[123] With complementary assets, the acquiring firm can maintain its focus on core businesses and leverage the complementary assets and capabilities from the acquired firm. Often, targets were selected and "groomed" by establishing a working relationship prior to the acquisition.[124] As discussed in Chapter 9, strategic alliances are sometimes used to test the feasibility of a future merger or acquisition between the involved firms.[125]

The study's results also show that friendly acquisitions facilitate integration of the firms involved in an acquisition. Through friendly acquisitions, firms work together to find ways to integrate their operations to create synergy.[126] The acquisition of Ocean Energy Inc. by Devon Energy Corp. represents a friendly acquisition. The $5.3 billion deal created the country's largest independent oil company and gives Oklahoma City–based Devon Energy the near-term production growth it needed. Also, the premium paid was lower because the deal was friendly.[127] In hostile takeovers, animosity often results between the two top-management teams, a condition that in turn affects working relationships in the newly created firm. As a result, more key personnel in the acquired firm may be lost, and those who remain may resist the changes necessary to integrate the two firms.[128] With effort, cultural clashes can be overcome, and fewer key managers and employees will become discouraged and leave.[129]

Additionally, effective due-diligence processes involving the deliberate and careful selection of target firms and an evaluation of the relative health of those firms (financial health, cultural fit, and the value of human resources) contribute to successful acquisitions.[130] Financial slack in the form of debt equity or cash, in both the acquiring and acquired firms, also has frequently contributed to success in acquisitions. While financial slack provides access to financing for the acquisition, it is still important to maintain a low or moderate level of debt after the acquisition to keep debt costs low. When substantial debt was used to finance the acquisition, companies with successful acquisitions reduced the debt quickly, partly by selling off assets from the acquired firm, especially noncomplementary or poorly performing assets. For these firms, debt costs do not prevent long-term investments such as R&D, and managerial discretion in the use of cash flow is relatively flexible.

Another attribute of successful acquisition strategies is an emphasis on innovation, as demonstrated by continuing investments in R&D activities. Significant R&D investments show a strong managerial commitment to innovation, a characteristic that is increasingly important to overall competitiveness, as well as acquisition success.

Berkshire Hathaway is a conglomerate holding company owned by Warren Buffett, one of the world's richest men. Here Mr. Buffett talks to members of the media at a Berkshire Hathaway shareholders meeting. Looking at Table 7.1, you will see that he owes his wealth, in part, to observance of these seven attributes of successful acquisitions.

Flexibility and adaptability are the final two attributes of successful acquisitions. When executives of both the acquiring and the target firms have experience in managing change and learning from acquisitions, they will be more skilled at adapting their capabilities to new environments.[131] As a result, they will be more adept at integrating the two organizations, which is particularly important when firms have different organizational cultures.

Efficient and effective integration may quickly produce the desired synergy in the newly created firm. Effective integration allows the acquiring firm to keep valuable human resources in the acquired firm from leaving.[132]

The attributes and results of successful acquisitions are summarized in Table 7.1. Managers seeking acquisition success should emphasize the seven attributes that are listed. Berkshire Hathaway is a conglomerate holding company for Warren Buffett, one of the world's richest men. The company operates widely in the insurance industry and also has stakes in gems, candy, apparel, pilot training, and shoes. The company owns an interest in such well-known firms as Wal-Mart, American Express, Coca-Cola, Gillette, The Washington Post Company, and Wells Fargo, among others. Recently, Buffett has bought an interest in a Chinese energy firm, PetroChina.[133] His acquisition strategy in insurance has been particularly successful because he has followed many of the suggestions in Table 7.1.

As we have learned, some acquisitions enhance strategic competitiveness. However, the majority of acquisitions that took place from the 1970s through the 1990s did not enhance firms' strategic competitiveness. In fact, "history shows that anywhere between one-third [and] more than half of all acquisitions are ultimately divested or

Attributes of Successful Acquisitions — Table 7.1

Attributes	Results
1. Acquired firm has assets or resources that are complementary to the acquiring firm's core business	1. High probability of synergy and competitive advantage by maintaining strengths
2. Acquisition is friendly	2. Faster and more effective integration and possibly lower premiums
3. Acquiring firm conducts effective due diligence to select target firms and evaluate the target firm's health (financial, cultural, and human resources)	3. Firms with strongest complementarities are acquired and overpayment is avoided
4. Acquiring firm has financial slack (cash or a favorable debt position)	4. Financing (debt or equity) is easier and less costly to obtain
5. Merged firm maintains low to moderate debt position	5. Lower financing cost, lower risk (e.g., of bankruptcy), and avoidance of trade-offs that are associated with high debt
6. Acquiring firm has sustained and consistent emphasis on R&D and innovation	6. Maintain long-term competitive advantage in markets
7. Acquiring firm manages change well and is flexible and adaptable	7. Faster and more effective integration facilitates achievement of synergy

spun-off."[134] Thus, firms often use restructuring strategies to correct for the failure of a merger or an acquisition.

Restructuring

Defined formally, **restructuring** is a strategy through which a firm changes its set of businesses or financial structure.[135] From the 1970s into the 2000s, divesting businesses from company portfolios and downsizing accounted for a large percentage of firms' restructuring strategies. Restructuring is a global phenomenon.[136]

The failure of an acquisition strategy often precedes a restructuring strategy. Softbank, a Japanese telecommunications and Internet holding company built through acquisitions and partnering, has about 40 percent of the consumer broadband market in Japan, and sees itself within striking distance of the 3 million customers needed to break even on its digital subscriber line (DSL) service. However, the effect of the high cost of acquiring new customers (approximately $250 per customer) was obvious in the company's balance sheet, when it posted an $833 million loss in 2002. To keep the company liquid and to pay down its debt, Softbank is restructuring its holdings by selling its stakes in several companies, namely E*Trade, Yahoo!, and UTStarcom, as well as its stake in Aozora Bank, a national bank in Japan.[137]

In other instances, however, firms use a restructuring strategy because of changes in their external and internal environments. For example, opportunities sometimes surface in the external environment that are particularly attractive to the diversified firm in light of its core competencies. In such cases, restructuring may be appropriate to position the firm to create more value for stakeholders, given the environmental changes.[138]

As discussed next, there are three restructuring strategies that firms use: downsizing, downscoping, and leveraged buyouts.

Downsizing

Once thought to be an indicator of organizational decline, downsizing is now recognized as a legitimate restructuring strategy. *Downsizing* is a reduction in the number of a firm's employees and, sometimes, in the number of its operating units, but it may or may not change the composition of businesses in the company's portfolio. Thus, downsizing is an intentional proactive management strategy, whereas "decline is an environmental or organizational phenomenon that occurs involuntarily and results in erosion of an organization's resource base."[139]

In the late 1980s, early 1990s, and early 2000s, thousands of jobs were lost in private and public organizations in the United States. One study estimates that 85 percent of *Fortune* 1000 firms have used downsizing as a restructuring strategy.[140] Moreover, *Fortune* 500 firms laid off more than one million employees, or 4 percent of their collective workforce, in 2001 and into the first few weeks of 2002.[141] This trend continued in many industries in 2003. In particular, the airlines downsized in response to decreases in traffic caused by the SARS epidemic and the war in Iraq. For instance, Continental laid off 1,200 people in an effort to cut costs.[142] Firms use downsizing as a restructuring strategy for different reasons. The most frequently cited reason is that the firm expects improved profitability from cost reductions and more efficient operations, as exemplified by the Continental Airlines layoffs.

Downscoping

Compared to downsizing, downscoping has a more positive effect on firm performance.[143] *Downscoping* refers to divestiture, spin-off, or some other means of eliminating businesses that are unrelated to a firm's core businesses. Commonly, downscoping is described as a set of actions that causes a firm to strategically refocus on its core businesses.[144]

A firm that downscopes often also downsizes simultaneously. However, it does not eliminate key employees from its primary businesses in the process, because such action could lead to a loss of one or more core competencies. Instead, a firm that is simultaneously downscoping and downsizing becomes smaller by reducing the diversity of businesses in its portfolio.[145]

By refocusing on its core businesses, the firm can be managed more effectively by the top management team. Managerial effectiveness increases because the firm has become less diversified, allowing the top management team to better understand and manage the remaining businesses.[146]

In general, U.S. firms use downscoping as a restructuring strategy more frequently than do European companies, while the trend in Europe, Latin America, and Asia has been to build conglomerates. In Latin America, these conglomerates are called *grupos*. Many Asian and Latin American conglomerates have begun to adopt Western corporate strategies in recent years and have been refocusing on their core businesses. This downscoping has occurred simultaneously with increasing globalization and with more open markets that have greatly enhanced the competition. By downscoping, these firms have been able to focus on their core businesses and improve their competitiveness.[147]

Downscoping has been practiced recently by many Korean chaebol, large diversified business groups. Samsung has been very successful using this strategy. Lucky Goldstar (LG) Group is Korea's second largest chaebol with $92 billion in revenue in 2002. LG Group has been controlled by two families, the Koos and the Huhs, since its initiation in 1947. Since 1998, the two families have engaged in a major restructuring program. They have eliminated most of the cross-holding (an arrangement in which major subsidiaries held ownership in each other), which has been typical of Korean chaebol. In place of the cross-holding arrangement, they have created a holding company with more separation between subsidiaries. Although this has been a boon to investors, a shareholder lawsuit has been threatened, which suggests that the families have been shorting shareholders in many of the deals the holding company has completed. One of the major problems is that many of the diversified businesses are being sold to Koos and Huh family members as stand-alone companies. This has allowed the families, through the holding company structure, to continue in firm control of the group. Thus, although shareholders have gained from the restructuring, there is still a concern about too much family control and possible self-dealing.[148]

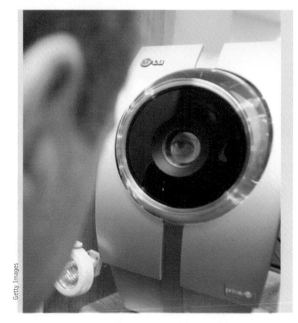

The Korean firm Lucky Goldstar (LG) Group has been heavily restructured through downscoping, as have other Korean chaebol that have previously been highly diversified. Shareholders are still expressing concern, however, about too much family control and self-interest. Pictured here is one of its products, a new iris scanning device (shown at Boston's Logan airport) manufactured by LG Electronics' Iris Technology Division.

Leveraged Buyouts

Leveraged buyouts are commonly used as a restructuring strategy to correct for managerial mistakes or because the firm's managers are making decisions that primarily serve their own interests rather than those of shareholders.[149] A *leveraged buyout* (LBO) is a restructuring strategy whereby a party buys all of a firm's assets in order to take the firm private. Once the transaction is completed, the company's stock is no longer traded publicly. As the Strategic Focus on an LBO revival indicates, these deals have many purposes.

Usually, significant amounts of debt are incurred to finance a buyout; hence the term "leveraged" buyout. To support debt payments and to downscope the company to concentrate on the firm's core businesses, the new owners may

Getty Images

Leveraged Buyouts and Private Equity Restructuring Deals Experience a Revival

Leveraged buyout associations receive funds from investors to invest in firms interested in being privately owned; as such, they are often labeled private equity funds. As the name implies, this is often done through the "leverage" of debt investment devices. Because of the Enron debacle and firms being under financial distress, assets sales through leveraged buyouts had increased. The *Wall Street Journal* indicated: "U.S. LBO volume doubled to $23 billion in 2002 from $11 billion the previous year, although it still remains below 2000 levels of $39 billion. The number of transactions held steady at 181. Worldwide LBOs increased to $81 billion, up 36% from 2001, with the number of deals falling 19.8% to 814." In commenting on the prospects of private equity funds, one analyst predicted: "With LBO shops having sufficient cash on hand, and there being a large number of distressed companies due to an adverse economic climate, there is ample reason to believe that 2003 will be a big year for LBOs."

Both investment and commercial banks often participate in these funds through syndicated arrangements to reduce risk. For example, Bain Capital, Texas Pacific Group, and Goldman Sachs helped to finance the $1.5 billion purchase of Burger King from Diageo PLC through syndicated loans among these banks.

Many firms are considering going private through leveraged buyouts through the help of private equity funds because of the increased safeguards for shareholders against corporate malfeasance. Some feel that the Sarbanes-Oxley Act of 2002 is too strict and does not allow enough flexibility for many firms, especially fast-moving technology firms and many small firms considering being listed on the NASDAQ stock exchange. Many of these firms, instead of going through an IPO, are choosing to receive funding from a private equity firm. For example, Quintiles, a pharmaceutical-testing company, pursued a private equity deal because it allowed the firm more flexibility to pursue its long-term growth, which requires expensive investments now. Dennis Gillings, the company founder, felt that market analysts of public companies were too focused on quarterly earnings and would fail to grasp his long-term strategy. Accordingly, he received $1.7 billion from Bank One's private equity arm to move forward with his strategy.

Wilbur Ross runs a private equity fund that has had significant success by buying distressed firms in mature businesses, such as textiles, carpet making, optical networking, and, lately, integrated steel mills. Ross has been steadfast in his pursuit of bankrupt and distressed companies, whether in boom or bust economic times. Carl Icahn says of Ross, "He has the abilities to see opportunities other investment bankers miss." In the past several years, Ross has bought 70 distressed properties, the largest of which are Burlington Industries in carpet making, 360 Networks in optical networking, and, most recently, Bethlehem Steel. He will seek to integrate Bethlehem Steel with previous acquisitions of LTV and Acme, which he brought together into the International Steel Group (ISG). Subsequent to the Bethlehem purchase, these steel operations will be responsible for more than 20 percent of U.S. production.

In searching for possible deals, Ross examines industries with a large concentration of high-yield financing, which he considers a red flag. Once these are identified, he tries to pick the survivors that will be able to overcome their difficulties and be successfully restructured. Regarding his steel investments, he believed that steel was "too vital to the economy and national security" to allow domestic production to disappear. Shortly after his investments, the Bush administration imposed a 30 percent tariff on foreign steel. Although ISG faces competitors from Japan, Russia, Mexico, and the European Union that are contesting the legality of U.S. tariffs at the World Trade Organization, Ross is confident that his integrated steel operations will be able to compete, given the restructuring that has been and will continue to be undertaken through the auspices of ISG managers. He is now continuing his search in real estate, energy, and other sectors for distressed firms that can be taken private through his large private equity fund.

SOURCES: J. Kahn, 2003, The burden of being public, *Fortune*, May 26, 35–36; K. Scannell, 2003, Year-end review of markets & finance 2002—LBO shops profit from scandals—buyouts accounted for 5% of 2002's M&A volume, *Wall Street Journal*, January 2, R8; N. Stein, 2003, Wilbur Ross is a man of steel, *Fortune*, May 26, 121–122; M. Sikora, 2003, Syndicated bank loans may fuel upturn in LBO deals expected in 2003, *Mergers and Acquisitions*, March, 18.

immediately sell a number of assets.[150] It is not uncommon for those buying a firm through an LBO to restructure the firm to the point that it can be sold at a profit within a five- to eight-year period.

Management buyouts (MBOs), employee buyouts (EBOs), and whole-firm buyouts, in which one company or partnership purchases an entire company instead of a part of it, are the three types of LBOs. In part because of managerial incentives, MBOs, more so than EBOs and whole-firm buyouts, have been found to lead to downscoping, an increased strategic focus, and improved performance.[151] Research has shown that management buyouts can also lead to greater entrepreneurial activity and growth.[152]

While there may be different reasons for a buyout, one is to protect against a capricious financial market, allowing the owners to focus on developing innovations and bringing them to the market.[153] As such, buyouts can represent a form of firm rebirth to facilitate entrepreneurial efforts and stimulate strategic growth.[154]

Restructuring Outcomes

The short-term and long-term outcomes resulting from the three restructuring strategies are shown in Figure 7.2. As indicated, downsizing does not commonly lead to a

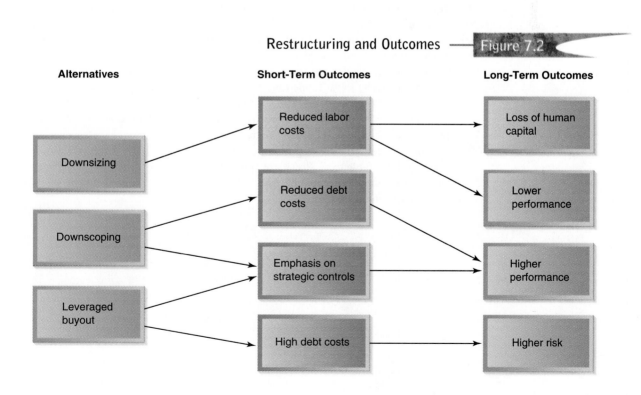

Restructuring and Outcomes — Figure 7.2

higher firm performance.[155] Still, in free-market-based societies at large, downsizing has generated an incentive for individuals who have been laid off to start their own businesses.

Research has shown that downsizing contributed to lower returns for both U.S. and Japanese firms. The stock markets in the firms' respective nations evaluated downsizing negatively. Investors concluded that downsizing would have a negative effect on companies' ability to achieve strategic competitiveness in the long term. Investors also seem to assume that downsizing occurs as a consequence of other problems in a company.[156] This is clear in the Continental Airlines layoffs mentioned above.

An unintentional outcome of downsizing, however, is that often, laid-off employees start new businesses in order to live through the disruption in their lives. Accordingly, downsizing has generated a host of entrepreneurial new ventures. For example, Richard Sheridan, a former vice-president of software development at Interface Systems, founded a software consulting business with a few other colleagues after being laid off in January 2001. His company, Menlo Innovations, broke even in 2001 and was profitable in 2002.[157]

As shown in Figure 7.2, downsizing tends to result in a loss of human capital in the long term. Losing employees with many years of experience with the firm represents a major loss of knowledge. As noted in Chapter 3, knowledge is vital to competitive success in the global economy.[158] Thus, in general, research evidence and corporate experience suggest that downsizing may be of more tactical (or short-term) value than strategic (or long-term) value.

Downscoping generally leads to more positive outcomes in both the short and the long term than does downsizing or engaging in a leveraged buyout (see Figure 7.2). Downscoping's desirable long-term outcome of higher performance is a product of reduced debt costs and the emphasis on strategic controls derived from concentrating on the firm's core businesses. In so doing, the refocused firm should be able to increase its ability to compete.

While whole-firm LBOs have been hailed as a significant innovation in the financial restructuring of firms, there can be negative trade-offs. First, the resulting large debt increases the financial risk of the firm, as is evidenced by the number of companies that filed for bankruptcy in the 1990s after executing a whole-firm LBO. Sometimes, the intent of the owners to increase the efficiency of the bought-out firm and then sell it within five to eight years creates a short-term and risk-averse managerial focus.[159] As a result, these firms may fail to invest adequately in R&D or take other major actions designed to maintain or improve the company's core competence.[160] Research also suggests that in firms with an entrepreneurial mind-set, buyouts can lead to greater innovation, especially if the debt load is not too great.[161] However, because buyouts more often result in significant debt, most LBOs have taken place in mature industries where stable cash flows are possible. This enables the buyout firm to meet the recurring debt payments as exemplified by Wilbur Ross' buyouts in the steel industry described in the Strategic Focus.

Summary

- Acquisition strategies are increasingly popular. Because of globalization, deregulation of multiple industries in many different economies, and favorable legislation, the number and size of domestic and cross-border acquisitions continues to increase.

- Firms use acquisition strategies to (1) increase market power, (2) overcome entry barriers to new markets or regions, (3) avoid the costs of developing new products and increase the speed of new market entries, (4) reduce the risk of entering a new business, (5) become more diversified, (6) reshape their competitive scope by developing a different portfolio of businesses, and (7) enhance their learning, thereby adding to their knowledge base.

- Among the problems associated with the use of an acquisition strategy are (1) the difficulty of effectively integrating the firms involved, (2) incorrectly evaluating the target firm's value, (3) creating debt loads that preclude adequate long-term investments (e.g., R&D), (4) overestimating the potential for synergy, (5) creating a firm that is too diversified, (6) creating an internal environment in which managers devote increasing amounts of their time and energy to analyzing and completing the acquisition, and (7) developing a combined firm that is too large, necessitating extensive use of bureaucratic, rather than strategic, controls.

- Effective acquisitions have the following characteristics: (1) the acquiring and target firms have complementary resources that can be the basis of core competencies in the newly created firm, (2) the acquisition is friendly thereby facilitating integration of the two firms' resources, (3) the target firm is selected and purchased based on thorough due diligence, (4) the acquiring and target firms have considerable slack in the form of cash or debt capacity, (5) the merged firm maintains a low or moderate level of debt by selling off portions of the acquired firm or some of the acquiring firm's poorly performing units, (6) the acquiring and acquired firms have experience in terms of adapting to change, and (7) R&D and innovation are emphasized in the new firm.

- Restructuring is used to improve a firm's performance by correcting for problems created by ineffective management. Restructuring by downsizing involves reducing the number of employees and hierarchical levels in the firm. Although it can lead to short-term cost reductions, they may be realized at the expense of long-term success, because of the loss of valuable human resources (and knowledge).

- The goal of restructuring through downscoping is to reduce the firm's level of diversification. Often, the firm divests unrelated businesses to achieve this goal. Eliminating unrelated businesses makes it easier for the firm and its top-level managers to refocus on the core businesses.

- Leveraged buyouts (LBOs) represent an additional restructuring strategy. Through an LBO, a firm is purchased so that it can become a private entity. LBOs usually are financed largely through debt. There are three types of LBOs: management buyouts (MBOs), employee buyouts (EBOs), and whole-firm LBOs. Because they provide clear managerial incentives, MBOs have been the most successful of the three. Often, the intent of a buyout is to improve efficiency and performance to the point where the firm can be sold successfully within five to eight years.

- Commonly, restructuring's primary goal is gaining or reestablishing effective strategic control of the firm. Of the three restructuring strategies, downscoping is aligned the most closely with establishing and using strategic controls.

Review Questions

1. Why are acquisition strategies popular in many firms competing in the global economy?

2. What reasons account for firms' decisions to use acquisition strategies as one means of achieving strategic competitiveness?

3. What are the seven primary problems that affect a firm's efforts to successfully use an acquisition strategy?

4. What are the attributes associated with a successful acquisition strategy?

5. What is the restructuring strategy and what are its common forms?

6. What are the short- and long-term outcomes associated with the different restructuring strategies?

Determining the Best Path to Firm Growth

You are on the executive board of an information technology firm that provides trafficking software to the trucking industry. One of the firm's managers feels the company should grow and has suggested expanding by creating trafficking software for rail shipments or by offering trucking trafficking services online. You know your firm is in a position to expand but are not sure about the best way to do so.

Part One. Should the firm consider a merger with or an acquisition of a firm that offers the suggested services, or should it develop them internally? List the advantages and disadvantages of each strategic option.

Part Two. Based on your findings and other information, assume that your firm decides to obtain trafficking software for rail shipments through an acquisition of an existing firm. Predict some general problems your firm might encounter in an acquisition and how they might be resolved.

Mergers and Acquisitions

Merger and acquisition activity is increasingly common, both domestically and internationally. However, such activity does not always result in the intended outcomes. In general, shareholders of acquired firms often enjoy above-average returns, while shareholders of acquiring firms are less likely to do so.

Identify a recent major merger or acquisition, such as one that made the front page of the *Wall Street Journal* or was a feature story in a business periodical such as *Fortune, Business Week,* or *The Economist.* Then find two or three other comprehensive articles about this merger or acquisition from more than one source, especially over a period of several weeks as the merger/acquisition events unfolded. This process of triangulation will provide a better understanding of any business activity and its results, as well as help substantiate the facts of the case.

1. What are the primary reasons for the merger or acquisition of study? Is this a horizontal, vertical, or related integration? How do you know? How is the firm's market power affected?

2. Was the merger or acquisition a success? To what extent do analysts anticipate problems in achieving success with this merger or acquisition? What issues appear to be of concern?

3. What happened to the stock prices of the involved firms before, during, and after the merger/acquisition? What actions could have been taken to make the integration more efficient and effective in achieving the acquiring firm's goals?

Notes

1. L. Capron & N. Pistre, 2002, When do acquirers earn abnormal returns? *Strategic Management Journal*, 23: 781–794.

2. K. Fuller, J. Netter, & M. Stegemoller, 2002, What do returns to acquiring firms tell us? Evidence from firms that make many acquisitions, *Journal of Finance*, 57: 1763–1793; M. A. Hitt, J. S. Harrison, & R. D. Ireland, 2001, *Mergers and Acquisitions: A Guide to Creating Value for Stakeholders*, New York: Oxford University Press.

3. G. K. Deans, F. Kroeger, & S. Zeisel, 2002, The consolidation curve, *Harvard Business Review*, 80(12): 20–21; 2000, How M&As will navigate the turn into a new century, *Mergers and Acquisitions*, January, 29–35.

4. J. A. Schmidt, 2002, Business perspective on mergers and acquisitions, in J. A. Schmidt (ed.), *Making Mergers Work*, Alexandria, VA: Society for Human Resource Management, 23–46.

5. E. R. Auster & M. L. Sirower, 2002, The dynamics of merger and acquisition waves: A three-stage conceptual framework with implications for practice, *Journal of Applied Behavioral Science*, 38: 216–244.

6. M. A. Hitt, R. D. Ireland, & J. S. Harrison, 2001, Mergers and acquisitions: A value creating or a value destroying strategy? in M. A. Hitt, R. E. Freeman, & J. S. Harrison, *Handbook of Strategic Management*, Oxford, UK: Blackwell Publishers, 385–408.

7. L. Saigol, 2002, Thin pickings in dismal year for dealmaking, *Financial Times*, http://www.ft.com, January 2; 2001, Waiting for growth, *The Economist*, http://www.economist.com, April 27.

8. 2002, Mergers snapshot: 2001 deal volume, *Wall Street Journal*, January 4, C12; 2001, The great merger wave breaks, *The Economist*, January 27, 59–60.

9. R. Sidel, 2002, Volatile U.S. markets and global slowdown cool corporate desire to merge, *Wall Street Journal*, January 2, R10.

10. J. Keough, 2003, M&A activity to rise in 2003, *Industrial Distribution*, February, 19–20.

11. L. Himelstein, L. Lee, J. Kerstetter, & P. Burrows, 2003, Let's make a deal: After a long M&A drought, corporate America is shopping around again, *Business Week*, April 21, 82–83.

12. R. Coff, 2003, Bidding wars over R&D-intensive firms: Knowledge, opportunism, and the market for corporate control, *Academy of Management Journal*, 46: 74–85; P. Chattopadhyay, W. H. Glick, & G. P. Huber, 2001, Organizational actions in response to threats and opportunities, *Academy of Management Journal*, 44: 937–955.

13. A. E. Bernardo & B. Chowdhry, 2002, Resources, real options, and corporate strategy, *Journal of Financial Economics*, 63: 211–234; M. A. Schilling & H. K. Steensma, 2002, Disentangling the theories of firm boundaries: A path model and empirical test, *Organization Science*, 13: 387–401; H. T. J. Smit, 2001, Acquisition strategies as option games, *Journal of Applied Corporate Finance*, 14(2): 79–89.

14. A. Bednarski, 2003, From diversity to duplication: Mega-mergers and the failure of the marketplace model under the Telecommunications Act of 1996, *Federal Communications Law Journal*, 55(2): 273–295.

15. L. Selden & G. Colvin, 2003, M&A needn't be a losers game, *Harvard Business Review*, 81(6): 70–73; J. P. Hughes, W. W. Lang, L. J. Mester, C.-G. Moon, & M. S. Pagano, 2003, Do bankers sacrifice value to build empires? Managerial incentives, industry consolidation, and financial performance, *Journal of Banking & Finance*, 27: 417–447.

16. K. Gugler, D. C. Mueller, R. B. Yurtoglu, & C. Zulehner, 2003, The effects of mergers: An international comparison, *International Journal of Industrial Organization*, 21: 625–653.

17. M. M. Cornett, G. Hovakimian, D. Palia, & H. Tehranian, 2003, The impact of the manager-shareholder conflict on acquiring bank returns, *Journal of Banking & Finance*, 27: 103–131; M. C. Jensen, 1988, Takeovers: Their causes and consequences, *Journal of Economic Perspectives*, 1(2): 21–48.

18. T. Wright, M. Kroll, A. Lado, & B. Van Ness, 2002, The structure of ownership and corporate acquisition strategies, *Strategic Management Journal*, 23: 41–53; Selden & Colvin, M&A needn't be a losers game; A. Rappaport & M.

19. L. Sirower, 1999, Stock or cash? *Harvard Business Review*, 77(6): 147–158.

A. Keeton, 2003, Class-action is approved against DaimlerChrysler, *Wall Street Journal*, June 13, B2.

20. J. Hall, 2003, Deals & deal makers: Kohlberg Kravis drops Safeway from shopping list, cites risk, *Wall Street Journal*, February 25, C5.

21. E. Thornton, F. Keesnan, C. Palmeri, & L. Himelstein, 2002, It sure is getting hostile, *Business Week*, January 14, 28–30.

22. R. Grover, 2003, Getting MGM off the back lot: Can Yemenidjian transform the studio into a media giant? *Business Week*, March 3, 101–102; J. Harding & C. Grimes, 2002, MGM owner sounds out possible suitors, *Financial Times*, http://www.ft.com, January 16; B. Pulley, 2001, The wizard of MGM, *Forbes*, May 28, 122–128.

23. P. Haspeslagh, 1999, Managing the mating dance in equal mergers, "Mastering Strategy" (Part Five), *Financial Times*, October 25, 14–15.

24. P. Wright, M. Kroll, & D. Elenkov, 2002, Acquisition returns, increase in firm size and chief executive officer compensation: The moderating role of monitoring, *Academy of Management Journal*, 45: 599–608.

25. G. Anders, 2002, Lessons from WaMu's M&A playbook, *Fast Company*, January, 100–107.

26. P. Starobin, 2003, A Russian oilman's global ambitions, *BusinessWeek Online*, http://www.businessweek.com, May 21.

27. Capron & Pistre, When do acquirers earn abnormal returns?; L. Capron, 1999, Horizontal acquisitions: The benefits and risks to long-term performance, *Strategic Management Journal*, 20: 987–1018.

28. M. Lubatkin, W. S. Schulze, A. Mainkar, & R. W. Cotterill, 2001, Ecological investigation of firm effects in horizontal mergers, *Strategic Management Journal*, 22: 335–357; K. Ramaswamy, 1997, The performance impact of strategic similarity in horizontal mergers: Evidence from the U.S. banking industry, *Academy of Management Journal*, 40: 697–715.

29. L. Capron, W. Mitchell, & A. Swaminathan, 2001, Asset divestiture following horizontal acquisitions: A dynamic view, *Strategic Management Journal*, 22: 817–844.

30. J. Markoff, 2003, Deal reunites early makers of handhelds, *New York Times*, http://www.nytimes.com, June 5.

31. M. R. Subramani & N. Venkatraman, 2003, Safeguarding investments in asymmetric interorganizational relationships: Theory and evidence, *Academy of Management Journal*, 46: 46–62; T. S. Gabrielsen, 2003, Conglomerate mergers: Vertical mergers in disguise? *International Journal of the Economics of Business*, 10(1): 1–16.

32. 2003, Special Report: The complete home entertainer? Sony, *The Economist*, March 1, 62–64.

33. W. Zellner, 2003, Tyson: Is there life outside the chicken coop? *Business Week*, March 10, 77.

34. D. Gupta & Y. Gerchak, 2002, Quantifying operational synergies in a merger/acquisition, *Management Science*, 48: 517–533.

35. D. E. M. Sappington, 2003, Regulating horizontal diversification, *International Journal of Industrial Organization*, 21: 291–315.

36. A. Barrett, 2003, "In the credibility penalty box": Can Honeywell CEO Cote restore investors' confidence? *Business Week*, April 28, 80–81.

37. A. R. Sorkin, 2003, Three's a crowd to air cargo giants, *New York Times*, http://www.nytimes.com, June 1.

38. M. Lerner, 2001, Israeli Antitrust Authority's general director David Tadmor on corporate mergers, *Academy of Management Executive*, 15(1): 8–11.

39. S. J. Chang & P. M. Rosenzweig, 2001, The choice of entry mode in sequential foreign direct investment, *Strategic Management Journal*, 22: 747–776.

40. N. Dawar & A. Chattopadhyay, 2002, Rethinking marketing programs for emerging markets, *Long Range Planning*, 35(5): 457–474; J. A. Gingrich, 1999, Five rules for winning emerging market consumers, *Strategy & Business*, 15: 19–33.

41. J. A. Doukas & L. H. P. Lang, 2003, Foreign direct investment, diversification and firm performance, *Journal of International Business Studies*, 34: 153–172; Hitt, Harrison, & Ireland, *Mergers and Acquisitions*, Chapter 10; D. Angwin &

B. Savill, 1997, Strategic perspectives on European cross–border acquisitions: A view from the top European executives, *European Management Review*, 15: 423–435.

42. A. Seth, K. P. Song, & R. R. Pettit, 2002, Value creation and destruction in cross-border acquisitions: An empirical analysis of foreign acquisitions of U.S. firms, *Strategic Management Journal*, 23: 921–940.

43. Schmidt, Business perspective on mergers and acquisitions.

44. A. M. Agami, 2002, The role that foreign acquisitions of Asian companies played in the recovery of the Asian financial crisis, *Multinational Business Review*, 10(1): 11–20.

45. 2002, Cleary Gottlieb acts in largest US cross-border deal of the year, *International Financial Law Review*, 21(12): 13.

46. D. Bilefsky, 2003, Miller Beer aims to be icon in Europe, *Wall Street Journal*, June 13, B7.

47. J. K. Sebenius, 2002, The hidden challenge of cross-border negotiations, *Harvard Business Review*, 80(3): 76–85.

48. W. Vanhaverbeke, G. Duysters, & N. Noorderhaven, 2002, External technology sourcing through alliances or acquisitions: An analysis of the application-specific integrated circuits industry, *Organization Science*, 6: 714–733; J. K. Shank & V. Govindarajan, 1992, Strategic cost analysis of technological investments, *Sloan Management Review*, 34(3): 39–51.

49. H. Gatignon, M. L. Tushman, W. Smith, & P. Anderson, 2002, A structural approach to assessing innovation: Construct development of innovation locus, type, and characteristics, *Management Science*, 48: 1103–1122; Hitt, Harrison, & Ireland, *Mergers and Acquisitions*.

50. M. A. Hitt, R. E. Hoskisson, R. A. Johnson, & D. D. Moesel, 1996, The market for corporate control and firm innovation, *Academy of Management Journal*, 39: 1084–1119.

51. Coff, Bidding wars over R&D-intensive firms: Knowledge, opportunism, and the market for corporate control.

52. 2003, Pharma and biotech M&A deal activity up in 2002, *Chemical Week*, April 2, 43.

53. T. Yoshikawa, 2003, Technology development and acquisition strategy, *International Journal of Technology Management*, 25(6,7): 666–674; K. F. McCardle & S. Viswanathan, 1994, The direct entry versus takeover decision and stock price performance around takeovers, *Journal of Business*, 67: 1–43.

54. Y. Luo, O. Shenkar, & M.-K. Nyaw, 2002, Mitigating liabilities of foreignness: Defensive versus offensive approaches, *Journal of International Management*, 8: 283–300; J. W. Lu & P. W. Beamish, 2001, The internationalization and performance of SMEs, *Strategic Management Journal*, 22(Special Issue): 565–586.

55. C. W. L. Hill & F. T. Rothaermel, 2003, The performance of incumbent firms in the face of radical technological innovation, *Academy of Management Review*, 28: 257–274; G. Ahuja & C. Lampert, 2001, Entrepreneurship in the large corporation: A longitudinal study of how established firms create breakthrough inventions, *Strategic Management Journal*, 22 (Special Issue): 521–543.

56. F. Rothaermel, 2001, Incumbent's advantage through exploiting complementary assets via interfirm cooperation, *Strategic Management Journal*, 22(Special Issue): 687–699.

57. K. Capell, 2003, Novartis CEO Daniel Vasella has a hot cancer drug and billions in the bank. What's his next big move? *Business Week*, May 26, 54.

58. G. Ahuja & R. Katila, 2001, Technological acquisitions and the innovation performance of acquiring firms: A longitudinal study, *Strategic Management Journal*, 22: 197–220; M. A. Hitt, R. E. Hoskisson, & R. D. Ireland, 1990, Mergers and acquisitions and managerial commitment to innovation in M-form firms, *Strategic Management Journal*, 11(Special Issue): 29–47.

59. Hitt, Hoskisson, Johnson, & Moesel, The market for corporate control.

60. Hill & Rothaermel, The performance of incumbent firms in the face of radical technological innovation.

61. M. A. Hitt, R. E. Hoskisson, R. D. Ireland, & J. S. Harrison, 1991, Effects of acquisitions on R&D inputs and outputs, *Academy of Management Journal*, 34: 693–706.

62. Capron, Mitchell, & Swaminathan, Asset divestiture following horizontal acquisitions; D. D. Bergh, 1997, Predicting divestiture of unrelated acquisitions: An integrative model of ex ante conditions, *Strategic Management Journal*, 18: 715–731.

63. A. L. Velocci, Jr., 2003, Goodrich curbs appetite, focuses on TRW integration, *Aviation Week & Space Technology*, February 24, 33–34.

64. C. Park, 2003, Prior performance characteristics of related and unrelated acquirers, *Strategic Management Journal*, 24: 471–480; C. Park, 2002, The effects of prior performance on the choice between related and unrelated acquisitions: Implications for the performance consequences of diversification strategy, *Journal of Management Studies*, 39: 1003–1019.

65. P. L. Moore, 2001, The most aggressive CEO, *Business Week*, May 28, 67–77.

66. A. Raghavan & R. Sidel, 2003, Deals & deal makers: United Technologies seals deal, *Wall Street Journal*, June 12, C5.

67. Hitt, Harrison, & Ireland, *Mergers and Acquisitions*.

68. J. Anand & H. Singh, 1997, Asset redeployment, acquisitions and corporate strategy in declining industries, *Strategic Management Journal*, 18(Special Issue): 99–118.

69. W. J. Ferrier, 2001, Navigating the competitive landscape: The drivers and consequences of competitive aggressiveness, *Academy of Management Journal*, 44: 858–877.

70. S. Lohr, 2003, PeopleSoft bid mirrors lofty goals of Oracle chief executive, *New York Times*, http://www.nytimes.com, June 11.

71. M. Warner, 2002, Can GE light up the market again? *Fortune*, November 11, 108–117; R. E. Hoskisson & M. A. Hitt, 1994, *Downscoping: How to Tame the Diversified Firm*, New York: Oxford University Press.

72. J. Anand & A. Delios, 2002, Absolute and relative resources as determinants of international acquisitions, *Strategic Management Journal*, 23(2): 119–134; F. Vermeulen & H. Barkema, 2001, Learning through acquisitions, *Academy of Management Journal*, 44: 457–476.

73. M. L. A. Hayward, 2002, When do firms learn from their acquisition experience? Evidence from 1990–1995, *Strategic Management Journal*, 23: 21–39.

74. J. S. Harrison, M. A. Hitt, R. E. Hoskisson, & R. D. Ireland, 2001, Resource complementarity in business combinations: Extending the logic to organizational alliances, *Journal of Management*, 27: 679–690.

75. S. Thurm, 2003, After the boom: A go-go giant of Internet age, Cisco is learning to go slow, *Wall Street Journal*, May 7, A1.

76. Schmidt, Business perspective on mergers and acquisitions.

77. Hitt, Harrison, & Ireland, *Mergers and Acquisitions*.

78. R. A. Weber & C. F. Camerer, 2003, Cultural conflict and merger failure: An experimental approach, *Management Science*, 49: 400–415; J. Vester, 2002, Lessons learned about integrating acquisitions, *Research Technology Management*, 45(3): 33–41; D. K. Datta, 1991, Organizational fit and acquisition performance: Effects of post-acquisition integration, *Strategic Management Journal*, 12: 281–297.

79. Y. Weber & E. Menipaz, 2003, Measuring cultural fit in mergers and acquisitions, *International Journal of Business Performance Management*, 5(1): 54–72.

80. M. Zollo, 1999, M&A — The challenge of learning to integrate, "Mastering Strategy" (Part Eleven), *Financial Times*, December 6, 14–15.

81. C. Haddad, A. Weintraub, & B. Grow, 2003, Too good to be true, *Business Week*, April 14, 70–72.

82. M. A. Hitt, L. Bierman, K. Shimizu, & R. Kochhar, 2001, Direct and moderating effects of human capital on strategy and performance in professional service firms, *Academy of Management Journal*, 44: 13–28.

83. J. A. Krug, 2003, Why do they keep leaving? *Harvard Business Review*, 81(2): 14–15; H. A. Krishnan & D. Park, 2002, The impact of workforce reduction on subsequent performance in major mergers and acquisitions: An exploratory study, *Journal of Business Research*, 55(4): 285–292; G. G. Dess & J. D. Shaw, 2001, Voluntary turnover, social capital and organizational performance, *Academy of Management Review*, 26: 446–456.

84. R. G. Baptiste, 2002, The merger of ACE and CARE: Two Caribbean banks, *Journal of Applied Behavioral Science*, 38: 466–480; J. A. Krug & H. Hegarty,

2001, Predicting who stays and leaves after an acquisition: A study of top managers in multinational firms, *Strategic Management Journal*, 22: 185–196.

85. L. B. Nygaard, 2002, Mergers and acquisitions: Beyond due diligence, *Internal Auditor*, 59(2): 36–43.

86. Rappaport & Sirower, Stock or cash? 149.

87. E. Thornton, 2003, Bypassing the street, *Business Week*, June 2, 79.

88. G. Yago, 1991, *Junk Bonds: How High Yield Securities Restructured Corporate America*, New York: Oxford University Press, 146–148.

89. M. C. Jensen, 1986, Agency costs of free cash flow, corporate finance, and takeovers, *American Economic Review*, 76: 323–329.

90. A. Fass, 2003, AOL Time over? *Forbes*, June 23, 49.

91. M. A. Hitt & D. L. Smart, 1994, Debt: A disciplining force for managers or a debilitating force for organizations? *Journal of Management Inquiry*, 3: 144–152.

92. Hitt, Harrison, & Ireland, *Mergers and Acquisitions*.

93. T. N. Hubbard, 1999, Integration strategies and the scope of the company, "Mastering Strategy" (Part Eleven), *Financial Times*, December 6, 8–10.

94. Hitt, Harrison, & Ireland, *Mergers and Acquisitions*.

95. Ibid.

96. Harrison, Hitt, Hoskisson, & Ireland, Resource complementarity in business combinations; J. B. Barney, 1988, Returns to bidding firms in mergers and acquisitions: Reconsidering the relatedness hypothesis, *Strategic Management Journal*, 9(Special Issue): 71–78.

97. O. E. Williamson, 1999, Strategy research: Governance and competence perspectives, *Strategic Management Journal*, 20: 1087–1108.

98. Hitt, Hoskisson, Johnson, & Moesel, The market for corporate control.

99. G. Khermouch, 2003, Interpublic Group: Synergy—or sinkhole? *Business Week*, April 21, 76–77.

100. B. Einhorn, F. Balfour, & K. Capell, 2002, More Virgin territory, *Business Week*, April 8, 25.

101. C. W. L. Hill & R. E. Hoskisson, 1987, Strategy and structure in the multiproduct firm, *Academy of Management Review*, 12: 331–341.

102. R. A. Johnson, R. E. Hoskisson, & M. A. Hitt, 1993, Board of director involvement in restructuring: The effects of board versus managerial controls and characteristics, *Strategic Management Journal*, 14(Special Issue): 33–50; C. C. Markides, 1992, Consequences of corporate refocusing: Ex ante evidence, *Academy of Management Journal*, 35: 398–412.

103. G. Garai, 2002, Take our outfit—Please! How do you start a small business? Maybe by relieving a corporation of a rashly acquired division, as our expert explains, *BusinessWeek Online*, http://www.businessweek.com, December 18.

104. D. Palmer & B. N. Barber, 2001, Challengers, elites and families: A social class theory of corporate acquisitions, *Administrative Science Quarterly*, 46: 87–120.

105. Hitt, Harrison, & Ireland, *Mergers and Acquisitions*.

106. Ibid.

107. Hughes, Lang, Mester, Moon, & Pagano, Do bankers sacrifice value to build empires? Managerial incentives, industry consolidation, and financial performance; Hitt, Hoskisson, Johnson, & Moesel, The market for corporate control.

108. M. L. A. Hayward & D. C. Hambrick, 1997. Explaining the premiums paid for large acquisitions: Evidence of CEO hubris, *Administrative Science Quarterly* 42: 103–127; R. Roll, 1986, The hubris hypothesis of corporate takeovers, *Journal of Business*, 59: 197–216.

109. J. Pfeffer, 2003, The human factor: Curbing the urge to merge, *Business 2.0*, July, 58.

110. Hayward, When do firms learn from their acquisition experience?

111. Weber & Camerer, Cultural conflict and merger failure: An experimental approach.

112. 2003, Business: Corus of disapproval; steel, *The Economist*, March 15, 61–62.

113. Hitt, Harrison, & Ireland, *Mergers and Acquisitions*; Hitt, Hoskisson, Ireland, & Harrison, Effects of acquisitions on R&D inputs and outputs.

114. R. E. Hoskisson, M. A. Hitt, & R. D. Ireland, 1994, The effects of acquisitions and restructuring (strategic refocusing) strategies on innovation, in G. von Krogh, A. Sinatra, and H. Singh (eds.), *Managing Corporate Acquisitions*, London: Macmillan Press, 144–169.

115. H. Greenberg, 2002, The buy-'em-up boondoggle, *Fortune*, July 22, 210.

116. R. M. Cyert, S.-H. Kang, and P. Kumar, 2002, Corporate governance, takeovers, and top-management compensation: Theory and evidence, *Management Science*, 48:453–469.

117. A. P. Dickerson, H. D. Gibson, & E. Tsakalotos, 2003, Is attack the best form of defence? A competing risks analysis of acquisition activity in the UK, *Cambridge Journal of Economics*, 27: 337–357.

118. Hitt, Harrison, & Ireland, *Mergers and Acquisitions*.

119. A. P. Dickerson, H. D. Gibson, and E. Tsakalotos, 2002. Takeover risk and the market for corporate control: The experience of British firms in the 1970s and 1980s, *International Journal of Industrial Organization*, 20: 1167–1195.

120. R. M. Di Gregorio, 2003, Making mergers and acquisitions work: What we know and don't know—Part II, *Journal of Change Management*, 3(3): 259–274; R. M. Di Gregorio, 2002, Making mergers and acquisitions work: What we know and don't know—Part I, *Journal of Change Management*, 3(2): 134–148.

121. B. Musler, 2002, Requiem for a predator, *Computerworld*, December 2, 25.

122. M. A. Hitt, R. D. Ireland, J. S. Harrison, & A. Best, 1998, Attributes of successful and unsuccessful acquisitions of U.S. firms, *British Journal of Management*, 9: 91–114.

123. Harrison, Hitt, Hoskisson, & Ireland, Resource complementarity in business combinations.

124. J. Hagedoorn & G. Dysters, 2002, External sources of innovative capabilities: The preference for strategic alliances or mergers and acquisitions, *Journal of Management Studies*, 39: 167–188.

125. J. Reuer, 2001, From hybrids to hierarchies: Shareholder wealth effects of joint venture partner buyouts, *Strategic Management Journal*, 22: 27–44.

126. R. J. Aiello & M. D. Watkins, 2000, The fine art of friendly acquisition, *Harvard Business Review*, 78(6): 100–107.

127. J. Wetuski, 2003, Devon-Ocean combination to be stronger than parts, *Oil & Gas Investor*, 23(4): 119–120.

128. D. D. Bergh, 2001, Executive retention and acquisition outcomes: A test of opposing views on the influence of organizational tenure, *Journal of Management*, 27: 603–622; J. P. Walsh, 1989, Doing a deal: Merger and acquisition negotiations and their impact upon target company top management turnover, *Strategic Management Journal*, 10: 307–322.

129. M. L. Marks & P. H. Mirvis, 2001, Making mergers and acquisitions work: Strategic and psychological preparation, *Academy of Management Executive*, 15(2): 80–92.

130. S. Rovit & C. Lemire, 2003, Your best M&A strategy, *Harvard Business Review*, 81(3): 16–17.

131. Hitt, Harrison, & Ireland, *Mergers and Acquisitions*; Q. N. Huy, 2001, Time, temporal capability and planned change, *Academy of Management Review*, 26: 601–623; L. Markoczy, 2001, Consensus formation during strategic change, *Strategic Management Journal*, 22: 1013–1031.

132. R. W. Coff, 2002, Human capital, shared expertise, and the likelihood of impasse in corporate acquisitions, *Journal of Management*, 28: 107–128.

133. S. McBride, 2003, China offers challenge for Buffett, *Wall Street Journal*, May 2, C11.

134. J. Anand, 1999, How many matches are made in heaven, Mastering Strategy (Part Five), *Financial Times*, October 25, 6–7.

135. R. A. Johnson, 1996, Antecedents and outcomes of corporate refocusing, *Journal of Management*, 22: 437–481; J. E. Bethel & J. Liebeskind, 1993, The effects of ownership structure on corporate restructuring, *Strategic Management Journal*, 14(Special Issue): 15–31.

136. R. E. Hoskisson, R. A. Johnson, D. Yiu, & W. P. Wan, 2001, Restructuring strategies of diversified groups: Differences associated with country institutional environments, in M. A. Hitt, R. E. Freeman, & J. S. Harrison (eds.), *Handbook of Strategic Management*, Oxford, UK: Blackwell Publishers, 433–463; S. R. Fisher & M. A. White, 2000, Downsizing in a learning

organization: Are there hidden costs? *Academy of Management Review*, 25: 244–251; E. Bowman & H. Singh, 1990, Overview of corporate restructuring: Trends and consequences, in L. Rock & R. H. Rock (eds.), *Corporate Restructuring*, New York: McGraw-Hill.

137. 2003, Business: Hard times; Softbank's woes, *The Economist*, May 17: 78.

138. T. A. Kruse, 2002, Asset liquidity and the determinants of asset sales by poorly performing firms, *Financial Management*, 31(4): 107–129.

139. G. J. Castrogiovanni & G. D. Bruton, 2000, Business turnaround processes following acquisitions: Reconsidering the role of retrenchment, *Journal of Business Research*, 48: 25–34; W. McKinley, J. Zhao, & K. G. Rust, 2000, A sociocognitive interpretation of organizational downsizing, *Academy of Management Review*, 25: 227–243.

140. W. McKinley, C. M. Sanchez, & A. G. Schick, 1995, Organizational downsizing: Constraining, cloning, learning, *Academy of Management Executive*, 9(3): 32–44.

141. P. Patsuris, 2002, Forbes.com layoff tracker surpasses 1M mark, *Forbes*, http://www.forbes.com, January 16.

142. A. G. Keane, 2003, Up is down, *Traffic World*, May 12, 26–27.

143. Hoskisson & Hitt, *Downscoping*.

144. L. Dranikoff, T. Koller, & A. Schneider, 2002, Divestiture: Strategy's missing link, *Harvard Business Review*, 80(5): 74–83.

145. M. Rajand & M. Forsyth, 2002, Hostile bidders, long-term performance, and restructuring methods: Evidence from the UK, *American Business Review*, 20(1): 71–81.

146. Johnson, Hoskisson, & Hitt, Board of director involvement; R. E. Hoskisson & M. A. Hitt, 1990, Antecedents and performance outcomes of diversification: A review and critique of theoretical perspectives, *Journal of Management*, 16: 461–509.

147. Hoskisson, Johnson, Yiu, & Wan, Restructuring strategies.

148. J. Doebele, 2003, Ends and means: Is the restructuring of LG aimed at benefiting investors—or its family members? *Forbes*, February 17, 68–70.

149. D. D. Bergh & G. F. Holbein, 1997, Assessment and redirection of longitudinal analysis: Demonstration with a study of the diversification and divestiture relationship, *Strategic Management Journal*, 18: 557–571; C. C. Markides & H. Singh, 1997, Corporate restructuring: A symptom of poor governance or a solution to past managerial mistakes? *European Management Journal*, 15: 213–219.

150. M. F. Wiersema & J. P. Liebeskind, 1995, The effects of leveraged buyouts on corporate growth and diversification in large firms, *Strategic Management Journal*, 16: 447–460.

151. S. C. Bae & H. Jo, 2002, Consolidating corporate control: Divisional versus whole-company leveraged buyouts, *Journal of Financial Research*, 25(2): 247–262; A. Seth & J. Easterwood, 1995, Strategic redirection in large management buyouts: The evidence from post-buyout restructuring activity, *Strategic Management Journal*, 14: 251–274; P. H. Phan & C. W. L. Hill, 1995, Organizational restructuring and economic performance in leveraged buyouts: An ex-post study, *Academy of Management Journal*, 38: 704–739.

152. C. M. Daily, P. P. McDougall, J. G. Covin, & D. R. Dalton, 2002, Governance and strategic leadership in entrepreneurial firms, *Journal of Management*, 3: 387–412.

153. M. Wright, R. E. Hoskisson, L. W. Busenitz, & J. Dial, 2000, Entrepreneurial growth through privatization: The upside of management buyouts, *Academy of Management Review*, 25: 591–601.

154. M. Wright, R. E. Hoskisson, & L. W. Busenitz, 2001, Firm rebirth: Buyouts as facilitators of strategic growth and entrepreneurship, *Academy of Management Executive*, 15(1): 111–125.

155. Bergh, Executive retention and acquisition outcomes: A test of opposing views on the influence of organizational tenure.

156. H. A. Krishnan & D. Park, 2002, The impact of work force reduction on subsequent performance in major mergers and acquisitions: An exploratory study, *Journal of Business Research*, 55(4): 285–292; P. M. Lee, 1997, A comparative analysis of layoff announcements and stock price reactions in the United States and Japan, *Strategic Management Journal*, 18: 879–894.

157. L. Kroll and E. Lambert, 2003, The accidental entrepreneur, *Forbes*, May 12, 90–96.

158. Fisher & White, Downsizing in a learning organization.

159. P. Desbrieres & A. Schatt, 2002, The impacts of LBOs on the performance of acquired firms: The French case, *Journal of Business Finance & Accounting*, 29(5,6): 695–729.

160. G. D. Bruton, J. K. Keels, & E. L. Scifres, 2002, Corporate restructuring and performance: An agency perspective on the complete buyout cycle, *Journal of Business Research*, 55: 709–724; W. F. Long & D. J. Ravenscraft, 1993, LBOs, debt, and R&D intensity, *Strategic Management Journal*, 14(Special Issue): 119–135.

161. Wright, Hoskisson, Busenitz, & Dial, Entrepreneurial growth through privatization; S. A Zahra, 1995, Corporate entrepreneurship and financial performance: The case of management leveraged buyouts, *Journal of Business Venturing*, 10: 225–248.

International Strategy

Knowledge Objectives

Studying this chapter should provide you with the strategic management knowledge needed to:

1. Explain traditional and emerging motives for firms to pursue international diversification.

2. Explore the four factors that lead to a basis for international business-level strategies.

3. Define the three international corporate-level strategies: multidomestic, global, and transnational.

4. Discuss the environmental trends affecting international strategy, especially liability of foreignness and regionalization.

5. Name and describe the five alternative modes for entering international markets.

6. Explain the effects of international diversification on firm returns and innovation.

7. Name and describe two major risks of international diversification.

8. Explain why the positive outcomes from international expansion are limited.

South-Western Publishing

Since joining the World Trade Organization, China has attracted a large amount of foreign direct investment, especially from manufacturing firms. Volkswagen, for example, has a bigger operation in China than it does in Germany, and it is still growing!

China, since the signing of the World Trade Organization (WTO) agreement, has accumulated a significant amount of foreign direct investment (FDI). Most of this foreign direct investment has come from manufacturing firms looking for low wages, and thereby lower costs, especially in labor-intensive industries. For example, China now manufactures 60 percent of the world's bicycles; 86 percent of those are sold in the United States. Rival manufacturers in Latin America and Africa are thus struggling to survive. One analyst suggests that the bicycle industry is the symbol of what most of the world fears about China: "Its phenomenally fast growth can be sustained only at the expense of other economies, both developed and developing." Another analyst suggested that China's exports could exceed those of Japan by 2005. Furthermore, it was suggested that part of the deflation threat in other countries might be because of China's industrialization: "China's industrialization devalues manufacturing assets outside of China." In fact, in 2002, China displaced Japan as the third largest trading partner with the United States, behind Canada and Mexico.

As export quotas in the textile industry expire in 2004, it is expected that China's share of the world's garment exports will increase from 20 percent to about 50 percent by the end of the decade. Other labor-intensive industries, such as shoes, semiconductors, and televisions, are likely to follow. This is due to the very low wages and seemingly endless supply of labor of China. This supply is also increased because, as large, state-owned enterprises restructure, they lay off people who then have the opportunity to be hired in newly developing, foreign capitalized manufacturing plants. For instance, average wages in the garment industry in China are forty cents an hour, less than a third of that of Mexico.

On the other hand, one explanation for the success of bicycle exporting is that China's bicycle manufacturers have lost half their domestic market; 20 percent fewer bicycles are being sold in China whereas more cars are being sold. In 2002, one million cars were sold for the first time, and that number was expected to rise by 20 percent in 2003. The point is that these cars are being produced in China by firms such as Volkswagen and General Motors. For example, "Volkswagen is already bigger in China than it is in Germany, and it is looking to add more capacity." Also, Ford expects China to become a bigger market for its vehicles than both Germany and Japan within five years. As such, as China grows, it becomes a bigger market for other people's goods. Thus, besides representing a threat, it also represents an opportunity for sales growth.

Due to the increased trade, China's economy is already very significant. In terms of GDP, it is the sixth largest economy in the world, just somewhat smaller than France. In 2002, China had a growth rate approaching 8 percent, by far the most dynamic large economy in the world. In fact, in 2002, China surpassed the United States as the world's largest recipient of FDI, with $53 billion. (This had to do more with collapse of investment in the United States, however; in 1999 and 2000, FDI in the United States was $283 billion and $301 billion, respectively. Nonetheless, FDI has been growing over the last three years in China.)

Not only is labor-intensive manufacturing being moved to China, but also high-value manufacturing has increasingly been locating in China. This is evidenced by the battle between DHL, FedEx, and UPS, all seeking to have operations in China. These companies do a lot of business for high-value (high-technology) manufacturing that is relocating to mainland China.

In summary, the WTO agreement has led to the acceleration of firms locating to China, first to reduce expenses, but also to take advantage of a larger market, such as the auto companies and the express delivery companies mentioned. It is a significant draw for FDI for the expected future growth given the possible size of its market as its people become more able to buy high-valued goods. China will also be a significant economic player as one of the top-producing economies in the world within this decade, barring unforeseen problems that may derail its growth prospects.

SOURCES: 2003, Special Report: Is the wakening giant a monster? China's economy, *The Economist*, February 15, 63–65; J. T. Areddy, 2003, China is allowing companies more flexibility over the yuan, *Wall Street Journal Online*, http//:www.wsj.com, June 22; J. Flint, 2003, China: How big, how fast, how dangerous? *Forbes*, http://www.forbes.com, July 1; F. Hansen, 2003, China in the WTO, *Business Credit*, May, 59–62; F. Hu, 2003, The Zhu Rongji's decade, *Wall Street Journal Online*, http//:www.wsj.com, March 10; G. Ip, 2003, The economy: Trade gap widens to record level—monthly deficit combines with other data to point to trouble for recovery, *Wall Street Journal*, February 21, A2; P. M. Norton & K. Almstedt, 2003, China joins the trade wars, *China Business Review*, January/February, 22–29; L. Weymouth, 2003, What's right, not popular, *Newsweek*, June 2, 32; L. Wozniak, 2003, DHL and FedEx race to integrate China, *Far Eastern Economic Review*, February 27, 42–44.

As the Opening Case indicates, China's entry into the World Trade Organization (WTO) has brought change not only to China and its trading partners, but also to firms in other countries such as Mexico that have depended on labor-intensive industry foreign direct investment to employ its people. Many of the potential investments in Mexican firms are losing out to Chinese firms.[1] While many firms have entered and will enter China in the coming years, foreign firms who have done so have found it difficult to manage the risk and establish legitimacy.[2]

China and its entrance into the WTO clearly illustrate how entering international markets features both opportunities and threats for firms that choose to compete in global markets. This chapter examines opportunities facing firms as they seek to develop and exploit core competencies by diversifying into global markets. In addition, we discuss different problems, complexities, and threats that might accompany use of the firm's international strategies.[3] Although national boundaries, cultural differences, and geographical distances all pose barriers to entry into many markets, significant opportunities draw businesses into the international arena. A business that plans to operate globally must formulate a successful strategy to take advantage of these global opportunities.[4] Furthermore, to mold their firms into truly global companies, managers must develop global mind-sets.[5] Especially in regard to managing human resources, traditional means of operating with little cultural diversity and without global sourcing are no longer effective.[6]

As firms move into international markets, they develop relationships with suppliers, customers, and partners, and then learn from these relationships. Such activity is evident in the pharmaceuticals industry as firms compete against each other in global markets and invest in all areas of the world in order to learn about new markets and new potential drugs.[7]

In this chapter, as illustrated in Figure 1.1, we discuss the importance of international strategy as a source of strategic competitiveness and above-average returns. The chapter focuses

©Reuters NewMedia Inc.

Signing an agreement for China's entry into the World Trade Organization.

on the incentives to internationalize. Once a firm decides to compete internationally, it must select its strategy and choose a mode of entry into international markets. It may enter international markets by exporting from domestic-based operations, licensing some of its products or services, forming joint ventures with international partners, acquiring a foreign-based firm, or establishing a new subsidiary. Such international diversification can extend product life cycles, provide incentives for more innovation, and produce above-average returns. These benefits are tempered by political and economic risks and the problems of managing a complex international firm with operations in multiple countries.

Figure 8.1 provides an overview of the various choices and outcomes. The relationships among international opportunities, and the exploration of resources and capabilities that result in strategies and modes of entry that are based on core competencies as well as strategic competitiveness outcomes, are explored in this chapter.

Opportunities and Outcomes of International Strategy — Figure 8.1

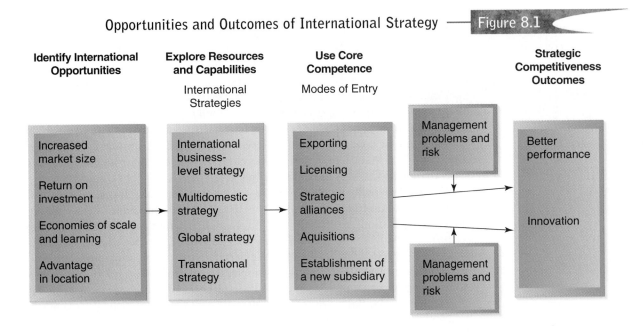

An international strategy is a strategy through which the firm sells its goods or services outside its domestic market.

An **international strategy** is a strategy through which the firm sells its goods or services outside its domestic market.[8] One of the primary reasons for implementing an international strategy (as opposed to a strategy focused on the domestic market) is that international markets yield potential new opportunities.[9]

Raymond Vernon captured the classic rationale for international diversification.[10] He suggested that, typically, a firm discovers an innovation in its home-country market, especially in an advanced economy such as that of the United States. Some demand for the product may then develop in other countries, and exports are provided by domestic operations. Increased demand in foreign countries justifies direct foreign investment in production capacity abroad, especially because foreign competitors also organize to meet increasing demand. As the product becomes standardized, the firm may rationalize its operations by moving production to a region with low manufacturing costs.[11] Vernon, therefore, suggests that firms pursue international diversification to extend a product's life cycle.

Another traditional motive for firms to become multinational is to secure needed resources. Key supplies of raw material—especially minerals and energy—are important in some industries. For instance, aluminum producers need a supply of bauxite, tire firms need rubber, and oil companies scour the world to find new petroleum reserves. Other industries, such as clothing, electronics, watch making, and many others, seek low-cost factors of production, and have moved portions of their operations to foreign locations in pursuit of lower costs as illustrated in the Opening Case on China.

Although these traditional motives persist, other emerging motivations also drive international expansion (see Chapter 1). For instance, pressure has increased for a global integration of operations, mostly driven by more universal product demand. As nations industrialize, the demand for some products and commodities appears to become more similar. This "nation-less," or borderless, demand for globally branded products may be due to similarities in lifestyle in developed nations. Increases in global communication media also facilitate the ability of people in different countries to visualize and model lifestyles in different cultures.[12] Benetton, an Italian casual-wear apparel company, although it has been forced to restructure given the global economic downturn, has used its global brand and well-established retail presence to more effectively manage its worldwide supply and manufacturing networks with improved communications technology.[13]

In some industries, technology drives globalization because the economies of scale necessary to reduce costs to the lowest level often require an investment greater than that needed to meet domestic market demand. The major Korean car manufacturers Daewoo, Hyundai, and Kia certainly found this to be true; accordingly, they have sought to enhance their operations in the United States and elsewhere.[14] There is also pressure for cost reductions, achieved by purchasing from the lowest-cost global suppliers. For instance, research and development expertise for an emerging business start-up may not exist in the domestic market.[15]

New large-scale, emerging markets, such as China and India, provide a strong internationalization incentive because of the potential demand in them.[16] Because of currency fluctuations, firms may also choose to distribute their operations across many countries, including emerging ones, in order to reduce the risk of devaluation in one country.[17] However, the uniqueness of emerging markets presents both opportunities and challenges.[18] While India, for example, differs from Western countries in many respects, including culture, politics, and the precepts of its economic system,[19] it also offers a huge potential market. Many international firms perceive Chinese markets as almost untouched markets, without exposure to many modern and sophisticated products. Once China is exposed to these products, these firms believe that demand will develop. However, the differences between China and Western countries pose serious challenges to Western competitive paradigms that emphasize the skills needed to manage financial, economic, and political risks.[20]

A large majority of U.S.-based companies' international business is in European markets, where 60 percent of U.S. firms' assets that are located outside the domestic market are invested.[21] Companies seeking to internationalize their operations in Europe, as elsewhere, need to understand the pressure on them to respond to local, national, or regional customs, especially where goods or services require customization because of cultural differences or effective marketing to entice customers to try a different product.[22]

Of course, all firms encounter challenges when using an international strategy. For example, Unilever is a large European-centered global food and consumer products firm that adapts its products to local tastes as it moves into new national markets.[23] Its investors expect Unilever executives to create global mega-brands, which have the most growth potential and margins, even though most of Unilever's growth has come through acquisition and the selling of the acquired, unique local brands. Establishing mega-brands while also dealing with the forces for localization is difficult.[24]

Local repair and service capabilities are another factor influencing an increased desire for local country responsiveness.[25] This localization may even affect industries that are seen as needing more global economies of scale, for example, white goods (home appliances, such as refrigerators). Alternatively, suppliers often follow their customers, particularly large ones, into international markets, which eliminates the firm's need to find local suppliers.[26] The transportation costs of large products and their parts, such as heavy earthmoving equipment, are significant, which may preclude a firm's suppliers from following the firm to an international market.

Employment contracts and labor forces differ significantly in international markets. For example, it is more difficult to lay off employees in Europe than in the United States because of employment contract differences. In many cases, host governments demand joint ownership, which allows the foreign firm to avoid tariffs. Also, host governments frequently require a high percentage of procurements, manufacturing, and R&D to use local sources. These issues increase the need for local investment and responsiveness compared to seeking global economies of scale.[27]

We've discussed incentives influencing firms to use international strategies. When successful, firms can derive four basic benefits from using international strategies: (1) increased market size; (2) greater returns on major capital investments or on investments in new products and processes; (3) greater economies of scale, scope, or learning; and (4) a competitive advantage through location (for example, access to low-cost labor, critical resources, or customers). We examine these benefits in terms of both their costs (such as higher coordination expenses and limited access to knowledge about host country political influences[28]) and their managerial challenges.

Increased Market Size

Firms can expand the size of their potential market—sometimes dramatically—by moving into international markets. Qualcomm, a chip maker for cell phones, views the large-scale, emerging markets in Asia as an incentive for its international strategy. Qualcomm holds a 90 percent market share for its chip technology, CDMA, and has aggressively and profitably pursued expansion into Asia. The company has been especially successful in China, where the telephone infrastructure has become mostly digital. Qualcomm has also devoted much research money to the next generation of CDMA, called WCDMA, which is becoming popular in Europe. The enormous market potential around the world has led to Qualcomm's pursuit of its international strategy.[29]

Although changing consumer tastes and practices linked to cultural values or traditions is not simple, following an international strategy is a particularly attractive option to firms competing in domestic markets that have limited growth opportunities. For example, firms in the beer industry lack significant growth opportunities in their domestic markets. Accordingly, as discussed in Chapter 7, most large global brewers have pursued a strategy of acquiring other brewers, both in developed markets and in emerging economies. For instance, Miller Brewing was purchased by South African Breweries (SAB) to form SABMiller, and Anheuser-Busch acquired a controlling interest in China's Tsingtao Brewery, a top volume brewer in China.[30]

The size of an international market also affects a firm's willingness to invest in R&D to build competitive advantages in that market.[31] Larger markets usually offer higher potential returns and thus pose less risk for a firm's investments. The strength of the science base in the country in question also can affect a firm's foreign R&D investments. Most firms prefer to invest more heavily in those countries with the scientific knowledge and talent to produce value-creating products and processes from their R&D activities.[32]

Return on Investment

Large markets may be crucial for earning a return on significant investments, such as plant and capital equipment or R&D. Therefore, most R&D-intensive industries such as electronics are international. This can be exampled by firms in the electronics-manufacturing services industry such as Flextronics. Before the electronics industry experienced a recent downturn, Flextronics flourished by buying "underused factories around the world from the likes of Hewlett-Packard, Siemens, and IBM."[33] Flextronics survived the downturn better than some of its competitors "by cutting the workforce in high-cost locations and adding in low-cost places."[34] However, because the firm moved a significant amount of capacity to China, its productivity was threatened by the SARS epidemic.[35] In addition to the need for a large market to recoup heavy investment in R&D, the development pace for new technology is increasing. As a result, new products become obsolete more rapidly. Therefore, investments need to be recouped more quickly. Moreover, firms' abilities to develop new technologies are expanding, and because of different patent laws across country borders, imitation by competitors is more likely. Through reverse engineering, competitors are able to take apart a product, learn the new technology, and develop a similar product that imitates the new technology. Because their competitors can imitate the new technology relatively quickly, firms need to recoup new product development costs even more rapidly. Consequently, the larger markets provided by international expansion are particularly attractive in many industries such as computer hardware, because they expand the opportunity for the firm to recoup significant capital investments and large-scale R&D expenditures.[36]

Regardless of other issues, however, the primary reason for investing in international markets is to generate above-average returns on investments. Still, firms from different countries have different expectations and use different criteria to decide whether to invest in international markets.[37] Turkey, for example, has experienced significant growth due to foreign direct investment over the last several decades because it has a fairly large market, but concerns about too much bureaucracy and instability have recently lowered levels of investment, especially due to the Iraq conflict.[38]

Economies of Scale and Learning

By expanding their markets, firms may be able to enjoy economies of scale, particularly in their manufacturing operations. To the extent that a firm can standardize its products across country borders and use the same or similar production facilities, thereby coordinating critical resource functions, it is more likely to achieve optimal economies of scale.[39]

Economies of scale are critical in the global auto industry. China's decision to join the World Trade Organization will allow carmakers from other countries to enter the country and lower tariffs to be charged (in the past, Chinese carmakers have had an advantage over foreign carmakers due to tariffs). Ford, Honda, General Motors, and Volkswagen are each producing an economy car to compete with the existing cars in China. Because of global economies of scale, all of these companies are likely to obtain market share in China.[40] As the Opening Case indicates, Ford expects to sell more cars in China than in both Germany and Japan within five years. Volkswagen already sells more cars in China than in Germany.[41] As a result, Chinese carmakers will have to change the way they do business to effectively compete against foreign carmakers.

Firms may also be able to exploit core competencies in international markets through resource and knowledge sharing between units across country borders.[42] This sharing generates synergy, which helps the firm produce higher-quality goods or services at lower cost. In addition, working across international markets provides the firm with new learning opportunities.[43] Multinational firms have substantial occasions to learn from the different practices they encounter in separate international markets. Even firms based in developed markets can learn from operations in emerging markets.[44]

Location Advantages

Firms may locate facilities in other countries to lower the basic costs of the goods or services they provide. These facilities may provide easier access to lower-cost labor, energy, and other natural resources. Other location advantages include access to critical supplies and to customers.[45] Once positioned favorably with an attractive location, firms must manage their facilities effectively to gain the full benefit of a location advantage.[46]

China's Internet portals have found their location to be a great advantage in reaching customers. All three of the major Chinese portals are profitable because they have focused less on computer Internet users and more on cell phone Internet users by building their business around text message updates sent to cell phones and sold on subscription. Even the SARS epidemic has been helpful—subscriptions to news updates increased 25 percent between March and June 2003.[47]

International Strategies

Firms choose to use one or both of two basic types of international strategies: business-level international strategy and corporate-level international strategy. At the business level, firms follow generic strategies: cost leadership, differentiation, focused cost leadership, focused differentiation, or integrated cost leadership/differentiation. There are three corporate-level international strategies: multidomestic, global, or transnational (a combination of multidomestic and global). To create competitive advantage, each strategy must realize a core competence based on difficult-to-duplicate resources and capabilities.[48] As discussed in Chapters 4 and 6, firms expect to create value through the implementation of a business-level strategy and a corporate-level strategy.[49]

International Business-Level Strategy

Each business must develop a competitive strategy focused on its own domestic market. We discuss business-level generic strategies in Chapter 4 and competitive rivalry and competitive dynamics in Chapter 5. International business-level strategies have some unique features. In an international business-level strategy, the home country of operation is often the most important source of competitive advantage.[50] The resources

©Stephanie Maze/CORBIS

Italy has become the leader in the shoe industry because of related and supporting industries such as leather processing, distribution through tourism in Italy, leather working, and design.

and capabilities established in the home country frequently allow the firm to pursue the strategy into markets located in other countries. However, as a firm continues its growth into multiple international locations, research indicates that the country of origin diminishes in importance as the dominant factor.[51]

Ikea, a furniture manufacturer and retailer, initiated its business-level strategy in its home market in Sweden in 1963. Later, Ikea entered the U.S. market in the mid-1980s. Currently, Ikea has 70,000 employees globally with 150 stores in over 30 countries; its sales total over $11 billion. Ikea's international success could not have been achieved in its domestic market alone, although it developed a strong culture and brand identity in its domestic market.[52]

Michael Porter's model, illustrated in Figure 8.2, describes the factors contributing to the advantage of firms in a dominant global industry and associated with a specific country or regional environment.[53] The first dimension in Porter's model is *factors of production*. This dimension refers to the inputs necessary to compete in any industry—labor, land, natural resources, capital, and infrastructure (such as transportation, postal, and communication systems). There are basic (for example, natural and labor resources) and advanced (such as digital communication systems and a highly educated workforce) factors. Other production factors are generalized (highway systems and the supply of debt capital) and specialized (skilled personnel in a specific industry, such as the workers in a port that specialize in handling bulk chemicals). If a country has both advanced

Figure 8.2 — **Determinants of National Advantage**

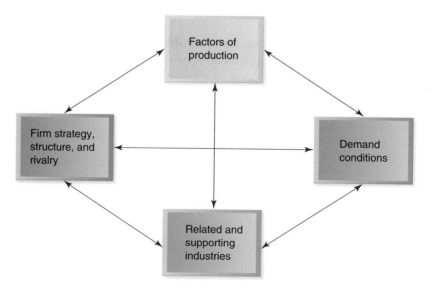

SOURCE: Adapted with the permission of The Free Press, an imprint of Simon & Schuster Adult Publishing Group, from *Competitive Advantage of Nations*, by Michael E. Porter, p. 72. Copyright ©1990, 1998 by Michael E. Porter.

and specialized production factors, it is likely to serve an industry well by spawning strong home-country competitors that also can be successful global competitors.

Ironically, countries often develop advanced and specialized factors because they lack critical basic resources. For example, some Asian countries, such as South Korea, lack abundant natural resources but offer a strong work ethic, a large number of engineers, and systems of large firms to create an expertise in manufacturing. Similarly, Germany developed a strong chemical industry, partially because Hoechst and BASF spent years creating a synthetic indigo dye to reduce their dependence on imports, unlike Britain, whose colonies provided large supplies of natural indigo.[54]

The second dimension in Porter's model, *demand conditions,* is characterized by the nature and size of buyers' needs in the home market for the industry's goods or services. The sheer size of a market segment can produce the demand necessary to create scale-efficient facilities.

Chinese manufacturing companies have spent years focused on building their businesses in China, and only recently are beginning to look at markets beyond their borders. Companies such as Legend (personal computers) and Haier (small appliances) have begun the difficult process of building their brand equity in other countries, beginning in the Far East and seeking to make subsequent moves into the West. These companies have been helped by China's entry to the World Trade Organization and are looking to overseas markets to increase market share and profits.[55] The efficiency built in a large-scale market could help lead to ultimate domination of the industry in other countries, although this could be difficult for firms coming from an emerging economy.

Specialized demand may also create opportunities beyond national boundaries. For example, Swiss firms have long led the world in tunneling equipment because of the need to tunnel through mountains for rail and highway passage in Switzerland. Japanese firms have created a niche market for compact, quiet air conditioners, which are important in Japan because homes are often small and close together.[56]

Related and supporting industries are the third dimension in Porter's model. Italy has become the leader in the shoe industry because of related and supporting industries; a well-established leather-processing industry provides the leather needed to construct shoes and related products. Also, many people travel to Italy to purchase leather goods, providing support in distribution. Supporting industries in leather-working machinery and design services also contribute to the success of the shoe industry. In fact, the design services industry supports its own related industries, such as ski boots, fashion apparel, and furniture. In Japan, cameras and copiers are related industries. Similarly, it is argued that the "creative resources nurtured by [the] popular cartoons and animation sector, combined with technological knowledge accumulated in the consumer electronics industry, facilitated the emergence of a successful video game industry in Japan."[57]

Firm strategy, structure, and rivalry make up the final country dimension and also foster the growth of certain industries. The dimension of strategy, structure, and rivalry among firms varies greatly from nation to nation. Because of the excellent technical training system in Germany, there is a strong emphasis on methodical product and process improvements. In Japan, unusual cooperative and competitive systems have facilitated the cross-functional management of complex assembly operations. In Italy, the national pride of the country's designers has spawned strong industries in sports cars, fashion apparel, and furniture. In the United States, competition among computer manufacturers and software producers has favored the development of these industries.

The four basic dimensions of the "diamond" model in Figure 8.2 emphasize the environmental or structural attributes of a national economy that contribute to national advantage. Government policy also clearly contributes to the success and failure of many firms and industries. DHL Worldwide Express seeks to enter the U.S.

domestic shipping market through the acquisition of Airborne, a Seattle-based air cargo firm, which would cause it to be in competition with UPS and FedEx. The combined company is hoping to take market share from UPS' and FedEx's small and mid-sized business accounts, which tend to have higher margins than large corporate accounts that are typically heavily discounted. UPS and FedEx are afraid that Deutsche Post (the German post office monopoly that controls DHL) will subsidize DHL-Airborne, allowing it to offer discount prices and thus gain market share. As such, UPS and FedEx have banded together to lobby the U.S. government to prohibit DHL's Airborne acquisition.[58]

Although each firm must create its own success, not all firms will survive to become global competitors—not even those operating with the same country factors that spawned the successful firms. The actual strategic choices managers make may be the most compelling reason for success or failure. Accordingly, the factors illustrated in Figure 8.2 are likely to produce competitive advantages only when the firm develops and implements an appropriate strategy that takes advantage of distinct country factors. Thus, these distinct country factors are necessary to consider when analyzing the business-level strategies (i.e., cost leadership, differentiation, focused cost leadership, focused differentiation, and integrated cost leadership/differentiation discussed in Chapter 4) in an international context.

International Corporate-Level Strategy

The international business-level strategies are based at least partially on the type of international corporate-level strategy the firm has chosen. Some corporate strategies give individual country units the authority to develop their own business-level strategies; other corporate strategies dictate the business-level strategies in order to standardize the firm's products and sharing of resources across countries.[59]

International corporate-level strategy focuses on the scope of a firm's operations through both product and geographic diversification.[60] International corporate-level strategy is required when the firm operates in multiple industries and multiple countries or regions.[61] The headquarters unit guides the strategy, although business or country-level managers can have substantial strategic input, given the type of international corporate level strategy followed. The three international corporate-level strategies are multidomestic, global, and transnational, as shown in Figure 8.3.

MULTIDOMESTIC STRATEGY

A **multidomestic strategy** is an international strategy in which strategic and operating decisions are decentralized to the strategic business unit in each country so as to allow that unit to tailor products to the local market.[62] A multidomestic strategy focuses on competition within each country. It assumes that the markets differ and therefore are segmented by country boundaries. In other words, consumer needs and desires, industry conditions (e.g., the number and type of competitors), political and legal structures, and social norms vary by country. With multidomestic strategies, the firm can customize its products to meet the specific needs and preferences of local customers. Therefore, these strategies should maximize a firm's competitive response to the idiosyncratic requirements of each market.[63]

The use of multidomestic strategies usually expands the firm's local market share because the firm can pay attention to the needs of the local clientele.[64] However, the use of these strategies results in more uncertainty for the corporation as a whole, because of the differences across markets and thus the different strategies employed by local country units.[65] Moreover, multidomestic strategies do not allow for the achievement of economies of scale and can be more costly. As a result, firms employing a multidomestic strategy decentralize their strategic and operating decisions to the business

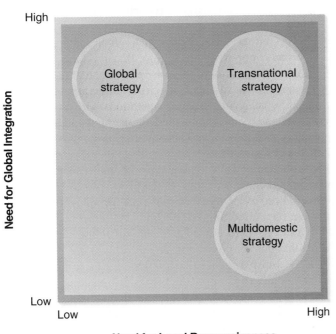

High

Global
strategy

Transnational
strategy

Multidomestic
strategy

Need for Global Integration

Low

Low   High

Need for Local Responsiveness

units operating in each country. Historically, Unilever has had a very decentralized approach to managing its international operations.[66] Although firms have expected the Internet to facilitate global integration across borders, research suggests that firms need to pay attention to local aspects of its use,[67] as the example about Chinese Internet portals noted above illustrates. The multidomestic strategy has been more commonly used by European multinational firms because of the variety of cultures and markets found in Europe.[68]

In the brewing industry, many firms have been following a multidomestic strategy by making acquisitions in regions of interest. Belgian brewer Interbrew, for example, bought 70 percent of K.K. Brewery, the leading beer maker in Zhejiang Province, in the Yangtze Delta in China. Interbrew is bringing its brewing skills to this facility to establish a strong competitive position in a highly fragmented, rapidly growing market that it believes is very attractive.[69] Similarly, Diageo PLC, the giant U.K.-based spirits and beer group (it owns the Guinness brand), is expanding aggressively in many countries and regions.[70] Viewing its expansion's outcomes favorably, some analysts think that "Diageo could easily mop up 10 points of market share over the next five years in the U.S."[71] Diageo's bold entry into U.S. markets could, however, engender strong competitive responses from Anheuser Busch and SABMiller.

GLOBAL STRATEGY

In contrast to a multidomestic strategy, a global strategy assumes more standardization of products across country markets.[72] As a result, a global strategy is centralized and controlled by the home office. The strategic business units operating in each country are assumed to be interdependent, and the home office attempts to achieve integration across these businesses.[73] A **global strategy** is an international strategy through which the firm offers standardized products across country markets, with competitive strategy being dictated by the home office. Thus, a global strategy emphasizes economies

A global strategy is an international strategy through which the firm offers standardized products across country markets, with competitive strategy being dictated by the home office.

of scale and offers greater opportunities to utilize innovations developed at the corporate level or in one country in other markets. This strategy is being facilitated through improved global accounting and financial reporting standards.[74]

While a global strategy produces lower risk, the firm may forgo growth opportunities in local markets, either because those markets are less likely to be identified as opportunities or because opportunities require that products be adapted to the local market.[75] The global strategy is not as responsive to local markets and is difficult to manage because of the need to coordinate strategies and operating decisions across country borders. Consequently, achieving efficient operations with a global strategy requires sharing of resources and coordination and cooperation across country boundaries, which in turn require centralization and headquarters control. Many Japanese firms have successfully used the global strategy.[76]

Cemex, a Monterrey, Mexico-based cement maker, is the world's third largest cement manufacturer, behind France's Lafarge and Switzerland's Holcim. Cemex's aggressive acquisition strategy was noticed more prominently by the media in the United States when it acquired Southdown, the U.S. cement company, for $3 billion at the end of 2001 and began to consolidate this operation with its other U.S. assets. Cemex has the leading market position in Spain with around 72 percent of the production capacity in the Spanish cement industry. Besides its significant assets in North and South America and southern Europe, the firm is also making inroads in Asia through acquisitions. Notwithstanding its presence in developed markets, "its real specialty lies in supplying cement in places that lack easy-to-navigate roads, solid telephone networks and highly skilled workers."[77] Accordingly, Cemex specializes "in supplying cement in countries such as Bangladesh, Thailand and Venezuela."[78] In these places, cement "can be sold at higher margins in bags for small-scale building, rather than in mixed ready-made quantities."[79]

To integrate its businesses globally, Cemex uses the Internet as one way of increasing revenue and lowering its cost structure. By using the Internet to improve logistics and manage an extensive supply network, Cemex can significantly reduce costs. "The advent of technology meant that every truck had a computer and a global-positioning system receiver. By combining the trucks' positions with the output at the plants and the order from customers, Cemex has been able to produce a system that not only calculates which truck should go where, but also lets dispatchers redirect trucks en route. Delivery time is now down to 20 minutes."[80] Thus, Cemex is using a global strategy to integrate many aspects of its worldwide operations.[81]

TRANSNATIONAL STRATEGY

A **transnational strategy** is an international strategy through which the firm seeks to achieve both global efficiency and local responsiveness. Realizing these goals is difficult: one requires close global coordination while the other requires local flexibility. "Flexible coordination"—building a shared vision and individual commitment through an integrated network—is required to implement the transnational strategy.[82] In reality, it is difficult to successfully use the transnational strategy because of the conflicting

A transnational strategy is an international strategy through which the firm seeks to achieve both global efficiency and local responsiveness.

New York Stock Exchange President William Johnson (third from left) joined executives from Cemex, S.A. de C.V. of Mexico, the third largest cement company in the world, as they rang the opening bell at the NYSE in New York. Chairman Lorenzo Zambrano (fourth from left) is the architect of the company's global strategy.

©Reuters NewMedia Inc./CORBIS

Large U.S. Auto Manufacturers and the Transnational Strategy

The Big Three auto manufacturers—General Motors, Ford, and Chrysler (now part of DaimlerChrysler)—found their sales, market share, and revenues were hurt so much by the globalization of competition that their dominance in the crucial North American market was significantly diminished. For 60 years these three companies controlled the American car market. As recently as the late 1990s, these companies earned record profits. However, the market shares of foreign car manufacturers have grown from their original, anemic level, and these firms are now serious competitors to domestic U.S. dominance. As Ford considered its centennial celebration, it learned that Toyota had overtaken Ford as the number two global market share leader. "Toyota is well on its way to achieving its audacious goal of grabbing 15 percent of the world's auto market by early in the next decade," up from 10 percent in 2001 and 11.7 percent in the first quarter of 2003. Although Ford's sales rose to 1.58 million, Toyota's increased more—to 1.66 million.

General Motors has long fought an image that it does not build quality vehicles. Despite its ranking in a recent survey as being the most reliable domestic U.S. carmaker after sales, GM still placed behind Toyota, Honda, and Nissan overall. "Japanese automakers continue to lead in durability, with 228 problems per 100 cars for the average Japanese brand, 282 for the average Big Three [U.S.] brand, 331 for European brands and 406 for Korean brands." For many consumers, quality is one of the major factors affecting their car purchase.

Manufacturing efficiency is also a problem. Toyota's "not-so-secret weapons are its plants, at home and, increasingly, abroad, which consistently rank among the world's most efficient."

Although domestic U.S. companies are improving, some foreign carmakers already have a good reputation and a known reliability rating. At the low end of the market, companies such as Hyundai and Kia are capturing market share. As price competition increases, domestic automakers have seen their market share shrink proportionately.

In response to this situation, U.S. firms and other large automakers are using international corporate-level strategies. For example, General Motors has invested billions of dollars in foreign car companies, moving toward a more transnational strategy for its automobiles. The company owns Saab and Opel and also has stakes in Daewoo, Fiat, Subaru, and Suzuki Motor. In the past, GM used a multidomestic strategy by which its foreign business units were managed in a decentralized way and each unit could decide what cars to design and build. This laissez-faire management approach produced poor financial results.

GM CEO G. Richard Wagoner Jr. decided to overcome this problem by implementing a transnational strategy. The senior managers from its partners' headquarters and product development centers now report directly to a top-ranking GM executive in the relevant region of the world. Thus, GM's top management team has more control over events in each of its foreign car companies but can continue to be responsive to regional or country needs. In particular, GM has focused on the Asia Pacific region because it expects the global market for cars to increase 12 million units by 2012 with half of that coming from the region (particularly from China, India, South Korea, and Thailand). However, the firm realizes it is important to maintain a country focus as well. Thus, GM has sought to balance efficiency and responsiveness through the transnational strategy.

SOURCES: J. Flint, 2003, China: How big, how fast, how dangerous? *Forbes*, http//:www.forbes.com, July 1; K. Greenberg, 2003, Imports look for big gains in minivan market, *Brandweek*, March 3; D. Hakim, 2003, American cars show gains in a survey of dependability, *New York Times*, http//:nytimes.com, July 9, 12; J. Palmer, 2003, Taking on the world, *Barron's*, May 5, 15–16; A. Taylor III, 2003, And it's Toyota by a nose! *Fortune*, June 9, 34; F. Warner, 2003, Learning how to speak to Gen Y, *Fast Company*, July, 36–37; S. A. Webster, 2003, GM alters strategy in Asia Pacific; Its global leadership position is at stake as it focuses more on China, less on Japan, *Detroit News*, June 12, 1.

goals (see Chapter 11 for more on implementation of this and other corporate-level international strategies). On the positive side, effective implementation of a transnational strategy often produces higher performance than does implementation of either the multidomestic or global international corporate-level strategies.[83]

The Strategic Focus on the global auto industry suggests that many large auto manufacturers choose the transnational strategy to deal with global trends. Renault has used this strategy to reinvigorate Nissan, in which Renault bought a controlling interest in 1999. Since then, Carlos Ghosn, CEO of Nissan, has brought Nissan back from being a very poor performer to achieving a "10.8 percent operating margin, the highest of any major carmaker, and a 19.5 percent return on invested capital."[84] The business units of Renault cooperate to achieve efficiencies and adapt to local market conditions. "For example, diesel engines have zero penetration in the Japanese market, but they power more than a third of the cars sold in Europe. So Nissan equips diesel cars it sells in Europe with Renault engines."[85]

Environmental Trends

Although the transnational strategy is difficult to implement, emphasis on global efficiency is increasing as more industries begin to experience global competition. To add to the problem, there is also an increased emphasis on local requirements: global goods and services often require some customization to meet government regulations within particular countries or to fit customer tastes and preferences. In addition, most multinational firms desire coordination and sharing of resources across country markets to hold down costs, as illustrated by the Cemex example above.[86] Furthermore, some products and industries may be more suited than others for standardization across country borders.

As a result, most large multinational firms with diverse products employ a multidomestic strategy with certain product lines and a global strategy with others. Many multinational firms may require this type of flexibility if they are to be strategically competitive, in part due to trends that change over time. Two important trends are the liability of foreignness, which has increased after the terrorist attacks and the war in Iraq, and regionalization.

Liability of Foreignness

The dramatic success of Japanese firms such as Toyota and Sony in the United States and other international markets in the 1980s was a powerful jolt to U.S. managers and awakened them to the importance of international competition in what were rapidly becoming global markets. In the 1990s, Eastern Europe and China represented potential major international market opportunities for firms from many countries, including the United States, Japan, Korea, and European nations.[87] However, as described in the Strategic Focus, there are legitimate concerns about the relative attractiveness of global strategies. Research shows that global strategies are not as prevalent as once thought and are very difficult to implement, even when using Internet-based strategies.[88] The September 11, 2001, attacks and the war in Iraq in 2003 are two explanations for these concerns.[89]

In the 21st century, firms may focus less on truly global markets and more on regional adaptation. Although parallel developments in the Internet and mobile telecommunication facilitate communications across the globe, as noted earlier, the implementation of Web-based strategies also requires local adaptation.

The globalization of businesses with local strategies is demonstrated by the online operation of Lands' End, Inc., using local Internet portals to offer its products for sale. Lands' End, formerly a direct-mail catalog business and now a part of Sears,

Uncertainty, Liability of Foreignness, and Regionalization

The U.S. economy is the biggest in the world, twice the size of the second largest. When certainty regarding the initiation of conflict in Iraq began to escalate in the United States, the uncertainty of the outcome negatively affected consumer spending, and large-scale capital investment and other potential creators of economic wealth in the global economy were affected. Easing concerns about the hostilities in Iraq provided "some lift to business and consumer confidence," but "the effect has not been dramatic." Until the U.S. economy improves, it is unlikely that the global economy will pick up as well. Political maneuvering and conflicts have also affected trade relations between the United States and Europe. American executives visiting France were scolded by their French counterparts for the aggressive Bush administration policy toward Iraq. European firms were reluctant to invest in the United States for fear of American retaliation.

Other countries will probably bear the economic effects of the war in Iraq differently. Japan's economy continues to shrink, only mildly exacerbated by the war, and China's continues to grow, also relatively unaffected by the war and higher oil prices. South Korea, besides its neighbor North Korea's nuclear threat, is also threatened by its dependence on imported oil. However, it has built formidable financial reserves, and its large companies have reduced their debt loads. Already suffering from enormous debt and increased oil prices, Turkey probably faces the worst repercussions. Tourism, a major source of revenue, is expected to drop off, and Turkey's unwilling support of U.S. armed forces lessens its chances of receiving an aid package from the American government.

Similarly, the September 11, 2001, terrorist attacks as well as the war in Afghanistan created uncertainty about the progress of globalization. Although these shocks put a short-term damper on increased globalization, research also suggests that globalization is not as pervasive as once believed. In only a few sectors, such as consumer electronics, is a global strategy as defined above economically viable. For most manufacturing (such as automobiles), national responsiveness and implementation of the transnational strategy are increasingly important.

In fact, even in a service sector such as banking and retailing, the more successful multinationals design their strategies on a regional basis, while the less successful multinationals pursue global strategies. Also, research suggests that geography still matters in regard to competition and rivalry of firms who use the Internet. Although events such as war and terrorist attacks that create shocks of uncertainty are likely to slow the process of globalization, they are not likely to reverse it. Furthermore, even though innovations such as the Internet may foster globalization, they are not likely to do away with the need for local responsiveness or regionalization. For example, although Internet commerce has reduced the need for local sales outlets, firms with local physical outlets still have an advantage.

SOURCES: B. Davis, 2003, For global economy, much rides on how the U.S. war plays out, *Wall Street Journal*, March 20, A1; G. Ip, 2003, Fed find few signs economy picked up after end of Iraq war, *Wall Street Journal*, June 12, A2; P. Magnusson, 2003, Ire over Iraq starts tripping up trade with Europe, *Business Week*, March 17, 51; R. L. Mecham III, 2003, Success for the new global manager: What you need to know to work across distances, countries, and cultures, *Leadership Quarterly*, 14: 347–352; A. Rugman & S. Girod, 2003, Retail multinationals and globalization: The evidence is regional, *European Management Journal*, 21(1): 24–37; A. M. Rugman & A. Verbeke, 2003, Extending the theory of the multinational enterprise: Internalization and strategic management perspectives, *Journal of International Business Studies*, 34: 125–137; J. Stell, 2003, War uncertainties delay construction projects, *Oil & Gas Journal*, April 14, 66–73; E. Scardino, 2003, Does a fast war mean a fast economic recovery? Not so fast, *DSN Retailing Today*, April 21, 30–34; L. Walczak, S. Crock, & P. Dwyer, 2003, America and the world, *BusinessWeek Online*, http://www.businessweek.com, April 21; D. Xu & O. Shenkar, 2002, Institutional distance and the multinational enterprise, *Academy of Management Review*, 27: 608–618.

Roebuck and Co., launched its web-based business in 1995. The firm established websites in the United Kingdom and Germany in 1999, and in France, Italy, and Ireland in 2000 prior to initiating a catalog business in those countries. With limited online advertising and word-of-mouth, a website business can be built in a foreign country without a lot of initial marketing expenses. Once the online business is large enough, a catalog business can be launched with mailing targeted to customers who have used the business online. Thus, even smaller companies can sell their goods and services globally when facilitated by electronic infrastructure without having significant (brick-and-mortar) facilities outside of their home location. But significant local adaptation is still needed in each country or region.[90]

Regionalization

Regionalization is a second trend that has become more common in global markets. Because a firm's location can affect its strategic competitiveness,[91] it must decide whether to compete in all or many global markets, or to focus on a particular region or regions. Competing in all markets provides economies that can be achieved because of the combined market size. Research suggests that firms that compete in risky emerging markets can also have higher performance.[92]

However, a firm that competes in industries where the international markets differ greatly (in which it must employ a multidomestic strategy) may wish to narrow its focus to a particular region of the world. In so doing, it can better understand the cultures, legal and social norms, and other factors that are important for effective competition in those markets. For example, a firm may focus on Far East markets only rather than competing simultaneously in the Middle East, Europe, and the Far East. Or, the firm may choose a region of the world where the markets are more similar and some coordination and sharing of resources would be possible. In this way, the firm may be able not only to better understand the markets in which it competes, but also to achieve some economies, even though it may have to employ a multidomestic strategy. For instance, research suggests that most large retailers are better at focusing on a particular region rather than being truly global.[93]

Countries that develop trade agreements to increase the economic power of their regions may promote regional strategies. The European Union (EU) and South America's Organization of American States (OAS) are country associations that developed trade agreements to promote the flow of trade across country boundaries within their respective regions.[94] However, the European Union is moving closer to unity, with a draft constitution on the table and plans for a more powerful president and foreign minister. If the EU's planned enlargement in 2004 succeeds, it will contain 25 countries and about 450 million people, and have about the same amount of wealth as the United States.[95] Many European firms acquire and integrate their businesses in Europe to better coordinate pan-European brands as the EU creates more unity in European markets. With a more united Europe, this process is likely to continue as new countries are added to the agreement.

The North American Free Trade Agreement (NAFTA), signed by the United States, Canada, and Mexico, facilitates free trade across country borders in North America and may be expanded to include other countries in South America, such as Argentina, Brazil, and Chile.[96] NAFTA loosens restrictions on international strategies within a region and provides greater opportunity for international strategies. NAFTA does not exist for the sole purpose of U.S. businesses moving across its borders. In fact, Mexico is the number two trading partner of the United States, and NAFTA greatly increased Mexico's exports to this country. Research suggests that managers of small and medium-sized firms are influenced by the strategy they implement (those with a differentiation strategy are more positively disposed to the agreement than are those pursuing a cost leadership strategy) and by their experience and rivalry with exporting firms.[97] Although Vicente Fox's election as president of Mexico and Mexico's new spirit of democracy have created opportunity for change, the poor U.S. economy and the September 11, 2001, attacks have lowered the economic outlook for Mexico. However, the Iraq War was a boon for Mexico as the price of oil was driven higher and trade became more regionally focused during the conflict. However, as the Opening Case indicates, China threatens to displace Mexico as the second largest U.S. trading partner. China displaced Japan as the third largest trading partner in 2002.[98]

Most firms enter regional markets sequentially, beginning in markets with which they are more familiar. They also introduce their largest and strongest lines of business into these markets first, followed by their other lines of business once the first lines are successful.[99]

After the firm selects its international strategies and decides whether to employ them in regional or world markets, it must choose a market entry mode.[100]

Choice of International Entry Mode

International expansion is accomplished by exporting products, participating in licensing arrangements, forming strategic alliances, making acquisitions, and establishing new wholly owned subsidiaries. These means of entering international markets and their characteristics are shown in Table 8.1. Each means of market entry has its advantages and disadvantages. Thus, choosing the appropriate mode or path to enter international markets affects the firm's performance in those markets.[101]

Exporting

Many industrial firms begin their international expansion by exporting goods or services to other countries.[102] Exporting does not require the expense of establishing operations in the host countries, but exporters must establish some means of marketing and distributing their products. Usually, exporting firms develop contractual arrangements with host-country firms.

The disadvantages of exporting include the often high costs of transportation and possible tariffs placed on incoming goods. Furthermore, the exporter has less control over the marketing and distribution of its products in the host country and must either pay the distributor or allow the distributor to add to the price to recoup its costs and earn a profit.[103] As a result, it may be difficult to market a competitive product

Global Market Entry: Choice of Entry Mode — Table 8.1

Type of Entry	Characteristics
Exporting	High cost, low control
Licensing	Low cost, low risk, little control, low returns
Strategic alliances	Shared costs, shared resources, shared risks, problems of integration (e.g., two corporate cultures)
Acquisition	Quick access to new market, high cost, complex negotiations, problems of merging with domestic operations
New wholly owned subsidiary	Complex, often costly, time consuming, high risk, maximum control, potential above-average returns

through exporting or to provide a product that is customized to each international market.[104] However, evidence suggests that cost leadership strategies enhance the performance of exports in developed countries, whereas differentiation strategies are more successful in emerging economies.[105]

Firms export mostly to countries that are closest to their facilities because of the lower transportation costs and the usually greater similarity between geographic neighbors. For example, U.S. NAFTA partners Mexico and Canada account for more than half of the goods exported from Texas. The Internet has also made exporting easier as illustrated by the Lands' End system described earlier.[106] Even small firms can access critical information about foreign markets, examine a target market, research the competition, and find lists of potential customers. Governments also use the Internet to facilitate applications for export and import licenses. Although the terrorist threat is likely to slow its progress, high-speed technology is still the wave of the future.[107]

Small businesses are most likely to use the exporting mode of international entry.[108] Currency exchange rates are one of the most significant problems small businesses face. The Bush administration has supported a dollar weak against the euro, which makes imports more expensive and U.S. goods less costly to foreign buyers, thus providing some economic relief for U.S. exporters.[109]

Licensing

Licensing is one of the forms of organizational networks that are becoming common, particularly among smaller firms.[110] A licensing arrangement allows a foreign firm to purchase the right to manufacture and sell the firm's products within a host country or set of countries.[111] The licenser is normally paid a royalty on each unit produced and sold. The licensee takes the risks and makes the monetary investments in facilities for manufacturing, marketing, and distributing the goods or services. As a result, licensing is possibly the least costly form of international expansion.

Licensing is also a way to expand returns based on previous innovations. Even if product life cycles are short, licensing may be a useful tool. For instance, because the toy industry faces relentless change and an unpredictable buying public, licensing is used and contracts are often completed in foreign markets where labor may be less expensive.[112]

Licensing also has disadvantages. For example, it gives the firm very little control over the manufacture and marketing of its products in other countries. Thus, license deals must be structured properly.[113] In addition, licensing provides the least potential returns, because returns must be shared between the licenser and the licensee. Worse, the international firm may learn the technology and produce and sell a similar competitive product after the license expires. Komatsu, for example, first licensed much of its technology from International Harvester, Bucyrus-Erie, and Cummins Engine to compete against Caterpillar in the earthmoving equipment business. Komatsu then dropped these licenses and developed its own products using the technology it had gained from the U.S. companies.[114]

In addition, if a firm wants to move to a different ownership arrangement, licensing may create some inflexibility. Thus, it is important that a firm think ahead and consider sequential forms of entry in international markets.[115]

Strategic Alliances

In recent years, strategic alliances have become a popular means of international expansion.[116] Strategic alliances allow firms to share the risks and the resources required to enter international markets.[117] Moreover, strategic alliances can facilitate the development of new core competencies that contribute to the firm's future strategic competitiveness.[118]

Most strategic alliances are formed with a host-country firm that knows and understands the competitive conditions, legal and social norms, and cultural idiosyncrasies of the country, which should help the expanding firm manufacture and market a competitive product. In return, the host-country firm may find its new access to the expanding firm's technology and innovative products attractive. Each partner in an alliance brings knowledge or resources to the partnership.[119] Indeed, partners often enter an alliance with the purpose of learning new capabilities. Common among those desired capabilities are technological skills.[120]

China is home to several large energy companies that are finally forming a global strategy. China's increasing petroleum needs and dependence on the Middle East are spurring the companies to seek out foreign oil sources and joint ventures with other companies. Recently, the oil companies have acquired stakes in the Caspian Sea region, Indonesia, and Australia, and are working to develop a joint venture with Russian companies to build a pipeline that would bring Russian crude oil to the northeast corner of China. The Caspian Sea deal in particular illustrates China's rising presence. "This gives us a firm foothold in probably the most prolific oil and gas basin outside the Middle East," says Mark Qiu, CFO of China National Offshore Oil Corporation (CNOOC).[121]

Not all alliances are successful; in fact, many fail.[122] The primary reasons for failure include incompatible partners and conflict between the partners.[123] International strategic alliances are especially difficult to manage.[124] Several factors may cause a relationship to sour. Trust between the partners is critical and is affected by at least four fundamental issues: the initial condition of the relationship, the negotiation process to arrive at an agreement, partner interactions, and external events.[125] Trust is also influenced by the country cultures involved in the alliance or joint venture.[126]

Research has shown that equity-based alliances, over which a firm has more control, tend to produce more positive returns[127] (strategic alliances are discussed in greater depth in Chapter 9). However, if conflict in a strategic alliance or joint venture will not be manageable, an acquisition may be a better option.[128] Research suggests that alliances are more favorable in the face of high uncertainty and where cooperation is needed to share knowledge between partners and where strategic flexibility is important, such as with small and medium-sized firms.[129] Acquisitions are better in situations with less need for strategic flexibility and when the transaction is used to maintain economies of scale or scope.[130]

Acquisitions

As free trade has continued to expand in global markets, cross-border acquisitions have also been increasing significantly. In recent years, cross-border acquisitions have comprised more than 45 percent of all acquisitions completed worldwide.[131] As explained in Chapter 7, acquisitions can provide quick access to a new market. In fact, acquisitions may provide the fastest, and often the largest, initial international expansion of any of the alternatives.[132]

Although acquisitions have become a popular mode of entering international markets, they are not without costs. International acquisitions carry some of the disadvantages of domestic acquisitions (see Chapter 7). In addition, they can be expensive and often require debt financing, which also carries an extra cost. International negotiations for acquisitions can be exceedingly complex and are generally more complicated than for domestic acquisitions. For example, it is estimated that only 20 percent of the cross-border bids made lead to a completed acquisition, compared to 40 percent for domestic acquisitions.[133] Dealing with the legal and regulatory requirements in the target firm's country and obtaining appropriate information to negotiate an agreement frequently present significant problems.[134] Finally, the problems of merging the new firm into the acquiring firm often are more complex than in domestic acquisitions. The acquiring firm must deal not only with different corporate cultures, but also with potentially different social cultures and practices. Therefore, while international acquisitions have been popular because of the rapid access to new markets they provide, they also carry with them important costs and multiple risks.

An ice cream rivalry is taking shape in the United States, but not between two U.S. firms. Through international acquisitions, Swiss-headquartered Nestlé and Anglo-Dutch giant Unilever have sought a strong presence in the U.S. ice cream market. Unilever holds 17 percent of the U.S. market through its Good Humor, Ben & Jerry's, and Breyers brands, while Nestlé's acquisition of Dreyer will allow it to own a similar market share by adding this brand to its Häagen-Dazs and Drumstick brands. Because this market requires freezer technology and a lot of ice cream is sold at scoop shops, "distribution headaches long made ice cream the province of small local dairies."[135] However, these two firms have exploited a strategy in Europe where branded ice cream freezers are visible everywhere. They expect to do the same in the United States by "exploiting on-the-go outlets, such as convenience stores, gas stations, video shops and vending machines."[136] "Unilever already sells ice cream in hundreds of Toys 'R' Us, True Value, Blockbuster and Family Dollar stores out of branded freezers."[137] Each firm will also exploit its well-known candy brands by mixing these candies with ice cream to create new flavors, such as "Nestlé's Butterfinger ice cream or Unilever's Klondike Caramel & Peanut bars with Planters peanuts."[138] The firms also expect to create licensing opportunities, such as Dreyer's deal with Walt Disney Co. for a *Finding Nemo* ice cream product that can be promoted with the movie. Acquisitions have allowed both firms to increase their presence quickly while obtaining distribution assets. Distribution to "on-the-go outlets" can be added to distribution runs to supermarkets.[139] Because the ice cream market is quite mature, an acquisition strategy worked well, although there are always integration difficulties as described in Chapter 7, and these only increase with cross-border deals.

New Wholly Owned Subsidiary

The establishment of a new wholly owned subsidiary is referred to as a **greenfield venture.** This process is often complex and potentially costly, but it affords maximum control to the firm and has the most potential to provide above-average returns. This potential is especially true of firms with strong intangible capabilities that might be leveraged through a greenfield venture.[140]

The risks are also high, however, because of the costs of establishing a new business operation in a new country. The firm may have to acquire the knowledge and expertise of the existing market by hiring either host-country nationals, possibly from competitors, or consultants, which can be costly. Still, the firm maintains control over the technology, marketing, and distribution of its products.[141] Alternatively, the company must build new manufacturing facilities, establish distribution networks, and learn and implement appropriate marketing strategies to compete in the new market.[142]

As the consumer electronics industry began to globalize, this trend had implications for electronic component distribution companies such as Avnet and Arrow, which sell parts to

The establishment of a new wholly owned subsidiary is referred to as a greenfield venture.

Unilever, a European-centered global food and consumer products firm, offers ice cream brands in the United States such as Good Humor, Ben & Jerry's, and Breyers. Its strongest rival in the United States is not a U.S. firm but, rather, the Swiss-headquartered European Nestlé.

PART 2 / Strategic Actions: Strategy Formulation

AP Photo

OEMs as well as to retail distributors. At first they expanded to Europe, mainly by making acquisitions, and then sought to integrate them by creating a centralized information system. This was difficult and often done in stages. However, a pure acquisition strategy has been more difficult to accomplish in Asia as component distributors have expanded into this region because there was more fragmentation among the existing distributors relative to Europe. As such, they have been doing more greenfield investment. Also, both TTI and Future, small distributors relative to Avnet and Arrow, have mostly used a greenfield approach because "they have a unique business model they want to preserve as they expand and staying on a single IT platform has its advantages."[143] Such an approach allows more centralized control, but takes longer to implement and longer to build local relationships than through acquiring a local distributor as in the ice cream example above.

Dynamics of Mode of Entry

A firm's choice of mode of entry into international markets is affected by a number of factors.[144] Initially, market entry will often be achieved through export, which requires no foreign manufacturing expertise and investment only in distribution. Licensing can facilitate the product improvements necessary to enter foreign markets, as in the Komatsu example. Strategic alliances have been popular because they allow a firm to connect with an experienced partner already in the targeted market. Strategic alliances also reduce risk through the sharing of costs. All three modes therefore are best for early market development tactics. Also, the strategic alliance is often used in more uncertain situations, such as an emerging economy.[145] However, if intellectual property rights in the emerging economy are not well protected, the number of firms in the industry is growing fast, and the need for global integration is high, the wholly owned entry mode is preferred.[146]

To secure a stronger presence in international markets, acquisitions or greenfield ventures may be required. Large aerospace firms Airbus and Boeing have used joint ventures, while military equipment firms such as Lockheed Martin have used acquisitions to build a global presence.[147] Many Japanese auto manufacturers, such as Honda, Nissan, and Toyota, have gained a presence in the United States through both greenfield ventures and joint ventures.[148] Toyota has particularly strong intangible production capabilities that it has been able to transfer through greenfield ventures.[149] Both acquisitions and greenfield ventures are likely to come at later stages in the development of an international strategy. In addition, both strategies tend to be more successful when the firm making the investment possesses valuable core competencies.[150] Large diversified business groups, often found in emerging economies, not only gain resources through diversification, but also have specialized abilities in managing differences in inward and outward flows of foreign direct investment. In particular, Korean *chaebol* have been adept at making acquisitions in emerging economies.[151]

Thus, to enter a global market, a firm selects the entry mode that is best suited to the situation at hand. In some instances, the various options will be followed sequentially, beginning with exporting and ending with greenfield ventures.[152] In other cases, the firm may use several, but not all, of the different entry modes, each in different markets. The decision regarding which entry mode to use is primarily a result of the industry's competitive conditions, the country's situation and government policies, and the firm's unique set of resources, capabilities, and core competencies.

Strategic Competitiveness Outcomes

Once its international strategy and mode of entry have been selected, the firm turns its attention to implementation issues (see Chapter 11). It is important to do this, because as explained next, international expansion is risky and may not result in a competitive advantage (see Figure 8.1). The probability the firm will achieve success by using an international strategy increases when that strategy is effectively implemented.

International Diversification and Returns

As noted earlier, firms have numerous reasons to diversify internationally. **International diversification** is a strategy through which a firm expands the sales of its goods or services across the borders of global regions and countries into different geographic locations or markets. Because of its potential advantages, international diversification should be related positively to firms' returns. Research has shown that, as international diversification increases, firms' returns increase.[153] In fact, the stock market is particularly sensitive to investments in international markets. Firms that are broadly diversified into multiple international markets usually achieve the most positive stock returns, especially when they diversify geographically into core business areas.[154] There are also many reasons for the positive effects of international diversification, such as potential economies of scale and experience, location advantages, increased market size, and the opportunity to stabilize returns. The stabilization of returns helps reduce a firm's overall risk.[155] All of these outcomes can be achieved by smaller and newer ventures, as well as by larger and established firms. New ventures can also enjoy higher returns when they learn new technologies from their international diversification.[156]

Firms in the Japanese auto industry, especially Toyota (as indicated in the Strategic Focus on the global auto industry), have found that international diversification may allow them to better exploit their core competencies, because sharing knowledge resources between operations can produce synergy. Also, a firm's returns may affect its decision to diversify internationally. For example, poor returns in a domestic market may encourage a firm to expand internationally in order to enhance its profit potential. In addition, internationally diversified firms may have access to more flexible labor markets, as the Japanese do in the United States, and may thereby benefit from global scanning for competition and market opportunities. Also, through global networks with assets in many countries, firms can develop more flexible structures to adjust to changes that might occur.[157] Petronas has developed such a strong global network and, even though it is a state-owned oil company in Malaysia, its operations are profitable, which is counter to most state-owned monopolies. Because Malaysia's oil reserves have dwindled and because few domestic opportunities exist to drill for new reserves, Petronas expanded its operations abroad to fill the potentially growing reserve challenge. It has done so successfully; it "established itself as the developing world's most aggressive foreign investor, with operations in 32 countries."[158] It has gone to Iraq and the Sudan, among other places, where more technologically developed "Western rivals have feared to tread."[159] In the process, Petronas has become a truly global company. However, it must still deal with Malaysian politics because of its state-owned status, which can cause problems during political transitions.[160] Multinational firms, such as Petronas, with efficient and competitive operations are more likely to produce above-average returns for their investors and better products for their customers than are solely domestic firms. However, as explained later, international diversification can be carried too far.

International Diversification and Innovation

In Chapter 1, we indicated that the development of new technology is at the heart of strategic competitiveness. As noted in Porter's model (see Figure 8.2), a nation's competitiveness depends, in part, on the capacity of its industry to innovate. Eventually and inevitably, competitors outperform firms that fail to innovate and improve their operations and products. Therefore, the only way to sustain a competitive advantage is to upgrade it continually.[161]

International diversification provides the potential for firms to achieve greater returns on their innovations (through larger or more numerous markets) and lowers the often substantial risks of R&D investments. Therefore, international diversification provides incentives for firms to innovate.[162]

In addition, international diversification may be necessary to generate the resources required to sustain a large-scale R&D operation. An environment of rapid technological obsolescence makes it difficult to invest in new technology and the capital-intensive operations required to take advantage of such investment. Firms operating solely in domestic markets may find such investments problematic because of the length of time required to recoup the original investment. If the time is extended, it may not even be possible to recover the investment before the technology becomes obsolete.[163] As a result, international diversification improves a firm's ability to appropriate additional and necessary returns from innovation before competitors can overcome the initial competitive advantage created by the innovation. In addition, firms moving into international markets are exposed to new products and processes. If they learn about those products and processes and integrate this knowledge into their operations, further innovation can be developed.[164]

The relationship among international diversification, innovation, and returns is complex. Some level of performance is necessary to provide the resources to generate international diversification, which in turn provides incentives and resources to invest in research and development. The latter, if done appropriately, should enhance the returns of the firm, which then provides more resources for continued international diversification and investment in R&D.[165]

Because of the potential positive effects of international diversification on performance and innovation, such diversification may even enhance returns in product-diversified firms. International diversification would increase market potential in each of these firms' product lines, but the complexity of managing a firm that is both product diversified and internationally diversified is significant. Research suggests that firms in less developed countries gain from being product diversified when partnering with multinational firms from a more developed country that are looking to enter a less developed country in pursuit of increased international diversification.[166]

Asea Brown Boveri (ABB) demonstrates these relationships. This firm's operations involve high levels of both product and international diversification, yet ABB's performance was strong until the recent downturn. Weaknesses have appeared, however. Some believe that the firm's inability to effectively implement the transnational strategy was ultimately due to overdiversification in both product and geographic markets. ABB assembled culturally diverse corporate and divisional management teams that facilitated the simultaneous achievement of global integration and local responsiveness, but too much diversification, especially in emerging markets such as Korea, forced a reorganization. ABB also bought companies that created "huge liabilities from asbestos litigation."[167] Although the firm's strategy failed, many local companies benefited, especially those that were already product diversified, such as those in Korea.

Evidence suggests that more culturally diverse top-management teams often have a greater knowledge of international markets and their idiosyncrasies[168] (top-management teams are discussed further in Chapter 12). Moreover, an in-depth understanding of diverse markets among top-level managers facilitates intrafirm coordination and the use of long-term, strategically relevant criteria to evaluate the performance of managers and their units.[169] In turn, this approach facilitates improved innovation and performance.[170]

Complexity of Managing Multinational Firms

Although firms can realize many benefits by implementing an international strategy, doing so is complex and can produce greater uncertainty.[171] For example, multiple risks are involved when a firm operates in several different countries. Firms can grow only so large and diverse before becoming unmanageable, or before the costs of managing them exceed their benefits.[172] Other complexities include the highly competitive nature of global markets, multiple cultural environments, potentially rapid shifts in the value of different currencies, and the possible instability of some national governments.

Risks in an International Environment

International diversification carries multiple risks.[173] Because of these risks, international expansion is difficult to implement and manage. The chief risks are political and economic. Taking these risks into account, highly internationally diversified firms are accustomed to market conditions yielding competitive situations that differ from what was predicted. Sometimes, these situations contribute to the firm's strategic competitiveness; on other occasions, they have a negative effect on the firm's efforts.[174] Specific examples of political and economic risks are shown in Figure 8.4.

Political Risks

Political risks are risks related to instability in national governments and to war, both civil and international. Instability in a national government creates numerous problems, including economic risks and uncertainty created by government regulation; the existence of many, possibly conflicting, legal authorities or corruption; and the potential nationalization of private assets.[175] Foreign firms that invest in another country may have concerns about the stability of the national government and what might happen to their investments or assets because of unrest and government instability.[176]

Economic Risks

As illustrated in the Strategic Focus on intellectual property rights, economic risks are interdependent with political risks. If firms cannot protect their intellectual property, foreign direct investment decreases. Countries therefore need to create and sustain strong intellectual property rights and their enforcement, or they risk losing their reputation in the eyes of potential investing firms and might also risk sanctions from international political bodies such as the WTO.

As noted earlier, foremost among the economic risks of international diversification are the differences and fluctuations in the value of different currencies.[177] The value of the dollar relative to other currencies determines the value of the international assets and earnings of U.S. firms; for example, an increase in the value of the U.S. dollar can reduce the value of U.S. multinational firms' international assets and earnings in other countries. Furthermore, the value of different currencies can also, at times, dramatically affect a firm's competitiveness in global markets because of its effect on the prices of goods manufactured in different countries.[178]

An increase in the value of the dollar can harm U.S. firms' exports to international markets because of the price differential of the products. Currently the dollar is weak, meaning that overseas profits for American companies do not look as good as they might in other years. A weak dollar could also contribute eventually to a slide into deeper recession for the American economy, another major risk for companies that invest in America.[179]

Limits to International Expansion: Management Problems

Firms tend to earn positive returns on early international diversification, but the returns often level off and become negative as the diversification increases past some point.[180] There are several reasons for the limits to the positive effects of international diversification. First, greater geographic dispersion across country borders increases the costs

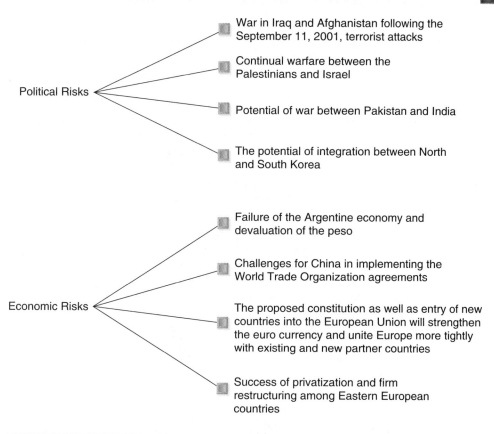

Political Risks
- War in Iraq and Afghanistan following the September 11, 2001, terrorist attacks
- Continual warfare between the Palestinians and Israel
- Potential of war between Pakistan and India
- The potential of integration between North and South Korea

Economic Risks
- Failure of the Argentine economy and devaluation of the peso
- Challenges for China in implementing the World Trade Organization agreements
- The proposed constitution as well as entry of new countries into the European Union will strengthen the euro currency and unite Europe more tightly with existing and new partner countries
- Success of privatization and firm restructuring among Eastern European countries

SOURCES: 2003, Finance and economics: The perils of convergence; Economics focus, *The Economist*, April 5, 71; K. D. Brouthers, 2003, Institutional, cultural and transaction cost influences on entry mode choice and performance, *Journal of International Business Studies*, 33: 203–221; F. Bruni, 2003, With a constitution to ponder, Europeans gather in Greece, *New York Times*, http://www.nytimes.com, June 20; B. Davis, R. Buckman, & C. Rhoads, 2003, A global journal report: For global economy, much rides on how the U.S. war plays out, *Wall Street Journal*, March 20, A1; J. Flint, 2003, China: How big, how fast, how dangerous? *Forbes*, http://www.forbes.com, July 1; G. A. Fowler, 2003, Copies 'R' Us—Pirates in China move fast to pilfer toy makers' ideas, *Wall Street Journal*, January 31, B1; W. Rugg, 2003, A down dollar's lure—and peril, *Business-Week Online*, http://www.businessweek.com, May 22; J. H. Zhao, S. H. Kim, & J. Du, 2003, The impact of corruption and transparency on foreign direct investment: An empirical analysis, *Management International Review*, 43(1): 41–62; M. Kripalani, N. Mangi, F. Balfour, P. Magnusson, & R. Brady, 2002, Now, will India and Pakistan get serious about peace? *Business Week*, January 14, 51; M. Wallin, 2002, Argentina grapples with postdevaluation, *Wall Street Journal*, January 10, A8; P. Engardio, R. Miller, G. Smith, D. Brady, M. Kripalani, A. Borrus, & D. Foust, 2001, What's at stake: How terrorism threatens the global economy, *Business Week*, October 22, 33–34; D. Eisenberg, 2001, Arafat's dance of death, *Time*, December 24, 64–65; B. Fulford, 2001, Another enemy, *Forbes*, October 29, 117; K. E. Myer, 2001, Institutions, transaction costs, and entry model choice in Eastern Europe, *Journal of International Business Studies*, 32: 357–367.

of coordination between units and the distribution of products. Second, trade barriers, logistical costs, cultural diversity, and other differences by country (e.g., access to raw materials and different employee skill levels) greatly complicate the implementation of an international diversification strategy.[181]

Institutional and cultural factors can present strong barriers to the transfer of a firm's competitive advantages from one country to another. Marketing programs often have to be redesigned and new distribution networks established when firms expand into new countries. In addition, firms may encounter different labor costs and capital charges. In general, it is difficult to effectively implement, manage, and control a firm's international operations.[182]

Intellectual Property Rights in China and Southeast Asia

The lack of protection for intellectual property in China and Southeast Asia has made it very difficult for Western firms to be successful there, and it includes all sorts of industries, from movies and music to software and textiles.

General Motors has a Chinese joint venture partner named SAIC. Together, they built Buicks and other models in China. GM developed a new car called the Matiz, which was to be released in China. Rumors surfaced that SAIC had produced a very similar subcompact car called the QQ. Government officials commented on the cars' similarity. When GM approached its partner with its concerns, SAIC denied imitating the design from GM's plans. GM has not decided yet what it is going to do to resolve its concern. Despite the growth in the auto industry in China (sales increased 50 percent from 2002 to 2003), GM is not alone in its piracy concerns. Toyota has filed suit against Geely Auto Group, a private Chinese auto company, for trademark infringement.

Toy makers have also encountered problems in China. The toy industry has evolved such that the molds used for casting can be copied within a few hours, and toy makers at conventions to showcase new toys find themselves face-to-face with copies at these conventions. China produces 70 percent of the world's toys, and as a manufacturing hub, it is very open to design theft. The big toy companies, Mattel and Hasbro, don't attend toy fairs to showcase new toys; instead, they hold their own invitation-only fairs once a year. Small toy companies can't afford to do that. They also can't afford to legally register their toys, although the law does not provide much relief from imposters. For example, the penalty for piracy doesn't include jail time. One owner reports having chased away would-be copiers with cameras, sketch pads, and Palm Pilots from her booth. Another retailer keeps its toys locked in hotel rooms, where only invited guests may see them.

Software is undeniably one of the most commonly pirated items in China. It is estimated that 92 percent of all software in China was counterfeit in 2001. This includes not only disks sold to end consumers, but also preinstalled software that comes with computers. As a result, companies such as Microsoft struggle to be profitable in China. Microsoft, attracted by a growing number of computer owners and the opening market in China, moved in through Taiwan and Hong Kong starting in 1989. The dream is that computers and software will follow the same trajectory as the mobile phone in China: 24 million cell phones in 1998 increased to 200 million cell phones in 2003.

Unfortunately, Microsoft began with an overconfident attitude unappealing to the Chinese. It followed that with an aggressive attack of lawsuits against pirates, which made it look like a foreign bully thrashing small Chinese companies. Microsoft has invested millions of dollars already in China and has yet to earn a profit, nor does it look likely that the firm will achieve profitability any time soon. Having evaluated its approach, Microsoft is now trying to rebuild its reputation by investing heavily in China, spending approximately $750 million. This includes sponsoring research at universities and forming joint ventures with Chinese companies as well as training Chinese software engineers and building research labs.

Cisco Systems filed suit in February 2003 against the Chinese company Huawei, alleging that Huawei had stolen its designs and software code for

Steamroller crushes approximately two million illegal CDs, DVDs, and videocassettes of local and foreign films during a ceremony highlighting the Philippine government's fight against piracy in suburban Quezon City. The pirated CDs, including music and pornographic movies, were seized in three days of raids by police of sidewalk stalls and shops in the city.

©Reuters NewMedia Inc./CORBIS

routers. For years, customers had wondered at the similarities, right down to the layout of the user handbook and the keyboard programming commands. 3Com, a Cisco rival that recently formed a joint venture with Huawei, was unalarmed at the suit, and said that Huawei had done its best to appease its own and Cisco's concerns with the venture, including a clause in the agreement that guarantees there is no pirated software in what will be produced.

China has begun taking steps to protect intellectual property rights, especially because of requirements for entry into the World Trade Organization. As China seeks to become a global player in the software industry, like India, it wants to overcome its reputation for piracy. It continues to stiffen its laws, making it easier for companies to sue and applying hefty fines to violators. Progress has been made in Hong Kong especially since 1999, when the city's Intellectual Property Investigation Bureau established a special antipiracy unit. China has amended its laws so that even offers to sell pirated products, not just actual sales, are illegal. And in February 2003, a Chinese court handed down a remarkable decision in favor of Lego, the Danish toy company, which clearly protected Lego's intellectual property rights.

Despite legal steps, enforcement remains scanty. Local governments might own the factory producing pirated products and choose Chinese jobs over the potential of foreign lawsuits. Progress will mostly come as the Chinese begin to see themselves as the creators of intellectual property and seek intellectual property rights in their own interest.

SOURCES: S. M. Andrews, 2003, Design thieves menace survival, *Home Textiles Today,* January 27, 10; G. A. Fowler, 2003, Copies `R' Us—Pirates in China move fast to pilfer toy makers' ideas, *Wall Street Journal,* January 31, B1; B. Einhorn, 2003, Cisco: Making a federal case out of it, *Business Week,* February 10, 36; B. Einhorn, 2003, China learns to say, "Stop, thief!" *BusinessWeek Online,* http//:www.businessweek.com, February 10; D. Ackman, 2003, Building blocks of Chinese IP law, *Forbes,* http//:www.forbes.com, February 11; R. Meredith, 2003, Microsoft's long march, *Forbes,* February 17, 78–86; P. D. Henig, 2003, Cross border IP hits the spotlight: With more tech startups operating in India and China, protecting IP has become ever more critical, *Venture Capital Journal,* March 1, 1; S. Thurm, 2003, China's Huawei, 3Com to form venture to compete with Cisco, *Wall Street Journal,* March 20, B5; P. Burrows, 2003, Cisco: In hot pursuit of a Chinese rival, *Business-Week Online,* http//:www.businessweek.com, May 19; K. Leggett, 2003, U.S. auto makers find promise—and peril—in China, *Wall Street Journal,* June 19, B1.

Wal-Mart made significant mistakes in markets around the world as it internationalized. For example, its first Mexican stores carried ice skates, riding lawn mowers, fishing tackle—even clay pigeons for skeet shooting. To get rid of the clay pigeons, they would be radically discounted, "only to have automated inventory systems linked to Wal-Mart's corporate headquarters in Bentonville, Arkansas, order a fresh batch."[183] As Wal-Mart began to get the right mix of products, the Mexican currency was devalued in 1994. However, over time, Wal-Mart has become very successful in Latin America, especially in Mexico, and elsewhere in the world. It has been able to increase its market share by taking advantage of local sourcing, and especially by taking advantage of the lower wages, for instance, in Mexico through NAFTA. It has made acquisitions in Europe and will have increased the number of stores in 2003 from 25 to 40 in China alone.[184]

The amount of international diversification that can be managed varies from firm to firm and according to the abilities of each firm's managers. The problems of central coordination and integration are mitigated if the firm diversifies into more friendly countries that are geographically close and have cultures similar to its own country's culture. In that case, there are likely to be fewer trade barriers, the laws and customs are better understood, and the product is easier to adapt to local markets.[185] For example, U.S. firms may find it less difficult to expand their operations into Mexico, Canada, and Western European countries than into Asian countries.

Management must also be concerned with the relationship between the host government and the multinational corporation.[186] Although government policy and regulations are often barriers, many firms, such as Toyota and General Motors, have turned to strategic alliances to overcome those barriers. By forming interorganizational networks, such as strategic alliances, firms can share resources and risks but also build flexibility.[187]

Summary

- The use of international strategies is increasing not only because of traditional motivations, but also for emerging reasons. Traditional motives include extending the product life cycle, securing key resources, and having access to low-cost labor. Emerging motivations focus on the combination of the Internet and mobile telecommunications, which facilitates global transactions. Also, there is increased pressure for global integration as the demand for commodities becomes borderless, and yet pressure is also increasing for local country responsiveness.

- An international strategy usually attempts to capitalize on four benefits: increased market size; the opportunity to earn a return on large investments; economies of scale and learning; and advantages of location.

- International business-level strategies are usually grounded in one or more home-country advantages, as Porter's diamond model suggests. The diamond model emphasizes four determinants: factors of production; demand conditions; related and supporting industries; and patterns of firm strategy, structure, and rivalry.

- There are three types of international corporate-level strategies. A multidomestic strategy focuses on competition within each country in which the firm competes. Firms using a multidomestic strategy decentralize strategic and operating decisions to the business units operating in each country, so that each unit can tailor its goods and services to the local market. A global strategy assumes more standardization of products across country boundaries; therefore, competitive strategy is centralized and controlled by the home office. A transnational strategy seeks to combine aspects of both multidomestic and global strategies in order to emphasize both local responsiveness and global integration and coordination. This strategy is difficult to implement, requiring an integrated network and a culture of individual commitment.

- Although the transnational strategy's implementation is a challenge, environmental trends are causing many multinational firms to consider the need for both global efficiency and local responsiveness. Many large multinational firms—particularly those with many diverse products—use a multidomestic strategy with some product lines and a global strategy with others.

- The threat of wars and terrorist attacks increases the risks and costs of international strategies. Furthermore, research suggests that the liability of foreignness is more difficult to overcome than once thought.

- Some firms decide to compete only in certain regions of the world, as opposed to viewing all markets in the world as potential opportunities. Competing in regional markets allows firms and managers to focus their learning on specific markets, cultures, locations, resources, etc.

- Firms may enter international markets in one of several ways, including exporting, licensing, forming strategic alliances, making acquisitions, and establishing new wholly owned subsidiaries, often referred to as greenfield ventures. Most firms begin with exporting or licensing, because of their lower costs and risks, but later may expand to strategic alliances and acquisitions. The most expensive and risky means of entering a new international market is through the establishment of a new wholly owned subsidiary. On the other hand, such subsidiaries provide the advantages of maximum control by the firm and, if they are successful, the greatest returns.

- International diversification facilitates innovation in a firm, because it provides a larger market to gain more and faster returns from investments in innovation. In addition, international diversification may generate the resources necessary to sustain a large-scale R&D program.

- In general, international diversification is related to above-average returns, but this assumes that the diversification is effectively implemented and that the firm's international operations are well managed. International diversification provides greater economies of scope and learning, which, along with greater innovation, help produce above-average returns.

- Several risks are involved with managing multinational operations. Among these are political risks (e.g., instability of national governments) and economic risks (e.g., fluctuations in the value of a country's currency).

- There are also limits to the ability to manage international expansion effectively. International diversification increases coordination and distribution costs, and management problems are exacerbated by trade barriers, logistical costs, and cultural diversity, among other factors.

1. What are the traditional and emerging motives that cause firms to expand internationally?

2. What four factors provide a basis for international business-level strategies?

3. What are the three international corporate-level strategies? How do they differ from each other? What factors lead to their development?

4. What environmental trends are affecting international strategy?

5. What five modes of international expansion are available, and what is the normal sequence of their use?

6. What is the relationship between international diversification and innovation? How does international diversification affect innovation? What is the effect of international diversification on a firm's returns?

7. What are the risks of international diversification? What are the challenges of managing multinational firms?

8. What factors limit the positive outcomes of international expansion?

Experiential Exercises

Modes of Entry into China

As pointed out in the Opening Case, China's 2001 entry into the World Trade Organization (WTO) is potentially one of the most significant international trade events in recent times. Substantial business discussion has focused on China's relative competitive advantage with regard to labor, which allows the production and exportation of vast quantities of goods at very low costs. Conversely, Chinese markets provide a substantial potential opportunity for non-Chinese firms to export into them. The huge market size (1.2 billion plus in population) is a key factor, as are virtually untapped consumer markets for many goods and services for increasingly sophisticated Chinese needs and tastes, which are often modest by Western standards. However, conflicting business and social goals in the macro Chinese environment have underscored the liability of foreignness. That is, being a foreign firm often increases the difficulty of management and the likelihood of failure. This is primarily due to unfamiliarity with cultural, political, economic, and other environmental differences and their potential effect on business operations, as well as to the need for coordination across geographic distance, among other factors. Organizational and strategic influences on firm survival in foreign banking and financial services markets have been linked to levels of technology adaptations, mode of internal control, and intensity of competition, as well as general levels of competitiveness of both the home and the host country. Furthermore, variance in the degree to which former state-owned businesses have been encouraged, or even allowed, to approach free-market status has caused further difficulties. For instance, before September 2003, certification for import/export business activity was tightly controlled by the Ministry of Commerce at the national level and generally limited to large, well-connected firms that could satisfy relatively high capitalization and operational requirements. These requirements were relaxed in response to WTO commitments, while primary responsibility for examination and registration of firms was delegated to the local government level. This should permit more (smaller) firms across industries to engage in import/export business activity but also is likely to create potential discrepancies in the certification process for import/export status.

Chinese and U.S. businesses have an inverse relationship concerning import and export patterns for goods and services. China is a net exporter of goods to the United States, while the United States is a net exporter of services to China. Based on this and chapter information, your own knowledge of Chinese and Western business practices, as well as Internet resources, explore the differences between Western and Chinese business practices. Using this information, evaluate the most appropriate mode of entry (see Table 8.1) *into* China by:

1. A U.S. financial services firm, such as a bank; and

2. A U.S. manufacturer of heavy goods, such as an auto company.

Developing and Implementing International Mode of Entry Strategies

In the late 1990s, Motorola Inc., a leading U.S. telecom supplier, viewed the telecommunication market in Turkey as promising. The rapidly growing Turkish economy presented substantial growth potential to U.S. firms seeking entry into this market, where subscribers grew from two to nine million during 1999–2001 alone, in a country of sixty-five million. Likewise, opportunity abounded for those awarded lucrative Turkish wireless telecom licenses, such as Telsim, a local (domestic) firm. Telsim was and is controlled by the powerful Turkish Uzan family. This family has substantial affiliations across construction, banking, media, and politics. In general, Telsim reportedly needed a strong partner to take advantage of market opportunities, and Motorola sought to enter the potentially lucrative telecommunication market in Turkey.

In February 2000, Motorola and Telsim announced an agreement for Motorola to expand wireless telephone service in Turkey by providing infrastructure, handsets, and associated services to supplement Telsim's global satellite network. As part of the agreement, Telsim named Motorola as its exclusive regional supplier of most equipment over the next three years. Motorola estimated that revenues from this supplier agreement would be at least $1.5 billion USD. In October 2000, Motorola and Telsim signed another agreement for the supply and deployment of a third generation (3G) mobile network capable of providing advanced multimedia services. Motorola estimated the potential value of the contract to be in excess of $2 billion USD. During the course of these interactions, Motorola loaned nearly $2 billion USD to Telsim (mostly in the form of cash and some equipment).

By the middle of 2001, the initially excellent business relations between Motorola and Telsim became troubled and were viewed by many as less than successful. This came during a general downturn in the global telecom market, making the industry as a whole less attractive. On January 28, 2002, Motorola filed a lawsuit against Telsim in the U.S. District Court for the Southern District of New York alleging criminal actions, including diversion of funds and fraud, on the part of Telsim. This lawsuit was filed under the Racketeer Influenced and Corrupt Organizations (RICO) Act. Motorola sought more than $2 billion USD in compensatory damages as well as unspecified punitive damages.

1. Briefly discuss various choices of market entry modes originally available to Motorola in this case. Table 8.1 provides a summary of market entry modes.

2. Working in small groups, students should update this case by developing and defending an approach to deal with this situation. What should Motorola do next? Pull out of the Turkish market? Find another licensing company? Wait until the lawsuits are completely settled in the courts? Change the mode of entry?

3. Can such disputes influence other firms interested in developing business relationships in Turkey? How? Class discussion will follow.

Understanding International Strategies

Divide the class into small groups. For each company in the table, indicate the international strategy being implemented. You may support your determination by using the content of Chapter 8, as it gives some clues regarding possible strategies used. Groups will discuss the selection with the class.

Company	Strategy	Supporting the Choice of Strategy
Unilever		1. 2. 3.
Coca-Cola		1. 2. 3.
Tricon Global Restaurants		1. 2. 3.
Flextronics		1. 2. 3.
Cemex		1. 2. 3.
DaimlerChrysler		1. 2. 3.
Lands' End		1. 2. 3.
General Motors		1. 2. 3.
Wal-Mart		1. 2. 3.

Company	Strategy	Supporting the Choice of Strategy
British American Tobacco (BAT)		1. 2. 3.
Asea Brown Boveri (ABB)		1. 2. 3.

Notes

1. G. Smith, 2003, Wasting away: Despite SARS, Mexico is still losing export ground to China, *Business Week*, June 2, 42–44.

2. H. Chen, M. Y. Hu, & P. S. Hu, 2002, Ownership strategy of multinationals from ASEAN: The case of their investment in Sino-foreign joint ventures, *Management International Review*, 42(3): 309–326; D. Ahlstrom & G. D. Bruton, 2001, Learning from successful local private firms in China: Establishing legitimacy, *Academy of Management Executive*, 15(4): 72–83.

3. S. Werner, 2002, Recent developments in international management research: A review of 20 top management journals, *Journal of Management*, 28: 277–305.

4. R. A. Kapp, 2003, Internationalizing China: Domestic interests and global linkages, *China Business Review*, 30(2): 80; A. K. Gupta & V. Govindarajan, 2001, Converting global presence into global competitive advantage, *Academy of Management Executive*, 15(2): 45–57.

5. T. M. Begley & D. P. Boyd, 2003, The need for a corporate global mind-set, *MIT Sloan Management Review*, 44(2): 25–32.

6. R. L. Mecham III, 2003, Success for the new global manager: What you need to know to work across distances, countries, and cultures, *Leadership Quarterly*, 14: 347–352; R. J. Trent & R. M. Monczka, 2002, Pursuing competitive advantage through integrated global sourcing, *Academy of Management Executive*, 16(2): 66–80; A. McWilliams, D. D. Van Fleet, & P. M. Wright, 2001, Strategic management of human resources for global competitive advantage, *Journal of Business Strategies*, 18(1): 1–24; B. L. Kedia & A. Mukherji, 1999, Global managers: Developing a mindset for global competitiveness, *Journal of World Business*, 34(3): 230–251.

7. D. M. De Carolis, 2003, Competencies and imitability in the pharmaceutical industry: An analysis of their relationship with firm performance, *Journal of Management*, 29: 27–50; J. S. Childers, Jr., R. L. Somerly, & K. E. Bass, 2002, Competitive environments and sustained economic rents: A theoretical examination of country-specific differences within the pharmaceutical industry, *International Journal of Management*, 19(1): 89–98; G. Bottazzi, G. Dosi, M. Lippi, F. Pammolli, & M. Riccaboni, 2001, Innovation and corporate growth in the evolution of the drug industry, *International Journal of Industrial Organization*, 19: 1161–1187.

8. S. Tallman & K. Fladmoe-Lindquist, 2002, Internationalization, globalization, and capability-based strategy, *California Management Review*, 45(1): 116–135; S. Tallman, 2001, Global strategic management, in M. A. Hitt, R. E. Freeman, & J. S. Harrison (eds.), *Handbook of Strategic Management*, Oxford, UK: Blackwell Publishers, 462–490; C. W. L. Hill, 2000, *International Business: Competing in the Global Marketplace*, 3d ed., Boston: Irwin/McGraw Hill, 378–380.

9. W. Hejazi & P. Pauly, 2003, Motivations for FDI and domestic capital formation, *Journal of International Business Studies*, 34: 282–289.

10. R. Vernon, 1996, International investment and international trade in the product cycle, *Quarterly Journal of Economics*, 80: 190–207.

11. H. F. Lau, C. C. Y. Kwok, & C. F. Chan, 2000, Filling the gap: Extending international product life cycle to emerging economies, *Journal of Global Marketing*, 13(4): 29–51.

12. L. Yu, 2003, The global-brand advantage, *MIT Sloan Management Review*, 44(3): 13.

13. G. Edmondson & C. Passariello, 2003, Has Benetton stopped unraveling? Its new boss plans sweeping changes, and investors are happy, *Business Week*, June 23, 22.

14. J. Flint, 2003, Too much globalism, *Forbes*, February 17, 96; Y. S. Pak, J. Lee, & J. M. An, 2002, Lessons learned from Daewoo Motors' experience in emerging markets, *Multinational Business Review*, 10(2): 122–128; B. Kim & Y. Lee, 2001, Global capacity expansion strategies: Lessons learned from two Korean carmakers, *Long Range Planning*, 34(3): 309–333.

15. D. Rigby & C. Zook, 2003, Open-market innovation, *Harvard Business Review*, 89(10): 80–89; J.-R. Lee & J.-S. Chen, 2003, Internationalization, local adaptation and subsidiary's entrepreneurship: An exploratory study on Taiwanese manufacturing firms in Indonesia and Malaysia, *Asia Pacific Journal of Management*, 20: 51–72; K. Macharzina, 2001, The end of pure global strategies? *Management International Review*, 41(2): 105.

16. Y. Luo, 2003, Market-seeking MNEs in an emerging market: How parent-subsidiary links shape overseas success, *Journal of International Business Studies*, 34: 290–309; 2003, Special Report: Two systems, one grand rivalry—India and China, *The Economist*, June 21, 66–68; Y. Luo, 2000, Entering China today: What choices do we have? *Journal of Global Marketing*, 14(2): 57–82.

17. C. C. Y. Kwok & D. M. Reeb, 2000, Internationalization and firm risk: An upstream-downstream hypothesis, *Journal of International Business Studies*, 31: 611–629; J. J. Choi & M. Rajan, 1997, A joint test of market segmentation and exchange risk factor in international capital markets, *Journal of International Business Studies*, 28: 29–49.

18. R. E. Hoskisson, L. Eden, C. M. Lau, & M. Wright, 2000, Strategy in emerging economies, *Academy of Management Journal*, 43: 249–267; D. J. Arnold & J. A. Quelch, 1998, New strategies in emerging markets, *Sloan Management Review*, 40: 7–20.

19. P. Engardio, A. Bernstein, & M. Kripalani, 2003, Is your job next? *Business Week*, February 3, 50–60; M. Wright, A. Lockett, & S. Pruthi, 2002, Internationalization of Western venture capitalists into emerging markets: Risk assessment and information in India, *Small Business Economics*, 19(1): 13–29.

20. M. Peng, 2003, Institutional transitions and strategic choices, *Academy of Management Review*, 28: 275–296.

21. T. Aeppel, 2003, Manufacturers spent much less abroad last year—U.S. firms cut investing overseas by estimated 37 percent; the "high-wage paradox," *Wall Street Journal*, May 9, A8.

22. W. Kuemmerle, 2001, Go global—or not? *Harvard Business Review*, 79(6): 37–49; Y. Luo & M. W. Peng, 1999, Learning to compete in a transition economy: Experience, environment and performance, *Journal of International Business Studies*, 30: 269–295.

23. G. Jones, 2002, Control, performance, and knowledge transfers in large multinationals: Unilever in the United States, 1945–1980, *Business History Review*, 76(3): 435–478.

24. A. P. Raman, 2003, HBR case study: The global brand face-off, *Harvard Business Review*, 81(6): 35–46.

25. Lee & Chen, Internationalization, local adaptation and subsidiary's entrepreneurship.

26. D. Skarmeas, C. S. Katsikeas, & B. B. Schlegelmilch, 2002, Drivers of commitment and its impact on performance in cross-cultural buyer-seller relationships: The importer's perspective, *Journal of International Business Studies*, 33: 757–783; X. Martin, A. Swaminathan, & W. Mitchell, 1999, Organizational evolution in the interorganizational environment: Incentives and constraints on international expansion strategy, *Administrative Science Quarterly*, 43: 566–601.

27. P. Ghemawat, 2001, Distance still matters: The hard reality of global expansion, *Harvard Business Review*, 79(8): 137–147.

28. S. R. Miller & A. Parkhe, 2002, Is there a liability of foreignness in global banking? An empirical test of banks' x-efficiency, *Strategic Management Journal*, 23: 55–75; T. Kostova & S. Zaheer, 1999, Organizational legitimacy under conditions of complexity: The case of the multinational enterprise, *Academy of Management Review*, 24: 64–81; S. Zaheer & E. Mosakowski, 1997, The dynamics of the liability of foreignness: A global study of survival in financial services, *Strategic Management Journal*, 18: 439–464.

29. O. Kharif, 2003, Qualcomm's mixed signals, *BusinessWeek Online*, http://www.businessweek.com, May 8.

30. A. Caplan, 2003, Global beer: Tapping into growth, *Beverage World*, February 15, 24–29.

31. K. Asakawa & M. Lehrer, 2003, Managing local knowledge assets globally: The role of regional innovation relays, *Journal of World Business*, 38: 31–42.

32. W. Chung & J. Alcacer, 2002, Knowledge seeking and location choice of foreign direct investment in the United States, *Management Science*, 48(12): 1534–1554.

33. 2003, Weathering the tech storm: How Michael Marks boosted efficiency at contract manufacturer Flextronics, *Business Week*, May 5, B24.

34. Ibid.

35. M. L. Clifford & P. Engardio, 2003, Standing guard: How a big factory is keeping SARS out, *Business Week*, May 5, 46–48.

36. C. R. Gowen III & W. J. Tallon, 2002, Turnaround strategies of American and Japanese electronics corporations—How do they differ in formulating plans and achieving results? *Journal of High Technology Management Research*, 13(2): 225–248; W. Shan & J. Song, 1997, Foreign direct investment and the sourcing of technological advantage: Evidence from the biotechnology industry, *Journal of International Business Studies*, 28: 267–284.

37. W. Chung, 2001, Identifying technology transfer in foreign direct investment: Influence of industry conditions and investing firm motives, *Journal of International Business Studies*, 32: 211–229.

38. B. Davis, R. Buckman, & C. Rhoads, 2003, A global journal report: For global economy, much rides on how the U.S. war plays out, *Wall Street Journal*, March 20, A1; F. Erdal & E. Tatoglu, 2002, Locational determinants of foreign direct investment in an emerging market economy: Evidence from Turkey, *Multinational Business Review*, 10(1): 21–28.

39. A. J. Mauri & A. V. Phatak, 2001, Global integration as inter-area product flows: The internalization of ownership and location factors influencing product flows across MNC units, *Management International Review*, 41(3): 233–249.

40. 2003, Business: The great leap forward; cars in China, *The Economist*, February 1, 53–56.

41. J. Flint, 2003, China: How big, how fast, how dangerous? *Forbes*, http://www.forbes.com, July 1.

42. W. Kuemmerle, 2002, Home base and knowledge management in international ventures, *Journal of Business Venturing*, 2: 99–122; H. Bresman, J. Birkinshaw, & R. Nobel, 1999, Knowledge transfer in international acquisitions, *Journal of International Business Studies*, 30: 439–462; J. Birkinshaw, 1997, Entrepreneurship in multinational corporations: The characteristics of subsidiary initiatives, *Strategic Management Journal*, 18: 207–229.

43. S. Makino, C. M. Lau, & R. S. Yeh, 2002, Asset-exploitation versus asset-seeking: Implications for location choice of foreign direct investment from newly industrialized economies, *Journal of International Business Studies*, 33(3): 403–421.

44. K. Uhlenbruck, K. E. Meyer, & M. A. Hitt, 2003, Organizational transformation in transition economies: Resource-based and organizational learning perspectives, *Journal of Management Studies*, 40: 257–282; Ahlstrom & Bruton, Learning from successful local private firms in China; S. A. Zahra, R. D. Ireland, & M. A. Hitt, 2000, International expansion by new venture firms: International diversity, mode of market entry, technological learning, and performance, *Academy of Management Journal*, 43: 925–950.

45. K. Ito & E. L. Rose, 2002, Foreign direct investment location strategies in the tire industry, *Journal of International Business Studies*, 33(3): 593–602.

46. J. Bernstein & D. Weinstein, 2002, Do endowments predict the location of production? Evidence from national and international data, *Journal of International Economics*, 56(1): 55–76.

47. B. Einhorn, 2003, China's homegrown stars, *BusinessWeek Online*, http://www.businessweek.com, May 12.

48. Tallman & Fladmoe-Lindquist, Internationalization, globalization, and capability-based strategy; D. A. Griffith & M. G. Harvey, 2001, A resource perspective of global dynamic capabilities, *Journal of International Business Studies*, 32: 597–606; D. J. Teece, G. Pisano, & A. Shuen, 1997, Dynamic capabilities and strategic management, *Strategic Management Journal*, 18: 509–533.

49. Y. Luo, 2000, Dynamic capabilities in international expansion, *Journal of World Business*, 35(4): 355–378.

50. H. W.-C. Zhao, 2002, Entrepreneurship in international business: An institutional perspective, *Asia Pacific Journal of Management*, 19: 29–61.

51. L. Nachum, 2001, The impact of home countries on the competitiveness of advertising TNCs, *Management International Review*, 41(1): 77–98.

52. K. Kling & I. Goteman, 2003, IKEA CEO Anders Dahlvig on international growth and IKEA's unique corporate culture and brand identity, *Academy of Management Executive*, 17(1): 31–37.

53. M. E. Porter, 1990, *The Competitive Advantage of Nations*, New York: The Free Press.

54. Porter, *The Competitive Advantage of Nations*, 84.

55. G. Khermouch, B. Einhorn, & D. Roberts, 2003, Breaking into the name game, *Business Week*, April 7, 54.

56. Porter, *The Competitive Advantage of Nations*, 89.

57. Y. Aoyama & H. Izushi, 2003, Hardware gimmick or cultural innovation? Technological, cultural, and social foundations of the Japanese video game industry, *Research Policy*, 32: 423–443.

58. Khermouch, Einhorn, & Roberts, Breaking into the name game.

59. J. Birkinshaw, 2001, Strategies for managing internal competition, *California Management Review*, 44(1): 21–38.

60. W. P. Wan & R. E. Hoskisson, 2003, Home country environments, corporate diversification strategies and firm performance, *Academy of Management Journal*, 46: 27–45; J. M. Geringer, S. Tallman, & D. M. Olsen, 2000, Product and international diversification among Japanese multinational firms, *Strategic Management Journal*, 21: 51–80.

61. Wan and Hoskisson, Home country environments, corporate diversification strategies and firm performance; M. A. Hitt, R. E. Hoskisson, & R. D. Ireland, 1994, A mid-range theory of the interactive effects of international and product diversification on innovation and performance, *Journal of Management*, 20: 297–326.

62. J. Pla-Barber, 2002, From Stopford and Wells's model to Bartlett and Ghoshal's typology: New empirical evidence, *Management International Review*, 42(2): 141–156; J. Sheth, 2001, From international to integrated marketing, *Journal of Business Research*, 9: 5–9; A.-W. Harzing, 2000, An empirical analysis and extension of the Bartlett and Ghoshal typology of multinational companies, *Journal of International Business Studies*, 32: 101–120; S. Ghoshal, 1987, Global strategy: An organizing framework, *Strategic Management Journal*, 8: 425–440.

63. L. Nachum, 2003, Does nationality of ownership make any difference and if so, under what circumstances? Professional service MNEs in global competition, *Journal of International Management*, 9: 1–32; Sheth, From international to integrated marketing; J. Taggart & N. Hood, 1999, Determinants of autonomy in multinational corporation subsidiaries, *European Management Journal*, 17: 226–236.

64. Y. Luo, 2001, Determinants of local responsiveness: Perspectives from foreign subsidiaries in an emerging market, *Journal of Management*, 27: 451–477.

65. M. Geppert, K. Williams, & D. Matten, 2003, The social construction of contextual rationalities in MNCs: An Anglo-German comparison of subsidiary choice, *Journal of Management Studies*, 40: 617–641; M. Carpenter & J. Fredrickson, 2001, Top management teams, global strategic posture, and the moderating role of uncertainty, *Academy of Management Journal*, 44: 533–545; T. T. Herbert, 1999, Multinational strategic planning: Matching central expectations to local realities, *Long Range Planning*, 32: 81–87.

66. Jones, Control, performance, and knowledge transfers in large multinationals: Unilever in the United States, 1945–1980.

67. A. Afuah, 2003, Redefining firm boundaries in the face of the Internet: Are firms really shrinking? *Academy of Management Review*, 28: 34–53; M. F. Guillen, 2002, What is the best global strategy for the Internet? *Business Horizons*, 45(3): 39–46.

68. A.-W. Harzing & A. Sorge, 2003, The relative impact of country of origin and universal contingencies in internationalization strategies and corporate control in multinational enterprises: Worldwide and European perspectives, *Organization Studies*, 24: 187–214.

69. 2003, Masks off, down the hatch, *The Economist*, May 17, 57.

70. G. Khermouch & K. Capell, 2003, Spiking the booze business, *Business Week*, May 19, 77–78.

71. C. Lawton & D. Ball, 2003, Diageo mixes it up—liquor giant targets system dating to end of prohibition, *Wall Street Journal Online*, http://www.wsj.com, May 8.

72. Harzing, An empirical analysis and extension of the Bartlett and Ghoshal typology.

73. I. C. MacMillan, A. B. van Putten, & R. G. McGrath, 2003, Global gamesmanship, *Harvard Business Review*, 81(5): 62–71.

74. R. G. Barker, 2003, Trend: Global accounting is coming, *Harvard Business Review*, 81(4): 24–25.

75. A. Yaprak, 2002, Globalization: Strategies to build a great global firm in the new economy, *Thunderbird International Business Review*, 44(2): 297–302; D. G. McKendrick, 2001, Global strategy and population level learning: The case of hard disk drives, *Strategic Management Journal*, 22: 307–334.

76. H. D. Hopkins, 2003, The response strategies of dominant US firms to Japanese challengers, *Journal of Management*, 29: 5–25; S. Massini, A. Y. Lewin, T. Numagami, & A. Pettigrew, 2002, The evolution of organizational routines among large Western and Japanese firms, *Research Policy*, 31(8,9): 1333–1348; M. W. Peng, S. H. Lee, & J. J. Tan, 2001, The keiretsu in Asia: Implications for multilevel theories of competitive advantage, *Journal of International Management*, 7: 253–276; A. Bhappu, 2000, The Japanese family: An institutional logic for Japanese corporate networks and Japanese management, *Academy of Management Review*, 25: 409–415; J. K. Johansson & G. S. Yip, 1994, Exploiting globalization potential: U.S. and Japanese strategies, *Strategic Management Journal*, 15: 579–601.

77. S. Roy, 2003, Cementing global success, *Strategic Direct Investor*, March, 12–13.

78. Ibid.

79. Ibid.

80. Ibid.

81. J. Barham, 2002, From local manufacturer to global player, *LatinFinance*, April, 25–26.

82. Y. Doz, J. Santos, & P. Williamson, 2001, *From Global to Metanational: How Companies Win in the Knowledge Economy*, Boston: Harvard Business School Press; C. A. Bartlett & S. Ghoshal, 1989, *Managing across Borders: The Transnational Solution*, Boston: Harvard Business School Press.

83. J. Child & Y. Yan, 2001, National and transnational effects in international business: Indications from Sino-foreign joint ventures, *Management International Review*, 41(1): 53–75.

84. B. James, 2003, Ghosn's local vision plays on a world stage, *International Herald Tribune*, May 3, 9.

85. Ibid.

86. A. M. Rugman & A. Verbeke, 2003, Extending the theory of the multinational enterprise: Internalization and strategic management perspectives, *Journal of International Business Studies*, 34: 125–137.

87. T. Isobe, S. Makino, & D. B. Montgomery, 2000, Resource commitment, entry timing and market performance of foreign direct investments in emerging economies: The case of Japanese international joint ventures in China, *Academy of Management Journal*, 43: 468–484.

88. S. Zaheer & A. Zaheer, 2001, Market microstructure in a global B2B network, *Strategic Management Journal*, 22: 859–873.

89. J. A. Trachtenberg & B. Steinberg, 2003, Plan B for Marketers–in a time of global conflict, companies consider changing how they push products, *Wall Street Journal*, March 20, B7.

90. S. Reda, 2003, Retailers take multi-faceted approaches to multi-channel success, *Stores*, June, 22–26.

91. F. X. Molina-Morales, 2001, European industrial districts: Influence of geographic concentration on performance of the firm, *Journal of International Management*, 7: 277–294; M. E. Porter & S. Stern, 2001, Innovation: Location matters, *Sloan Management Review*, 42(4): 28–36.

92. C. Pantzalis, 2001, Does location matter? An empirical analysis of geographic scope and MNC market valuation, *Journal of International Business Studies*, 32: 133–155.

93. A. Rugman & S. Girod, 2003, Retail multinationals and globalization: The evidence is regional, *European Management Journal*, 21(1): 24–37.

94. R. D. Ludema, 2002, Increasing returns, multinationals and geography of preferential trade agreements, *Journal of International Economics*, 56: 329–358; L. Allen & C. Pantzalis, 1996, Valuation of the operating flexibility of multinational corporations, *Journal of International Business Studies*, 27: 633–653.

95. F. Bruni, 2003, With a constitution to ponder, Europeans gather in Greece, *New York Times*, http://www.nytimes.com, June 20.

96. J. I. Martinez, J. A. Quelch, & J. Ganitsky, 1992, Don't forget Latin America, *Sloan Management Review*, 33(Winter): 78–92.

97. T. L. Pett & J. A. Wolff, 2003, Firm characteristic and managerial perceptions of NAFTA: An assessment of export implications for U.S. SMEs, *Journal of Small Business Management*, 41(2): 117–132.

98. G. Ip, 2003, The economy: Trade gap widens to record level–monthly deficit combines with other data to point to trouble for recovery, *Wall Street Journal*, February 21, A2.

99. D. Xu & O. Shenkar, 2002, Institutional distance and the multinational enterprise, *Academy of Management Review*, 27(4): 608–618; J. Chang & P. M. Rosenzweig, 1998, Industry and regional patterns in sequential foreign market entry, *Journal of Management Studies*, 35: 797–822.

100. K. D. Brouthers, L. E. Brouthers, & S. Werner, 2003, Industrial sector, perceived environmental uncertainty and entry mode strategy, *Journal of Business Research*, 55: 495–507; S. Zahra, J. Hayton, J. Marcel, & H. O'Neill, 2001, Fostering entrepreneurship during international expansion: Managing key challenges, *European Management Journal*, 19: 359–369.

101. K. D. Brouthers, 2003, Institutional, cultural and transaction cost influences on entry mode choice and performance, *Journal of International Business Studies*, 33: 203–221; R. Konopaske, S. Werner, & K. E. Neupert, 2002, Entry mode strategy and performance: The role of FDI staffing, *Journal of Business Research*, 55: 759–770; Zahra, Ireland, & Hitt, International expansion by new venture firms.

102. R. Isaak, 2002, Using trading firms to export: What can the French experience teach us? *Academy of Management Executive*, 16(4): 155–156; M. W. Peng, C. W. L. Hill, & D. Y. L. Wang, 2000, Schumpeterian dynamics versus Williamsonian considerations: A test of export intermediary performance, *Journal of Management Studies*, 37: 167–184.

103. Y. Chui, 2002, The structure of the multinational firm: The role of ownership characteristics and technology transfer, *International Journal of Management*, 19(3): 472–477.

104. Luo, Determinants of local responsiveness.

105. L. E. Brouthers & K. Xu, 2002, Product stereotypes, strategy and performance satisfaction: The case of Chinese exporters, *Journal of International Business Studies*, 33: 657–677; M. A. Raymond, J. Kim, & A. T. Shao, 2001, Export strategy and performance: A comparison of exporters in a developed market and an emerging market, *Journal of Global Marketing*, 15(2): 5–29; P. S. Aulakh, M. Kotabe, & H. Teegen, 2000, Export strategies and performance of firms from emerging economies: Evidence from Brazil, Chile and Mexico, *Academy of Management Journal*, 43: 342–361.

106. W. Dou, U. Nielsen, & C. M. Tan, 2003, Using corporate Websites for export marketing, *Journal of Advertising Research*, 42(5): 105–115.

107. B. Walker & D. Luft, 2001, Exporting tech from Texas, *Texas Business Review*, August, 1–5.

108. P. Westhead, M. Wright, & D. Ucbasaran, 2001, The internationalization of new and small firms: A resource-based view, *Journal of Business Venturing*, 16: 333–358.

109. W. Rugg, 2003, A down dollar's lure—and peril, *BusinessWeek Online*, http://www.businessweek.com, May 22.

110. D. Kline, 2003, Sharing the corporate crown jewels, *MIT Sloan Management Review*, 44(3): 83–88; M. A. Hitt & R. D. Ireland, 2000, The intersection of entrepreneurship and strategic management research, in D. L. Sexton & H. Landstrom (eds.), *Handbook of Entrepreneurship*, Oxford, UK: Blackwell Publishers, 45–63.

111. A. Arora & A. Fosfuri, 2000, Wholly owned subsidiary versus technology licensing in the worldwide chemical industry, *Journal of International Business Studies*, 31: 555–572.

112. M. Johnson, 2001, Learning from toys: Lessons in managing supply chain risk from the toy industry, *California Management Review*, 43(3): 106–124.

113. Rigby & Zook, Open-market innovation.

114. C. A. Bartlett & S. Rangan, 1992, Komatsu limited, in C. A. Bartlett & S. Ghoshal (eds.), *Transnational Management: Text, Cases and Readings in Cross-Border Management*, Homewood, IL: Irwin, 311–326.

115. Chang & Rosenzweig, The choice of entry mode in sequential foreign direct investment; B. Petersen, D. E. Welch, & L. S. Welch, 2000, Creating meaningful switching options in international operations, *Long Range Planning*, 33(5): 688–705.

116. R. Larsson, K. R. Brousseau, M. J. Driver, & M. Homqvist, 2003, International growth through cooperation: Brand-driven strategies, leadership, and career development in Sweden, *Academy of Management Executive*, 17(1): 7–21; J. W. Lu & P. W. Beamish, 2001, The internationalization and performance of SMEs, *Strategic Management Journal*, 22 (Special Issue): 565–586; M. Koza & A. Lewin, 2000, Managing partnerships and strategic alliances: Raising the odds of success, *European Management Journal*, 18(2): 146–151.

117. J. S. Harrison, M. A. Hitt, R. E. Hoskisson, & R. D. Ireland, 2001, Resource complementarity in business combinations: Extending the logic to organization alliances, *Journal of Management*, 27: 679–690; T. Das & B. Teng, 2000, A resource-based theory of strategic alliances, *Journal of Management*, 26: 31–61.

118. M. A. Hitt, D. Ahlstrom, M. T. Dacin, E. Levitas, & L. Svobodina, 2004, The institutional effects on strategic alliance partner selection in transition economies: China versus Russia, *Organization Science*, in press; M. Peng, 2001, The resource-based view and international business, *Journal of Management*, 27: 803–829.

119. H. Chen & T. Chen, 2003, Governance structures in strategic alliances: Transaction cost versus resource-based perspective, *Journal of World Business*, 38(1): 1–14; E. W. K. Tsang, 2002, Acquiring knowledge by foreign partners for international joint ventures in a transition economy: Learning-by-doing and learning myopia, *Strategic Management Journal*, 23(9): 835–854; P. J. Lane, J. E. Salk, & M. A. Lyles, 2002, Absorptive capacity, learning, and performance in international joint ventures, *Strategic Management Journal*, 22: 1139–1161; B. L. Simonin, 1999, Transfer of marketing know-how in international strategic alliances: An empirical investigation of the role and antecedents of knowledge ambiguity, *Journal of International Business Studies*, 30: 463–490; M. A. Lyles & J. E. Salk, 1996, Knowledge acquisition from foreign parents in international joint ventures: An empirical examination in the Hungarian context, *Journal of International Business Studies*, 27 (Special Issue): 877–903.

120. P. Almeida, J. Song, & R. M. Grant, 2002, Are firms superior to alliances and markets? An empirical test of cross-border knowledge building, *Organization Science*, 13(2): 147–161; Shrader, Collaboration and performance in foreign markets; M. A. Hitt, M. T. Dacin, E. Levitas, J. L. Arregle, & A. Borza, 2000, Partner selection in emerging and developed market contexts: Resource based and organizational learning perspectives, *Academy of Management Journal*, 43: 449–467.

121. P. Engardio & D. Roberts, 2003, Growing up fast, *Business Week*, March 31, 52–53.

122. M. W. Peng & O. Shenkar, 2002, Joint venture dissolution as corporate divorce, *Academy of Management Executive*, 16(2): 92–105; O. Shenkar & A. Yan, 2002, Failure as a consequence of partner politics: Learning from the life and death of an international cooperative venture, *Human Relations*, 55: 565–601.

123. J. A. Robins, S. Tallman, & K. Fladmoe-Lindquist, 2002, Autonomy and dependence of international cooperative ventures: An exploration of the strategic performance of U.S. ventures in Mexico, *Strategic Management Journal*, 23(10): 881–901; Y. Gong, O. Shenkar, Y. Luo, & M-K. Nyaw, 2001, Role conflict and ambiguity of CEOs in international joint ventures: A transaction cost perspective, *Journal of Applied Psychology*, 86: 764–773.

124. D. C. Hambrick, J. Li, K. Xin, & A. S. Tsui, 2001, Compositional gaps and downward spirals in international joint venture management groups, *Strategic Management Journal*, 22: 1033–1053; M. T. Dacin, M. A. Hitt, & E. Levitas, 1997, Selecting partners for successful international alliances: Examination of U.S. and Korean Firms, *Journal of World Business*, 32: 3–16.

125. J. Child & Y. Yan, 2003, Predicting the performance of international joint ventures: An investigation in China, *Journal of Management Studies*, 40(2): 283–320; J. P. Johnson, M. A. Korsgaard, & H. J. Sapienza, 2002, Perceived fairness, decision control, and commitment in international joint venture management teams, *Strategic Management Journal*, 23(12): 1141–1160; A. Arino, J. de la Torre, & P. S. Ring, 2001, Relational quality: Managing trust in corporate alliances, *California Management Review*, 44(1): 109–131.

126. L. Huff & L. Kelley, 2003, Levels of organizational trust in individualist versus collectivist societies: A seven-nation study, *Organization Science*, 14(1): 81–90.

127. Y. Pan & D. K. Tse, 2000, The hierarchical model of market entry modes, *Journal of International Business Studies*, 31: 535–554; Y. Pan, S. Li, & D. K. Tse, 1999, The impact of order and mode of market entry on profitability and market share, *Journal of International Business Studies*, 30: 81–104.

128. J. J. Reuer, 2002, Incremental corporate reconfiguration through international joint venture buyouts and selloffs, *Management International Review*, 42: 237–260.

129. G. A. Knight & P. W. Liesch, 2002, Information internalisation in internationalising the firm, *Journal of Business Research*, 55(12): 981–995; M. Supphellen, S. A. Haugland, & T. Korneliussen, 2002, SMBs in search of international strategic alliances: Perceived importance of personal information sources, *Journal of Business Research*, 55(9): 785–795.

130. W. H. Hoffmann & W. Schaper-Rinkel, 2001, Acquire or ally? A strategy framework for deciding between acquisition and cooperation, *Management International Review*, 41(2): 131–159.

131. M. A. Hitt, J. S. Harrison, & R. D. Ireland, 2001, *Creating Value through Mergers and Acquisitions*, New York: Oxford University Press.

132. M. A. Hitt & V. Pisano, 2003, The cross-border merger and acquisition strategy, *Management Research*, 1: 133–144.

133. 1999, French dressing, *The Economist*, July 10, 53–54.

134. Xu & Shenkar, Institutional distance and the multinational enterprise.

135. D. Ball, 2003, Ice cream rivals prepare to wage a new cold war, *Wall Street Journal*, June 26, B1.

136. Ibid.

137. Ibid.

138. Ibid.

139. Ibid.

140. A.-W. Harzing, 2002, Acquisitions versus greenfield investments: International strategy and management of entry modes, *Strategic Management Journal*, 23: 211–227; K. D. Brouthers & L. E. Brouthers, 2000, Acquisition or greenfield start-up? Institutional, cultural and transaction cost influences, *Strategic Management Journal*, 21: 89–97.

141. P. Deng, 2003, Determinants of full-control mode in China: An integrative approach, *American Business Review*, 21(1): 113–123.

142. R. Belderbos, 2003, Entry mode, organizational learning, and R&D in foreign affiliates: Evidence from Japanese firms, *Strategic Management Journal*, 34: 235–259.

143. B. Jorgensen, 2003, Act global, think local, *Electronic Business*, April 15, 42–50.

144. V. Gaba, Y. Pan, & G. R. Ungson, 2002, Timing of entry in international market: An empirical study of U.S. Fortune 500 firms in China, *Journal of International Business Studies*, 33(1): 39–55; S.-J. Chang & P. Rosenzweig, 2001, The choice of entry mode in sequential foreign direct investment, *Strategic Management Journal*, 22: 747–776.

145. K. E. Myer, 2001, Institutions, transaction costs, and entry mode choice in Eastern Europe, *Journal of International Business Studies*, 32: 357–367.

146. Deng, Determinants of full-control mode in China; Y. Luo, 2001, Determinants of entry in an emerging economy: A multilevel approach, *Journal of Management Studies*, 38: 443–472.

147. A. Antoine, C. B. Frank, H. Murata, & E. Roberts, 2003, Acquisitions and alliances in the aerospace industry: An unusual triad, *International Journal of Technology Management*, 25(8): 779–790.

148. L. J. Howell & J. C. Hsu, 2002, Globalization within the auto industry, *Research Technology Management*, 45(4): 43–49; A. Takeishi, 2001, Bridging inter- and intra-firm boundaries: Management of supplier involvement in automobile product development, *Strategic Management Journal*, 22: 403–433.

149. D. K Sobek II, A. C. Ward, & J. K. Liker, 1999, Toyota's principles of set-based concurrent engineering, *Sloan Management Review*, 40(2): 53–83.

150. J. Hagedoorn & G. Dysters, 2002, External sources of innovative capabilities: The preference for strategic alliances or mergers and acquisitions, *Journal of Management Studies*, 39: 167–188; H. Chen, 1999, International performance of multinationals: A hybrid model, *Journal of World Business*, 34: 157–170.

151. H. S. Tu, S. Y. Kim, & S. E. Sullivan, 2002, Global strategy lessons from Japanese and Korean business groups, *Business Horizons*, 45(2): 39–46; S.-J. Chang & J. Hong, 2002, How much does the business group matter in Korea? *Strategic Management Journal*, 23: 265–274.

152. J. Song, 2002, Firm capabilities and technology ladders: Sequential foreign direct investments of Japanese electronics firms in East Asia, *Strategic Management Journal*, 23: 191–210.

153. Wan & Hoskisson, Home country environments, corporate diversification strategies and firm performance; M. Ramirez-Aleson & M. A. Espitia-Escuer, 2001, The effect of international diversification strategy on the performance of Spanish-based firms during the period 1991–1995, *Management International Review*, 41(3): 291–315; A. Delios & P. W. Beamish, 1999, Geographic scope, product diversification, and the corporate performance of Japanese firms, *Strategic Management Journal*, 20: 711–727.

154. J. A. Doukas & L. H. P. Lang, 2003, Foreign direct investment, diversification and firm performance, *Journal of International Business Studies*, 34: 153–172; Pantzalis, Does location matter?; C. Y. Tang & S. Tikoo, 1999,

Operational flexibility and market valuation of earnings, *Strategic Management Journal*, 20: 749–761.

155. Kwok & Reeb, 2000, Internationalization and firm risk; J. M. Geringer, P. W. Beamish, & R. C. daCosta, 1989, Diversification strategy and internationalization: Implications for MNE performance, *Strategic Management Journal*, 10: 109–119; R. E. Caves, 1982, *Multinational Enterprise and Economic Analysis*, Cambridge, MA: Cambridge University Press.

156. Zahra, Ireland, & Hitt, International expansion by new venture firms.

157. T. W. Malnight, 2002, Emerging structural patterns within multinational corporations: Toward process-based structures, *Academy of Management Journal*, 44: 1187–1210.

158. L. Lopez, 2003, A well-oiled money machine, *Far Eastern Economic Review*, March 13, 40–43.

159. Ibid.

160. Ibid.

161. Hagedoorn & Dysters, External sources of innovative capabilities; G. Hamel, 2000, *Leading the Revolution*, Boston: Harvard Business School Press.

162. L. Tihanyi, R. A. Johnson, R. E. Hoskisson, & M. A. Hitt, 2003, Institutional ownership differences and international diversification: The effects of board of directors and technological opportunity, *Academy of Management Journal*, 46: 195–211.

163. F. Bradley & M. Gannon, 2000, Does the firm's technology and marketing profile affect foreign market entry? *Journal of International Marketing*, 8(4): 12–36; M. Kotabe, 1990, The relationship between off-shore sourcing and innovativeness of U.S. multinational firms: An empirical investigation, *Journal of International Business Studies*, 21: 623–638.

164. Asakawa & Lehrer, Managing local knowledge assets globally: The role of regional innovation relays; I. Zander & O. Solvell, 2000, Cross border innovation in the multinational corporation: A research agenda, *International Studies of Management and Organization*, 30(2): 44–67; Y. Luo, 1999, Time-based experience and international expansion: The case of an emerging economy, *Journal of Management Studies*, 36: 505–533.

165. O. E. M. Janne, 2002, The emergence of corporate integrated innovation systems across regions: The case of the chemical and pharmaceutical industry in Germany, the UK and Belgium, *Journal of International Management*, 8: 97–119; N. J. Foss & T. Pedersen, 2002, Transferring knowledge in MNCs: The role of sources of subsidiary knowledge and organizational context, *Journal of International Management*, 8: 49–67; Z. Liao, 2001, International R&D project evaluation by multinational corporations in the electronics and IT industry of Singapore, *R&D Management*, 31: 299–307.

166. Wan & Hoskisson, Home country environments, corporate diversification strategies and firm performance.

167. S. Reed & M. Arndt, 2003, Working his magic: Can Dormann bring ABB back? *Business Week*, February 10, 26; D. Bilefsky & A. Raghavan, 2003, Blown fuse: How "Europe's GE" and its star CEO tumbled to earth—Percy Barnevik's leadership made ABB a global name, but also may have hurt it—lingering asbestos woes, *Wall Street Journal*, January 23, A1.

168. P. Herrmann, 2002, The influence of CEO characteristics on the international diversification of manufacturing firms: An empirical study in the United States, *International Journal of Management*, 19(2): 279–289; M. Carpenter & J. Fredrickson, 2001, Top management teams, global strategic posture, and the moderating role of uncertainty, *Academy of Management Journal*, 44: 533–545; S. Finkelstein & D. C. Hambrick, 1996, *Strategic Leadership: Top Executives and Their Effects on Organizations*, St. Paul, MN: West Publishing Company.

169. H. A. Krishnan & D. Park, 2003, Power in acquired top management teams and post-acquisition performance: A conceptual framework, *International Journal of Management*, 20: 75–80; A. McWilliams, D. D. Van Fleet, & P. M. Wright, 2001, Strategic management of human resources for global competitive advantage, *Journal of Business Strategies*, 18(1): 1–24.

170. M. A. Hitt, R. E. Hoskisson, & H. Kim, 1997, International diversification: Effects on innovation and firm performance in product-diversified firms, *Academy of Management Journal*, 40: 767–798.

171. J. Child, L. Chung, & H. Davies, 2003, The performance of cross-border units in China: A test of natural selection, strategic choice and contingency theories, *Journal of International Business Studies*, 34: 242–254; D. Rondinelli,

B. Rosen, & I. Drori, 2001, The struggle for strategic alignment in multinational corporations: Managing readjustment during global expansion, *European Management Journal*, 19: 404–405; Carpenter & Fredrickson, Top management teams, global strategic posture, and the moderating role of uncertainty.

172. Y.-H. Chiu, 2003, The impact of conglomerate firm diversification on corporate performance: An empirical study in Taiwan, *International Journal of Management*, 19: 231–237; Luo, Market-seeking MNEs in an emerging market: How parent-subsidiary links shape overseas success.

173. A. Delios & W. J. Henisz, 2003, Policy uncertainty and the sequence of entry by Japanese firms, 1980–1998, *Journal of International Business Studies*, 34: 227–241; D. M. Reeb, C. C. Y. Kwok, & H. Y. Baek, 1998, Systematic risk of the multinational corporation, *Journal of International Business Studies*, 29: 263–279.

174. C. Pompitakpan, 1999, The effects of cultural adaptation on business relationships: Americans selling to Japanese and Thais, *Journal of International Business Studies*, 30: 317–338.

175. J. H. Zhao, S. H. Kim, & J. Du, 2003, The impact of corruption and transparency on foreign direct investment: An empirical analysis, *Management International Review*, 43(1): 41–62.

176. S. Globerman & D. Shapiro, 2003, Governance infrastructure and US foreign direct investment, *Journal of International Business Studies*, 34(1): 19–39.

177. L. L. Jacque & P. M. Vaaler, 2001, The international control conundrum with exchange risk: An EVA framework, *Journal of International Business Studies*, 32: 813–832.

178. S. Mudd, R. Grosse, & J. Mathis, 2002, Dealing with financial crises in emerging markets, *Thunderbird International Business Review*, 44(3): 399–430.

179. Rugg, A down dollar's lure—and peril.

180. Wan & Hoskisson, Home country environments, corporate diversification strategies and firm performance; Hitt, Hoskisson, & Kim, International diversification; S. Tallman & J. Li, 1996, Effects of international diversity and product diversity on the performance of multinational firms, *Academy of Management Journal*, 39: 179–196; Hitt, Hoskisson, & Ireland, A mid-range theory of interactive effects; Geringer, Beamish, & daCosta, Diversification strategy.

181. A. K. Rose & E. van Wincoop, 2001, National money as a barrier to international trade: The real case for currency union, *American Economic Review*, 91: 386–390.

182. I. M. Manev & W. B. Stevenson, 2001, Nationality, cultural distance, and expatriate status: Effects on the managerial network in a multinational enterprise, *Journal of International Business Studies*, 32: 285–303.

183. D. Luhnow, 2001, How NAFTA helped Wal-Mart transform the Mexican market. *Wall Street Journal*, August 31, A1, A2.

184. B. Saporito, 2003, Can Wal-Mart get any bigger? (Yes, a lot bigger . . . here's how), *Time*, January 13, 38–43.

185. V. Miroshnik, 2002, Culture and international management: A review, *Journal of Management Development*, 21(7,8): 521–544; P. Ghemawat, 2001, Distance still matters, *Harvard Business Review*, 79(8): 137–147; D. E. Thomas & R. Grosse, 2001, Country-of-origin determinants of foreign direct investment in an emerging market: The case of Mexico, *Journal of International Management*, 7: 59–79.

186. T. P. Blumentritt & D. Nigh, 2002, The integration of subsidiary political activities in multinational corporations, *Journal of International Business Studies*, 33: 57–77; J. Feeney & A. Hillman, 2001, Privatization and the political economy of strategic trade policy, *International Economic Review*, 42: 535–556; R. Vernon, 2001, Big business and national governments: Reshaping the compact in a globalizing economy, *Journal of International Business Studies*, 32: 509–518; B. Shaffer & A. J. Hillman, 2000, The development of business-government strategies by diversified firms, *Strategic Management Journal*, 21: 175–190.

187. U. Andersson, M. Forsgren, & U. Holm, 2002, The strategic impact of external networks: Subsidiary performance and competence development in the multinational corporation, *Strategic Management Journal*, 23: 979–996; B. Barringer & J. Harrison, 2000, Walking the tightrope: Creating value through interorganizational relationships, *Journal of Management*, 26: 367–404.

Cooperative Strategy

Knowledge Objectives

Studying this chapter should provide you with the strategic management knowledge needed to:

1. Define cooperative strategies and explain why firms use them.

2. Define and discuss three types of strategic alliances.

3. Name the business-level cooperative strategies and describe their use.

4. Discuss the use of corporate-level cooperative strategies in diversified firms.

5. Understand the importance of cross-border strategic alliances as an international cooperative strategy.

6. Describe cooperative strategies' risks.

7. Describe two approaches used to manage cooperative strategies.

©Getty Images

Phone companies and satellite TV providers have formed both business- and corporate-level alliances, allowing them to respond effectively to cable company offerings in phone services. The alliance between EchoStar and SBC, for example, will allow customers to sign up for as many as five services (local, long distance, and cellular phone plus satellite TV and broadband). The newly formed SBC DISH Network should please customers, who will receive one bill for several diverse services.

Demand for broadband Internet connections has surged in the United States, and telephone companies have scrambled to maintain pace with the cable companies as they respond to the demand. The phone companies are relative latecomers to broadband. Cable operators, which invested heavily in the 1990s in expanding and modernizing their networks, dominate the market. Comcast, the biggest provider, had 4.1 million subscribers at the end of March 2003, far ahead of the leading phone companies—SBC Communications with 2.5 million, Verizon with 1.8 million, and BellSouth with 1.1 million.

Offering broadband also allowed the cable companies to offer phone service (once regulatory agencies allowed it) through cable, something they have aggressively pursued. In 2003, cable operators had registered over three million phone customers, often offering discounts if a customer subscribed to more than one service (cable television, phone, broadband). In response to the competition, phone companies formed alliances to better contend with the cable companies' aggressive moves into phone service.

SBC Communications has agreed to an alliance with EchoStar Communications Corp. EchoStar offers satellite TV services (DISH Network). Under the SBC plan, starting early in 2004 the phone company's customers were able to sign up for EchoStar TV services by calling SBC sales representatives. Customers could receive as many as five services—local phone, long distance, cellular phone, satellite TV, and broadband—consolidated on one SBC bill. SBC and EchoStar intended to brand their service "SBC DISH Network." In return, SBC will invest $500 million in EchoStar's convertible debt. Qwest is building a similar alliance with DirecTV, another satellite TV provider.

The SBC-EchoStar alliance builds on "bundling," the practice of selling diverse kinds of services under a single bill, which one analyst declares is the future of telecommunications. Bundling services is more profitable for the telecommunication companies than giving a customer a single service, because it creates switching costs for the customer. As another analyst noted: "When customers use multiple services, it becomes increasingly difficult to compare and contrast to competitive offerings so they tend to stay put." As phone companies seek to defend themselves, "you'll see more and more bundled deals," adds Michael Bowen, a telecommunication analyst at SoundView Technology Group.

SBC has made other alliances to diversify the services it offers. For example, a deal announced with Yahoo! Inc. made the popular site part of SBC's broadband package. SBC subscribers who sign up for the service automatically reach the Web through a Yahoo! portal. Users can check their e-mail through Yahoo! Mail and customize their home screen with special Yahoo!

content. Under the terms of the deal, SBC will pay Yahoo! an estimated $5 a month for each subscriber; Yahoo!, in return, will give SBC an undisclosed percentage of any premium services subscribers purchase beyond the basic package, like real-time stock quotes or expanded e-mail storage.

The competition response alliances (defined later in this chapter) between phone companies and satellite TV providers have not only allowed them to respond to cable companies' strategic moves into phone services, but have also allowed phone companies to diversify their service offerings. Thus, these examples represent both business- as well as corporate-level alliances, which are discussed in this chapter.

SOURCES: A. Latour & P. Grant, 2003, SBC, Qwest strike partnerships with providers of satellite TV, *Wall Street Journal Online*, http://www.wsj.com, July 22; L. J. Flynn, 2003, EchoStar deal lets SBC offer satellite TV in phone bill, *New York Times*, http://www.nytimes.com, July 22; 2003, SBC, Qwest in satellite TV partnerships, *New York Times*, http://www.nytimes.com, July 21; B. Simon, 2003, Some bet the future of broadband belongs to regional Bells, not cable, *New York Times*, http://www.nytimes.com, July 21; A. Latour, 2003, BellSouth unveils DSL Lite service as Bells step up subscriber battle, *Wall Street Journal Online*, www.http://www.wsj.com, July 8; D. Roth, 2002, Terry Semel thinks Yahoo should grow up already, *Fortune*, September 30, 107–110; B. Elgin, 2002, Can Yahoo make them pay? *BusinessWeek Online*, http://www.businessweek.com, September 9.

A cooperative strategy is a strategy in which firms work together to achieve a shared objective.

Pursuing internal opportunities (doing better than competitors through strategic execution or innovation) and merging with or acquiring other companies are the two primary means by which firms grow that we have discussed to this point in the book. In this chapter, we examine cooperative strategies, which are the third major alternative firms use to grow, develop value-creating competitive advantages, and create differences between themselves and competitors.[1] Defined formally, a **cooperative strategy** is a strategy in which firms work together to achieve a shared objective.[2] Thus, cooperating with other firms is another strategy that is used to create value for a customer that exceeds the cost of constructing that value in other ways[3] and to establish a favorable position relative to competition (see Chapters 2, 4, 5, and 8).[4] The Opening Case provides an example of SBC Communications and EchoStar Communications forming an alliance. This partnership will provide SBC, a phone service company, with a stronger position against cable companies' thrust into phone services by giving SBC a satellite TV service offering. The increasing importance of cooperative strategies as a growth engine shouldn't be underestimated. Increasingly, cooperative strategies are formed by firms competing against one another,[5] as illustrated by the number of alliances between rivals in the auto industry.[6] This means that effective competition in the 21st-century landscape results when the firm learns how to cooperate with as well as compete against competitors.[7]

Because they are the primary type of cooperative strategy that firms use, strategic alliances (defined in the next section) are this chapter's focus. Although not frequently used, collusive strategies are another type of cooperative strategy discussed in this chapter. In a *collusive strategy*, two or more firms cooperate to raise prices above the fully competitive level.[8]

We examine several topics in this chapter. First, we define and offer examples of different strategic alliances as primary types of cooperative strategies. Next, we discuss the extensive use of cooperative strategies in the global economy and reasons for this use. In succession, we then describe business-level (including collusive strategies), corporate-level, international, and network cooperative strategies—most in the form of strategic alliances. The chapter closes with discussions of the risks of using cooperative strategies as well as how effective management of them can reduce those risks.

Strategic Alliances as a Primary Type of Cooperative Strategy

Strategic alliances are increasingly popular.[9] Two researchers describe this popularity by noting that an "unprecedented number of strategic alliances between firms are being formed each year. [These] strategic alliances are a logical and timely response to intense and rapid changes in economic activity, technology, and globalization, all of which have cast many corporations into two competitive races: one for the world and the other for the future."[10]

A **strategic alliance** is a cooperative strategy in which firms combine some of their resources and capabilities to create a competitive advantage.[11] Thus, as linkages between them, strategic alliances involve firms with some degree of exchange and sharing of resources and capabilities to co-develop or distribute goods or services.[12] Strategic alliances let firms leverage their existing resources and capabilities while working with partners to develop additional resources and capabilities as the foundation for new competitive advantages.[13]

A strategic alliance is a cooperative strategy in which firms combine some of their resources and capabilities to create a competitive advantage.

Many firms, especially large global competitors, establish multiple strategic alliances. General Motors' alliances, for example, include collaboration with Honda on internal combustion engines, with Toyota on advanced propulsion, with Renault on medium- and heavy-duty vans for Europe and, in the United States, with AM General on the brand and distribution rights for the Hummer.[14] Focusing on developing advanced technologies, Lockheed Martin has formed over 250 alliances with firms in more than 30 countries as it concentrates on its primary business of defense modernization.[15] In general, strategic alliance success requires cooperative behavior from all partners. Actively solving problems, being trustworthy, and consistently pursuing ways to combine partners' resources and capabilities to create value are examples of cooperative behavior known to contribute to alliance success.[16]

A competitive advantage developed through a cooperative strategy often is called a collaborative or relational advantage.[17] As previously discussed, particularly in Chapter 4, competitive advantages significantly influence the firm's marketplace success.[18] Rapid technological changes and the global economy are examples of factors challenging firms to constantly upgrade current competitive advantages while they develop new ones to maintain strategic competitiveness.[19]

Three Types of Strategic Alliances

There are three major types of strategic alliances—joint venture, equity strategic alliance, and nonequity strategic alliance.

A **joint venture** is a strategic alliance in which two or more firms create a legally independent company to share some of their resources and capabilities to develop a competitive advantage. Joint ventures are effective in establishing long-term relationships and in transferring tacit knowledge. Because it can't be codified, tacit knowledge is learned through experiences[20] such as those taking place when people from partner firms work together in a joint venture. As discussed in Chapter 3, tacit knowledge is an important source of competitive advantage for many firms.[21]

A joint venture is a strategic alliance in which two or more firms create a legally independent company to share some of their resources and capabilities to develop a competitive advantage.

Typically, partners in a joint venture own equal percentages and contribute equally to its operations. In China, Shui On Construction and entrepreneur Paul S. P. Tung created a 50-50 joint venture called TH Group to invest in cement factories. Cement is big business in China as the government seeks to develop the infrastructure (ports, highways, etc.) of the western provinces. Mr. Tung contributed money, and Shui On the expertise, necessary to develop a large, well-run cement company.[22] Overall, evidence suggests that a joint venture may be the optimal alliance when firms need to combine their resources and capabilities to create a competitive advantage that is substantially different from any they possess individually and when the partners intend to enter highly uncertain markets.[23]

An **equity strategic alliance** is an alliance in which two or more firms own different percentages of the company they have formed by combining some of their resources and capabilities to create a competitive advantage. Many foreign direct investments, such as those made by Japanese and U.S. companies in China, are completed through equity strategic alliances.[24]

For example, Citigroup Inc. is forming a strategic alliance with Shanghai Pudong Development Bank Co. It is doing so through an initial equity investment totaling 5 percent. However, it was allowed to raise that stake to almost 25 percent and will be the first foreign bank to own more than 20 percent of a bank in the PRC (People's Republic of China). Shanghai Pudong Development Bank is China's ninth largest bank, and Citigroup's investment will make it a significant shareholder. This equity strategic alliance "will serve as a launchpad for Citigroup to enter the Chinese credit-card business."[25]

A **nonequity strategic alliance** is an alliance in which two or more firms develop a contractual relationship to share some of their unique resources and capabilities to create a competitive advantage. In this type of strategic alliance, firms do not establish a separate independent company and therefore don't take equity positions. Because of this, nonequity strategic alliances are less formal and demand fewer partner commitments than do joint ventures and equity strategic alliances.[26] The relative informality and lower commitment levels characterizing nonequity strategic alliances make them unsuitable for complex projects where success requires effective transfers of tacit knowledge between partners.[27]

However, firms today increasingly use this type of alliance in many different forms, such as licensing agreements, distribution agreements, and supply contracts.[28] For example, Sears, Roebuck and Co. recently announced an agreement to outsource its credit card business to Citigroup Inc. for $3 billion. Sears was one of the few companies that still held total control over its private-label credit cards, as most department stores favored co-branding nonequity alliances with financial institutions. The terms of the deal allow Sears to outsource its financing business by forming an alliance with Citigroup to manage its credit card operations. Under a ten-year marketing-and-servicing agreement, Citigroup will absorb costs associated with Sears' 0 percent financing program, which Sears said will save it more than $200 million a year. Sears also said that it expects to receive approximately $200 million in annual performance payments from Citigroup under the agreement. This strategic alliance will give Sears a chance to refocus on its struggling retail business.[29] A key reason for the growth in types of cooperative strategies is the complexity and uncertainty that characterize most global industries such as the global agrochemical industry, making it difficult for firms to be successful without partnerships.[30]

Typically, outsourcing commitments take the form of a nonequity strategic alliance.[31] Discussed in Chapter 3, *outsourcing* is the purchase of a value-creating primary or support activity from another firm. Johnson Controls, Inc. (JCI) has become a leading manufacturer of automotive interior systems, automotive batteries, and automated building control systems. A wide range of cooperative strategies has served as the engine of its growth. JCI has used a cooperative strategy with many of its suppliers. For example, it worked out an agreement with IKON Office Solutions to provide networked copiers for its offices and plants nationwide. Instead of paying a flat fee, however, it pays per use, and this arrangement has cut printing and copying costs by 35 percent.[32]

Reasons Firms Develop Strategic Alliances

As previously noted, the use of cooperative strategies as a path to strategic competitiveness is on the rise[33] in for-profit firms of all sizes as well as in public organizations.[34] Thus, cooperative strategies are becoming more important to companies. For

---

An equity strategic alliance is an alliance in which two or more firms own different percentages of the company they have formed by combining some of their resources and capabilities to create a competitive advantage.

A nonequity strategic alliance is an alliance in which two or more firms develop a contractual relationship to share some of their unique resources and capabilities to create a competitive advantage.

example, recently surveyed executives of technology companies stated that strategic alliances are central to their firms' success.[35] Speaking directly to the issue of technology acquisition and development for these firms, a manager noted that "you have to partner today or you will miss the next wave. You cannot possibly acquire the technology fast enough, so partnering is essential."[36]

Some even suggest that strategic alliances "may be the most powerful trend that has swept American business in a century."[37] Among other benefits, strategic alliances allow partners to create value that they couldn't develop by acting independently[38] and to enter markets more quickly.[39] Moreover, most (if not all) firms lack the full set of resources and capabilities needed to reach their objectives, which indicates that partnering with others will increase the probability of reaching them.[40]

©Myrleen Ferguson Cate/PhotoEdit

Strategic alliances through outsourcing allow partners to create value they couldn't otherwise develop on their own. Ann Taylor, for example, has improved its marketing through testing data it receives from its partner, a proprietary credit network.

For example, Ann Taylor and its owner, United Retail Group, have partnered with a private-label credit service to build and strengthen their existing credit card programs. The firms worked with Alliance Data's proprietary credit network to provide credit processing at each store, which allowed Ann Taylor to link all of its stores and receive critical market testing data, thereby providing "a new way to communicate and market messages to its customers."[41]

The effects of the greater use of cooperative strategies—particularly in the form of strategic alliances—are noticeable. In large firms, for example, alliances now account for more than 20 percent of revenue.[42] Booz Allen Hamilton, Inc. predicted that by 2003, alliances would account for as much as 35 percent of revenue for the 1,000 largest U.S. companies.[43] Supporting this expectation is the belief of many senior-level executives that alliances are a prime vehicle for firm growth.[44]

In some industries, alliance versus alliance is becoming more prominent than firm against firm as a point of competition. In the global airline industry, for example, competition is increasingly between large alliances rather than between airlines.[45] This increased use of cooperative strategies and its results are not surprising in that the mid-1990s and early 21st century saw predictions that cooperative strategies were the wave of the future.[46]

The individually unique competitive conditions of slow-cycle, fast-cycle, and standard-cycle markets[47] find firms using cooperative strategies to achieve slightly different objectives (see Table 9.1). We discuss these three market types in Chapter 5, where we study competitive rivalry and competitive dynamics. *Slow-cycle markets* are markets where the firm's competitive advantages are shielded from imitation for relatively long periods of time and where imitation is costly. These markets are close to monopolistic conditions. Railroads and, historically, telecommunications, utilities, and financial services are examples of industries characterized as slow-cycle markets. In *fast-cycle markets,* the firm's competitive advantages aren't shielded from imitation, preventing their long-term sustainability. Competitive advantages are moderately shielded from imitation in *standard-cycle markets,* typically allowing them to be sustained for a longer period of time compared to fast-cycle market situations, but for a shorter period of time than in slow-cycle markets.

Table 9.1

Reasons for Strategic Alliances by Market Type

Market	Reason
Slow-Cycle	• Gain access to a restricted market
	• Establish a franchise in a new market
	• Maintain market stability (e.g., establishing standards)
Fast-Cycle	• Speed up development of new goods or services
	• Speed up new market entry
	• Maintain market leadership
	• Form an industry technology standard
	• Share risky R&D expenses
	• Overcome uncertainty
Standard-Cycle	• Gain market power (reduce industry overcapacity)
	• Gain access to complementary resources
	• Establish better economies of scale
	• Overcome trade barriers
	• Meet competitive challenges from other competitors
	• Pool resources for very large capital projects
	• Learn new business techniques

SLOW-CYCLE MARKETS

Firms in slow-cycle markets often use strategic alliances to enter restricted markets or to establish franchises in new markets. For example, due to consolidating acquisitions, the American steel industry has three major players: U.S. Steel, ISG, and Nucor. In an effort to compete in a global steel market, these companies are looking overseas. They have made strategic alliances in Europe and Asia and are investing in ventures in South America and Australia. U.S. Steel, for example, bought a Slovakian steel producer, VSZ, in 2000. ISG is bidding for a Korean steel producer, Kia Steel Co., and Nucor is investing in joint ventures in Brazil and Australia. While the global consolidation continues, these companies are increasing their competitiveness through their strategic alliances overseas.[48]

In another example, the opening of India's previously restricted insurance market prompted a number of international insurers to enter this large potential market. "Most are joint ventures between Indian companies and international insurers like AIG, MetLife, and Prudential, all eager to get in at the ground floor of what they believe will be a huge opportunity."[49] For example, American International Group (AIG) formed a joint venture—Tata AIG—with Mumbai-based Tata Group, one of the country's largest conglomerates.[50] Prior to the privatization process in India, state-operated insurers had played a monopolistic role for decades.

Slow-cycle markets are becoming rare in the 21st-century competitive landscape for several reasons, including the privatization of industries and economies, the rapid expansion of the Internet's capabilities in terms of the quick dissemination of information, and the speed with which advancing technologies make quickly imitating even complex products possible.[51] Firms competing in slow-cycle markets should recognize the future likelihood that they'll encounter situations in which their competitive advantages become partially sustainable (in the instance of a standard-cycle market) or unsustainable (in the case of a fast-cycle market). Cooperative strategies can be helpful to firms making the transition from relatively sheltered markets to more competitive ones.[52]

FAST-CYCLE MARKETS

Fast-cycle markets tend to be unstable, unpredictable, and complex.[53] Combined, these conditions virtually preclude the establishment of long-lasting competitive advantages, forcing firms to constantly seek sources of new competitive advantages while creating value by using current ones. Alliances between firms with current excess resources and capabilities and those with promising capabilities help companies competing in fast-cycle markets to make an effective transition from the present to the future and also to gain rapid entry to new markets.

The information technology (IT) industry is a fast-cycle market. The IT landscape will continue to change rapidly as businesses are becoming more focused on selecting a handful of strategic partners to help drive down costs, integrate technologies that provide significant business advantage or productivity gains, and aggressively look for applications that can be shifted to more flexible and cost-effective platforms. For example, Dell Inc. is striving to maintain its market leadership through responsiveness to customers. As a result of customers' requests, it is making servers and storage more modular and more customizable. It also sees wireless as the next technology that will be demanded by corporations, and thus is making it a standard feature on all corporate laptops by 2004. Strategic partners who help Dell remain on top of new innovations accomplish much of this work.[54]

Sometimes, companies establish venture capital programs to facilitate changes that occur rapidly in an industry.[55] Even after significant write-offs after the technology "bubble" burst in 2000, Intel continues to make venture capital partnership investments through its Intel Capital operation. In the first six months of 2003, Intel's venture unit made ten deals, including five in the United States and five abroad. "In addition to its interest in wireless, Intel says its new deals will fall into three other major categories: the digital home, network infrastructure and the enterprise market."[56]

Henry Liu, who works for MTV Online, does some work using free wireless high-speed Internet access on his laptop in Bryant Park in New York City. The Bryant Park Wireless Network provides free high-speed Wi-Fi (short for wireless fidelity) Internet access to users anywhere in the park at up to 11 megabits per second, faster than DSL or cable modem lines. Wireless communication on laptops is becoming standard, and Dell Inc. is taking advantage of this through alliances.

STANDARD-CYCLE MARKETS

In standard-cycle markets, which are often large and oriented toward economies of scale (e.g., commercial aerospace), alliances are more likely to be made by partners with complementary resources and capabilities. While airline alliances were originally set up to increase revenue, airlines have recently realized that they could also be used to reduce costs. SkyTeam (chaired by Delta and Air France) has set up an internal website to speed joint-buying and let member carriers swap tips on pricing. Managers at Oneworld (American Airlines and British Airways) believe the alliance's members have already saved up to $200 million through joint purchasing, and Star (United and Lufthansa) estimates that its member airlines save up to 25 percent on joint orders. Some airlines have taken this new buying power up to their biggest-ticket item: airplanes. Four airlines (Air Canada, Lufthansa, Austrian Airlines, and Scandinavian Airlines System) are seeking to buy together as many as 100 planes. Alitalia and Air France are attempting to purchase regional jets together. Airplane makers are intrigued and pleased by the new arrangements. "Group buys are something that we have envisioned for years," says Kent Fisher, vice-president for future customers and markets at Boeing. The trick will be getting the airlines to agree on things that previously were points of differentiation:

cabin décor, galley layout, cockpit arrangement. If the airlines succeed in agreeing upon a common plan, they will possibly realize even greater savings than just the cost of the plane. If, for example, members in the same alliance used exactly the same plane, there would be international economies of scale in equipment and training previously unrealized. Thus, this example illustrates that alliances of companies in this standard-cycle market are often geared toward obtaining potential economies of scale.[57]

Companies also may cooperate in standard-cycle markets to gain market power. As discussed in Chapter 6, market power allows the firm to sell its product above the existing competitive level or to reduce its costs below the competitive level, or both. Vivendi Universal, in a bid to avoid insolvency, signaled that it was selling many of its entertainment assets and has attracted many bidders. NBC, a television network owned by General Electric, instead of seeking an outright purchase of the assets, wanted to form an alliance with Vivendi. In 2003, NBC did complete a transaction to combine its broadcast and cable television operations with Vivendi Universal's entertainment assets in an arrangement that would give NBC majority control, but also much more market share, increasing its market power.[58] The alliance may avoid significant government scrutiny relative to an acquisition and would allow NBC to reduce excess capacity without an outright purchase.

Business-Level Cooperative Strategy

A **business-level cooperative strategy** is used to help the firm improve its performance in individual product markets. As discussed in Chapter 4, business-level strategy details what the firm intends to do to gain a competitive advantage in specific product markets. Thus, the firm forms a business-level cooperative strategy when it believes that combining its resources and capabilities with those of one or more partners will create competitive advantages that it can't create by itself and that will lead to success in a specific product market. There are four business-level cooperative strategies (see Figure 9.1).

Complementary Strategic Alliances

Complementary strategic alliances are business-level alliances in which firms share some of their resources and capabilities in complementary ways to develop competitive advantages.[59] There are two types of complementary strategic alliances—vertical and horizontal (see Figure 9.1).

VERTICAL COMPLEMENTARY STRATEGIC ALLIANCE
In a *vertical complementary strategic alliance,* firms share their resources and capabilities from different stages of the value chain to create a competitive advantage (see

> *A business-level cooperative strategy is used to help the firm improve its performance in individual product markets.*

> *Complementary strategic alliances are business-level alliances in which firms share some of their resources and capabilities in complementary ways to develop competitive advantages.*

Figure 9.1 — Business-Level Cooperative Strategies

- Complementary strategic alliances
  - Vertical
  - Horizontal
- Competition response strategy
- Uncertainty reducing strategy
- Competition reducing strategy

Figure 9.2).[60] Universal Music Group (UMG), a division of Vivendi Universal, has put together a vertical strategic alliance by forming a venture to create a new label in the music business, recruiting executives who have relationships with music artists. The "all-star" team includes executives from Interscope, Island Def Jam, Universal Motown, and Bad Boy Entertainment. Tommy Mottola, formerly of Sony Music, has agreed to serve as CEO of the new venture. UMG will fund the new label, called Casablanca, with about $15 million over the next five years. By putting together talent from several labels, UMG hopes to develop hits and improve its bottom line. In the

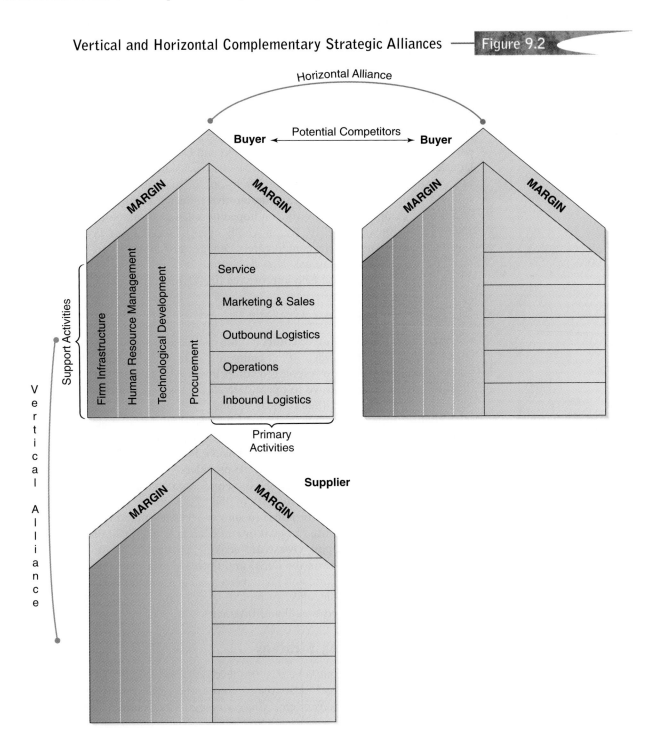

Vertical and Horizontal Complementary Strategic Alliances — Figure 9.2

words of UMG CEO Doug Morris, "It's so similar to a sports team, it's unbelievable. If you have no one on your team who can get hits, you're out of business."[61] This is a vertical alliance because of the executives' relationships to suppliers of music.

HORIZONTAL COMPLEMENTARY ALLIANCE

A *horizontal complementary strategic alliance* is an alliance in which firms share some of their resources and capabilities from the same stage of the value chain to create a competitive advantage (see Figure 9.2). Commonly, firms use this type of alliance to focus on long-term product development and distribution opportunities.[62] Bell Canada and Microsoft Canada have entered into an alliance to provide Internet services in Canada through a new portal. Although they will share the day-to-day operations of the portal, Bell Canada will be responsible for content development and for customer support, billing, and marketing. Microsoft will provide access to its portal infrastructure and to online services such as Hotmail and MSN Messenger.[63]

Hyundai Motor Company has seen its sales increase across the globe, and has set an ambitious goal to move from being the world's number nine automaker to being number five. Horizontal complementary strategic alliances and joint ventures are a key part of its strategy. In February 2003, Hyundai and DaimlerChrysler were scheduled to launch a joint venture in Korea to build 90,000 trucks annually. Hyundai has also set up strategic relationships to allow it to reach China's huge emerging market. In 2002, it set up a joint venture with Beijing Automotive Industry Holding Co., China's sixth largest auto company, through which it hoped to sell 50,000 cars in 2003, increasing to 500,000 cars annually by 2010. Kia, a wholly owned subsidiary of Hyundai, also has agreements with Chinese car manufacturers Dongfeng Motor Co. and Yueda Automobile Co., and was poised to sell 50,000 cars in China in 2003. Hyundai's strategic alliances have done much to help improve the firm's growth potential.[64]

Competition Response Strategy

As discussed in Chapter 5, competitors initiate competitive actions to attack rivals and launch competitive responses to their competitors' actions. Strategic alliances can be used at the business level to respond to competitors' attacks. Because they can be difficult to reverse and expensive to operate, strategic alliances are primarily formed to respond to strategic rather than tactical actions.

As the Opening Case indicates, because cable services continue to lead the telephone companies as broadband Internet providers, BellSouth has entered into an alliance with Movielink (see the Strategic Focus). BellSouth has been offering its service at a cheaper rate to compete with cable providers. "By becoming more aggressive in the broadband arena, the Bells hope to achieve two goals: to compete better with cable operators and to make customers of their core phone services more loyal."[65] Accordingly, the alliance is a response to similar services offered by cable companies but will not require BellSouth "to own or run content itself."[66] Similarly, as noted in the Opening Case, SBC and Qwest are striking partnerships with EchoStar and DirecTV, respectively, who run the DISH and DirecTV satellite TV networks, to offer billing services. The cable companies have been moving aggressively into phone service. This will allow SBC, for instance, to bundle local phone, long distance, cell phone, satellite TV, and high-speed broadband Internet service.[67]

Uncertainty Reducing Strategy

Particularly in fast-cycle markets, business-level strategic alliances are used to hedge against risk and uncertainty.[68] Also, they are used where uncertainty exists, such as in entering new product markets or emerging economies. For example, Dutch bank ABN

Competition Response Alliances in the Media Content, Internet, Software, and Cell Phone Equipment Industries

In highly competitive markets, companies often form alliances in response to competitors' actions. Telecommunication companies such as SBC Communications and Verizon Communications are battling with cable companies like Comcast to be chosen as Internet broadband providers for households and businesses. In addition to cutting prices and offering special services, the telecommunication companies are reaching out to form alliances in response to the competition with cable companies, which have traditionally offered more services.

For example, BellSouth has entered into an alliance with Movielink. Movielink LLC, headquartered in Santa Monica, California, is an Internet-based movie-rental service formed as a joint venture that is owned by Metro-Goldwyn-Mayer Studios, Paramount Pictures, Sony Pictures Entertainment, Universal, and Warner Bros. Movielink, because of its affiliation with its owners, can offer recently released movies as well as films owned by members of the closely held joint venture. Movielink offers a downloadable service that allows appropriately formatted films to be played on television sets. The aim of the Movielink alliance with BellSouth is to store movies closer to the customer on BellSouth's network, thus shortening the download time for the customer and making BellSouth's Internet service more appealing.

In another example, in response to competition from Microsoft, RealNetworks recently announced an alliance agreement with Vodafone, the mobile-phone operator, to use its software. RealNetworks makes audio and video software in competition with Microsoft. It hopes that by pushing into the mobile-phone market, it will persuade content owners to make audio and video available in its format, rather than in Microsoft's, or in other popular formats such as MPEG. RealNetworks pioneered the delivery of audio and video over the Internet and is seeking to strengthen its weakening position. Vodafone controls operations in 16 countries, and it says it plans to use RealNetworks' server software to deliver video and audio clips of its Vodafone Live! suite of multimedia services. It will also ask handset suppliers to include RealNetworks' phone software on their products. An analyst with International Data Corporation says that mobile-phone users are less likely than PC owners to download additional video players, and therefore suppliers of video software are "scrambling to sign up as many partners and devices as possible."

Nokia Corporation, the world's largest cell phone maker, is mounting a comeback in the U.S. market that is largely connected to its alliance relationship with Sprint PCS, one of the United States' largest mobile-phone operators. Motorola overtook Nokia in 2002 in North America and had a 32 percent U.S. market share by unit sales in the first quarter of 2003, compared with 29 percent for Nokia. Pekka Vartiainen, general manager of Nokia Mobile Phones–Americas, says that Nokia's 3585i handset is the top-selling low-end phone in the Sprint PCS portfolio of handsets, and an analyst attributes Nokia's market-share gains in the second quarter of 2003 to "a strong showing at Sprint." This is important for Nokia, because Sprint hadn't sold Nokia phones for three years prior to the launch of the 3585i in February 2003. These examples illustrate that to maintain competitiveness, alliances are often used to respond to rivals' competitive moves.

SOURCES: 2003, The generation game, *The Economist*, http://www.economist.com, May 30; D. Pringle, 2003, RealNetworks beats Microsoft in Vodafone clip-delivery deal, *Wall Street Journal Online*, http://www.wsj.com, June 30; A. Latour, 2003, BellSouth unveils DSL Lite service as Bells step up subscriber battle, *Wall Street Journal Online*, http://www.wsj.com, July 8; D. Pringle, 2003, Nokia spurs comeback in U.S. with new handsets, promotions, *Wall Street Journal Online*, http://www.wsj.com, July 10; S. Alsop, 2002, Hollywood's latest flop, *Fortune*, December 9, 56.

AMRO signed on to a venture called ShoreCap International. This commercial company is a multisector partnership of organizations, including private businesses, financial institutions, development funds, and foundations. ShoreCap will invest capital in and advise local financial institutions that do small and microbusiness lending in developing economies, targeting Asia, Africa, and Central and Eastern Europe. The venture's leading sponsor, ShoreBank Corporation, is a for-profit community development and environmental bank. It has a history of collaboration with financial institutions and other partners, including the World Bank. Through this cooperative strategy with other financial institutions, ShoreBank hopes to be able to reduce the risk of providing credit to smaller borrowers in disadvantaged regions. It also hopes to reduce poverty in the regions where it invests.[69]

In other instances, firms form business-level strategic alliances to reduce the uncertainty associated with developing new products or establishing a technology standard. Wind Infostrada SpA, Italy's third largest telecom company, recently signed an agreement with Japan's NTT DoCoMo Inc. to become the sole provider of DoCoMo's i-mode technology. I-mode technology, which allows users to access the Internet on their mobile-phone handsets, has been a noteworthy success in Japan. DoCoMo sees this relationship as an opportunity to establish a foothold for its standard in cell phone technology, and Wind is going to share the risk with DoCoMo, as they test to see if i-mode will also be a successful standard in Europe.[70] Thus, the uncertainty and risk of the 21st-century landscape finds firms, such as those competing in the cell phone and telecommunication industries, forming multiple strategic alliances to increase their strategic competitiveness.

Competition Reducing Strategy

Used to reduce competition, collusive strategies differ from strategic alliances in that collusive strategies are often an illegal type of cooperative strategy. There are two types of collusive strategies—explicit collusion and tacit collusion.

Explicit collusion "exists when firms directly negotiate production output and pricing agreements in order to reduce competition."[71] Explicit collusion strategies are illegal in the United States and most developed economies (except in regulated industries).

Firms that use explicit collusion strategies may face litigation and may be found guilty of noncompetitive actions. For instance, in 2003, cosmetics firms, including Estée Lauder, and a group of retail firms settled a price-fixing lawsuit out of court for a $175-million cosmetic products giveaway program. In regard to the suit, one of the winning attorneys stated: "Virtually every woman who buys cosmetics knows that department-store cosmetics are never discounted, never go on sale and are priced identically in any department store in any city. This kind of conduct does not happen in a competitive environment without collusion."[72]

Tacit collusion exists when several firms in an industry indirectly coordinate their production and pricing decisions by observing each other's competitive actions and responses.[73] Tacit collusion results in below fully competitive production output and prices that are above fully competitive levels. Unlike explicit collusion, firms engaging in tacit collusion do not directly negotiate output and pricing decisions.

Discussed in Chapter 6, *mutual forbearance* is a form of tacit collusion "in which firms avoid competitive attacks against those rivals they meet in multiple markets."[74] Rivals learn a great deal about each other when engaging in multimarket competition, including how to deter the effects of their rival's competitive attacks and responses. Given what they know about each other as a competitor, firms choose not to engage in what could be destructive competitions in multiple product markets.[75]

AOL dominates the instant-messaging (IM) business, with almost 60 million users. Yahoo! and MSN also operate IM services, but unlike e-mail, instant messages cannot cross over programs, which irritates many users. AOL and Microsoft quietly announced in 2003 that they would make their IM services work together. MSN has the next largest group of IM users (23.6 million) and through this strategic agreement with AOL will be able to reduce the level of competition.[76]

Tacit collusion tends to be used as a business-level competition reducing strategy in highly concentrated industries, such as breakfast cereals. Firms in these industries recognize that they are interdependent and that their competitive actions and responses significantly affect competitors' behavior toward them. Understanding this interdependence and carefully observing competitors because of it tend to lead to tacit collusion.

Four firms (Kellogg, General Mills, Post, and Quaker) have accounted for as much as 80 percent of sales volume in the ready-to-eat segment of the U.S. cereal market.[77] Some believe that this high degree of concentration results in "prices for branded cereals that are well above [the] costs of production."[78] Prices above the competitive level in this industry suggest the possibility that the dominant firms use a tacit collusion cooperative strategy.

At a broad level in free-market economies, governments need to determine how rivals can collaborate to increase their competitiveness without violating established regulations.[79] Reaching this determination is challenging when evaluating collusive strategies, particularly tacit ones. For example, regulation of pharmaceutical and biotech firms who must collaborate to meet global competition might lead to too much price fixing and, therefore, regulation is required to make sure that the balance is right, although sometimes the regulation gets in the way of good market functioning.[80] For individual companies, the issue is to understand the effect of a competition reducing strategy on their performance and competitiveness.

Assessment of Business-Level Cooperative Strategies

Firms use business-level strategies to develop competitive advantages that can contribute to successful positioning and performance in individual product markets. For a competitive advantage to be developed by using an alliance, the particular set of resources and capabilities that is combined and shared in a particular manner through the alliance must be valuable, rare, imperfectly imitable, and nonsubstitutable (see Chapter 3).

Evidence suggests that complementary business-level strategic alliances, especially vertical ones, have the greatest probability of creating a sustainable competitive advantage.[81] Horizontal complementary alliances are sometimes difficult to maintain because they are often between rivalrous competitors. The international airline industry, in an effort to skirt laws blocking international mergers, as noted earlier, has been forming global partnerships for a number of years. The largest is Star, built around United Airlines, Lufthansa, and All Nippon Airways. The fact that United entered Chapter 11 bankruptcy proceedings in 2003 and threatened Chapter 7 bankruptcy (liquidation) has destabilized these partnerships. KLM, based in the Netherlands, has been mainly on the outside of the big partnerships, its only joint venture being with Northwest Airlines on transatlantic routes. However, Northwest recently won approval to work with Delta and Continental on joint domestic flights, which would make it logical for KLM and Northwest to join SkyTeam, the partnership anchored by Delta and Air France. KLM is also considering joining Oneworld, partnering with British Airways and American Airlines. If United does go into Chapter 7 bankruptcy, which would dissolve its assets, the Star alliance will probably strive to lure either Delta or American into the fold to replace United. This would in turn destabilize the alliance to which they formerly belonged. Because of the high rivalry among partners in the airline industry, the horizontal alliances formed are often unstable.[82]

Although strategic alliances designed to respond to competition and to reduce uncertainty can also create competitive advantages, these advantages tend to be more temporary than those developed through complementary (both vertical and horizontal) strategic alliances. The primary reason is that complementary alliances have a stronger focus on the creation of value compared to competition reducing and uncertainty reducing alliances, which tend to be formed to respond to competitors' actions or reduce uncertainty rather than to attack competitors.

Of the four business-level cooperative strategies, the competition reducing strategy has the lowest probability of creating a sustainable competitive advantage. Research suggests that firms following a foreign direct investment strategy using alliances can be due to a follow-the-leader imitation approach without regard to strong strategic or learning goals. Thus, such investment may be attributable to tacit collusion, or interdependence, among the participating firms rather than for obtaining significant strategic or competitive advantage.[83] This suggests that companies using such competition reducing business-level strategic alliances should carefully monitor them as to the degree to which they are facilitating the firm's efforts to develop and successfully create competitive advantages.

Corporate-Level Cooperative Strategy

A corporate-level cooperative strategy is used by the firm to help it diversify in terms of products offered or markets served, or both.

A firm uses a **corporate-level cooperative strategy** to help it diversify in terms of products offered or markets served, or both. Diversifying alliances, synergistic alliances, and franchising are the most commonly used corporate-level cooperative strategies (see Figure 9.3).

Firms use diversifying alliances and synergistic alliances to grow and diversify their operations through a means other than a merger or an acquisition.[84] When a firm seeks to diversify into markets in which the host nation's government prevents mergers and acquisitions, alliances become an especially appropriate option. Corporate-level strategic alliances are also attractive compared to mergers and particularly acquisitions, because they require fewer resource commitments[85] and permit greater flexibility in terms of efforts to diversify partners' operations.[86] An alliance can be used as a way to determine if the partners might benefit from a future merger or acquisition between them. This "testing" process often characterizes alliances completed to combine firms' unique technological resources and capabilities.[87]

Diversifying Strategic Alliance

A diversifying strategic alliance is a corporate-level cooperative strategy in which firms share some of their resources and capabilities to diversify into new product or market areas.

A **diversifying strategic alliance** is a corporate-level cooperative strategy in which firms share some of their resources and capabilities to diversify into new product or market areas. Shell Petrochemicals and China National Offshore Oil Corporation (CNOOC) have announced a joint venture focused on the construction of a $4.3 billion petrochemicals complex in southern China. The emphasis will be to produce products for

Figure 9.3 — Corporate-Level Cooperative Strategies

- Diversifying alliances
- Synergistic alliances
- Franchising

"Guangdong and high-consumption areas along the country's coastal economic zones."[88] CNOOC's business has been mainly upstream, especially in offshore oil production. "For CNOOC, the development is part of its continuing diversification from its core upstream business."[89]

Besides creating more diversification, cooperative ventures are also used to reduce diversification in firms that have overdiversified. Japanese chipmakers Fujitsu, Mitsubishi Electric, Hitachi, NEC, and Toshiba have been using joint ventures to consolidate and then spin off diversified businesses that were a drag on earnings. Hitachi and Mitsubishi Electric created a joint venture called Renesas that focuses on producing large-scale integrated circuits. Hitachi further entered a joint venture with NEC called Elpida, which is considered the last Japanese DRAM maker. Toshiba and Fujitsu announced an alliance last year. Fujitsu, realizing that memory chips were becoming a financial burden, dumped its flash-memory business into a joint venture company controlled by Advanced Micro Devices. These alliances resulted in the involved firms being able to refocus on their core businesses, reduce excessive diversification, and add value to their firm.[90]

©Philip Gould/CORBIS

Synergistic Strategic Alliance

A **synergistic strategic alliance** is a corporate-level cooperative strategy in which firms share some of their resources and capabilities to create economies of scope. Similar to the business-level horizontal complementary strategic alliance, synergistic strategic alliances create synergy across multiple functions or multiple businesses between partner firms.

Grupo Televisa SA, a Mexican entertainment company, is seeking an alliance with Univision Communications Inc., the largest U.S. Spanish-language television network. Univision captures four-fifths of the U.S. Spanish-language cable audience, and it already licenses Televisa's shows. Such a large and relatively wealthy market is very appealing to Emilio Azcarraga Jean, head of Televisa. Since Univision has not shown interest in allying with Televisa, another way for Televisa to increase its U.S. market exposure would be through purchasing an equity stake in Entravision Communications Corp., which owns a large group of Univision affiliates as well as Spanish-language radio stations, billboards, and a newspaper. An alliance with either company would create economies of scope for Grupo Televisa and hence is an example of a potential synergistic alliance.[91] The Opening Case also illustrated how SBC Communications and EchoStar Communications were synergistically diversified by the arrangement to offer satellite TV billing services through SBC's system. Thus, a synergistic strategic alliance is different from a complementary business-level alliance in that it diversifies both firms into a new business, but in a synergistic way.

Franchising

Franchising is a corporate-level cooperative strategy in which a firm (the franchisor) uses a franchise as a contractual relationship to describe and control the sharing of its resources and capabilities with partners (the franchisees).[92] A *franchise* is a "contractual

Shell Petrochemicals and China National Offshore Oil Corporation (CNOOC) have announced a joint venture focused on the construction of a petrochemicals complex in south China. This venture helps diversify both firms: CNOOC experiences increased product diversification, while Shell Petrochemicals experiences increased international diversification.

A **synergistic strategic alliance** *is a corporate-level cooperative strategy in which firms share some of their resources and capabilities to create economies of scope.*

Franchising *is a corporate-level cooperative strategy in which a firm (the franchisor) uses a franchise as a contractual relationship to describe and control the sharing of its resources and capabilities with partners (the franchisees).*

agreement between two legally independent companies whereby the franchisor grants the right to the franchisee to sell the franchisor's product or do business under its trademarks in a given location for a specified period of time."[93]

Franchising is a popular strategy: companies using it account for $1 trillion in annual U.S. retail sales and compete in more than 75 industries. As the Cendant strategy outlined in a Strategic Focus in Chapter 6 indicates, franchising can be used successfully across a number of businesses. Cendant has used franchising in real estate, for example, through its Century 21 and ERA brands. Already frequently used in developed nations, franchising is expected to account for significant portions of growth in emerging economies in the 21st century's first two decades.[94] As with diversifying and synergistic strategic alliances, franchising is an alternative to pursuing growth through mergers and acquisitions.

McDonald's, Hilton International, and Krispy Kreme are well-known examples of firms that use the franchising corporate-level cooperative strategy. 7-Eleven, Inc., the convenience store company, has successfully used franchising in its expansion, both domestically and internationally. The chain now has over 25,000 outlets worldwide and sales of $3 billion. 7-Eleven is especially popular in Asia, where convenience stores are more like pantries for city dwellers short on space. There are 77 stores per million people in Japan and 148 per million in Taiwan, far more than the 20 per million in the United States.[95]

In the most successful franchising strategy, the partners (the franchisor and the franchisees) closely work together.[96] A primary responsibility of the franchisor is to develop programs to transfer to the franchisees the knowledge and skills that are needed to successfully compete at the local level.[97] In return, franchisees should provide feedback to the franchisor regarding how their units could become more effective and efficient.[98] Working cooperatively, the franchisor and its franchisees find ways to strengthen the core company's brand name, which is often the most important competitive advantage for franchisees operating in their local markets.[99]

Franchising is a particularly attractive strategy to use in fragmented industries, such as retailing and commercial printing. In fragmented industries, a large number of small and medium-sized firms compete as rivals; however, no firm or small set of firms has a dominant share, making it possible for a company to gain a large market share by consolidating independent companies through contractual relationships.[100] La Quinta Inns decided to use franchising as a corporate-level cooperative strategy in order to increase its market share. Even though the lodging industry isn't as fragmented as it once was, La Quinta's decision to franchise has been viewed favorably. It is seeking to have 1,000 La Quinta Inn and La Quinta Inn & Suites properties by 2010, which would represent significant growth from its 353 branded properties in 2003. Alan Talis, executive vice-president at La Quinta, speaking of the relationship to its franchisees, said, "There is absolutely no difference between our company-owned properties and our franchised properties. They are not our customers. They are our operating partners."[101]

Assessment of Corporate-Level Cooperative Strategies

Costs are incurred with each type of cooperative strategy.[102] Compared to those at the business-level, corporate-level cooperative strategies commonly are broader in scope and more complex, making them relatively more costly. Those forming and using cooperative strategies, especially corporate-level ones, should be aware of alliance costs and carefully monitor them.

In spite of these costs, firms can create competitive advantages and value when they effectively form and use corporate-level cooperative strategies.[103] The likelihood of this being the case increases when successful alliance experiences are internalized.

In other words, those involved with forming and using corporate-level cooperative strategies can also use them to develop useful knowledge about how to succeed in the future. To gain maximum value from this knowledge, firms should organize it and verify that it is always properly distributed to those involved with the formation and use of alliances.[104]

We explain in Chapter 6 that firms answer two questions to form a corporate-level strategy—in which businesses will the diversified firm compete, and how will those businesses be managed? These questions are also answered as firms form corporate-level cooperative strategies. Thus, firms able to develop corporate-level cooperative strategies and manage them in ways that are valuable, rare, imperfectly imitable, and nonsubstitutable (see Chapter 3) develop a competitive advantage that is in addition to advantages gained through the activities of individual cooperative strategies. Later in the chapter, we further describe alliance management as a source of competitive advantage.

International Cooperative Strategy

A **cross-border strategic alliance** is an international cooperative strategy in which firms with headquarters in different nations combine some of their resources and capabilities to create a competitive advantage. For example, British Petroleum (BP) agreed to invest over $6 billion in a joint venture with Russian oil company Tyumen Oil. The venture will combine BP's Russian assets, a stake in Russian oil company Sidanco, with Tyumen. The new company will be the tenth largest oil producer in the world, increasing its competitive advantage against other, smaller oil companies.[105] Taking place in virtually all industries, the number of cross-border alliances being completed continues to increase,[106] in some cases at the expense of mergers and acquisitions.[107] However, as the Strategic Focus on cross-border aerospace industry alliances illustrates, although cross-border alliances can be complex, they may be necessary to improve technology as well as win government support for new orders in the aerospace industry.

There are several reasons for the increasing use of cross-border strategic alliances. In general, multinational corporations outperform firms operating on only a domestic basis,[108] so a firm may form cross-border strategic alliances to leverage core competencies that are the foundation of its domestic success to expand into international markets.[109] Nike has used its core competence with celebrity marketing as it expands overseas, especially because its U.S. business growth has slowed. It has sought to duplicate its marketing strategy in international markets, signing big-name athletes to sell shoes and apparel. In the United States, Nike's focus has been on basketball, while in other nations, soccer is more popular, and Nike has alliance agreements with Brazilian soccer star Ronaldo and the world's most popular soccer team, Manchester United. As a result of these alliances, Nike's global soccer business generated $720 million in sales in 2003, up from $500 million in fiscal year 2002.[110]

A cross-border strategic alliance is an international cooperative strategy in which firms with headquarters in different nations combine some of their resources and capabilities to create a competitive advantage.

In the United States, Nike has focused on marketing its shoes through celebrity basketball players who use and endorse its products. That celebrity marketing strategy is adapted abroad. In Europe and Central and South America, soccer is more popular than in the United States, and Nike has sought alliance agreements with soccer players such as Brazilian star Ronaldo (center) and Manchester United, the world's most popular soccer team.

AP Photo/Laurent Rebours

Cross-Border Alliances Battle to Win the President's Entourage: S-92 versus EH101 Helicopters

An analyst speaking about firms in the aerospace industry said, "If an aerospace company is not good at alliances, it's not in business." Commonly, these alliances are formed across borders. Aerospace is one of the industries in which highly diversified United Technologies competes. The firm is involved with over 100 worldwide cooperative strategies, including cross-border alliances and joint ventures. One of United Technologies' cooperative strategies was the cross-border alliance formed by the firm's Sikorsky business unit to produce the S-92 helicopter. Five firms from four continents joined Sikorsky to form this alliance.

This alliance's partners (called "Team S-92") and their responsibilities were: (1) Japan's Mitsubishi Heavy Industries (main cabin section), (2) Jingdezhen Helicopter Group/CATIC of the People's Republic of China (vertical tail fin and stabilizer), (3) Spain's Gamesa Aeronautica (main rotor pylon, engine nacelles, aft tail transition section, and cabin interior), (4) Aerospace Industrial Development Corporation of Taiwan (the electrical harnesses, flight controls, hydraulic lines, and environmental controls forming the cockpit), and (5) Embraer of Brazil (main landing gear and fuel system). As the sixth member of the alliance, Sikorsky was responsible for the main and tail rotor head components and the S-92's transmissions, along with final assembly and launch-ready certification.

The FAA certified the S-92 in December 2002. The Air Force is seeking to revitalize its search-and-rescue operations, and as part of that wants to replace aging helicopters. It has chosen the S-92 as the "front-runner," according to Maj. General Randall M. Schmidt. The Navy has decided to replace the fleet of 1970s helicopters that transport the American president. Although the contract is small in scope (11 helicopters in all), the prestige is enormous, and could translate into marketing gains for the winner.

However, the S-92 faces stiff competition from other helicopter manufacturers for the Navy contract, including AgustaWestland. AgustaWestland is a joint venture by a British company, GKN, and an Italian company, Finmeccanica. The venture was created in 2001 to strengthen the product range and increase the global reach of both companies. In July 2002, AgustaWestland signed an agreement with American company Lockheed Martin to jointly market the EH101 helicopter for American government applications. In May 2003, it also chose an American partner, Bell Helicopter, a division of Textron, a large diversified conglomerate, to build the machine should it win the contracts.

In the contest for the president's entourage of helicopters, some say that the American president should not fly in a foreign helicopter. Stephen C. Moss, president of AgustaWestland's U.S. subsidiary, noted that the foreign pedigree of the EH101 won't matter, largely because much of the Sikorsky helicopter was built by foreign partners.

Both Sikorsky and AgustaWestland are using cross-border alliances to facilitate doing business. Sikorsky's Team S-92 alliance smoothed the development of a new helicopter. AgustaWestland itself is a product of a cross-border alliance, and it is building strategic alliance relationships with American companies in order to win contracts from the American government.

SOURCES: R. Wall, 2003, Coming to America: AgustaWestland expands U.S. ties in pursuit of Pentagon programs, facing Sikorsky in heated competition for new presidential helo, *Aviation Week & Space Technology*, May 19, 32; J. L. Lunsford, 2003, Should U.S. president use a foreign copter? *Wall Street Journal*, May 12, B1; 2003, AgustaWestland Company History, http://www.agustawestland.com, July 19; M. A. Taverna, 2002, AgustaWestland teams with Lockheed Martin, Thales, *Aviation Week & Space Technology*, July 29, 39; R. Wall, 2002, USAF to bolster pilot rescue ability, *Aviation Week & Space Technology*, August 12, 30–32; 2002, Sikorsky S-92 awarded FAA type certification, United Technologies, http://www.utc.com, December 19.

Limited domestic growth opportunities are another reason firms use cross-border alliances. Hewlett-Packard has formed an alliance with NEC, a large computer manufacturer, to help NEC manage information-technology systems of Japanese companies. The alliance also has plans to target other customers in Asia. "Joe Hogan, H-P's vice president of marketing for managed services, said the pact is likely to generate more than $1 billion in revenues over the next few years." The alliance will likely increase the growth rates for both companies.[111]

Another reason for forming cross-border alliances is government economic policies. As discussed in Chapter 8, local ownership is an important national policy objective in some nations. In India and China, for example, governmental policies reflect a strong preference to license local companies. Morgan Stanley has created a joint venture with China Construction Bank to dispose of mainland China's nonperforming loans, the first foreign bank to do so. China Construction Bank sees the deal as an opportunity to use Western banking expertise to clean up its bad loan problem, while Morgan Stanley views this as an opportunity to move further into China's opening market. "But the communist bureaucracy isn't known for its quickness in instituting ground-breaking reforms. For instance, Morgan Stanley's new bad loan deal has yet to be cleared by the bureaucrats at the People's Bank of China, the China Banking Regulatory Commission, or the Ministry of Finance."[112] Thus, in spite of Morgan Stanley's efforts, it may not be able to follow up fully on this joint venture,[113] indicating that in some countries, the full range of entry mode choices that we describe in Chapter 8 may not be available to firms wishing to internationally diversify. Indeed, investment by foreign firms in these instances may be allowed only through a partnership with a local firm, such as in a cross-border alliance. A cross-border strategic alliance can also be helpful to foreign partners from an operational perspective, because the local partner has significantly more information about factors contributing to competitive success such as local markets, sources of capital, legal procedures, and politics.[114]

Firms also use cross-border alliances to help transform themselves or to better use their advantages to benefit from opportunities surfacing in the rapidly changing global economy. Starbucks, the Seattle-based purveyor of gourmet coffee, has been expanding quickly into China and Japan. In China, the firm hopes to benefit from improved income of the emerging middle class. Although China is a nation of tea drinkers who generally don't care for coffee, Starbucks is counting on its image of relaxed affluence to attract the Chinese. In Japan, Starbucks has opened 470 stores in seven years, and is reaching the saturation point in several cities. Japanese consumers eagerly embrace new ideas, and as a result Starbucks views Japan as an ideal test market. It now offers alcohol at one store and assorted new coffee drinks at other stores. In 2003, the chain began serving food in some Japanese stores. Products that are popular in Japan can often be exported to the United States, like Starbucks' green tea Frappucino, which was devised in Japan and Taiwan and may soon be sold in the United States. Thus, the firm expects to learn a great deal from its ventures in Asia, which may be costly initially but ultimately may help improve performance in the United States and in other markets around the world.[115]

In general, cross-border alliances are more complex and risky than domestic strategic alliances. However, the fact that firms competing internationally tend to outperform domestic-only competitors suggests the importance of learning how to diversify into international markets. Compared to mergers and acquisitions, cross-border alliances may be a better way to learn this process, especially in the early stages of the firms' geographic diversification efforts. As mentioned earlier, when Starbucks was looking to expand overseas, it wanted to do so quickly in order to keep its first-mover advantage. Thus, it agreed to a complex series of joint ventures in many countries in the interest of speed. Lately, its overseas stores have been unprofitable, and it seems that the complexity of the joint ventures is partly to blame. While the company gets a slice of revenues and profits as well as licensing fees for supplying its coffee, controlling costs abroad is more difficult than in the United States.[116] However, as noted above, the firm hopes to learn a great deal from serving multiple markets. Careful and thorough study of a proposed cross-border alliance contributes to success[117] as do precise specifications of each partner's alliance role.[118] These points are explored later in our discussion of how to best manage alliances.

Network Cooperative Strategy

A network cooperative strategy is a cooperative strategy wherein several firms agree to form multiple partnerships to achieve shared objectives.

Increasingly, firms are involved with more than one cooperative strategy. In addition to forming their own alliances with individual companies, a growing number of firms are joining forces in multiple cooperative strategies. A **network cooperative strategy** is a cooperative strategy wherein several firms agree to form multiple partnerships to achieve shared objectives.

A network cooperative strategy is particularly effective when it is formed by geographically clustered firms,[119] as in California's Silicon Valley and Singapore's Silicon Island.[120] Effective social relationships and interactions among partners while sharing their resources and capabilities make it more likely that a network cooperative strategy will be successful,[121] as does having a productive *strategic center firm* (discussed further in Chapter 11). In Europe, there has recently been an increased emphasis on joint venture film production. As the European Union prepared for its expansion to 25 countries in 2004, production houses across Europe were learning to use film festivals such as Cannes to strike alliances and pool their resources. With these joint ventures, firms from countries with minimal film budgets, such as Portugal, can get off the ground. For example, in May 2003, RAI Cinema and Europa Corp., from Italy and France, respectively, signed a coproduction and distribution agreement through 2005. The geographic closeness of the members of the European Union facilitates effective use of this strategy.[122]

The early research evidence suggests the positive financial effects of network cooperative strategies will make these strategies important contributors to the 21st-century success of both supplier and buyer partners involved.[123]

Alliance Network Types

Joint venture film production benefits countries with smaller film budgets, as production houses pool their resources. Film festivals, such as the one pictured here in Cannes, foster these alliances.

An important advantage of a network cooperative strategy is that firms gain access "to their partners' partners."[124] Having access to multiple collaborations increases the likelihood that additional competitive advantages will be formed as the set of resources and capabilities being shared expands.[125] In turn, increases in competitive advantages further stimulate the development of product innovations that are so critical to strategic competitiveness in the global economy.[126]

The set of partnerships, such as strategic alliances, that result from the use of a network cooperative strategy is commonly called an *alliance network.* The alliance networks that companies develop vary by industry conditions. A *stable alliance network* is formed in mature industries where demand is relatively constant and predictable. Through a stable alliance network, firms try to extend their competitive advantages to other settings while con-

Getty Images

PART 2 / Strategic Actions: Strategy Formulation

tinuing to profit from operations in their core, relatively mature industry. Thus, stable networks are built for *exploitation* of the economies (scale and/or scope) available between firms.[127] *Dynamic alliance networks* are used in industries characterized by frequent product innovations and short product life cycles.[128] For instance, the pace of innovation in the information technology (IT) industry is too fast for any one company to maintain success over time. Therefore, the ability to develop and nurture strategic partnerships can make the difference between success and failure. As such, independent software vendors earn more than 40 percent of their revenue through successful partnering. After IBM's "near-death experience" in the early 1990s, the power of its alliances with more than 90,000 business partners helped shape its turnaround. By partnering, companies play on "teams," fielding the best players at every position and thus providing stamina and flexibility for customers. Through partnerships, a company can offer a broader range of IT solutions and improve the probability of market success.[129]

Thus, dynamic alliance networks are primarily used to stimulate rapid, value-creating product innovations and subsequent successful market entries, demonstrating that their purpose is often *exploration* of new ideas.[130] Often, large firms in such industries as software and pharmaceuticals create networks of smaller entrepreneurial start-up firms to accomplish this goal.[131] Small firms also build credibility faster by being engaged in such joint network relationships.[132]

Competitive Risks with Cooperative Strategies

Stated simply, many cooperative strategies fail.[133] In fact, evidence shows that two-thirds of cooperative strategies have serious problems in their first two years and that as many as 70 percent of them fail.[134] This failure rate suggests that even when the partnership has potential complementarities and synergies, alliance success is elusive.[135] We describe two failed alliances, MusicNet and Pressplay, in the Strategic Focus.

Although failure is undesirable, it can be a valuable learning experience. Certainly, it appears that MusicNet and Pressplay have learned from the more positive results and customer demand experienced by Apple's iTunes venture, as the Strategic Focus indicates. Companies willing to carefully study a cooperative strategy's failure may gain insights that can be used to successfully develop and use future cooperative strategies.[136] Thus, companies should work equally hard to avoid cooperative strategy failure and to learn from failure if it occurs. In the construction industry, cooperation on a project between the main contractor and subcontractors is very important. Without managing areas of mistrust, including suspected incompetence and potential dishonesty, success can be elusive, and failure of the alliance can be very costly.[137] Prominent cooperative strategy risks are shown in Figure 9.4.

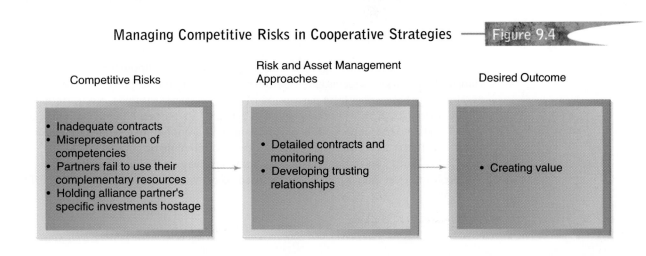

Managing Competitive Risks in Cooperative Strategies — Figure 9.4

Competitive Risks

- Inadequate contracts
- Misrepresentation of competencies
- Partners fail to use their complementary resources
- Holding alliance partner's specific investments hostage

Risk and Asset Management Approaches

- Detailed contracts and monitoring
- Developing trusting relationships

Desired Outcome

- Creating value

Rivalry and Mistrust: Failure and Success of Music Industry Alliances

The music industry is in the middle of a significant change. Increasingly, music is being pirated online and industry executives are having a hard time finding a viable way to curtail the losses associated with the illegal behavior. Napster, the biggest online music swap service, was shut down by a lawsuit filed by the music companies. The music companies promised to launch paid services with the same ease of access. Accordingly, Warner Music, BMG, EMI, and RealNetworks started an alliance called MusicNet, while Sony and Vivendi Universal formed a joint venture called Pressplay. Instead of making digital music easier to obtain legally, however, these two joint ventures apparently increased the difficulty.

The record companies were afraid of cannibalizing CD sales and decided to "rent" music to customers through the Internet. Customers were expected to pay a monthly subscription fee for songs from MusicNet and Pressplay. However, MusicNet tunes could be downloaded only onto a computer, but not burned onto CDs, and they disappeared off the computer (through the downloading software) if the customer's bill was not paid. To make matters worse for the consumer, the two joint ventures fought over who would dominate instead of trying to work together on a standard to attract customers. Pressplay wouldn't share its songs with MusicNet, and MusicNet withheld its tunes from Pressplay. As a result, neither service had enough songs to attract paying customers. All of these factors contributed to the ventures' lack of success. Although their executives insist otherwise, both could be considered initial failures.

Apple, on the other hand, opened an online music store called iTunes as a venture with most major record companies and artists. It is not a subscription service like MusicNet and Pressplay. Instead, an iTunes customer pays 99 cents per song and from then on owns the music, although sharing with others is still illegal. Also, the purchased tune can be downloaded to portable MP3 players, burned on a CD, or arranged in a play list for the PC, and it never goes away. In its first week, iTunes sold over one million songs, in contrast to the subscribership of MusicNet and Pressplay, estimated at 225,000 altogether since their initiation. Another sign of iTunes' success is that both the MusicNet and Pressplay joint ventures have scrambled to add a service like Apple's to their offerings.

SOURCES: J. Ellis, 2003, Digital squared: Living in an iTunes world, *Fast Company*, August, 59; C. Haddad, 2003, How Apple spells future: i-P-O-D, *BusinessWeek Online*, http://www.businessweek.com, July 2; D. Leonard, 2003, Songs in the key of Steve, *Fortune*, http://www.fortune.com, April 28; D. Leonard, 2003, Leader of the digital music pack? *Fortune*, http://www.fortune.com, April 28; D. Leonard, 2003, Apple takes a big bite, *Fortune*, http://www.fortune.com, May 13; N. Wingfield & A. W. Matthews, 2003, Behind the missing music, *Wall Street Journal*, July 2, D1.

One cooperative strategy risk is that a partner may act opportunistically. Opportunistic behaviors surface either when formal contracts fail to prevent them or when an alliance is based on a false perception of partner trustworthiness. Not infrequently, the opportunistic firm wants to acquire as much of its partner's tacit knowledge as it can.[138] Full awareness of what a partner wants in a cooperative strategy reduces the likelihood that a firm will suffer from another's opportunistic actions.[139]

TVS Motor, an Indian motorcycle company, was created as a joint venture with Suzuki Motor Co., but when Suzuki refused to provide financial guarantees for TVS after a devastating strike, TVS initiated a strategy to become independent. Having learned much from Suzuki, including the implementation of Japanese-style quality programs, Venu Srinivasan, CEO of TVS, improved the company's situation through upgrading plants, nurturing in-house design, and investing in new technology. When sales of its new Victor motorcycle took off in 2001, TVS decided to go its own way and ended its relationship with Suzuki.[140]

Some cooperative strategies fail when it is discovered that a firm has misrepresented the competencies it can bring to the partnership. 3Com Corporation recently agreed to a joint venture with Huawei Technologies, China's equivalent to Cisco Systems for developing network infrastructure that supports the Internet. On paper, the combination of Huawei and 3Com appears very promising. It provides Huawei with 3Com's global distribution system, along with a strong base in the United States, and it lets 3Com fill gaps in its product line and exploit Huawei's low-cost operations in China. Unfortunately, Cisco, 3Com's major rival, has accused Huawei of stealing its intellectual property and has filed suit against the company. For years, others have noticed how similar Huawei's products were to Cisco's, down to the model number and manual. Now Cisco says that it has found some of its own bugs in Huawei's software, which would be an extremely unlikely coincidence. 3Com CEO Bruce Claflin says the company agreed to the joint venture only after a detailed investigation of Huawei's source code. Terms of the venture include warranties by Huawei that its products do not infringe intellectual rights. Even if certain Huawei products turn out to have Cisco code, Claflin believes it was not done with management's blessing and has confidence in the company's future offerings. The furor already endangers the joint venture, however: Cisco has threatened to sue 3Com as well as Huawei.[141] The risk of competence misrepresentation is more common when the partner's contribution is grounded in some of its intangible assets. Superior knowledge of local conditions is an example of an intangible asset that partners often fail to deliver. Asking the partner to provide evidence that it does possess the resources and capabilities (even when they are largely intangible) it is to share in the cooperative strategy may be an effective way to deal with this risk.

Another risk is that a firm won't actually make available to its partners the resources and capabilities (such as its most sophisticated technologies) that it committed to the cooperative strategy. This risk surfaces most commonly when firms form an international cooperative strategy.[142] In these instances, different cultures can result in different interpretations of contractual terms or trust-based expectations.

A final risk is that the firm may make investments that are specific to the alliance while its partner does not. For example, the firm might commit resources and capabilities to develop manufacturing equipment that can be used only to produce items coming from the alliance. If the partner isn't also making alliance-specific investments, the firm is at a relative disadvantage in terms of returns earned from the alliance compared to investments made to earn the returns.

For example, Pixar and Disney have partnered to release several computer graphics animated features, including *Toy Story, Monsters Inc.*, and *A Bug's Life*, all of which have been box-office hits. Disney is seeing the risks in its partnership as the firm's managers consider the possible expiration of the agreement with Pixar. Pixar may have more bargaining power to strike another deal—with Disney or with someone else. All of Pixar's films have done better at the box office than have Disney's recent animated features, and Pixar contributed 35 percent of Disney's studio operating profits in 2002. Pixar's chairman Steve Jobs has been meeting with executives from other studios, which puts pressure on Disney to sweeten its offer for continued partnership, perhaps by allowing Pixar to keep more of its profits.[143] If Disney had more of a commitment in the form of equity ownership in Pixar, it would have more control due to such investment.

As our discussion has shown, cooperative strategies are an important option for firms competing in the global economy.[144] However, our study of cooperative strategies also shows that they are complex.[145]

Firms gain the most benefit from cooperative strategies when they are effectively managed. Being able to flexibly adapt partnerships is a crucial aspect of managing cooperative strategies.[146] The firm that learns how to manage cooperative strategies better than its competitors do may develop a competitive advantage in terms of this activity.[147] Because the ability to effectively manage cooperative strategies is unevenly distributed across organizations in general, assigning managerial responsibility for a firm's cooperative strategies to a high-level executive or to a team improves the likelihood that the strategies will be well managed.

Those responsible for managing the firm's set of cooperative strategies coordinate activities, categorize knowledge learned from previous experiences, and make certain that what the firm knows about how to effectively form and use cooperative strategies is in the hands of the right people at the right time. Firms use one of two primary approaches to manage cooperative strategies—cost minimization and opportunity maximization[148] (see Figure 9.4). This is the case whether the firm has formed a separate cooperative strategy management function or not.

In the *cost minimization* management approach, the firm develops formal contracts with its partners. These contracts specify how the cooperative strategy is to be monitored and how partner behavior is to be controlled. The goal of this approach is to minimize the cooperative strategy's cost and to prevent opportunistic behavior by a partner. The focus of the second managerial approach—*opportunity maximization*—is on maximizing a partnership's value-creation opportunities. In this case, partners are prepared to take advantage of unexpected opportunities to learn from each other and to explore additional marketplace possibilities. Less formal contracts, with fewer constraints on partners' behaviors, make it possible for partners to explore how their resources and capabilities can be shared in multiple value-creating ways.

Firms can successfully use either approach to manage cooperative strategies. However, the costs to monitor the cooperative strategy are greater with cost minimization, in that writing detailed contracts and using extensive monitoring mechanisms is expensive, even though the approach is intended to reduce alliance costs. Although monitoring systems may prevent partners from acting in their own best interests, they also preclude positive responses to those situations where opportunities to use the alliance's competitive advantages surface unexpectedly. Thus, formal contracts and extensive monitoring systems tend to stifle partners' efforts to gain maximum value from their participation in a cooperative strategy and require significant resources to put into place and use.[149]

For example, Sony Ericsson Mobile Communications was a joint venture formed by Sony and Ericsson to become the top seller of multimedia mobile-phone handsets. Although it was growing at three times the overall market rate in its core areas, the venture posted a loss for the second quarter of 2003. Notably, the loss was attributed to costs from job cuts and closing units, such as research parks in Munich, Germany, and North Carolina. Such cost-cutting activities may create difficulties for strategic alliances built to explore opportunities. "The question is whether they can continue such an exceptional performance given that they are cutting costs rather than growing."[150]

The relative lack of detail and formality that is a part of the contract developed by firms using the second management approach of opportunity maximization means that firms need to trust each other to act in the partnership's best interests. A psychological state, *trust* is a willingness to be vulnerable because of the expectations of positive behavior from the firm's alliance partner.[151] When partners trust each other, there is less need to write detailed formal contracts to specify each firm's alliance behaviors,[152] and the cooperative relationship tends to be more stable.[153] On a relative basis, trust tends to be more difficult to establish in international cooperative strategies compared to domestic ones. Differences in trade policies, cultures, laws, and politics that are part of cross-border alliances account for the increased difficulty.[154] When trust exists, partners' monitoring costs are reduced and opportunities to create value are maximized.[155]

Research showing that trust between partners increases the likelihood of alliance success[156] seems to highlight the benefits of the opportunity maximization approach to managing cooperative strategies. Trust may also be the most efficient way to influence and control alliance partners' behaviors.[157] Research indicates that trust can be a capability that is valuable, rare, imperfectly imitable, and often nonsubstitutable.[158] Thus, firms known to be trustworthy can have a competitive advantage in terms of how they develop and use cooperative strategies both internally and externally.[159] One reason is that it is impossible to specify all operational details of a cooperative strategy in a formal contract. Confidence that its partner can be trusted reduces the firm's concern about the inability to contractually control all alliance details.

Summary

- A cooperative strategy is one in which firms work together to achieve a shared objective. Strategic alliances, cooperative strategies in which firms combine some of their resources and capabilities to create a competitive advantage, are the primary form of cooperative strategies. Joint ventures (where firms create and own equal shares of a new venture that is intended to develop competitive advantages), equity strategic alliances (where firms own different shares of a newly created venture), and non-equity strategic alliances (where firms cooperate through a contractual relationship) are the three basic types of strategic alliances. Outsourcing, discussed in Chapter 3, commonly occurs as firms form nonequity strategic alliances.

- Collusive strategies are the second type of cooperative strategies (with strategic alliances being the other). In many economies and certainly developed ones, explicit collusive strategies are illegal unless sanctioned by government policies. With increasing globalization, fewer government-sanctioned situations of explicit collusion exist. Tacit collusion, also called mutual forbearance, is a cooperative strategy through which firms tacitly cooperate to reduce industry output below the potential competitive output level, thereby raising prices above the competitive level.

- Reasons firms use cooperative strategies vary by slow-cycle, fast-cycle, and standard-cycle market conditions. To enter restricted markets (slow-cycle), to move quickly from one competitive advantage to another (fast-cycle), and to gain market power (standard-cycle) demonstrate the differences among reasons by market type for use of cooperative strategies.

- There are four business-level cooperative strategies (a business-level cooperative strategy is used to help the firm improve its performance in individual product markets). Through vertical and horizontal complementary alliances, companies combine their resources and capabilities to create value in different parts (vertical) or the same parts (horizontal) of the value chain. Competition responding strategies are formed to respond to competitors' actions, especially strategic ones. Competition reducing strategies are used to avoid excessive competition while the firm marshals its resources and capabilities to improve its competitiveness. Uncertainty reducing strategies are used to hedge against the risks created by the conditions of uncertain competitive environments (such as new product markets). Complementary alliances have the highest probability of yielding a sustainable competitive advantage; competition reducing alliances have the lowest probability of doing so.

- Corporate-level cooperative strategies are used when the firm wants to pursue product and/or geographic diversification. Through diversifying strategic alliances, firms agree to share some of their resources and capabilities to enter new markets or produce new products. Synergistic alliances are ones where firms share resources and capabilities to develop economies of scope. This alliance is similar to the business-level horizontal complementary alliance in which firms try to develop operational synergy whereas synergistic alliances are used to develop synergy at the corporate level. Franchising is a corporate-level cooperative strategy where the franchisor uses a franchise as a contractual relationship to describe the sharing of its resources and capabilities with franchisees.

- As an international cooperative strategy, a cross-border alliance is used for several reasons, including the performance superiority of firms competing in markets outside their domestic market and governmental restrictions on growth through mergers and acquisitions. Cross-border alliances tend to be riskier than their domestic counterparts, particularly when partners aren't fully aware of each other's purpose for participating in the partnership.

- A network cooperative strategy is one wherein several firms agree to form multiple partnerships to achieve shared objectives. One of the primary benefits of a network cooperative strategy is the firm's opportunity to gain access "to its partner's other partnerships." When this happens, the probability greatly increases that partners will find unique ways to uniquely share their resources and capabilities to form competitive advantages. Network cooperative strategies are used to form either a stable alliance network or a dynamic alliance network. Used in mature industries, partners use stable networks to extend competitive advantages into new areas. In rapidly changing environments where frequent product innovations occur, dynamic networks are primarily used as a tool of innovation.

- Cooperative strategies aren't risk free. If a contract is not developed appropriately, or if a partner misrepresents its competencies or fails to make them available, failure is likely. Furthermore, a firm may be held hostage through asset-specific investments made in conjunction with a partner, which may be exploited.

- Trust is an increasingly important aspect of successful cooperative strategies. Firms recognize the value of partnering with companies known for their trustworthiness. When trust exists, a cooperative strategy is managed to maximize the pursuit of opportunities between partners. Without trust, formal contracts and extensive monitoring systems are used to manage cooperative strategies. In this case, the interest is to minimize costs rather than to maximize opportunities by participating in a cooperative strategy.

Review Questions

1. What is the definition of cooperative strategy and why is this strategy important to firms competing in the 21st-century competitive landscape?

2. What is a strategic alliance? What are the three types of strategic alliances firms use to develop a competitive advantage?

3. What are the four business-level cooperative strategies and what are the differences among them?

4. What are the three corporate-level cooperative strategies? How do firms use each one to create a competitive advantage?

5. Why do firms use cross-border strategic alliances?

6. What risks are firms likely to experience as they use cooperative strategies?

7. What are the differences between the cost-minimization approach and the opportunity-maximization approach to managing cooperative strategies?

Alliance Strategy

Assume that you are the CEO of Century Pharmaceuticals, Inc., seeking a strategic alliance with Excel Research, an independent, full-service research organization. Excel Research specializes in working with pharmaceutical companies to efficiently and effectively navigate the regulatory approval process and bring new drug therapies to market. Century will be consulting with Excel about submissions to the Food and Drug Administration (FDA) for new and current products as well as general development projects. As CEO, you believe that Century Pharmaceuticals and Excel Research can successfully work together to create novel therapies to fill unmet needs in dermatology and other therapeutic arenas.

You expect that the strategic alliance between Century Pharmaceuticals and Excel Research will provide enhanced benefits for both companies. Century, under your leadership, is committed to continuing to grow by implementing its differentiation strategy, which specifies the objectives of acquiring new products, extending the product life cycle of existing products, and introducing new uses for therapies in specific markets. Excel Research has an established and proven track record of success in supporting and providing the evaluation required to bring new therapies and new uses for existing therapies to market.

Based on this information, determine answers to the following questions and make a brief presentation to the class as the Board of Directors:

1. Is the above case a complementary strategic alliance? If so, what kind of complementary strategic alliance?

2. Is it a competition response strategy? If so, who are the competitors and what are they doing?

3. Is it an uncertainty reducing strategy? If so, how can uncertainty be reduced?

4. Is it a competition reducing strategy? If so, explain how it works.

Cooperative Strategy Risk

Your firm manufactures fasteners for industrial applications. As the senior vice president of sales, you have developed several long-term relationships with your customers. Your main competitor has recently approached you about establishing a strategic alliance with your firm.

1. Because you are not sure if this alliance would be beneficial to your firm, you decide to bring the proposal to your firm's executive committee for a preliminary discussion. You anticipate that the committee will ask several basic questions. What information should you be able to provide?

2. After several weeks of investigating the value of an alliance, your firm decides that it would be financially beneficial, but the executive committee now wants you to present the risks that an alliance might entail and how you would suggest minimizing them. What risks do you foresee? How can they be prevented?

3. Before a contract between your firm and your competitor can be signed, you begin negotiations with one of your competitor's largest customers to provide new products based on a new technology your firm has developed. In your opinion, does the alliance raise legal or ethical issues that your firm should consider before proceeding with your negotiations?

1. J. Hagedoorn & G. Dysters, 2002, External sources of innovative capabilities: The preference for strategic alliances or mergers and acquisitions, *Journal of Management Studies*, 39: 167–188; K. M. Eisenhardt, 2002, Has strategy changed? *MIT Sloan Management Review*, 43(2): 88–91; T. B. Lawrence, C. Hardy, & N. Phillips, 2002, Institutional effects of interorganizational collaborations: The emergence of proto-institutions, *Academy of Management Journal*, 45: 281–290; E. B. Roberts & W. K. Liu, 2002, Ally or acquire? *MIT Sloan Management Review*, 43(1): 26–34.

2. T. A. Hemphill, 2003, Cooperative strategy, technology innovation and competition policy in the United States and the European Union, *Technology Analysis & Strategic Management*, 15(1): 93–101; J. B. Barney, 2002, *Gaining and Sustaining Competitive Advantage*, 2nd ed., Upper Saddle River, NJ: Prentice-Hall, 339.

3. M. Takayama, C. Watanabe, & C. Griffy-Brown, 2002, Alliance strategy as a competitive strategy for successively creative new product development: The proof of the co-evolution of creativity and efficiency in the Japanese pharmaceutical industry, *Technovation*, 22(10): 607–614; W. S. Desarbo, K. Jedidi, & I. Sinha, 2001, Customer value in a heterogeneous market, *Strategic Management Journal*, 22: 845–857.

4. C. Young-Ybarra & M. Wiersema, 1999, Strategic flexibility in information technology alliances: The influence of transaction cost economics and social exchange theory, *Organization Science*, 10: 439–459; M. E. Porter & M. B. Fuller, 1986, Coalitions and global strategy, in M. E. Porter (ed.), *Competition in Global Industries*, Boston: Harvard Business School Press, 315–344.

5. M. A. Hitt, R. D. Ireland, S. M. Camp, & D. L. Sexton, 2002, Strategic entrepreneurship: Integrating entrepreneurial and strategic management perspectives, in M. A. Hitt, R. D. Ireland, S. M. Camp, & D. L. Sexton (eds.), *Strategic Entrepreneurship: Creating a New Mindset*, Oxford, UK: Blackwell Publishers, 8.

6. C. Garcia-Pont & N. Nohria, 2002, Local versus global mimetism: The dynamics of alliance formation in the automobile industry, *Strategic Management Journal*, 23: 307–321; S. Royer, 2002, Successful horizontal alliances between competitors: Evidence from the automobile industry, *International Journal of Human Resources Development and Management*, 2(3,4): 445–462.

7. J. Bowser, 2001, Strategic co-opetition: The value of relationships in the networked economy, *IBM Business Strategy Consulting*, http://www.ibm.com, March 12.

8. Barney, *Gaining and Sustaining Competitive Advantage*, 339.

9. D. Rigby & C. Zook, 2003, Open-market innovation, *Harvard Business Review*, 89(10): 80–89.

10. Y. L. Doz & G. Hamel, 1998, *Alliance Advantage: The Art of Creating Value through Partnering*, Boston: Harvard Business School Press, xiii.

11. R. D. Ireland, M. A. Hitt, & D. Vaidyanath, 2002, Alliance management as a source of competitive advantage, *Journal of Management*, 28: 413–446; J. G. Coombs & D. J. Ketchen, 1999, Exploring interfirm cooperation and performance: Toward a reconciliation of predictions from the resource-based view and organizational economics, *Strategic Management Journal*, 20: 867–888.

12. M. R. Subramani & N. Venkatraman, 2003, Safeguarding investments in asymmetric interorganizational relationships: Theory and evidence, *Academy of Management Journal*, 46(1): 46–62; P. Kale, H. Singh, & H. Perlmutter, 2000, Learning and protection of proprietary assets in strategic alliances: Building relational capital, *Strategic Management Journal*, 21: 217–237.

13. P. Kale, J. H. Dyer, & H. Singh, 2002, Alliance capability, stock market response, and long-term alliance success: The role of the alliance function, *Strategic Management Journal*, 23: 747–767; D. F. Kuratko, R. D. Ireland, & J. S. Hornsby, 2001, Improving firm performance through entrepreneurial actions: Acordia's corporate entrepreneurship strategy, *Academy of Management Executive*, 15(4): 60–71.

14. 2002, Borrego blurs traditional lines, *Dallas Morning News*, February 24, M4.

15. A. Antoine, C. B. Frank, H. Murata, & E. Roberts, 2003, Acquisitions and alliances in the aerospace industry: An unusual triad, *International Journal of Technology Management*, 25(8): 779–790; 2002, Lockheed Martin, Responsive global partnerships, http://www.lockheedmartin.com, March 17.

16. Ireland, Hitt, & Vaidyanath, Alliance management as a source of competitive advantage; J. H. Tiessen & J. D. Linton, 2000, The JV dilemma: Cooperating and competing in joint ventures, *Revue Canadienne des Sciences de l'Administration*, 17(3): 203–216.

17. M. Harvey, M. B. Myers, & M. M. Novicevic, 2003, The managerial issues associated with global account management: A relational contract perspective, *Journal of Management Development*, 22(1,2): 103–129; T. K. Das & B.-S. Teng, 2001, A risk perception model of alliance structuring, *Journal of International Management*, 7: 1–29; J. H. Dyer & H. Singh, 1998, The relational view: Cooperative strategy and sources of interorganizational competitive advantage, *Academy of Management Review*, 23: 660–679.

18. A. Afuah, 2002, Mapping technological capabilities into product markets and competitive advantage: The case of cholesterol drugs, *Strategic Management Journal*, 23: 171–179; A. Arino, 2001, To do or not to do? Non-cooperative behavior by commission and omission in interfirm ventures, *Group & Organization Management*, 26(1): 4–23; C. Holliday, 2001, Sustainable growth, the DuPont way, *Harvard Business Review*, 79(8): 129–134.

19. Y. Kim & K. Lee, 2003, Technological collaboration in the Korean electronic parts industry: Patterns and key success factors, *R&D Management*, 33(1): 59–77; M. A. Geletkanycz & S. S. Black, 2001, Bound by the past? Experience-based effects on commitment to the strategic status quo, *Journal of Management*, 27: 3–21.

20. S. L. Berman, J. Down, & C. W. L. Hill, 2002, Tacit knowledge as a source of competitive advantage in the National Basketball Association, *Academy of Management Journal*, 45: 13–31.

21. Tiessen & Linton, The JV dilemma, 206; P. E. Bierly III & E. H. Kessler, 1999, The timing of strategic alliances, in M. A. Hitt, P. G. Clifford, R. D. Nixon, & K. P. Coyne (eds.), *Dynamic Strategic Resources: Development, Diffusion and Integration*, Chichester: John Wiley & Sons, 299–345.

22. M. Clifford, 2003, Concrete lessons in reform, *BusinessWeek Online*, http://www.businessweek.com, June 16.

23. R. E. Hoskisson & L. W. Busenitz, 2002, Market uncertainty and learning distance in corporate entrepreneurship entry mode choice, in M. A. Hitt, R. D. Ireland, S. M. Camp, & D. L. Sexton (eds.), *Strategic Entrepreneurship: Creating a New Mindset*, Oxford, UK: Blackwell Publishers, 151–172.

24. A.-W. Harzing, 2002, Acquisitions versus greenfield investments: International strategy and management of entry modes, *Strategic Management Journal*, 23: 211–227; S.-J. Chang & P. M. Rosenzweig, 2001, The choice of entry mode in sequential foreign direct investment, *Strategic Management Journal*, 22: 747–776; Y. Pan, 1997, The formation of Japanese and U.S. equity joint ventures in China, *Strategic Management Journal*, 18: 247–254.

25. J. T. Areddy, 2003, Citigroup may bolster 5% stake in Pudong Development Bank, *Wall Street Journal*, January 6, C7; 2003, Citibank can boost China stake, *Wall Street Journal*, April 28, C11.

26. S. Das, P. K. Sen, & S. Sengupta, 1998, Impact of strategic alliances on firm valuation, *Academy of Management Journal*, 41: 27–41.

27. Bierly & Kessler, The timing of strategic alliances, 303.

28. T. B. Folta & K. D. Miller, 2002, Real options in equity partnerships, *Strategic Management Journal*, 23: 77–88; Barney, *Gaining and Sustaining Competi-*

tive Advantage, 339; S. D. Hunt, C. J. Lambe, & C. M. Wittmann, 2002, A theory and model of business alliance success, *Journal of Relationship Marketing*, 1(1): 17–35.

29. M. Pacelle, R. Sidel, & A. Merrick, 2003, Citigroup agrees to buy Sears's credit-card unit, *Wall Street Journal Online*, http://www.wsj.com, July 15.

30. A. Hinterhuber, 2002, Value chain orchestration in action and the case of the global agrochemical industry, *Long Range Planning*, 35(6): 615–635; A. C. Inkpen, 2001, Strategic alliances, in M. A. Hitt, R. E. Freeman, & J. S. Harrison (eds.), *Handbook of Strategic Management*, Oxford, UK: Blackwell Publishers, 409–432.

31. M. Delio, 1999, Strategic outsourcing, *Knowledge Management*, 2(7): 62–68.

32. E. Chabrow, 2003, Creative pressure, *InformationWeek*, June 16, 38–44.

33. J. J. Reuer, M. Zollo, & H. Singh, 2002, Post-formation dynamics in strategic alliances, *Strategic Management Journal*, 23: 135–151.

34. D. Campbell, 2001, High-end strategic alliances as fundraising opportunities, *Nonprofit World*, 19(5): 8–12; M. D. Hutt, E. R. Stafford, B. A. Walker, & P. H. Reingen, 2000, Case study: Defining the social network of a strategic alliance, *Sloan Management Review*, 41(2): 51–62.

35. M. J. Kelly, J.-L. Schaan, & H. Jonacas, 2002, Managing alliance relationships: Key challenges in the early stages of collaboration, *R&D Management*, 32(1): 11–22.

36. A. C. Inkpen & J. Ross, 2001, Why do some strategic alliances persist beyond their useful life? *California Management Review*, 44(1): 132–148.

37. M. Schifrin, 2001, Partner or perish, *Forbes*, May 21, 28.

38. C. Hardy, N. Phillips, & T. B. Lawrence, 2003, Resources, knowledge and influence: The organizational effects of interorganizational collaboration, *Journal of Management Studies*, 40(2): 321–347; Inkpen, Strategic alliances, 411.

39. L. Fuentelsaz, J. Gomez, & Y. Polo, 2002, Followers' entry timing: Evidence from the Spanish banking sector after deregulation, *Strategic Management Journal*, 23: 245–264.

40. K. R. Harrigan, 2001, Strategic flexibility in the old and new economies, in M. A. Hitt, R. E. Freeman, & J. S. Harrison (eds.), *Handbook of Strategic Management*, Oxford, UK: Blackwell Publishers, 97–123.

41. D. M. Amato-McCoy, 2003, Outsourced private label credit card program brings flexibility in-house, *Stores*, 85(2): 38–40.

42. G. W. Dent, Jr., 2001, Gap fillers and fiduciary duties in strategic alliances, *Business Lawyer*, 57(1): 55–104.

43. S. Ulfelder, 2001, Partners in profit, *Computerworld*, July/August, 24–28.

44. M. Gonzalez, 2001, Strategic alliances, *Ivey Business Journal*, 66(1): 47–51.

45. M.-J. Oesterle & K. Macharzina, 2002, Editorial: De-regulation, liberalization, and concentration in the airline industry, *Management International Review*, 42(2): 115–119; M. Johnson, 2001, Airlines rush for comfort alliances, *Global Finance*, 15(11): 119–120.

46. J. Child & D. Faulkner, 1998, *Strategies of Co-operation: Managing Alliances, Networks, and Joint Ventures*, New York: Oxford University Press.

47. J. R. Williams, 1998, *Renewable Advantage: Crafting Strategy through Economic Time*, New York: The Free Press.

48. M. Arndt, 2003, Up from the scrap heap, *BusinessWeek Online*, http://www.businessweek.com, July 21.

49. J. Slater, 2002, India seeds a new market, *Far Eastern Economic Review*, October 31, 50–51.

50. Ibid.; V. Kumari, 2001, Joint ventures bolster credibility of new players in India, *National Underwriter*, 105(14): 46.

51. S. A. Zahra, R. D. Ireland, I. Gutierrez, & M. A. Hitt, 2000, Privatization and entrepreneurial transformation: Emerging issues and a future research agenda, *Academy of Management Review*, 25: 509–524.

52. I. Filatotchev, M. Wright, K. Uhlenbruck, L. Tihanyi, & R. E. Hoskisson, 2003, Governance, organizational capabilities, and restructuring in transition economies, *Journal of World Business*, in press.

53. Eisenhardt, Has strategy changed? 88.

54. M. Dell, 2003, Collaboration equals innovation, *InformationWeek*, January 27, 24–26; H. D'Antoni, 2003, Behind the numbers: Business alliances merit closer examination, *InformationWeek*, January 27, 88.

55. H. W. Chesbrough, 2002, Making sense of corporate venture capital, *Harvard Business Review*, 80(3): 90–99.

56. C. Braunschweig, 2003, Big write-downs won't slow Intel Capital, *Venture Capital Journal*, March 1, 1.

57. D. Michaels & J. L. Lunsford, 2003, Airlines move toward buying planes jointly, *Wall Street Journal*, May 20, A3.

58. E. Nelson & M. Peros, 2003, Vivendi, GE sign pact, shift focus to acquiring Diller stakes, *Wall Street Journal*, October 9, B6.

59. D. R. King, J. G. Covin, & H. Hegarty, 2003, Complementary resources and the exploitation of technological innovations, *Journal of Management*, 29: 589–606; J. S. Harrison, M. A. Hitt, R. E. Hoskisson, & R. D. Ireland, 2001, Resource complementarity in business combinations: Extending the logic to organizational alliances, *Journal of Management*, 27: 679–699; S. H. Park & G. R. Ungson, 1997, The effect of national culture, organizational complementarity, and economic motivation on joint venture dissolution, *Academy of Management Journal*, 40: 297–307.

60. Subramani & Venkatraman, Safeguarding investments in asymmetric interorganizational relationships.

61. 2003, Mottola joins Universal all-stars, *New York Times*, http://www.nytimes.com, July 13.

62. M. Kotabe & K. S. Swan, 1995, The role of strategic alliances in high technology new product development, *Strategic Management Journal*, 16: 621–636.

63. J. Li, 2003, Bell Canada, Microsoft in Internet service alliance, *Wall Street Journal Online*, http://www.wsj.com, June 16.

64. M. Ihlwan, L. Armstrong, & G. Edmondson, 2003, Hyundai's hurdles, *BusinessWeek Online*, http://www.businessweek.com, July 21.

65. A. Latour, 2003, BellSouth unveils DSL Lite service as Bells step up subscriber battle, *Wall Street Journal Online*, http://www.wsj.com, July 8.

66. Ibid.

67. A. Latour & P. Grant, 2003, SBC, Qwest strikes partnership with providers of satellite TV; alliances with EchoStar, DirecTV aim to fend off rivalry from cable firms, *Wall Street Journal*, July 22, B11.

68. S. Chatterjee, R. M. Wiseman, A. Fiegenbaum, & C. E. Devers, 2003, Integrating behavioural and economic concepts of risk into strategic management: The twain shall meet, *Long Range Planning*, 36(1), 61–80; Hitt, Ireland, Camp, & Sexton, Strategic Entrepreneurship, 9; R. G. McGrath, 1999, Falling forward: Real options reasoning and entrepreneurial failure, *Academy of Management Journal*, 22: 13–30.

69. Dow Jones, 2003, ABN, ShoreBank set up co to invest in developing economies, *Wall Street Journal Online*, http://www.wsj.com, July 10.

70. V. Alessio & L. Di Leo, 2003, Wind, NTT DoCoMo set up strategic alliance, *Wall Street Journal Online*, http://www.wsj.com, June 25.

71. Barney, *Gaining and Sustaining Competitive Advantage*, 339.

72. 2003, Cosmetics makers agree to give-aways, *Wall Street Journal*, July 21, B2.

73. D. Leahy & S. Pavelin, 2003, Follow-my-leader and tacit collusion, *International Journal of Industrial Organization*, 21(3): 439–454.

74. S. Jayachandran, J. Gimeno, & P. Rajan, 1999, Theory of multimarket competition: A synthesis and implications for marketing strategy, *Journal of Marketing*, 63(3): 49–66.

75. B. R. Golden & H. Ma, 2003, Mutual forbearance: The role of intrafirm integration and rewards, *Academy of Management Review*, 28: 479–493.

76. 2003, AOL, Microsoft vow messaging cooperation, *New York Times*, http://www.nytimes.com, June 4.

77. G. K. Price & J. M. Connor, 2003, Modeling coupon values for ready-to-eat breakfast cereals, *Agribusiness*, 19(2): 223–244.

78. G. K. Price, 2000, Cereal sales soggy despite price cuts and reduced couponing, *Food Review*, 23(2): 21–28.

79. S. B. Garland & A. Reinhardt, 1999, Making antitrust fit high tech, *Business Week*, March 22, 34–36.

80. E. G. Rogoff & H. S. Guirguis, 2002, Legalized price-fixing, *Forbes*, December 9, 48.

81. G. Gari, 1999, Leveraging the rewards of strategic alliances, *Journal of Business Strategy*, 20(2): 40–43.

82. 2003, Who gains if United should die? *The Economist*, May 10, 56.

83. Leahy & Pavelin, Follow-my-leader and tacit collusion.

84. Harrison, Hitt, Hoskisson, & Ireland, Resource complementarity, 684–685; S. Chaudhuri & B. Tabrizi, 1999, Capturing the real value in high-tech acquisitions, *Harvard Business Review*, 77(5): 123–130; J.-F. Hennart & S. Reddy, 1997, The choice between mergers/acquisitions and joint ventures in the United States, *Strategic Management Journal*, 18: 1–12.

85. A. E. Bernardo & B. Chowdhry, 2002, Resources, real options, and corporate strategy, *Journal of Financial Economics*, 63: 211–234; Inkpen, Strategic alliances, 413.

86. J. L. Johnson, R. P.-W. Lee, A. Saini, & B. Grohmann, 2003, Market-focused strategic flexibility: Conceptual advances and an integrative model, *Academy of Marketing Science Journal*, 31: 74–90; Young-Ybarra & Wiersema, Strategic flexibility, 439.

87. Folta & Miller, Real options in equity partnerships, 77.

88. 2002, CNOOC adds petrochemicals to downstream strategy, *Petroleum Economist*, December, 39.

89. Ibid.

90. J. Yang, 2003, One step forward for Japan's chipmakers, *BusinessWeek Online*, http://www.businessweek.com, July 7.

91. M. Allen & E. Porter, 2003, Grupo Televisa chief considers U.S. citizenship to pursue bid, *Wall Street Journal Online*, http://www.wsj.com, July 1.

92. J. G. Combs & D. J. Ketchen, Jr., 2003, Why do firms use franchising as an entrepreneurial strategy? A meta-analysis, *Journal of Management*, 29: 427–443; S. A. Shane, 1996, Hybrid organizational arrangements and their implications for firm growth and survival: A study of new franchisers, *Academy of Management Journal*, 39: 216–234.

93. F. Lafontaine, 1999, Myths and strengths of franchising, "Mastering Strategy" (Part Nine), *Financial Times*, November 22, 8–10.

94. G. G. Marcial, 2003, Cendant comes back, *Business Week*, May 12, 110; L. Fenwick, 2001, Emerging markets: Defining global opportunities, *Franchising World*, 33(4): 54–55.

95. J. Wilgoren, 2003, In the urban 7-Eleven, the Slurpee looks sleeker, *New York Times*, http://www.nytimes.com, July 13.

96. S. C. Michael, 2002, Can a franchise chain coordinate? *Journal of Business Venturing*, 17: 325–342; R. P. Dant & P. J. Kaufmann, 1999, Franchising and the domain of entrepreneurship research, *Journal of Business Venturing*, 14: 5–16.

97. M. Gerstenhaber, 2000, Franchises can teach us about customer care, *Marketing*, March 16, 18.

98. P. J. Kaufmann & S. Eroglu, 1999, Standardization and adaptation in business format franchising, *Journal of Business Venturing*, 14: 69–85.

99. S. C. Michael, 2002, First mover advantage through franchising, *Journal of Business Venturing*, 18: 61–81; L. Wu, 1999, The pricing of a brand name product: Franchising in the motel services industry, *Journal of Business Venturing*, 14: 87–102.

100. Barney, *Gaining and Sustaining Competitive Advantage*, 110–111.

101. D. Blank, 2003, La Quinta moves ahead with long-term plans, *Hotel and Motel Management*, 218(8): 28; J. Higley, 2000, La Quinta jumps into franchising, *Hotel and Motel Management*, 215(13): 1, 54.

102. M. Zollo, J. J. Reuer, & H. Singh, 2002, Interorganizational routines and performance in strategic alliances, *Organization Science*, 13: 701–714; P. J. Buckley & M. Casson, 1996, An economic model of international joint venture strategy, *Journal of International Business Studies*, 27: 849–876; M. J. Dowling & W. L. Megginson, 1995, Cooperative strategy and new venture performance: The role of business strategy and management experience, *Strategic Management Journal*, 16: 565–580.

103. Ireland, Hitt, & Vaidyanath, Alliance management.

104. P. Almeida, G. Dokko, & L. Rosenkopf, 2003, Startup size and the mechanisms of external learning: Increasing opportunity and decreasing ability? *Research Policy*, 32(2): 301–316; B. L. Simonin, 1997, The importance of collaborative know-how: An empirical test of the learning organization, *Academy of Management Journal*, 40: 1150–1174.

105. H. Timmons, 2003, BP signs deal with Russian firm for venture in oil and gas, *New York Times*, June 27, W1.

106. M. A. Hitt, M. T. Dacin, E. Levitas, J.-L. Arregle, & A. Borza, 2000, Partner selection in emerging and developed market contexts: Resource-based and organizational learning perspectives, *Academy of Management Journal*, 43: 449–467; M. D. Lord & A. L. Ranft, 2000, Organizational learning about new international markets: Exploring the internal transfer of local market knowledge, *Journal of International Business Studies*, 31: 73–589.

107. D. Kovaleski, 2003, More firms shaking hands on strategic partnership agreements, *Pensions & Investments*, February 3, 20; A. L. Velocci, Jr., 2001, U.S.-Euro strategic alliances will outpace company mergers, *Aviation Week & Space Technology*, 155(23): 56.

108. I. M. Manev, 2003, The managerial network in a multinational enterprise and the resource profiles of subsidiaries, *Journal of International Management*, 9: 133–152; M. A. Hitt, R. E. Hoskisson, & H. Kim, 1997, International diversification: Effects on innovation and firm performance in product diversified firms, *Academy of Management Journal*, 40: 767–798; R. N. Osborn & J. Hagedoorn, 1997, The institutionalization and evolutionary dynamics of interorganizational alliances and networks, *Academy of Management Journal*, 40: 261–278.

109. L. Nachum & D. Keeble, 2003, MNE linkages and localized clusters: Foreign and indigenous firms in the media cluster of Central London, *Journal of International Management*, 9: 171–192; J. Hagedoorn, 1995, A note on international market leaders and networks of strategic technology partnering, *Strategic Management Journal*, 16: 241–250.

110. S. Holmes, 2003, The real Nike news is happening abroad, *BusinessWeek Online*, http://www.businessweek.com, July 21.

111. 2002, H-P says it has alliance with NEC in Asia, *Wall Street Journal*, December 12, B2; A. Rogers, 2002, NEC, HP to form outsourcing services alliance, *CRN*, December 23–30, 70.

112. D. Roberts & M. L. Clifford, 2003, Morgan Stanley: What great wall? *BusinessWeek Online*, http://www.businessweek.com, July 28.

113. Ibid.

114. S. R. Miller & A. Parkhe, 2002, Is there a liability of foreignness in global banking? An empirical test of banks' x-efficiency, *Strategic Management Journal*, 23: 55–75; Y. Luo, 2001, Determinants of local responsiveness: Perspectives from foreign subsidiaries in an emerging market, *Journal of Management*, 27: 451–477.

115. G. A. Fowler, 2003, Starbucks' road to China, *Wall Street Journal Online*, http://www.wsj.com, July 14; J. Singer & M. Fackler, 2003, In Japan, adding beer, wine to the latte list, *Wall Street Journal Online*, http://www.wsj.com, July 14.

116. S. Holmes, 2003, For Starbucks, there's no place like home, *BusinessWeek Online*, http://www.businessweek.com, June 9.

117. H. J. Teegen & J. P. Doh, 2002, US-Mexican alliance negotiations: Impact of culture on authority, trust, performance, *Thunderbird International Business Review*, 44(6): 749–775; P. Ghemawat, 2001, Distance matters: The hard reality of global expansion, *Harvard Business Review*, 79(8): 137–147.

118. J. K. Sebenius, 2002, The hidden challenge of cross-border negotiations, *Harvard Business Review*, 80(3): 76–85.

119. C. B. Copp & R. L. Ivy, 2001, Networking trends of small tourism businesses in post-socialist Slovakia, *Journal of Small Business Management*, 39: 345–353.

120. M. Ferrary, 2003, Managing the disruptive technologies life cycle by externalising the research: Social network and corporate venturing in the Silicon Valley, *International Journal of Technology Management*, 25(1,2): 165–180; S. S. Cohen & G. Fields, 1999, Social capital and capital gains in Silicon Valley, *California Management Review*, 41(2): 108–130; J. A. Matthews, 1999, A silicon island of the east: Creating a semiconductor

industry in Singapore, *California Management Review*, 41(2): 55–78; M. E. Porter, 1998, Clusters and the new economics of competition, *Harvard Business Review*, 78(6): 77–90; R. Pouder & C. H. St. John, 1996, Hot spots and blind spots: Geographical clusters of firms and innovation, *Academy of Management Review*, 21: 1192–1225.

121. A. C. Cooper, 2001, Networks, alliances, and entrepreneurship, in M. A. Hitt, R. D. Ireland, S. M. Camp, & D. L. Sexton (eds.), *Strategic Entrepreneurship: Creating a New Mindset*, Oxford, UK: Blackwell Publishers, 203–222.

122. C. Passariello, 2003, Doing the continental at Cannes, *BusinessWeek Online*, http://www.businessweek.com, May 23.

123. S. Chung & G. M. Kim, 2003, Performance effects of partnership between manufacturers and suppliers for new product development: The supplier's standpoint, *Research Policy*, 32: 587–604.

124. R. S. Cline, 2001, Partnering for strategic alliances, *Lodging Hospitality*, 57(9): 42.

125. M. Rudberg & J. Olhager, 2003, Manufacturing networks and supply chains: An operations strategy perspective, *Omega*, 31(1): 29–39.

126. G. J. Young, M. P. Charns, & S. M. Shortell, 2001, Top manager and network effects on the adoption of innovative management practices: A study of TQM in a public hospital system, *Strategic Management Journal*, 22: 935–951.

127. E. Garcia-Canal, C. L. Duarte, J. R. Criado, & A. V. Llaneza, 2002, Accelerating international expansion through global alliances: A typology of cooperative strategies, *Journal of World Business*, 37(2): 91–107; F. T. Rothaermel, 2001, Complementary assets, strategic alliances, and the incumbent's advantage: An empirical study of industry and firm effects in the biopharmaceutical industry, *Research Policy*, 30: 1235–1251.

128. V. Shankar & B. L. Bayus, 2003, Network effects and competition: An empirical analysis of the home video game industry, *Strategic Management Journal*, 24: 375–384.

129. B. Duncan, 2003, Five steps to successful strategic partnering, *InformationWeek*, http://www.informationweek.com, July 21.

130. Z. Simsek, M. H. Lubatkin, & D. Kandemir, 2003, Inter-firm networks and entrepreneurial behavior: A structural embeddedness perspective, *Journal of Management*, 29: 401–426; H. W. Volberda, C. Baden-Fuller, & F. A. J. van den Bosch, 2001, Mastering strategic renewal: Mobilising renewal journeys in multi-unit firms, *Long Range Planning*, 34(2): 159–178.

131. King, Covin, & Hegarty, Complementary resources and the exploitation of technological innovations.

132. A. I. Goldberg, G. Cohen, & A. Fiegenbaum, 2003, Reputation building: Small business strategies for successful venture development, *Journal of Small Business Management*, 41(2): 168–186; S. Das, P. K. Sen, & S. Sengupta, 2003, Strategic alliances: A valuable way to manage intellectual capital? *Journal of Intellectual Capital*, 4(1): 10–19.

133. D. C. Hambrick, J. Li, K. Xin, & A. S. Tsui, 2001, Compositional gaps and downward spirals in international joint venture management groups, *Strategic Management Journal*, 22: 1033–1053; T. K. Das & B.-S. Teng, 2000, Instabilities of strategic alliances: An internal tensions perspective, *Organization Science*, 11: 77–101.

134. M. P. Koza & A. Y. Lewin, 1999, Putting the S-word back in alliances, "Mastering Strategy" (Part Six), *Financial Times*, November 1, 12–13; S. H. Park & M. Russo, 1996, When cooperation eclipses competition: An event history analysis of joint venture failures, *Management Science*, 42: 875–890.

135. A. Madhok & S. B. Tallman, 1998, Resources, transactions and rents: Managing value through interfirm collaborative relationships, *Organization Science*, 9: 326–339.

136. D. De Cremer & D. van Knippenberg, 2002, How do leaders promote cooperation? The effects of charisma and procedural fairness, *Journal of Applied Psychology*, 87: 858–867.

137. S.-O. Cheung, T. S. T. Ng, S.-P. Wong, & H. C. H. Suen, 2003, Behavioral aspects in construction partnering, *International Journal of Project Management*, 21: 333–344.

138. P. M. Norman, 2002, Protecting knowledge in strategic alliances—Resource and relational characteristics, *Journal of High Technology Management Research*, 13(2): 177–202; P. M. Norman, 2001, Are your secrets safe? Knowledge protection in strategic alliances, *Business Horizons*, November/December, 51–60.

139. M. A. Hitt, M. T. Dacin, B. B. Tyler, & D. Park, 1997, Understanding the differences in Korean and U.S. executives strategic orientations, *Strategic Management Journal*, 18: 159–168.

140. 2003, Venu Srinivasan, *BusinessWeek Online*, http://www.businessweek.com, June 9.

141. P. Burrows, 2003, Cisco: In hot pursuit of a Chinese rival, *BusinessWeek Online*, http://www.businessweek.com, May 19.

142. R. Abratt & P. Motlana, 2002, Managing co-branding strategies: Global brands into local markets, *Business Horizons*, 45(5): 43–50; P. Lane, J. E. Salk, & M. A. Lyles, 2001, Absorptive capacity, learning, and performance in international joint ventures, *Strategic Management Journal*, 22: 1139–1161.

143. R. Grover, 2003, Is Steve about to move his cheese? *Business Week*, February 10, 72.

144. R. Larsson, K. R. Brousseau, M. J. Driver, & M. Homqvist, 2003, International growth through cooperation: Brand-driven strategies, leadership, and career development in Sweden, *Academy of Management Executive*, 17(1): 7–21; R. Larsson, L. Bengtsson, K. Henriksson, & J. Sparks, 1998, The interorganizational learning dilemma: Collective knowledge development in strategic alliances, *Organization Science*, 9: 285–305.

145. Ireland, Hitt, & Vaidyanath, Alliance management.

146. Reuer, Zollo, & Singh, Post-formation dynamics, 148.

147. J. H. Dyer, P. Kale, & H. Singh, 2001, How to make strategic alliances work, *MIT Sloan Management Review*, 42(4): 37–43.

148. J. H. Dyer, 1997, Effective interfirm collaboration: How firms minimize transaction costs and maximize transaction value, *Strategic Management Journal*, 18: 535–556.

149. J. H. Dyer & C. Wujin, 2003, The role of trustworthiness in reducing transaction costs and improving performance: Empirical evidence from the United States, Japan, and Korea, *Organization Science*, 14: 57–69.

150. 2003, Sony Ericsson venture to close sites and cut 500 jobs, *New York Times*, http://www.nytimes.com, June 25; J. L. Schenker, 2003, Sony Ericsson posts loss despite sales gain, *New York Times*, http://www.nytimes.com, July 16.

151. Hutt, Stafford, Walker, & Reingen, Case study: Defining the social network, 53.

152. D. L. Ferrin & K. T. Dirks, 2003, The use of rewards to increase and decrease trust: Mediating processes and differential effects, *Organization Science*, 14(1): 18–31; D. F. Jennings, K. Artz, L. M. Gillin, & C. Christodouloy, 2000, Determinants of trust in global strategic alliances: Amrad and the Australian biomedical industry, *Competitiveness Review*, 10(1): 25–44.

153. V. Perrone, A. Zaheer, & B. McEvily, 2003, Free to be trusted? Boundary constraints on trust in boundary spanners, *Organization Science*, 14: 422–439; H. K. Steensma, L. Marino, & K. M. Weaver, 2000, Attitudes toward cooperative strategies: A cross-cultural analysis of entrepreneurs, *Journal of International Business Studies*, 31: 591–609.

154. J. Child & Y. Yan, 2003, Predicting the performance of international joint ventures: An investigation in China, *Journal of Management Studies*, 40(2): 283–320.

155. L. Huff & L. Kelley, 2003, Levels of organizational trust in individualist versus collectivist societies: A seven-nation study, *Organization Science*, 14(1): 81–90.

156. S. J. Carson, A. Madhok, R. Varman, & G. John, 2003, Information processing moderators of the effectiveness of trust-based governance in inter-firm R&D collaboration, *Organization Science*, 14(1): 45–56; A. Arino & J. de la Torre, 1998, Learning from failure: Towards an evolutionary model of collaborative ventures, *Organization Science*, 9: 306–325; J. B. Barney & M. H. Hansen, 1994, Trustworthiness: Can it be a source of competitive advantage? *Strategic Management Journal*, 15(Special Issue): 175–203.

157. Dyer & Wujin, The role of trustworthiness in reducing transaction costs and improving performance; R. Gulati & H. Singh, 1998, The architecture of cooperation: Managing coordination costs and appropriation concerns in strategic alliances, *Administrative Science Quarterly*, 43: 781–814; R. Gulati, 1996, Social structure and alliance formation patterns: A longitudinal analysis, *Administrative Science Quarterly*, 40: 619–652.

158. J. H. Davis, F. D. Schoorman, R. C. Mayer, & H. H. Tan, 2000, The trusted general manager and business unit performance: Empirical evidence of a competitive advantage, *Strategic Management Journal*, 21: 563–576; R. C. Mayer, J. H. Davis, & F. D. Schoorman, 1995, An integrative model of organizational trust, *Academy of Management Review*, 20: 709–734.

159. B. Hillebrand & W. G. Biemans, 2003, The relationship between internal and external cooperation: literature review and propositions, *Journal of Business Research*, 56: 735–744.

Part Three

Chapter 10
Corporate Governance

Chapter 11
Organizational Structure and Controls

Chapter 12
Strategic Leadership

Chapter 13
Strategic Entrepreneurship

Strategic Actions: Strategy Implementation

Corporate Governance

Chapter Ten 10

Knowledge Objectives

Studying this chapter should provide you with the strategic management knowledge needed to:

1. Define corporate governance and explain why it is used to monitor and control managers' strategic decisions.

2. Explain why ownership has been largely separated from managerial control in the modern corporation.

3. Define an agency relationship and managerial opportunism and describe their strategic implications.

4. Explain how three internal governance mechanisms—ownership concentration, the board of directors, and executive compensation—are used to monitor and control managerial decisions.

5. Discuss the types of compensation executives receive and their effects on strategic decisions.

6. Describe how the external corporate governance mechanism—the market for corporate control—acts as a restraint on top-level managers' strategic decisions.

7. Discuss the use of corporate governance in international settings, in particular in Germany and Japan.

8. Describe how corporate governance fosters ethical strategic decisions and the importance of such behaviors on the part of top-level executives.

Boards of directors are now under pressure to better control CEO pay and compensation. Given the amount of money involved, these decisions are integral to the strategic management process.

In light of the corporate scandals among large U.S. firms, the poor economy and bad performance of many companies, and the substantial layoffs and high unemployment engendered by the economy and poor corporate performance, high executive pay, especially for CEOs, has been controversial in the last few years. Given the substantial media publicity about CEO pay, scandals, and layoffs, many (e.g., union leaders, major investors, congressional representatives, and compensation experts) have questioned what they believe to be excessive pay received by CEOs. The question is, has this controversy and the heavy publicity changed pay practices in major corporations? The answer is twofold. In selected companies, changes have been made in pay practices, but in the aggregate, overall pay for CEOs remains largely unchanged.

Executive pay is difficult to compare because of the multiple components and comparison group. CEO pay, for example, is often composed of salary, bonuses, stock issued, and stock options. And, should total compensation include stock options valued at the time issued or the value when exercised? Also, average pay depends on the firms and the executives included in the group. For example, the *Wall Street Journal* reported that the top CEO pay in 2002 was $116.4 million given to Jeffrey Barbakow, CEO of Tenet Healthcare. The *Journal* focused on direct pay, however, including only the value of stock options exercised. Alternatively, *USA Today* reported the top CEO income for 2002 to be $188.8 million, given to Jeffrey Barbakow; but that figure included the value of options issued but not exercised. The *New York Times* reported that total CEO compensation declined by 20 percent in 2002 to an average $10.83 million, yet salaries, amount of stock received (not options), and other perquisites increased such that the median direct compensation grew by almost 17 percent. Therefore, the value of options decreased because of declines in the stock market, but boards of directors tried to "compensate" for this decline by increasing CEOs' direct compensation. These actions suggest that there have been few material changes in the CEO compensation practices in large U.S. firms.

Overall, CEO pay has remained high; the changes are relatively small. And, some CEOs are cashing out their stock holdings (or exercising options and then selling). In fact, if cashing out were included in the pay, Lee Raymond, CEO of ExxonMobil, would have been among those receiving the most compensation in 2002. And, Bill Gates sold $2.6 billion of Microsoft stock in 2002. But, some believe that potentially major changes are on the horizon. For example, some boards of directors are barring executives from making large sales of stock at one time. James Rogers, executive with Cinergy Corp., acquired 239,894 shares of stock by exercising options, but he is barred by policy from selling until 90 days after he leaves the company. Boards are now under strong pressure to better control CEO compensation and thus are more likely to take action than at any time in the past.

SOURCES: G. Strauss & B. Hansen, 2003, Bubble hasn't burst yet on CEO salaries despite the times, *USA Today,* http://www.usatoday.com, July 3; 2003, How CEO salary and bonus packages compare, *USA Today,* http://www.usatoday.com, July 3; 2003, How CEO compensation packages compare, *USA Today,* http://www.usatoday.com, July 3; 2003, Who made the biggest bucks, *Wall Street Journal Online,* http://www.wsj.com, April 14; J. Lublin, 2003, Why the get-rich-quick days for executives may be over, *Wall Street Journal Online,* http://www.wsj.com, April 14; J. Lublin, 2003, Under the radar, *Wall Street Journal Online,* http://www.wsj.com, April 14; L. Browning, 2003, The perks still flow (but with less fizz), *New York Times,* http://www.nytimes.com, April 6; D. Leonhardt, 2003, Is that your CEO cashing out? *New York Times,* http://www.nytimes.com, April 6; P. McGeehan, 2003, Again, money follows the pinstripes, *New York Times,* http://www.nytimes.com, April 6; S. Craig, 2003, Wall Street's CEOs still get fat paychecks despite woes, *Wall Street Journal Online,* http://www.wsj.com, March 4.

As the Opening Case illustrates, corporate governance is an increasingly important part of the strategic management process.[1] If the board makes the wrong decision in compensating the firm's strategic leader, the CEO, the shareholders, and the firm suffer. Compensation is used to motivate CEOs to act in the best interests of the firm—in particular, the shareholders. When they do, the firm's value should increase.

What are a CEO's actions worth? The Opening Case suggests that they are worth a significant amount in the United States. While some critics argue that U.S. CEOs are paid too much, the hefty increases in their compensation in recent years ostensibly have come from linking their pay to their firms' performance, and U.S. firms have performed better than many companies in other countries. However, research suggests that firms with a smaller pay gap between the CEO and other top executives perform better, especially when collaboration among top management team members is more important.[2] The performance improvement is attributed to better cooperation among the top management team members. Other research suggests that CEOs receive excessive compensation when corporate governance is the weakest.[3] Also, as noted in the Opening Case, there has been little change in the compensation practices used for top executives over the last several years despite increasing criticism. However, it appears that some changes in policy are beginning to occur, such as the restriction barring the selling of stock gained from options until after the executive's employment with the company ends.

Corporate governance represents the relationship among stakeholders that is used to determine and control the strategic direction and performance of organizations.[4] At its core, corporate governance is concerned with identifying ways to ensure that strategic decisions are made effectively.[5] Governance can also be thought of as a means corporations use to establish order between parties (the firm's owners and its top-level managers) whose interests may conflict. Thus, corporate governance reflects and enforces the company's values.[6] In modern corporations—especially those in the United States and the United Kingdom—a primary objective of corporate governance is to ensure that the interests of top-level managers are aligned with the interests of the shareholders. Corporate governance involves oversight in areas where owners, managers, and members of boards of directors may have conflicts of interest. These areas include the election of directors, the general supervision of CEO pay and more focused supervision of director pay, and the corporation's overall structure and strategic direction.[7]

Corporate governance has been emphasized in recent years because, as the Opening Case illustrates, corporate governance mechanisms occasionally fail to adequately monitor and control top-level managers' decisions. This situation has resulted in changes in governance mechanisms in corporations throughout the world, especially with respect to efforts intended to improve the performance of boards of directors. A second and more positive reason for this interest is that evidence suggests that a well-

Corporate governance *represents the relationship among stakeholders that is used to determine and control the strategic direction and performance of organizations.*

functioning corporate governance and control system can create a competitive advantage for an individual firm.[8] For example, one governance mechanism—the board of directors—has been suggested to be rapidly evolving into a major strategic force in U.S. business firms.[9] Thus, in this chapter, we describe actions designed to implement strategies that focus on monitoring and controlling mechanisms, which can help to ensure that top-level managerial actions contribute to the firm's strategic competitiveness and its ability to earn above-average returns.

Effective corporate governance is also of interest to nations.[10] As stated by one scholar, "Every country wants the firms that operate within its borders to flourish and grow in such ways as to provide employment, wealth, and satisfaction, not only to improve standards of living materially but also to enhance social cohesion. These aspirations cannot be met unless those firms are competitive internationally in a sustained way, and it is this medium- and long-term perspective that makes good corporate governance so vital."[11]

Corporate governance, then, reflects company standards, which in turn collectively reflect societal standards.[12] In many individual corporations, shareholders hold top-level managers accountable for their decisions and the results they generate. As with these individual firms and their boards, nations that effectively govern their corporations may gain a competitive advantage over rival countries. In a range of countries, but especially in the United States and the United Kingdom, the fundamental goal of business organizations is to maximize shareholder value.[13] Traditionally, shareholders are treated as the firm's key stakeholders, because they are the company's legal owners. The firm's owners expect top-level managers and others influencing the corporation's actions (for example, the board of directors) to make decisions that will result in the maximization of the company's value and, hence, of the owners' wealth.[14]

In the first section of this chapter, we describe the relationship providing the foundation on which the modern corporation is built: the relationship between owners and managers. The majority of this chapter is used to explain various mechanisms owners use to govern managers and to ensure that they comply with their responsibility to maximize shareholder value.

Three internal governance mechanisms and a single external one are used in the modern corporation (see Table 10.1). The three internal governance mechanisms we describe in this chapter are (1) ownership concentration, as represented by types of shareholders and their different incentives to monitor managers, (2) the board of directors, and (3) executive compensation. We then consider the market for corporate control, an external corporate governance mechanism. Essentially, this market is a set of potential owners seeking to acquire undervalued firms and earn above-average returns on their investments by replacing ineffective top-level management teams.[15] The chapter's focus then shifts to the issue of international corporate governance. We briefly describe governance approaches used in German and Japanese firms whose traditional governance structures are being affected by the realities of global competition. In part, this discussion suggests the possibility that the structures used to govern global companies in many different countries, including Germany, Japan, the United Kingdom, and the United States, are becoming more, rather than less, similar. Closing our analysis of corporate governance is a consideration of the need for these control mechanisms to encourage and support ethical behavior in organizations.

Importantly, the mechanisms discussed in this chapter can positively influence the governance of the modern corporation, which has placed significant responsibility and authority in the hands of top-level managers. The most effective managers understand their accountability for the firm's performance and respond positively to corporate governance mechanisms.[16] In addition, the firm's owners should not expect any single mechanism to remain effective over time. Rather, the use of several mechanisms allows owners to govern the corporation in ways that maximize strategic competitiveness and

Table 10.1

Corporate Governance Mechanisms

Internal Governance Mechanisms

Ownership Concentration

- Relative amounts of stock owned by individual shareholders and institutional investors

Board of Directors

- Individuals responsible for representing the firm's owners by monitoring top-level managers' strategic decisions

Executive Compensation

- Use of salary, bonuses, and long-term incentives to align managers' interests with shareholders' interests

External Governance Mechanism

Market for Corporate Control

- The purchase of a company that is underperforming relative to industry rivals in order to improve the firm's strategic competitiveness

increase the financial value of their firm. With multiple governance mechanisms operating simultaneously, however, it is also possible for some of the governance mechanisms to be in conflict.[17] Later, we review how these conflicts can occur.

Separation of Ownership and Managerial Control

Historically, the founder-owners and their descendants managed U.S. firms. In these cases, corporate ownership and control resided in the same persons. As firms grew larger, "the managerial revolution led to a separation of ownership and control in most large corporations, where control of the firm shifted from entrepreneurs to professional managers while ownership became dispersed among thousands of unorganized stockholders who were removed from the day-to-day management of the firm."[18] These changes created the modern public corporation, which is based on the efficient separation of ownership and managerial control. Supporting the separation is a basic legal premise suggesting that the primary objective of a firm's activities is to increase the corporation's profit and, thereby, the financial gains of the owners (the shareholders).[19]

The separation of ownership and managerial control allows shareholders to purchase stock, which entitles them to income (residual returns) from the firm's operations after paying expenses. This right, however, requires that they also take a risk that the firm's expenses may exceed its revenues. To manage this investment risk, shareholders maintain a diversified portfolio by investing in several companies to reduce their overall risk.[20] As shareholders diversify their investments over a number of corporations, their risk declines. The poor performance or failure of any one firm in which they invest has less overall effect. Thus, shareholders specialize in managing their investment risk.

In small firms, managers often are high percentage owners, so there is less separation between ownership and managerial control. In fact, there are a large number of family-owned firms in which ownership and managerial control are not separated. In the United States, families have a substantial ownership of at least one-third of the S&P top 500 firms. Furthermore, families own about 18 percent of the outstanding equity. And, family-owned firms perform better when a member of the family is CEO than when the CEO is an outsider.[21] In many countries outside the United States, such as in Latin America, Asia, and some European countries, family-owned firms represent the dominant form.[22] The primary purpose of most of these firms is to increase the family's wealth, which explains why a family CEO often is better than an outside CEO.[23] There are at least two critical issues for family-controlled firms. First, as they grow, they may not have access to all of the skills needed to effectively manage the firm and maximize its returns for the family. Thus, they may need outsiders. Also, as they grow, they may need to seek outside capital and thus give up some of the ownership. In these cases, protection of the minority owners' rights becomes important.[24] To avoid these potential problems, when these firms grow and become more complex, their owner-managers may contract with managerial specialists. These managers make major decisions in the owner's firm and are compensated on the basis of their decision-making skills. As decision-making specialists, managers are agents of the firm's owners and are expected to use their decision-making skills to operate the owners' firm in ways that will maximize the return on their investment.[25]

Without owner (shareholder) specialization in risk bearing and management specialization in decision making, a firm may be limited by the abilities of its owners to manage and make effective strategic decisions. Thus, the separation and specialization of ownership (risk bearing) and managerial control (decision making) should produce the highest returns for the firm's owners.

Shareholder value is reflected by the price of the firm's stock. As stated earlier, corporate governance mechanisms, such as the board of directors or compensation based on the performance of a firm, is the reason that CEOs show general concern about the firm's stock price. For example, Cisco earned the dubious honor in 2001 of losing the most in shareholder value: $156 billion for the year. Furthermore, it lost $456 billion between March 2000 and December 2001. On a more positive note, it is fair to report that over its lifetime, Cisco has created significant wealth for its investors and managers; it ranks 11th overall in regard to wealth creation.[26] And, while Cisco experienced a net loss of slightly over $1 billion in fiscal 2001, it had a net profit of more than $1.8 billion in fiscal 2002. And, its stock price in July 2003 (the end of its fiscal year) was approximately 8.5 percent higher than the highest price achieved in its fourth quarter of fiscal 2002.[27] As a result, Cisco's future is looking much brighter, and it is beginning to rebuild shareholder value.

*An **agency relationship** exists when one or more persons (the principal or principals) hire another person or persons (the agent or agents) as decision-making specialists to perform a service.*

Agency Relationships

The separation between owners and managers creates an agency relationship. An **agency relationship** exists when one or more persons (the principal or principals) hire another person or persons (the agent or agents) as decision-making specialists to perform a service.[28] Thus, an agency relationship exists when one party delegates decision-making responsibility to a second party for compensation (see Figure 10.1).[29] In addition to shareholders and top executives, other examples of agency relationships are consultants and clients and insured and insurer. Moreover, within organizations, an agency relationship exists between managers and their employees, as well as between top executives and the firm's owners.[30] In the modern corporation, managers must understand the links between these relationships and the firm's effectiveness.[31] Although the agency relationship between managers and their employees is important, in this chapter we focus on the agency relationship between the firm's owners (the principals) and top-level managers (the principals' agents), because this relationship is related directly to how the firm's strategies are implemented.

CEO John Chambers is helping to rebuild Cisco's lost shareholder value.

©Reuters NewMedia Inc./CORBIS

Figure 10.1 — An Agency Relationship

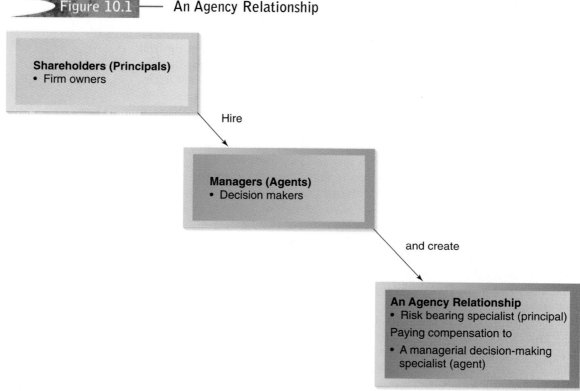

The separation between ownership and managerial control can be problematic. Research evidence documents a variety of agency problems in the modern corporation.[32] Problems can surface because the principal and the agent have different interests and goals, or because shareholders lack direct control of large publicly traded corporations. Problems also arise when an agent makes decisions that result in the pursuit of goals that conflict with those of the principals. Thus, the separation of ownership and control potentially allows divergent interests (between principals and agents) to surface, which can lead to managerial opportunism.

Managerial opportunism *is the seeking of self-interest with guile (i.e., cunning or deceit).*

Managerial opportunism is the seeking of self-interest with guile (i.e., cunning or deceit).[33] Opportunism is both an attitude (e.g., an inclination) and a set of behaviors (i.e., specific acts of self-interest).[34] It is not possible for principals to know beforehand which agents will or will not act opportunistically. The reputations of top executives are an imperfect predictor, and opportunistic behavior cannot be observed until it has occurred. Thus, principals establish governance and control mechanisms to prevent agents from acting opportunistically, even though only a few are likely to do so.[35] Any time that principals delegate decision-making responsibilities to agents, the opportunity for conflicts of interest exists. Top executives, for example, may make strategic decisions that maximize their personal welfare and minimize their personal risk.[36] Decisions such as these prevent the maximization of shareholder wealth. Decisions regarding product diversification demonstrate these possibilities.

Product Diversification as an Example of an Agency Problem

As explained in Chapter 6, a corporate-level strategy to diversify the firm's product lines can enhance a firm's strategic competitiveness and increase its returns, both of which serve the interests of shareholders and the top executives. However, product diversification can result in two benefits to managers that shareholders do not enjoy, so top executives may prefer more product diversification than do shareholders.[37]

First, diversification usually increases the size of a firm, and size is positively related to executive compensation. Also, diversification increases the complexity of managing a firm and its network of businesses and may thus require more pay because of this complexity.[38] Thus, increased product diversification provides an opportunity for top executives to increase their compensation.[39]

Second, product diversification and the resulting diversification of the firm's portfolio of businesses can reduce top executives' employment risk. Managerial employment risk is the risk of job loss, loss of compensation, and loss of managerial reputation.[40] These risks are reduced with increased diversification, because a firm and its upper-level managers are less vulnerable to the reduction in demand associated with a single or limited number of product lines or businesses. For example, Gemplus International named Antonio Perez as its CEO in 2000. With his 25-year career at Hewlett-Packard, Perez had a good reputation in the business world and his Hewlett-Packard experience seemed to be perfect preparation for his new position. Gemplus, headquartered at the time in France, is the world's top producer of smart cards (microchips used in telephones and credit cards), and is highly focused on a narrow product market. Perez' appointment was met with outrage by the French media over the $97 million worth of stock and options he received when he was hired. This focus has positive attributes, but the substantial downturn in telecommunications, the major market for smart cards, and the economic slump led to a major reduction in Gemplus' revenues and large net losses. Perez gave back the options trying to appease shareholders. However, the poor performance and a battle with the company founder led to Perez' resignation, forced by the firm's major shareholders. Perez' employment risk was higher because the firm lacked significant product diversification, which is probably why he received significant compensation in the form of stock and options when he began his tenure with Gemplus.[41] In fact, Gemplus has had two CEOs in the short time since Perez left, and has engaged in significant restructuring, showing the risks of low diversification.[42]

Another concern that may represent an agency problem is a firm's free cash flows over which top executives have control. Free cash flows are resources remaining after the firm has invested in all projects that have positive net present values within its current businesses.[43] In anticipation of positive returns, managers may decide to invest these funds in products that are not associated with the firm's current lines of business to increase the firm's level of diversification. The managerial decision to use free cash flows to overdiversify the firm is an example of self-serving and opportunistic managerial behavior. In contrast to managers, shareholders may prefer that free cash flows be distributed to them as dividends, so they can control how the cash is invested.[44]

Curve S in Figure 10.2 depicts the shareholders' optimal level of diversification. Owners seek the level of diversification that reduces the risk of the firm's total failure while simultaneously increasing the company's value through the development of economies of scale and scope (see Chapter 6). Of the four corporate-level diversification strategies shown in Figure 10.2, shareholders likely prefer the diversified position noted by point A on curve S—a position that is located between the dominant business and related-constrained diversification strategies. Of course, the optimum level of diversification owners seek varies from firm to firm.[45] Factors that affect shareholders' preferences include the firm's primary industry, the intensity of rivalry among competitors in that industry, and the top management team's experience with implementing diversification strategies.

As do principals, upper-level executives—as agents—also seek an optimal level of diversification. Declining performance resulting from too much product diversification increases the probability that corporate control of the firm will be acquired in the market. After a firm is acquired, the employment risk for the firm's top executives

Figure 10.2 —— Manager and Shareholder Risk and Diversification

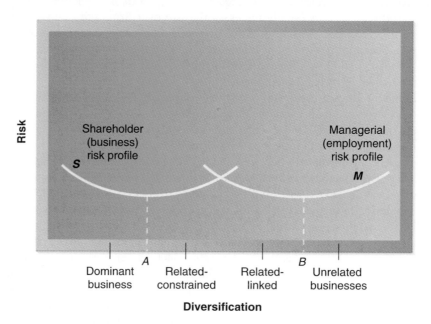

increases substantially. Furthermore, a manager's employment opportunities in the external managerial labor market (discussed in Chapter 12) are affected negatively by a firm's poor performance. Therefore, top executives prefer diversification, but not to a point that it increases their employment risk and reduces their employment opportunities.[46] Curve *M* in Figure 10.2 shows that executives prefer higher levels of product diversification than do shareholders. Top executives might prefer the level of diversification shown by point *B* on curve *M*.

In general, shareholders prefer riskier strategies and more focused diversification. They reduce their risk through holding a diversified portfolio of equity investments. Alternatively, managers obviously cannot balance their employment risk by working for a diverse portfolio of firms. Therefore, top executives may prefer a level of diversification that maximizes firm size and their compensation and that reduces their employment risk. Product diversification, therefore, is a potential agency problem that could result in principals incurring costs to control their agents' behaviors.

Agency Costs and Governance Mechanisms

The potential conflict illustrated by Figure 10.2, coupled with the fact that principals do not know which managers might act opportunistically, demonstrates why principals establish governance mechanisms. However, the firm incurs costs when it uses one or more governance mechanisms. **Agency costs** are the sum of incentive costs, monitoring costs, enforcement costs, and individual financial losses incurred by principals, because governance mechanisms cannot guarantee total compliance by the agent. If a firm is diversified, governance costs increase because it is more difficult to monitor what is going on inside the firm.[47]

In general, managerial interests may prevail when governance mechanisms are weak, as is exemplified by allowing managers a significant amount of autonomy to make strategic decisions. If, however, the board of directors controls managerial autonomy, or if other strong governance mechanisms are used, the firm's strategies should better reflect the interests of the shareholders.

Agency costs *are the sum of incentive costs, monitoring costs, enforcement costs, and individual financial losses incurred by principals, because governance mechanisms cannot guarantee total compliance by the agent.*

Research suggests that even using more governance mechanisms may produce major changes in strategies. Firms acquired unrelated businesses at approximately the same rate in the 1980s as they did in the 1960s, even though more governance mechanisms were employed in the 1980s. Thus, governance mechanisms are an imperfect means of controlling managerial opportunism.[48] Alternatively, other evidence suggests that active shareholders, especially institutional investors, are more willing to try to remove the CEO leading a firm that is performing poorly. The actions taken at Gemplus International, as explained above, demonstrate this willingness.[49]

Next, we explain the effects of different governance mechanisms on the decisions managers make about the choice and the use of the firm's strategies.

Ownership Concentration

Both the number of large-block shareholders and the total percentage of shares they own define **ownership concentration. Large-block shareholders** typically own at least 5 percent of a corporation's issued shares. Ownership concentration as a governance mechanism has received considerable interest because large-block shareholders are increasingly active in their demands that corporations adopt effective governance mechanisms to control managerial decisions.[50]

In general, diffuse ownership (a large number of shareholders with small holdings and few, if any, large-block shareholders) produces weak monitoring of managers' decisions. Among other problems, diffuse ownership makes it difficult for owners to effectively coordinate their actions. Diversification of the firm's product lines beyond the shareholders' optimum level can result from ineffective monitoring of managers' decisions. Higher levels of monitoring could encourage managers to avoid strategic decisions that harm shareholder value. In fact, research evidence shows that ownership concentration is associated with lower levels of firm product diversification.[51] Thus, with high degrees of ownership concentration, the probability is greater that managers' strategic decisions will be intended to maximize shareholder value. Much of this concentration has come from increasing equity ownership by institutional investors.

> Ownership concentration *is defined by both the number of large-block shareholders and the total percentage of shares they own.*

> Large-block shareholders *typically own at least 5 percent of a corporation's issued shares.*

The Growing Influence of Institutional Owners

A classic work published in the 1930s argued that the "modern" corporation had become characterized by a separation of ownership and control.[52] This change occurred primarily because growth prevented founders-owners from maintaining their dual positions in their increasingly complex companies. More recently, another shift has occurred: ownership of many modern corporations is now concentrated in the hands of institutional investors rather than individual shareholders.[53]

Institutional owners are financial institutions such as stock mutual funds and pension funds that control large-block shareholder positions. Because of their prominent ownership positions, institutional owners, as large-block shareholders, are a powerful governance mechanism. Institutions of these types now own more than 50 percent of the stock in large U.S. corporations, and of the top 1,000 corporations, they own, on average, 56 percent of the stock. Pension funds alone control at least one-half of corporate equity.[54]

> Institutional owners *are financial institutions such as stock mutual funds and pension funds that control large-block shareholder positions.*

These ownership percentages suggest that as investors, institutional owners have both the size and the incentive to discipline ineffective top-level managers and can significantly influence a firm's choice of strategies and overall strategic decisions.[55] Research evidence indicates that institutional and other large-block shareholders are becoming more active in their efforts to influence a corporation's strategic decisions. Initially, these shareholder activists and institutional investors concentrated on the performance and accountability of CEOs and contributed to the ouster of a number of them. They are now targeting what they believe are ineffective boards of directors.[56]

For example, CalPERS provides retirement and health coverage to over 1.3 million current and retired public employees.[57] As the largest public employee pension fund in the United States, CalPERS is generally thought to act aggressively to promote decisions and actions that it believes will enhance shareholder value in companies in which it invests. As noted in the Strategic Focus, CalPERS is currently focusing on problems with executive compensation as exemplified by the addition of executive pay to its corporate governance principles. However, CalPERS has also become a target because of concerns about its own governance. As a result, it announced in 2003 that it would begin releasing information on the performance of fund-of-fund investments (e.g., on Grove Street Advisors, which manages about $2 billion of CalPERS monies).[58] The largest institutional investor, TIAA-CREF, has taken actions similar to those of CalPERS, but with a less publicly aggressive stance. To date, research suggests that these institutions' activism may not have a direct effect on firm performance, but that its influence may be indirect through its effects on important strategic decisions, such as those concerned with international diversification and innovation.[59]

The Strategic Focus suggests that institutional investors are not the only ones who have become active. Small investors, such as in the case of John Hancock Financial Services, and large investors, such as KKR, a buyout firm that forced out a CEO with which it disagreed on strategy, are becoming more active on governance issues. Thus, shareholder activism has become an important issue related to corporate governance.

Shareholder Activism: How Much Is Possible?

The U.S. Securities and Exchange Commission (SEC) has issued several rulings that support shareholder involvement and control of managerial decisions. For example, the SEC eased its rule regarding communications among shareholders. Historically, shareholders could communicate among themselves only through a cumbersome and expensive filing process. Now, with a simple notification to the SEC of an upcoming meeting, shareholders can convene to discuss a corporation's strategic direction. If a consensus on an issue exists, shareholders can vote as a block. As a result of the new policies, proxy fights are becoming more common.[60]

Some argue that greater latitude should be extended to those managing the funds of large institutional investor groups, believing that allowing these individuals to hold positions on boards of firms in which their organizations have significant investments might enable fund managers to better represent the interests of those they serve.[61] However, the actions of traditionally activist institutional investor CalPERS were potentially compromised by investments it had in Enron. Institutional activism should create a premium for companies with good corporate governance. However, trustees for these funds sometimes have other relationships that compromise their effectiveness, as apparently was the case for CalPERS. It is more often the case that large *private* pension funds, which have other business relationships with companies in their fund's portfolio, reduce effective monitoring.[62] Alternatively, mutual funds such as the Vanguard Group also have increasing influence because of their substantial equity holdings.

Also, the degree to which institutional investors can effectively monitor the decisions being made in all of the companies in which they have investments is questionable. Historically, CalPERS targeted 12 companies at a time for improvement. The New York State Teachers' Retirement System, another activist institutional investor, focuses on 25 of the 1,300-plus companies in its investment portfolio. Given limited resources, even large-block shareholders tend to concentrate on corporations in which they have significant investments. Thus, although shareholder activism has increased, institutional investors face barriers to the amount of active governance they can realistically employ.[63] Furthermore, at times, activist institutional shareholders may have conflicting goals.[64] Other means of corporate governance are needed.

In addition to institutional owners, other owners are able to influence the decisions managers make as agents. Although other investors have significant influence, battles are

The Growing Activism of Shareholders

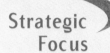

Institutional Shareholder Services Inc. (ISS) has developed a service that evaluates companies and ranks them based on the quality of their governance. ISS provides advice and information to institutional investors on proxy issues. It is a powerful organization that has over $40 million in revenue. An ISS rating results in a numerical score, but the criteria used provide guidelines for improving a firm's governance. Some of the criteria used for the evaluation include the percentage of outside board members, the independence of key board committees, the existence of poison pill defenses against takeovers, and the type and amount of executive compensation. Others provide these services, and some criteria in the ISS evaluation scheme have been criticized for lack of a basis in research. The ISS tool, called the Corporate Governance Quotient, has become influential, and many companies are buying access to it to improve their governance and ratings.

CalPERS (California Public Employees Retirement System) is a large institutional investor known for its activism. For example, in June 2003, it announced actions to ensure that firms carefully consider shareholders' interests when they develop executive compensation plans. These actions are designed to focus on abusive executive compensation. The leadership at CalPERS is especially concerned about practices that provide incentives, purposeful or otherwise, for short-term oriented or self-interested behavior on the part of executives. As an example, CalPERS actively opposed the planned $35 million "golden farewell" for the CEO of GlaxoSmithKline, Jean-Pierre Garnier, at the firm's annual shareholders' meeting held in 2003. While the vote was purely advisory to the board, it forced the board to publicly defend its actions.

Other shareholders are following CalPERS lead and taking up the gauntlet. For example, Halliburton shareholders expressed dissatisfaction that the board had developed severance agreements that shareholders considered excessive. Although a vote to require all future agreements to have shareholder approval failed, 36.5 percent voted for the measure, putting the board on notice. A lawsuit was filed against John Hancock Financial Services regarding excessive pay to its CEO and other senior executives. Highfields Capital Management, the largest shareholder in the Janus Capital Group, opposed a $15 million bonus for five executives because of the lack of disclosure in the 2002 proxy statement regarding significant compensation paid to top executives. Other top executives have been pressured by major shareholders to take specific actions. For example, shareholders pressured the CEO of Hollinger International, Lord Black, to restructure the shareholder voting procedures and to accept less compensation. More extreme, KKR, as a major shareholder, pressured the CEO of Primedia, Thomas Rogers, to resign.

Other institutional investors have become active in a different way. Jack Brennan is CEO of Vanguard Group, the second largest mutual fund with approximately $557 billion in assets in 2003. Brennan wrote a letter to 450 companies in which it owns at least 3 percent of the stock to express the emphasis that Vanguard now places on effective governance and honest accounting processes (and outcomes). Brennan believes that incentive pay for executives should be linked to long-term performance of the firm. His advice is being sought by such firms as General Electric on ways to make boards of directors more independent.

SOURCES: J. B. Treaster, 2003, Shareholder sues John Hancock over executive pay levels, *New York Times*, http://www.nytimes.com, May 29; S. Kirchgaessner & A. Beard, 2003, Hollinger chief bows to investor pressure, *Financial Times*, http://www.ft.com, May 23; 2003, Revolting shareholders, *The Economist*, http://www.economist.com, May 22; S. McNulty, 2003, Halliburton investors kick against pay, *Financial Times*, http://www.ft.com, May 21; G. Dyer, 2003, CalPERS to take stance on executive pay at GSK, *Financial Times*, http://www.ft.com, May 9; J. Earle, 2003, Investors oppose Janus bosses' $15m bonuses, *Financial Times*, http://www.ft.com, May 8; M. Rose, 2003, Pressured by KKR, Primedia CEO resigns, *Wall Street Journal*, April 18, B1, B3; J. Sonnenfeld, 2003, Some research is missing in governance quotients, *Wall Street Journal Online*, http://www.wsj.com, April 1; A. Lucchetti, 2003, Vanguard CEO Jack Brennan makes his demands heard, *Wall Street Journal Online*, http://www.wsj.com, February 6; M. Langley, 2003, Want to lift your firm's rating on governance? Buy the test, *Wall Street Journal*, June 6, A1, A6.

not likely to be won or lost unless institutional investors are involved because they currently are such significant shareholders. Texas billionaire Sam Wyly sold his company, Sterling Software, to Computer Associates in 2000. Wyly fought to elect a new Computer Associates board that would in turn elect him to be Computer Associates' chairman. He argued that Computer Associates, the fourth largest software company in the world, had not performed well since 1996 and had alienated customers and employees.[65] Wyly was unsuccessful in his attempt to take over the leadership of Computer Associates, but his revised plan won the support of CalPERS and other investors. Even though Wyly lost his attempt at leadership, Computer Associates made significant improvements in its corporate governance procedures. It made a commitment to financial transparency and to using "state-of-the-art" corporate governance principles. For example, it developed a policy of having 75 percent of the board members be independent outsiders and established a lead director position.[66]

Corporate governance may also by affected by the recent phenomenon of increased managerial ownership of the firm's stock. There are many positive reasons for managerial ownership. However, an unexpected outcome of managerial ownership has been reduced support for shareholder-sponsored proposals to repeal anti-takeover provisions. Institutional owners generally support the repeal of these provisions because shareholder wealth is typically increased if a takeover is offered, while managerial owners, whose jobs are at risk if a takeover is executed, generally oppose their repeal. Thus, managerial ownership provides managers with power to protect their own interests.[67]

Board of Directors

Typically, shareholders monitor the managerial decisions and actions of a firm through the board of directors. Shareholders elect members to their firm's board. Those who are elected are expected to oversee managers and to ensure that the corporation is operated in ways that will maximize its shareholders' wealth. Even with large institutional investors having major equity ownership in U.S. firms, diffuse ownership continues to exist in most firms, which means that monitoring and control of managers by individual shareholders is limited in large corporations. Furthermore, large financial institutions, such as banks, are prevented from directly owning stock in firms and from having representatives on companies' boards of directors, although this is not the case in Europe and elsewhere.[68] These conditions highlight the importance of the board of directors for corporate governance. Unfortunately, over time, boards of directors have not been highly effective in monitoring and controlling top management's actions.[69] As noted in the Strategic Focus, boards are experiencing increasing pressure from shareholders, lawmakers, and regulators to become more forceful in their oversight role and thereby forestall inappropriate actions by top executives. While boards of directors are imperfect, they have the potential to positively influence both managers and the companies they serve.[70] If changes are instituted as recommended by the panel described in the Strategic Focus, boards will have even more power to influence the actions of managers and the directions of their companies. Furthermore, boards not only serve a monitoring role, but they also provide resources to firms. These resources include their personal knowledge and expertise as well as their access to resources of other firms through their external contacts and relationships.[71]

The **board of directors** is a group of elected individuals whose primary responsibility is to act in the owners' interests by formally monitoring and controlling the corporation's top-level executives.[72] Boards have power to direct the affairs of the organization, punish and reward managers, and protect shareholders' rights and interests.[73] Thus, an appropriately structured and effective board of directors protects owners from managerial opportunism. Board members are seen as stewards of their company's resources, and the way they carry out these responsibilities affects the society in which their firm operates.[74]

The board of directors *is a group of elected individuals whose primary responsibility is to act in the owners' interests by formally monitoring and controlling the corporation's top-level executives.*

Generally, board members (often called directors) are classified into one of three groups (see Table 10.2). *Insiders* are active top-level managers in the corporation who are elected to the board because they are a source of information about the firm's day-to-day operations.[75] *Related outsiders* have some relationship with the firm, contractual or otherwise, that may create questions about their independence, but these individuals are not involved with the corporation's day-to-day activities. *Outsiders* provide independent counsel to the firm and may hold top-level managerial positions in other companies or may have been elected to the board prior to the beginning of the current CEO's tenure.[76]

Recently, a number of critics have argued that many boards are not fulfilling their primary fiduciary duty to protect shareholders. Among other possibilities, it may be that boards represent a managerial tool: they do not question managers' actions, and they readily approve managers' self-serving initiatives.[77] In general, those critical of boards as a governance mechanism believe that inside managers dominate boards and exploit their personal ties with them. A widely accepted view is that a board with a significant percentage of its membership from the firm's top executives tends to provide relatively weak monitoring and control of managerial decisions.[78]

Critics advocate reforms to ensure that independent outside directors represent a significant majority of the total membership of a board.[79] Critics have become highly vocal as indicated in the Strategic Focus. As suggested in the Strategic Focus, changes are likely to be made that strengthen the boards and weaken the power of CEOs, in particular. For example, Cendant Corporation has instituted major changes, including the requirement that two-thirds of the directors be independent outsiders. Recent research suggests that firms with more independent outside directors tend to make higher-quality strategic decisions.[80] Alternatively, others argue that having outside directors is not enough to resolve the problems; it depends on the power of the CEO. In some cases, the CEO's power reduces the effectiveness of outside board members.[81]

One criticism of boards has been that some have not been vigilant enough in hiring and then monitoring the behavior of CEOs. For example, Albert Dunlap, the former CEO at Sunbeam, agreed to settle a shareholder lawsuit brought against him (and other former executives) for $15 million out of his own pocket. A number of questionable acquisitions had been made by the Dunlap team, ultimately spreading the company too thin and causing Sunbeam to file for Chapter 11 bankruptcy.[82] The Sunbeam board must share the blame in the failure for two reasons. First, it selected the CEO. Second, the board should have been actively involved in the development of the firm's strategy—if the strategy fails, the board has failed.[83] Sunbeam emerged from bankruptcy in late 2002 and changed its name to American Household. The firm is not in good financial shape (its stock sold at less than four cents when it came out of bankruptcy). The former CEO and the board of Sunbeam obviously failed the shareholders.[84]

| Classifications of Boards of Directors' Members | Table 10.2 |

Insiders
- The firm's CEO and other top-level managers

Related outsiders
- Individuals not involved with the firm's day-to-day operations, but who have a relationship with the company

Outsiders
- Individuals who are independent of the firm in terms of day-to-day operations and other relationships

Other issues, in addition to criticisms of their work, affect today's corporate boards. For example, there is some disagreement about the most appropriate role of outside directors in a firm's strategic decision-making process.[85] In 1984, the New York Stock Exchange started requiring that listed firms have board audit committees composed solely of outside directors.[86] As a result of external pressures, boards of large corporations have more outside members. Therefore, there are potential strategic implications associated with the movement toward having corporate boards dominated by outsiders. But, with the recent scandals, the Sarbanes-Oxley corporate governance bill was passed and signed into law. It requires CEOs and chief financial officers (CFOs) to sign their accounting reports, certifying the reports' accuracy. They are threatened with criminal prosecution if they knowingly certify false documents. Thus, top executives have pressure to hire audit help to ensure the accuracy of their reports. Furthermore, their desire for a strong audit committee on the board of directors is increased.[87]

Alternatively, a large number of outside board members can also create some problems. Outsiders do not have contact with the firm's day-to-day operations and typically do not have easy access to the level of information about managers and their skills that is required to effectively evaluate managerial decisions and initiatives. Outsiders can, however, obtain valuable information through frequent interactions with inside board members, during board meetings and otherwise. Insiders possess such information by virtue of their organizational positions. Thus, boards with a critical mass of insiders typically are better informed about intended strategic initiatives, the reasons for the initiatives, and the outcomes expected from them.[88] Without this type of information, outsider-dominated boards may emphasize the use of financial, as opposed to strategic, controls to gather performance information to evaluate managers' and business units' performances. A virtually exclusive reliance on financial evaluations shifts risk to top-level managers, who, in turn, may make decisions to maximize their interests and reduce their employment risk. Reductions in R&D investments, additional diversification of the firm, and the pursuit of greater levels of compensation are some of the results of managers' actions to achieve financial goals set by outsider-dominated boards.[89]

Enhancing the Effectiveness of the Board of Directors

Because of the importance of boards of directors in corporate governance and as a result of increased scrutiny from shareholders—in particular, large institutional investors—the performances of individual board members and of entire boards are being evaluated more formally and with greater intensity.[90] Given the demand for greater accountability and improved performance, many boards have initiated voluntary changes. Among these changes are (1) increases in the diversity of the backgrounds of board members (for example, a greater number of directors from public service, academic, and scientific settings; a greater percentage of boards with ethnic minorities and women; and members from different countries on boards of U.S. firms), (2) the strengthening of internal management and accounting control systems, and (3) the establishment and consistent use of formal processes to evaluate the board's performance.[91] Additional changes suggested in the

Renault board of directors during a typical business meeting. Increased pressure is being applied to all boards of directors for greater accountability and improved performance. One of the many cited areas in need of improvement is increased diversity, because many boards are still composed primarily of Caucasian males.

©PITCHAL FREDERIC/CORBIS SYGMA

Controversy in the Boardroom

According to a special report on corporate governance published in the *Wall Street Journal*, "Boards of directors have been put on notice." Because of the major scandals in U.S. corporations, shareholders, congressional representatives, and regulators are placing strong pressure on boards of directors to make a number of changes that, in effect, shift the power from CEOs to directors. This pressure includes expectations that directors will be more conscientious in the discharge of their responsibilities.

Institutional investors are placing pressures on firms and boards to separate the roles of chairman of the board and CEO. CEOs who hold both positions have substantial power. They can largely control the agenda of the board and, many times, its membership as well. And, in almost two-thirds of the major U.S. companies, the CEO also is chairman of the board. A blue-ribbon panel, the Commission on Public Trust and Private Enterprise, created by the Conference Board, recommended separating these two roles. The panel also recommended creating the position of "lead director," an action that would weaken the CEO's power over the board. The lead director would set the board agenda, oversee executive sessions of nonmanagement directors, and have the authority to call board meetings. In addition, there are calls for more outside and independent directors, and for more diversity on boards that are overwhelmingly male and Caucasian. Data suggest that the few women and minorities on boards are outside directors and are independent: approximately 86 percent of women directors and 82 percent of minority directors are independent.

What is needed is a board that is not afraid to confront senior management if needed. To do so, the board must be strong and independent, and have a good working relationship among the directors. Trying to create such a board, Cendant Corporation announced major changes to its board of directors. One of the new policies requires that two-thirds of the board members be independent. Additionally, stock options have been eliminated as compensation for directors, and directors on major governance committees can have no other relationship with the company for which they are compensated. Cendant has also appointed a "lead director" to manage executive sessions of nonmanagement directors. The lead director idea is being adopted at other major U.S. companies, such as GE and Walt Disney.

The fervor for change has even extended to the New York Stock Exchange (NYSE), which has pushed for governance change itself. External parties have expressed criticism of the composition of the NYSE board, the compensation of its top executives, and potential inappropriate practices on the trading floor. Therefore, the NYSE board announced a major review of its governance process to be completed by the end of 2003. Governance experts argue that the NYSE governance processes require more transparency. The primary catalyst for this review was the controversy that occurred over the nomination for the NYSE board of Sanford Weill, CEO and chairman of Citigroup Inc. Weill became a subject of controversy because of questionable actions in his job. After substantial criticism, the nomination was withdrawn. The pressure for change has reached beyond U.S. companies. For example, Toyota Motor Corporation announced that its board would be reduced in size by 50 percent, and foreign managers would be added. The firm hopes these moves will speed the decision process and enrich its globalization efforts.

SOURCES: C. Hymowitz, 2003, In the U.S., what will it take to create diverse boardrooms? *Wall Street Journal*, July 8, B1; V. Boland, 2003, NYSE probe will focus on the boardroom, *Financial Times*, http://www.ft.com, May 25; 2003, Have fat cats had their day? *The Economist*, http://www.economist.com, May 22; M. O'Neal, 2003, Expectations (and pay) climb for directors, *New York Times*, http://www.nytimes.com, April 6; C. Hymowitz, 2003, Changing the rules, *Wall Street Journal Online*, http://www.wsj.com, February 24; M. Rich, 2003, Cendant makes major changes to corporate governance rules, *Wall Street Journal Online*, http://www.wsj.com, February 7; J. S. Lublin, 2003, Separating top posts trims CEO's power, some believe, *Wall Street Journal Online*, http://www.wsj.com, January 10; C. Hymowitz, 2002, Building a board that's independent, strong and effective, *Wall Street Journal*, November 19, B1.

Strategic Focus include (4) the creation of a "lead director" role that has strong powers with regard to the board agenda and oversight of nonmanagement board member activities, and (5) changes in the compensation of directors, especially reducing or eliminating stock options as a part of the package.

Boards have become more involved in the strategic decision-making process, so they must work collaboratively. Research shows that boards working collaboratively make higher-quality strategic decisions, and they make them faster.[92] In fact, some argue that improving the processes used by boards to make decisions and monitor managers and firm outcomes is the key to increasing board effectiveness.[93] Moreover, because of the increased pressure from owners and the potential conflict among board members, procedures are necessary to help boards function effectively in facilitating the strategic decision-making process.[94] In addition to being increasingly involved in important strategic decisions, boards also are becoming more active in expressing their view about CEO succession, as opposed to readily supporting the incumbent's choice. In general, however, boards have relied on precedence (past decisions) for guidance in the selection process. Also, they are most likely to consider inside candidates before looking for outside candidates.[95] Outside directors have the power to facilitate the firm's transition to a new CEO. When an internal heir apparent CEO candidate is associated with a high-performing firm, outside directors are likely to help the heir apparent make the transition. However, if firm performance is problematic, outside directors are less likely to support the chosen successor and are often skeptical of someone chosen to follow in the footsteps of the former CEO.[96]

Increasingly, outside directors are being required to own significant equity stakes as a prerequisite to holding a board seat. In fact, some research suggests that firms perform better if outside directors have such a stake.[97] Director compensation has increased partly because of their need to perform more work. The average director annual pay is slightly over $152,000.[98] Additionally, while critics have argued that directors serving on several boards cannot be effective, research suggests that directors have the opportunity to serve on more boards when they are on the board of firms that perform well. Research also shows that directors on boards where poor strategic decisions are made (i.e., not in the best interests of the shareholders) are less likely to serve on multiple boards.[99] Other research suggests that diverse boards help firms make more effective strategic decisions and perform better over time.[100] One activist concludes that boards need three foundational characteristics to be effective: director stock ownership, executive meetings to discuss important strategic issues, and a serious nominating committee that truly controls the nomination process to strongly influence the selection of new board members.[101]

Executive Compensation

As the Opening Case illustrates, the compensation of top-level managers, and especially of CEOs, generates a great deal of interest and strongly held opinions. One reason for this widespread interest can be traced to a natural curiosity about extremes and excesses. Another stems from a more substantive view, that CEO pay is tied in an indirect but tangible way to the fundamental governance processes in large corporations: Who has power? What are the bases of power? How and when do owners and managers exert their relative preferences? How vigilant are boards? Who is taking advantage of whom?[102]

Executive compensation is a governance mechanism that seeks to align the interests of managers and owners through salaries, bonuses, and long-term incentive compensation, such as stock awards and options.[103] Long-term incentive plans are becoming a critical part of compensation packages in U.S. firms. The use of longer-term pay helps firms cope with or avoid potential agency problems.[104] Because of this, the stock

Executive compensation *is a governance mechanism that seeks to align the interests of managers and owners through salaries, bonuses, and long-term incentive compensation, such as stock options.*

market generally reacts positively to the introduction of a long-range incentive plan for top executives.[105]

Sometimes the use of a long-term incentive plan prevents major stockholders (e.g., institutional investors) from pressing for changes in the composition of the board of directors, because they assume that the long-term incentives will ensure that top executives will act in shareholders' best interests. Alternatively, stockholders largely assume that top-executive pay and the performance of a firm are more closely aligned when firms have boards that are dominated by outside members.[106]

Effectively using executive compensation as a governance mechanism is particularly challenging to firms implementing international strategies. For example, the interests of owners of multinational corporations may be best served when there is less uniformity among the firm's foreign subsidiaries' compensation plans.[107] Developing an array of unique compensation plans requires additional monitoring and increases the firm's potential agency costs. Importantly, levels of pay vary by regions of the world. For example, managers receive the highest compensation in the United States, while managerial pay is much lower in Asia. Compensation is lower in India partly because many of the largest firms have strong family ownership and control.[108] As corporations acquire firms in other countries, the managerial compensation puzzle becomes more complex and may cause additional executive turnover.[109]

A Complicated Governance Mechanism

For several reasons, executive compensation—especially long-term incentive compensation—is complicated. First, the strategic decisions made by top-level managers are typically complex and nonroutine, so direct supervision of executives is inappropriate for judging the quality of their decisions. The result is a tendency to link the compensation of top-level managers to measurable outcomes, such as the firm's financial performance. Second, an executive's decision often affects a firm's financial outcomes over an extended period, making it difficult to assess the effect of current decisions on the corporation's performance. In fact, strategic decisions are more likely to have long-term, rather than short-term, effects on a company's strategic outcomes. Third, a number of other factors affect a firm's performance besides top-level managerial decisions and behavior. Unpredictable economic, social, or legal changes (see Chapter 2) make it difficult to discern the effects of strategic decisions. Thus, although performance-based compensation may provide incentives to top management teams to make decisions that best serve shareholders' interests,[110] such compensation plans alone are imperfect in their ability to monitor and control managers.[111] Still, annual bonuses as incentive compensation represent a significant portion of many executives' total pay. For example, the ten highest CEO salaries and bonuses in 2002 ranged from $5.5 million to just under $8 million.[112]

Although incentive compensation plans may increase the value of a firm in line with shareholder expectations, such plans are subject to managerial manipulation. For instance, annual bonuses may provide incentives to pursue short-run objectives at the expense of the firm's long-term interests. Supporting this conclusion, some research has found that bonuses based on annual performance were negatively related to investments in R&D when the firm was highly diversified, which may affect the firm's long-term strategic competitiveness.[113] However, research has found a positive relationship between investments in R&D and long-term compensation in non-family firms.[114]

Although long-term, performance-based incentives may reduce the temptation to underinvest in the short run, they increase executive exposure to risks associated with uncontrollable events, such as market fluctuations and industry decline. The longer the focus of incentive compensation, the greater are the long-term risks borne by top-level managers. Also, because long-term incentives tie a manager's overall wealth to the firm in a way that is inflexible, such incentives and ownership may not be valued as highly by a manager as by outside investors who have the opportunity to diversify their wealth in a number of other financial investments.[115] Thus, firms may have to overcompensate managers using long-term incentives, as the next section suggests.

The Effectiveness of Executive Compensation

The compensation recently received by some top-level managers, especially CEOs, has angered many stakeholders, including shareholders. Table 10.3 lists the compensation received by the highest-paid U.S. CEOs in 2002. The table shows those receiving the largest direct compensation (including exercised options) and those receiving the largest total compensation, including stock and stock options, for the same time period. As the table shows, Jeffrey Barbakow received the highest direct compensation as well as the highest total compensation including the value of stock and stock options awarded. However, Steven Jobs, CEO of Apple Computer, received the highest total compensation and value of stock options granted, with $381 million and $872 million, respectively, in 2000. Thus, the value of his total compensation that year was over $1 billion.[116] As Table 10.3 indicates, stock and stock options are the primary component of large compensation packages.

The primary reason for compensating executives in stock is that the practice affords them an incentive to keep the stock price high and hence aligns managers' interests with shareholders' interests. However, there may be some unintended consequences. Managers who own more than 1 percent of their firm's stock may be less

Table 10.3

Highest Paid CEOs in 2002

Executive	Company	Total Pay Received (Millions)	Total Pay with Options Granted (Millions)
J. C. Barbakow	Tenet Healthcare	$116.4	$188.8
D. M. Cote	Honeywell	3.2	145.5
R. I. Lipp	Travelers P&C	1.8	129.8
P. T. Stokes	Anheuser-Busch	17.9	125.6
M. S. Dell	Dell	82.3	119.7
E. D. Breen	Tyco	4.1	103.5
J. T. Chambers	Cisco	0.0	99.2
E. E. Whitacre	SBC Comm.	6.1	88.4
A. G. Lafley	Procter & Gamble	5.0	87.7
S. G. McNealy	Sun Microsystems	25.8	87.1

Considering only compensation received without the value of options granted (but not exercised), the following people would be in the above list:

I. M. Jacobs	Qualcomm	63.2	
C. M. Cawley	MBNA	48.3	
O. C. Smith	Starbucks	38.8	
R. S. Fuld	Lehman Brothers	28.7	
V. D. Coffman	Lockheed Martin	23.9	

SOURCES: 2003, Who made the biggest bucks?, *Wall Street Journal Online*, http://www.wsj.com, April 14; 2003, How CEO compensation packages compare, *USA Today*, http://www.usatoday.com, March 31.

likely to be forced out of their jobs, even when the firm is performing poorly.[117] Furthermore, a review of the research suggests that over time, firm size has accounted for more than 50 percent of the variance in total CEO pay, while firm performance has accounted for less than 5 percent of the variance.[118] Thus, the effectiveness of pay plans as a governance mechanism is suspect.

Another way that boards may compensate executives is through loans with favorable, or no, interest for the purpose of buying company stock. If appropriately used, this practice can be a governance tool, since it aligns executives' priorities with those of the shareholders in that the executives hold stock, instead of only options on the stock. They gain or lose money along with the shareholders. "When people exercise most stock options, they pay the regular income-tax rate—close to 40 percent for executives—on the difference between the option's exercise price and the share price at that time. But if executives buy shares with borrowed money instead of receiving options, the government considers their profit to be an investment gain, not a part of their salary, and they pay only the capital-gains tax of 20 percent or less."[119]

While some stock option–based compensation plans are well designed with option strike prices substantially higher than current stock prices, too many have been designed simply to give executives more wealth that will not immediately show up on the balance sheet.[120] Research of stock option repricing where the strike price value of the option has been lowered from its original position suggests that action is taken more frequently in high-risk situations. However, it also happens when firm performance was poor to restore the incentive effect for the option. Evidence also suggests that politics are often involved.[121] Additionally, research has found that repricing stock options does not appear to be a function of management entrenchment or ineffective governance. These firms often have had sudden and negative changes to their growth and profitability. They also frequently lose their top managers.[122] Interestingly, institutional investors prefer compensation schemes that link pay with performance, including the use of stock options.[123] Again, this evidence shows that no internal governance mechanism is perfect.

While stock options became highly popular as a means of compensating top executives and linking pay with performance, they also have become controversial of late. It seems that option awards became a means of providing large compensation packages, and the options awarded did not relate to the firm's performance, particularly when boards showed a propensity to reprice options at a lower strike price when stock prices fell precipitously.[124] Because of the large number of options granted in recent years and the increasingly common practice of repricing them, several analysts, compensation experts, and politicians have called for expensing the options by the firm at the time they are awarded. This action could be quite costly to many firms' stated profits. Thus, some firms have begun to move away from granting stock options. In fact, Microsoft announced in July 2003 that it would no longer grant stock options to its employees. The firm is replacing options with awards of restricted stock that will vest over a five-year period. Some suggest that Microsoft's action may spell the end of stock options as a means of compensation.[125]

Market for Corporate Control

The **market for corporate control** is an external governance mechanism that becomes active when a firm's internal controls fail.[126] The market for corporate control is composed of individuals and firms that buy ownership positions in or take over potentially undervalued corporations so they can form new divisions in established diversified companies or merge two previously separate firms. Because the undervalued firm's executives are assumed to be responsible for formulating and implementing the strategy that led to poor performance, they are usually replaced. Thus, when the market for

*The **market for corporate control** is an external governance mechanism that becomes active when a firm's internal controls fail.*

corporate control operates effectively, it ensures that managers who are ineffective or act opportunistically are disciplined.[127]

The market for corporate control governance mechanism should be triggered by a firm's poor performance relative to industry competitors. A firm's poor performance, often demonstrated by the firm's earning below-average returns, is an indicator that internal governance mechanisms have failed; that is, their use did not result in managerial decisions that maximized shareholder value. This market has been active for some time. As noted in Chapter 7, the decade of the 1990s produced the largest number and value of mergers and acquisitions. The major reduction in the stock market resulted in a significant drop in acquisition activity in the first part of the 21st century. However, the number of mergers and acquisitions began to increase in 2003, with the number expected to reach almost 25,000 by the end of the year.[128] And, the market for corporate control has become increasingly international with over 40 percent of the merger and acquisition activity involving two firms from different countries.[129]

While some acquisition attempts are intended to obtain resources important to the acquiring firm, most of the hostile takeover attempts are due to the target firm's poor performance.[130] Therefore, target firm managers and members of the boards of directors are highly sensitive about hostile takeover bids. First, it frequently means that they have not done an effective job in managing the company because of the performance level inviting the bid. If they accept the offer, they are likely to lose their jobs; the acquiring firm will insert its own management. If they reject the offer and fend off the takeover attempt, they must improve the performance of the firm or risk losing their jobs as well.[131]

In 2003, the increasing number of hostile bids provided evidence of the merger and acquisition market heating up. For example, Oracle made a hostile bid for PeopleSoft; PeopleSoft rejected the offer, but Oracle remained in the takeover battle. The takeover attempt invited considerable attention from regulatory authorities in both the United States and Europe.[132] Also in 2003, smaller rival ArvinMeritor launched a hostile takeover attempt of its larger competitor, Dana, with a cash bid of $4.4 billion. But, analysts believed that the attempt would encourage others to make bids as well, making the takeover more expensive.[133] In fact, the takeover attempt of Safeway involved six bidders, but some were disapproved because of the potential concentration that might be created by the acquisition.[134]

Jean-Marie Messier, former CEO of Vivendi Universal, won an arbitration award for his severance pay package of $23.3 million. However, in late 2003, the SEC filed a suit to stop payment.

AP Photo/Jacques Brinon

Managerial Defense Tactics

Hostile takeovers are the major activity in the market for corporate control governance mechanism. Not all hostile takeovers are prompted by poorly performing targets, and firms targeted for hostile takeovers may use multiple defense tactics to fend off the takeover attempt. Historically, the increased use of the market for corporate control has enhanced the sophistication and variety of managerial defense tactics that are used to reduce the influence of this governance mechanism. The market for corporate control tends to increase risk for managers. As a result, managerial pay is often augmented indirectly through golden parachutes (wherein a CEO can receive up to three years' salary if his or her firm is taken over). Golden parachutes, similar to most other defense tactics, are controversial. For example, Jean-Marie Messier was given a golden parachute near the end of his tenure as CEO of Vivendi Universal, presumably to encourage him to resign. The package involved a $23.3 million payment, but it was delayed by court tests after he departed. The board claimed that no vote was taken to approve the severance payment. While the American Arbitration Association ruled in favor of Messier, Vivendi appealed the ruling to the French supreme court, which suspended the payment. Thus, the payment remains in litigation.[135]

Among other outcomes, takeover defenses increase the costs of mounting a takeover, causing the incumbent management to become entrenched, while reducing the chances of introducing a new management team.[136] Some defense tactics require asset restructuring created by divesting one or more divisions in the diversified firm's portfolio. Others necessitate only changes in the financial structure of the firm, such as repurchasing shares of the firm's outstanding stock.[137] Some tactics (e.g., reincorporation of the firm in another state) require shareholder approval, but the greenmail tactic, wherein money is used to repurchase stock from a corporate raider to avoid the takeover of the firm, does not. These defense tactics are controversial, and the research on their effects is inconclusive. Alternatively, most institutional investors oppose the use of defense tactics. TIAA-CREF and CalPERS have taken actions to have several firms' poison pills eliminated.[138] Hewlett-Packard's board adopted a policy that a poison pill could not be established in the future without taking a shareholder vote for approval. The stockholders also wanted approval on future executive severance pay packages.[139] But, there can be advantages to severance packages because they may encourage executives to accept takeover bids that are attractive to shareholders. Also, as in the case of Messier, it may encourage a CEO doing a poor job to depart.[140]

A potential problem with the market for corporate control is that it may not be totally efficient. A study of several of the most active corporate raiders in the 1980s showed that approximately 50 percent of their takeover attempts targeted firms with above-average performance in their industry—corporations that were neither undervalued nor poorly managed.[141] The targeting of high-performance businesses may lead to acquisitions at premium prices and to decisions by managers of the targeted firm to establish what may prove to be costly takeover defense tactics to protect their corporate positions.[142]

Although the market for corporate control lacks the precision of internal governance mechanisms, the fear of acquisition and influence by corporate raiders is an effective constraint on the managerial-growth motive.[143] The market for corporate control has been responsible for significant changes in many firms' strategies and, when used appropriately, has served shareholders' interests.[144] But this market and other means of corporate governance vary by region of the world and by country. Accordingly, we next address the topic of international corporate governance.

International Corporate Governance

Understanding the corporate governance structure of the United Kingdom and the United States is inadequate for a multinational firm in today's global economy.[145] The Strategic Focus suggests that the governance systems in many countries have been affected by the realities of the global economy. While the stability associated with German and Japanese governance structures has historically been viewed as an asset, some believe that it may now be a burden.[146] And the governance in Germany and Japan is changing, just as it is in other parts of the world. As suggested in the Strategic Focus, the corporate governance systems are becoming more similar. These changes are partly the

Corporate Governance Is Changing across the World

The pressures to change corporate governance practices have extended well beyond the United States. For example, a new report commissioned by the British government recommends significant changes in the governance practices of British companies. The report has a number of recommendations but two are especially important. First, the report suggests that firms should designate a nonexecutive director to attend regular management meetings with major shareholders. Second, it recommends that instead of the chairperson of the board, a nonexecutive director should chair the nomination committee. British top executives have expressed serious concerns about the changes.

Similarly, there have been calls for changes in the governance of French firms. The emphasis in France has been on increasing the number of independent directors on corporate boards. The most recent recommendation is to increase the number of independent directors to 50 percent of the total number of directors on the board. However, a major problem is that most "independent" directors (nonmanagement, outside members) are not truly independent. They have connections to the top executives in the company or to other board members or both. Thus, they are selected based on these connections instead of their expertise or independence.

Changes are also occurring in Switzerland and Japan. Similar to the United States, Switzerland has experienced corporate scandals in recent years. The bankruptcy of Swiss Air and the government rescue of it have created a public furor. Additionally, the disclosure that ABB awarded $170 million in pensions and other benefits to two former CEOs produced calls for governance changes. As a result, the Swiss stock market leaders have issued new regulations requiring disclosure of board members' total stock holdings and options, the highest paid director, and the names of all boards on which directors serve (to avoid conflicts of interest).

Even in Japan, changes in governance similar to those taking place in Europe are moving Japanese firms toward the U.S. system. For example, Sony announced that it would appoint more outsiders to its board and would have a majority of outsiders on the three critical board committees—compensation, audit, and nominating. In a similar move, Toyota announced that its board would be reduced by 50 percent and that the firm would simultaneously appoint more foreign managers. Its stated reasons are different from Sony's. Sony suggested that its changes are designed to make the firm's corporate governance more similar to that of U.S. firms. Toyota says that its moves are designed to help it compete in global markets, yet the changes also make Toyota's governance slightly more similar to that in the United States.

While there have been changes in Latin American firms' governance systems, they have been minor, largely because of the severe economic problems occurring in many Latin American countries. For example, shareholders do not have to be concerned about excessive executive compensation in Argentina. Because of the severe recession coupled with a devaluation of the peso and an increasing inflation rate, executives have received an average 30 percent pay cut. The job market for top executives in Argentina is highly limited.

SOURCES: T. Smith, 2003, Shrinking salaries hit home in Argentina, *New York Times*, http://www.nytimes.com, April 6; T. Zaun, 2003, Toyota to halve board, add foreign managers, *Wall Street Journal Online*, http://www.wsj.com, March 31; 2003, Hating Higgs, *The Economist*, http://www.economist.com, March 15; 2003, Independent? Moi? *The Economist*, http://www. economist.com, March 15; G. Mijuk, 2003, Money talks a little, *Wall Street Journal Online*, http://www.wsj.com, February 24; R. A. Guth, 2003, Sony's board will divide up its responsibilities in future, *Wall Street Journal Online*, http://www.wsj.com, January 29.

result of multinational firms operating in many different countries and attempting to develop a more global governance system.[147] While the similarity is increasing, differences remain evident, and firms employing an international strategy must understand these differences in order to operate effectively in different international markets.[148]

Corporate Governance in Germany

In many private German firms, the owner and manager may still be the same individual. In these instances, there is no agency problem.[149] Even in publicly traded German corporations, there is often a dominant shareholder. Thus, the concentration of ownership is an important means of corporate governance in Germany, as it is in the United States.[150]

Historically, banks have been at the center of the German corporate governance structure, as is also the case in many other European countries, such as Italy and France. As lenders, banks become major shareholders when companies they financed earlier seek funding on the stock market or default on loans. Although the stakes are usually under 10 percent, the only legal limit on how much of a firm's stock banks can hold is that a single ownership position cannot exceed 15 percent of the bank's capital. Through their shareholdings, and by casting proxy votes for individual shareholders who retain their shares with the banks, three banks in particular—Deutsche, Dresdner, and Commerzbank—exercise significant power. Although shareholders can tell the banks how to vote their ownership position, they generally do not do so. A combination of their own holdings and their proxies results in majority positions for these three banks in many German companies. Those banks, along with others, monitor and control managers, both as lenders and as shareholders, by electing representatives to supervisory boards.

German firms with more than 2,000 employees are required to have a two-tiered board structure. Through this structure, the supervision of management is separated from other duties normally assigned to a board of directors, especially the nomination of new board members. Germany's two-tiered system places the responsibility for monitoring and controlling managerial (or supervisory) decisions and actions in the hands of a separate group.[151] While all the functions of direction and management are the responsibility of the management board (the Vorstand), appointment to the Vorstand is the responsibility of the supervisory tier (the Aufsichtsrat). Employees, union members, and shareholders appoint members to the Aufsichtsrat.

Because of the role of local government (through the board structure) and the power of banks in Germany's corporate governance structure, private shareholders rarely have major ownership positions in German firms. Large institutional investors, such as pension funds and insurance companies, are also relatively insignificant owners of corporate stock. Thus, at least historically, German executives generally have not been dedicated to the maximization of shareholder value that is occurring in many countries.

Volkswagen (VW) made an amazing turnaround in the latter half

Volkswagen's foray into manufacturing luxury cars such as the $70,000 Phaeton has not proven successful. The internal corporate governance system at the company has failed to control costly strategic errors and has put Volkswagen's survival in jeopardy. Here an employee polishes a Phaeton at its factory in Dresden, eastern Germany.

AP Photo/Matthias Rietschel

of the 1990s. The company became much more profitable than it had been, and it appeared to be headed to new heights. Despite these promising signs, many investors had uneasy feelings about VW. The company would not release financial data, including operating profits that investors wanted to examine. In 2001, VW's market capitalization was less than Bayerische Motoren Werke's (BMW's), another German carmaker, in spite of the fact that VW generated twice as much revenue as did BMW.

As we learned in Chapter 2, Volkswagen invested billions of dollars to develop and introduce several new luxury automobiles, only to find that they were not in demand in the marketplace. One of these new cars, the Phaeton, is priced at $70,000 and its sales reached only 25 percent of the expected number in 2002, its year of introduction. The competition is fierce in the premium auto market. Lack of attention to Volkswagen's primary midpriced auto market allowed competitors to gain market share. Thus, Volkswagen's financial results have suffered, and unless it regains a competitive advantage, its performance will continue to suffer. The internal corporate governance system in Volkswagen has not controlled managerial behavior, allowing serious strategic errors. As a result, Volkswagen's survival may be in question.[152]

Corporate governance in Germany is changing, at least partially, because of the increasing globalization of business. Many German firms are beginning to gravitate toward the U.S. system. Recent research suggests that the traditional system produced some agency costs because of a lack of external ownership power. Alternatively, firms with stronger external ownership power were less likely to undertake governance reforms. Firms that adopted governance reforms often divested poorly performing units and achieved higher levels of market performance.[153]

Corporate Governance in Japan

Attitudes toward corporate governance in Japan are affected by the concepts of obligation, family, and consensus.[154] In Japan, an obligation "may be to return a service for one rendered or it may derive from a more general relationship, for example, to one's family or old alumni, or one's company (or Ministry), or the country. This sense of particular obligation is common elsewhere but it feels stronger in Japan."[155] As part of a company family, individuals are members of a unit that envelops their lives; families command the attention and allegiance of parties throughout corporations. Moreover, a *keiretsu* (a group of firms tied together by cross-shareholdings) is more than an economic concept; it, too, is a family. Consensus, an important influence in Japanese corporate governance, calls for the expenditure of significant amounts of energy to win the hearts and minds of people whenever possible, as opposed to top executives issuing edicts.[156] Consensus is highly valued, even when it results in a slow and cumbersome decision-making process.

As in Germany, banks in Japan play an important role in financing and monitoring large public firms. The bank owning the largest share of stocks and the largest amount of debt—the main bank—has the closest relationship with the company's top executives. The main bank provides financial advice to the firm and also closely monitors managers. Thus, Japan has a bank-based financial and corporate governance structure, whereas the United States has a market-based financial and governance structure.[157]

Aside from lending money, a Japanese bank can hold up to 5 percent of a firm's total stock; a group of related financial institutions can hold up to 40 percent. In many cases, main-bank relationships are part of a horizontal keiretsu. A keiretsu firm usually owns less than 2 percent of any other member firm; however, each company typically has a stake of that size in every firm in the keiretsu. As a result, somewhere between 30 and 90 percent of a firm is owned by other members of the keiretsu. Thus, a keiretsu is a system of relationship investments.

As is the case in Germany, Japan's structure of corporate governance is changing. For example, because of Japanese banks' continuing development as economic organizations, their role in the monitoring and control of managerial behavior and firm outcomes is less significant than in the past.[158] The Asian economic crisis in the latter part of the 1990s made the governance problems in Japanese corporations apparent. The problems were readily evidenced in the large and once-powerful Mitsubishi keiretsu. Many of its core members lost substantial amounts of money in the late 1990s.[159]

Still another change in Japan's governance system has occurred in the market for corporate control, which was nonexistent in past years. Japan experienced three recessions in the 1990s and is dealing with another early in the 21st century. As a whole, managers are unwilling to make the changes necessary to turn their companies around. As a result, many firms in Japan are performing poorly, but could, under the right guidance, improve their performance. Still, recent research suggests that the Japanese stewardship management approach leads to greater investments in long-term R&D projects than does the more financially oriented system in the United States.[160]

Global Corporate Governance

The 21st-century competitive landscape is fostering the creation of a relatively uniform governance structure that will be used by firms throughout the world.[161] As markets become more global and customer demands more similar, shareholders are becoming the focus of managers' efforts in an increasing number of companies. Investors are becoming more and more active throughout the world as evidenced by the shareholder outrage at the severance package given to Jean-Marie Messier, former CEO of Vivendi Universal.

Changes in governance are evident in many countries and are moving the governance models closer to that of the United States, as suggested in the Strategic Focus. Firms in Europe, especially in France and the United Kingdom, are developing boards of directors with more independent members. Similar actions are occurring in Japan, where the boards are being reduced in size and foreign members added.

Even in transitional economies, such as those of China and Russia, changes in corporate governance are occurring.[162] However, changes are implemented more slowly in these economies. Chinese firms have found it helpful to use stock-based compensation plans, thereby providing an incentive for foreign companies to invest in China.[163] Because Russia has reduced controls on the economy and on business activity much faster than China has, the country needs more effective governance systems to control its managerial activities. In fact, research suggests that ownership concentration leads to lower performance in Russia, primarily because minority shareholder rights are not well protected through adequate governance controls.[164]

Governance Mechanisms and Ethical Behavior

The governance mechanisms described in this chapter are designed to ensure that the agents of the firm's owners—the corporation's top executives—make strategic decisions that best serve the interests of the entire group of stakeholders, as described in Chapter 1. In the United States, shareholders are recognized as a company's most significant stakeholder. Thus, governance mechanisms focus on the control of managerial decisions to ensure that shareholders' interests will be served, but product market stakeholders (e.g., customers, suppliers, and host communities) and organizational stakeholders (e.g., managerial and nonmanagerial employees) are important as well.[165] Therefore, at least the minimal interests or needs of all stakeholders must be satisfied through the firm's actions. Otherwise, dissatisfied stakeholders will withdraw their support from one firm and provide it to another (for example, customers will purchase products from a supplier offering an acceptable substitute).

The firm's strategic competitiveness is enhanced when its governance mechanisms take into consideration the interests of all stakeholders. Although the idea is subject to debate, some believe that ethically responsible companies design and use governance mechanisms that serve all stakeholders' interests. There is, however, a more critical relationship between ethical behavior and corporate governance mechanisms. The Enron disaster illustrates the devastating effect of poor ethical behavior not only on a firm's stakeholders, but also on other firms.

In addition to Enron, recent scandals at WorldCom, HealthSouth, and Ahold NV show that all corporate owners are vulnerable to unethical behaviors by their employees, including top-level managers—the agents who have been hired to make decisions that are in shareholders' best interests. The decisions and actions of a corporation's board of directors can be an effective deterrent to these behaviors. In fact, some believe that the most effective boards participate actively to set boundaries for their firms' business ethics and values.[166] Once formulated, the board's expectations related to ethical decisions and actions of all of the firm's stakeholders must be clearly communicated to its top-level managers. Moreover, as shareholders' agents, these managers must understand that the board will hold them fully accountable for the development and support of an organizational culture that results in ethical decisions and behaviors. As explained in Chapter 12, CEOs can be positive role models for ethical behavior.

Only when the proper corporate governance is exercised can strategies be formulated and implemented that will help the firm achieve strategic competitiveness and earn above-average returns. As the discussion in this chapter suggests, corporate governance mechanisms are a vital, yet imperfect, part of firms' efforts to select and successfully use strategies.

Summary

- Corporate governance is a relationship among stakeholders that is used to determine a firm's direction and control its performance. How firms monitor and control top-level managers' decisions and actions affects the implementation of strategies. Effective governance that aligns managers' decisions with shareholders' interests can help produce a competitive advantage.

- There are three internal governance mechanisms in the modern corporation—ownership concentration, the board of directors, and executive compensation. The market for corporate control is the single external governance mechanism influencing managers' decisions and the outcomes resulting from them.

- Ownership is separated from control in the modern corporation. Owners (principals) hire managers (agents) to make decisions that maximize the firm's value. As risk-bearing specialists, owners diversify their risk by investing in multiple corporations with different risk profiles. As decision-making specialists, owners expect their agents (the firm's top-level managers) to make decisions that will lead to maximization of the value of their firm. Thus, modern corporations are characterized by an agency relationship that is created when one party (the firm's own-

ers) hires and pays another party (top-level managers) to use its decision-making skills.

- Separation of ownership and control creates an agency problem when an agent pursues goals that conflict with principals' goals. Principals establish and use governance mechanisms to control this problem.

- Ownership concentration is based on the number of large-block shareholders and the percentage of shares they own. With significant ownership percentages, such as those held by large mutual funds and pension funds, institutional investors often are able to influence top executives' strategic decisions and actions. Thus, unlike diffuse ownership, which tends to result in relatively weak monitoring and control of managerial decisions, concentrated ownership produces more active and effective monitoring. Institutional investors are an increasingly powerful force in corporate America and actively use their positions of concentrated ownership to force managers and boards of directors to make decisions that maximize a firm's value.

- In the United States and the United Kingdom, a firm's board of directors, composed of insiders, related outsiders, and outsiders, is a governance mechanism expected to represent shareholders' collective interests. The percentage of outside directors on many boards now exceeds the percentage of inside directors. Outsiders are expected to be more independent of a firm's top-level managers compared to those selected from inside the firm.

- Executive compensation is a highly visible and often criticized governance mechanism. Salary, bonuses, and long-term incentives are used to strengthen the alignment between managers' and shareholders' interests. A firm's board of directors is responsible for determining the effectiveness of the firm's executive compensation system. An effective system elicits managerial decisions that are in shareholders' best interests.

- In general, evidence suggests that shareholders and boards of directors have become more vigilant in their control of managerial decisions. Nonetheless, these mechanisms are insufficient to govern managerial behavior in many large companies. Therefore, the market for corporate control is an important governance mechanism. Although it, too, is imperfect, the market for corporate control has been effective in causing corporations to combat inefficient diversification and to implement more effective strategic decisions.

- Corporate governance structures used in Germany and Japan differ from each other and from that used in the United States. Historically, the U.S. governance structure has focused on maximizing shareholder value. In Germany, employees, as a stakeholder group, have a more prominent role in governance. By contrast, until recently, Japanese shareholders played virtually no role in the monitoring and control of top-level managers. However, all of these systems are becoming increasingly similar, as are many governance systems both in developed countries, such as France and Spain, and in transitional economies, such as Russia and China.

- Effective governance mechanisms ensure that the interests of all stakeholders are served. Thus, long-term strategic success results when firms are governed in ways that permit at least minimal satisfaction of capital market stakeholders (e.g., shareholders), product market stakeholders (e.g., customers and suppliers), and organizational stakeholders (managerial and nonmanagerial employees; see Chapter 2). Moreover, effective governance produces ethical behavior in the formulation and implementation of strategies.

Review Questions

Review Questions Review Questions

1. What is corporate governance? What factors account for the considerable amount of attention corporate governance receives from several parties, including shareholder activists, business press writers, and academic scholars? Why is governance necessary to control managers' decisions?

2. What does it mean to say that ownership is separated from managerial control in the modern corporation? Why does this separation exist?

3. What is an agency relationship? What is managerial opportunism? What assumptions do owners of modern corporations make about managers as agents?

4. How is each of the three internal governance mechanisms—ownership concentration, boards of directors, and executive compensation—used to align the interests of managerial agents with those of the firm's owners?

5. What trends exist regarding executive compensation? What is the effect of the increased use of long-term incentives on executives' strategic decisions?

6. What is the market for corporate control? What conditions generally cause this external governance mechanism to become active? How does the mechanism constrain top executives' decisions and actions?

7. What is the nature of corporate governance in Germany and Japan?

8. How can corporate governance foster ethical strategic decisions and behaviors on the part of managers as agents?

Experiential Exercises

Experiential Exercise

Corporate Governance and the Board of Directors

The composition and actions of the firm's board of directors have a profound effect on the firm. "The most important thing a board can ask itself today is whether it is professionally managed in the same way that the company itself is professionally managed," says Carolyn Brancato, director of the Global Corporate Governance Research Center at The Conference Board, which creates and disseminates knowledge about management and the marketplace. "The collegial nature of boards must give way to a new emphasis on professionalism, and directors must ask management the hard questions."

Following are several questions about boards of directors and corporate governance. Break into small groups and use the content of this chapter to discuss these questions. Be prepared to defend your answers.

1. How can corporate governance keep a company viable and maintain its shareholders' confidence?

2. How should boards evaluate CEOs? How can the board learn of problems in the CEO's performance? How does a board decide when a CEO needs to be replaced? How should succession plans be put in place?

3. Who should serve on a board? What human factors affect board members' interactions with each other, and how can those factors be used to best advantage?

4. Should independent directors meet on a regular basis without management present? Does the board have a role in setting corporate strategy?

5. What should a CEO expect of directors? How can a CEO move unproductive participants off a board?

6. What processes can be put in place to help make the board more aware of problems in company operations? How can the board be assured of receiving appropriate information? How can the board fulfill its monitoring role while relying on information provided by management and external accountants?

Developing and Analyzing Executive Compensation Packages

To date, A. G. Lafley, the chairman, president, and chief executive officer (CEO) of Procter & Gamble (P&G) can be proud of the company's financial performance under his leadership. Procter & Gamble's net income rose 19 percent in the fiscal year ended June 30, 2003, while unit volume grew 8 percent and net sales rose 8 percent to $43.38 billion. In general, the shareholders were pleased with wealth creation based on these performance-related outcomes. The board of directors carefully listens to presentations by Mr. Lafley and the Compensation Committee concerning CEO

compensation for the next year. The fiduciary duty of the board requires that its members make decisions that are in the best interest of P&G shareholders.

Break the class into three groups.

Phase 1: Group Work

- Group A will represent Mr. Lafley. This group should develop a list of three to five major changes in executive compensation that will be presented to the P&G board of directors for approval. The list should contain some changes that are primarily beneficial to shareholders and other changes that are primarily beneficial to Mr. Lafley and other senior managers (it's important to have both). The list could be created using this chapter's contents or other sources. Students may refer to the P&G website at http://www.pg.com to gather useful information.

- Group B will represent the Compensation Committee. This group believes that Mr. Lafley deserves a compensation increase, largely because his incentives lagged the industry average. The group will prepare a new compensation offer for Mr. Lafley. Use this chapter's contents for ideas of executive compensation incentives.

- Group C will act as a Board of Directors. To prepare for phase 2 of the exercise, this group will discuss various aspects of managerial opportunism, various ways to compensate top managers, and the importance to all stakeholders of retaining competent CEOs.

Phase 2: Role Playing

A representative of group A presents the list of major changes that Mr. Lafley proposes. Group C listens to the proposal and approves or disapproves each item. The discussion is in front of the class. Members may differ in opinions—there is no right or wrong position. Items that do not benefit shareholders should not be approved.

A representative of group B presents a new compensation plan for Mr. Lafley. Group C discusses the plan and approves it, disapproves it, or suggests changes.

Phase 3: Analysis and Feedback

The instructor leads the entire class in an analysis of what has transpired while completing this exercise.

▌Notes

1. M. Carpenter & J. Westphal, 2001, Strategic context of external network ties: Examining the impact of director appointments on board involvement in strategic decision making, *Academy of Management Journal*, 44: 639–660.

2. A. Henderson & J. Fredrickson, 2001, Top management team coordination needs and the CEO pay gap: A competitive test of economic and behavioral views, *Academy of Management Journal*, 44: 96–117.

3. F. Elloumi & J.-P. Gueyie, 2001, CEO compensation, IOS and the role of corporate governance, *Corporate Governance*, 1(2): 23–33; J. E. Core, R. W.

Holthausen, & D. F. Larcker, 1999, Corporate governance, chief executive officer compensation, and firm performance, *Journal of Financial Economics*, 51: 371–406.

4. M. D. Lynall, B. R. Golden, & A. J. Hillman, 2003, Board composition from adolescence to maturity: A multitheoretic view, *Academy of Management Review*, 28: 416–431; A. J. Hillman, G. D. Keim, & R. A. Luce, 2001, Board composition and stakeholder performance: Do stakeholder directors make a difference? *Business and Society*, 40: 295–314.

5. C. M. Daily, D. R. Dalton, & A. A. Cannella, 2003, Corporate governance: Decades of dialogue and data, *Academy of Management Review*, 28: 371–382; P. Stiles, 2001, The impact of the board on strategy: An empirical examination, *Journal of Management Studies*, 38: 627–650.

6. D. Finegold, E. E. Lawler III, & J. Conger, 2001, Building a better board, *Journal of Business Strategy*, 22(6): 33–37.

7. E. F. Fama & M. C. Jensen, 1983, Separation of ownership and control, *Journal of Law and Economics*, 26: 301–325.

8. J. Henderson & K. Cool, 2003, Corporate governance, investment bandwagons and overcapacity: An analysis of the worldwide petrochemical industry, 1975–95, *Strategic Management Journal*, 24: 393–413; R. Charan, 1998, *How Corporate Boards Create Competitive Advantage*, San Francisco: Jossey-Bass.

9. A. Cannella, Jr., A. Pettigrew, & D. Hambrick, 2001, Upper echelons: Donald Hambrick on executives and strategy, *Academy of Management Executive*, 15(3): 36–52; J. D. Westphal & E. J. Zajac, 1997, Defections from the inner circle: Social exchange, reciprocity and diffusion of board independence in U.S. corporations, *Administrative Science Quarterly*, 42: 161–212.

10. J. McGuire & S. Dow, 2002, The Japanese keiretsu system: An empirical analysis, *Journal of Business Research*, 55: 33–40.

11. J. Charkham, 1994, *Keeping Good Company: A Study of Corporate Governance in Five Countries*, New York: Oxford University Press, 1.

12. A. Cadbury, 1999, The future of governance: The rules of the game, *Journal of General Management*, 24: 1–14.

13. R. Aguilera & G. Jackson, 2003, The cross-national diversity of corporate governance: Dimensions and determinants, *Academy of Management Review*, 28: 447–465; Cadbury Committee, 1992, *Report of the Cadbury Committee on the Financial Aspects of Corporate Governance*, London: Gee.

14. C. K. Prahalad & J. P. Oosterveld, 1999, Transforming internal governance: The challenge for multinationals, *Sloan Management Review*, 40(3): 31–39.

15. M. A. Hitt, R. A. Harrison, & R. D. Ireland, 2001, *Mergers and Acquisitions: A Guide to Creating Value for Stakeholders*, New York: Oxford University Press; M. A. Hitt, R. E. Hoskisson, R. A. Johnson, & D. D. Moesel, 1996, The market for corporate control and firm innovation, *Academy of Management Journal*, 39: 1084–1119.

16. K. Ramaswamy, M. Li, & R. Veliyath, 2002, Variations in ownership behavior and propensity to diversify: A study of the Indian context, *Strategic Management Journal*, 23: 345–358.

17. R. E. Hoskisson, M. A. Hitt, R. A. Johnson, & W. Grossman, 2002, Conflicting voices: The effects of ownership heterogeneity and internal governance on corporate strategy, *Academy of Management Journal*, 45: 697–716.

18. G. E. Davis & T. A. Thompson, 1994, A social movement perspective on corporate control, *Administrative Science Quarterly*, 39: 141–173.

19. R. Bricker & N. Chandar, 2000, Where Berle and Means went wrong: A reassessment of capital market agency and financial reporting, *Accounting, Organizations and Society*, 25: 529–554; M. A. Eisenberg, 1989, The structure of corporation law, *Columbia Law Review*, 89(7): 1461 as cited in R. A. G. Monks & N. Minow, 1995, *Corporate Governance*, Cambridge, MA: Blackwell Business, 7.

20. R. M. Wiseman & L. R. Gomez-Mejia, 1999, A behavioral agency model of managerial risk taking, *Academy of Management Review*, 23: 133–153.

21. R. C. Anderson & D. M. Reeb, 2003, Founding-family ownership and firm performance: Evidence from the S&P 500, *Journal of Finance*, 58: in press.

22. N. Anthanassiou, W. F. Crittenden, L. M. Kelly, & P. Marquez, 2002, Founder centrality effects on the Mexican family firm's top management group: Firm culture, strategic vision and goals and firm performance, *Journal of World Business*, 37: 139–150.

23. G. Redding, 2002, The capitalist business system of China and its rationale, *Asia Pacific Journal of Management*, 19: 221–249.

24. M. Carney & E. Gedajlovic, 2003, Strategic innovation and the administrative heritage of East Asian family business groups, *Asia Pacific Journal of Management*, 20: 5–26; D. Miller & I. Le Breton-Miller, 2003, Challenge versus advantage in family business, *Strategic Organization*, 1: 127–134.

25. E. E. Fama, 1980, Agency problems and the theory of the firm, *Journal of Political Economy*, 88: 288–307.

26. D. Stires, 2001, America's best & worst wealth creators, *Fortune*, December 10, 137–142.

27. 2003, Information obtained from Cisco's financial data presented on its website, http://www.cisco.com, July.

28. D. Dalton, C. Daily, T. Certo, & R. Roengpitya, 2003, Meta-analyses of financial performance and equity: Fusion or confusion? *Academy of Management Journal*, 46: 13–26; M. Jensen & W. Meckling, 1976, Theory of the firm: Managerial behavior, agency costs, and ownership structure, *Journal of Financial Economics*, 11: 305–360.

29. L. R. Gomez-Mejia, M. Nunez-Nickel, & I. Gutierrez, 2001, The role of family ties in agency contracts, *Academy of Management Journal*, 44: 81–95.

30. M. G. Jacobides & D. C. Croson, 2001, Information policy: Shaping the value of agency relationships, *Academy of Management Review*, 26: 202–223.

31. R. Mangel & M. Useem, 2001, The strategic role of gainsharing, *Journal of Labor Research*, 2: 327–343; T. M. Welbourne & L. R. Gomez-Mejia, 1995, Gainsharing: A critical review and a future research agenda, *Journal of Management*, 21: 577.

32. A. J. Hillman & T. Dalziel, 2003, Boards of directors and firm performance: Integrating agency and resource dependence perspectives, *Academy of Management Review*, 28: 383–396; Jacobides & Croson, Information policy: Shaping the value of agency relationships.

33. Hoskisson, Hitt, Johnson, & Grossman, Conflicting voices; O. E. Williamson, 1996, *The Mechanisms of Governance*, New York: Oxford University Press, 6.

34. C. C. Chen, M. W. Peng, & P. A. Saparito, 2002, Individualism, collectivism, and opportunism: A cultural perspective on transaction cost economics, *Journal of Management*, 28: 567–583; S. Ghoshal & P. Moran, 1996, Bad for practice: A critique of the transaction cost theory, *Academy of Management Review*, 21: 13–47.

35. K. H. Wathne & J. B. Heide, 2000, Opportunism in interfirm relationships: Forms, outcomes, and solutions, *Journal of Marketing*, 64(4): 36–51.

36. L. Tihanyi, R. A. Johnson, R. E. Hoskisson, & M. A. Hitt, 2003, Institutional ownership differences and international diversification: The effects of boards of directors and technological opportunity, *Academy of Management Journal*, 46: 195–211; Y. Amihud & B. Lev, 1981, Risk reduction as a managerial motive for conglomerate mergers, *Bell Journal of Economics*, 12: 605–617.

37. R. C. Anderson, T. W. Bates, J. M. Bizjak, & M. L. Lemmon, Corporate governance and firm diversification, *Financial Management*, 29(1): 5–22; R. E. Hoskisson & T. A. Turk, 1990, Corporate restructuring: Governance and control limits of the internal market, *Academy of Management Review*, 15: 459–477.

38. M. A. Geletkanycz, B. K. Boyd, & S. Finkelstein, 2001, The strategic value of CEO external directorate networks: Implications for CEO compensation, *Strategic Management Journal*, 9: 889–898.

39. P. Wright, M. Kroll, & D. Elenkov, 2002, Acquisition returns, increase in firm size and chief executive officer compensation: The moderating role of monitoring, *Academy of Management Journal*, 45: 599–608; S. Finkelstein & D. C. Hambrick, 1989, Chief executive compensation: A study of the intersection of markets and political processes, *Strategic Management Journal*, 16: 221–239.

40. Gomez-Mejia, Nunez-Nickel, & Gutierrez, The role of family ties in agency contracts.

41. C. Matlack, 2001, Gemplus: No picnic in Provence, *BusinessWeek Online*, http://www.businessweek.com, August 6; C. Matlack, 2001, A global clash at France's Gemplus, *BusinessWeek Online*, http://www.businessweek.com, December 21.

42. 2003, Gemplus Profile and Company Information, http://www.gemplus. com, July.

43. M. S. Jensen, 1986, Agency costs of free cash flow, corporate finance, and takeovers, *American Economic Review*, 76: 323–329.

44. T. H. Brush, P. Bromiley, & M. Hendrickx, 2000, The free cash flow hypothesis for sales growth and firm performance, *Strategic Management Journal*, 21: 455–472; H. DeAngelo & L. DeAngelo, 2000, Controlling stockholders and the disciplinary role of corporate payout policy: A study of the Times Mirror Company, *Journal of Financial Economics*, 56: 153–207.

45. Ramaswamy, Li, & Veliyath, Variations in ownership behavior and propensity to diversify.

46. P. Wright, M. Kroll, A. Lado, & B. Van Ness, 2002, The structure of ownership and corporate acquisition strategies, *Strategic Management Journal*, 23: 41–53.

47. R. Rajan, H. Servaes, & L. Zingales, 2001, The cost of diversity: The diversification discount and inefficient investment, *Journal of Finance*, 55: 35–79; A. Sharma, 1997, Professional as agent: Knowledge asymmetry in agency exchange, *Academy of Management Review*, 22: 758–798.

48. P. Lane, A. A. Cannella, Jr., & M. H. Lubatkin, 1999, Agency problems as antecedents to unrelated mergers and diversification: Amihud and Lev reconsidered, *Strategic Management Journal*, 19: 555–578.

49. David Champion, 2001, Off with his head? *Harvard Business Review*, 79(9): 35–46.

50. J. Coles, N. Sen, & V. McWilliams, 2001, An examination of the relationship of governance mechanisms to performance, *Journal of Management*, 27: 23–50.

51. S.-S. Chen & K. W. Ho, 2000, Corporate diversification, ownership structure, and firm value: The Singapore evidence, *International Review of Financial Analysis*, 9: 315–326; R. E. Hoskisson, R. A. Johnson, & D. D. Moesel, 1994, Corporate divestiture intensity in restructuring firms: Effects of governance, strategy, and performance, *Academy of Management Journal*, 37: 1207–1251.

52. A. Berle & G. Means, 1932, *The Modern Corporation and Private Property*, New York: Macmillan.

53. P. A. Gompers & A. Metrick, 2001, Institutional investors and equity prices, *Quarterly Journal of Economics*, 116: 229–259; M. P. Smith, 1996, Shareholder activism by institutional investors: Evidence from CalPERS, *Journal of Finance*, 51: 227–252.

54. Hoskisson, Hitt, Johnson, & Grossman, Conflicting voices; C. M. Dailey, 1996, Governance patterns in bankruptcy reorganizations, *Strategic Management Journal*, 17: 355–375.

55. Hoskisson, Hitt, Johnson, & Grossman, Conflicting voices; R. E. Hoskisson & M. A. Hitt, 1994, *Downscoping: How to Tame the Diversified Firm*, New York: Oxford University Press.

56. K. Rebeiz, 2001, Corporate governance effectiveness in American corporations: A survey, *International Management Journal*, 18(1): 74–80.

57. 2002, CalPERS at a glance, http://www.calpers.com, April 24.

58. A. Grimes, 2003, Calpers is to widen disclosure on its private-equity returns, *Wall Street Journal Online*, http://www.wsj.com, March 18; 2003, Cronyism at Calpers, *Wall Street Journal Online*, http://www.wsj.com, January 31.

59. Tihanyi, Johnson, Hoskisson, & Hitt, Institutional ownership differences and international diversification; Hoskisson, Hitt, Johnson, & Grossman, Conflicting voices; P. David, M. A. Hitt, & J. Gimeno, 2001, The role of institutional investors in influencing R&D, *Academy of Management Journal*, 44: 144–157.

60. 2001, Shareholder activism is rising, *Investor Relations Business*, August 6, 8.

61. M. J. Roe, 1993, Mutual funds in the boardroom, *Journal of Applied Corporate Finance*, 5(4): 56–61.

62. R. A. G. Monks, 1999, What will be the impact of active shareholders? A practical recipe for constructive change, *Long Range Planning*, 32(1): 20–27.

63. B. S. Black, 1992, Agents watching agents: The promise of institutional investor's voice, *UCLA Law Review*, 39: 871–893.

64. Hoskisson, Hitt, Johnson, & Grossman, Conflicting voices; T. Woidtke, 2002, Agents watching agents: Evidence from pension fund ownership and firm value, *Journal of Financial Economics*, 63: 99–131.

65. A. Berenson, 2001, The fight for control of Computer Associates, *New York Times*, http://www.nytimes.com, June 25.

66. 2003, Computer Associates corporate governance and financial transparency initiatives 2002: Year in review, http://www.ca.com/governance/2002_review.htm, January.

67. C. Sundaramurthy & D. W. Lyon, 1998, Shareholder governance proposals and conflict of interests between inside and outside shareholders, *Journal of Managerial Issues*, 10: 30–44.

68. S. Thomsen & T. Pedersen, 2000, Ownership structure and economic performance in the largest European companies, *Strategic Management Journal*, 21: 689–705.

69. D. R. Dalton, C. M. Daily, A. E. Ellstrand, & J. L. Johnson, 1998, Meta-analytic reviews of board composition, leadership structure, and financial performance, *Strategic Management Journal*, 19: 269–290; M. Huse, 1998, Researching the dynamics of board-stakeholder relations, *Long Range Planning*, 31: 218–226.

70. A. Dehaene, V. De Vuyst, & H. Ooghe, 2001, Corporate performance and board structure in Belgian companies, *Long Range Planning*, 34(3): 383–398.

71. Hillman & Dalziel, Boards of directors and firm performance.

72. Rebeiz, Corporate governance effectiveness in American corporations; J. K. Seward & J. P Walsh, 1996, The governance and control of voluntary corporate spinoffs, *Strategic Management Journal*, 17: 25–39.

73. S. Young, 2000, The increasing use of non-executive directors: Its impact on UK board structure and governance arrangements, *Journal of Business Finance & Accounting*, 27(9/10): 1311–1342; P. Mallete & R. L. Hogler, 1995, Board composition, stock ownership, and the exemption of directors from liability, *Journal of Management*, 21: 861–878.

74. J. Chidley, 2001, Why boards matter, *Canadian Business*, October 29, 6; D. P. Forbes & F. J. Milliken, 1999, Cognition and corporate governance:

75. Understanding boards of directors as strategic decision-making groups, *Academy of Management Review*, 24: 489–505.

Hoskisson, Hitt, Johnson, & Grossman, Conflicting voices; B. D. Baysinger & R. E. Hoskisson, 1990, The composition of boards of directors and strategic control: Effects on corporate strategy, *Academy of Management Review*, 15: 72–87.

76. Carpenter & Westphal, Strategic context of external network ties: Examining the impact of director appointments on board involvement in strategic decision making; E. J. Zajac & J. D. Westphal, 1996, Director reputation, CEO-board power, and the dynamics of board interlocks, *Administrative Science Quarterly*, 41: 507–529.

77. A. Hillman, A. Cannella, Jr., & R. Paetzold, 2000, The resource dependence role of corporate directors: Strategic adaptation of board composition in response to environmental change, *Journal of Management Studies*, 37: 235–255; J. D. Westphal & E. J. Zajac, 1995, Who shall govern? CEO/board power, demographic similarity, and new director selection, *Administrative Science Quarterly*, 40: 60–83.

78. J. S. Lublin, 2003, More work, more pay, *Wall Street Journal Online*, http://www.wsj.com, February 24; J. Westphal & L. Milton, 2000, How experience and network ties affect the influence of demographic minorities on corporate boards, *Administrative Science Quarterly*, June, 45(2): 366–398.

79. 2003, The hot seat, *Wall Street Journal Online*, http://www.wsj.com, February 24; 2001, The fading appeal of the boardroom series, *The Economist*, February 10 (Business Special): 67–69.

80. G. Kassinis & N. Vafeas, 2002, Corporate boards and outside stakeholders as determinants of environmental litigation, *Strategic Management Journal*, 23: 399–415.

81. H. L. Tosi, W. Shen, & R. J. Gentry, 2003, Why outsiders on boards can't solve the corporate governance problem, *Organizational Dynamics*, 32: 180–192.

82. K. Greene, 2002, Dunlap agrees to settle suit over Sunbeam, *Wall Street Journal*, January 15, A3, A8.

83. P. Stiles, The impact of the board on strategy: An empirical examination, *Journal of Management Studies*, 38: 627–650; J. A. Byrne, 1999, Commentary: Boards share the blame when the boss fails, *BusinessWeek Online*, http://www.businessweek.com, December 27.

84. 2002, Sunbeam emerges from Chapter 11 bankruptcy, *Muzi News*, http://www.latelinenews.com, December 12; J. S. Lublin, 2002, Sunbeam's chief tells how he kept afloat amid crisis, *Wall Street Journal Online*, http://www.wsj.com, November 12.

85. E. Perotti & S. Gelfer, 2001, Red barons or robber barons? Governance and investment in Russian financial-industrial groups, *European Economic Review*, 45(9): 1601–1617; I. M. Millstein, 1997, Red herring over independent boards, *New York Times*, April 6, F10; W. Q. Judge, Jr., & G. H. Dobbins, 1995, Antecedents and effects of outside directors' awareness of CEO decision style, *Journal of Management*, 21: 43–64.

86. I. E. Kesner, 1988, Director characteristics in committee membership: An investigation of type, occupation, tenure and gender, *Academy of Management Journal*, 31: 66–84.

87. The hot seat.

88. J. Coles & W. Hesterly, 2000, Independence of the chairman and board composition: Firm choices and shareholder value, *Journal of Management*, 26: 195–214; S. Zahra, 1996, Governance, ownership and corporate entrepreneurship among the *Fortune* 500: The moderating impact of industry technological opportunity, *Academy of Management Journal*, 39: 1713–1735.

89. Hoskisson, Hitt, Johnson, & Grossman, Conflicting voices.

90. A. Conger, E. E. Lawler, & D. L. Finegold, 2001, *Corporate Boards: New Strategies for Adding Value at the Top*, San Francisco: Jossey-Bass; J. A. Conger, D. Finegold, & E. E. Lawler III, 1998, Appraising boardroom performance, *Harvard Business Review*, 76(1): 136–148.

91. J. Marshall, 2001, As boards shrink, responsibilities grow, *Financial Executive*, 17(4): 36–39.

92. C. A. Simmers, 2000, Executive/board politics in strategic decision making, *Journal of Business and Economic Studies*, 4: 37–56.

93. S. Finkelstein & A. C. Mooney, 2003, Not the usual suspects: How to use board process to make boards better, *Academy of Management Executive*, 17: 101–113.

94. Hoskisson, Hitt, Johnson, & Grossman, Conflicting voices.

95. W. Ocasio, 1999, Institutionalized action and corporate governance, *Administrative Science Quarterly*, 44: 384–416.

96. A. A. Cannella, Jr. & W. Shen, 2001, So close and yet so far: Promotion versus exit for CEO heirs apparent, *Academy of Management Journal*, 44: 252–270.

97. M. Gerety, C. Hoi, & A. Robin, 2001, Do shareholders benefit from the adoption of incentive pay for directors? *Financial Management*, 30: 45–61; D. C. Hambrick & E. M. Jackson, 2000, Outside directors with a stake: The linchpin in improving governance, *California Management Review*, 42(4): 108–127.

98. Lublin, More work, more pay.

99. J. L. Coles & C.-K. Hoi, 2003, New evidence on the market for directors: Board membership and Pennsylvania Bill 1310, *Journal of Finance*, 58: 197–230; S. P. Ferris, M. Jagannathan, & A. C. Pritchard, 2003, Too busy to mind the business? Monitoring by directors with multiple board appointments, *Journal of Finance*, 58: in press.

100. I. Filatotchev & S. Toms, 2003, Corporate governance, strategy and survival in a declining industry: A study of UK cotton textile companies, *Journal of Management Studies*, 40: 895–920.

101. J. Kristie, 2001, The shareholder activist: Nell Minow, *Directors and Boards*, 26(1): 16–17.

102. M. A. Carpenter & W. G. Sanders, 2002, Top management team compensation: The missing link between CEO pay and firm performance, *Strategic Management Journal*, 23: 367–375; D. C. Hambrick & S. Finkelstein, 1995, The effects of ownership structure on conditions at the top: The case of CEO pay raises, *Strategic Management Journal*, 16: 175.

103. J. S. Miller, R. M. Wiseman, & L. R. Gomez-Mejia, 2002, The fit between CEO compensation design and firm risk, *Academy of Management Journal*, 45: 745–756; L. Gomez-Mejia & R. M. Wiseman, 1997, Reframing executive compensation: An assessment and outlook, *Journal of Management*, 23: 291–374.

104. J. McGuire & E. Matta, 2003, CEO stock options: The silent dimension of ownership, *Academy of Management Journal*, 46: 255–265; W. G. Sanders & M. A. Carpenter, 1998, Internationalization and firm governance: The roles of CEO compensation, top team composition and board structure, *Academy of Management Journal*, 41: 158–178.

105. N. T. Hill & K. T. Stevens, 2001, Structuring compensation to achieve better financial results, *Strategic Finance*, 9: 48–51; J. D. Westphal & E. J. Zajac, 1999, The symbolic management of stockholders: Corporate governance reform and shareholder reactions, *Administrative Science Quarterly*, 43: 127–153.

106. L. Gomez-Mejia, M. Larraza-Kintana, & M. Makri, 2003, The determinants of executive compensation in family-controlled public corporations, *Academy of Management Journal*, 46: 226–237; Elloumi & Gueyie, CEO compensation, IOS and the role of corporate governance; M. J. Conyon & S. I. Peck, 1998, Board control, remuneration committees, and top management compensation, *Academy of Management Journal*, 41: 146–157.

107. S. O'Donnell, 2000, Managing foreign subsidiaries: Agents of headquarters, or an interdependent network? *Strategic Management Journal*, 21: 521–548; K. Roth & S. O'Donnell, 1996, Foreign subsidiary compensation: An agency theory perspective, *Academy of Management Journal*, 39: 678–703.

108. K. Ramaswamy, R. Veliyath, & L. Gomes, 2000, A study of the determinants of CEO compensation in India, *Management International Review*, 40(2): 167–191.

109. J. Krug & W. Hegarty, 2001, Predicting who stays and leaves after an acquisition: A study of top managers in multinational firms, *Strategic Management Journal*, 22: 185–196.

110. Carpenter & Sanders, Top management team compensation.

111. S. Bryan, L. Hwang, & S. Lilien, 2000, CEO stock-based compensation: An empirical analysis of incentive-intensity, relative mix, and economic determinants, *Journal of Business*, 73: 661–693.

112. 2003, How CEO salary and bonus packages compare, *USA Today*, http://www.usatoday.com, March 31.

113. R. E. Hoskisson, M. A. Hitt, & C. W. L. Hill, 1993, Managerial incentives and investment in R&D in large multiproduct firms, *Organization Science*, 4: 325–341.

114. Gomez-Mejia, Larraza-Kintana, & Makri, 2003, The determinants of executive compensation in family-controlled public corporations.

115. L. K. Meulbroek, 2001, The efficiency of equity-linked compensation: Understanding the full cost of awarding executive stock options, *Financial Management*, 30(2): 5–44.

116. G. Colvin, 2001, The great CEO pay heist, *Fortune*, June 25, 67.

117. J. Dahya, A. A. Lonie, & D. A. Power, 1998, Ownership structure, firm performance and top executive change: An analysis of UK firms, *Journal of Business Finance & Accounting*, 25: 1089–1118.

118. L. Gomez-Mejia, 2003, What should be done about CEO pay? *Academy of Management Issues Forum*, July; H. Tosi, S. Werner, J. Katz, & L. Gomez-Mejia, 2000, How much does performance matter? A meta-analysis of CEO pay studies, *Journal of Management*, 26: 301–339.

119. D. Leonhardt, 2002, It's called a "loan," but it's far sweeter, *New York Times*, http://www.nytimes.com, February 3.

120. G. Strom, Even last year, option spigot was wide open, *New York Times*, http://www.nytimes.com, February 3.

121. T. G. Pollock, H. M. Fischer, & J. B. Wade, 2002, The role of politics in repricing executive options, *Academy of Management Journal*, 45: 1172–1182; M. E. Carter and L. J. Lynch, 2001, An examination of executive stock option repricing, *Journal of Financial Economics*, 59: 207–225; D. Chance, R. Kumar, & R. Todd, 2001, The "repricing" of executive stock options, *Journal of Financial Economics*, 59: 129–154.

122. N. K. Chidambaran & N. R. Prabhala, 2003, Executive stock option repricing, internal governance mechanisms and management turnover, *Journal of Financial Economics*, 61: in press.

123. J. C. Hartzell & L. T. Starks, 2003, Institutional investors and executive compensation, *Journal of Finance*, 61: in press.

124. P. Brandes, R. Dharwadkar, & G. V. Lemesis, 2003, Effective stock option design: Reconciling stakeholder, strategic and motivational factors, *Academy of Management Executive*, 17(1): 77–93.

125. J. Greene, C. Edwards, S. Hamm, D. Henry, & L. Lavelle, 2003, Will stock options lose their sex appeal? *Business Week*, July 21, 23–24.

126. R. Coff, 2002, Bidding wars over R&D intensive firms: Knowledge, opportunism and the market for corporate control, *Academy of Management Journal*, 46: 74–85; Hitt, Hoskisson, Johnson, & Moesel, The market for corporate control and firm innovation; J. P. Walsh & R. Kosnik, 1993, Corporate raiders and their disciplinary role in the market for corporate control, *Academy of Management Journal*, 36: 671–700.

127. D. Goldstein, 2000, Hostile takeovers as corporate governance? Evidence from 1980s, *Review of Political Economy*, 12: 381–402.

128. R. Sidel & A. Raghavan, 2003, Merger activity sizzles again, *Wall Street Journal*, July 9, C1, C5.

129. M. A. Hitt & V. Pisano, 2003, The cross-border merger and acquisition strategy, *Management Research*, 1: 133–144; B. Venard, 2003, Les acquisitions transnationales en hongrie: Vers une taxonomie des attitudes face au changement, *Management International*, 7: 19–30.

130. J. Anand & A. Delios, 2002, Absolute and relative resources as determinants of international acquisitions, *Strategic Management Journal*, 23: 119–134.

131. J. Harford, 2003, Takeover bids and target directors' incentives: The impact of a bid on directors' wealth and board seats, *Journal of Financial Economics*, 61: in press; S. Chatterjee, J. S. Harrison, & D. D. Bergh, 2003, Failed takeover attempts, corporate governance and refocusing, *Strategic Management Journal*, 24: 87–96.

132. F. Guerrera & R. Waters, 2003, EU probe looms over Oracle merger plans, *Financial Times*, http://www.ft.com, July 2; M. Lander, 2003, Ringside at PeopleSoft bout, SAP hopes to share in the prize, *New York Times*, http://www.nytimes.com, June 30.

133. M. Maynard & F. Warner, 2003, Rival makes hostile bid for Dana, *New York Times*, http://www.nytimes.com, July 9; J. Grant, 2003, ArvinMeritor launches hostile bid for Dana, *Financial Times*, http://www.ft.com, July 8.

134. D. Ball, J. R. Hagerly, & R. Sidel, 2003, List of Safeway suitors keeps growing, *Wall Street Journal*, January 23, C1, C9.

135. J. Johnson, 2003, Ex-Vivendi chief in transatlantic legal battle, *Financial Times*, http://www.ft.com, July 11; A. R. Sorkin, 2003, Arbitrators say Vivendi owes Messier millions, *New York Times*, http://www.nytimes.com, July 1.

136. C. Sundaramurthy, J. M. Mahoney, & J. T. Mahoney, Board structure, anti-takeover provisions, and stockholder wealth, *Strategic Management Journal*, 18: 231–246.

137. J. Westphal & E. Zajac, 2001, Decoupling policy from practice: The case of stock repurchase programs, *Administrative Science Quarterly*, 46: 202–228.

138. H. W. Jenkins, 2003, Don't sweat it, *Wall Street Journal*, http://www.wsj.com, February 24; J. A. Byrne, 1999, Poison pills: Let shareholders decide, *Business Week*, May 17, 104.

139. P.-W. Tam, 2003, H-P severance curbs get support, *Wall Street Journal*, April 3, B5.

140. A. Almanzan & J. Suarez, 2003, Entrenchment and severance pay in optimal governance structures, *Journal of Finance*, 58: 519–548.

141. Walsh & Kosnik, Corporate raiders.

142. A. Chakraborty & R. Arnott, 2001, Takeover defenses and dilution: A welfare analysis, *Journal of Financial and Quantitative Analysis*, 36: 311–334.

143. A. Portlono, 2000, The decision to adopt defensive tactics in Italy, *International Review of Law and Economics*, 20: 425–452.

144. C. Sundaramurthy, 2000, Antitakeover provisions and shareholder value implications: A review and a contingency framework, *Journal of Management*, 26: 1005–1030.

145. B. Kogut, G. Walker, & J. Anand, 2002, Agency and institutions: National divergence in diversification behavior, *Organization Science*, 13: 162–178; D. Norburn, B. K. Boyd, M. Fox, & M. Muth, 2000, International corporate governance reform, *European Business Journal*, 12(3): 116–133; M. Useem, 1998, Corporate leadership in a globalizing equity market, *Academy of Management Executive*, 12(3): 43–59.

146. Y. Yafeh, 2000, Corporate governance in Japan: Past performance and future prospects, *Oxford Review of Economic Policy*, 16(2): 74–84; H. Kim & R. E. Hoskisson, 1996, Japanese governance systems: A critical review, in B. Prasad (ed.), *Advances in International Comparative Management*, Greenwich, CT: JAI Press, 165–189.

147. L. Nanchum, 2003, Does nationality of ownership make any difference and if so, under what circumstances? Professional service MNEs in global competition, *Journal of International Management*, 9: 1–32.

148. Aguilera & Jackson, The cross-national diversity of corporate governance: Dimensions and determinants.

149. S. Klein, 2000, Family businesses in Germany: Significance and structure, *Family Business Review*, 13: 157–181.

150. J. Edwards & M. Nibler, 2000, Corporate governance in Germany: The role of banks and ownership concentration, *Economic Policy*, 31: 237–268; E. R. Gedajlovic & D. M. Shapiro, 1998, Management and ownership effects: Evidence from five countries, *Strategic Management Journal*, 19: 533–553.

151. S. Douma, 1997, The two-tier system of corporate governance, *Long Range Planning*, 30(4): 612–615.

152. N. E. Boudette, 2003, Volkswagen stalls on several fronts after luxury drive, *Wall Street Journal*, May 8, A1, A17; C. Tierney, 2001, Volkswagen, *BusinessWeek Online*, http://www.businessweek.com, July 23.

153. A. Tuschke & W. G. Sanders, 2003, Antecedents and consequences of corporate governance reform: The case of Germany, *Strategic Management Journal*, 24: 631–649.

154. T. Hoshi, A. K. Kashyap, & S. Fischer, 2001, *Corporate Financing and Governance in Japan*, Boston: MIT Press.

155. Charkham, *Keeping Good Company*, 70.

156. M. A. Hitt, H. Lee, & E. Yucel, 2002, The importance of social capital to the management of multinational enterprises: Relational networks among Asian and Western Firms, *Asia Pacific Journal of Management*, 19: 353–372.

157. P. M. Lee & H. M. O'Neill, 2003, Ownership structures and R&D investments of U.S. and Japanese firms: Agency and stewardship perspectives, *Academy of Management Journal*, 46: 212–225.

158. B. Bremner, 2001, Cleaning up the banks—finally, *Business Week*, December 17, 86; 2000, Business: Japan's corporate-governance u-turn, *The Economist*, November 18, 73.

159. B. Bremner, E. Thornton, & I. M. Kunii, 1999, Fall of a keiretsu, *Business Week*, March 15, 87–92.

160. Lee & O'Neill, Ownership structures and R&D investments of U.S. and Japanese firms.

161. J. B. White, 2000, The company we'll keep, *Wall Street Journal Online*, http://www.wsj.com, January 17.

162. K. Uhlenbruck, K. E. Meyer, & M. A. Hitt, 2003, Organizational transformation in transition economies: Resource-based and organizational learning perspectives, *Journal of Management Studies*, 40: 257–282; P. Mar & M. Young, 2001, Corporate governance in transition economies: A case study of 2 Chinese airlines, *Journal of World Business*, 36(3): 280–302.

163. L. Chang, 1999, Chinese firms find incentive to use stock-compensation plans, *Wall Street Journal*, November 1, A2; T. Clarke & Y. Du, 1998, Corporate governance in China: Explosive growth and new patterns of ownership, *Long Range Planning*, 31(2): 239–251.

164. M. A. Hitt, D. Ahlstrom, M. T. Dacin, E. Levitas, & L. Svobodina, 2004, The institutional effects on strategic alliance partner selection in transition economies: China versus Russia, *Organization Science*, in press; I. Filatotchev, R. Kapelyushnikov, N. Dyomina, & S. Aukutsionek, 2001, The effects of ownership concentration on investment and performance in privatized firms in Russia, *Managerial and Decision Economics*, 22(6): 299–313; E. Perotti & S. Gelfer, 2001, Red barons or robber barons? Governance and investment in Russian financial-industrial groups, *European Economic Review*, 45(9): 1601–1617.

165. Hillman, Keim, & Luce, Board composition and stakeholder performance; R. Oliver, 2000, The board's role: Driver's seat or rubber stamp? *Journal of Business Strategy*, 21: 7–9.

166. A. Felo, 2001, Ethics programs, board involvement, and potential conflicts of interest in corporate governance, *Journal of Business Ethics*, 32: 205–218.

Organizational Structure and Controls

Chapter Eleven

Knowledge Objectives

Studying this chapter should provide you with the strategic management knowledge needed to:

1. Define organizational structure and controls and discuss the difference between strategic and financial controls.

2. Describe the relationship between strategy and structure.

3. Discuss the functional structures used to implement business-level strategies.

4. Explain the use of three versions of the multidivisional (M-form) structure to implement different diversification strategies.

5. Discuss the organizational structures used to implement three international strategies.

6. Define strategic networks and strategic center firms.

©Reuters NewMedia Inc./Corbis

The success of Amaze Entertainment, creator of Sony's Playstation2, is partly a function of the match between its corporate-level strategy and organizational structure.

Amaze Entertainment: Bringing Video-Game Excitement Directly to You!

Amaze Entertainment was founded in 1996. It has become one of the world's largest and most successful independent developers of interactive video-game entertainment. The firm believes that it is quite skilled at "creating reliable, solid, interactive experiences for platforms ranging from PCs and Macs to handheld devices and gaming consoles—including next-generation systems like the Nintendo Game Cube, Microsoft X-Box and Sony Playstation2." As this array of products suggests, Microsoft, Mattel, Sony, and Electronic Arts are but a few of Amaze's clients. Designing and producing games linked to Holly-wood blockbusters is an important source of the firm's profitable growth. Amaze's games based on *Harry Potter and the Sorcerer's Stone*, *The Lord of the Rings: The Two Towers*, *Finding Nemo*, and *Daredevil*, for example, have been highly successful.

Although relatively small (with approximately 220 employees in mid-2003), Amaze Entertainment is a diversified company with an organizational structure featuring five core business units (called studios) serving different markets. Each specialized studio is guided by a unique vision and has its own culture. However, all the studios rely on technical sophistication and skilled designers to produce their products. The goal of the Adrenium studio is to surprise, amuse, and captivate even the most seasoned gamer. Azurik is one of its popular games. Griptonite is Amaze's handheld entertainment studio. In addition to *Harry Potter*, Griptonite has produced handheld games based on *Star Wars*, Barbie, and Ren and Stimpy, among others. The PC entertainment studio is called KnowWonder. Oriented to family fun, KnowWonder creates digital entertainment products for use on PCs. Titles produced by KnowWon-der are intended to educate as well as entertain. The Fizz Factor studio was acquired by Amaze. The "Fizz" unit seeks to be a premiere developer of orig-inal character-driven console and handheld titles for customers such as Has-bro and Nickelodeon. Black Ship studios is the newest Amaze business unit. After gaining success in its U.S. domestic market, Amaze decided to expand into what it envisions to be a lucrative Asian market, starting with Japan. The former president of Nintendo Software USA is heading Black Ship, which is focused on developing partnerships and superior products by work-ing with the best publishers in Asia. Amaze believes that Black Ship has the potential to eventually account for as much as 33 percent of the firm's total revenues.

Amaze Entertainment is using a related constrained corporate-level strategy, with each of its five studios implementing a differentiation business-level strategy. The cooperative multidivisional organizational structure (dis-cussed later in the chapter) is used at Amaze to support its related constrained corporate-level strategy. This structure means that while Amaze's studios work independently, all five of them share the firm's strength in innovative game technologies as well as its ability to share knowledge among its employees regarding their game development skills. The corporate office centralizes strategic planning and marketing efforts to foster cooperation among the five studios. This proper match between corporate-level strategy and structure has contributed to the firm's ability to establish a niche with Hollywood producers. Indeed, as an Amaze executive says, "There really isn't another studio in the world that can do what we do. With one contract, publishers can get a great PC game, a great Game Boy game and a great console game—nobody that I know of offers that." Family-oriented games form the other market niche analysts believe Amaze dominates.

SOURCES: 2003, Amaze Entertainment, http://www.amazeentertainment.com, July 7; 2003, One market at a time, *Business Week Online*, http://www.businessweek.com, April 15; S. Ernst, Fast-growing Amaze builds on its Hollywood ties, *Puget Sound Business Journal*, 23(41): 12; L. Hawkins, 2003, Computer-game maker puts Fizz back into Austin, Texas, industry, *Austin American-Statesman*, June 23.

As described in Chapter 4, all firms use one or more business-level strategies. In Chapters 6–9, we discuss the other strategies that might be used (corporate-level, international, and cooperative strategies). Once selected, strategies can't be implemented in a vacuum. Organizational structure and controls, this chapter's topic, provide the framework within which strategies are used in both for-profit organizations and not-for-profit agencies.[1] However, as we explain, separate structures and controls are required to successfully implement different strategies. For example, Amaze Entertainment uses a form of the multidivisional structure to support use of its related constrained corporate-level strategy, while each of its business units or studios employs a version of the functional structure to effectively implement the differentiation business-level strategy. Top-level managers have the final responsibility for ensuring that the firm has matched each of its strategies with the appropriate organizational structure and that changes to both take place when needed.[2] The match or degree of fit between strategy and structure influences the firm's attempts to earn above-average returns.[3] Thus, the ability to select an appropriate strategy and match it with the appropriate structure is an important characteristic of effective strategic leadership.[4]

This chapter opens with an introduction to organizational structure and controls. We then provide more details about the need for the firm's strategy and structure to be properly matched. Executives at Amaze Entertainment are aware of this need and are committed to maintaining a proper match between its corporate-level strategy and the structure used to implement it. Affecting firms' efforts to match strategy and structure is the fact that they influence each other.[5] As we discuss, strategy has a more important influence on structure, although once in place, structure influences strategy.[6]

The chapter then describes the relationship between growth and structural change that successful firms experience. This is followed with discussions of the different organizational structures that firms use to implement the separate business-level, corporate-level, international, and cooperative strategies. A series of figures highlights the different structures firms match with strategies. Across time and based on their experiences, organizations, especially large and complex ones, customize these general structures to meet their unique needs.[7] Typically, the firm tries to form a structure that is complex enough to facilitate use of its strategies but simple enough for all to effectively implement.[8] For example, the main priority of the organizational structure developed by DnB NOR, Norway's largest commercial bank, was "to adapt the functional organization as far as possible to our customer activities, making sure that the chosen structure will enable us to realize potential synergies."[9]

Organizational Structure and Controls

Research shows that organizational structure and the controls that are a part of it affect firm performance.[10] In particular, when the firm's strategy isn't matched with the most appropriate structure and controls, performance declines.[11] An ineffective match between strategy and structure is thought to account for Zurich Financial Services' recent performance declines.[12] Recognizing this mismatch, the firm is restructuring its business portfolio to focus on its core non-life insurance programs. Less diversification and a renewed concentration on its core business area are expected to result in a match between corporate-level strategy and structure.[13] Even though mismatches between strategy and structure do occur, such as the one at Zurich Financial Services, research evidence suggests that managers try to act rationally when forming or changing their firm's structure.[14]

Organizational Structure

Organizational structure specifies the firm's formal reporting relationships, procedures, controls, and authority and decision-making processes.[15] Developing an organizational structure that effectively supports the firm's strategy is difficult,[16] especially because of the uncertainty (or unpredictable variation[17]) about cause-effect relationships in the global economy's rapidly changing and dynamic competitive environments.[18] When a structure's elements (e.g., reporting relationships, procedures, and so forth) are properly aligned with one another, that structure facilitates effective implementation of the firm's strategies.[19] Thus, organizational structure is a critical component of effective strategy implementation processes.[20]

A firm's structure specifies the work to be done and how to do it, given the firm's strategy or strategies.[21] Thus, organizational structure influences how managers work and the decisions resulting from that work.[22] Supporting the implementation of strategies,[23] structure is concerned with processes used to complete organizational tasks.[24] Effective structures provide the stability a firm needs to successfully implement its strategies and maintain its current competitive advantages, while simultaneously providing the flexibility to develop competitive advantages that will be needed for its future strategies.[25] Thus, *structural stability* provides the capacity the firm requires to consistently and predictably manage its daily work routines,[26] while *structural flexibility* provides the opportunity to explore competitive possibilities and then allocate resources to activities that will shape the competitive advantages the firm will need to be successful in the future.[27] An effective organizational structure allows the firm to *exploit* current competitive advantages while *developing* new ones.[28]

Modifications to the firm's current strategy or selection of a new strategy call for changes to its organizational structure. However, research shows that once in place, organizational inertia often inhibits efforts to change structure, even when the firm's performance suggests that it is time to do so.[29] In his pioneering work, Alfred Chandler found that organizations change their structures only when inefficiencies force them to do so.[30] Firms seem to prefer the structural status quo and its familiar working relationships until the firm's performance declines to the point where change is absolutely necessary.[31] In addition, top-level managers hesitate to conclude that there are problems with the firm's structure (or its strategy, for that matter), in that doing so suggests that their previous choices weren't the best ones.[32] Because of these inertial tendencies, structural change is often induced instead by the actions of stakeholders

Organizational structure specifies the firm's formal reporting relationships, procedures, controls, and authority and decision-making processes.

who are no longer willing to tolerate the firm's performance. For example, continuing losses of customers who have become dissatisfied with the value created by the firm's products could force change, as could reactions from capital market stakeholders (see Chapter 2). This appears to be the case for Sears, Roebuck and Co. Because of dissatisfactions expressed by those it tried to serve, Sears recently changed its organizational structure in ways that it believes allows it to better satisfy customers' needs.[33]

In spite of the timing of structural change described above, many companies make changes prior to substantial performance declines. Appropriate timing of structural change happens when top-level managers quickly recognize that a current organizational structure no longer provides the coordination and direction needed for the firm to successfully implement its strategies.[34] As we discuss in the Strategic Focus, Eastman Chemical Company has made various changes to its organizational structure prior to significant performance declines. Indeed, in commenting about one of the changes to the firm's structure, a company official asserted, "This was not a company that reorganized in response to plummeting sales, laying off thousands of workers to stay afloat. This was restructuring from strength."[35]

As we discuss next, effective organizational controls help managers recognize when it is time to change the firm's structure. Eastman Chemical Company uses a mixture of strategic and financial controls to judge its overall performance. In addition, the controls in place at Eastman help the firm determine when to make changes to its organizational structure.

Organizational Controls

Organizational controls *guide the use of strategy, indicate how to compare actual results with expected results, and suggest corrective actions to take when the difference between actual and expected results is unacceptable.*

Organizational controls are an important aspect of structure.[36] **Organizational controls** guide the use of strategy, indicate how to compare actual results with expected results, and suggest corrective actions to take when the difference between actual and expected results is unacceptable. The fewer the differences between actual and expected outcomes, the more effective are the organization's controls.[37] It is hard for the company to successfully exploit its competitive advantages without effective organizational controls.[38] Properly designed organizational controls provide clear insights regarding behaviors that enhance firm performance.[39] Firms rely on strategic controls and financial controls as part of their structures to support use of their strategies.[40]

Strategic controls *are largely subjective criteria intended to verify that the firm is using appropriate strategies for the conditions in the external environment and the company's competitive advantages.*

Strategic controls are largely subjective criteria intended to verify that the firm is using appropriate strategies for the conditions in the external environment and the company's competitive advantages. Thus, strategic controls are concerned with examining the fit between what the firm *might do* (as suggested by opportunities in its external environment) and what it *can do* (as indicated by its competitive advantages; see Figure 3.1). Effective strategic controls help the firm understand what it takes to be successful.[41] Strategic controls demand rich communications between managers responsible for using them to judge the firm's performance and those with primary responsibility for implementing the firm's strategies (such as middle- and first-level managers). These frequent exchanges are both formal and informal in nature.[42]

Strategic controls are also used to evaluate the degree to which the firm focuses on the requirements to implement its strategies. For a business-level strategy, for example, the strategic controls are used to study primary and support activities (see Tables 3.8 and 3.9) to verify that those critical to successful execution of the business-level strategy are being properly emphasized and executed. With related corporate-level strategies, strategic controls are used to verify the sharing of appropriate strategic factors such as knowledge, markets, and technologies across businesses. To effectively use strategic controls when evaluating related diversification strategies, executives must have a deep understanding of each unit's business-level strategy.[43]

Partly because strategic controls are difficult to use with extensive diversification,[44] financial controls are emphasized to evaluate the performance of the firm following the

Effective Timing of Structural Change at Eastman Chemical Company

Founded in 1920 to supply basic photographic materials to Eastman Kodak Company, Eastman Chemical Company (ECC) was spun off and became an independently traded public company in 1994. A global firm with sales exceeding $5 billion annually and with production operations in 17 countries, ECC manufactures and markets more than 1,200 plastics, chemicals, and fibers products. Collectively, this array of products and their success has resulted in ECC becoming the world's largest supplier of polyester plastics for packaging, a leading supplier of coatings, raw materials, specialty chemicals, and plastics, and a major supplier of cellulose acetate fibers and basic chemicals.

On September 1, 1999, ECC announced that it had created two major business groups—one for its polymers business and one for its chemicals business. From 1994 until the 1999 reorganization, ECC had operated through a functional structure. However, the functional structure was no longer capable of dealing with the firm's increasing product and market complexity and diversity. Following analysis of the situation, executives concluded that organizing the firm around two core product divisions would lead to stronger relationships with customers. Increased efficiency, primarily in the form of quicker response to customers' needs, and greater accountability for performance were other benefits expected from the new structure in addition to an enhanced focus on customers. With the new structure, each business group was given direct responsibility for manufacturing, sales, and pricing and product management decisions. Thus, the polymers and chemicals businesses were each to operate with an independent set of organizational functions.

ECC's structure was changed again in 2002. In this instance, 1994's product divisions were changed to create the Eastman Division and the Voridian Division. The purpose of this structural change was to allow ECC to "strategically focus on the unique needs of individual markets." The Eastman Division consists of three product segments—coatings, adhesives, specialty polymers, and inks; specialty plastics; and performance chemicals and intermediates. Polymers and fibers, the product groups formed in 1999, became Voridian's two core segments in 2002. In general, Voridian uses the cost leadership business-level strategy while the differentiation strategy is used in the Eastman Division, primarily to continuously develop innovative products.

In 2003, Developing Businesses became the third division in ECC's multidivisional structure. Soon after its formation, this division had 20 to 30 projects in the pipeline in various stages of development. The purpose of creating this division was to provide a unique environment to "leverage Eastman's technology expertise, intellectual property and know-how into business models that extend to new customers and markets." For the most part, Developing Businesses focuses on service businesses that are less capital intensive compared to the products that are the mainstay of the Eastman and Voridian Divisions.

Eastman Chemical Company was originally a division of Eastman Kodak Company, a supplier of photographic materials. Eastman Chemical now produces a variety of consumer goods, some of which are featured here. The organizational controls that led to Eastman Chemical's independence from its parent company allow each company to better handle its own market complexities and customer needs.

Photo courtesy of the Eastman Chemical Company

SOURCES: 2003, Eastman introduces new business unit, *Chemical Market Reporter*, 263(13): 3; 2003, Eastman Chemical Company, *Standard & Poor's Stock Reports*, http://www.standardandpoors.com, June 3; 2003, The company profile, http://www.eastmanchemicals.com, July 10; 2003, Eastman facts, http://www.eastmanchemicals.com, July 9; 1999, Eastman announces management reorganization, http://www.eastmanchemicals.com, July 27.

Financial controls *are largely objective criteria used to measure the firm's performance against previously established quantitative standards.*

unrelated diversification strategy. The unrelated diversification strategy's focus on financial outcomes (see Chapter 6) requires the use of standardized financial controls to compare performances between units and managers.[45] **Financial controls** are largely objective criteria used to measure the firm's performance against previously established quantitative standards. Accounting-based measures, such as return on investment and return on assets, and market-based measures, such as economic value added, are examples of financial controls.

When using financial controls, firms evaluate their current performance against previous outcomes as well as their performance compared to competitors and industry averages. In the global economy, technological advances are being used to develop highly sophisticated financial controls, making it possible for firms to more thoroughly analyze their performance results and to assure compliance with regulations. For example, Oracle Corp. developed software tools that automate processes firms can use to meet the financial reporting requirements specified by the Sarbanes-Oxley Act.[46] (This act requires a firm's principal executive and financial officers to certify corporate financial and related information in quarterly and annual reports submitted to the Securities and Exchange Commission.) Pfizer Inc.'s expectations of sophisticated financial controls are that they will: "(1) safeguard the firm's assets, (2) ensure that transactions are properly authorized, and (3) provide reasonable assurance, at reasonable cost, of the integrity, objectivity, and reliability of the financial information."[47]

Both strategic and financial controls are important aspects of each organizational structure, and any structure's effectiveness is determined by using a combination of strategic and financial controls. However, the relative use of controls varies by type of strategy. For example, companies and business units of large diversified firms using the cost leadership strategy emphasize financial controls (such as quantitative cost goals), while companies and business units using the differentiation strategy emphasize strategic controls (such as subjective measures of the effectiveness of product development teams).[48] As explained above, a corporate-wide emphasis on sharing among business units (as called for by related diversification strategies) results in an emphasis on strategic controls, while financial controls are emphasized for strategies in which activities or capabilities aren't shared (e.g., in an unrelated diversification).

Relationships between Strategy and Structure

Strategy and structure have a reciprocal relationship.[49] This relationship highlights the interconnectedness between strategy formulation (Chapter 4 and Chapters 6–9) and strategy implementation (Chapters 10–13). In general, this reciprocal relationship finds structure flowing from or following the selection of the firm's strategy. Once in place, structure can influence current strategic actions as well as choices about future strategies. The general nature of the strategy/structure relationship means that changes to the firm's strategy create the need to change how the organization completes its work. In the "structure influences strategy" direction, firms must be vigilant in their efforts to verify that how their structure calls for work to be completed remains consistent with the implementation requirements of chosen strategies. Research shows, however, that "strategy has a much more important influence on structure than the reverse."[50]

Regardless of the strength of the reciprocal relationships between strategy and structure, those choosing the firm's strategy and structure should be committed to matching each strategy with a structure that provides the stability needed to use current competitive advantages as well as the flexibility required to develop future advantages. This means, for example, that when changing strategies, the firm should simultaneously consider the structure that will be needed to support use of the new strategy. Aware of this mandate, executives at the new Hewlett-Packard continue to adjust the firm's structure in light of the strategies being used following the combining of the former Hewlett-

Packard and Compaq Computer Corp.[51] The fact that a proper strategy/structure match can be a competitive advantage[52] supports actions such as those being taken at Hewlett-Packard. When the firm's strategy/structure combination is a competitive advantage, it contributes to the earning of above-average returns.[53]

Evolutionary Patterns of Strategy and Organizational Structure

Research suggests that most firms experience a certain pattern of relationships between strategy and structure. Chandler[54] found that firms tended to grow in somewhat predictable patterns: "first by volume, then by geography, then integration (vertical, horizontal) and finally through product/business diversification"[55] (see Figure 11.1). Chandler interpreted his findings to indicate that the firm's growth patterns determine its structural form.

As shown in Figure 11.1, sales growth creates coordination and control problems that the existing organizational structure can't efficiently handle. Organizational growth

Strategy and Structure Growth Pattern — Figure 11.1

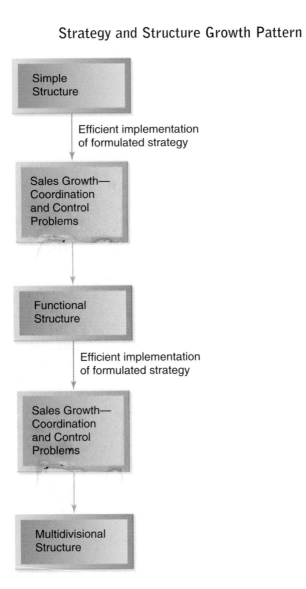

creates the opportunity for the firm to change its strategy to try to become even more successful. However, the existing structure's formal reporting relationships, procedures, controls, and authority and decision-making processes lack the sophistication required to support use of the new strategy. A new structure is needed to help decision makers gain access to the knowledge and understanding required to effectively integrate and coordinate actions to implement the new strategy.[56]

Three major types of organizational structures are used to implement strategies: simple structure, functional structure, and multidivisional structure.

Simple Structure

The **simple structure** is a structure in which the owner-manager makes all major decisions and monitors all activities while the staff serves as an extension of the manager's supervisory authority.[57] Typically, the owner-manager actively works in the business on a daily basis. Informal relationships, few rules, limited task specialization, and unsophisticated information systems describe the simple structure. Frequent and informal communications between the owner-manager and employees make it relatively easy to coordinate the work that is to be done. The simple structure is matched with focus strategies and business-level strategies as firms commonly compete by offering a single product line in a single geographic market. Local restaurants, repair businesses, and other specialized enterprises are examples of firms relying on the simple structure to implement their strategy.

As the small firm grows larger and becomes more complex, managerial and structural challenges emerge. For example, the amount of competitively relevant information requiring analysis substantially increases, placing significant pressure on the owner-manager. Additional growth and success may cause the firm to change its strategy. Even if the strategy remains the same, the firm's larger size dictates the need for more sophisticated workflows and integrating mechanisms. At this evolutionary point, firms tend to move from the simple structure to a functional organizational structure.[58]

Casketfurniture.com, a firm mentioned in Chapter 4 as an example of a company using the focus differentiation strategy, may soon move from the simple structure to a functional structure. Family-owned and managed, this venture is a new part of MHP Enterprises Ltd.'s operations. As a small family firm, MHP has long been managed through the simple structure. In 1997, MHP decided to expand its distribution by establishing Casketfurniture.com. Using the Internet, this venture sells what it believes are creative products throughout the world. The continuing success of Casketfurniture.com could create coordination and control problems for MHP that may be solved only by the firm changing from the simple to the functional structure.[59]

Functional Structure

The **functional structure** is a structure consisting of a chief executive officer and a limited corporate staff, with

Courtesy of MHP Enterprises, LTD

functional line managers in dominant organizational areas, such as production, accounting, marketing, R&D, engineering, and human resources.[60] This structure allows for functional specialization,[61] thereby facilitating active sharing of knowledge within each functional area. Knowledge sharing facilitates career paths as well as the professional development of functional specialists. However, a functional orientation can have a negative effect on communication and coordination among those representing different organizational functions. Because of this, the CEO must work hard to verify that the decisions and actions of individual business functions promote the entire firm rather than a single function.[62] The functional structure supports implementation of business-level strategies and some corporate-level strategies (e.g., single or dominant business) with low levels of diversification.

Multidivisional Structure

With continuing growth and success, firms often consider greater levels of diversification. However, successful diversification requires analysis of substantially greater amounts of data and information when the firm offers the same products in different markets (market or geographic diversification) or offers different products in several markets (product diversification). In addition, trying to manage high levels of diversification through functional structures creates serious coordination and control problems.[63] Thus, greater diversification leads to a new structural form.[64]

The **multidivisional (M-form) structure** consists of operating divisions, each representing a separate business or profit center in which the top corporate officer delegates responsibilities for day-to-day operations and business-unit strategy to division managers. Each division represents a distinct, self-contained business with its own functional hierarchy.[65] As initially designed, the M-form was thought to have three major benefits: "(1) it enabled corporate officers to more accurately monitor the performance of each business, which simplified the problem of control; (2) it facilitated comparisons between divisions, which improved the resource allocation process; and (3) it stimulated managers of poorly performing divisions to look for ways of improving performance."[66] Active monitoring of performance through the M-form increases the likelihood that decisions made by managers heading individual units will be in shareholders' best interests. Diversification is a dominant corporate-level strategy in the global economy, resulting in extensive use of the M-form.[67]

The multidivisional (M-form) structure consists of operating divisions, each representing a separate business or profit center in which the top corporate officer delegates responsibilities for day-to-day operations and business-unit strategy to division managers.

Used to support implementation of related and unrelated diversification strategies, the M-form helps firms successfully manage the many demands (including those related to processing vast amounts of information) of diversification.[68] Chandler viewed the M-form as an innovative response to coordination and control problems that surfaced during the 1920s in the functional structures then used by large firms such as DuPont and General Motors.[69] Research shows that the M-form is appropriate when the firm grows through diversification.[70] Partly because of its value to diversified corporations, some consider the multidivisional structure to be one of the 20th century's most significant organizational innovations.[71]

No organizational structure (simple, functional, or multidivisional) is inherently superior to the other structures.[72] In Peter Drucker's words: "There is no one right organization. . . . Rather, the task . . . is to select the organization for the particular task and mission at hand."[73] In our context, Drucker is saying that the firm must select a structure that is "right" for the particular strategy that has been selected to pursue the firm's strategic intent and strategic mission. Because no single structure is optimal in all instances, managers concentrate on developing proper matches between strategies and organizational structures rather than searching for an "optimal" structure.

We now describe the strategy/structure matches that evidence shows positively contribute to firm performance.

Matches between Business-Level Strategies and the Functional Structure

Different forms of the functional organizational structure are used to support implementation of the cost leadership, differentiation, and integrated cost leadership/differentiation strategies. The differences in these forms are accounted for primarily by different uses of three important structural characteristics or dimensions—*specialization* (concerned with the type and number of jobs required to complete work[74]), *centralization* (the degree to which decision-making authority is retained at higher managerial levels[75]), and *formalization* (the degree to which formal rules and procedures govern work[76]).

USING THE FUNCTIONAL STRUCTURE TO IMPLEMENT THE COST LEADERSHIP STRATEGY

Firms using the cost leadership strategy want to sell large quantities of standardized products to an industry's or a segment's typical customer. Simple reporting relationships, few layers in the decision-making and authority structure, a centralized corporate staff, and a strong focus on process improvements through the manufacturing function rather than the development of new products through an emphasis on product R&D characterize the cost leadership form of the functional structure[77] (see Figure 11.2). This structure contributes to the emergence of a low-cost culture—a culture in which all employees constantly try to find ways to reduce the costs incurred to complete their work.

In terms of centralization, decision-making authority is centralized in a staff function to maintain a cost-reducing emphasis within each organizational function (for example, engineering, marketing, etc.). While encouraging continuous cost reductions, the centralized staff also verifies that further cuts in costs in one function won't adversely affect the productivity levels in other functions.

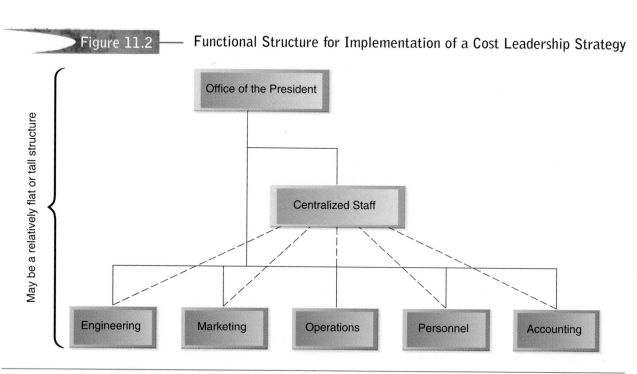

Figure 11.2 — Functional Structure for Implementation of a Cost Leadership Strategy

Notes:
• Operations is the main function
• Process engineering is emphasized rather than new product R&D
• Relatively large centralized staff coordinates functions
• Formalized procedures allow for emergence of a low-cost culture
• Overall structure is mechanistic; job roles are highly structured

Jobs are highly specialized in the cost leadership functional structure. Job specialization is accomplished by dividing work into homogeneous subgroups. Organizational functions are the most common subgroup, although work is sometimes batched on the basis of products produced or clients served. Specializing in their work allows employees to increase their efficiency, reducing the firm's costs as a result. Highly formalized rules and procedures, often emanating from the centralized staff, guide the work completed in the cost leadership form of the functional structure. Predictably following formal rules and procedures creates cost-reducing efficiencies. Known for its commitment to EDLP ("everyday low price"), Wal-Mart's functional organizational structures in both its retail (e.g., Wal-Mart Stores, Supercenters, Sam's Club) and specialty (e.g., Wal-Mart Vacations, Used Fixture Auctions) divisions are formed to continuously drive costs lower.[78] As discussed in Chapter 4, competitors' efforts to duplicate the success of Wal-Mart's cost leadership strategies have failed, partly because of the effective strategy/structure matches in Wal-Mart's business units.

USING THE FUNCTIONAL STRUCTURE TO IMPLEMENT THE DIFFERENTIATION STRATEGY

Firms using the differentiation strategy produce products that customers perceive as being different in ways that create value for them. With this strategy, the firm wants to sell nonstandardized products to customers with unique needs. Relatively complex and flexible reporting relationships, frequent use of cross-functional product development teams, and a strong focus on marketing and product R&D rather than manufacturing and process R&D (as with the cost leadership form of the functional structure) characterize the differentiation form of the functional structure (see Figure 11.3). This structure contributes to the emergence of a development-oriented culture—a culture in which employees try to find ways to further differentiate current products and to develop new, highly differentiated products.

Functional Structure for Implementation of a Differentiation Strategy — Figure 11.3

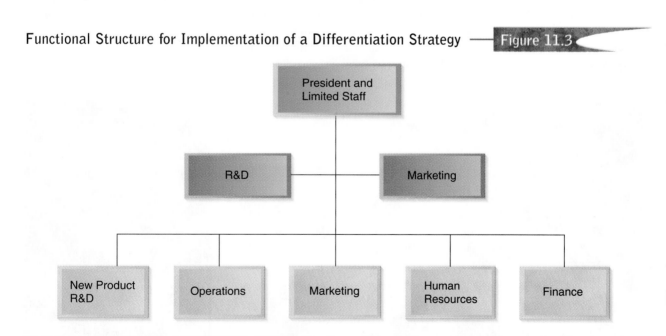

Notes: • Marketing is the main function for keeping track of new product ideas
- New product R&D is emphasized
- Most functions are decentralized, but R&D and marketing may have centralized staffs that work closely with each other
- Formalization is limited so that new product ideas can emerge easily and change is more readily accomplished
- Overall structure is organic; job roles are less structured

Thinking Globally, Acting Locally: The Foundations of Procter & Gamble's Multidivisional Structure

Consumer giant Procter & Gamble (P&G) has a bold self-perception, believing that its rightful place in corporate America is as a company that is admired, imitated, and uncommonly profitable. Historical successes suggest that this perception is reasonably consistent with reality. Across time, P&G has been quite profitable while analysts have viewed the firm's management techniques as setting "the gold standard" for others to emulate. Two of the innovations and subsequent skills for which P&G is recognized are brand management and excellence in managerial training. CEOs Jeff Immelt (GE), Meg Whitman (eBay) and W. James McNerney, Jr. (3M) are just a few of the alumni who have achieved great success following their P&G careers.

As with all successful firms, P&G is challenged to continuously reinvent itself while striving to outperform its competitors. Rivals such as Unilever are launching intense campaigns to improve their competitive positions relative to P&G. Unilever began restructuring in 1999 to deliver on the promises of its "Path to Growth" agenda. Unilever's five-year restructuring involves a major overhaul of its portfolio. The firm "has sold low-growth businesses and acquired new-growth drivers, most notably Best-foods, which it bought for $24 billion in 2000. The company also snapped up diet brand SlimFast and Ben & Jerry's ice cream."

P&G also restructured its operations in 1999. Framed around the objective of having an organizational structure that would allow the firm to "think globally and act locally," P&G formed a unique version of the cooperative multidivisional structure to support use of its related constrained diversification strategy. This structure, which P&G officials believe is a source of competitive advantage for the firm, features five global business product units (GBUs) (baby, feminine and family care, fabric and home care, food and beverage, and health and beauty care) and seven market development organizations (MDOs), each formed around a region of the world, such as Northeast Asia. Using the five global product units to create strong brand equities through ongoing innovation is how P&G thinks globally; interfacing with customers to ensure that a division's marketing plans fully capitalize on local opportunities is how P&G acts locally. Information is shared between the product-oriented and the marketing-oriented efforts to enhance the corpora-

Well-known CEOs Jeff Immelt, Meg Whitman, and W. James McNerney may owe their current success to the skills acquired during their employment at P&G, which is known for its excellence in managerial training.

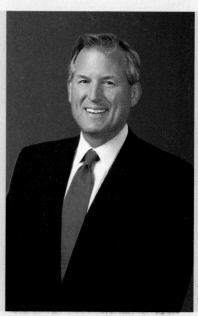

tion's performance. Indeed, some corporate staff members are responsible for focusing on making certain that knowledge is meaningfully categorized and then rapidly transferred throughout P&G's businesses. Those working to achieve this objective are part of P&G's Global Business Services (GBS) group. Last, the Corporate Functions group is essentially a set of consultants ready to assist those working in the global business units and the market development organizations in their efforts to use "best practices" in terms of organizational functions, such as external relations, information technology management, and human resources practices. In summary, P&G's cooperative structure uses GBUs to define a brand's equity, MDOs to adapt a brand to local preferences, the GBS group to support operations through infrastructure services such as accounting and employee benefits and payroll, and Corporate Functions to assure that the latest and most effective methodologies are being used to conduct the firm's product- and marketing-oriented operations.

SOURCES: 2003, Procter & Gamble Home Page, http://www.procter&gamble.com, July 5; 2003, Procter & Gamble corporate structure, http://www.procter&gamble.com, July 9; D. Ball, 2003, Unilever cuts sales estimates as U.S. competition stiffens, *Wall Street Journal Online*, http://www.wsj.com, June 23; R. Berner, 2003, P&G: New and improved, *Business Week*, July 7, 52–63.

Continuous product innovation demands that people throughout the firm be able to interpret and take action based on information that is often ambiguous, incomplete, and uncertain. With a strong focus on the external environment to identify new opportunities, employees often gather this information from people outside the firm, such as customers and suppliers. Commonly, rapid responses to the possibilities indicated by the collected information are necessary, suggesting the need for decision-making responsibility and authority to be decentralized. To support creativity and the continuous pursuit of new sources of differentiation and new products, jobs in this structure are not highly specialized. This lack of specialization means that workers have a relatively large number of tasks in their job descriptions. Few formal rules and procedures are also characteristics of this structure. Low formalization, decentralization of decision-making authority and responsibility, and low specialization of work tasks combine to create a structure in which people interact frequently to exchange ideas about how to further differentiate current products while developing ideas for new products that can be differentiated to create value for customers.

USING THE FUNCTIONAL STRUCTURE TO IMPLEMENT THE INTEGRATED COST LEADERSHIP/DIFFERENTIATION STRATEGY

Firms using the integrated cost leadership/differentiation strategy want to sell products that create value because of their relatively low cost and reasonable sources of differentiation. The cost of these products is low "relative" to the cost leader's prices while their differentiation is "reasonable" compared to the clearly unique features of the differentiator's products.

The integrated cost leadership/differentiation strategy is used frequently in the global economy, although it is difficult to successfully implement. This difficulty is due largely to the fact that different primary and support activities (see Chapter 3) must be emphasized when using the cost leadership and differentiation strategies. To achieve the cost leadership position, emphasis is placed on production and process engineering, with infrequent product changes. To achieve a differentiated position, marketing and new product R&D are emphasized while production and process engineering are not. Thus, effective use of the integrated strategy results when the firm successfully combines activities intended to reduce costs with activities intended to create additional differentiation features. As a result, the integrated form of the functional structure must have decision-making patterns that are partially centralized and partially decentralized. Additionally, jobs are semispecialized, and rules and procedures call for some formal and some informal job behavior.

Matches between Corporate-Level Strategies and the Multidivisional Structure

As explained earlier, Chandler's research showed that the firm's continuing success leads to product or market diversification or both.[79] The firm's level of diversification is a function of decisions about the number and type of businesses in which it will compete as well as how it will manage the businesses (see Chapter 6). Geared to managing individual organizational functions, increasing diversification eventually creates information processing, coordination, and control problems that the functional structure can't handle. Thus, use of a diversification strategy requires the firm to change from the functional structure to the multidivisional structure to develop an appropriate strategy/structure match.

As defined in Figure 6.1 in Chapter 6, corporate-level strategies have different degrees of product and market diversification. The demands created by different levels of diversification highlight the need for each strategy to be implemented through a unique organizational structure (see Figure 11.4).

USING THE COOPERATIVE FORM OF THE MULTIDIVISIONAL STRUCTURE TO IMPLEMENT THE RELATED CONSTRAINED STRATEGY

The cooperative form is a structure in which horizontal integration is used to bring about interdivisional cooperation.

The **cooperative form** is a structure in which horizontal integration is used to bring about interdivisional cooperation. The divisions in the firm using the related constrained diversification strategy commonly are formed around products, markets, or both. We discuss related constrained firm Procter & Gamble's (P&G's) cooperative form of the multidivisional structure in the Strategic Focus. As we explain, P&G's organizational structure is intended to allow the firm to "think globally, yet act locally."

In Figure 11.5, we use product divisions as part of the representation of the cooperative form of the multidivisional structure, although as the P&G example in the Strategic Focus suggests, market divisions could be used instead of or in addition to product divisions to develop the figure. Thus, P&G has modified the core cooperative form of the multidivisional structure to satisfy its unique strategy/structure match requirements.

Figure 11.4 — Three Variations of the Multidivisional Structure

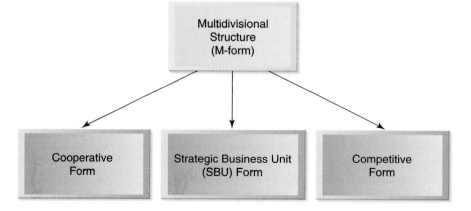

Figure 11.5

Cooperative Form of the Multidivisional Structure for Implementation of a Related Constrained Strategy

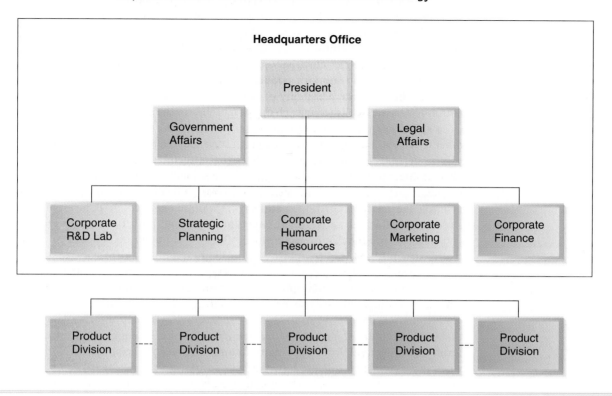

Notes: • Structural integration devices create tight links among all divisions
   • Corporate office emphasizes centralized strategic planning, human resources, and marketing to foster cooperation between divisions
   • R&D is likely to be centralized
   • Rewards are subjective and tend to emphasize overall corporate performance in addition to divisional performance
   • Culture emphasizes cooperative sharing

All of the related constrained firm's divisions share one or more corporate strengths. Production competencies, marketing competencies, or channel dominance are examples of strengths that the firm's divisions might share.[80] Production expertise is one of the strengths shared across P&G's divisions. At Halliburton Co., the world's largest oilfield services company, the firm's competence in the development and application of sophisticated technologies is shared between its two major divisions.[81]

The sharing of divisional competencies facilitates the corporation's efforts to develop economies of scope. As explained in Chapter 6, economies of scope (cost savings resulting from the sharing of competencies developed in one division with another division) are linked with successful use of the related constrained strategy. Interdivisional sharing of competencies depends on cooperation, suggesting the use of the cooperative form of the multidivisional structure.[82] Increasingly, it is important that the links resulting from effective use of integration mechanisms support the cooperative sharing of both intangible resources (such as knowledge) as well as tangible resources (such as facilities and equipment).[83]

Different characteristics of structure are used as integrating mechanisms by the cooperative structure to facilitate interdivisional cooperation. Defined earlier in the discussion of functional organizational structures, centralization is one of these mechanisms. Centralizing some organizational functions (human resource management, R&D, marketing, and finance) at the corporate level allows the linking of activities among divisions. Work completed in these centralized functions is managed by the firm's central office with the purpose of exploiting common strengths among divisions by sharing competencies. The intent is to develop a competitive advantage in the divisions as they implement their cost leadership, differentiation, or integrated cost leadership/differentiation business-unit strategies that exceeds the value created by the advantages used by nondiversified rivals' implementation of these strategies.[84]

Frequent, direct contact between division managers, another integrating mechanism, encourages and supports cooperation and the sharing of either competencies or resources that have the possibility of being used to create new advantages. Sometimes, liaison roles are established in each division to reduce the amount of time division managers spend integrating and coordinating their unit's work with the work occurring in other divisions. Temporary teams or task forces may be formed around projects whose success depends on sharing competencies that are embedded within several divisions. Formal integration departments might be established in firms frequently using temporary teams or task forces. Ultimately, a matrix organization may evolve in firms implementing the related constrained strategy. A *matrix organization* is an organizational structure in which there is a dual structure combining both functional specialization and business product or project specialization.[85] Although complicated, an effective matrix structure can lead to improved coordination among a firm's divisions.[86]

The success of the cooperative multidivisional structure is significantly affected by how well information is processed among divisions. But because cooperation among divisions implies a loss of managerial autonomy, division managers may not readily commit themselves to the type of integrative information-processing activities that this structure demands. Moreover, coordination among divisions sometimes results in an unequal flow of positive outcomes to divisional managers. In other words, when managerial rewards are based at least in part on the performance of individual divisions, the manager of the division that is able to benefit the most by the sharing of corporate competencies might be viewed as receiving relative gains at others' expense. Strategic controls are important in these instances, as divisional managers' performance can be evaluated at least partly on the basis of how well they have facilitated interdivisional cooperative efforts. Furthermore, using reward systems that emphasize overall company performance, besides outcomes achieved by individual divisions, helps overcome problems associated with the cooperative form.

USING THE STRATEGIC BUSINESS UNIT FORM OF THE MULTIDIVISIONAL STRUCTURE TO IMPLEMENT THE RELATED LINKED STRATEGY

When the firm has fewer links or less constrained links among its divisions, the related linked diversification strategy is used. The strategic business unit form of the multidivisional structure supports implementation of this strategy. The **strategic business unit (SBU) form** is a structure consisting of three levels: corporate headquarters, strategic business units (SBUs), and SBU divisions (see Figure 11.6).

The divisions within each SBU are related in terms of shared products or markets or both, but the divisions of one SBU have little in common with the divisions of the other SBUs. Divisions within each SBU share product or market competencies to develop economies of scope and possibly economies of scale. The integration mechanisms used by the divisions in a cooperative structure can be equally well used by the divisions within the individual strategic business units that are part of the SBU form of the multidivisional structure. In the SBU structure, each SBU is a profit center that is controlled and evaluated by the headquarters office. Although both financial and strategic controls are important, on a relative basis, financial controls are vital to headquarters' evaluation of each SBU; strategic controls are critical when the heads of SBUs evaluate their divisions' performance. Strategic controls are also critical to the

The strategic business unit (SBU) form is a structure consisting of three levels: corporate headquarters, strategic business units (SBUs), and SBU divisions.

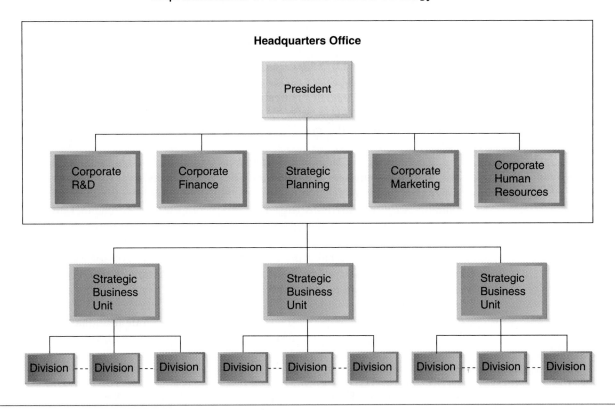

Notes: • Structural integration among divisions within SBUs, but independence across SBUs
   • Strategic planning may be the most prominent function in headquarters for managing the strategic planning approval process of SBUs for the president
   • Each SBU may have its own budget for staff to foster integration
   • Corporate headquarters staff serve as consultants to SBUs and divisions, rather than having direct input to product strategy, as in the cooperative form

headquarters' efforts to determine if the company has chosen an effective portfolio of businesses and if those businesses are being successfully managed.

Used by large firms, the SBU structure can be complex, with the complexity reflected by the organization's size and product and market diversity. Related linked firm GE, for example, has over 20 strategic business units, each with multiple divisions. GE Aircraft Engines, Appliances, Power Systems, NBC, and GE Capital are a few of the firm's SBUs. As is frequently the case with large diversified corporations, the scale of GE's business units is striking. GE Aircraft Engines, for example, is the world's leading manufacturer of jet engines for civil and military aircraft. With almost 30 divisions, GE Capital is a diversified financial services company creating comprehensive solutions to increase client productivity and efficiency. The GE Power Systems business unit has 21 divisions, including GE Energy Rentals, GE Distributed Power, and GE Water Technologies.[87]

In many of GE's SBUs, efforts are undertaken to form competencies in services and technology as a source of competitive advantage. Recently, technology was identified as an advantage for the GE Medical Systems SBU, as that unit's divisions share technological competencies to produce an array of sophisticated equipment, including computed tomography (CT) scanners, magnetic resonance imaging (MRI) systems, nuclear medicine cameras, and ultrasound systems.[88] Once a competence is developed in one of GE Medical Systems' divisions, it is quickly transferred to the other divisions in that SBU so that the competence can be leveraged to increase the unit's overall performance.[89] The sharing of competencies among units within an SBU is an important characteristic of the SBU form of the multidivisional structure (see the legend to Figure 11.6).

USING THE COMPETITIVE FORM OF THE MULTIDIVISIONAL STRUCTURE TO IMPLEMENT THE UNRELATED DIVERSIFICATION STRATEGY

Firms using the unrelated diversification strategy want to create value through efficient internal capital allocations or by restructuring, buying, and selling businesses.[90] The competitive form of the multidivisional structure supports implementation of this strategy.

The **competitive form** is a structure in which there is complete independence among the firm's divisions (see Figure 11.7). Unlike the divisions included in the cooperative structure, the divisions that are part of the competitive structure do not share common corporate strengths (e.g., marketing competencies or channel dominance). Because strengths aren't shared, integrating devices aren't developed for use by the divisions included in the competitive structure.

The efficient internal capital market that is the foundation for use of the unrelated diversification strategy requires organizational arrangements that emphasize divisional competition rather than cooperation.[91] Three benefits are expected from the internal competition that the competitive form of the multidivisional structure facilitates. First, internal competition creates flexibility—corporate headquarters can have divisions working on different technologies to identify those with the greatest future

The competitive form is a structure in which there is complete independence among the firm's divisions.

Figure 11.7 — Competitive Form of the Multidivisional Structure for Implementation of an Unrelated Strategy

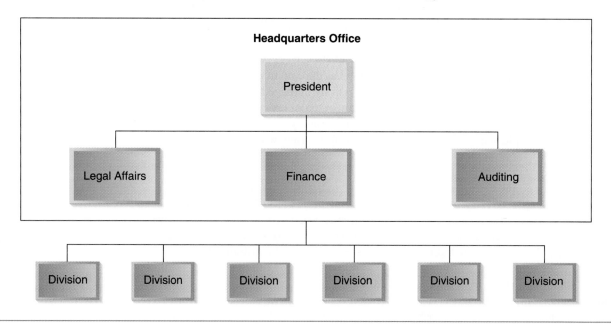

Notes:
- Corporate headquarters has a small staff
- Finance and auditing are the most prominent functions in the headquarters office to manage cash flow and assure the accuracy of performance data coming from divisions
- The legal affairs function becomes important when the firm acquires or divests assets
- Divisions are independent and separate for financial evaluation purposes
- Divisions retain strategic control, but cash is managed by the corporate office
- Divisions compete for corporate resources

United Technologies Corp.: Where Strategy and Structure Are Matched

United Technologies is a diversified corporation providing high-technology products to the aerospace and building systems industries throughout the world. Operating in over 180 countries and employing more than 155,000 people worldwide and with annual sales revenue of approximately $28 billion, the firm's recent market capitalization exceeded $33 billion. United Technologies' multidivisional structure features six business units (Sikorsky, Pratt & Whitney, Hamilton Sundstrand, UTC Fuel Cells, Otis, and Carrier) as well as a corporate-level research center. Operating independently, these units compete against one another for resources that are allocated from corporate headquarters. The firm spends more than $2.5 billion annually on R&D, with the clear majority of these funds allocated to the corporate-level research center. This center's primary responsibility is to work individually with the six units to assist in developing product and process innovations that are unique to each unit's operations.

During the 1990s, United Technologies' unrelated diversification strategy was implemented very successfully as demonstrated by the fact that the firm's stock outperformed the S&P 500 index, rising at a ten-year average annual rate of 21 percent versus 15 percent for the index. However, the aftermath of the September 11, 2001 attacks has affected the firm's independent business units. As analysts noted, "Ongoing cuts in Boeing and Airbus commercial aircraft production should continue to temper near-term demand for UTX's Pratt & Whitney jet engines and Hamilton Sundstrand aircraft components." The Otis Elevator business unit has cushioned the firm's bottom line while these other two units continue to be affected by the worst slump in aviation history. Between 2002 and 2003, for example, the percentage of the firm's operating profits accounted for by Otis grew from 24.8 percent to 27.4 percent while Pratt & Whitney's percentage of total operating profits declined from 38.3 percent to 33.2 percent.

To continue reducing its dependence on the volatile airline industry, United Technologies acquired Chubb PLC for $1 billion in 2003. Based in the United Kingdom, Chubb specializes in electronic security products (e.g., hotel locks and burglar alarms) and services (e.g., security guards). A cross-border transaction, this strategic acquisition reflects United Technologies' desire to build a portfolio of businesses that are more stable and less cyclical compared to those competing in the aviation industry. In addition to being available at an attractive price, Chubb appealed to United Technologies because electronic security is one of the few sectors of the global economy that emerged stronger after the September 11, 2001 attacks. Company officials anticipate that in the current environment, Chubb will join Otis as a primary contributor to the corporation's operating profits. As part of United Technologies, Chubb will compete with all other business units for corporate resources and will operate independently from them as called for by the competitive form of the multidivisional structure.

SOURCES: J. L. Lunsford, 2003, United Technologies' formula: A powerful lift from elevators, *Wall Street Journal Online*, http://www.wsj.com, July 2; A. Raghavan, 2003, U.S. firms are shopping for European M&A deals, *Wall Street Journal Online*, http://www.wsj.com, June 30; A. Raghavan & R. Sidel, 2003, United Technologies to buy Chubb PLC for $1 billion, *Wall Street Journal Online*, http://www.wjs.com, June 12; 2003, United Tech gets U.S. clearance to buy Chubb, *Reuters*, http://www.reuters.com, July 1; 2003, United Technologies, *Standard & Poor's Stock Reports*, http://www.standardandpoors.com, July 3; 2003, UTC Fuel Cells, United Technologies Home Page, http://www.unitedtechnologies.com, July 10.

357

potential, for example. Resources can then be allocated to the division that is working with the most promising technology to fuel the entire firm's success. Second, internal competition challenges the status quo and inertia, because division heads know that future resource allocations are a product of excellent current performance as well as superior positioning of their division in terms of future performance. Last, internal competition motivates effort. The challenge of competing against internal peers can be as great as the challenge of competing against external marketplace competitors.[92]

Independence among divisions, as shown by a lack of sharing of corporate strengths and the absence of integrating devices, allows the firm using the unrelated diversification strategy to form specific profit performance expectations for each division to stimulate internal competition for future resources. The benefits of internal capital allocations or restructuring cannot be fully realized unless divisions are held accountable for their own independent performance. In the competitive structure, organizational controls (primarily financial controls) are used to emphasize and support internal competition among separate divisions and as the basis for allocating corporate capital based on divisions' performances. At Textron Inc., for example, return on invested capital is the primary measure used to assess the performance of the firm's unrelated business units. According to the firm, "return on invested capital serves as both a compass to guide every investment decision and a measurement of Textron's success."[93]

To emphasize competitiveness among divisions, the headquarters office maintains an arms-length relationship with them and does not intervene in divisional affairs, except to audit operations and discipline managers whose divisions perform poorly. In this situation, the headquarters office relies on strategic controls to set rate-of-return targets and financial controls to monitor divisional performance relative to those targets. The headquarters office then allocates cash flow on a competitive basis, rather than automatically returning cash to the division that produced it. Thus, the focus of the headquarters' work is on performance appraisal, resource allocation, and long-range planning to verify that the firm's portfolio of businesses will lead to financial success.[94]

As explained in the Strategic Focus, United Technologies Corp. uses the competitive form of the multidivisional structure to support use of its unrelated diversification strategy.

The three major forms of the multidivisional structure should each be paired with a particular corporate-level strategy. As explained in the Strategic Focus, United Technologies uses the competitive form of the multidivisional structure to implement the unrelated diversification strategy. Table 11.1 shows these structures' characteristics. Differences are seen in the degree of centralization, the focus of the performance appraisal, the horizontal structures (integrating mechanisms), and the incentive compensation schemes. The most centralized and most costly structural form is the cooperative structure. The least centralized, with the lowest bureaucratic costs, is the competitive structure. The SBU structure requires partial centralization and involves some of the mechanisms necessary to implement the relatedness between divisions. Also, the divisional incentive compensation awards are allocated according to both SBUs and corporate performance.

Matches between International Strategies and Worldwide Structures

As explained in Chapter 8, international strategies are becoming increasingly important for long-term competitive success.[95] Among other benefits, international strategies allow the firm to search for new markets, resources, core competencies, and technologies as part of its efforts to outperform competitors.[96]

As with business-level and corporate-level strategies, unique organizational structures are necessary to successfully implement the different international strategies.[97] Forming proper matches between international strategies and organizational structures facilitates the firm's efforts to effectively coordinate and control its global operations.[98] More importantly, recent research findings confirm the validity of the international strategy/structure matches we discuss here.[99]

Characteristics of the Structures Necessary to Implement — Table 11.1
the Related Constrained, Related Linked, and
Unrelated Diversification Strategies

Structural Characteristics	Overall Structural Form		
	Cooperative M-Form (Related Constrained Strategy)[a]	SBU M-Form (Related Linked Strategy)[a]	Competitive M-Form (Unrelated Diversification Strategy)[a]
Centralization of operations	Centralized at corporate office	Partially centralized (in SBUs)	Decentralized to divisions
Use of integration mechanisms	Extensive	Moderate	Nonexistent
Divisional performance appraisals	Emphasize subjective (strategic) criteria and objective (financial) criteria	Use a mixture of subjective (strategic)	Emphasize objective (financial) criteria
Divisional incentive compensation	Linked to overall corporate performance	Mixed linkage to corporate, SBU, and divisional performance	Linked to divisional performance

[a]Strategy implemented with structural form.

USING THE WORLDWIDE GEOGRAPHIC AREA STRUCTURE TO IMPLEMENT THE MULTIDOMESTIC STRATEGY

The *multidomestic strategy* decentralizes the firm's strategic and operating decisions to business units in each country so that product characteristics can be tailored to local preferences. Firms using this strategy try to isolate themselves from global competitive forces by establishing protected market positions or by competing in industry segments that are most affected by differences among local countries. The worldwide geographic area structure is used to implement this strategy. The **worldwide geographic area structure** is a structure emphasizing national interests and facilitating the firm's efforts to satisfy local or cultural differences (see Figure 11.8).

Because using the multidomestic strategy requires little coordination between different country markets, integrating mechanisms among divisions in the worldwide geographic area structure aren't needed. Hence, formalization is low, and coordination among units in a firm's worldwide geographic area structure is often informal.

The multidomestic strategy/worldwide geographic area structure match evolved as a natural outgrowth of the multicultural European marketplace. Friends and family members of the main business who were sent as expatriates into foreign countries to develop the independent country subsidiary often implemented this type of structure for the main business. The relationship to corporate headquarters by divisions took place through informal communication among "family members."[100]

Unilever, the giant Dutch consumer products firm and major competitor for Procter & Gamble, has refocused its business operations.[101] As a result, the firm grouped its worldwide operations into two global divisions—foods, and home and personal care. The firm uses the worldwide geographic area structure. For the foods division (known as Unilever Bestfoods), regional presidents are responsible for results from operations in the region to which they have been assigned. Asia, Europe, North America, Africa, the Middle East and Turkey, and Latin America are the regions of

*The **worldwide geographic area structure** is a structure emphasizing national interests and facilitating the firm's efforts to satisfy local or cultural differences.*

Notes: • The perimeter circles indicate decentralization of operations
• Emphasis is on differentiation by local demand to fit an area or country culture
• Corporate headquarters coordinates financial resources among independent subsidiaries
• The organization is like a decentralized federation

Unilever's worldwide geographic structure has regionalized its food division, allowing it to be in better touch with customers in each area.

the foods division. The firm describes the match between the multidomestic strategy and Unilever's worldwide geographic structure (in terms of the firm's foods division): "Unilever Bestfoods' strength lies in our ability to tailor products to different markets as well as to anticipate consumer trends and demands. This comes from our deep understanding of the countries in which we operate and our policy of listening to our customers."[102]

A key disadvantage of the multidomestic strategy/worldwide geographic area structure match is the inability to create global efficiency. With an increasing emphasis on lower-cost products in international markets, the need to pursue worldwide economies of scale has also increased. These changes have fostered the use of the global strategy and its structural match, the worldwide product divisional structure.

USING THE WORLDWIDE PRODUCT DIVISIONAL STRUCTURE TO IMPLEMENT THE GLOBAL STRATEGY

With the corporation's home office dictating competitive strategy, the *global strategy* is one through which the firm offers standardized products

AP Photo/Greg Baker

across country markets. The firm's success depends on its ability to develop and take advantage of economies of scope and scale on a global level. Decisions to outsource some primary or support activities to the world's best providers are particularly helpful when the firm tries to develop economies of scale.

The worldwide product divisional structure supports use of the global strategy. In the **worldwide product divisional structure,** decision-making authority is centralized in the worldwide division headquarters to coordinate and integrate decisions and actions among divisional business units (see Figure 11.9). This structure is often used in rapidly growing firms seeking to manage their diversified product lines effectively, as in Japan's Kyowa Hakko. With businesses in pharmaceuticals, chemicals, biochemicals, and liquor and food, this company uses the worldwide product divisional structure to facilitate its decisions about how to successfully compete in what it believes are rapidly shifting global competitive environments.[103]

Integrating mechanisms are important to effective use of the worldwide product divisional structure. Direct contact between managers, liaison roles between departments, and temporary task forces as well as permanent teams are examples of these mechanisms. One researcher describes the use of these mechanisms in the worldwide structure: "There is extensive and formal use of task forces and operating committees to supplement communication and coordination of worldwide operations."[104] The evolution of a shared vision of the firm's strategy and how structure supports its implementation is one of the important outcomes resulting from these mechanisms' effective use. The disadvantages of the global strategy/worldwide structure combination are the difficulty involved with coordinating decisions and actions across country borders and the inability to quickly respond to local needs and preferences.

The worldwide product divisional structure is a structure in which decision-making authority is centralized in the worldwide division headquarters to coordinate and integrate decisions and actions among divisional business units.

Worldwide Product Divisional Structure for Implementation of a Global Strategy — Figure 11.9

Notes: • The headquarters' circle indicates centralization to coordinate information flow among worldwide products
   • Corporate headquarters uses many intercoordination devices to facilitate global economies of scale and scope
   • Corporate headquarters also allocates financial resources in a cooperative way
   • The organization is like a centralized federation

USING THE COMBINATION STRUCTURE TO IMPLEMENT THE TRANSNATIONAL STRATEGY

The *transnational strategy* calls for the firm to combine the multidomestic strategy's local responsiveness with the global strategy's efficiency. Thus, firms using this strategy are trying to gain the advantages of both local responsiveness and global efficiency.[105] The combination structure is used to implement the transnational strategy. The **combination structure** is a structure drawing characteristics and mechanisms from both the worldwide geographic area structure and the worldwide product divisional structure.

The fits between the multidomestic strategy and the worldwide geographic area structure and between the global strategy and the worldwide product divisional structure are apparent. However, when a firm wants to implement both the multidomestic and the global strategies simultaneously through a combination structure, the appropriate integrating mechanisms for the two structures are less obvious. The structure used to implement the transnational strategy must be simultaneously centralized and decentralized; integrated and nonintegrated; formalized and nonformalized. These seemingly opposite characteristics must be managed by an overall structure that is capable of encouraging all employees to understand the effects of cultural diversity on a firm's operations.

This requirement highlights the need for a strong educational component to change the whole culture of the organization. If the cultural change is effective, the combination structure should allow the firm to learn how to gain competitive benefits in local economies by adapting its core competencies, which often have been developed and nurtured in less culturally diverse competitive environments. As firms globalize and move toward the transnational strategy, the idea of a corporate headquarters has become increasingly important in fostering leadership and a shared vision to create a stronger company identity.[106]

Matches between Cooperative Strategies and Network Structures

As discussed in Chapter 9, a network strategy exists when partners form several alliances in order to improve the performance of the alliance network itself through cooperative endeavors.[107] The greater levels of environmental complexity and uncertainty companies face in today's competitive environment are causing increasing numbers of firms to use cooperative strategies such as strategic alliances and joint ventures.[108]

The breadth and scope of firms' operations in the global economy create many opportunities for firms to cooperate.[109] In fact, the firm can develop cooperative relationships with many of its stakeholders, including customers, suppliers, and competitors.[110] When the firm becomes involved with combinations of cooperative relationships, it is part of a strategic network, or what others call an alliance constellation.[111]

A *strategic network* is a group of firms that has been formed to create value by participating in multiple cooperative arrangements, such as alliances and joint ventures. An effective strategic network facilitates the discovery of opportunities beyond those identified by individual network participants.[112] A strategic network can be a source of competitive advantage for its members when its operations create value that is difficult for competitors to duplicate and that network members can't create by themselves.[113] Strategic networks are used to implement business-level, corporate-level, and international cooperative strategies.

Commonly, a strategic network is a loose federation of partners who participate in the network's operations on a flexible basis. At the core or center of the strategic network, the *strategic center firm* is the one around which the network's cooperative relationships revolve (see Figure 11.10).

Because of its central position, the strategic center firm is the foundation for the strategic network's structure. Concerned with various aspects of organizational struc-

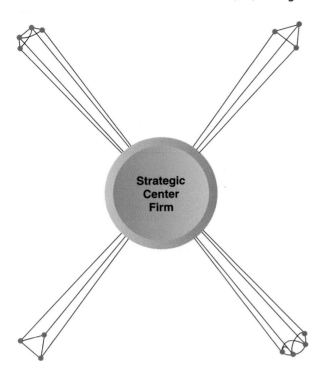

ture, such as formal reporting relationships and procedures, the strategic center firm manages what are often complex, cooperative interactions among network partners. The strategic center firm is engaged in four primary tasks as it manages the strategic network and controls its operations:[114]

> *Strategic outsourcing.* The strategic center firm outsources and partners with more firms than do other network members. At the same time, the strategic center firm requires network partners to be more than contractors. Members are expected to find opportunities for the network to create value through its cooperative work.
>
> *Competencies.* To increase network effectiveness, the strategic center firm seeks ways to support each member's efforts to develop core competencies that can benefit the network.
>
> *Technology.* The strategic center firm is responsible for managing the development and sharing of technology-based ideas among network members. The structural requirement that members submit formal reports detailing the technology-oriented outcomes of their efforts to the strategic center firm facilitates this activity.
>
> *Race to learn.* The strategic center firm emphasizes that the principal dimensions of competition are between value chains and between networks of value chains. Because of this, the strategic network is only as strong as its weakest value-chain link. With its centralized decision-making authority and responsibility, the strategic center firm guides participants in efforts to form network-specific competitive advantages. The need for each participant to have capabilities that can be the foundation for the network's competitive advantages encourages friendly rivalry among participants seeking to develop the skills needed to quickly form new capabilities that create value for the network.[115]

As noted in Chapter 9, there are two types of business-level complementary alliances: vertical and horizontal. Firms with competencies in different stages of the value chain form a vertical alliance to cooperatively integrate their different, but complementary, skills. Firms that agree to combine their competencies to create value in the same stage of the value chain form a horizontal alliance. Vertical complementary strategic alliances, such as those developed by Toyota Motor Company, are formed more frequently than horizontal alliances. Acting as the strategic center firm, Toyota fashioned its lean production system around a network of supplier firms.[116]

A strategic network of vertical relationships, such as the network in Japan between Toyota and its suppliers, often involves a number of implementation issues.[117] First, the strategic center firm encourages subcontractors to modernize their facilities and provides them with technical and financial assistance to do so, if necessary. Second, the strategic center firm reduces its transaction costs by promoting longer-term contracts with subcontractors, so that supplier-partners increase their long-term productivity. This approach is diametrically opposed to that of continually negotiating short-term contracts based on unit pricing. Third, the strategic center firm enables engineers in upstream companies (suppliers) to have better communication with those companies with whom it has contracts for services. As a result, suppliers and the strategic center firm become more interdependent and less independent.[118]

The lean production system pioneered by Toyota has been diffused throughout the Japanese and U.S. auto industries. However, no auto company has learned how to duplicate the manufacturing effectiveness and efficiency Toyota derives from the cooperative arrangements in its strategic network.[119] A key factor accounting for Toyota's manufacturing-based competitive advantage is the cost other firms would incur to imitate the structural form used to support Toyota's application. In part, then, the structure of Toyota's strategic network that it created as the strategic center firm facilitates cooperative actions among network participants that competitors can't fully understand or duplicate.

In vertical complementary strategic alliances, such as the one between Toyota and its suppliers, the strategic center firm is obvious, as is the structure that firm establishes. However, this is not always the case with horizontal complementary strategic alliances where firms try to create value in the same part of the value chain, as with airline alliances that are commonly formed to create value in the marketing and sales primary activity segment of the value chain (see Table 3.6). Because air carriers commonly participate in multiple vertical complementary alliances, it is difficult to select the strategic center firm. Moreover, participation in several alliances can cause firms to question partners' true loyalties and intentions. For these reasons, horizontal complementary alliances are used less frequently than their vertical counterpart.

Strategic networks have been important to Cisco Systems Inc. The worldwide leader in networking for the Internet, Cisco provides a broad line of solutions for transporting data, voice, and video in multiple settings[120] and has been involved with a number of strategic networks in its pursuit of competitive success. Cisco recently announced that it was changing its organizational structure. Historically, the firm's structure featured three primary business units—enterprise, service provider, and commercial. In late 2001, Cisco changed its structure to create 11 technology areas.[121] Will cooperative strategies be as critical to the firm as it completes its work through the dictates of a new organizational structure? In all likelihood, this will be the case, although the evolution of strategy and structure at Cisco will ultimately decide this issue.

Implementing Corporate-Level Cooperative Strategies

Corporate-level cooperative strategies (such as franchising) are used to facilitate product and market diversification. As a cooperative strategy, franchising allows the firm to use its competencies to extend or diversify its product or market reach, but without completing a merger or an acquisition. For example, McDonald's, the largest fast-food company in the world, has more than 50 percent of its almost 31,000 restaurants outside the United States and serves more than 46 million customers daily.[122]

The McDonald's franchising system is a strategic network. McDonald's headquarters office serves as the strategic center firm for the network's franchisees. The headquarters office uses strategic controls and financial controls to verify that the franchisees' operations create the greatest value for the entire network. One strategic control issue is the location of franchisee units. McDonald's believes that its greatest expansion opportunities are outside the United States. Density percentages seem to support this conclusion. "While in the United States there are 22,000 people per McDonald's, in the rest of the world there is only one McDonald's for every 605,000 people."[123] As a result, as the strategic center firm, McDonald's is devoting its capital expenditures (over 70 percent in the last three years) primarily to develop units in non–U.S. markets. Financial controls are framed around requirements an interested party must satisfy to become a McDonald's franchisee as well as performance standards that are to be met when operating a unit.[124]

Implementing International Cooperative Strategies

Strategic networks formed to implement international cooperative strategies result in firms competing in several countries.[125] Differences among countries' regulatory environments increase the challenge of managing international networks and verifying that at a minimum, the network's operations comply with all legal requirements.[126]

Distributed strategic networks are the organizational structure used to manage international cooperative strategies. As shown in Figure 11.11, several regional strategic

A Distributed Strategic Network — Figure 11.11

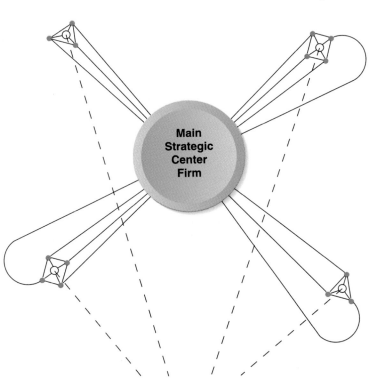

Distributed Strategic Center Firms

center firms are included in the distributed network to manage partner firms' multiple cooperative arrangements.[127] Strategic centers for Ericsson (telecommunications exchange equipment) and Electrolux (white goods, washing machines) are located in countries throughout the world, instead of only in Sweden where the firms are headquartered. Ericsson, for example, is active in more than 140 countries and employs more than 90,000 people. Using the SBU structure, Ericsson has five strategic business units and has formed cooperative agreements with companies throughout the world in each unit. As a founding member of an Ethernet alliance (Intel and Cisco are also members), Ericsson acts as the strategic center firm for this cooperative arrangement, which seeks to solve the wireline access bottleneck by promoting open industry standards.[128]

Summary

- Organizational structure specifies the firm's formal reporting relationships, procedures, controls, and authority and decision-making processes. Influencing managerial work, structure essentially details the work to be done and how that work is to be accomplished. Organizational controls guide the use of strategy, indicate how to compare actual and expected results, and suggest actions to take to improve performance when it falls below expectations. When properly matched with the strategy for which they were intended, structure and controls can be a competitive advantage.

- Strategic controls (largely subjective criteria) and financial controls (largely objective criteria) are the two types of organizational controls used to successfully implement the firm's chosen strategy. Both types of controls are critical, although their degree of emphasis varies based on individual matches between strategy and structure.

- Strategy and structure influence each other, although strategy has an overall stronger influence on structure. Research indicates that firms tend to change structure when declining performance forces them to do so. Effective managers anticipate the need for structural change, quickly modifying structure to better accommodate the firm's strategy implementation needs when evidence calls for that action.

- Business-level strategies are implemented through the functional structure. The cost leadership strategy requires a centralized functional structure—one in which manufacturing efficiency and process engineering are emphasized. The differentiation strategy's functional structure decentralizes implementation-related decisions, especially those concerned with marketing, to those involved with individual organizational functions. Focus strategies, often used in small firms, require a simple structure until such time that the firm diversifies in terms of products and/or markets.

- Unique combinations of different forms of the multidivisional structure are matched with different corporate-level diversification strategies to properly implement these strategies. The cooperative M-form, used to implement the related constrained corporate-level strategy, has a centralized corporate office and extensive integrating mechanisms. Divisional incentives are linked to overall corporate performance. The related linked SBU M-form structure establishes separate profit centers within the diversified firm. Each profit center may have divisions offering similar products, but the centers are unrelated to each other. The competitive M-form structure, used to implement the unrelated diversification strategy, is highly decentralized, lacks integrating mechanisms, and utilizes objective financial criteria to evaluate each unit's performance.

- The multidomestic strategy, implemented through the worldwide geographic area structure, emphasizes decentralization and locates all functional activities in the host country or geographic area. The worldwide product divisional structure is used to implement the global strategy. This structure is centralized in order to coordinate and integrate different functions' activities so as to gain global economies of scope and scale. Decision-making authority is centralized in the firm's worldwide division headquarters.

- The transnational strategy—a strategy through which the firm seeks the local responsiveness of the multidomestic strategy and the global efficiency of the global strategy—is implemented through the combination structure. Because it must be simultaneously centralized and decentralized, integrated and nonintegrated, and formalized and nonformalized, the combination structure is difficult to organize and manage successfully.

- Increasingly important to competitive success, cooperative strategies are implemented through organizational structures framed around strategic networks. Strategic center firms are critical to the management of strategic networks.

1. What is organizational structure and what are organizational controls? What are the differences between strategic controls and financial controls?

2. What does it mean to say that strategy and structure have a reciprocal relationship?

3. What are the characteristics of the functional structures that are used to implement the cost leadership, differentiation, integrated cost leadership/differentiation, and focused business-level strategies?

4. What are the differences among the three versions of the multidivisional (M-form) organizational structures that are used to implement the related constrained, related linked, and unrelated corporate-level diversification strategies?

5. What organizational structures are used to implement the multidomestic, global, and transnational international strategies?

6. What is a strategic network? What is a strategic center firm?

Experiential Exercises

Organizational Structure and Controls

As an executive board member for a successful 50-partner firm that provides accounting services to corporate clients, you are interested in expanding to offer management consulting services to these clients. Another possibility for your firm is offering both types of services to smaller clients.

Part One. You are concerned about how your organizational structure may need to change to support these services. Based on the material in the chapter, use the chart to rank each type of organizational structure against the activities—information processing, coordination, and control—that you anticipate will need to be strengthened.

Part Two. You are also very concerned that there may be a potential conflict of interest if your firm provides both accounting and management consulting services to the same client. In small groups, discuss whether it is possible for a firm to use organizational structure and controls to achieve its strategic objectives but also to prevent conflicts of interest among its divisions.

	Information processing	Coordination	Control
Simple structure			
Functional structure			
Multidivisional structure			

Structural Issues of Related Diversification

For years, Kodak used the cooperative form of the multidivisional structure to implement the related-constrained diversification strategy. Following this structure, primary organizational functions such as manufacturing, customer care, and strategic planning were centralized, which allowed such

expertise to be shared among Kodak's seven product divisions. The cooperative structure worked well for Kodak as it used the related-constrained strategy to compete in what for many years had been relatively stable markets. However, innovative technologies and increased competition disrupted these markets, making the sharing of the firm's technologies and related skills across product divisions less competitively valuable. Moreover, sharing key resources and their corresponding costs across many business units with increased competition in unstable markets made it difficult for Kodak to assess the profitability of its product divisions (Consumer Imaging, Digital and Applied Imaging, Kodak Professional, Health Imaging, Document Imaging, Entertainment Imaging) and operational divisions (Commercial and Government, Federal Government Contracts, and Worldwide Transportation).

Analysis of the external environment as well as of Kodak's resources, capabilities, and core competencies resulted in management concluding that the firm should reduce the number of links between its business units and their products and services. Kodak subsequently made two consecutive changes to the SBU structure. First, Kodak moved to a three SBU structure in October 2000 (see Figure 11.12). This combined the previous seven product divisions into two broad customer-oriented SBUs (Consumer and Commercial), while the third (Global Operations) handled Kodak's governmental contracts along with various supply chain and operational needs. The resulting structure was viewed as less than optimal by Kodak executives, who concluded that another form of the SBU structure might be necessary. A new version of the SBU structure was implemented by Kodak in November 2001 (see Figure 11.13).

1. How might these rapid, consecutive, and fundamental changes in the corporate structure both facilitate and hinder Kodak's ability to realistically implement its corporate-level strategy?

2. Do either of the newest Kodak organizational charts match well with the related-constrained or related-linked corporate strategies? Why or why not?

Figure 11.12

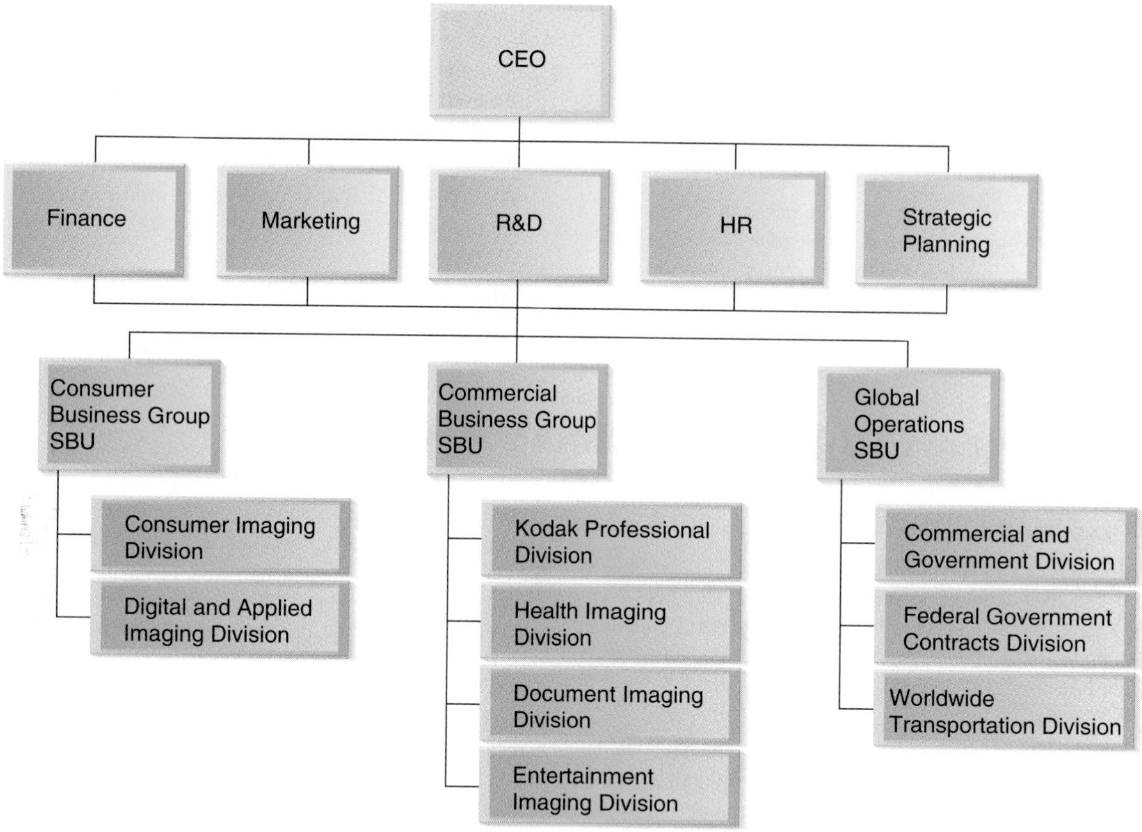

CEO

Finance | Marketing | R&D | HR | Strategic Planning

Consumer Business Group SBU
- Consumer Imaging Division
- Digital and Applied Imaging Division

Commercial Business Group SBU
- Kodak Professional Division
- Health Imaging Division
- Document Imaging Division
- Entertainment Imaging Division

Global Operations SBU
- Commercial and Government Division
- Federal Government Contracts Division
- Worldwide Transportation Division

Figure 11.13

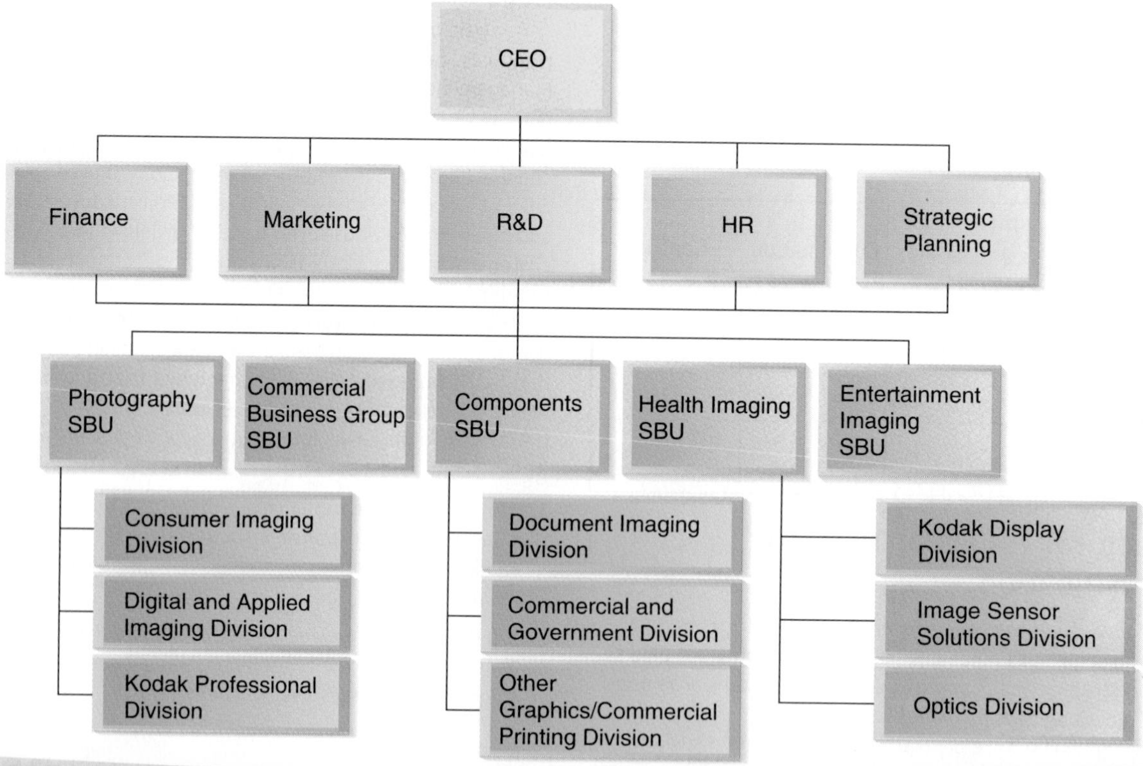

CEO

Finance | Marketing | R&D | HR | Strategic Planning

Photography SBU
- Consumer Imaging Division
- Digital and Applied Imaging Division
- Kodak Professional Division

Commercial Business Group SBU

Components SBU
- Document Imaging Division
- Commercial and Government Division
- Other Graphics/Commercial Printing Division

Health Imaging SBU

Entertainment Imaging SBU
- Kodak Display Division
- Image Sensor Solutions Division
- Optics Division

Notes

1. J. Hauser, 2003, Organizational lessons for nonprofits, *The McKinsey Quarterly*, Special Edition: 60–69.

2. R. J. Herbold, 2002, Inside Microsoft: Balancing creativity and discipline, *Harvard Business Review*, 80(1): 73–79.

3. R. E. Miles & C. C. Snow, 1978, *Organizational Strategy, Structure and Process*, New York: McGraw-Hill.

4. N. Nohria, W. Joyce, & B. Roberson, 2003, What really works, *Harvard Business Review*, 81(7): 42–52.

5. T. Amburgey & T. Dacin, 1994, As the left foot follows the right? The dynamics of strategic and structural change, *Academy of Management Journal*, 37: 1427–1452.

6. B. Keats & H. O'Neill, 2001, Organizational structure: Looking through a strategy lens, in M. A. Hitt, R. E. Freeman, & J. S. Harrison (eds.), *Handbook of Strategic Management*, Oxford, UK: Blackwell Publishers, 520–542.

7. R. E. Hoskisson, C. W. L. Hill, & H. Kim, 1993, The multidivisional structure: Organizational fossil or source of value? *Journal of Management*, 19: 269–298.

8. F. Warner, 2002, Think lean, *Fast Company*, February, 40–42.

9. 2003, DnB, Gjensidige NOR outline merged bank's structure, *Wall Street Journal Online*, http://www.wsj.com, June 11.

10. T. Burns & G. M. Stalker, 1961, *The Management of Innovation*, London: Tavistok; P. R. Lawrence & J. W. Lorsch, 1967, *Organization and Environment*, Homewood, IL: Richard D. Irwin; J. Woodward, 1965, *Industrial Organization: Theory and Practice*, London: Oxford University Press.

11. M. Bower, 2003, Organization: Helping people pull together, *The McKinsey Quarterly*, Number 2, http://www.premium.mckinseyquarterly.com; P. Jenster & D. Hussey, 2001, *Company Analysis: Determining Strategic Capability*, Chichester: John Wiley & Sons, 135–171.

12. B. Rigby & T. Johnson, 2002, Zurich scraps plan to see U.S. unit, *Reuters Business News*, http://www.fidelity.com, January 9.

13. 2003, Zurich sells U.S. life unit for $500 million, *Reuters Business News*, http://www.fidelity.com, May 30.

14. Keats & O'Neill, Organizational structure, 520–542; J. R. Galbraith, 1995, *Designing Organizations*, San Francisco: Jossey-Bass, 6.

15. Keats & O'Neill, Organizational structure, 533; Galbraith, *Designing Organizations*, 6.

16. H. J. Leavitt, 2003, Why hierarchies thrive, *Harvard Business Review*, 81(3): 96–102.

17. R. L. Priem, L. G. Love, & M. A. Shaffer, 2002, Executives' perceptions of uncertainty sources: A numerical taxonomy and underlying dimensions, *Journal of Management*, 28: 725–746.

18. J. D. Day, 2003, The value in organization, *The McKinsey Quarterly*, Number 2: 4–5; V. P. Rindova & S. Kotha, 2001, Continuous "morphing": Competing through dynamic capabilities, form, and function, *Academy of Management Journal*, 44: 1263–1280.

19. H. Barth, 2003, Fit among competitive strategy, administrative mechanisms, and performance: A comparative study of small firms in mature and new industries, *Journal of Small Business Management*, 41: 133–147; J. G. Covin, D. P. Slevin, & M. B. Heeley, 2001, Strategic decision making in an intuitive vs. technocratic mode: Structural and environmental considerations, *Journal of Business Research*, 52: 51–67.

20. H. Barkema, J. A. C. Baum, & E. A. Mannix, 2002, Management challenges in a new time, *Academy of Management Journal*, 45: 916–930.

21. Jenster & Hussey, *Company Analysis*, 169; L. Donaldson, 1997, A positivist alternative to the structure-action approach, *Organization Studies*, 18: 77–92.

22. M. A. Schilling & H. K. Steensma, 2001, The use of modular organizational forms: An industry-level analysis, *Academy of Management Journal*, 44: 1149–1168.

23. C. B. Dobni & G. Luffman, 2003, Determining the scope and impact of market orientation profiles on strategy implementation and performance, *Strategic Management Journal*, 24: 577–585; D. C. Hambrick & J. W. Fredrickson, 2001, Are you sure you have a strategy? *Academy of Management Executive*, 15(4): 48–59.

24. C. M. Fiol, 2003, Organizing for knowledge-based competitiveness: About pipelines and rivers, in S. E. Jackson, M. A. Hitt, & A. S. DeNisi (eds.), *Managing Knowledge for Sustained Competitive Advantage*, San Francisco: Jossey-Bass, 64–93; G. G. Dess & G. T. Lumpkin, 2001, Emerging issues in strategy process research, in M. A. Hitt, R. E. Freeman, & J. S. Harrison (eds.), *Handbook of Strategic Management*, Oxford, UK: Blackwell Publishers, 3–34.

25. R. D. Ireland, J. G. Covin, & D. F. Kuratko, 2003, Antecedents, elements and consequences of corporate entrepreneurship as strategy, *Proceedings of the Sixty-third Annual Meeting of the Academy of Management (CD)*, ISSN 1543-8643.

26. G. A. Bigley & K. H. Roberts, 2001, The incident command system: High-reliability organizing for complex and volatile task environments, *Academy of Management Journal*, 44: 1281–1299.

27. J. Child & R. M. McGrath, 2001, Organizations unfettered: Organizational form in an information-intensive economy, *Academy of Management Journal*, 44: 1135–1148.

28. T. W. Malnight, 2001, Emerging structural patterns within multinational corporations: Toward process-based structures, *Academy of Management Journal*, 44: 1187–1210; A. Sharma, 1999, Central dilemmas of managing innovation in firms, *California Management Review*, 41(3): 146–164; H. A. Simon, 1991, Bounded rationality and organizational learning, *Organization Science*, 2: 125–134.

29. B. W. Keats & M. A. Hitt, 1988, A causal model of linkages among environmental dimensions, macroorganizational characteristics, and performance, *Academy of Management Journal*, 31: 570–598.

30. A. Chandler, 1962, *Strategy and Structure*, Cambridge, MA: MIT Press.

31. J. D. Day, E. Lawson, & K. Leslie, 2003, When reorganization works, *The McKinsey Quarterly*, Number 2, 20–29.

32. M. Robb, P. Todd, & D. Turnbull, 2003, Untangling underperformance, *The McKinsey Quarterly*, Number 2, 52–59; Keats & O'Neill, Organizational structure, 535.

33. C. Sloan, 2003, Sears revamps home management, *Furniture Today*, 27(36): 2.

34. C. H. Noble, 1999, The eclectic roots of strategy implementation research, *Journal of Business Research*, 45: 119–134.

35. J. Lyne, 1992, Eastman Chemical CEO Earnest Deavenport: Restructuring to become a major global player, *Site Selection*, August, 1–5.

36. P. K. Mills & G. R. Ungson, 2003, Reassessing the limits of structural empowerment: Organizational constitution and trust as controls, *Academy of Management Review*, 28: 143–153.

37. S. Venkataraman & S. D. Sarasvathy, 2001, Strategy and entrepreneurship: Outlines of an untold story, in M. A. Hitt, R. E. Freeman, & J. S. Harrison (eds.), *Handbook of Strategic Management*, Oxford, UK: Blackwell Publishers, 650–668.

38. C. Sundaramurthy & M. Lewis, 2003, Control and collaboration: Paradoxes of governance, *Academy of Management Review*, 28: 397–415.

39. D. F. Kuratko, R. D. Ireland, & J. S. Hornsby, 2001, Improving firm performance through entrepreneurial actions: Acordia's corporate entrepreneurship strategy, *Academy of Management Executive*, 15(4): 60–71.

40. J. S. Harrison & C. H. St. John, 2002, *Foundations in Strategic Management*, 2nd ed., Cincinnati: South-Western College Publishing, 118–129.

41. S. D. Julian & E. Scifres, 2002, An interpretive perspective on the role of strategic control in triggering strategic change, *Journal of Business Strategies*, 19: 141–159.

42. R. E. Hoskisson, M. A. Hitt, & R. D. Ireland, 1994, The effects of acquisitions and restructuring strategies (strategic refocusing) on innovation, in G. von Krogh, A. Sinatra, & H. Singh (eds.), *Managing Corporate Acquisition*, London: MacMillan, 144–169.

43. M. A. Hitt, R. E. Hoskisson, R. A. Johnson, & D. D. Moesel, 1996, The market for corporate control and firm innovation, *Academy of Management Journal*, 39: 1084–1119.

44. R. E. Hoskisson & M. A. Hitt, 1988, Strategic control and relative R&D investment in multiproduct firms, *Strategic Management Journal*, 9: 605–621.

45. D. J. Collis, 1996, Corporate strategy in multibusiness firms, *Long Range Planning*, 29: 416–418.

46. M. L. Songini, 2003, Oracle tools designed to help monitor financial controls, *Computerworld*, 37(22): 49.

47. 2002, Pfizer Inc., Management's report, http://www.pfizer.com, January 27.

48. J. B. Barney, 2002, *Gaining and Sustaining Competitive Advantage*, 2nd ed., Upper Saddle River, NJ: Prentice-Hall.

49. M. Sengul, 2001, Divisionalization: Strategic effects of organizational structure, Paper presented during the 21st Annual Strategic Management Society Conference.

50. Keats & O'Neill, Organizational structure, 531.

51. 2003, Fitch affirms Hewlett-Packard; outlook stable, *Wall Street Journal Online*, http://www.wsj.com, June 27.

52. D. Miller & J. O. Whitney, 1999, Beyond strategy: Configuration as a pillar of competitive advantage, *Business Horizons*, 42(3): 5–17.

53. S. Tallman, 2001, Global strategic management, in M. A. Hitt, R. E. Freeman, & J. S. Harrison (eds.), *Handbook of Strategic Management*, Oxford, UK: Blackwell Publishers, 464–490.

54. Chandler, *Strategy and Structure*.

55. Keats & O'Neill, Organizational structure, 524.

56. G. M. McNamara, R. A. Luce, & G. H. Thompson, 2002, Examining the effect of complexity in strategic group knowledge structures on firm performance, *Strategic Management Journal*, 23: 153–170; J. P. Walsh, 1995, Managerial and organizational cognition: Notes from a trip down memory lane, *Organization Science*, 6: 280–321.

57. C. Levicki, 1999, *The Interactive Strategy Workout*, 2nd ed., London: Prentice-Hall.

58. J. J. Chrisman, A. Bauerschmidt, & C. W. Hofer, 1998, The determinants of new venture performance: An extended model, *Entrepreneurship Theory & Practice*, 23(3): 5–29; H. M. O'Neill, R. W. Pouder, & A. K. Buchholtz, 1998, Patterns in the diffusion of strategies across organizations: Insights from the innovation diffusion literature, *Academy of Management Review*, 23: 98–114.

59. 2003, Casketfurniture.com, About our company, http://www.casketfurniture.com, July 7.

60. Galbraith, *Designing Organizations*, 25.

61. Keats & O'Neill, Organizational structure, 539.

62. Lawrence & Lorsch, *Organization and Environment*.

63. O. E. Williamson, 1975, *Markets and Hierarchies: Analysis and Anti-trust Implications*, New York: The Free Press.

64. Chandler, *Strategy and Structure*.

65. J. Greco, 1999, Alfred P. Sloan, Jr. (1875–1966): The original organizational man, *Journal of Business Strategy*, 20(5): 30–31.

66. Hoskisson, Hill, & Kim, The multidivisional structure, 269–298.

67. W. G. Rowe & P. M. Wright, 1997, Related and unrelated diversification and their effect on human resource management controls, *Strategic Management Journal*, 18: 329–338; D. C. Galunic & K. M. Eisenhardt, 1996, The evolution of intracorporate domains: Divisional charter losses in high-technology, multidivisional corporations, *Organization Science*, 7: 255–282.

68. A. D. Chandler, 1994, The functions of the HQ unit in the multibusiness firm, in R. P. Rumelt, D. E. Schendel, & D. J. Teece (eds.), *Fundamental Issues in Strategy*, Cambridge, MA: Harvard Business School Press, 327.

69. O. E. Williamson, 1994, Strategizing, economizing, and economic organization, in R. P. Rumelt, D. E. Schendel, & D. J. Teece (eds.), *Fundamental Issues in Strategy*, Cambridge, MA: Harvard Business School Press, 361–401.

70. R. M. Burton & B. Obel, 1980, A computer simulation test of the M-form hypothesis, *Administrative Science Quarterly*, 25: 457–476.

71. O. E. Williamson, 1985, *The Economic Institutions of Capitalism: Firms, Markets, and Relational Contracting*, New York: Macmillan.

72. Keats & O'Neill, Organizational structure, 532.

73. M. F. Wolff, 1999, In the organization of the future, competitive advantage will be inspired, *Research Technology Management*, 42(4): 2–4.

74. R. H. Hall, 1996, *Organizations: Structures, Processes, and Outcomes*, 6th ed., Englewood Cliffs, NJ: Prentice-Hall, 13; S. Baiman, D. F. Larcker, & M. V. Rajan, 1995, Organizational design for business units, *Journal of Accounting Research*, 33: 205–229.

75. L. G. Love, R. L. Priem, & G. T. Lumpkin, 2002, Explicitly articulated strategy and firm performance under alternative levels of centralization, *Journal of Management*, 28: 611–627.

76. Hall, *Organizations*, 64–75.

77. Barney, *Gaining and Sustaining Competitive Advantage*, 257.

78. 2002, Wal-Mart stores pricing policy, http://www.walmart.com, February 2.

79. Chandler, *Strategy and Structure*.

80. R. Rumelt, 1974, *Strategy, Structure and Economic Performance*, Boston: Harvard University Press.

81. 2002, Halliburton Co., http://www.halliburton.com, February 1.

82. C. C. Markides & P. J. Williamson, 1996, Corporate diversification and organizational structure: A resource-based view, *Academy of Management Journal*, 39: 340–367; C. W. L. Hill, M. A. Hitt, & R. E. Hoskisson, 1992, Cooperative versus competitive structures in related and unrelated diversified firms, *Organization Science*, 3: 501–521.

83. P. F. Drucker, 2002, They're not employees, they're people, *Harvard Business Review*, 80(2): 70–77; J. Robins & M. E. Wiersema, 1995, A resource-based approach to the multibusiness firm: Empirical analysis of portfolio interrelationships and corporate financial performance, *Strategic Management Journal*, 16: 277–299.

84. C. C. Markides, 1997, To diversify or not to diversify, *Harvard Business Review*, 75(6): 93–99.

85. J. G. March, 1994, *A Primer on Decision Making: How Decisions Happen*, New York: The Free Press, 117–118.

86. P. Walter, 2003, Executive Agenda Column, *Bangkok Post*, http://www.proquest.umi.com, May 1.

87. 2002, GE businesses, http://www.ge.com, February 4.

88. 2002, General Electric Co., Argus Research, http://argusresearch.com, February 4.

89. J. Welch with J. A. Byrne, 2001, *Jack: Straight from the Gut*, New York: Warner Business Books.

90. R. E. Hoskisson & M. A. Hitt, 1990, Antecedents and performance outcomes of diversification: A review and critique of theoretical perspectives, *Journal of Management*, 16: 461–509.

91. Hill, Hitt, & Hoskisson, Cooperative versus competitive structures, 512.

92. J. Birkinshaw, 2001, Strategies for managing internal competition, *California Management Review*, 44(1): 21–38.

93. 2002, Textron profile, http://www.textron.com, February 4.

94. T. R. Eisenmann & J. L. Bower, 2000, The entrepreneurial M-form: Strategic integration in global media firms, *Organization Science*, 11: 348–355.

95. Y. Luo, 2002, Product diversification in international joint ventures: Performance implications in an emerging market, *Strategic Management Journal*, 23: 1–20.

96. T. M. Begley & D. P. Boyd, 2003, The need for a corporate global mindset, *MIT Sloan Management Review*, 44(2): 25–32; Tallman, Global strategic management, 467.

97. T. Kostova & K. Roth, 2003, Social capital in multinational corporations and a micro-macro model of its formation, *Academy of Management Review*, 28: 297–317.

98. Malnight, Emerging structural patterns, 1188.

99. J. Wolf & W. G. Egelhoff, 2002, A reexamination and extension of international strategy-structure theory, *Strategic Management Journal*, 23: 181–189.

100. C. A. Bartlett & S. Ghoshal, 1989, *Managing across Borders: The Transnational Solution*, Boston: Harvard Business School Press.

101. I. C. MacMillan, A. B. van Putten, & R. G. McGrath, 2003, Global gamesmanship, *Harvard Business Review*, 81(5): 62–71.

102. 2002, Unilever today, http://www.unilever.com, February 5.

103. 2001, Kyowa Hakko, Semiannual report, September 30.

104. Malnight, Emerging structural patterns, 1197.

105. Barney, *Gaining and Sustaining Competitive Advantage*, 533.

106. R. J. Kramer, 1999, Organizing for global competitiveness: The corporate headquarters design, *Chief Executive Digest*, 3(2): 23–28.

107. Y. L. Doz & G. Hamel, 1998, *Alliance Advantage: The Art of Creating Value through Partnering*, Boston: Harvard Business School Press, 222.

108. S. X. Li & T. J. Rowley, 2002, Inertia and evaluation mechanisms in interorganizational partner selection: Syndicate formation among U.S. investment banks, *Academy of Management Journal*, 45: 1104–1119; A. C. Inkpen, 2001, Strategic alliances, in M. A. Hitt, R. E. Freeman, & J. S. Harrison (eds.), *Handbook of Strategic Management*, Oxford, UK: Blackwell Publishers, 409–432.

109. Luo, Product diversification in international joint ventures, 2.

110. M. Sawhney, E. Prandelli, & G. Verona, 2003, The power of innomediation, *MIT Sloan Management Review*, 44(2): 77–82; R. Gulati, N. Nohria, & A. Zaheer, 2000, Strategic networks, *Strategic Management Journal*, 21(Special Issue): 203–215; B. Gomes-Casseres, 1994, Group versus group: How alliance networks compete, *Harvard Business Review*, 72(4): 62–74.

111. T. K. Das & B.-S. Teng, 2002, Alliance constellations: A social exchange perspective, *Academy of Management Review*, 27: 445–456.

112. C. Lee, K. Lee, & J. M. Pennings, 2001, Internal capabilities, external networks, and performance: A study on technology-based ventures, *Strategic Management Journal* 22(Special Issue): 615–640.

113. M. B. Sarkar, R. Echambadi, & J. S. Harrison, 2001, Alliance entrepreneurship and firm market performance, *Strategic Management Journal*, 22(Special Issue): 701–711.

114. S. Harrison, 1998, *Japanese Technology and Innovation Management*, Northampton, MA: Edward Elgar.

115. P. Dussauge, B. Garrette, & W. Mitchell, 2000, Learning from competing partners: Outcomes and duration of scale and link alliances in Europe, North America and Asia, *Strategic Management Journal*, 21: 99–126; G. Lorenzoni & C. Baden-Fuller, 1995, Creating a strategic center to manage a web of partners, *California Management Review*, 37(3): 146–163.

116. J. H. Dyer & K. Nobeoka, 2000, Creating and managing a high-performance knowledge-sharing network: The Toyota case, *Strategic Management Journal*, 21(Special Issue): 345–367; J. H. Dyer, 1997, Effective interfirm collaboration: How firms minimize transaction costs and maximize transaction value, *Strategic Management Journal*, 18: 535–556.

117. M. Kotabe, X. Martin, & H. Domoto, 2003, Gaining from vertical partnerships: Knowledge transfer, relationship duration and supplier performance improvement in the U.S. and Japanese automotive industries, *Strategic Management Journal*, 24: 293–316.

118. T. Nishiguchi, 1994, *Strategic Industrial Sourcing: The Japanese Advantage*, New York: Oxford University Press.

119. W. M. Fruin, 1992, *The Japanese Enterprise System*, New York: Oxford University Press.

120. 2003, News @ Cisco, http://www.cisco.com, July 9.

121. 2002, Q&A with John Chambers, http://www.cisco.com, February 10.

122. 2003, McDonald's Corp., *Standard & Poor's Stock Reports*, http://www.fidelity.com, July 5.

123. Ibid.

124. 2003, McDonald's USA franchising, http://www.mcdonalds.com, July 9.

125. C. Jones, W. S. Hesterly, & S. P. Borgatti, 1997, A general theory of network governance: Exchange conditions and social mechanisms, *Academy of Management Review*, 22: 911–945.

126. J. M. Mezias, 2002, Identifying liabilities of foreignness and strategies to minimize their effects: The case of labor lawsuit judgments in the United States, *Strategic Management Journal*, 23: 229–244.

127. R. E. Miles, C. C. Snow, J. A. Mathews, G. Miles, & J. J. Coleman, Jr., 1997, Organizing in the knowledge age: Anticipating the cellular form, *Academy of Management Executive*, 11(4): 7–20.

128. 2002, Ericsson NewsCenter, http://www.ericsson.com, February 10.

Strategic Leadership

Chapter Twelve **12**

Knowledge Objectives

Studying this chapter should provide you with the strategic management knowledge needed to:

1. Define strategic leadership and describe top-level managers' importance as a resource.

2. Define top management teams and explain their effects on firm performance.

3. Describe the internal and external managerial labor markets and their effects on developing and implementing strategies.

4. Discuss the value of strategic leadership in determining the firm's strategic direction.

5. Describe the importance of strategic leaders in managing the firm's resources, with emphasis on exploiting and maintaining core competencies, human capital, and social capital.

6. Define organizational culture and explain what must be done to sustain an effective culture.

7. Explain what strategic leaders can do to establish and emphasize ethical practices.

8. Discuss the importance and use of organizational controls.

Andrea Jung, CEO of Avon Products (center), in New York's Central Park. Emphasizing women's health and self-esteem, Avon Products recently launched "Avon Running—Global Women's Circuit," a series of 10K and 5K fitness walks and prerace clinics in 11 U.S. cities and 16 countries. Andrea Jung, together with Susan Kropf (COO), have strengthened Avon domestically and abroad.

"The truth is that CEOs are flawed individuals who are operating in a complex and imperfect world. . . . They are intensely driven to achieve and they operate in a marketplace that measures achievement almost wholly in the short term. They confront a world that moves faster than ever before, and really, there is little about their unwieldy organizations that they easily control." Despite the major scandals and poor performance of corporations, the current crop of CEOs is no worse overall than previous CEOs. According to Keith Hammonds, the difference is that they now play in a different "sandbox" than they did ten years ago. In 1993, the CEOs of American Express, IBM, and Westinghouse were all forced to resign in the same week. Their companies were performing poorly. Today, a number of companies are performing poorly and a good number of CEOs have resigned because of their company's performance (or because of unethical practices that have come to light).

Regardless of the challenges, some effective and successful strategic leaders do exist. For example, the team of Andrea Jung, CEO, and Susan Kropf, COO, of Avon Products deftly avoided a potential disaster for the company in the economic free fall experienced in Argentina, and have taken other actions to solidify Avon's position in domestic and international markets. While 5 percent of Avon's sales came from Argentina, Jung and Kropf have effectively expanded sales in other parts of the world. They have made Avon a major player in the $500 million market in Central and Eastern Europe and have increased sales by 30 percent in China. In 2002, Avon achieved its third consecutive year in which its earnings per share increased by more than 10 percent (an accomplishment in a very weak economy).

Another successful strategic leader is James Morgan, recently retired CEO of Applied Materials. Before his retirement, Morgan had the distinction of being the longest-serving CEO in Silicon Valley, having held the position for 25 years. Morgan was thought of as a forward thinker, but actions leading to this description caused some analysts to question his strategies. Morgan took bold actions in slow economic times, a strategy that often produced revenue and market share growth when the economic turnaround began. In the 1980s, he moved into Asian markets before most U.S. firms perceived the opportunities there. Although Morgan's action was heavily criticized, he was active in China ten years before his competitors, and his firm recently received a $200 million contract there. In fact, Morgan's goal was to have 5 percent of the firm's revenue come from China by 2005. The company's stock has appreciated in value by 5,600 percent during the previous 20 years, compared to a 500 percent increase in the Standard & Poor's Stock Index for the same time period.

A number of other successful strategic leaders exist. For example, Lindsay Owen-Jones, CEO of L'Oréal, claims part of his success comes from allowing employees to make mistakes and to learn from those mistakes. He also believes if no one makes mistakes, the firm is taking no risks and likely is overlooking opportunities. Fujio Cho, CEO of Toyota, has been highly successful in changing the firm to become a global automaker by expanding into Eastern Europe and China. Toyota's goal is to achieve a 15 percent share of the global auto market, up from 10 percent today. Cho nurtures a culture of managing costs and simultaneously achieving high quality. Michael O'Leary, CEO of Ryanair, transferred the concept of a low-cost airline from the United States (and Southwest Airlines) to Europe. Ryanair's fares on average are about 50 percent lower than those of its competitors. The firm provides low levels of service in terms of food and other amenities on flights, but has fast turnarounds on the ground (20 minutes). The firm's revenues increased by 32 percent and profits grew by 49 percent in 2002. Many of the successful executives can be described as pathfinders and pragmatists, and as having the right value set.

The list of failing strategic leaders is too long to present. Recent failures include William Smithburg, former CEO of Quaker Oats; Jean-Marie Messier, former CEO of Vivendi Universal; Dennis Kozlowski, former CEO of Tyco; Jill Barad, former CEO of Mattel; George Shaheen, former CEO of Webvan; and Samuel Waksal, former CEO of ImClone. The reasons for their failures vary, but identification of those reasons may help others avoid similar pitfalls. According to Sydney Finkelstein, these leaders and many others fail for one or more of the following reasons: they overestimate their ability to control the firm's external environment; there is no boundary between their interests and the company's; they believe that they can answer all questions; they eliminate all who disagree with them; they become obsessed with the company's image; and they underestimate obstacles and rely on what worked in the past. Many of these reasons can be summarized by the terms *arrogance* or *managerial hubris*. There is at least one other critical reason not in the preceding list: a lack of strong ethical values. While Dennis Kozlowski and Sam Waksal suffered from several of the characteristics noted above, both have been charged with crimes, and Waksal has already been convicted and sentenced.

"And so, the razor's edge. You are a CEO. You have the title, the visibility, and the responsibility. You're also isolated. You're under extraordinary pressure to deliver results. And, you're deathly afraid of failing." Being CEO is a very difficult job.

SOURCES: S. Finkelstein, 2003, 7 habits of spectacularly unsuccessful executives, *Fast Company*, July, 84–89; C. Hymowitz, 2003, CEOs value pragmatists with broad, positive views, *Wall Street Journal Online*, http://www.wsj.com, January 28; C. Hymowitz, 2003, CEOs raised in affluence confront new vulnerability, *Wall Street Journal Online*, http://www.wsj.com, January 21; 2003, The best and worst managers of the year, *Business Week*, January 13, 58–92; K. H. Hammonds & J. Collins, 2002, The secret life of the CEO, *Fast Company*, October, 81–86; N. Byrnes, J. A. Byrne, C. Edwards, & L. Lee, 2002, The good CEO, *Business Week*, September 23, 80–88.

As the Opening Case illustrates, all CEOs encounter significant risk, but they also can make a significant difference in how a firm performs. If a strategic leader can create a strategic vision for the firm using the forward thinking that was evident during James Morgan's leadership of Applied Materials, and then energize the firm's human capital, positive outcomes can be achieved. Although the challenge of strategic leadership is significant, the Opening Case provides examples of several highly successful CEOs. However, it is difficult to build and maintain success over a sustained period of time. Some of the CEOs who failed miserably, as described in the Opening Case, had been recognized for their previous success (e.g., Dennis Kozlowski of Tyco).

As this chapter makes clear, it is through effective strategic leadership that firms are able to successfully use the strategic management process. As strategic leaders, top-level managers must guide the firm in ways that result in the formation of a strategic intent and strategic mission. This guidance may lead to goals that stretch everyone in the organization to improve their performance.[1] Moreover, strategic leaders must facilitate the development of appropriate strategic actions and determine how to implement them. These actions on the part of strategic leaders culminate in strategic competitiveness and above-average returns,[2] as shown in Figure 12.1.

Strategic Leadership and the Strategic Management Process — Figure 12.1

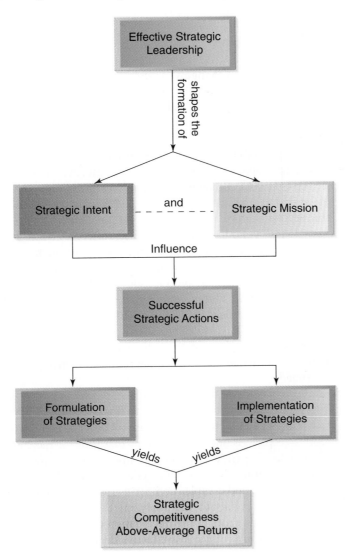

As noted in the Opening Case, there are a number of successful strategic leaders and several who have been highly unsuccessful. The Opening Case also suggests that the job of CEO is challenging and stressful, even more so than it was in previous years. Research suggests that CEO tenure on the job is likely to be three to ten years. The average tenure of a CEO in 1995 was 9.5 years. In the early 21st century, the average had decreased to 7.3 years. Additionally, the boards of directors of companies are showing an increased tendency to go outside the firm for new CEOs or to select "dark horses" from within the firm. They seem to be searching for an executive who is unafraid to make changes in the firm's traditional practices. Still, many new CEOs fail (as we learn later in this chapter).[3]

This chapter begins with a definition of strategic leadership and its importance as a potential source of competitive advantage. Next, we examine top management teams and their effects on innovation, strategic change, and firm performance. Following this discussion is an analysis of the internal and external managerial labor markets from which strategic leaders are selected. Closing the chapter are descriptions of the five key components of effective strategic leadership: determining a strategic direction, effectively managing the firm's resource portfolio, sustaining an effective organizational culture, emphasizing ethical practices, and establishing balanced organizational control systems.

Strategic Leadership

Strategic leadership *is the ability to anticipate, envision, maintain flexibility, and empower others to create strategic change as necessary.*

Strategic leadership is the ability to anticipate, envision, maintain flexibility, and empower others to create strategic change as necessary. Multifunctional in nature, strategic leadership involves managing through others, managing an entire enterprise rather than a functional subunit, and coping with change that continues to increase in the 21st-century competitive landscape, as suggested in the Opening Case. Because of this landscape's complexity and global nature, strategic leaders must learn how to effectively influence human behavior, often in uncertain environments. By word or by personal example, and through their ability to envision the future, effective strategic leaders meaningfully influence the behaviors, thoughts, and feelings of those with whom they work.[4]

The ability to manage human capital may be the most critical of the strategic leader's skills.[5] In the 21st century, intellectual capital, including the ability to manage knowledge and create and commercialize innovation, affects a strategic leader's success.[6] Competent strategic leaders also establish the context through which stakeholders (such as employees, customers, and suppliers) can perform at peak efficiency.[7] "When a public company is left with a void in leadership, for whatever reason, the ripple effects are widely felt both within and outside the organization. Internally, a company is likely to suffer a crisis of morale, confidence and productivity among employees and, similarly, stockholders may panic when a company is left rudderless and worry about the safety and future of their investment."[8] The crux of strategic leadership is the ability to manage the firm's operations effectively and sustain high performance over time.[9]

A firm's ability to achieve strategic competitiveness and earn above-average returns is compromised when strategic leaders fail to respond appropriately and quickly to changes in the complex global competitive environment. The inability to respond or to identify the need to respond is one of the reasons that some of the CEOs mentioned in the Opening Case failed. A firm's "long-term competitiveness depends on managers' willingness to challenge continually their managerial frames."[10] Strategic leaders must learn how to deal with diverse and complex competitive situations. Individual judgment is an important part of learning about and analyzing the firm's external conditions.[11] However, managers also make errors in their evaluation of the competitive conditions. These errors in perception can produce less-effective decisions. But, usually, it means that managers must make decisions under more uncertainty. Some can do this well, but some cannot. Those who cannot are likely to be ineffective and short-term managers. However, to survive, managers do not have to make optimal decisions. They only need to make better decisions than their competitors.[12] Effective strategic leaders are willing to make candid and courageous, yet pragmatic, decisions—decisions that may be difficult, but necessary—through foresight as they reflect on external conditions facing the firm. They also need to understand how such decisions will affect the internal systems currently in use in the firm. Effective strategic leaders use visioning to motivate employees. They often solicit corrective feedback from peers, superiors, and employees about the value of their difficult decisions and vision. Ultimately, they develop strong partners internally and externally to facilitate execution of their strategic vision.[13]

The primary responsibility for effective strategic leadership rests at the top, in particular, with the CEO. Other commonly recognized strategic leaders include members of the board of directors, the top management team, and divisional general managers. Regardless of their title and organizational function, strategic leaders have substantial decision-making responsibilities that cannot be delegated.[14] Strategic leadership is an extremely complex, but critical, form of leadership. Strategies cannot be formulated and implemented to achieve above-average returns without effective strategic leaders. Because strategic leadership is a requirement of strategic success, and because organizations may be poorly led and over-managed, firms competing in the 21st-century competitive landscape are challenged to develop effective strategic leaders.[15]

Managers as an Organizational Resource

As we have suggested, top-level managers are an important resource for firms seeking to formulate and implement strategies effectively.[16] The strategic decisions made by top-level managers influence how the firm is designed and whether or not goals will be achieved. Thus, a critical element of organizational success is having a top management team with superior managerial skills.[17]

Managers often use their discretion (or latitude for action) when making strategic decisions, including those concerned with the effective implementation of strategies.[18] Managerial discretion differs significantly across industries. The primary factors that determine the amount of decision-making discretion a manager (especially a top-level manager) has include (1) external environmental sources (such as the industry structure, the rate of market growth in the firm's primary industry, and the degree to which products can be differentiated), (2) characteristics of the organization (including its size, age, resources, and culture), and (3) characteristics of the manager (including commitment to the firm and its strategic outcomes, tolerance for ambiguity, skills in working with different people, and aspiration levels) (see Figure 12.2). Because strategic leaders' decisions are intended to help the firm gain a competitive advantage, how managers exercise discretion when determining appropriate strategic actions is critical to the firm's success.[19] Top executives must be action oriented; thus, the decisions that they make should spur the company to action.

A top-level executive leads a discussion at a Nike Ethnic Diversity Council meeting. Top executives can have a major effect on a firm's culture and cultural values.

©Mark Richards/PhotoEdit

Figure 12.2 — Factors Affecting Managerial Discretion

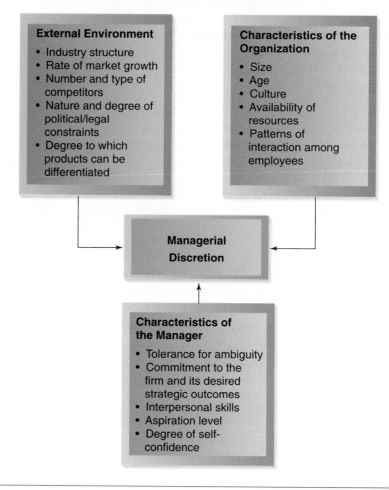

SOURCE: Adapted from S. Finkelstein & D. C. Hambrick, 1996, *Strategic Leadership: Top Executives and Their Effects on Organizations*, St. Paul, MN: West Publishing Company.

In addition to determining new strategic initiatives, top-level managers develop the appropriate organizational structure and reward systems of a firm. In Chapter 11, we described how the organizational structure and reward systems affect strategic actions taken to implement different strategies. Top executives also have a major effect on a firm's culture. Evidence suggests that managers' values are critical in shaping a firm's cultural values.[20] Accordingly, top-level managers have an important effect on organizational activities and performance.[21]

The effects of strategic leaders on the firm's performance are evident at Avon, described in the Opening Case. Avon received approximately 5 percent of its revenue from Argentina before the country experienced an economic disaster. Top executives Andrea Jung and Susan Kropf acted quickly to avoid revenue and cash problems for the firm. In short, they promoted and enhanced Avon's sales in Eastern Europe and in China to overcome the revenue losses in Argentina.

The decisions and actions of strategic leaders can make them a source of competitive advantage for the firm. In accordance with the criteria of sustainability discussed in Chapter 3, strategic leaders can be a source of competitive advantage only when their work is valuable, rare, costly to imitate, and nonsubstitutable. Effective strategic leaders become a source of competitive advantage when they focus their work on the key issues that ultimately shape the firm's ability to earn above-average returns.[22]

Top Management Teams

The complexity of the challenges faced by the firm and the need for substantial amounts of information and knowledge require teams of executives to provide the strategic leadership of most firms. The **top management team** is composed of the key managers who are responsible for selecting and implementing the firm's strategies. Typically, the top management team includes the officers of the corporation, defined by the title of vice-president and above or by service as a member of the board of directors.[23] The quality of the strategic decisions made by a top management team affects the firm's ability to innovate and engage in effective strategic change.[24]

TOP MANAGEMENT TEAM, FIRM PERFORMANCE, AND STRATEGIC CHANGE

The job of top-level executives is complex and requires a broad knowledge of the firm's operations, as well as the three key parts of the firm's external environment— the general, industry, and competitor environments, as discussed in Chapter 2. Therefore, firms try to form a top management team that has the appropriate knowledge and expertise to operate the internal organization, yet also can deal with all the firm's stakeholders as well as its competitors.[25] This normally requires a heterogeneous top management team. A **heterogeneous top management team** is composed of individuals with different functional backgrounds, experience, and education. The more heterogeneous a top management team is, with varied expertise and knowledge, the more capacity it has to provide effective strategic leadership in *formulating* strategy.[26]

Members of a heterogeneous top management team benefit from discussing the different perspectives advanced by team members. In many cases, these discussions increase the quality of the top management team's decisions, especially when a synthesis emerges from the diverse perspectives that is generally superior to any one individual perspective.[27] For example, heterogeneous top management teams in the airline industry have the propensity to take stronger competitive actions and reactions than do more homogeneous teams.[28] The net benefit of such actions by heterogeneous teams has been positive in terms of market share and above-average returns. Research shows that more heterogeneity among top management team members promotes debate, which often leads to better strategic decisions. In turn, better strategic decisions produce higher firm performance.[29]

It is also important that the top management team members function cohesively. In general, the more heterogeneous and larger the top management team is, the more difficult it is for the team to effectively implement strategies.[30] Comprehensive and long-term strategic plans can be inhibited by communication difficulties among top executives who have different backgrounds and different cognitive skills.[31] Alternatively, communication among diverse top management team members can be facilitated through electronic communications, sometimes reducing the barriers before face-to-face meetings.[32] As a result, a group of top executives with diverse backgrounds may inhibit the process of decision making if it is not effectively managed. In these cases, top management teams may fail to comprehensively examine threats and opportunities, leading to a sub-optimal strategic decision.

Having members with substantive expertise in the firm's core functions and businesses is also important to the effectiveness of a top management team. In a high-technology industry, it may be critical for a firm's top management team to have R&D expertise, particularly when growth strategies are being implemented.[33]

The characteristics of top management teams are related to innovation and strategic change.[34] For example, more heterogeneous top management teams are associated

The top management team *is composed of the key managers who are responsible for selecting and implementing the firm's strategies.*

A heterogeneous top management team *is composed of individuals with different functional backgrounds, experience, and education.*

positively with innovation and strategic change. The heterogeneity may force the team or some of the members to "think outside of the box" and thus be more creative in making decisions.[35] Therefore, firms that need to change their strategies are more likely to do so if they have top management teams with diverse backgrounds and expertise. When a new CEO is hired from outside the industry, the probability of strategic change is greater than if the new CEO is from inside the firm or inside the industry.[36] While hiring a new CEO from outside the industry adds diversity to the team, the top management team must be managed effectively to use the diversity in a positive way. Thus, to create strategic change, the CEO should exercise transformational leadership.[37] A top management team with various areas of expertise is more likely to identify environmental changes (opportunities and threats) or changes within the firm that require a different strategic direction.[38]

THE CEO AND TOP MANAGEMENT TEAM POWER

As noted in Chapter 10, the board of directors is an important governance mechanism for monitoring a firm's strategic direction and for representing stakeholders' interests, especially those of shareholders. In fact, higher performance normally is achieved when the board of directors is more directly involved in shaping a firm's strategic direction.[39]

Boards of directors, however, may find it difficult to direct the strategic actions of powerful CEOs and top management teams.[40] It is not uncommon for a powerful CEO to appoint a number of sympathetic outside board members or have inside board members who are also on the top management team and report to the CEO.[41] In either case, the CEO may have significant control over the board's actions. "A central question is whether boards are an effective management control mechanism . . . or whether they are a 'management tool,' . . . a rubber stamp for management initiatives . . . and often surrender to management their major domain of decision-making authority, which includes the right to hire, fire, and compensate top management."[42]

In the poor performance of Vivendi Universal and Tyco mentioned in the Opening Case, the board of directors can clearly be faulted. In both firms, the CEOs, Jean-Marie Messier (Vivendi Universal) and Dennis Kozlowski (Tyco) made multiple acquisitions that eventually greatly harmed the financial strength of the companies. The boards should have stopped these actions before they caused such harm. Alternatively, recent research shows that social ties between the CEO and board members may actually increase board members' involvement in strategic decisions. Thus, strong relationships between the CEO and the board of directors may have positive or negative outcomes.[43]

CEOs and top management team members can achieve power in other ways. A CEO who also holds the position of chairman of the board usually has more power than the CEO who is not simultaneously serving as chairman of the firm's board.[44] Although this practice of CEO duality (when the CEO and the chairperson of the board are the same) has become more common in U.S. businesses, it has come under heavy criticism. Duality has been blamed for poor performance and slow response to change in a number of firms.[45]

DaimlerChrysler CEO Jürgen Schrempp, who holds the dual positions of chairman of the board and CEO, has substantial power in the firm. In fact, insiders suggest that he was purging those individuals who are outspoken and who represent potential threats to his dominance. In particular, many former Chrysler executives left the firm, although research suggests that retaining key employees after an acquisition contributes to improved post-acquisition performance.[46] Thus, it has been particularly difficult to turn around the U.S. operations.[47] Dieter Zetsche, a German who is likely next in line to be CEO at DaimlerChrysler, is leading the team that is seeking to reverse Chrysler's fortunes. However, Chrysler's fortunes have not been reversed since the acquisition in 1998. In July 2003, Zetsche called on Joe Eberhardt, manager of the company's operations in the United Kingdom, to try to fix Chrysler's sales and marketing strategy problems and thereby reverse its performance. Simultaneous with Eberhardt's appointment was an announcement of a $1.2 billion loss by Chrysler in the second quarter of 2003.[48]

Although it varies across industries, duality occurs most commonly in the largest firms. Increased shareholder activism, however, has brought CEO duality under scrutiny and attack in both U.S. and European firms. Historically, an independent board leadership structure in which the same person did not hold the positions of CEO and chair was believed to enhance a board's ability to monitor top-level managers' decisions and actions, particularly in terms of the firm's financial performance.[49] And, as reported in Chapter 10, many believe these two positions should be separate in most companies today in order to make the board more independent from the CEO. Stewardship theory, on the other hand, suggests that CEO duality facilitates effective decisions and actions. In these instances, the increased effectiveness gained through CEO duality accrues from the individual who wants to perform effectively and desires to be the best possible steward of the firm's assets. Because of this person's positive orientation and actions, extra governance and the coordination costs resulting from an independent board leadership structure would be unnecessary.[50]

Top management team members and CEOs who have long tenure—on the team and in the organization—have a greater influence on board decisions.[51] And, CEOs with greater influence may take actions in their own best interests, the outcomes of which increase their compensation from the company.[52] Long tenure is known to restrict the breadth of an executive's knowledge base. With the limited perspectives associated with a restricted knowledge base, long-tenured top executives typically develop fewer alternatives to evaluate in making strategic decisions.[53] However, long-tenured managers also may be able to exercise more effective strategic control, thereby obviating the need for board members' involvement because effective strategic control generally produces higher performance.[54]

To strengthen the firm, boards of directors should develop an effective relationship with the firm's top management team. The relative degrees of power held by the board and top management team members should be examined in light of an individual firm's situation. For example, the abundance of resources in a firm's external environment and the volatility of that environment may affect the ideal balance of power between boards and top management teams.[55] Moreover, a volatile and uncertain environment may create a situation where a powerful CEO is needed to move quickly, but a diverse top management team may create less cohesion among team members and prevent or stall a necessary strategic move.[56] Through the development of effective working relationships, boards, CEOs, and other top management team members are able to serve the best interests of the firm's stakeholders.[57]

Managerial Labor Market

The choice of top executives—especially CEOs—is a critical organizational decision with important implications for the firm's performance.[58] Many companies use leadership screening systems to identify individuals with managerial and strategic leadership potential. The most effective of these systems assess people within the firm and gain valuable information about the capabilities of other companies' managers, particularly their strategic leaders.[59] Based on the results of these assessments, training and development programs are provided for current managers in an attempt to preselect and shape the skills of people who may become tomorrow's leaders. The "ten-step talent" management development program at GE, for example, is considered one of the most effective in the world.[60]

Organizations select managers and strategic leaders from two types of managerial labor markets—internal and external.[61] An **internal managerial labor market** consists of

An internal managerial labor market consists of the opportunities for managerial positions within a firm.

The Times Are Changing: Is Wonder Woman Still Required for Top Executive Positions in the 21st Century?

Total employment in the United States is expected to increase by 22.2 million jobs during the period 2000–2010. The number of women in the workforce is expected to increase by 15.1 percent to 75.5 million, while the number of men in the workforce is projected to climb by 9.3 percent to 82.2 million. As such, women should compose approximately 48 percent of the workforce in 2010. However, despite gains, only a few of the major U.S. corporations have women CEOs. Do they have to be wonder women to attain such positions? To receive consideration for a CEO position requires an exceptional record. Still, corporate America seems to be highly underutilizing a valuable asset, female human capital. But, times are changing. Ten percent of the *Fortune* 500 companies have women in 25 percent of their corporate officer teams. This represents an increase from 5 percent of the *Fortune* 500 in 1995. And, most of the women who now hold officer positions no longer refer to their gender. However, important issues remain in the gender gap. For example, a wage gap between men and women holding the same jobs is prevalent in most industries. This gap exists not only in the United States, but also in Europe. The gap is smallest in Luxembourg (11 percent) and largest in Austria (33 percent). However, the women who are members of top management teams enjoy more pay equity than women in other positions.

Anne Mulcahy, CEO of Xerox, has quietly but successfully turned around the financial performance of the firm she leads. Currently only 10 percent of *Fortune* 500 companies have women in 25 percent of their corporate officer teams—that represents an increase of only 5 percent since 1995.

There are many more examples of successful women executives in the current corporate environment than in the past. Well-known women CEOs include Carly Fiorina (Hewlett-Packard), Anne Mulcahy (Xerox), and Meg Whitman (eBay). But there are others who might be considered as "trail blazers" who should also receive recognition. For example, Catherine Elizabeth Hughes began her career in 1969 and became the first African American woman to head a firm that was publicly traded on a U.S. stock exchange. Muriel Siebert began her career in 1954 and in 1967 became the first woman to purchase a seat on the New York Stock Exchange. Judith Regan started as a secretary and then became a reporter for the *National Enquirer* in the late 1970s. She then developed a highly successful series of books for Simon and Schuster in the 1980s on celebrities such as Rush Limbaugh and Howard Stern. In 1994, she was given her own imprint at HarperCollins called ReganBooks, along with a TV show on Fox News. Today, two of the highest-profile women CEOs are Anne Mulcahy and Carly Fiorina.

Anne Mulcahy was promoted to president and COO of Xerox only a short time before it encountered significant difficulties and performance declined precipitously. Many questioned whether or not Xerox could survive. But, it has done so under Mulcahy's steady guidance. Because of her leadership, Xerox has returned to profitability, and she has become the chairman and CEO of the company. As CEO, she has several priorities for Xerox. Her first priority is to provide value to customers and growth for Xerox. Her second priority is people, those who work for the company. In fact, she argues that the success of Xerox is fully based on the Xerox human capital. Her third priority is shareholder value; many CEOs have this as their first and only priority. Her fourth priority is corporate governance. She has taken several important actions to improve the governance processes at Xerox. And, her fifth priority is to provide effective leadership. She claims that the most successful leaders are self-effacing and give credit to others. Yet, they have a strong resolve to take whatever actions

Getty Images

are necessary to see that the firm succeeds. The future of Xerox looks bright with Anne Mulcahy as the CEO.

Carly Fiorina is perhaps the highest-profile woman strategic leader as CEO of Hewlett-Packard. She has had many challenges during her relatively short tenure as CEO, the most prominent of which was the contested acquisition of Compaq. With each of these challenges, beginning with her appointment as CEO, analysts argued that she would fail. To date, although sometimes scarred in battle, she has overcome all of the major challenges. Fiorina was hired as CEO of HP in 1998 with a mandate from the board to transform the firm and breathe new life into it. To do so, she has had to take on and change long-standing practices and traditions as well as revise and revive the innovative culture that once existed. Fiorina has made shrewd strategic moves and has shown that she can "play the game" with the best of them and win. She has made HP more nimble and lean and a company that is active and on the move. Time will tell if HP and Fiorina will be truly successful, but there is little doubt that Fiorina has also been a trail blazer. Because of her leadership as CEO, few are likely to question if a woman CEO knows how to fight and win. She has shown that she can do both.

SOURCES: J. Gettings & D. Johnson, 2003, Wonder Women: Profiles of leading female CEOs and business executives, *Infoplease*, http://www.infoplease.com, July 13; 2003, Online Fact Book, Xerox at a glance, http://www.xerox.com, July 13; 2003, Facts on Working Women, U.S. Department of Labor, http://www.dol.gov/wb, May; 2003, Remarks by Anne M. Mulcahy, chairman and chief executive officer, http://www.uschamber.com, April 2; 2003, Equality through pay equity, *Trade Union World*, http://www.dol.gov/wb, March; 2003, Showdown, *Business Week*, February 17, 70–72; G. Anders, 2003, The Carly chronicle, *Fast Company*, February, 66–73; 2003, Carly Fiorina, up close, *Wall Street Journal*, January 13, B1, B6.

the opportunities for managerial positions within a firm, whereas an **external managerial labor market** is the collection of career opportunities for managers in organizations other than the one for which they work currently. Several benefits are thought to accrue to a firm when the internal labor market is used to select an insider as the new CEO. Because of their experience with the firm and the industry environment in which it competes, insiders are familiar with company products, markets, technologies, and operating procedures. Also, internal hiring produces lower turnover among existing personnel, many of whom possess valuable firm-specific knowledge. When the firm is performing well, internal succession is favored to sustain high performance. It is assumed that hiring from inside keeps the important knowledge necessary to sustain the performance.

Given the phenomenal success of GE and its highly effective management development program, an insider, Jeffrey Immelt, was chosen to succeed Jack Welch.[62] As noted in a later Strategic Focus, Immelt is making a number of changes in GE. This is surprising because new CEOs from inside the firm are less likely to make changes, and GE has performed better than many other firms over the last two decades. However, changes in the economic and competitive environments have produced needs for changes in the firm. Thus, Immelt is trying to create a new strategy and ensure continued success for the firm. One of his actions has been to create a more independent board and improve the governance system. For an inside move to the top to occur successfully, firms must develop and implement effective succession management programs. In that way, managers can be developed so that one will eventually be prepared to ascend to the top.[63] Immelt was well prepared to take over the CEO job at GE.

It is not unusual for employees to have a strong preference for the internal managerial labor market to be used to select top management team members and the CEO. In the past, companies have also had a preference for insiders to fill top-level management positions because of a desire for continuity and a continuing commitment to the firm's current strategic intent, strategic mission, and chosen strategies.[64] However,

*An **external managerial labor market** is the collection of career opportunities for managers in organizations other than the one for which they work currently.*

because of a changing competitive landscape and varying levels of performance, even at companies such as GE, an increasing number of boards of directors have been going to outsiders to succeed CEOs.[65] A firm often has valid reasons to select an outsider as its new CEO. For example, research suggests that executives who have spent their entire career with a particular firm may become "stale in the saddle."[66] Long tenure with a firm seems to reduce the number of innovative ideas top executives are able to develop to cope with conditions facing their firm. Given the importance of innovation for a firm's success in today's competitive landscape (see Chapter 13), an inability to innovate or to create conditions that stimulate innovation throughout a firm is a liability for a strategic leader. Figure 12.3 shows how the composition of the top management team and CEO succession (managerial labor market) may interact to affect strategy. For example, when the top management team is homogeneous (its members have similar functional experiences and educational backgrounds) and a new CEO is selected from inside the firm, the firm's current strategy is unlikely to change.

On the other hand, when a new CEO is selected from outside the firm and the top management team is heterogeneous, there is a high probability that strategy will change. When the new CEO is from inside the firm and a heterogeneous top management team is in place, the strategy may not change, but innovation is likely to continue. An external CEO succession with a homogeneous team creates a more ambiguous situation.

To have an adequate number of top managers, firms must take advantage of a highly qualified labor pool, including one source of managers that has often been overlooked: women. Firms are beginning to utilize women's potential managerial talents with substantial success, as described in the Strategic Focus. As noted in the Strategic Focus, women, such as Catherine Elizabeth Hughes, Muriel Siebert, and Judith Regan, have made important contributions as strategic leaders. A few firms have gained value by using the significant talents of women leaders. But many more have not done so, which represents an opportunity cost to them. Alternatively, the Strategic Focus explains that women are being recognized for their leadership skill and are being selected for prominent strategic leadership positions, such as those held by Anne Mulcahy, CEO of Xerox, and Carly Fiorina, CEO of Hewlett-Packard.

Figure 12.3 — **Effects of CEO Succession and Top Management Team Composition on Strategy**

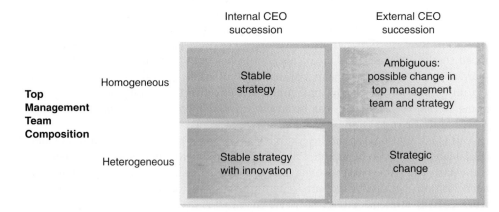

More women are now being appointed to the boards of directors for organizations in both the private and public sectors. These additional appointments suggest that women's ability to represent stakeholders' and especially shareholders' best interests in for-profit companies at the level of the board of directors is being more broadly recognized. However, in addition to appointments to the board of directors, firms competing in the complex and challenging global economy—an economy demanding the best of an organization—may be well served by adding more female executives to their top management teams. It is important for firms to create diversity in leadership positions. Organizations such as Johnson & Johnson, the World Bank, and Royal Dutch Shell are creating more diverse leadership teams in order to deal with complex, heterogeneous, and ambiguous environments.[67] To build diverse teams, firms must break down their glass ceilings to allow all people regardless of gender or ethnicity to move into key leadership positions.[68] In so doing, firms more effectively use the human capital in their workforce. They also provide more opportunities for all people in the firm to satisfy their needs, such as their need for self-actualization; therefore, employees should be more highly motivated, leading to higher productivity for the firm.[69]

Key Strategic Leadership Actions

Several identifiable actions characterize strategic leadership that positively contributes to effective use of the firm's strategies.[70] We present the most critical of these actions in Figure 12.4. Many of the actions interact with each other. For example, managing the firm's resources effectively includes developing human capital and contributes to establishing a strategic direction, fostering an effective culture, exploiting core competencies, using effective organizational control systems, and establishing ethical practices.

Determining Strategic Direction

Determining the strategic direction of a firm involves developing a long-term vision of the firm's strategic intent. A long-term vision typically looks at least five to ten years into the future. A philosophy with goals, this vision consists of the image and character the firm seeks.[71]

Determining the strategic direction of a firm involves developing a long-term vision of the firm's strategic intent.

Exercise of Effective Strategic Leadership — Figure 12.4

©Keith Dannemiller/CORBIS SABA

The ideal long-term vision has two parts: a core ideology and an envisioned future. While the core ideology motivates employees through the company's heritage, the envisioned future encourages employees to stretch beyond their expectations of accomplishment and requires significant change and progress in order to be realized.[72] The envisioned future serves as a guide to many aspects of a firm's strategy implementation process, including motivation, leadership, employee empowerment, and organizational design.

Matthew D. Heyman came out of Harvard Business School in 1993 with a vision of building lavish movie theaters in Mexico City, a city with 20 million inhabitants. The Mexican theater industry was in shambles because of government price controls, and so a vacuum existed for quality movie theaters. After finding financial backing for his company, Cinemex, Heyman and his partners began constructing movie theaters. Heyman decided early on to target the largest market in Mexico City, the working poor. His theaters charged about half as much for tickets in poor areas of the city as did theaters in wealthy areas, even though they were just as extravagant. In 2001, Cinemex generated a profit of approximately $40 million.[73] In 2002, Cinemex was sold for $286 million to a Canadian partnership that owned Loews Cineplex, the fourth largest theater chain in the United States. At the time of the sale, Cinemex had 31 theaters with 349 screens.[74]

A former Cinemex movie theatre in Mexico City, Mexico. In 2001, the year prior to its sale to Loews Cineplex, Cinemex generated a profit of $40 million. Its success came from recognizing a need for quality movie theaters in a huge potential market.

Most changes in strategic direction are difficult to design and implement, but Jeffrey Immelt has an even greater challenge at GE. As explained in the Strategic Focus, GE performed exceptionally well under Jack Welch's leadership. While there is need for a change because the competitive landscape is shifting, stakeholders accustomed to Jack Welch and high performance may not readily accept Immelt's changes, especially in strategy. Immelt is trying to effect critical changes in strategy and governance and simultaneously gain stakeholders' commitment to them. A charismatic CEO may foster stakeholders' commitment to a new vision and strategic direction. Nonetheless, it is important not to lose sight of the strengths of the organization in making changes required by a new strategic direction. Immelt must use the strengths of GE to ensure continued positive performance. The goal is to pursue the firm's short-term need to adjust to a new vision while maintaining its long-term survivability by managing its portfolio of resources effectively.

Effectively Managing the Firm's Resource Portfolio

Probably the most important task for strategic leaders is effectively managing the firm's portfolio of resources. Firms have multiple resources that can be categorized into one of the following: financial capital, human capital, social capital, and organizational capital (including organizational culture).[75] Strategic leaders manage the firm's portfolio of resources by organizing them into capabilities, structuring the firm to use the capabilities, and developing and implementing a strategy to leverage those resources to achieve a competitive advantage.[76] In particular, strategic leaders must exploit and maintain the firm's core competencies and develop and retain the firm's human and social capital.

Changing the House That Jack Built—A New GE

Jack Welch built an incredibly successful company during his tenure as CEO of GE. In 2002, the firm enjoyed revenues of $131.7 billion, 40 percent of which came from international operations. Thus, it is a truly global company. In 2002, the return on sales was 11.5 percent with earnings per share of $1.51. GE was chosen by the *Financial Times* as the world's most respected company in 1999, 2000, 2001, 2002, and 2003. However, the competitive landscape has been changing; the sands are shifting. With the economy down and political uncertainties around the world, GE is unable to grow as quickly as it has in the past. And, many argue that Welch fueled growth by reducing jobs and costs, making acquisitions, and developing a large and powerful financial services unit. Unfortunately, the same opportunities no longer exist. As a result, analysts predict that GE is likely to grow between 3 and 13 percent in the foreseeable future, with growth under 10 percent most of the time. Jeffrey Immelt, who succeeded Welch, will need to achieve growth largely by emphasizing the core industrial companies that Welch deemphasized. Thus, the job is even more challenging.

In 2002, GE's net income grew by 7.1 percent. This is clearly respectable growth in poor economic and uncertain times. But, net income grew at more than 10 percent for the ten preceding years. GE also has come under criticism for its accounting practices, suggesting some of the previous growth reported may have been the result of questionable accounting practices related to acquisitions. Therefore, Immelt faces substantial challenges and is making changes as a result. He is emphasizing the industrial and consumer goods businesses. Thus, he must refocus the firm's marketing and innovation capabilities. Immelt does have some bright areas on which he can build, one of which is the jet engine business. GE controls approximately 64 percent of the global jet engine market. It has done so by emphasizing quality, innovation, and vision. For example, while it has monopolized the engine market for large jets, executives predicted the development of the small, regional jet market. Therefore, they invested in R&D to develop an excellent engine for the small jet market. The timing was almost perfect as the number of regional jets in service grew from 85 in 1993 to 1,300 in 2003. Immelt has to strongly support this type of vision and innovation in all of GE's major businesses.

Immelt is emphasizing more transparency in accounting practices and is developing a more independent board of directors. Additionally, he expects GE managers to excel in many areas including exercising high personal integrity while simultaneously gaining high sales. It is very difficult to follow an icon, especially a highly respected and successful CEO such as Jack Welch. However, the challenge is even greater when the firm's performance is suffering and the new CEO must make major changes in the firm's strategy and managerial practices. While the environment is requiring that firms such as GE seek growth in ways different from the recent past, and GE's performance is lower than in the previous decade, GE's board seems satisfied with Immelt's performance to date. He received pay and stock options valued at $43 million for 2002. In taking this action, the GE board emphasized Immelt's integrity, his commitment to effective corporate governance (including changes in the board membership), and his determination to take actions that enhance long-term shareholder value.

SOURCES: G. Strauss & B. Hansen, 2003, Bubble hasn't burst yet on CEO salaries despite the times, *USA Today*, http://www.usatoday.com, July 3; 2003, Fact Sheet, http://www.ge.com, June 20; K. Kranhold, 2003, GE appliances don't wash with "growth," *Wall Street Journal Online*, http://www.wsj.com, April 3; A. Slywotzky & R. Wise, 2003, Double digit growth in no-growth times, *Fast Company*, April, 66–72; M. Murray, 2003, GE's Immelt starts renovations on the house that Jack built, *Wall Street Journal*, February 6, A1, A6; S. Holmes, 2003, GE: Little engines that could, *Business Week*, January 20, 62–63; C. Hymowitz, 2002, Resolving to let the new year be a year of better leadership, *Wall Street Journal Online*, http://www.wsj.com, December 31.

EXPLOITING AND MAINTAINING CORE COMPETENCIES

Examined in Chapters 1 and 3, *core competencies* are resources and capabilities that serve as a source of competitive advantage for a firm over its rivals. Typically, core competencies relate to an organization's functional skills, such as manufacturing, finance, marketing, and research and development. As shown by the descriptions that follow, firms develop and exploit core competencies in many different functional areas. Strategic leaders must verify that the firm's competencies are emphasized in strategy implementation efforts. Intel, for example, has core competencies of *competitive agility* (an ability to act in a variety of competitively relevant ways) and *competitive speed* (an ability to act quickly when facing environmental and competitive pressures).[77]

The Heart and Soul-Mates Support Network jointly promotes Tropicana Pure Premium and Quaker Oatmeal products, representing PepsiCo's exploitation of core competencies across organizational units.

In many large firms, and certainly in related diversified ones, core competencies are effectively exploited when they are developed and applied across different organizational units (see Chapter 6). For example, PepsiCo purchased Quaker Oats, which makes the sports drink Gatorade. PepsiCo uses its competence in distribution systems to exploit the Quaker assets. For example, Pepsi soft drinks (e.g., Pepsi Cola and Mountain Dew) and Gatorade share the logistics activity. Similarly, PepsiCo uses this competence to distribute Quaker Oats' healthy snacks and Frito Lay's salty snacks through the same channels. In 2003, PepsiCo launched the Heart and Soul-Mates Support Network offering nutritional tips, motivational messages, and coaching advice to jointly promote its Tropicana Pure Premium and Quaker Oatmeal products.[78]

Firms must continuously develop or even change their core competencies to stay ahead of the competition. If they have a competence that provides an advantage but do not change it, competitors will eventually imitate that competence and reduce or eliminate the firm's competitive advantage. Additionally, firms must guard against the competence becoming a liability thereby preventing change. If this occurs, competitors will eventually develop a more valuable competence, eliminating the firm's competitive advantage and taking its market share away.[79] Most core competencies require high-quality human capital.

DEVELOPING HUMAN CAPITAL AND SOCIAL CAPITAL

Human capital refers to the knowledge and skills of a firm's entire workforce. From the perspective of human capital, employees are viewed as a capital resource that requires investment.[80] These investments are productive, in that much of the development of U.S. industry can be attributed to the effectiveness of its human capital. This fact suggests that "as the dynamics of competition accelerate, people are perhaps the only truly sustainable source of competitive advantage."[81] Human capital's increasing importance suggests a significant role for the firm's human resource management activities.[82] As a support activity (see Chapter 2), human resource management practices facilitate people's efforts to successfully select and especially to use the firm's strategies.[83]

Human capital is important in all types of organizations, large and small, new and established. For example, a major factor in the decision by venture capitalists to

Human capital *refers to the knowledge and skills of a firm's entire workforce.*

PART 3 / Strategic Actions: Strategy Implementation

invest in an entrepreneurial venture is the quality of the human capital involved. In fact, it may be of equal or more importance to the quality of the entrepreneurial opportunity.[84] J. W. Marriott, Jr., CEO of Marriott International, argued strongly that the primary reason for the long-term success of the company has been the belief that its human capital is the most important asset of the firm. Thus, the company built and maintained a homelike and friendly environment that supports the growth and development of its employees, called "associates in Marriott." He also suggested that the firm invests significant effort in hiring caring and dependable people who are ethical and trustworthy. The firm then trains and rewards them for high-quality performance.[85]

Effective training and development programs increase the probability that a manager will be a successful strategic leader. These programs have grown progressively important to the success of firms as knowledge has become more integral to gaining and sustaining a competitive advantage.[86] Additionally, such programs build knowledge and skills, inculcate a common set of core values, and offer a systematic view of the organization, thus promoting the firm's strategic vision and organizational cohesion. The programs also contribute to the development of core competencies.[87] Furthermore, they help strategic leaders improve skills that are critical to completing other tasks associated with effective strategic leadership, such as determining the firm's strategic direction, exploiting and maintaining the firm's core competencies, and developing an organizational culture that supports ethical practices. Thus, building human capital is vital to the effective execution of strategic leadership.[88]

Strategic leaders must acquire the skills necessary to help develop human capital in their areas of responsibility. When human capital investments are successful, the result is a workforce capable of learning continuously. Continuous learning and leveraging the firm's expanding knowledge base are linked with strategic success.[89] Learning also can preclude making errors. Strategic leaders tend to learn more from their failures than their successes because they sometimes make the wrong attributions for the successes.[90] It is important to learn from both successes and failures.

Learning and building knowledge are important for creating innovation in firms.[91] And, innovation leads to competitive advantage.[92] Overall, firms that create and maintain greater knowledge usually achieve and maintain competitive advantages. However, as noted with core competencies, strategic leaders must guard against allowing high levels of knowledge in one area to lead to myopia and overlooking knowledge development opportunities in other important areas of the business.[93]

Programs that achieve outstanding results in the training of future strategic leaders become a competitive advantage for a firm. As noted earlier, GE's system of training and development of future strategic leaders is comprehensive and thought to be among the best.[94] Accordingly, it may be a source of competitive advantage for the firm.

Because of the economic downturn in 2001–2002 and the continuing economic malaise for some time thereafter, many firms laid off key people. Layoffs can result in a significant loss of the knowledge possessed by a firm's human capital. Research has shown that moderate-sized layoffs may improve firm performance, but large layoffs produce stronger performance downturns in firms because of the loss of human capital.[95] Although it is also not uncommon for restructuring firms to reduce their expenditures on, or investments in, training and development programs, restructuring may actually be an important time to increase investments in these programs. Restructuring firms have less slack and cannot absorb as many errors; moreover, the employees who remain after layoffs may find themselves in positions without all of the skills or knowledge they need to perform the required tasks effectively.[96] Improvements in information technology can facilitate better use of human resources when a downsizing event occurs.[97]

Viewing employees as a resource to be maximized rather than a cost to be minimized facilitates the successful implementation of a firm's strategies. The implementation of such strategies also is more effective when strategic leaders approach layoffs in a manner that employees believe is fair and equitable.[98]A critical issue for employees is the fairness in the layoffs and in treatment in their jobs.[99]

Social capital involves relationships inside and outside the firm that help the firm accomplish tasks and create value for customers and shareholders.[100] Social capital is a critical asset for a firm. Inside the firm, employees and units must cooperate to get the work done. In multinational organizations, units often must cooperate across country boundaries on activities such as R&D to produce outcomes needed by the firm (e.g., new products).[101]

External social capital has become critical to firm success in the last several years. Few, if any, firms have all of the resources that they need to compete in global (or domestic) markets. Thus, they establish alliances with other firms that have complementary resources in order to gain access to them. These relationships must be effectively managed to ensure that the partner trusts the firm and is willing to share the desired resources.[102] In fact, the success of many types of firms may partially depend on social capital. Large multinational firms often must establish alliances in order to enter new foreign markets. Likewise, entrepreneurial firms often must establish alliances to gain access to resources, venture capital, or other types of resources (e.g., special expertise that the entrepreneurial firm cannot afford to maintain in-house.)[103] Retaining quality human capital and maintaining strong internal social capital can be affected strongly by the firm's culture.

Sustaining an Effective Organizational Culture

An **organizational culture** consists of a complex set of ideologies, symbols, and core values that is shared throughout the firm and influences the way business is conducted. Evidence suggests that a firm can develop core competencies in terms of both the capabilities it possesses and the way the capabilities are leveraged by strategies to produce desired outcomes. In other words, because the organizational culture influences how the firm conducts its business and helps regulate and control employees' behavior, it can be a source of competitive advantage.[104] Thus, shaping the context within which the firm formulates and implements its strategies—that is, shaping the organizational culture—is a central task of strategic leaders.[105] Ikea's CEO, Anders Dahlvig, attributes the success of his firm partly to its unique corporate culture.[106]

ENTREPRENEURIAL ORIENTATION

An organizational culture often encourages (or discourages) the pursuit of entrepreneurial opportunities, especially in large firms.[107] Entrepreneurial opportunities are an important source of growth and innovation.[108] In Chapter 13, we describe how large firms use strategic entrepreneurship to pursue entrepreneurial opportunities and to gain first-mover advantages. Medium- and small-sized firms also rely on strategic entrepreneurship when trying to develop innovations as the foundation for profitable growth. In firms of all sizes, strategic entrepreneurship is more likely to be successful when employees have an entrepreneurial orientation.[109] Five dimensions characterize a firm's entrepreneurial orientation: autonomy, innovativeness, risk taking, proactiveness, and competitive aggressiveness.[110] In combination, these dimensions influence the activities of a firm to be innovative and launch new ventures.

The first of an entrepreneurial orientation's five dimensions, *autonomy,* allows employees to take actions that are free of organizational constraints and permits individuals and groups to be self-directed. The second dimension, *innovativeness,* "reflects a firm's tendency to engage in and support new ideas, novelty, experimentation, and creative processes that may result in new products, services, or technological processes."[111] Cultures with a tendency toward innovativeness encourage employees to

Social capital *involves relationships inside and outside the firm that help the firm accomplish tasks and create value for customers and shareholders.*

An organizational culture *consists of a complex set of ideologies, symbols, and core values that is shared throughout the firm and influences the way business is conducted.*

think beyond existing knowledge, technologies, and parameters in efforts to find creative ways to add value. *Risk taking* reflects a willingness by employees and their firm to accept risks when pursuing entrepreneurial opportunities. These risks can include assuming significant levels of debt and allocating large amounts of other resources (e.g., people) to projects that may not be completed. The fourth dimension of an entrepreneurial orientation, *proactiveness,* describes a firm's ability to be a market leader rather than a follower. Proactive organizational cultures constantly use processes to anticipate future market needs and to satisfy them before competitors learn how to do so. Finally, *competitive aggressiveness* is a firm's propensity to take actions that allow it to consistently and substantially outperform its rivals.[112]

CHANGING THE ORGANIZATIONAL CULTURE AND RESTRUCTURING

Changing a firm's organizational culture is more difficult than maintaining it, but effective strategic leaders recognize when change is needed. Incremental changes to the firm's culture typically are used to implement strategies.[113] More significant and, sometimes, even radical changes to organizational culture are used to support the selection of strategies that differ from those the firm has implemented historically. Regardless of the reasons for change, shaping and reinforcing a new culture require effective communication and problem solving, along with the selection of the right people (those who have the values desired for the organization), effective performance appraisals (establishing goals and measuring individual performance toward goals that fit in with the new core values), and appropriate reward systems (rewarding the desired behaviors that reflect the new core values).[114]

Evidence suggests that cultural changes succeed only when the firm's CEO, other key top management team members, and middle-level managers actively support them.[115] To effect change, middle-level managers in particular need to be highly disciplined to energize the culture and foster alignment with the strategic vision.[116]

As noted earlier, selecting new top management team members from the external managerial labor market is a catalyst for changes to organizational culture. This is illustrated by the example of Carlos Ghosn, a Brazilian-born manager working for Renault. Ghosn was charged with turning around Nissan, partially owned by Renault, which was suffering from lost market share. But, transforming an organization and its culture is challenging. Ghosn implemented several major changes. He closed plants and significantly reduced costs. In so doing, however, he gave generous bonuses of over five months' pay to the employees who were laid off. He dismantled the keiretsu investments, allowing him to revise the supply chain relationships. As a result, he returned Nissan to profitability. Renault's CEO now sees Nissan as an important asset for his firm and is integrating Renault's and Nissan's complementary resources to create global growth for the firm.[117]

Because of the actions of executives like those at Tenet HealthCare, Ahold, HealthSouth, and the major Wall Street investment firms described in the Strategic Focus, the world of corporate governance is changing, as described in Chapter 10. These changes have significant implications for the strategic leadership in individual companies. This is evidenced by the action taken by Michael Capellas, CEO of MCI, to have his top 300 executives sign an ethics pledge.

Emphasizing Ethical Practices

The effectiveness of processes used to implement the firm's strategies increases when they are based on ethical practices. Ethical companies encourage and enable people at all organizational levels to act ethically when doing what is necessary to implement the firm's strategies. In turn, ethical practices and the judgment on which they are based

As Corporate Scandals and Ethical Dilemmas Proliferate, Heads Roll

Corporate scandals have created a crisis of confidence in the practices of major corporations worldwide. In the United States, the multiple scandals of major proportion caused Congress to pass the Sarbanes-Oxley Act. The primary goal is to prevent accounting manipulations by top executives. While the names of Enron, Tyco, and WorldCom are prominent in these scandals, there are others. For example, Tenet Healthcare was investigated by the U.S. Justice Department regarding allegations that the company overbilled the U.S. government for services provided to senior citizens under the Medicare program. The CEO at the time, Jeffrey Barbakow, who received the highest compensation of any CEO in 2002, was forced to resign by the board of Tenet. Prior to these problems, Tenet's stock price was greater than $50, but fell dramatically to less than $20 per share after the allegations came to light.

Scandal was not limited to U.S. companies. Royal Ahold NV, a large international supermarket chain headquartered in the Netherlands, had major accounting problems. Specifically, Ahold's U.S. Foodservice division overstated its earnings in 2001 and 2002. Ahold also discovered potentially illegal transactions in its Argentine subsidiary. Because of these problems, the CEO and chief financial officer of Ahold were discharged. The "accounting problems" caused Ahold to reduce its operating earnings by $500 million.

Federal prosecutors investigated massive accounting fraud at HealthSouth Corporation. The prosecutors negotiated plea arrangements with five HealthSouth employees in which they would testify that they were directed by the company's chairman and CEO, Richard Scrushy, to inflate the financial results. In fact, the Securities and Exchange Commission (SEC) accused the company (and Scrushy) of inflating the profits by $1.4 billion over the period 1999–2002. The government believes that these practices may have been common in the company since its founding in 1986, so the overstatement of profits may be much greater. According to the SEC, company managers falsified accounting entries, overstated cash and other assets, and created numbers to fill in the differences between actual and desired earnings. The board of directors for HealthSouth fired the CEO, Richard Scrushy, upon learning of further allegations that he may have established offshore bank accounts to avoid taxes.

The scandals also engulfed major Wall Street firms. In fact, the top ten investment firms on Wall Street settled an inquiry by the U.S. government into irregularities, such as potential conflicts of interest whereby firms received secret payments (supposedly for research conducted) from companies for which they gave potential investors strong recommendations to buy. Other firms were accused of gaining favor with corporate clients by selling hot stock offerings to their senior executives (who could then sell the shares for almost guaranteed profits).

To avoid problems similar to those noted above and those made by its predecessor company, WorldCom, the new MCI CEO, Michael Capellas (former CEO of Compaq), required the top 300 executives in the firm to sign an ethics pledge. His intent is to restore investor confidence in the company. He stated that "we will operate at a higher standard than the rest of the world. The burden of proof is on us."

SOURCES: S. Morrison & P. T. Larsen, 2003, MCI executives sign ethics pledge, *Financial Times*, http://www.ft.com, May 8; L. R. Roth & A. Hill, 2003, Tenet chief forced to quit, *Financial Times*, http://www.ft.com, May 27; S. Labaton, 2003, 10 Wall St. firms settle with U.S. in analyst inquiry, *New York Times*, http://www.nytimes.com, April 29; C. Terhune & C. Mollenkamp, 2003, Five HealthSouth employees may plead guilty to fraud, *Wall Street Journal Online*, http://www.wsj.com, March 31; M. Freudenheim, 2003, HealthSouth inquiry looks for accounts held offshore, *New York Times*, http://www.nytimes.com, March 31; M. Freudenheim, 2003, HealthSouth fires its embattled chairman, *New York Times*, http://www.nytimes.com, March 31; M. Wallin, L. Norman, & J. Quintanilha, 2003, Ahold replaces management at Argentine unit, ends probe, *Wall Street Journal Online*, http://www.wsj.com, February 28; D. Ball, J. S. Lublin, & M. Karnitschnig, 2003, Ahold scandal raises questions about directors' responsibilities, *Wall Street Journal Online*, http://www.wsj.com, February 27; D. Ball, A. Zimmerman, & M. Veen, 2003, Supermarket giant Ahold ousts CEO in big accounting scandal, *Wall Street Journal*, February 25, A1, A10.

create "social capital" in the organization in that "goodwill available to individuals and groups" in the organization increases.[118] Alternately, when unethical practices evolve in an organization, they become like a contagious disease.[119]

To properly influence employees' judgment and behavior, ethical practices must shape the firm's decision-making process and be an integral part of an organization's culture. In fact, research has found that a value-based culture is the most effective means of ensuring that employees comply with the firm's ethical requirements.[120] As discussed in Chapter 10, in the absence of ethical requirements, managers may act opportunistically, making decisions that are in their own best interests, but not in the firm's best interests. In other words, managers acting opportunistically take advantage of their positions, making decisions that benefit themselves to the detriment of the firm's owners (shareholders).[121]

Managerial opportunism may explain the behavior and decisions of a few key executives at HealthSouth, where, as described in the Strategic Focus, substantial accounting irregularities were discovered. In fact, the investigations suggested that the company overstated its performance for many years, thereby propping up its stock price. Firms that have been reported to have poor ethical behavior, such as perpetrating fraud or having to restate financial results, see their overall corporate value in the stock market drop precipitously.[122]

While the Strategic Focus also explains the accounting irregularities completed by Ahold, Tenet Healthcare overcharged the U.S. government for Medicare payments. Interestingly, Tenet's CEO, Jeffrey Barbakow, was the highest-paid CEO in 2002. Yet Barbakow and the CEO and CFO of Ahold lost their jobs when the irregularities came to light. Thus, in addition to the firms' shareholders, they paid a high price for the indiscretions.

These incidents suggest that firms need to employ ethical strategic leaders—leaders who include ethical practices as part of their long-term vision for the firm, who desire to do the right thing, and for whom honesty, trust, and integrity are important.[123] Strategic leaders who consistently display these qualities inspire employees as they work with others to develop and support an organizational culture in which ethical practices are the expected behavioral norms.[124]

The effects of white-collar fraud are substantial.[125] Estimates in the United States suggest that white-collar fraud ranges from $200 billion to as much as $600 billion annually. Furthermore, this fraud usually equals from 1 to 6 percent of the firm's sales, and white-collar crime causes as much as 30 percent of new venture firms to fail. These amounts are incredibly high when compared to the total cost of approximately $20 billion for street crime in the United States.[126] Certainly, executives in multinational firms must understand that there are differences in ethical values across cultures globally.[127] Beyond this, however, research has shown that a positive relationship exists between ethical values (character) and an executive's health. So, ethical practices have many possible benefits to the firm and the executive.[128] Strategic leaders are challenged to take actions that increase the probability that an ethical culture will prevail in their organizations. One action that has gained favor is to institute a formal program to manage ethics. Operating much like control systems, these programs help inculcate values throughout the organization.[129] Therefore, when these efforts are successful, the practices associated with an ethical culture become institutionalized in the firm; that is, they become the set of behavioral commitments and actions accepted by most of the firm's employees and other stakeholders with whom employees interact.

Additional actions strategic leaders can take to develop an ethical organizational culture include (1) establishing and communicating specific goals to describe the firm's ethical standards (e.g., developing and disseminating a code of conduct); (2) continuously revising and updating the code of conduct, based on inputs from people throughout the firm and from other stakeholders (e.g., customers and suppliers); (3) disseminating the code of conduct to all stakeholders to inform them of the firm's ethical standards and practices; (4) developing and implementing methods and procedures to use in achieving the firm's ethical standards (e.g., using internal auditing practices that are consistent with the standards); (5) creating and using explicit reward systems that recognize acts of courage (e.g., rewarding those who use proper channels and procedures to report observed wrongdoings); and (6) creating a work environment in which all people are treated with dignity.[130] The effectiveness of these actions increases when they are taken simultaneously, thereby making them mutually supportive. When managers and employees do not engage in such actions—perhaps because an ethical culture has not been created—problems are likely to occur. As we discuss next, formal organizational controls can help prevent further problems and reinforce better ethical practices.

Establishing Balanced Organizational Controls

Organizational controls are basic to a capitalistic system and have long been viewed as an important part of strategy implementation processes.[131] Controls are necessary to help ensure that firms achieve their desired outcomes.[132] Defined as the "formal, information-based . . . procedures used by managers to maintain or alter patterns in organizational activities," controls help strategic leaders build credibility, demonstrate the value of strategies to the firm's stakeholders, and promote and support strategic change.[133] Most critically, controls provide the parameters within which strategies are to be implemented, as well as corrective actions to be taken when implementation-related adjustments are required. In this chapter, we focus on two organizational controls—strategic and financial—that were introduced in Chapter 11. Our discussion of organizational controls here emphasizes strategic and financial controls because strategic leaders are responsible for their development and effective use.

Evidence suggests that, although critical to the firm's success, organizational controls are imperfect. *Control failures* have a negative effect on the firm's reputation and divert managerial attention from actions that are necessary to effectively use the strategic management process.

As explained in Chapter 11, financial control focuses on short-term financial outcomes. In contrast, strategic control focuses on the *content* of strategic actions, rather than their *outcomes.* Some strategic actions can be correct, but poor financial outcomes may still result because of external conditions, such as a recession in the economy, unexpected domestic or foreign government actions, or natural disasters.[134] Therefore, an emphasis on financial control often produces more short-term and risk-averse managerial decisions, because financial outcomes may be caused by events beyond managers' direct control. Alternatively, strategic control encourages lower-level managers to make decisions that incorporate moderate and acceptable levels of risk because outcomes are shared between the business-level executives making strategic proposals and the corporate-level executives evaluating them.

THE BALANCED SCORECARD

The **balanced scorecard** is a framework that firms can use to verify that they have established both strategic and financial controls to assess their performance.[135] This technique is most appropriate for use when dealing with business-level strategies, but can also apply to corporate-level strategies.

The underlying premise of the balanced scorecard is that firms jeopardize their future performance possibilities when financial controls are emphasized at the expense of strategic controls,[136] in that financial controls provide feedback about outcomes achieved from past actions, but do not communicate the drivers of the firm's future performance.[137] Thus, an overemphasis on financial controls could promote organizational behavior that has a net effect of sacrificing the firm's long-term value-creating potential for short-term performance gains.[138] An appropriate balance of strategic

The balanced scorecard is a framework that firms can use to verify that they have established both strategic and financial controls to assess their performance.

controls and financial controls, rather than an overemphasis on either, allows firms to effectively monitor their performance.

Four perspectives are integrated to form the balanced scorecard framework: *financial* (concerned with growth, profitability, and risk from the shareholders' perspective), *customer* (concerned with the amount of value customers perceive was created by the firm's products), *internal business processes* (with a focus on the priorities for various business processes that create customer and shareholder satisfaction), and *learning and growth* (concerned with the firm's effort to create a climate that supports change, innovation, and growth). Thus, using the balanced scorecard framework allows the firm to understand how it looks to shareholders (financial perspective), how customers view it (customer perspective), the processes it must emphasize to successfully use its competitive advantage (internal perspective), and what it can do to improve its performance in order to grow (learning and growth perspective).[139] Generally speaking, strategic controls tend to be emphasized when the firm assesses its performance relative to the learning and growth perspective, while financial controls are emphasized when assessing performance in terms of the financial perspective. Study of the customer and internal business processes perspectives often is completed through virtually an equal emphasis on strategic controls and financial controls.

Firms use different criteria to measure their standing relative to the scorecard's four perspectives. Sample criteria are shown in Figure 12.5. The firm should select the number of criteria that will allow it to have both a strategic understanding and a financial understanding of its performance without becoming immersed in too many details.[140]

Strategic Controls and Financial Controls in a Balanced Scorecard Framework — Figure 12.5

Perspectives	Criteria
Financial	• Cash flow • Return on equity • Return on assets
Customer	• Assessment of ability to anticipate customers' needs • Effectiveness of customer service practices • Percentage of repeat business • Quality of communications with customers
Internal Business Processes	• Asset utilization improvements • Improvements in employee morale • Changes in turnover rates
Learning and Growth	• Improvements in innovation ability • Number of new products compared to competitors' • Increases in employees' skills

Strategic leaders play an important role in determining a proper balance between strategic controls and financial controls for their firm. This is true in single-business firms as well as in diversified firms. A proper balance between controls is important, in that "wealth creation for organizations where strategic leadership is exercised is possible because these leaders make appropriate investments for future viability [through strategic control], while maintaining an appropriate level of financial stability in the present [through financial control]."[141] In fact, most corporate restructuring is designed to refocus the firm on its core businesses, thereby allowing top executives to reestablish strategic control of their separate business units.[142] Thus, as emphasized in Chapter 11, both strategic controls and financial controls support effective use of the firm's corporate-level strategy.

Successful use of strategic control by top executives frequently is integrated with appropriate autonomy for the various subunits so that they can gain a competitive advantage in their respective markets.[143] Strategic control can be used to promote the sharing of both tangible and intangible resources among interdependent businesses within a firm's portfolio. In addition, the autonomy provided allows the flexibility necessary to take advantage of specific marketplace opportunities. As a result, strategic leadership promotes the simultaneous use of strategic control and autonomy.[144]

Balancing strategic and financial controls in diversified firms can be difficult. Failure to maintain an effective balance between strategic controls and financial controls in these firms often contributes to a decision to restructure the company. For example, Jean-Pierre Garnier, CEO of GlaxoSmithKline, is trying to reinvent the company by streamlining its costs (financial controls) and simultaneously enhancing its development of innovative and valuable new drugs (strategic controls). In fact, the firm must achieve a balance in these controls in order to survive in the strongly competitive pharmaceuticals industry.[145]

Samsung provides another example of the need to achieve a balance in these types of control. Following the 1997 Southeast Asian currency crisis, Samsung Electronics, a large Korean firm, was heading into a significant crisis in its Chinese operations. It was a large diversified firm with businesses throughout the world. Its Chinese operations included selling everything from washing machines to VCRs. Each product division had established Chinese factories and a nationwide sales organization by the mid-1990s. However, in China, these divisions encountered significant losses, losing $37 million in 1998.

When Jong-Yong Yun took over as Samsung's CEO in 1997, he shut down all 23 sales offices and declared that each of the seven mainland factories would have to become profitable on its own to survive. Thus, he instituted strong financial controls that were to be followed to verify that each

The recent successes of Samsung, through the leadership of its CEO, Jong-Yong Yun, represent an effective use of the balanced scorecard, which helps put strategic and financial controls in balance.

HKGCC
Hong Kong General Chamber of Commerce
香港總商會 1861

©AFP/CORBIS

PART 3 / Strategic Actions: Strategy Implementation

division was operating profitably. Additionally, based on market survey results, Samsung executives decided that the firm would focus on ten major cities in China. Furthermore, the firm carefully selected products and supported them with intense marketing. Thus, the firm improved strategic controls using a "top-down marketing strategy." Overall, Samsung increased its revenue from $18.45 billion in 1998 to $40.51 billion in 2002. Its net income increased from $313 million in 1998 to $7.05 billion in 2002. A more effective balance between strategic and financial controls has helped Samsung to improve its performance and to make progress toward its goal of establishing marquee brands in China, comparable to Sony and Motorola.[146]

Summary

- Effective strategic leadership is a prerequisite to successfully using the strategic management process. Strategic leadership entails the ability to anticipate events, envision possibilities, maintain flexibility, and empower others to create strategic change.

- Top-level managers are an important resource for firms to develop and exploit competitive advantages. In addition, when they and their work are valuable, rare, imperfectly imitable, and nonsubstitutable, strategic leaders can themselves be a source of competitive advantage.

- The top management team is composed of key managers who play a critical role in the selection and implementation of the firm's strategies. Generally, they are officers of the corporation or members of the board of directors.

- There is a relationship among the top management team's characteristics, a firm's strategies, and its performance. For example, a top management team that has significant marketing and R&D knowledge positively contributes to the firm's use of growth strategies. Overall, most top management teams are more effective when they have diverse skills.

- When the board of directors is involved in shaping a firm's strategic direction, that firm generally improves its performance. However, the board may be less involved in decisions about strategy formulation and implementation when CEOs have more power. CEOs increase their power when they appoint people to the board and when they simultaneously serve as the CEO and board chair.

- Strategic leaders are selected from either the internal or the external managerial labor market. Because of their effect on performance, the selection of strategic leaders has implications for a firm's effectiveness. There are valid reasons to use either the internal or the external market when choosing the firm's strategic leaders. In most instances, the internal market is used to select the firm's CEO, but the number of outsiders chosen is increasing. Outsiders often are selected to initiate changes.

- Effective strategic leadership has five major components: determining the firm's strategic direction, effectively managing the firm's resource portfolio (including exploiting and maintaining core competencies and managing human capital and social capital), sustaining an effective organizational culture, emphasizing ethical practices, and establishing balanced organizational controls.

- A firm must develop a long-term vision of its strategic intent. A long-term vision is the driver of strategic leaders' behavior in terms of the remaining four components of effective strategic leadership.

- Strategic leaders must ensure that their firm exploits its core competencies, which are used to produce and deliver products that create value for customers, through the implementation of strategies. In related diversified and large firms in particular, core competencies are exploited by sharing them across units and products.

- A critical element of strategic leadership and the effective implementation of strategy is the ability to manage the firm's resource portfolio. This includes integrating resources to create capabilities and leveraging those capabilities through strategies to build competitive advantages. Perhaps the most important resources are human capital and social capital.

- As a part of managing the firm's resources, strategic leaders must develop a firm's human capital. Effective strategic leaders and firms view human capital as a resource to be maximized, rather than as a cost to be minimized. Resulting from this perspective is the development and use of programs intended to train current and future strategic leaders to build the skills needed to nurture the rest of the firm's human capital.

- Effective strategic leaders also build and maintain internal and external social capital. Internal social capital promotes cooperation and coordination within and across units in the firm. External social capital provides access to resources that the firm needs to compete effectively.

- Shaping the firm's culture is a central task of effective strategic leadership. An appropriate organizational culture encourages the development of an entrepreneurial orientation among employees and an ability to change the culture as necessary.

- In ethical organizations, employees are encouraged to exercise ethical judgment and to behave ethically at all times. Improved ethical practices foster social capital. Setting specific goals to describe the firm's ethical standards, using a code of conduct, rewarding ethical behaviors, and creating a work environment in which all people are treated with dignity are examples of actions that facilitate and support ethical behavior within the firm.

- Developing and using balanced organizational controls is the final component of effective strategic leadership. An effective balance between strategic and financial controls allows for the flexible use of core competencies, but within the parameters indicated by the firm's financial position. The balanced scorecard is a tool used by the firm and its strategic leaders to develop an appropriate balance between its strategic and financial controls.

Review Questions

1. What is strategic leadership? In what ways are top executives considered important resources for an organization?

2. What is a top management team, and how does it affect a firm's performance and its abilities to innovate and make appropriate strategic changes?

3. What are the differences between the internal and external managerial labor markets? What are the effects of each type of labor market on the formulation and implementation of strategies?

4. How does strategic leadership affect the determination of the firm's strategic direction?

5. How do strategic leaders effectively manage their firm's resource portfolio such that its core competencies are exploited, and the human capital and social capital are leveraged to achieve a competitive advantage?

6. What is organizational culture? What must strategic leaders do to develop and sustain an effective organizational culture?

7. As a strategic leader, what actions could you take to establish and emphasize ethical practices in your firm?

8. What are organizational controls? Why are strategic controls and financial controls important parts of the strategic management process?

Using the Balanced Scorecard Framework

This experiential exercise is based on the Balanced Scorecard Framework (Figure 12.5). Form groups of three or four students each. Assume that you are strategists for a multinational sportswear manufacturing and marketing company with millions of dollars in sales worldwide. In designing your business-level strategy (see Chapter 4), you are expected to

define the objectives associated with that strategy concerning financial performance, customer service, internal processes, and learning and growth. Additionally, your task is to define measures and initiatives necessary for each category of objectives. Measures refer to the definition of specific criteria for each objective, and initiatives refer to the specific actions that should be taken to achieve a particular objective. Use the table below to record your definitions.

Financial Performance:		
Objectives	Measures	Initiatives
1.	1.	1.1 1.2
2.	2.	2.1 2.2

Customer Service:		
Objectives	Measures	Initiatives
1.	1.	1.1 1.2
2.	2.	2.1 2.2

Internal Processes:		
Objectives	Measures	Initiatives
1.	1.	1.1 1.2
2.	2.	2.1 2.2

Learning and Growth:		
Objectives	Measures	Initiatives
1.	1.	1.1 1.2
2.	2.	2.1 2.2

Strategic Leadership

The executive board for a large company is concerned that the firm's future leadership needs to be developed. Several top-level managers are expected to leave the firm in the next three to seven years. You have been put in charge of a committee to determine how the firm should prepare for these departures.

Part 1 (individual). Use the information provided within this chapter and your own perceptions to complete the following chart. Be prepared to discuss in class.

Candidates	Internal Managerial Labor Market	External Managerial Labor Market
Strengths		
Weaknesses		

Part 2 (individually or in small groups). The firm's executive board feels that the external managerial labor market is beyond its control—the managerial resources the firm will need may or may not be available when they are needed. The board has then asked your committee to consider a program that would develop the firm's internal managerial labor market. Outline the objectives that you want your program to achieve, the steps you would take to reach them, and the time frame involved. Also consider potential problems in such a program and how they could be resolved.

Notes

1. R. D. Ireland, M. A. Hitt, S. M. Camp, & D. L. Sexton, 2001, Integrating entrepreneurship and strategic management actions to create firm wealth, *Academy of Management Executive*, 15(1): 49–63; K. R. Thompson, W. A. Hochwarter, & N. J. Mathys, 1997, Stretch targets: What makes them effective? *Academy of Management Executive*, 11(3): 48–59.

2. A. Cannella, Jr., A. Pettigrew, & D. Hambrick, 2001, Upper echelons: Donald Hambrick on executives and strategy, *Academy of Management Executive*, 15(3): 36–52; R. D. Ireland & M. A. Hitt, 1999, Achieving and maintaining strategic competitiveness in the 21st century: The role of strategic leadership, *Academy of Management Executive*, 12(1): 43–57; D. Lei, M. A. Hitt, & R. Bettis, 1996, Dynamic core competencies through meta-learning and strategic context, *Journal of Management*, 22: 547–567.

3. L. Greiner, T. Cummings, & A. Bhambri, 2002, When new CEOs succeed and fail: 4-D theory of strategic transformation, *Organizational Dynamics*, 32: 1–16.

4. S. Green, F. Hassan, J. Immelt, M. Marks, & D. Meiland, 2003, In search of global leaders, *Harvard Business Review*, 81(8): 38–45; T. J. Peters, 2001, Leadership: Sad facts and silver linings, *Harvard Business Review*, 79(11): 121–128.

5. M. A. Hitt & R. D. Ireland, 2002, The essence of strategic leadership: Managing human and social capital, *Journal of Leadership and Organizational Studies*, 9: 3–14; J. Collins, 2001, Level 5 leadership: The triumph of humility and fierce resolve, *Harvard Business Review*, 79(1): 66–76.

6. A. S. DeNisi, M. A. Hitt, & S. E. Jackson, 2003, The knowledge-based approach to sustainable competitive advantage, in S. E. Jackson, M. A. Hitt, & A. S. DeNisi (eds.), *Managing Knowledge for Sustained Competitive Advantage*, San Francisco: Jossey-Bass, 3–33; D. J. Teece, 2000, *Managing Intellectual Capital: Organizational, Strategic and Policy Dimensions*, Oxford: Oxford University Press.

7. J. E. Post, L. E. Preston, & S. Sachs, 2002, Managing the extended enterprise: The new stakeholder view, *California Management Review*, 45(1): 6–28.

8. D. C. Carey & D. Ogden, 2000, *CEO Succession: A Window on How Boards Can Get It Right When Choosing a New Chief Executive*, New York: Oxford University Press.

9. M. Maccoby, 2001, Making sense of the leadership literature, *Research Technology Management*, 44(5): 58–60; T. Kono, 1999, A strong head office makes a strong company, *Long Range Planning*, 32: 225–246.

10. G. Hamel & C. K. Prahalad, 1993, Strategy as stretch and leverage, *Harvard Business Review*, 71(2): 75–84.

11. C. L. Shook, R. L. Priem, & J. E. McGee, 2003, Venture creation and the enterprising individual: A review and synthesis, *Journal of Management*, 29: 379–399.

12. J. M. Mezias & W. H. Starbuck, 2003, Studying the accuracy of managers' perceptions: A research odyssey, *British Journal of Management*, 14: 3–17.

13. M. Maccoby, 2001, Successful leaders employ strategic intelligence, *Research Technology Management*, 44(3): 58–60.

14. S. Finkelstein & D. C. Hambrick, 1996, *Strategic Leadership: Top Executives and Their Effects on Organizations*, St. Paul, MN: West Publishing Company, 2.

15. Collins, Level 5 leadership.

16. R. Castanias & C. Helfat, 2001, The managerial rents model: Theory and empirical analysis, *Journal of Management*, 27: 661–678; H. P. Gunz & R. M. Jalland, 1996, Managerial careers and business strategy, *Academy of Management Review*, 21: 718–756.

17. M. Beer & R. Eisenstat, 2000, The silent killers of strategy implementation and learning, *Sloan Management Review*, 41(4): 29–40; C. M. Christensen, 1997, Making strategy: Learning by doing, *Harvard Business Review*, 75(6): 141–156; M. A. Hitt, B. W. Keats, H. E. Harback, & R. D. Nixon, 1994, Rightsizing: Building and maintaining strategic leadership and long-term competitiveness, *Organizational Dynamics*, 23: 18–32.

18. R. Whittington, 2003, The work of strategizing and organizing: For a practice perspective, *Strategic Organization*, 1: 117–125; M. Wright, R. E. Hoskisson, L. W. Busenitz, & J. Dial, 2000, Entrepreneurial growth through

privatization: The upside of management buyouts, *Academy of Management Review*, 25: 591–601; M. J. Waller, G. P. Huber, & W. H. Glick, 1995, Functional background as a determinant of executives' selective perception, *Academy of Management Journal*, 38: 943–974; N. Rajagopalan, A. M. Rasheed, & D. K. Datta, 1993, Strategic decision processes: Critical review and future directions, *Journal of Management*, 19: 349–384.

19. W. Rowe, 2001, Creating wealth in organizations: The role of strategic leadership, *Academy of Management Executive*, 15(1): 81–94; Finkelstein & Hambrick, *Strategic Leadership*, 26–34.

20. J. A. Petrick & J. F. Quinn, 2001, The challenge of leadership accountability for integrity capacity as a strategic asset, *Journal of Business Ethics*, 34: 331–343; R. C. Mayer, J. H. Davis, & F. D. Schoorman, 1995, An integrative model of organizational trust, *Academy of Management Review*, 20: 709–734.

21. S. Gove, D. Sirmon, & M. A. Hitt, 2003, Relative resource advantages: The effect of resources and resource management on organizational performance, Paper presented at the Strategic Management Society Conference, Baltimore; J. J. Sosik, 2001, Self-other agreement on charismatic leadership: Relationships with work attitudes and managerial performance, *Group & Organization Management*, 26: 484–511.

22. J. E. Dutton, S. J. Ashford, R. M. O'Neill, & K. A. Lawrence, 2001, Moves that matter: Issue selling and organizational change, *Academy of Management Journal*, 44: 716–736.

23. I. Goll, R. Sambharya, & L. Tucci, 2001, Top management team composition, corporate ideology, and firm performance, *Management International Review*, 41(2): 109–129.

24. J. Bunderson, 2003, Team member functional background and involvement in management teams: Direct effects and the moderating role of power and centralization, *Academy of Management Journal*, 46: 458–474; L. Markoczy, 2001, Consensus formation during strategic change, *Strategic Management Journal*, 22: 1013–1031.

25. Post, Preston, & Sachs, Managing the extended enterprise; C. Pegels, Y. Song, & B. Yang, 2000, Management heterogeneity, competitive interaction groups, and firm performance, *Strategic Management Journal*, 21: 911–923.

26. H. Lee, M. A. Hitt, & E. Jeong, 2003, The impact of CEO and TMT characteristics on strategic flexibility and firm performance, Working paper, Texas A&M University.

27. Markoczy, Consensus formation during strategic change; D. Knight, C. L. Pearce, K. G. Smith, J. D. Olian, H. P. Sims, K. A. Smith, & P. Flood, 1999, Top management team diversity, group process, and strategic consensus, *Strategic Management Journal*, 20: 446–465.

28. D. C. Hambrick, T. S. Cho, & M. J. Chen, 1996, The influence of top management team heterogeneity on firms' competitive moves, *Administrative Science Quarterly*, 41: 659–684.

29. J. J. Distefano & M. L. Maznevski, 2000, Creating value with diverse teams in global management, *Organizational Dynamics*, 29(1): 45–63; T. Simons, L. H. Pelled, & K. A. Smith, 1999, Making use of difference, diversity, debate, and decision comprehensiveness in top management teams, *Academy of Management Journal*, 42: 662–673.

30. Finkelstein & Hambrick, *Strategic Leadership*, 148.

31. S. Barsade, A. Ward, J. Turner, & J. Sonnenfeld, 2000, To your heart's content: A model of affective diversity in top management teams, *Administrative Science Quarterly*, 45: 802–836; C. C. Miller, L. M. Burke, & W. H. Glick, 1998, Cognitive diversity among upper-echelon executives: Implications for strategic decision processes, *Strategic Management Journal*, 19: 39–58.

32. B. J. Avolio & S. S. Kahai, 2002, Adding the "e" to e-leadership: How it may impact your leadership, *Organizational Dynamics*, 31: 325–338.

33. U. Daellenbach, A. McCarthy, & T. Schoenecker, 1999, Commitment to innovation: The impact of top management team characteristics, *R&D Management*, 29(3): 199–208; D. K. Datta & J. P. Guthrie, 1994, Executive succession: Organizational antecedents of CEO characteristics, *Strategic Management Journal*, 15: 569–577.

34. W. B. Werther, 2003, Strategic change and leader-follower alignment, *Organizational Dynamics*, 32: 32–45; S. Wally & M. Becerra, 2001, Top manage-

ment team characteristics and strategic changes in international diversification: The case of U.S. multinationals in the European community, *Group & Organization Management*, 26: 165–188.

35. A. Tomie, 2000, Fast pack 2000, *Fast Company Online*, http://www.fastcompany.com, March 1.

36. Y. Zhang & N. Rajagopalan, 2003, Explaining the new CEO origin: Firm versus industry antecedents, *Academy of Management Journal*, 46: 327–338.

37. T. Dvir, D. Eden, B. J. Avolio, & B. Shamir, 2002, Impact of transformational leadership on follower development and performance: A field experiment, *Academy of Management Journal*, 45: 735–744.

38. Wally & Becerra, Top management team characteristics and strategic changes in international diversification; L. Tihanyi, C. Daily, D. Dalton, & A. Ellstrand, 2000, Composition of the top management team and firm international diversification, *Journal of Management*, 26: 1157–1178.

39. L. Tihanyi, R. A. Johnson, R. E. Hoskisson, & M. A. Hitt, 2003, Institutional ownership and international diversification: The effects of boards of directors and technological opportunity, *Academy of Management Journal*, 46: 195–211; B. Taylor, 2001, From corporate governance to corporate entrepreneurship, *Journal of Change Management*, 2(2): 128–147.

40. B. R. Golden & E. J. Zajac, 2001, When will boards influence strategy? Inclination times power equals strategic change, *Strategic Management Journal*, 22: 1087–1111.

41. M. Carpenter & J. Westphal, 2001, Strategic context of external network ties: Examining the impact of director appointments on board involvement in strategic decision making, *Academy of Management Journal*, 44: 639–660.

42. J. D. Westphal & E. J. Zajac, 1995, Who shall govern? CEO/board power, demographic similarity, and new director selection, *Administrative Science Quarterly*, 40: 60.

43. J. D. Westphal, 1999, Collaboration in the boardroom: Behavioral and performance consequences of CEO-board social ties, *Academy of Management Journal*, 42: 7–24.

44. J. Roberts & P. Stiles, 1999, The relationship between chairmen and chief executives: Competitive or complementary roles? *Long Range Planning*, 32(1): 36–48.

45. J. Coles, N. Sen, & V. McWilliams, 2001, An examination of the relationship of governance mechanisms to performance, *Journal of Management*, 27: 23–50; J. Coles & W. Hesterly, 2000, Independence of the chairman and board composition: Firm choices and shareholder value, *Journal of Management*, 26: 195–214; B. K. Boyd, 1995, CEO duality and firm performance: A contingency model, *Strategic Management Journal*, 16: 301.

46. D. D. Bergh, 2001, Executive retention and acquisition outcomes: A test of opposing views on the influence of organizational tenure, *Journal of Management*, 27: 603–622.

47. J. Muller, J. Green, & C. Tierney, 2001, Chrysler's rescue team, *Business Week*, January 15, 48–50.

48. J. B. White & N. E. Boudette, 2003, His mission: Shift Chrysler out of reverse, *Wall Street Journal*, July 16, B1, B4.

49. C. M. Daily & D. R. Dalton, 1995, CEO and director turnover in failing firms: An illusion of change? *Strategic Management Journal*, 16: 393–400.

50. R. Albanese, M. T. Dacin, & I. C. Harris, 1997, Agents as stewards, *Academy of Management Review*, 22: 609–611; J. H. Davis, F. D. Schoorman, & L. Donaldson, 1997, Toward a stewardship theory of management, *Academy of Management Review*, 22: 20–47.

51. M. A. Carpenter, 2002, The implications of strategy and social context for the relationship between top management team heterogeneity and firm performance, *Strategic Management Journal*, 23: 275–284.

52. J. G. Combs & M. S. Skill, 2003, Managerialist and human capital explanations for key executive pay premiums: A contingency perspective, *Academy of Management Journal*, 46: 63–73.

53. N. Rajagopalan & D. Datta, 1996, CEO characteristics: Does industry matter? *Academy of Management Journal*, 39: 197–215.

54. R. A. Johnson, R. E. Hoskisson, & M. A. Hitt, 1993, Board involvement in restructuring: The effect of board versus managerial controls and characteristics, *Strategic Management Journal*, 14(Special Issue): 33–50.

55. Boyd, CEO duality and firm performance: A contingency model.

56. Lee, Hitt, & Jeong, The impact of CEO and TMT characteristics on strategic flexibility; M. Carpenter & J. Fredrickson, 2001, Top management teams, global strategic posture, and the moderating role of uncertainty, *Academy of Management Journal*, 44: 533–545.

57. M. Schneider, 2002, A stakeholder model of organizational leadership, *Organization Science*, 13: 209–220.

58. M. Sorcher & J. Brant, 2002, Are you picking the right leaders? *Harvard Business Review*, 80(2): 78–85; D. A. Waldman, G. G. Ramirez, R. J. House, & P. Puranam, 2001, Does leadership matter? CEO leadership attributes and profitability under conditions of perceived environmental uncertainty, *Academy of Management Journal*, 44: 134–143.

59. W. Shen & A. A. Cannella, 2002, Revisiting the performance consequences of CEO succession: The impacts of successor type, postsuccession senior executive turnover, and departing CEO tenure, *Academy of Management Journal*, 45: 717–734; A. Kakabadse & N. Kakabadse, 2001, Dynamics of executive succession, *Corporate Governance*, 1(3): 9–14.

60. R. Charan, 2000, GE's ten-step talent plan, *Fortune*, April 17, 232.

61. R. E. Hoskisson, D. Yiu, & H. Kim, 2000, Capital and labor market congruence and corporate governance: Effects on corporate innovation and global competitiveness, in S. S. Cohen & G. Boyd (eds.), *Corporate Governance and Globalization*, Northampton, MA: Edward Elgar, 129–154.

62. S. B. Shepard, 2002, A talk with Jeff Immelt: Jack Welch's successor charts a course for GE in the 21st century, *Business Week*, January 28, 102–104.

63. Carey & Ogden, *CEO Succession*.

64. W. Shen & A. A. Cannella, 2003, Will succession planning increase shareholder wealth? Evidence from investor reactions to relay CEO successions, *Strategic Management Journal*, 24: 191–198; V. Kisfalvi, 2000, The threat of failure, the perils of success and CEO character: Sources of strategic persistence, *Organization Studies*, 21: 611–639.

65. Greiner, Cummings, & Bhambri, When new CEOs succeed and fail.

66. D. Miller, 1991, Stale in the saddle: CEO tenure and the match between organization and environment, *Management Science*, 37: 34–52.

67. R. M. Fulmer & M. Goldsmith, 2000, *The Leadership Investment: Promoting Diversity in Leadership*, New York: American Management Association.

68. S. Foley, D. L. Kidder, & G. N. Powell, 2002, The perceived glass ceiling and justice perceptions: An investigation of Hispanic law associates, *Journal of Management*, 28: 471–496.

69. N. M. Carter, W. B. Gartner, K. G. Shaver, & E. J. Gatewood, 2003, The career reasons of nascent entrepreneurs, *Journal of Business Venturing*, 18: 13–39.

70. B. Dyck, M. Mauws, F. Starke, & G. Mischke, 2002, Passing the baton: The importance of sequence, timing, technique and communication in executive succession, *Journal of Business Venturing*, 17: 143–162.

71. M. A. Hitt, B. W. Keats, & E. Yucel, 2003, Strategic leadership in global business organizations, in W. H. Mobley & P. W. Dorfman (eds.), *Advances in Global Leadership*, Oxford, UK: Elsevier Science, Ltd., 9–35; J. J. Rotemberg & G. Saloner, 2000, Visionaries, managers, and strategic direction, *RAND Journal of Economics*, 31: 693–716.

72. I. M. Levin, 2000, Vision revisited, *Journal of Applied Behavioral Science*, 36: 91–107; J. C. Collins & J. I. Porras, 1996, Building your company's vision, *Harvard Business Review*, 74(5): 65–77.

73. G. Gori, 2001, An American directs Mexico City's cinema revival, *New York Times*, http://www.nytimes.com, July 15.

74. 2002, Onex slides into Mexico with Cinemex purchase, http://www.latinfilmnetwork.com, July 17.

75. J. Barney & A. M. Arikan, 2001, The resource-based view: Origins and implications, in M. A. Hitt, R. E. Freeman, & J. S. Harrison (eds.), *Handbook of Strategic Management*, Oxford, UK: Blackwell Publishers, 124–188.

76. D. G. Sirmon, M. A. Hitt, & R. D. Ireland, 2003, Managing firm resources for advantage: Creating value for stakeholders, Paper presented at the Academy of Management, Seattle, August.

77. R. A. Burgelman, 2001, *Strategy Is Destiny: How Strategy-Making Shapes a Company's Future*, New York: The Free Press.

78. 2003, History, http://www.pepsico.com, July; 2003, PepsiCo, Inc., http://www.hoovers.com, July; S. Jaffe, 2001, Do Pepsi and Gatorade mix? *BusinessWeek Online*, http://www.businessweek.com, August 14.

79. Barney & Arikan, The resource-based view.

80. C. A. Lengnick-Hall & J. A. Wolff, 1999, Similarities and contradictions in the core logic of three strategy research streams, *Strategic Management Journal*, 20: 1109–1132.

81. M. A. Hitt, L. Bierman, K. Shimizu, & R. Kochhar, 2001, Direct and moderating effects of human capital on strategy and performance in professional service firms: A resource-based perspective, *Academy of Management Journal*, 44: 13–28; S. A. Snell & M. A. Youndt, 1995, Human resource management and firm performance: Testing a contingency model of executive controls, *Journal of Management*, 21: 711–737.

82. S. E. Jackson, M. A. Hitt, & A. S. DeNisi (eds.), 2003, *Managing Knowledge for Sustained Competitive Advantage: Designing Strategies for Effective Human Resource Management*, Oxford, UK: Elsevier Science, Ltd.; P. Caligiuri & V. Di Santo, 2001, Global competence: What is it, and can it be developed through global assignments? *Human Resource Planning*, 24(3): 27–35.

83. A. McWilliams, D. D. Van Fleet, & P. M. Wright, 2001, Strategic management of human resources for global competitive advantage, *Journal of Business Strategies* 18(1): 1–24; J. Pfeffer, 1994, *Competitive Advantage through People*, Cambridge, MA: Harvard Business School Press, 4.

84. W. Watson, W. H. Stewart, & A. Barnir, 2003, The effects of human capital, organizational demography, and interpersonal processes on venture partner perceptions of firm profit and growth, *Journal of Business Venturing*, 18: 145–164.

85. H. B. Gregersen & J. S. Black, 2002, J. W. Marriott, Jr., on growing the legacy, *Academy of Management Executive*, 16(2): 33–39.

86. R. A. Noe, J. A. Colquitt, M. J. Simmering, & S. A. Alvarez, 2003, Knowledge management: Developing intellectual and social capital, in S. E. Jackson, M. A. Hitt, & A. S. DeNisi (eds.), 2003, *Managing Knowledge for Sustained Competitive Advantage: Designing Strategies for Effective Human Resource Management*, Oxford, UK: Elsevier Science, Ltd., 209–242; C. A. Bartlett & S. Ghoshal, 2002, Building competitive advantage through people, *MIT Sloan Management Review*, 43(2): 34–41.

87. G. P. Hollenbeck & M. W. McCall, Jr., 2003, Competence, not competencies: Making a global executive development work, in W. H. Mobley & P. W. Dorfman (eds.), *Advances in Global Leadership*, Oxford, UK: Elsevier Science, Ltd., 101–119; J. Sandberg, 2000, Understanding human competence at work: An interpretative approach, *Academy of Management Journal*, 43: 9–25.

88. Hitt, Keats, & Yucel, Strategic leadership in global business organizations; J. J. Distefano & M. L. Maznevski, 2003, Developing global managers integrating theory, behavior, data and performance, in W. H. Mobley & P. W. Dorfman (eds.), *Advances in Global Leadership*, Oxford, UK: Elsevier Science, Ltd., 341–371.

89. J. S. Bunderson & K. M. Sutcliffe, 2003, Management team learning orientation and business unit performance, *Journal of Applied Psychology*, 88: 552–560; C. R. James, 2003, Designing learning organizations, *Organizational Dynamics*, 32(1): 46–61; Bartlett & Ghoshal, Building competitive advantage through people.

90. J. D. Bragger, D. A. Hantula, D. Bragger, J. Kirnan, & E. Kutcher, 2003, When success breeds failure: History, Hysteresis, and delayed exit decisions, *Journal of Applied Psychology*, 88: 6–14.

91. J. W. Spencer, 2003, Firms' knowledge-sharing strategies in the global innovation system: Empirical evidence from the flat-panel display industry, *Strategic Management Journal*, 24: 217–233; M. Harvey & M. M. Novicevic, 2002, The hypercompetitive global marketplace: The importance of intuition and creativity in expatriate managers, *Journal of World Business*, 37: 127–138.

92. S. K. McEvily & B. Charavarthy, 2002, The persistence of knowledge-based advantage: An empirical test for product performance and technological knowledge, *Strategic Management Journal*, 23: 285–305.

93. K. D. Miller, 2002, Knowledge inventories and managerial myopia, *Strategic Management Journal*, 23: 689–706.

94. H. Collingwood & D. L. Coutu, 2002, Jack on Jack, *Harvard Business Review*, 80(2): 88–94.

95. R. D. Nixon, M. A. Hitt, H. Lee, & E. Jeong, 2003, Market reactions to corporate announcements of downsizing actions and implementation strategies, Unpublished working paper, University of Louisville.

96. J. Di Frances, 2002, 10 reasons why you shouldn't downsize, *Journal of Property Management*, 67(1): 72–73.

97. A. Pinsonneault & K. Kraemer, 2002, The role of information technology in organizational downsizing: A tale of two American cities, *Organization Science*, 13: 191–208.

98. Nixon, Hitt, Lee, & Jeong, Market reactions to corporate announcements of downsizing actions; M. David, 2001, Leadership during an economic slowdown, *Journal for Quality and Participation*, 24(3): 40–43.

99. T. Simons & Q. Roberson, 2003, Why managers should care about fairness: The effects of aggregate justice perceptions on organizational outcomes, *Journal of Applied Psychology*, 88: 432–443; M. L. Ambrose & R. Cropanzano, 2003, A longitudinal analysis of organizational fairness: An examination of reactions to tenure and promotion decisions, *Journal of Applied Psychology*, 88: 266–275.

100. P. S. Adler & S.-W. Kwon, 2002, Social capital: Prospects for a new concept, *Academy of Management Review*, 27: 17–40.

101. A. Mendez, 2003, The coordination of globalized R&D activities through project teams organization: An exploratory empirical study, *Journal of World Business*, 38: 96–109.

102. R. D. Ireland, M. A. Hitt, & D. Vaidyanath, 2002, Managing strategic alliances to achieve a competitive advantage, *Journal of Management*, 28: 413–446.

103. J. Florin, M. Lubatkin, & W. Schulze, 2003, *Academy of Management Journal*, 46: 374–384; P. Davidsson & B. Honig, 2003, The role of social and human capital among nascent entrepreneurs, *Journal of Business Venturing*, 18: 301–331.

104. A. K. Gupta & V. Govindarajan, 2000, Knowledge management's social dimension: Lessons from Nucor Steel, *Sloan Management Review*, 42(1): 71–80; C. M. Fiol, 1991, Managing culture as a competitive resource: An identity-based view of sustainable competitive advantage, *Journal of Management*, 17: 191–211; J. B. Barney, 1986, Organizational culture: Can it be a source of sustained competitive advantage? *Academy of Management Review*, 11: 656–665.

105. V. Govindarajan & A. K. Gupta, 2001, Building an effective global business team, *Sloan Management Review*, 42(4): 63–71; S. Ghoshal & C. A. Bartlett, 1994, Linking organizational context and managerial action: The dimensions of quality of management, *Strategic Management Journal*, 15: 91–112.

106. K. Kling & I. Goteman, 2003, IKEA CEO Anders Dahlvig on international growth and IKEA's unique corporate culture and brand identity, *Academy of Management Executive*, 17(1): 31–37.

107. D. F. Kuratko, R. D. Ireland, & J. S. Hornsby, 2001, Improving firm performance through entrepreneurial actions: Acordia's corporate entrepreneurship strategy, *Academy of Management Executive*, 15(4): 60–71.

108. A. Ardichvili, R. Cardoza, & S. Ray, 2003, A theory of entrepreneurial opportunity identification and development, *Journal of Business Venturing*, 18: 105–123; T. E. Brown, P. Davidsson, & J. Wiklund, 2001, An operationalization of Stevenson's conceptualization of entrepreneurship as opportunity-based firm behavior, *Strategic Management Journal*, 22: 953–968.

109. R. D. Ireland, M. A. Hitt, & D. Sirmon, 2003, A model of strategic entrepreneurship: The construct and its dimensions, *Journal of Management*, in press.

110. G. T. Lumpkin & G. G. Dess, 1996, Clarifying the entrepreneurial orientation construct and linking it to performance, *Academy of Management Review*, 21: 135–172.

111. Ibid., 142.

112. Ibid., 137.

113. R. R. Sims, 2000, Changing an organization's culture under new leadership, *Journal of Business Ethics*, 25: 65–78.

114. R. A. Burgelman & Y. L. Doz, 2001, The power of strategic integration, *Sloan Management Review*, 42(3): 28–38; P. H. Fuchs, K. E. Mifflin, D. Miller, & J. O. Whitney, 2000, Strategic integration: Competing in the age of capabilities, *California Management Review*, 42(3): 118–147.

115. J. S. Hornsby, D. F. Kuratko, & S. A. Zahra, 2002, Middle managers' perception of the internal environment for corporate entrepreneurship: Assessing a measurement scale, *Journal of Business Venturing*, 17: 253–273; J. E. Dutton, S. J. Ashford, R. M. O'Neill, E. Hayes, & E. E.

Wierba, 1997, Reading the wind: How middle managers assess the context for selling issues to top managers, *Strategic Management Journal*, 18: 407–425.

116. B. Axelrod, H. Handfield-Jones, & E. Michaels, 2002, A new game plan for C players, *Harvard Business Review*, 80(1): 80–88.

117. 2003, Louis Schweitzer: The interview, http://www.renault.com, July; C. Dawson, 2002, Nissan bets big on small, *BusinessWeek Online*, http://www.businessweek.com, March 4; C. Ghosn, 2002, Saving the business without losing the company, *Harvard Business Review*, 80(1): 37–45; M. S. Mayershon, 2002, Nissan's u-turn to profits, *Chief Executive*, January, 12–16; A. Raskin, 2002, Voulez-vous completely overhaul this big, slow company and start making some cars people actually want avec moi? *Business 2.0*, January, 61–67.

118. P. S. Adler & S.-W. Kwon, Social capital.

119. D. J. Brass, K. D. Butterfield, & B. C. Skaggs, 1998, Relationships and unethical behavior: A social network perspective, *Academy of Management Review*, 23: 14–31.

120. L. K. Trevino, G. R. Weaver, D. G. Toffler, & B. Ley, 1999, Managing ethics and legal compliance: What works and what hurts, *California Management Review*, 41(2): 131–151.

121. C. W. L. Hill, 1990, Cooperation, opportunism, and the invisible hand: Implications for transaction cost theory, *Academy of Management Review*, 15: 500–513.

122. W. Wallace, 2000, The value relevance of accounting: The rest of the story, *European Management Journal*, 18(6): 675–682.

123. C. J. Robertson & W. F. Crittenden, 2003, Mapping moral philosophies: Strategic implications for multinational firms, *Strategic Management Journal*, 24: 385–392; E. Soule, 2002, Managerial moral strategies—In search of a few good principles, *Academy of Management Review*, 27: 114–124.

124. L. M. Leinicke, J. A. Ostrosky, & W. M. Rexroad, 2000, Quality financial reporting: Back to the basics, *CPA Journal*, August, 69–71.

125. J. Ivancevich, T. N. Duening, J. A. Gilbert, & R. Konopaske, 2003, Deterring white-collar crime, *Academy of Management Executive*, 17(2): 114–127.

126. K. Schnatterly, 2003, Increasing firm value through detection and prevention of white-collar crime, *Strategic Management Journal*, 24: 587–614.

127. S. Watson & G. Weaver, 2003, How internationalization affects corporate ethics: Formal structures and informal management behavior, *Journal of International Management*, 9: 75–93.

128. J. H. Gavin, J. C. Quick, C. L. Cooper, & J. D. Quick, 2003, A spirit of personal integrity: The role of character in executive health, *Organizational Dynamics*, 32: 165–179.

129. J. R. Cohen, L. W. Pant, & D. J. Sharp, 2001, An examination of differences in ethical decision-making between Canadian business students and accounting professionals, *Journal of Business Ethics*, 30: 319–336; G. R. Weaver, L. K. Trevino, & P. L. Cochran, 1999, Corporate ethics programs as control systems: Influences of executive commitment and environmental factors, *Academy of Management Journal*, 42: 41–57.

130. P. E. Murphy, 1995, Corporate ethics statements: Current status and future prospects, *Journal of Business Ethics*, 14: 727–740.

131. G. Redding, 2002, The capitalistic business system of China and its rationale, *Asia Pacific Journal of Management*, 19: 221–249.

132. J. H. Gittell, 2000, Paradox of coordination and control, *California Management Review*, 42(3): 101–117; L. J. Kirsch, 1996, The management of complex tasks in organizations: Controlling the systems development process, *Organization Science*, 7: 1–21.

133. M. D. Shields, F. J. Deng, & Y. Kato, 2000, The design and effects of control systems: Tests of direct- and indirect-effects models, *Accounting, Organizations and Society*, 25: 185–202; R. Simons, 1994, How new top managers use control systems as levers of strategic renewal, *Strategic Management Journal*, 15: 170–171.

134. K. J. Laverty, 1996, Economic "short-termism": The debate, the unresolved issues, and the implications for management practice and research, *Academy of Management Review*, 21: 825–860.

135. R. S. Kaplan & D. P. Norton, 2001, The strategy-focused organization, *Strategy & Leadership*, 29(3): 41–42; R. S. Kaplan & D. P. Norton, 2000,

The *Strategy-Focused Organization: How Balanced Scorecard Companies Thrive in the New Business Environment*, Boston: Harvard Business School Press.

136. B. E. Becker, M. A. Huselid, & D. Ulrich, 2001, *The HR Scorecard: Linking People, Strategy, and Performance*, Boston: Harvard Business School Press, 21.

137. Kaplan & Norton, The strategy-focused organization.

138. R. S. Kaplan & D. P. Norton, 2001, Transforming the balanced scorecard from performance measurement to strategic management: Part I, *Accounting Horizons*, 15(1): 87–104.

139. R. S. Kaplan & D. P. Norton, 1992, The balanced scorecard—measures that drive performance, *Harvard Business Review*, 70(1): 71–79.

140. M. A. Mische, 2001, *Strategic Renewal: Becoming a High-Performance Organization*, Upper Saddle River, NJ: Prentice-Hall, 181.

141. Rowe, Creating wealth in organizations: The role of strategic leadership.

142. R. E. Hoskisson, R. A. Johnson, D. Yiu, & W. P. Wan, 2001, Restructuring strategies of diversified business groups: Differences associated with country institutional environments, in M. A. Hitt, R. E. Freeman, & J. S. Harrison (eds.), *Handbook of Strategic Management*, Oxford, UK: Blackwell Publishers, 433–463; R. A. Johnson, 1996, Antecedents and outcomes of corporate refocusing, *Journal of Management*, 22: 437–481; R. E. Hoskisson & M. A. Hitt, 1994, *Downscoping: How to Tame the Diversified Firm*, New York: Oxford University Press.

143. J. Birkinshaw & N. Hood, 2001, Unleash innovation in foreign subsidiaries, *Harvard Business Review*, 79(3): 131–137.

144. Ireland & Hitt, Achieving and maintaining strategic competitiveness.

145. R. C. Morais, 2003, Mind the gap, *Forbes*, http://www.forbes.com, July 21.

146. 2003, About Samsung, http://www.samsung.com, July; M. Ihlwan & D. Roberts, 2002, How Samsung plugged into China, *BusinessWeek Online*, http://www.businessweek.com, March 4.

Strategic Entrepreneurship

Knowledge Objectives

Studying this chapter should provide you with the strategic management knowledge needed to:

1. Define and explain strategic entrepreneurship.

2. Describe the importance of entrepreneurial opportunities, innovation, and entrepreneurial capabilities.

3. Discuss the importance of international entrepreneurship.

4. Describe autonomous and induced strategic behavior—the two forms of internal corporate venturing.

5. Discuss how cooperative strategies such as strategic alliances are used to develop innovation.

6. Explain how firms use acquisitions to increase their innovations and enrich their innovative capabilities.

7. Describe the importance of venture capital and initial public offerings to entrepreneurial activity.

8. Explain how strategic entrepreneurship creates value in all types of firms.

Getty/PhotoDisc, Inc.

Entrepreneurship involves taking unique actions to fulfill business and consumer needs as those opportunities become apparent. Anne Maxfield and Leslie Frank, for example, founded a company called Project Solvers, which acts as an agent by connecting firms and individuals involved in designing, making, and selling fashion clothing.

There is a wide variety of types of entrepreneurs, but no one formula for success. However, there are many successful entrepreneurs. For example, Marion McCaw Garrison was one of the first female accounting graduates of the University of Washington in 1939. While she was told that it was unlikely she could ever earn her CPA because she was a woman, she completed her degree in accounting anyway. At 22 years of age, she bought 40 acres of land and became a real estate developer, one of the first women to do so. After she married, she helped her husband manage their businesses, including radio and television stations and real estate. When her husband died suddenly, she took over the management of the businesses. She moved out of the radio business and entered cable television and wireless communications. The company went public in 1987, and in 1994, McCaw Cellular Communications was sold to AT&T for more than $11 billion. Garrison was successful because of her strong business knowledge and determination.

Clothing designers Anne Maxfield and Leslie Frank worked for a large fashion design company for more than a decade. Their assignments often found them assembling outside teams of illustrators, designers, and art directors to complete specific projects. Observing that "all creative people working in New York had agents except for fashion designers," Maxfield and Frank launched Project Solvers, Inc. Using their uniquely developed comprehensive database of people involved in all activities associated with designing, making, and selling fashion clothing, Project Solvers serves firms' needs to hire talented individuals/artists to complete specific projects. Their ability to envision an entrepreneurial opportunity that others hadn't seen is the foundation of the success achieved by entrepreneurs Maxfield and Frank.

Entrepreneurs sometimes establish new ventures from the base of an existing one. An entrepreneurial family business venture, International Visual Corp. (IVC) manufactures fixtures for department stores such as Nordstrom and JCPenney. By the end of the 1990s, declines in business with IVC's core department store customers had reduced the firm's profit margin from 40 percent to 20 percent. However, IVC continued to develop innovative products even as its margins declined. A thermoplastic wall panel became a valuable innovation for the firm. This innovative panel's modular design, strength, durability, and consistent color made it very attractive to department stores. But, IVC looked on with dismay as its sales, even of its valued new innovation, declined. Along with his partner, IVC's president, the founder's son, originated the idea of selling the panel to homeowners who could use the product as a base for attaching cabinets, shelves, and other components. Their idea appealed to home builders, and an innovative application of the firm's panel quickly became a success. After securing funding from a venture capital firm, the entrepreneurs established GarageTek and sold IVC to one of their former material suppliers (who retained the rights to sell the panel to retailers). Operating in an established firm, these entrepreneurs understood that proprietary technologies may have uses in multiple markets.

Each of these successful entrepreneurs took unique actions and had some special traits, but they all had a passion for the businesses they developed. According to Michael Dell, founder and CEO of Dell Inc., passion must be the driving force for starting a company. Dell also emphasizes the importance of identifying and exploiting opportunities. All of the entrepreneurs described identified opportunities and were passionate about exploiting them.

SOURCES: P. Thomas, 2003, A change of scenery boosts special project, *Wall Street Journal Online*, http://www.wsj.com, May 27; P. Thomas, 2003, When employees quit to become competitors, *Wall Street Journal Online*, http://www.wsj.com, April 29; 2001, Marion McCaw Garrison: An entrepreneurial woman, *Business*, University of Washington Business School, Fall, 40.

Several factors are important to the success of the entrepreneurs described in the Opening Case. They all have a passion for their business and a willingness to take calculated risks to pursue their entrepreneurial vision. Other factors, such as determination (Marion McCaw Garrison), an ability to see opportunities that others haven't seen (Maxfield and Frank) and a recognition that proprietary, innovative technology may have applications in several markets (IVC's leaders) also contributed to their success.

For several reasons, including the fact that entrepreneurship is the economic engine driving many nations' economies in the global competitive landscape,[1] it is important for firms' managers to understand how to act entrepreneurially. Entrepreneurship and innovation are important for young and old and for large and small firms, for service companies as well as manufacturing firms and high-technology ventures.[2] In the global competitive landscape, the long-term success of new ventures and established firms is a function of the ability to meld entrepreneurship with strategic management.[3]

This chapter focuses on strategic entrepreneurship. **Strategic entrepreneurship** is taking entrepreneurial actions using a strategic perspective. More specifically, strategic entrepreneurship involves engaging in simultaneous opportunity seeking and competitive advantage seeking behaviors to design and implement entrepreneurial strategies to create wealth.[4] These actions can be taken by individuals or by corporations and are of increasing importance in the evolving 21st-century competitive landscape.[5]

The competitive landscape that has evolved in the 21st century presents firms with substantial change, a global marketplace, and significant complexity and uncertainty.[6] Because of this uncertain environment, firms cannot easily predict the future.[7] As a result, they must develop strategic flexibility to have a range of strategic alternatives that they can implement as needed. To do so, they must acquire resources and build the capabilities that allow them to take necessary actions to adapt to a dynamic environment or to be proactive in that environment.[8] In this environment, entrepreneurs and entrepreneurial managers design and implement actions that capture more of existing markets from less aggressive and innovative competitors while creating new markets.[9] In effect, they are trying to create tomorrow's businesses.[10]

Creating tomorrow's businesses requires identifying opportunities, as argued by Michael Dell in the Opening Case, and developing innovation. In other words, firms must be entrepreneurial and innovative, yet strategic in their thinking and actions. Innovations are critical to companies' efforts to differentiate their goods or services from competitors in ways that create additional or new value for customers.[11] Thus,

Strategic entrepreneurship is taking entrepreneurial actions using a strategic perspective.

entrepreneurial competencies are important for firms to achieve and sustain competitive advantages.[12]

To describe how firms produce and manage innovation, we consider several topics in this chapter. First, we examine strategic entrepreneurship and innovation in a strategic context. Included as parts of this analysis are definitions of entrepreneurs and the entrepreneurial opportunities they pursue. Next, we discuss international entrepreneurship, a phenomenon reflecting the increased use of entrepreneurship in economies throughout the world. The chapter then shifts to discussions of the three ways firms innovate, with internal innovation being the first method. Most large, complex firms use all three methods to innovate. Internally, firms innovate through either autonomous or induced strategic behavior. We then describe actions firms take to implement the innovations resulting from those two types of strategic behavior. In addition to innovating through internal activities, firms can develop innovations by using cooperative strategies, such as strategic alliances, and by acquiring other companies to gain access to their innovations and innovative capabilities. The method the firm chooses to innovate can be affected by the firm's governance mechanisms. Research evidence suggests, for example, that inside board directors with equity positions favor internal innovation while outside directors with equity positions prefer acquiring innovation.[13] Descriptions of capital that is available to support entrepreneurial ventures and a final assessment of how firms use strategic entrepreneurship to create value and earn above-average returns close the chapter.

Strategic Entrepreneurship and Innovation

Joseph Schumpeter viewed entrepreneurship as a process of "creative destruction," through which existing products or methods of production are destroyed and replaced with new ones.[14] Thus, *entrepreneurship* is "concerned with the discovery and exploitation of profitable opportunities."[15] Entrepreneurial activity is an important mechanism for creating change, as well as for helping firms adapt to change created by others.[16] Firms that encourage entrepreneurship are risk takers, are committed to innovation, and act proactively in that they try to create opportunities rather than waiting to respond to opportunities created by others.[17]

Increasingly, entrepreneurship is viewed by some as a means of bringing about changes that have implications for broader societies. Called social entrepreneurship, different interpretations of the term and the actions associated with it remain.[18] In reading about social entrepreneurship in the Strategic Focus, notice that social entrepreneurs share some if not many of the traits associated with the entrepreneurs described in the Opening Case. In other words, strategic entrepreneurship is also appropriate for use by those wanting to be social entrepreneurs.

Entrepreneurial opportunities represent conditions in which new goods or services can satisfy a need in the market. The essence of entrepreneurship is to identify and exploit these opportunities.[19] Importantly, entrepreneurs or entrepreneurial managers must be able to identify opportunities not perceived by others. As explained in the Strategic Focus, social entrepreneurs find opportunities to fulfill socially oriented purposes to which others haven't committed.

Identifying opportunities in a dynamic and uncertain environment requires an entrepreneurial mind-set that entails the passionate pursuit of opportunities.[20] Discussed further later in the chapter, a mind-set can be a source of competitive advantage because of the actions resulting from its focus,[21] such as the actions taken when entrepreneurs passionately pursue opportunities. For example, three cofounders who had started other entrepreneurial ventures recently established Supply Marketing Inc. The firm sells advertising space on virtually all disposable items that are used in physicians' offices. Tongue depressors, bandages, sterile paper covering examining tables,

Entrepreneurial opportunities represent conditions in which new goods or services can satisfy a need in the market.

Social Entrepreneurship: Innovative, Proactive, Risk-oriented, and Purposeful

Coming primarily from countries or regions where entrepreneurship as a business model is well established (e.g., Asia, Latin America, and the United States), social entrepreneurs are passionate about their projects and have a single-minded focus in pursuing outcomes to which they are committed. Deliberate in their choices, social entrepreneurs work on projects throughout the world, believing that virtually all societies have groups who could benefit from their services. Those who for a variety of reasons aren't actively participating in formal economic markets, such as minorities, women, and disabled people, are social entrepreneurs' primary targets.

Social entrepreneurs practice social entrepreneurship, a process that "melds the enterprise and innovation often associated with the private sector with the grassroots accountability necessary to sustain solutions in the public sector." In slightly different words, "social entrepreneurship strives to combine the heart of business with the heart of the community through the creativity of the individual."

As we noted above, entrepreneurship is concerned with discovering and exploiting opportunities to earn profits. To do this, entrepreneurs commit to the importance of innovation, are willing to take risks, and are proactive in finding opportunities rather than waiting to respond to opportunities generated by others. In a like manner, social entrepreneurship is concerned with discovering and exploiting opportunities to achieve a social mission in the face of moral complexity. As decision makers, social entrepreneurs also commit to innovation's importance, take calculated risks, and seek opportunities to serve rather than waiting for others to act. Commonly, social entrepreneurs seek to help others establish ventures through which targeted individuals will be able to earn income. Because of growing successes, public policy makers in a variety of countries are evaluating the possibility of more actively supporting social entrepreneurship as an approach to alleviating social disadvantage.

The projects resulting from social entrepreneurship are diverse. Social entrepreneur Karen Tse, a lawyer and minister, is building networks of public defenders in China, Vietnam, and Cambodia. Located in the United Kingdom, Big Issue provides homeless individuals with an opportunity to earn income. The organization's profits are donated to a charity studying homelessness to determine how to eliminate its causes. ApproTEC creates and markets simple and inexpensive tools in Kenya and Tanzania. An irrigation pump called the MoneyMaker is the firm's most successful product. Costing only $38 for the standard size, this pump can be operated simply. The MoneyMaker "eliminates the need to haul water from a well with ropes and buckets and dramatically increases the productivity of rural gardens."

In the final analysis, social entrepreneurship "involves combining commercial aims with social objectives to reap strategic or competitive benefits." Thus, the most effective social entrepreneurs learn how to proactively use the strategic management process to create competitive advantages through which social purposes can be served. Sound strategic management practices are at the core of the social entrepreneur's success and are the foundation on which effective social entrepreneurship is built.

SOURCES: 2003, Social entrepreneurs: Playing the role of change agents in society, *Knowledge at Wharton*, http://www.knowledge.wharton.penn.edu, June 2; 2003, Globalization with a human face—and a social conscience, *Knowledge at Wharton*, http://www.knowledge.wharton.penn.edu, June 2; K. Hammonds, 2003, Investing in social change, *Fast Company*, June, 54; G. S. Mort, J. Weeawardena, & K. Carnegie, 2003, Social entrepreneurship: Toward a conceptualisation, *International Journal of Nonprofit and Voluntary Sector Marketing*, 8(1): 76–88; M. Pomerantz, 2003, The business of social entrepreneurship in a "down economy," *In Business*, 25(2): 25–28.

and rubber gloves are just a few of the products on which advertising can be placed. Financed with $250,000 in venture capital, Supply Marketing provides ad-covered products to physicians. Believing deeply in the potential of the entrepreneurial opportunity they've identified, the cofounders have contacted many companies to solicit their business. Wyeth Labs Inc., Schering-Plough Corp., Novartis AG, and Fujisawa Pharmaceutical Co., Ltd., are examples of companies that have placed orders with Supply Marketing to advertise their products on various disposable items.[22]

Getty Images

Supply Marketing Inc. sells advertising space on products used in doctors' offices, such as the tongue depressors shown here with the slogan "Fewer Coughs, Wetter Coughs."

After identifying opportunities, entrepreneurs must act to develop capabilities that will become the basis of their firm's core competencies and competitive advantages. The process of identifying opportunities is entrepreneurial, but this activity alone is not sufficient to create maximum wealth or even to survive over time.[23] As we learned in Chapter 3, to successfully exploit opportunities, a firm must develop capabilities that are valuable, rare, difficult to imitate, and nonsubstitutable. When capabilities satisfy these four criteria, the firm has one or more competitive advantages to exploit the identified opportunities (as described in Chapter 3). Without a competitive advantage, the firm's success will be only temporary (as explained in Chapter 1). An innovation may be valuable and rare early in its life, if a market perspective is used in its development. However, competitive actions must be taken to introduce the new product to the market and protect its position in the market against competitors to gain a competitive advantage. These actions combined represent strategic entrepreneurship.

Innovation

Peter Drucker argues that "innovation is the specific function of entrepreneurship, whether in an existing business, a public service institution, or a new venture started by a lone individual."[24] Moreover, Drucker suggests that innovation is "the means by which the entrepreneur either creates new wealth-producing resources or endows existing resources with enhanced potential for creating wealth."[25] Thus, entrepreneurship and the innovation resulting from it are important for large and small firms, as well as for start-up ventures, as they compete in the 21st-century competitive landscape.[26] Therefore, we can conclude that "entrepreneurship and innovation are central to the creative process in the economy and to promoting growth, increasing productivity and creating jobs."[27]

Innovation is a key outcome firms seek through entrepreneurship and is often the source of competitive success, especially in turbulent, highly competitive environments.[28] For example, research results show that firms competing in global industries that invest more in innovation also achieve the highest returns.[29] In fact, investors often react positively to the introduction of a new product, thereby increasing the price of a firm's stock. Innovation, then, is an essential feature of high-performance firms.[30] Furthermore, "innovation may be required to maintain or achieve competitive parity, much less a competitive advantage in many global markets."[31] The most innovative firms understand that financial slack should be available at all times to support the pursuit of entrepreneurial opportunities.[32]

Invention *is the act of creating or developing a new product or process.*

Innovation *is the process of creating a commercial product from an invention.*

Imitation *is the adoption of an innovation by similar firms.*

In his classic work, Schumpeter argued that firms engage in three types of innovative activity.[33] **Invention** is the act of creating or developing a new product or process. **Innovation** is the process of creating a commercial product from an invention. Thus, an invention brings something new into being, while an innovation brings something new into use. Accordingly, technical criteria are used to determine the success of an invention, whereas commercial criteria are used to determine the success of an innovation.[34] Finally, **imitation** is the adoption of an innovation by similar firms. Imitation usually leads to product or process standardization, and products based on imitation often are offered at lower prices, but without as many features.

In the United States in particular, innovation is the most critical of the three types of innovative activity that occur in firms. Many companies are able to create ideas that lead to inventions, but commercializing those inventions through innovation has, at times, proved difficult. Approximately 80 percent of R&D occurs in large firms, but these same firms produce fewer than 50 percent of the patents.[35] Patents are a strategic asset and the ability to regularly produce them can be an important source of competitive advantage, especially for firms competing in knowledge-intensive industries[36] (e.g., pharmaceuticals).

Corporate entrepreneurship *is a process whereby an individual or a group in an existing organization creates a new venture or develops an innovation.*

Innovations produced in large established firms are the products of **corporate entrepreneurship**, which is a process whereby an individual or a group in an existing organization creates a new venture or develops an innovation.[37] Corporate entrepreneurship practices are facilitated when the firm's human capital successfully uses the strategic management process.[38] Determining how to harness the ingenuity of a firm's employees and how to reward them for it while retaining some of the benefits of the entrepreneurial efforts for shareholders also supports corporate entrepreneurship.[39] The most successful firms remain aware of the continuing need for corporate entrepreneurship. Having formed an e-commerce powerhouse known as USA Interactive, for example, CEO Barry Diller is concentrating on creating synergies among his firm's businesses while leaving them entrepreneurial and independent as the basis for generating additional value for shareholders.[40]

Entrepreneurs and Entrepreneurial Capabilities

Entrepreneurs *are individuals, acting independently or as part of an organization, who create a new venture or develop an innovation and take risks entering it into the marketplace.*

Entrepreneurs are individuals, acting independently or as part of an organization, who create a new venture or develop an innovation and take risks entering it into the marketplace. Entrepreneurs can be independent individuals or serve in an organization at any level. Thus, top-level managers, middle- and first-level managers, staff personnel, and those producing the company's good or service can all be entrepreneurs.

Firms need employees who think entrepreneurially. Top-level managers should try to establish an entrepreneurial culture that inspires individuals and groups to engage in corporate entrepreneurship.[41] Apple Computer's Steve Jobs is committed to this effort, believing one of his key responsibilities is to help Apple become more entrepreneurial. And, as described in Chapter 6, Apple has introduced some innovative products, such as the iPod portable digital music player, thought to be the gold standard of the industry. Competitors "are feverishly working on iPod clones."[42] As a competitive response, Apple redesigned its product, making it thinner and lighter than the original version while being capable of packing in more songs.[43] Another Apple innovation is iTunes, an online music store. When launched, this website sold songs for 99 cents per download or roughly $10 per album. Users of iTunes can hear songs on an unlimited number of iPod digital-music players and burn as many as ten compact discs with the same playlists. Expecting to sell one million songs during the first month of iTunes' operation, Apple reached this initial sales target in the first week.[44]

Of course, to create and commercialize products such as the iPod and iTunes requires not only intellectual capital, but an entrepreneurial mind-set as well. An entrepreneurial mind-set finds individuals using a prevailing sense of uncertainty to develop unique products.[45] Entrepreneurial competence supports development and use of an entrepreneurial mind-set. In most cases, knowledge must be transferred to others in the organization, even in smaller ventures, to enhance the entrepreneurial competence of the firm. The transfer is likely to be more difficult in larger firms. Research has shown, however, that units within firms are more innovative if they have access to new knowledge.[46]

Transferring knowledge can be difficult, because the receiving party must have adequate absorptive capacity (or the ability) to learn the knowledge.[47] This requires that the new knowledge be linked to the existing knowledge. Thus, managers will need to develop the capabilities of their human capital to build on their current knowledge base while incrementally expanding that knowledge.[48]

Developing innovations and achieving success in the marketplace require effective human capital. In particular, firms must have strong intellectual capital in their R&D organization.[49] However, a firm must have strong human capital throughout its workforce if employees are to be innovative. For example, WinSpec West Manufacturing Inc. credits its positive market position to innovation produced by its strong employee base. In fact, the managers are very careful in hiring. Even in jobs with seemingly low challenges, they try to hire high-potential employees. For one secretarial position, the managers hired a person with an MBA in finance; that person went on to serve as the acting chief financial officer.[50]

©Chris Hardy/San Francisco Chronicle/Corbis

Steve Jobs demonstrates how to download favorite tunes with Apple's iTunes.

International Entrepreneurship

Entrepreneurship is a global phenomenon.[51] In general, internationalization leads to improved firm performance,[52] a fact influencing the practice of entrepreneurship on a global scale. Nonetheless, decision makers should recognize that the decision to internationalize exposes their firms to various risks, including those of unstable foreign currencies, problems with market efficiencies, insufficient infrastuctures to support businesses, and limitations on market size, among others.[53] Thus, the decision to engage in international entrepreneurship should be a product of careful analysis.

Because of its positive benefits, entrepreneurship is at the top of public policy agendas in many of the world's countries, including Finland, Germany, Israel, Ireland, and France, among others. Placing entrepreneurship on these agendas may be appropriate in that some argue that regulation hindering innovation and entrepreneurship is the root cause of Europe's productivity problems.[54] In Northern Ireland, the minister for enterprise, trade, and investment told businesspeople that their current and future commercial success would be affected by the degree to which they decided to emphasize R&D and innovation (critical components of entrepreneurship).[55]

While entrepreneurship is a global phenomenon, the rate of entrepreneurship differs across countries. A recent study of 29 countries found that the percentage of adults involved in entrepreneurial activity ranged from a high of more than 20 percent in Mexico to a low of approximately 5 percent in Belgium. The United States had a rate of about 13 percent. Importantly, this study also found a strong positive relationship between the rate of entrepreneurial activity and economic development in the country.[56]

Culture is one of the reasons for the differences in rates of entrepreneurship among different countries. For example, the tension between individualism and collectivism is important for entrepreneurship; research shows that entrepreneurship declines as collectivism is emphasized. Simultaneously, however, research results suggest that exceptionally high levels of individualism might be dysfunctional for entrepreneurship. Viewed collectively, these results appear to call for a balance between individual initiative and a spirit of cooperation and group ownership of innovation. For firms to be entrepreneurial, they must provide appropriate autonomy and incentives for individual initiative to surface, but also promote cooperation and group ownership of an innovation if it is to be implemented successfully. Thus, international entrepreneurship often requires teams of people with unique skills and resources, especially in cultures where collectivism is a valued historical norm.[57]

The level of investment outside of the home country made by young ventures is also an important dimension of international entrepreneurship. In fact, with increasing globalization, a greater number of new ventures have been "born global."[58] Research has shown that new ventures that enter international markets increase their learning of new technological knowledge and thereby enhance their performance.[59] Because of positive outcomes such as the ones we've described, the amount of international entrepreneurship has been increasing in recent years.[60]

The probability of entering international markets increases when the firm has top executives with international experience.[61] Furthermore, the firm has a higher likelihood of successfully competing in international markets when its top executives have international experience.[62] Because of the learning and economies of scale and scope afforded by operating in international markets, both young and established internationally diversified firms often are stronger competitors in their domestic market as well. Additionally, as research has shown, internationally diversified firms are generally more innovative.[63]

International entrepreneurship has been an important factor in the economic development of Asia. In fact, private companies owned by Chinese families outside of China compose the fourth largest economic power in the world. Significant learning from their international ventures occurs in these businesses, and this learning enhances their success with future ventures.[64] The learning that occurs contributes to a firm's knowledge of operating in international markets.[65] It also contributes knowledge that can enhance a firm's new product development, on which we focus in the next section.

New Product Development and Internal Corporate Ventures

Most corporate innovation is developed through research and development (R&D). In many industries, the competitive battle for the market begins in the R&D labs. In fact, R&D may be the most critical factor in gaining and sustaining a competitive advantage in some industries, such as pharmaceuticals. Larger, established firms use R&D labs to create the competence-destroying new technology and products envisioned by Schumpeter. Such radical innovation has become an important component of competition in many industries.[66] Although critical to long-term corporate success, the outcomes of R&D investments are uncertain and often not achieved in the short term,[67] meaning that patience is required as firms examine the benefits of their allocations to R&D.

Incremental and Radical Innovation

Firms can produce and manage incremental or radical innovations. Most innovations are *incremental*—that is, they build on existing knowledge bases and provide small improvements in the current product lines. Alternatively, *radical innovations* usually provide significant technological breakthroughs and create new knowledge.[68] Improving existing processes is an important aspect of incremental innovations.[69] In contrast, developing new processes is a critical part of producing radical innovations. Both types of innovation can create value, meaning that firms should determine when it is appropriate to emphasize either incremental or radical innovation.[70]

Radical innovations are rare because of the difficulty and risk involved in developing them.[71] There is substantial uncertainty with radical innovation regarding the technology and the market opportunities.[72] Because radical innovation creates new knowledge and uses only some or little of a firm's current product or technological knowledge, creativity is required. However, creativity does not create something from nothing. Rather, creativity discovers, combines, or synthesizes current knowledge, often from diverse areas.[73] This knowledge is then used to develop new products or services that can be used in an entrepreneurial manner to move into new markets, capture new customers, and gain access to new resources.[74] Such innovations are often developed in separate business units that start internal ventures.[75]

Internal corporate venturing is the set of activities used to create inventions and innovations through internal means.[76] Spending on R&D is linked to success in internal corporate venturing. Put simply, firms are unable to invent or innovate without significant R&D investments.

As shown in Figure 13.1, there are two forms of internal corporate venturing: autonomous strategic behavior and induced strategic behavior.

> *Internal corporate venturing is the set of activities used to create inventions and innovations through internal means.*

Autonomous Strategic Behavior

Autonomous strategic behavior is a bottom-up process in which product champions pursue new ideas, often through a political process, by means of which they develop and coordinate the commercialization of a new good or service until it achieves success in the marketplace. A *product champion* is an organizational member with an entrepreneurial vision of a new good or service who seeks to create support for its commercialization. Product champions play critical roles in moving innovations forward.[77] The primary reason for this is that "no business idea takes root purely on its own merits; it has to be sold."[78] Autonomous strategic behavior is based on a firm's wellsprings of knowledge and resources that are the sources of the firm's innovation.

> *Autonomous strategic behavior is a bottom-up process in which product champions pursue new ideas, often through a political process, by means of which they develop and coordinate the commercialization of a new good or service until it achieves success in the marketplace.*

Model of Internal Corporate Venturing — Figure 13.1

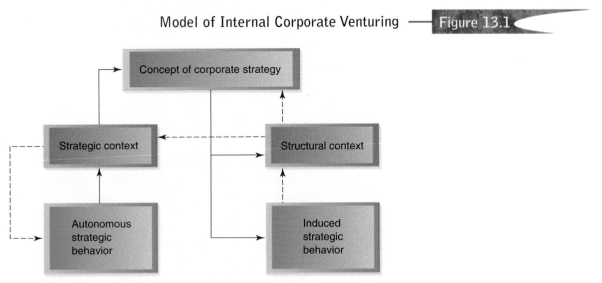

SOURCE: Adapted from R. A. Burgelman, 1983, A model of the interactions of strategic behavior, corporate context, and the concept of strategy, *Academy of Management Review*, 8: 65.

Thus, a firm's technological capabilities and competencies are the basis for new products and processes.[79] GE depends on autonomous strategic behavior on a regular basis to produce innovations. Essentially, "the search for marketable services can start in any of GE's myriad businesses. [For example], an operating unit seeks out appropriate technology to better do what it already does. Having mastered the technology, it then incorporates it into a service it can sell to others."[80]

Changing the concept of corporate-level strategy through autonomous strategic behavior results when a product is championed within strategic and structural contexts (see Figure 13.1). The strategic context is the process used to arrive at strategic decisions (often requiring political processes to gain acceptance). The best firms keep changing their strategic context and strategies because of the continuous changes in the current competitive landscape. Thus, some believe that the most competitively successful firms reinvent their industry or develop a completely new one across time as they compete with current and future rivals.[81]

To be effective, an autonomous process for developing new products requires that new knowledge be continuously diffused throughout the firm. In particular, the diffusion of tacit knowledge is important for development of more effective new products.[82] Interestingly, some of the processes important for the promotion of autonomous new product development behavior vary by the environment and country in which a firm operates. For example, the Japanese culture is high on uncertainty avoidance. As such, research has found that Japanese firms are more likely to engage in autonomous behaviors under conditions of low uncertainty.[83]

Induced Strategic Behavior

Induced strategic behavior *is a top-down process whereby the firm's current strategy and structure foster product innovations that are closely associated with that strategy and structure.*

The second of the two forms of internal corporate venturing, **induced strategic behavior,** is a top-down process whereby the firm's current strategy and structure foster product innovations that are closely associated with that strategy and structure. In this form of venturing, the strategy in place is filtered through a matching structural hierarchy.

The ability to substitute aluminum for steel in some parts used to manufacture Jaguar automobiles is an innovation that resulted from induced strategic behavior. Ford Motor Company bought Jaguar in 1990. Part of Ford's differentiation business-level strategy for Jaguar called for innovation to be the source of improved competitiveness for Jaguar cars. Because aluminum parts are roughly half the weight of their steel counterparts, "Jaguar's new $60,000 XJ sedan boasts a body as light as a Mini's, accelerates quicker than a Mercedes 430 and is put together using a clever assembly method that weds aircraft-style metal bonding to mass-production-style metal shaping."[84] Thus, by using the differentiation strategy and a particular form of the functional structure (see Chapter 11), Jaguar's strategy and structure have elicited value-creating innovations.

Implementing New Product Development and Internal Ventures

To be innovative and develop internal ventures requires an entrepreneurial mind-set. In Chapter 12, we discuss an entrepreneurial orientation that includes several dimensions, such as risk propensity. Clearly, firms and individuals must be willing to take risks to commercialize new products. While they must continuously attempt to identify opportunities, they must also select and pursue the best opportunities and do so with discipline. Thus, employing an entrepreneurial mind-set entails not only developing new products and markets but also placing an emphasis on execution. Those with an entrepreneurial mind-set "engage the energies of everyone in their domain," both inside and outside the organization.[85]

Having processes and structures in place through which a firm can successfully implement the outcomes of internal corporate ventures and commercialize the innovations is critical. Indeed, the successful introduction of innovations into the marketplace reflects implementation effectiveness.[86] In the context of internal corporate ventures, processes are the "patterns of interaction, coordination, communication, and decision making employees use" to convert the innovations resulting from either autonomous or induced strategic behaviors into successful market entries.[87] As we describe in Chapter 11, organizational structures are the sets of formal relationships supporting organizational processes.

A detailer at Jaguar polishes an aluminum Jaguar XJ-R concept car in preparation for the North American International Auto Show in Detroit, 2003. The use of aluminum to partly manufacture the new Jaguar is an innovation induced by Ford that has resulted in a lighter car.

Effective integration of the various functions involved in innovation processes—from engineering to manufacturing and, ultimately, market distribution—is required to implement the innovations resulting from internal corporate ventures.[88] Increasingly, product development teams are being used to integrate the activities associated with different organizational functions. Product development teams are commonly used to produce cross-functional integration. Such integration involves coordinating and applying the knowledge and skills of different functional areas in order to maximize innovation.[89] Effective product development teams also create value when they "pull the plug" on a project.[90] Although difficult, sometimes because of emotional commitments to innovation-based projects, effective teams recognize when conditions change in ways that preclude the innovation's ability to create value as originally anticipated.

Cross-Functional Product Development Teams

Cross-functional teams facilitate efforts to integrate activities associated with different organizational functions, such as design, manufacturing, and marketing. In addition, new product development processes can be completed more quickly and the products more easily commercialized when cross-functional teams work effectively.[91] Using cross-functional teams, product development stages are grouped into parallel or overlapping processes to allow the firm to tailor its product development efforts to its unique core competencies and to the needs of the market.

Horizontal organizational structures support the use of cross-functional teams in their efforts to integrate innovation-based activities across organizational functions.[92] Therefore, instead of being built around vertical hierarchical functions or departments, the organization is built around core horizontal processes that are used to produce and manage innovations. Some of the core horizontal processes that are critical to innovation efforts are formal; they may be defined and documented as procedures and practices. More commonly, however, these processes are informal: "They are routines or ways of working that evolve over time."[93] Often invisible, informal processes are critical to successful product innovations and are supported properly through horizontal organizational structures more so than through vertical organizational structures.

Two primary barriers that may prevent the successful use of cross-functional teams as a means of integrating organizational functions are independent frames of reference of team members and organizational politics.[94]

Team members working within a distinct specialization (i.e., a particular organizational function) may have an independent frame of reference typically based on common backgrounds and experiences. They are likely to use the same decision criteria to evaluate issues such as product development efforts as they do within their functional units. Research suggests that functional departments vary along four dimensions: time orientation, interpersonal orientation, goal orientation, and formality of structure.[95] Thus, individuals from different functional departments having different orientations on these dimensions can be expected to perceive product development activities in different ways. For example, a design engineer may consider the characteristics that make a product functional and workable to be the most important of the product's characteristics. Alternatively, a person from the marketing function may hold characteristics that satisfy customer needs most important. These different orientations can create barriers to effective communication across functions.[96]

Organizational politics is the second potential barrier to effective integration in cross-functional teams. In some organizations, considerable political activity may center on allocating resources to different functions. Interunit conflict may result from aggressive competition for resources among those representing different organizational functions. This dysfunctional conflict between functions creates a barrier to their integration.[97] Methods must be found to achieve cross-functional integration without excessive political conflict and without changing the basic structural characteristics necessary for task specialization and efficiency.

Facilitating Integration and Innovation

Shared values and effective leadership are important to achieve cross-functional integration and implement innovation.[98] Highly effective shared values are framed around the firm's strategic intent and mission, and become the glue that promotes integration between functional units. Thus, the firm's culture promotes unity and internal innovation.[99]

Strategic leadership is also highly important for achieving cross-functional integration and promoting innovation. Leaders set the goals and allocate resources. The goals include integrated development and commercialization of new goods and services. Effective strategic leaders also ensure a high-quality communication system to facilitate cross-functional integration. A critical benefit of effective communication is the sharing of knowledge among team members.[100] Effective communication thus helps create synergy and gains team members' commitment to an innovation throughout the organization. Shared values and leadership practices shape the communication systems that are formed to support the development and commercialization of new products.[101]

Creating Value from Innovation

The model in Figure 13.2 shows how firms can create value from the internal processes they use to develop and commercialize new goods and services. An entrepreneurial mind-set is necessary so that managers and employees will consistently try to identify entrepreneurial opportunities that the firm can pursue by developing new goods and services and new markets. Cross-functional teams are important to promote integrated new product design ideas and commitment to their implementation thereafter. Effective leadership and shared values promote integration and vision for innovation and commitment to it. The end result for the firm is the creation of value for the customers and shareholders by developing and commercializing new products.[102]

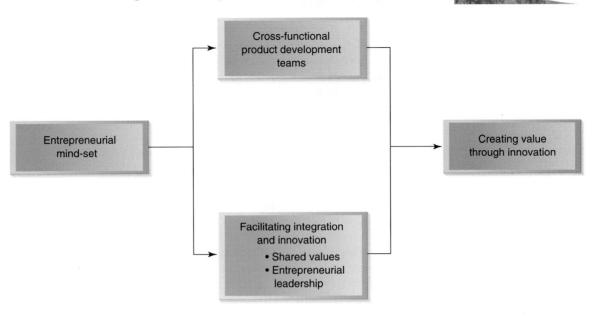

In the next two sections, we discuss the other ways firms can develop innovations—through use of cooperative strategies and acquisitions of other companies.

Cooperative Strategies for Entrepreneurship and Innovation

It is unlikely that a firm possesses all the knowledge and resources required for it to be entrepreneurial and innovative in dynamic competitive markets. Knowledge and resources are needed to develop new products and serve new markets.[103] To successfully commercialize inventions, firms may therefore choose to cooperate with other organizations and integrate their knowledge and resources.[104] Entrepreneurial new ventures, for example, may seek investment capital as well as the distribution capabilities of more established firms to implement a new product idea and introduce it to the market.[105] Alternatively, more established companies may need new technological knowledge and can gain access to it through alliances with start-up ventures.[106] Alliances between large pharmaceutical firms and biotechnology companies have increasingly been formed to integrate the knowledge and resources of both to develop new products and bring them to market.[107]

As suggested by the descriptions in the Strategic Focus, established firms also partner with one another to share their knowledge and skills in order to produce or manage innovations. Notice that the innovations described in the Strategic Focus all involve the combining of partners' unique skills. Commonly, the skills and knowledge contributed by each alliance partner are technology-based, a fact suggesting how rapidly technologies and their applications change in the 21st-century competitive landscape.

Because of the importance of alliances, particularly in the development of new technology and in commercializing innovations, firms are beginning to build networks of alliances that represent a form of social capital to them.[108] This social capital in the form of relationships with other firms helps them to obtain the knowledge and other resources necessary to develop innovations.[109] Knowledge from these alliances helps firms develop new capabilities.[110] Some firms now even allow other

Partnering to Innovate

GE Fleet Services is one of the largest fleet management companies in the world with more than 1.2 million commercial cars and trucks under lease and service management. Founded in the United Kingdom, Minorplanet Systems PLC serves close to 1,500 customers and has an installed base of 23,000 vehicles. Targeting similar customers, these firms formed a strategic alliance to develop and sell Vehicle Management Information (VMI) systems, initially in the United Kingdom and then in the United States as well. These products "provide innovative productivity solutions to help reduce fleet costs," according to officials involved with the alliance. In 2000, the firms won the "Innovation of the Year" award for productivity from *Fleet News*, the United Kingdom's leading fleet management trade publication. The award was given because one of the VMI products developed by the alliance partners was determined to radically improve the management of commercial fleets. Technologically sophisticated, this product leverages satellite and Internet technologies to help fleet operators plan routes, track vehicles on a live basis, and engage in intra-fleet text messaging, among other capabilities.

Especially early in its growth, Cisco Systems acquired innovations as it bought high-technology companies. However, Cisco also emphasizes strategic alliances to produce innovations. BearingPoint is one of the companies with which Cisco has an alliance that is designed to produce innovations. The alliance combines Cisco's expertise in network design and integrated IP-based solutions with BearingPoint's experience in assessing, designing, and implementing corporate networks. These firms combine their skills to develop what they consider to be innovative, end-to-end Internet-business solutions. Atlantic Health System (AHS) was one of the alliance's customers. To improve the reliability and performance of AHS's network, Cisco and BearingPoint developed a "state-of-the-art gigabit Ethernet infrastructure that enables digital medical-imaging and other high-bandwidth applications, increased collaboration between staff members at facilities within the group, and increased network reliability and performance."

Cisco also partners with KPMG Consulting to develop innovations. In this partnership, Cisco provides its intelligent enterprise-wide infrastructure solutions skills while KPMG offers its development and consulting expertise. Boise Cascade Office Products is a customer that the alliance served. In this instance, the alliance worked with its customer to design and implement the computer-telephony integration and Web collaboration aspects of Boise Cascade Office Products' new customer contact center. A business-to-business distributor of office products, Boise Cascade wanted to develop a differentiated, high-value-added customer contact center as a competitive advantage in what is essentially a highly competitive commodity-based business.

SOURCES: 2003, Boise Cascade thinks globally, sells locally, *Business Solutions*, http://www.business.cisco.com, June 6; 2003, Network transfusion for Atlantic Health System, *Welcome to IQ Magazine*, http://www.business.cisco.com, June 6; 2003, GE Fleet Services, UK's Minorplanet to extend strategic alliance to North America, *GE Fleet Services*, http://www.gefleet.com, June 8.

companies to participate in their internal new product development processes. It is not uncommon, for example, for firms to have supplier representatives on their cross-functional innovation teams because of the importance of the suppliers' input to ensure quality materials for any new product developed.[111]

However, alliances formed for the purpose of innovation are not without risks, including the risk that a partner will appropriate a firm's technology or knowledge and use it to enhance its own competitive abilities.[112] To prevent or at least minimize this risk, firms, particularly new ventures, need to select their partners carefully. The ideal partnership is one in which the firms have complementary skills as well as compatible strategic goals.[113] However, because firms are operating in a network of firms and thus may be participating in multiple alliances simultaneously, they encounter challenges in managing the alliances.[114] Research has shown that firms can become involved in too many alliances, which can harm rather than facilitate their innovation capabilities.[115] Thus, effectively managing the cooperative relationships to produce innovation is critical.

Acquisitions to Buy Innovation

As described in the Strategic Focus, firms sometimes acquire companies to gain access to their innovations and to their innovative capabilities. One of the reasons that firms turn to acquisitions is that the capital market values growth; acquisitions provide a means to rapidly extend the product line and increase the firm's revenues. Novartis AG likely cannot achieve its growth goal of becoming one of the world's pharmaceutical giants without acquiring other companies. Pfizer's acquisition of Pharmacia Corp. improves the likelihood that it will reach its goal of improving its percentage of converting experimental compounds into successful commercial applications that will lead to increased sales and profitability. Additional information about the relationship between acquisitions and innovation for these firms appears in the Strategic Focus.

Similar to internal corporate venturing and strategic alliances, acquisitions are not a risk-free approach to producing and managing innovations. A key risk of acquisitions is that a firm may substitute an ability to buy innovations for an ability to produce innovations internally. In support of this contention, research shows that firms engaging in acquisitions introduce fewer new products into the market.[116] This substitution may take place because firms lose strategic control and focus instead on financial control of their original and especially of their acquired business units.

We note in Chapter 7 that companies can also learn new capabilities from firms they acquire. As such, firms can gain capabilities to produce innovation from an acquired company. Additionally, firms that emphasize innovation and carefully select companies for acquisition that also emphasize innovation are likely to remain innovative.[117]

Capital for Entrepreneurial Ventures

Venture capital is a resource that is typically allocated to entrepreneurs who are involved in projects with high growth potential. The intent of venture capitalists is to achieve a high rate of return on the funds they invest.[118] In the late 1990s, the number of venture capital firms and the amount of capital invested in new ventures reached unprecedented levels with the amount of venture capital invested in new ventures reaching a high of $106 billion in 2000.[119] Venture capitalists desire to receive large returns on their investments and take major risks by investing in new ventures. Research has shown that venture capitalists may earn large returns or experience significant losses. For example, one study found that 34 percent of venture capitalists experienced a loss, while 23 percent gained a rate of return on their investments of 50 percent or greater.[120]

In addition to the benefit of financial resources, the firm receiving venture capital gains *legitimacy* (a social judgment of acceptance, appropriateness, and desirability). In turn, legitimacy increases the probability a new venture will appeal to other resources such as human capital.[121]

Venture capitalists place weight on the competence of the entrepreneur or the human capital in the firms in which they consider investing. They also weigh the expected scope of competitive rivalry the firm is likely to experience and the degree of instability in the market addressed.[122] However, the characteristics of the entrepreneur

Acquisitions as a Pathway to Innovation

Pfizer Inc. spent $14.4 billion on R&D during the three years prior to announcing in 2002 that it would acquire competitor Pharmacia. Although Pfizer spent more on R&D than any other company over that three-year period, it filed for Food and Drug Administration (FDA) approval for just three new medicines that were discovered by its own scientists. In response to this disappointing performance in its own labs, Pfizer chose to pay approximately $58 billion to acquire Pharmacia. This transaction was the third largest of all time in the pharmaceutical industry, exceeded in value only by Pfizer's previous acquisition in 2000 of Warner Lambert for $100 billion and by Glaxo Wellcome PLC's $77.26 billion purchase of SmithKline Beecham PLC. Almost ten months were required for regulatory approval to be completed in the United States and Europe. The largest hurdle to the acquisition was cleared when Pfizer agreed to sell an experimental incontinence drug to Novartis AG for $225 million. Officially, Pharmacia (formerly the world's ninth largest drugmaker) and Pfizer became a single entity in April 2003.

The newly created Pfizer intended to overhaul its R&D operations to enhance the "firm's ability to discover new medicines." Oncology research is one area in which Pharmacia excelled, resulting in a decision to lay off some Pfizer scientists working in that area. Pfizer officials believed that combining the two firms' areas of R&D expertise created a company with significant growth potential in three areas—eye care, growth disorders, and oncology. In addition to gaining access to Pharmacia's ability to develop innovative oncology drugs, Pfizer also acquired Pharmacia's eplerenone, a blood-pressure drug. In a major study, eplerenone improved "survival among heart-failure patients by 15% when tested against the best available current drug treatments." Because of a stretch of disappointing drug trials against heart disease, analysts viewed eplerenone's test results as a "home run." Thus, Pfizer's acquisition of Pharmacia allowed it to gain access to specific innovations (e.g., eplerenone) as well as to innovative capabilities, such as those concerned with oncology-related drugs.

Novartis AG also acquires innovations and innovative capabilities. Following what analysts call a "targeted acquisition" program, Novartis recently purchased a 51 percent controlling stake in Idenix Pharmaceuticals. A biotechnology company, Idenix had developed two promising hepatitis treatment drugs that interested Novartis. The acquisition of a controlling interest in Idenix gave Novartis "an instant entrée into antiviral hepatitis therapies, a market that's growing about 30% a year and in which Swiss rival Roche Holding AG is a big player." Committed to becoming one of the world's pharmaceutical giants, Novartis is trying to build a portfolio of superior drugs and is more than willing to acquire rivals to do so. In mid-2003, Schering-Plough was identified as a firm Novartis might acquire to expand its portfolio of innovative drugs as well as to enhance its innovative capabilities.

SOURCES: 2003, Novartis acquires hepatitis C franchise, *Chemical Market Reporter*, 263(13): 2; K. Capell, 2003, Novartis: CEO Daniel Vasella has a hot cancer drug and billions in the bank, *BusinessWeek Online*, http://www.businessweek.com, May 26; V. Fuhrmans, 2003, Novartis to acquire 51% of Idenix Pharmaceuticals, *Wall Street Journal Online*, http://www.wsj.com, March 27; S. Hensley, 2003, Pfizer to overhaul research following its Pharmacia deal, *Wall Street Journal Online*, http://www.wsj.com, April 30; S. Hensley, 2003, Pfizer to sell drug to Novartis to satisfy FTC, *Wall Street Journal Online*, http://www.wsj.com, March 18; R. Frank, 2002, Deals & deal makers: Pfizer's Pharmacia deal draws mixed opinions for M&A game, *Wall Street Journal Online*, http://www.wsj.com, July 16.

or firm in which venture capitalists invest as well as the rate of return expected will vary with the type of venture in which investments are made.[123]

Increasingly, venture capital is being used to support the acquisition of innovations. To provide such support, some firms establish their own venture-capital divisions. These divisions carefully evaluate other companies to identify those with innovations or innovative capabilities that might yield a competitive advantage. In other instances, a firm might decide to serve as an internal source of capital for innovative product ideas that can be spun off as independent or affiliated firms. New enterprises that are backed by venture capital provide an important source of innovation and new technology. The amount of corporate venture capital invested grew exponentially at the end of the 1990s and in 2000. For example, it grew from about $2 billion in 1998 to almost $11 billion in 1999. In 2000, the amount of corporate venture capital invested was slightly over $18 billion.[124]

Some relatively new ventures are able to obtain capital through initial public offerings (IPOs). Firms that offer new stock in this way must have high potential in order to sell their stock and obtain adequate capital to finance the growth and development of the firm. This form of capital can be substantial and is often much larger than the amounts obtained from venture capitalists. Investment bankers frequently play major roles in the development and offering of IPOs. Research has shown that founder-managed firms generally receive lower returns from IPOs than do professionally managed firms.[125] The IPO market values experienced managers more than founders who frequently do not have substantial managerial experience. JetBlue Airways created a lot of interest from investors because of its low costs, strong customer demand, and highly experienced CEO (who also happens to be the firm's founder).[126] Investors believe that the firm with an experienced CEO is more likely to succeed. Also, firms that have received venture capital backing usually receive greater returns from IPOs.[127]

Creating Value through Strategic Entrepreneurship

Newer entrepreneurial firms often are more effective than larger firms in identifying opportunities.[128] Some believe that these firms tend to be more innovative as well because of their flexibility and willingness to take risks. Alternatively, larger and well-established firms often have more resources and capabilities to exploit opportunities that are identified.[129] So, younger, entrepreneurial firms are generally opportunity seeking, and more established firms are advantage seeking. However, to compete effectively in the 21st century's competitive landscape, firms must identify and exploit opportunities, but do so while achieving and sustaining a competitive advantage.[130] Thus, newer entrepreneurial firms must learn how to gain a competitive advantage, and older, more established firms must relearn how to identify entrepreneurial opportunities.

Well-established Blockbuster Inc. recently created a new position called executive vice-president and president of emerging brands. Responsibilities attached to this position include those of finding entrepreneurial opportunities and then helping the firm decide if the innovations necessary to pursue them should be developed internally or acquired.[131] The concept of strategic entrepreneurship suggests that established and successful firms such as Blockbuster can be simultaneously entrepreneurial and strategic as can all firms, regardless of their size and age.

To be entrepreneurial, firms must develop an entrepreneurial mind-set among their managers and employees. Managers must emphasize the management of their resources, particularly human capital and social

Blockbuster Inc. is trying new innovations to expand its business. At a store in the Little Havana section of Miami, Florida, for example, it is targeting the growing Hispanic market by increasing its selection of Spanish-subtitled and dubbed movies.

Getty Images

capital.[132] The importance of knowledge to identify and exploit opportunities as well as to gain and sustain a competitive advantage suggests that firms must have strong human capital.[133] Social capital is critical for access to complementary resources from partners in order to compete effectively in domestic and international markets.[134]

Many entrepreneurial opportunities remain in international markets. Thus, firms should seek to enter and compete in international markets. Firms can learn new technologies and management practices from international markets and diffuse this knowledge throughout the firm. Furthermore, the knowledge firms gain can contribute to their innovations. Research has shown that firms operating in international markets tend to be more innovative.[135] Small and large firms are now regularly moving into international markets. Both types of firms must also be innovative to compete effectively. Thus, by developing resources (human and social capital), taking advantage of opportunities in domestic and international markets, and using the resources and knowledge gained in these markets to be innovative, firms achieve competitive advantages.[136] In so doing, they create value for their customers and shareholders.

Firms practicing strategic entrepreneurship contribute to a country's economic development. In fact, some countries such as Ireland have made dramatic economic progress by changing the institutional rules for businesses operating in the country. This could be construed as a form of institutional entrepreneurship. Likewise, firms that seek to establish their technology as a standard, also representing institutional entrepreneurship, are engaging in strategic entrepreneurship because creating a standard produces a sustainable competitive advantage for the firm.[137]

Research shows that because of its economic importance and individual motives, entrepreneurial activity is increasing across the globe. Furthermore, more women are becoming entrepreneurs because of the economic opportunity entrepreneurship provides and the individual independence it affords.[138] In future years, entrepreneurial activity may increase the wealth of less-affluent countries and continue to contribute to the economic development of the more-affluent countries. Regardless, the companies that practice strategic entrepreneurship are likely to be the winners in the 21st century.[139]

Summary

- Strategic entrepreneurship is taking entrepreneurial actions using a strategic perspective. More specifically, it involves engaging in simultaneous opportunity seeking and competitive advantage seeking behaviors to design and implement entrepreneurial strategies to create wealth.

- The concepts of entrepreneurial opportunity, innovation, and capabilities are important to firms. Entrepreneurial opportunities represent conditions in which new goods or services can satisfy a need in the market. The essence of entrepreneurship is to identify and exploit these opportunities. Innovation is the process of commercializing the products or processes that surfaced through invention. Entrepreneurial capabilities include building an entrepreneurial culture, having a passion for the business, and having a desire for measured risk.

- Increasingly, entrepreneurship is being practiced in many countries. As used by entrepreneurs, entrepreneurship and corporate entrepreneurship are strongly related to a nation's economic growth.

- Three basic approaches are used to produce and manage innovation: internal corporate venturing, cooperative strategies such as strategic alliances, and acquisitions. Autonomous strategic behavior and induced strategic behavior are the two processes of internal corporate venturing. Autonomous strategic behavior is a bottom-up process through which a product champion facilitates the commercialization of an innovative good or service. Induced strategic behavior is a top-down process in which a firm's current strategy and structure facilitate product or process innovations that are associated with them. Thus, induced strategic behavior is driven by the organization's current corporate strategy and structure.

- To create incremental and radical innovation requires effective innovation processes and practices. Increasingly, cross-functional integration is vital to a firm's efforts to develop and implement internal corporate venturing activities and to commercialize the resulting innovation. Additionally, integration and innovation can be facilitated by the development of shared values and the practice of entrepreneurial leadership.

- To gain access to the kind of specialized knowledge that often is required to innovate in the complex global economy, firms may form a cooperative relationship such as a strategic alliance with other firms, sometimes even with competitors.

- Acquisitions provide another means for firms to produce and manage innovation. Innovation can be acquired through direct acquisition, or firms can learn new capabilities from an acquisition, thereby enriching their internal innovation processes.

- Entrepreneurial activity requires capital for development. Venture capitalists are a prime source for this capital. The amount of venture capital available increased dramatically in the 1990s. While it decreased recently due to economic problems, it remains much higher than in earlier years. Initial public offerings (IPOs) also have become a common means of obtaining capital for new ventures.

- The practice of strategic entrepreneurship by all types of firms, large and small, new and more established, creates value for all stakeholders, especially for shareholders and customers. Strategic entrepreneurship also contributes to the economic development of entire nations.

Review Questions

Review Questions Review Questions

1. What is strategic entrepreneurship? What is its importance for firms competing in the global economy?

2. What are entrepreneurial opportunities, innovation, and entrepreneurial capabilities, and what is their importance?

3. What is international entrepreneurship and why is it increasingly being used in the global economy?

4. What is autonomous strategic behavior? What is induced strategic behavior?

5. How do firms use cooperative strategies such as strategic alliances to help them produce innovation?

6. How can a firm use acquisitions to increase the number of innovations it produces and improve its capability to produce innovations?

7. What is the importance of venture capital and initial public offerings to entrepreneurial activity?

8. How does strategic entrepreneurship create value for stakeholders and contribute to economic development?

Experiential Exercises

Experiential Exercises

Strategic Entrepreneurship

Assume that you are a partner in a new venture energy company called Currence. You have approached an investor group for capital to fund the first three years of your operation. Following the preliminary presentation, you find that the group is very impressed by Currence and by its six start-up partners, each of whom brings unique, yet critical skills, experience, contacts, and other knowledge to the venture. Before the investor group decides to fund your company, however, it has asked for a brief presentation about how the Currence partners will be rewarded.

Part 1 (complete individually). Indicate how Currence will determine the approximate salary, fringe benefits, and shares of stock (as a percentage) each partner will be allocated upon closing the financing of your new venture. Also indicate your rationale for these amounts.

Part 2 (in small groups). Compare your responses to Part 1 with others in your small group. Reach a consensus on the criteria your small group would use to determine how to

reward each partner. Appoint one small group member to present your consensus and how your team reached it to the class.

Part 3 (in small groups). Following the presentations in Part 2, discuss the following issues and indicate any important lessons and implications:

1. Why would an entrepreneurial venture such as Currence be asked to provide this type of information to an investor group?

2. What criteria did the groups use concerning salaries and stock? Why?

3. What patterns did you perceive in the approaches taken by each team?

4. Did the groups make salaries or stock equal for all Currence partners? Why or why not? What reasons would there be for providing different rewards for different partners?

5. How difficult was it for the small groups to reach a consensus?

Entrepreneurial Culture

One of your responsibilities as an entrepreneurial leader is to build shared values that will support entrepreneurial behavior. Describe the steps that you would follow to build an entrepreneurial culture.

Option A: Take the perspective of a manager within a large corporation who has just been given responsibility to lead a newly acquired business unit that has an innovative product. Prepare a report for the top management team that describes the steps you will take. Provide a brief rationale for your recommendations.

Option B: Take the perspective of an entrepreneur who has personally developed an innovation and is establishing a new start-up to produce and market the innovation. Prepare a report for investors about how you plan to build an entrepreneurial culture so that the investors will be willing to provide financial resources for your venture. Explain how your efforts to build an entrepreneurial culture will lead to strategic competitiveness.

Notes

1. R. G. Holcombe, 2003, The origins of entrepreneurial opportunities, *Review of Austrian Economics*, 16: 25–54; C. M. Daily, P. P. McDougall, J. G. Covin, & D. R. Dalton, 2002, Governance and strategic leadership in entrepreneurial firms, *Journal of Management*, 28: 387–412.
2. S. Thomke, 2003, R&D comes to services, *Harvard Business Review*, 81(4): 70–79.
3. R. D. Ireland, M. A. Hitt, & D. G. Sirmon, 2003, A model of strategic entrepreneurship: The construct and its dimensions, *Journal of Management*, in press.
4. M. A. Hitt, R. D. Ireland, S. M. Camp, & D. L. Sexton, 2002, Strategic entrepreneurship: Integrating entrepreneurial and strategic management perspectives, in M. A. Hitt, R. D. Ireland, S. M. Camp, & D. L. Sexton (eds.), *Strategic Entrepreneurship: Creating a New Mindset*, Oxford, UK: Blackwell Publishers, 1–16; M. A. Hitt, R. D. Ireland, S. M. Camp, & D. L. Sexton, 2001, Strategic entrepreneurship: Entrepreneurial strategies for wealth creation, *Strategic Management Journal*, 22(Special Issue): 479–491; R. D. Ireland, M. A. Hitt, S. M. Camp, & D. L. Sexton, 2001, Integrating entrepreneurship and strategic management actions to create firm wealth, *Academy of Management Executive*, 15(1): 49–63.
5. R. D. Ireland, D. F. Kuratko, & J. G. Covin, 2003, Antecedents, elements, and consequences of corporate entrepreneurship strategy, Working paper, University of Richmond.
6. B. Bowonder, J. J. Thomas, V. M. Rokkam, & A. Rokkam, 2003, The global pharmaceutical industry: Changing competitive landscape, *International Journal of Technology Management*, 25(3,4): 211–226; I. C. MacMillan, A. B. van Putten, & R. M. McGrath, 2003, Global gamesmanship, *Harvard Business Review*, 81(5): 62–71.
7. H. G. Barkema, J. A. C. Baum, & E. A. Mannix, 2002, Management challenges in a new time, *Academy of Management Journal*, 45: 916–930.
8. H. Lee, M. A. Hitt, & E. K. Jeong, 2003, The impact of CEO and TMT characteristics on strategic flexibility and firm performance, Working paper, Texas A&M University.
9. G. Hamel, 2000, *Leading the Revolution*, Boston, MA: Harvard Business School Press.
10. S. Michael, D. Storey, & H. Thomas, 2002, Discovery and coordination in strategic management and entrepreneurship, in M. A. Hitt, R. D. Ireland, S. M. Camp, & D. L. Sexton (eds.), *Strategic Entrepreneurship: Creating a New Mindset*, Oxford, UK: Blackwell Publishers, 45–65.
11. R. Katila & G. Ahuja, 2002, Something old, something new: A longitudinal study of search behavior and new product innovation, *Academy of Management Journal*, 45: 1183–1194.
12. T. W. Y. Man, T. Lau, & K. F. Chan, 2002, The competitiveness of small and medium enterprises: A conceptualization with focus on entrepreneurial competencies, *Journal of Business Venturing*, 17: 123–142.
13. R. E. Hoskisson, M. A. Hitt, R. A. Johnson, & W. Grossman, 2002, Conflicting voices: The effects of institutional ownership heterogeneity and internal governance on corporate innovation strategies, *Academy of Management Journal*, 45: 697–716.
14. J. Schumpeter, 1934, *The Theory of Economic Development*, Cambridge, MA: Harvard University Press.
15. S. Shane & S. Venkataraman, 2000, The promise of entrepreneurship as a field of research, *Academy of Management Review*, 25: 217–226.
16. E. Danneels, 2002, The dynamics of product innovation and firm competencies, *Strategic Management Journal*, 23: 1095–1121.
17. R. Katila, 2002, New product search over time: Past ideas in their prime? *Academy of Management Journal*, 45: 995–1010; B. R. Barringer & A. C. Bluedorn, 1999, The relationship between corporate entrepreneurship and strategic management, *Strategic Management Journal*, 20: 421–444.
18. J. L. Thompson, 2002, The world of the social entrepreneur, *The International Journal of Public Sector Management*, 15(4–5): 412–431.
19. G. D. Meyer, H. M. Neck, & M. D. Meeks, 2002, The entrepreneurship-strategic management interface, in M. A. Hitt, R. D. Ireland, S. M. Camp, & D. L. Sexton (eds.), *Strategic Entrepreneurship: Creating a New Mindset*, Oxford, UK: Blackwell Publishers, 19–44; I. Kirzner, 1997, Entrepreneurial discovery and the competitive market process: An Austrian approach, *Journal of Economic Literature*, 35(1): 60–85.
20. R. G. McGrath & I. MacMillan, 2000, *The Entrepreneurial Mindset*, Boston, MA: Harvard Business School Press.
21. T. M. Begley & D. P. Boyd, 2003, The need for a corporate global mind-set, *MIT Sloan Management Review*, 44(2): 25–32.
22. R. Kanaley, 2003, Advertising on bandages is just beginning for King of Prussia, Pa., firm, *The Philadelphia Inquirer*, April 28, B6.
23. C. W. L. Hill & F. T. Rothaermel, 2003, The performance of incumbent firms in the face of radical technological innovation, *Academy of Management Review*, 28: 257–274.
24. P. F. Drucker, 1998, The discipline of innovation, *Harvard Business Review*, 76(6): 149–157.
25. Ibid.
26. J. D. Wolpert, 2002, Breaking out of the innovation box, *Harvard Business Review*, 80(8): 77–83.
27. P. D. Reynolds, M. Hay, & S. M. Camp, 1999, *Global Entrepreneurship Monitor, 1999 Executive Report*, Babson Park, MA: Babson College.
28. J. E. Perry-Smith & C. E. Shalley, 2003, The social side of creativity: A static and dynamic social network perspective, *Academy of Management Review*, 28: 89–106.
29. R. Price, 1996, Technology and strategic advantage, *California Management Review*, 38(3): 38–56; L. G. Franko, 1989, Global corporate competition: Who's winning, who's losing and the R&D factor as one reason why, *Strategic Management Journal*, 10: 449–474.
30. J. W. Spencer, 2003, Firms' knowledge-sharing strategies in the global innovation system: Empirical evidence from the flat panel display industry, *Strategic Management Journal*, 24: 217–233; K. M. Kelm, V. K. Narayanan, &

G. E. Pinches, 1995, Shareholder value creation during R&D innovation and commercialization stages, *Academy of Management Journal*, 38: 770–786.

31. M. A. Hitt, R. D. Nixon, R. E. Hoskisson, & R. Kochhar, 1999, Corporate entrepreneurship and cross-functional fertilization: Activation, process and disintegration of a new product design team, *Entrepreneurship: Theory and Practice*, 23(3): 145–167.

32. J. P. O'Brien, 2003, The capital structure implications of pursuing a strategy of innovation, *Strategic Management Journal*, 24: 415–431.

33. Schumpeter, *The Theory of Economic Development*.

34. P. Sharma & J. L. Chrisman, 1999, Toward a reconciliation of the definitional issues in the field of corporate entrepreneurship, *Entrepreneurship: Theory and Practice*, 23(3): 11–27; R. A. Burgelman & L. R. Sayles, 1986, *Inside Corporate Innovation: Strategy, Structure, and Managerial Skills*, New York: Free Press.

35. R. E. Hoskisson & L. W. Busenitz, 2002, Market uncertainty and learning distance in corporate entrepreneurship entry mode choice, in M. A. Hitt, R. D. Ireland, S. M. Camp, & D. L. Sexton (eds.), *Strategic Entrepreneurship: Creating a New Mindset*, Oxford, UK: Blackwell Publishers, 151–172.

36. D. Somaya, 2003, Strategic determinants of decisions not to settle patent litigation, *Strategic Management Journal*, 24: 17–38.

37. G. G. Dess, R. D. Ireland, S. A. Zahra, S. W. Floyd, J. J. Janney, & P. J. Lane, 2003, Emerging issues in corporate entrepreneurship, *Journal of Management*, 29: 351–378.

38. J. S. Hornsby, D. F. Kuratko, & S. A. Zahra, 2002, Middle managers' perception of the internal environment for corporate entrepreneurship: Assessing a measurement scale, *Journal of Business Venturing*, 17: 253–273.

39. S. D. Sarasvathy, 2000, Seminar on research perspectives in entrepreneurship (1997), *Journal of Business Venturing*, 15: 1–57.

40. R. Grover, D. Foust, & B. Elgin, 2003, From media mogul to web warlord, *Business Week*, May 19, 46.

41. D. F. Kuratko, R. D. Ireland, & J. S. Hornsby, 2001, Improving firm performance through entrepreneurial actions: Acordia's corporate entrepreneurship strategy, *Academy of Management Executive*, 15(4): 60–71; J. Birkinshaw, 1999, The determinants and consequences of subsidiary initiative in multinational corporations, *Entrepreneurship: Theory and Practice*, 24(1): 9–36.

42. W. S. Mossberg, 2003, Apple's iPod just keeps getting better as top digital play, *Wall Street Journal*, Eastern edition, May 1, B1.

43. Ibid.

44. 2003, Apple Computer Inc.: In first week, iTunes web site sells over one million songs, *Wall Street Journal*, Eastern edition, May 6, C9.

45. S. Godin, 2003, What did you do during the 2000s? *Fast Company*, June, 70.

46. W. Tsai, 2001, Knowledge transfer in intraorganizational networks: Effects of network position and absorptive capacity on business unit innovation and performance, *Academy of Management Journal*, 44: 996–1004.

47. S. A. Zahra & G. George, 2002, Absorptive capacity: A review, reconceptualization, and extension, *Academy of Management Review*, 27: 185–203.

48. M. A. Hitt, L. Bierman, K. Shimizu, & R. Kochhar, 2001, Direct and moderating effects of human capital on strategy and performance in professional service firms: A resource-based perspective, *Academy of Management Journal*, 44: 13–28.

49. R. Belderbos, 2003, Entry mode, organizational learning, and R&D in foreign affiliates: Evidence from Japanese firms, *Strategic Management Journal*, 24: 235–259; I. Bouty, 2000, Interpersonal and interaction influences on informal resource exchanges between R&D researchers across organizational boundaries, *Academy of Management Journal*, 43: 5–65.

50. 2001, Some like it hot, *Entrepreneur.com*, October 30.

51. C. G. Brush, L. F. Edelman, & P. G. Greene, 2002, Internationalization of small firms: Personal factors revisited, *International Small Business Journal*, 20(1): 9–31; J. W. Lu & P. W. Beamish, 2001, The internationalization and performance of SMEs, *Strategic Management Journal*, 22(Special Issue): 565–585.

52. L. Tihanyi, R. A. Johnson, R. E. Hoskisson, & M. A. Hitt, 2003, Institutional ownership differences and international diversification: The effects of boards of directors and technological opportunity, *Academy of Management Journal*, 46: 195–211.

53. A. E. Ellstrand, L. Tihanyi, & J. L. Johnson, 2002, Board structure and international political risk, *Academy of Management Journal*, 45: 769–777.

54. D. Farrell, H. Fassbender, T. Kneip, S. Kriesel, & E. Labaye, 2003, Reviving French and German productivity, *The McKinsey Quarterly*, Number One, 40–53.

55. 2000, Business innovation urged, *Irish Times*, February 9, 23.

56. P. D. Reynolds, S. M. Camp, W. D. Bygrave, E. Autio, & M. Hay, 2002, *Global Entrepreneurship Monitor*, Kauffman Center for Entrepreneurial Leadership, Ewing Marion Kauffman Foundation.

57. M. H. Morris, 1998, *Entrepreneurial Intensity: Sustainable Advantages for Individuals, Organizations, and Societies*, Westport, CT: Quorum Books, 85–86.

58. S. A. Zahra & G. George, 2002, International entrepreneurship: The state of the field and future research agenda, in M. A. Hitt, R. D. Ireland, S. M. Camp, & D. L. Sexton (eds.), *Strategic Entrepreneurship: Creating a New Mindset*, Oxford, UK: Blackwell Publishers, 255–288.

59. S. A. Zahra, R. D. Ireland, & M. A. Hitt, 2000, International expansion by new venture firms: International diversity, mode of market entry, technological learning and performance, *Academy of Management Journal*, 43: 925–950.

60. P. P. McDougall & B. M. Oviatt, 2000, International entrepreneurship: The intersection of two paths, *Academy of Management Journal*, 43: 902–908.

61. A. Yan, G. Zhu, & D. T. Hall, 2002, International assignments for career building: A model of agency relationships and psychological contracts, *Academy of Management Review*, 27: 373–391.

62. H. Barkema & O. Chvyrkov, 2002, What sort of top management team is needed at the helm of internationally diversified firms? in M. A. Hitt, R. D. Ireland, S. M. Camp, & D. L. Sexton (eds.), *Strategic Entrepreneurship: Creating a New Mindset*, Oxford, UK: Blackwell Publishers, 290–305.

63. T. S. Frost, 2001, The geographic sources of foreign subsidiaries' innovations, *Strategic Management Journal*, 22: 101–122.

64. E. W. K. Tsang, 2002, Learning from overseas venturing experience: The case of Chinese family businesses, *Journal of Business Venturing*, 17: 21–40.

65. W. Kuemmerle, 2002, Home base and knowledge management in international ventures, *Journal of Business Venturing*, 17: 99–122.

66. C. D. Charitou & C. C. Markides, 2003, Responses to disruptive strategic innovation, *MIT Sloan Management Review*, 44(2): 55–63; R. Leifer, G. Colarelli, & M. Rice, 2001, Implementing radical innovation in mature firms: The role of hubs, *Academy of Management Executive*, 15(3): 102–113.

67. P. M. Lee & H. M. O'Neill, 2003, Ownership structures and R&D investments of U.S. and Japanese firms: Agency and stewardship perspectives, *Academy of Management Journal*, 46: 212–225.

68. G. Ahuja & M. Lampert, 2001, Entrepreneurship in the large corporation: A longitudinal study of how established firms create breakthrough inventions, *Strategic Management Journal*, 22(Special Issue): 521–543.

69. M. J. Benner & M. L. Tushman, 2003, Exploitation, exploration, and process management: The productivity dilemma revisited, *Academy of Management Review*, 28: 238–256.

70. J. E. Ashton, F. X. Cook, Jr., & P. Schmitz, 2003, Uncovering hidden value in a midsize manufacturing company, *Harvard Business Review*, 81(6): 111–119; L. Fleming & O. Sorenson, 2003, Navigating the technology landscape of innovation, *MIT Sloan Management Review*, 44(2): 15–23.

71. J. Goldenberg, R. Horowitz, A. Levav, & D. Mazursky, 2003, Finding your innovation sweet spot, *Harvard Business Review*, 81(3): 120–129.

72. G. C. O'Connor, R. Hendricks, & M. P. Rice, 2002, Assessing transition readiness for radical innovation, *Research Technology Management*, 45(6): 50–56.

73. R. I. Sutton, 2002, Weird ideas that spark innovation, *MIT Sloan Management Review*, 43(2): 83–87.

74. K. G. Smith & D. Di Gregorio, 2002, Bisociation, discovery, and the role of entrepreneurial action, in M. A. Hitt, R. D. Ireland, S. M. Camp, & D. L. Sexton (eds.), *Strategic Entrepreneurship: Creating a New Mindset*, Oxford, UK: Blackwell Publishers, 129–150.

75. Hoskisson & Busenitz, Market uncertainty and learning distance.

76. R. A. Burgelman, 1995, *Strategic Management of Technology and Innovation*, Boston: Irwin.

77. S. K. Markham, 2002, Moving technologies from lab to market, *Research Technology Management*, 45(6): 31–42.

78. T. H. Davenport, L. Prusak, & H. J. Wilson, 2003, Who's bringing you hot ideas and how are you responding? *Harvard Business Review*, 81(2): 58–64.

79. M. A. Hitt, R. D. Ireland, & H. Lee, 2000, Technological learning, knowledge management, firm growth and performance, *Journal of Engineering and*

Technology Management, 17: 231–246; D. Leonard-Barton, 1995, *Well-springs of Knowledge: Building and Sustaining the Sources of Innovation*, Cambridge, MA: Harvard Business School Press.

80. S. S. Rao, 2000, General Electric, software vendor, *Forbes*, January 24, 144–146.

81. H. W. Chesbrough, 2002, Making sense of corporate venture capital, *Harvard Business Review*, 80(3): 90–99.

82. M. Subramaniam & N. Venkatraman, 2001, Determinants of transnational new product development capability: Testing the influence of transferring and deploying tacit overseas knowledge, *Strategic Management Journal*, 22: 359–378.

83. M. Song & M. M. Montoya-Weiss, 2001, The effect of perceived technological uncertainty on Japanese new product development, *Academy of Management Journal*, 44: 61–80.

84. J. Turrettini, 2003, Beware of cat, *Forbes*, June 9, 164–168.

85. McGrath and MacMillan, *Entrepreneurial Mindset*.

86. 2002, Building scientific networks for effective innovation, *MIT Sloan Management Review*, 43(3): 14.

87. C. M. Christensen & M. Overdorf, 2000, Meeting the challenge of disruptive change, *Harvard Business Review*, 78(2): 66–77.

88. L. Yu, 2002, Marketers and engineers: Why can't we just get along? *MIT Sloan Management Review*, 43(1):13.

89. P. S. Adler, 1995, Interdepartmental interdependence and coordination: The case of the design/manufacturing interface, *Organization Science*, 6: 147–167.

90. I. Royer, 2003, Why bad projects are so hard to kill, *Harvard Business Review*, 81(2): 48–56.

91. B. L. Kirkman & B. Rosen, 1999, Beyond self-management: Antecedents and consequences of team empowerment, *Academy of Management Journal*, 42: 58–74; A. R. Jassawalla & H. C. Sashittal, 1999, Building collaborative cross-functional new product teams, *Academy of Management Executive*, 13(3): 50–63.

92. Hitt, Nixon, Hoskisson, & Kochhar, Corporate entrepreneurship.

93. Christensen & Overdorf, Meeting the challenge of disruptive change.

94. Hitt, Nixon, Hoskisson, & Kochhar, Corporate entrepreneurship.

95. A. C. Amason, 1996, Distinguishing the effects of functional and dysfunctional conflict on strategic decision making: Resolving a paradox for top management teams, *Academy of Management Journal*, 39: 123–148; P. R. Lawrence & J. W. Lorsch, 1969, *Organization and Environment*, Homewood, IL: Richard D. Irwin.

96. D. Dougherty, L. Borrelli, K. Muncir, & A. O'Sullivan, 2000, Systems of organizational sensemaking for sustained product innovation, *Journal of Engineering and Technology Management*, 17: 321–355; D. Dougherty, 1992, Interpretive barriers to successful product innovation in large firms, *Organization Science*, 3: 179–202.

97. Hitt, Nixon, Hoskisson, & Kochhar, Corporate entrepreneurship.

98. E. C. Wenger & W. M. Snyder, 2000, Communities of practice: The organizational frontier, *Harvard Business Review*, 78(1): 139–144.

99. Hamel, *Leading the Revolution*.

100. McGrath & MacMillan, *Entrepreneurial Mindset*.

101. Hamel, *Leading the Revolution*.

102. Hitt, Ireland, Camp, & Sexton, Strategic entrepreneurship; S. W. Fowler, A. W. King, S. J. Marsh, & B. Victor, 2000, Beyond products: New strategic imperatives for developing competencies in dynamic environments, *Journal of Engineering and Technology Management*, 17: 357–377.

103. R. K. Kazanjian, R. Drazin, & M. A. Glynn, 2002, Implementing strategies for corporate entrepreneurship: A knowledge-based perspective, in M. A. Hitt, R. D. Ireland, S. M. Camp, & D. L. Sexton (eds.), *Strategic Entrepreneurship: Creating a New Mindset*, Oxford, UK: Blackwell Publishers, 173–199.

104. R. Gulati & M. C. Higgins, 2003, Which ties matter when? The contingent effects of interorganizational partnerships on IPO success, *Strategic Management Journal*, 24: 127–144.

105. A. C. Cooper, 2002, Networks, alliances and entrepreneurship, in M. A. Hitt, R. D. Ireland, S. M. Camp, & D. L. Sexton (eds.), *Strategic Entrepreneurship: Creating a New Mindset*, Oxford, UK: Blackwell Publishers, 204–222.

106. S. A. Alvarez & J. B. Barney, 2001, How entrepreneurial firms can benefit from alliances with large partners, *Academy of Management Executive*, 15(1): 139–148; F. T. Rothaermel, 2001, Incumbent's advantage through exploiting complementary assets via interfirm cooperation, *Strategic Management Journal*, 22(Special Issue): 687–699.

107. J. Hagedoorn & N. Roijakkers, 2002, Small entrepreneurial firms and large companies in inter-firm R&D networks—the international biotechnology industry, in M. A. Hitt, R. D. Ireland, S. M. Camp, & D. L. Sexton (eds.), *Strategic Entrepreneurship: Creating a New Mindset*, Oxford, UK: Blackwell Publishers, 223–252.

108. D. Kline, 2003, Sharing the corporate crown jewels, *MIT Sloan Management Review*, 44(3): 89–93.

109. H. Yli-Renko, E. Autio, & H. J. Sapienza, 2001, Social capital, knowledge acquisition and knowledge exploitation in young technology-based firms, *Strategic Management Journal*, 22(Special Issue): 587–613.

110. C. Lee, K. Lee, & J. M. Pennings, 2001, Internal capabilities, external networks and performance: A study of technology-based ventures, *Strategic Management Journal*, 22(Special Issue): 615–640.

111. A. Takeishi, 2001, Bridging inter- and intra-firm boundaries: Management of supplier involvement in automobile product development, *Strategic Management Journal*, 22: 403–433.

112. R. D. Ireland, M. A. Hitt, & D. Vaidyanath, 2002, Strategic alliances as a pathway to competitive success, *Journal of Management*, 28: 413–446.

113. M. A. Hitt, M. T. Dacin, E. Levitas, J.-L. Arregle, & A. Borza, 2000, Partner selection in emerging and developed market contexts: Resource-based and organizational learning perspectives, *Academy of Management Journal*, 43: 449–467.

114. J. J. Reuer, M. Zollo, & H. Singh, 2002, Post-formation dynamics in strategic alliances, *Strategic Management Journal*, 23: 135–151.

115. F. Rothaermel & D. Deeds, 2002, More good things are not always necessarily better: An empirical study of strategic alliances, experience effects, and new product development in high-technology start-ups, in M. A. Hitt, R. Amit, C. Lucier, & R. Nixon (eds.), *Creating Value: Winners in the New Business Environment*, Oxford, UK: Blackwell Publishers, 85–103.

116. M. A. Hitt, R. E. Hoskisson, R. A. Johnson, & D. D. Moesel, 1996, The market for corporate control and firm innovation, *Academy of Management Journal*, 39: 1084–1119.

117. M. A. Hitt, J. S. Harrison, & R. D. Ireland, 2001, *Mergers and Acquisitions: A Guide to Creating Value for Stakeholders*, New York: Oxford University Press.

118. J. A. Timmons, 1999, *New Venture Creation: Entrepreneurship for the 21st Century*, 5th ed., New York: Irwin/McGraw-Hill.

119. L. Stern, 2003, VCs open the wallets, *Newsweek*, April 21, E2.

120. C. M. Mason & R. T. Harrison, 2002, Is it worth it? The rates of return from informal venture capital investments, *Journal of Business Venturing*, 17: 211–236.

121. M. A. Zimmerman & G. J. Zeitz, 2002, Beyond survival: Achieving new venture growth by building legitimacy, *Academy of Management Review*, 27: 414–431.

122. D. A. Shepherd & A. Zacharakis, 2002, Venture capitalists' expertise: A call for research into decision aids and cognitive feedback, *Journal of Business Venturing*, 17: 1–20.

123. S. Manigart, K. de Waele, M. Wright, K. Robbie, P. Desbrieres, H. J. Sapienza, & A. Beekman, 2002, Determinants of required return in venture capital investments: A five-country study, *Journal of Business Venturing*, 17: 291–312.

124. M. Maula & G. Murray, 2002, Corporate venture capital and the creation of U.S. public companies: The impact of sources of capital on the performance of portfolio companies, in M. A. Hitt, R. Amit, C. Lucier, & R. Nixon (eds.), *Creating Value: Winners in the New Business Environment*, Oxford, UK: Blackwell Publishers, 164–187.

125. S. T. Certo, J. G. Covin, C. M. Daily, & D. R. Dalton, 2001, Wealth and the effects of founder management among IPO-stage new ventures, *Strategic Management Journal*, 22(Special Issue): 641–658.

126. L. DeCarlo, 2002, JetBlue IPO will fly right for investors, *Forbes*, http://www.forbes.com, February, 13.

127. Maula & Murray, Corporate venture capital.

PART 3 / Strategic Actions: Strategy Implementation

128. Ireland, Hitt, & Sirmon, A model of strategic entrepreneurship.

129. Ibid.

130. Hitt, Ireland, Camp, & Sexton, Strategic entrepreneurship.

131. M. Halkias, 2003, Blockbuster seeking new ventures, *Dallas Morning News,* May 21, D2.

132. D. G. Sirmon, M. A. Hitt, & R. D. Ireland, 2003, Dynamically managing firm resources for competitive advantage: Creating value for stakeholders. Paper presented at the Academy of Management meeting, Seattle, August.

133. Hitt, Bierman, Shimizu, & Kochhar, Direct and moderating effects of human capital.

134. M. A. Hitt, H. Lee, & E. Yucel, 2002, The importance of social capital to the management of multinational enterprises: Relational networks among Asian and Western firms, *Asia Pacific Journal of Management,* 19: 353–372.

135. M. A. Hitt, R. E. Hoskisson, & H. Kim, 1997, International diversification: Effects on innovation and firm performance in product diversified firms, *Academy of Management Journal,* 40: 767–798.

136. M. A. Hitt & R. D. Ireland, 2002, The essence of strategic leadership: Managing human and social capital, *Journal of Leadership and Organization Studies,* 9(1): 3–14.

137. R. Garud, S. Jain, & A. Kumaraswamy, 2002, Institutional entrepreneurship in the sponsorship of common technological standards: The case of Sun Microsystems and JAVA, *Academy of Management Journal,* 45: 196–214.

138. Reynolds, Camp, Bygrave, Autio, & Hay, *Global Entrepreneurship Monitor.*

139. Hitt, Ireland, Camp, & Sexton, Strategic entrepreneurship.

Case Studies

Preparing an Effective Case Analysis

introduction

In most strategic management courses, cases are used extensively as a teaching tool.[1] A key reason is that cases provide active learners with opportunities to use the strategic management process to identify and solve organizational problems. Thus, by analyzing situations that are described in cases and presenting the results, active learners (i.e., students) become skilled at effectively using the tools, techniques, and concepts that combine to form the strategic management process.

The cases that follow are concerned with actual companies. Presented within the cases are problems and situations that managers and those with whom they work must analyze and resolve. As you will see, a strategic management case can focus on an entire industry, a single organization, or a business unit of a large, diversified firm. The strategic management issues facing not-for-profit organizations also can be examined using the case analysis method.

Basically, the case analysis method calls for a careful diagnosis of an organization's current conditions (as manifested by its external and internal environments) so that appropriate strategic actions can be recommended in light of the firm's strategic intent and strategic mission. Strategic actions are taken to develop and then use a firm's core competencies to select and implement different strategies, including business-level, corporate-level, acquisition and restructuring, international, and cooperative strategies. Thus, appropriate strategic actions help the firm to survive in the long run as it creates and uses competitive advantages as the foundation for achieving strategic competitiveness and earning above-average returns. The case method that we are recommending to you has a rich heritage as a pedagogical approach to the study and understanding of managerial effectiveness.[2]

As an active learner, your preparation is critical to successful use of the case analysis method. Without careful study and analysis, active learners lack the insights required to participate fully in the discussion of a firm's situation and the strategic actions that are appropriate.

Instructors adopt different approaches in their application of the case analysis method. Some require active learners/students to use a specific analytical procedure to examine an organization; others provide less structure, expecting students to learn by developing their own unique analytical method. Still other instructors believe that a moderately structured framework should be used to analyze a firm's situation and make appropriate recommendations. Your professor will determine the specific approach you take. The approach we are presenting to you is a moderately structured framework.

We divide our discussion of a moderately structured case analysis method framework into four sections. First, we describe the importance of understanding the skills active learners can acquire through effective use of the case analysis method. In the second section, we provide you with a process-oriented framework. This framework can be of value in your efforts to analyze cases and then present the results of your work. Using this framework in a classroom setting yields valuable experiences that can, in turn, help you successfully complete assignments that you will receive from your employer. The third section is where we describe briefly what you can expect to occur during in-class case discussions. As this description shows, the relationship and interactions between instructors and active learners/students during case discussions are different than they are during lectures. In the final section, we present a moderately structured framework that we believe can help you prepare effective oral and written presentations. Written and oral communication skills also are valued highly in many organizational settings; hence, their development today can serve you well in the future.

Skills Gained Through Use of the Case Analysis Method

The case analysis method is based on a philosophy that combines knowledge acquisition with significant involvement from students as active learners. In the words of Alfred North Whitehead, this philosophy "rejects the doctrine that students had first learned passively, and then, having learned should apply knowledge."[3] In contrast to this philosophy, the case analysis method is based on principles that were elaborated upon by John Dewey:

> Only by wrestling with the conditions of this problem at hand, seeking and finding his own way out, does [the student] think. . . . If he cannot devise his own solution (not, of course, in isolation, but in correspondence with the teacher and other pupils) and find his own way out he will not learn, not even if he can recite some correct answer with a hundred percent accuracy.[4]

The case analysis method brings reality into the classroom. When developed and presented effectively, with rich and interesting detail, cases keep conceptual discussions grounded in reality. Experience shows that simple fictional accounts of situations and collections of actual organizational data and articles from public sources are not as effective for learning as fully developed cases. A comprehensive case presents you with a partial clinical study of a real-life situation that faced managers as well as other stakeholders including employees. A case presented in narrative form provides motivation for involvement with and analysis of a specific situation. By framing alternative strategic actions and by confronting the complexity and ambiguity of the practical world, case analysis provides extraordinary power for your involvement with a personal learning experience. Some of the potential consequences of using the case method are summarized in Exhibit 1.

As Exhibit 1 suggests, the case analysis method can assist active learners in the development of their analytical and judgment skills. Case analysis also helps you learn how to ask the right questions. By this we mean questions that focus on the core strategic issues that are included in a case. Active learners/students with managerial aspirations can improve their ability to identify underlying problems rather than focusing on superficial symptoms as they develop skills at asking probing yet appropriate questions.

The collection of cases your instructor chooses to assign can expose you to a wide variety of organizations and decision situations. This approach vicariously broadens your experience base and provides insights into many types of managerial situations, tasks, and responsibilities. Such indirect experience can help you make a more informed career decision about the industry and managerial situation you believe will prove to be challenging and satisfying. Finally, experience in analyzing cases definitely enhances your problem-solving skills, and research indicates that the case method for this class is better than the lecture method.[5]

Furthermore, when your instructor requires oral and written presentations, your communication skills will be honed through use of the case method. Of course, these added skills depend on your preparation as well as your instructor's facilitation of learning. However, the primary responsibility for learning is yours. The quality of case discussion is generally acknowledged to require, at a minimum, a thorough mastery of case facts and some independent analysis of them. The case method therefore first requires that you read and think carefully about each case. Additional comments about the preparation you should complete to successfully discuss a case appear in the next section.

EXHIBIT 1   Consequences of Student Involvement with the Case Method

1. Case analysis requires students to practice important managerial skills—diagnosing, making decisions, observing, listening, and persuading—while preparing for a case discussion.

2. Cases require students to relate analysis and action, to develop realistic and concrete actions despite the complexity and partial knowledge characterizing the situation being studied.

3. Students must confront the *intractability of reality*—complete with absence of needed information, an imbalance between needs and available resources, and conflicts among competing objectives.

4. Students develop a general managerial point of view—where responsibility is sensitive to action in a diverse environmental context.

Source: 1993, C. C. Lundberg and C. Enz, A framework for student case preparation, *Case Research Journal*, 13 (Summer): 134.

STUDENT PREPARATION FOR CASE DISCUSSION

If you are inexperienced with the case method, you may need to alter your study habits. A lecture-oriented course may not require you to do intensive preparation for *each* class period. In such a course, you have the latitude to work through assigned readings and review lecture notes according to your own schedule. However, an assigned case requires significant and conscientious *preparation before class*. Without it, you will be unable to contribute meaningfully to in-class discussion. Therefore, careful reading and thinking about case facts, as well as reasoned analyses and the development of alternative solutions to case problems, are essential. Recommended alternatives should flow logically from core problems identified through study of the case. Exhibit 2 shows a set of steps that can help you familiarize yourself with a case, identify problems, and propose strategic actions that increase the probability that a firm will achieve strategic competitiveness and earn above-average returns.

GAINING FAMILIARITY

The first step of an effective case analysis process calls for you to become familiar with the facts featured in the case and the focal firm's situation. Initially, you should become familiar with the focal firm's general situation (e.g., who, what, how, where, and when). Thorough familiarization demands appreciation of the nuances as well as the major issues in the case.

Gaining familiarity with a situation requires you to study several situational levels, including interactions

An Effective Case Analysis Process	EXHIBIT 2

Step 1: *Gaining Familiarity*	a. In general—determine who, what, how, where, and when (the critical facts of the case). b. In detail—identify the places, persons, activities, and contexts of the situation. c. Recognize the degree of certainty/uncertainty of acquired information.
Step 2: *Recognizing Symptoms*	a. List all indicators (including stated "problems") that something is not as expected or as desired. b. Ensure that symptoms are not assumed to be the problem (symptoms should lead to identification of the problem).
Step 3: *Identifying Goals*	a. Identify critical statements by major parties (e.g., people, groups, the work unit, etc.). b. List all goals of the major parties that exist or can be reasonably inferred.
Step 4: *Conducting the Analysis*	a. Decide which ideas, models, and theories seem useful. b. Apply these conceptual tools to the situation. c. As new information is revealed, cycle back to substeps a and b.
Step 5: *Making the Diagnosis*	a. Identify predicaments (goal inconsistencies). b. Identify problems (discrepancies between goals and performance). c. Prioritize predicaments/problems regarding timing, importance, etc.
Step 6: *Doing the Action Planning*	a. Specify and prioritize the criteria used to choose action alternatives. b. Discover or invent feasible action alternatives. c. Examine the probable consequences of action alternatives. d. Select a course of action. e. Design an implementation plan/schedule. f. Create a plan for assessing the action to be implemented.

Source: 1993, C. C. Lundberg and C. Enz, A framework for student case preparation, *Case Research Journal*, 13 (Summer): 144.

between and among individuals within groups, business units, the corporate office, the local community, and the society at large. Recognizing relationships within and among levels facilitates a more thorough understanding of the specific case situation.

It is also important that you evaluate information on a continuum of certainty. Information that is verifiable by several sources and judged along similar dimensions can be classified as a *fact*. Information representing someone's perceptual judgment of a particular situation is referred to as an *inference*. Information gleaned from a situation that is not verifiable is classified as *speculation*. Finally, information that is independent of verifiable sources and arises through individual or group discussion is an *assumption*. Obviously, case analysts and organizational decision makers prefer having access to facts over inferences, speculations, and assumptions.

Personal feelings, judgments, and opinions evolve when you are analyzing a case. It is important to be aware of your own feelings about the case and to evaluate the accuracy of perceived "facts" to ensure that the objectivity of your work is maximized.

RECOGNIZING SYMPTOMS

Recognition of symptoms is the second step of an effective case analysis process. A symptom is an indication that something is not as you or someone else thinks it should be. You may be tempted to correct the symptoms instead of searching for true problems. True problems are the conditions or situations requiring solution before the performance of an organization, business unit, or individual can improve. Identifying and listing symptoms early in the case analysis process tends to reduce the temptation to label symptoms as problems. The focus of your analysis should be on the *actual causes* of a problem, rather than on its symptoms. Thus, it is important to remember that symptoms are indicators of problems; subsequent work facilitates discovery of critical causes of problems that your case recommendations must address.

IDENTIFYING GOALS

The third step of effective case analysis calls for you to identify the goals of the major organizations, business units, and/or individuals in a case. As appropriate, you should also identify each firm's strategic intent and strategic mission. Typically, these direction-setting statements (goals, strategic intents, and strategic missions) are derived from comments made by central characters in the organization, business unit, or top management team as described in the case and/or from public documents (e.g., an annual report).

Completing this step successfully sometimes can be difficult. Nonetheless, the outcomes you attain from this step are essential to an effective case analysis because identifying goals, intent, and mission helps you to clarify the major problems featured in a case and to evaluate alternative solutions to those problems. Direction-setting statements are not always stated publicly or prepared in written format. When this occurs, you must infer goals from other available factual data and information.

CONDUCTING THE ANALYSIS

The fourth step of effective case analysis is concerned with acquiring a systematic understanding of a situation. Occasionally cases are analyzed in a less-than-thorough manner. Such analyses may be a product of a busy schedule or the difficulty and complexity of the issues described in a particular case. Sometimes you will face pressures on your limited amounts of time and may believe that you can understand the situation described in a case without systematic analysis of all the facts. However, experience shows that familiarity with a case's facts is a necessary, but insufficient, step in the development of effective solutions—solutions that can enhance a firm's strategic competitiveness. In fact, a less-than-thorough analysis typically results in an emphasis on symptoms, rather than problems and their causes. To analyze a case effectively, you should be skeptical of quick or easy approaches and answers.

A systematic analysis helps you understand a situation and determine what can work and probably what will not work. Key linkages and underlying causal networks based on the history of the firm become apparent. In this way, you can separate causal networks from symptoms.

Also, because the quality of a case analysis depends on applying appropriate tools, it is important that you use the ideas, models, and theories that seem to be useful for evaluating and solving individual and unique situations. As you consider facts and symptoms, a useful theory may become apparent. Of course, having familiarity with conceptual models may be important in the effective analysis of a situation. Successful students and successful organizational strategists add to their intellectual tool kits on a continual basis.

MAKING THE DIAGNOSIS

The fifth step of effective case analysis—diagnosis—is the process of identifying and clarifying the roots of the problems by comparing goals to facts. In this step, it is useful to search for predicaments. Predicaments are situations in which goals do not fit with known facts. When you evaluate the actual performance of an organization, business unit, or individual, you may identify over- or underachievement (relative to established goals). Of course, single-problem situations are rare. Accordingly, you should recognize that the case situations you study probably will be complex in nature.

Effective diagnosis requires you to determine the problems affecting longer term performance and those requiring immediate handling. Understanding these issues will aid your efforts to prioritize problems and predicaments, given available resources and existing constraints.

DOING THE ACTION PLANNING

The final step of an effective case analysis process is called action planning. Action planning is the process of identifying appropriate alternative actions. In the action planning step you select the criteria you will use to evaluate the identified alternatives. You may derive these criteria from the analyses; typically, they are related to key strategic situations facing the focal organization. Furthermore, it is important that you prioritize these criteria to ensure a rational and effective evaluation of alternative courses of action.

Typically, managers "satisfice" when selecting courses of action; that is, they find *acceptable* courses of action that meet most of the chosen evaluation criteria. A rule of thumb that has proved valuable to strategic decision makers is to select an alternative that leaves other plausible alternatives available if the one selected fails.

Once you have selected the best alternative, you must specify an implementation plan. Developing an implementation plan serves as a reality check on the feasibility of your alternatives. Thus, it is important that you give thoughtful consideration to all issues associated with the implementation of the selected alternatives.

WHAT TO EXPECT FROM IN-CLASS CASE DISCUSSIONS

Classroom discussions of cases differ significantly from lectures. The case method calls for instructors to guide the discussion, encourage student participation, and solicit alternative views. When alternative views are not forthcoming, instructors typically adopt one view so students can be challenged to respond to it thoughtfully. Often students' work is evaluated in terms of both the quantity and the quality of their contributions to in-class case discussions. Students benefit by having their views judged against those of their peers and by responding to challenges by other class members and/or the instructor.

During case discussions, instructors listen, question, and probe to extend the analysis of case issues. In the course of these actions, peers or the instructor may challenge an individual's views and the validity of alternative perspectives that have been expressed. These challenges are offered in a constructive manner; their intent is to help students develop their analytical and communication skills. Instructors should encourage students to be innovative and original in the development and presentation of their ideas. Over the course of an individual discussion, students can develop a more complex view of the case, benefiting from the diverse inputs of their peers and instructor. Among other benefits, experience with multiple-case discussions should help students increase their knowledge of the advantages and disadvantages of group decision-making processes.

Student peers as well as the instructor value comments that contribute to the discussion. To offer *relevant* contributions, you are encouraged to use independent thought and, through discussions with your peers outside of class, to refine your thinking. We also encourage you to avoid using "I think," "I believe," and "I feel" to discuss your inputs to a case analysis process. Instead, consider using a less emotion-laden phrase, such as "My analysis shows." This highlights the logical nature of the approach you have taken to complete the six steps of an effective case analysis process.

When preparing for an in-class case discussion, you should plan to use the case data to explain your assessment of the situation. Assume that your peers and instructor know the case facts. In addition, it is good practice to prepare notes before class discussions and use them as you explain your view. Effective notes signal to classmates and the instructor that you are prepared to engage in a thorough discussion of a case. Moreover, thorough notes eliminate the need for you to memorize the facts and figures needed to discuss a case successfully.

The case analysis process just described can help you prepare to effectively discuss a case during class meetings. Adherence to this process results in consideration of the issues required to identify a focal firm's problems and to propose strategic actions through which the firm can increase the probability that it will achieve strategic competitiveness.

In some instances, your instructor may ask you to prepare either an oral or a written analysis of a particular case. Typically, such an assignment demands even more thorough study and analysis of the case contents. At your instructor's discretion, oral and written analyses may be completed by individuals or by groups of two or more people. The information and insights gained through completing the six steps shown in Exhibit 2 often are of value in the development of an oral or written analysis. However, when preparing an oral or written presentation, you must consider the overall framework in which your information and inputs will be presented. Such a framework is the focus of the next section.

PREPARING AN ORAL/WRITTEN CASE STRATEGIC PLAN

Experience shows that two types of thinking are necessary to develop an effective oral or written presentation (see Exhibit 3). The upper part of the model in Exhibit 3 outlines the *analysis* stage of case preparation.

In the analysis stage, you should first analyze the general external environmental issues affecting the firm. Next your environmental analysis should focus on the particular industry (or industries, in the case of a diversified company) in which a firm operates. Finally, you should examine the competitive environment of the focal firm. Through study of the three levels of the external environment, you will be able to identify a firm's opportunities and threats. Following the external environmental analysis is the analysis of the firm's internal environment, which results in the identification of the firm's strengths and weaknesses.

As noted in Exhibit 3, you must then change the focus from analysis to *synthesis*. Specifically, you must *synthesize* information gained from your analysis of the firm's internal and external environments. Synthesizing information allows you to generate alternatives that can resolve the significant problems or challenges facing the focal firm. Once you identify a best alternative, from an evaluation based on predetermined criteria and goals, you must explore implementation actions.

Exhibit 4 and Exhibit 5 outline the sections that should be included in either an oral or a written strategic plan presentation: introduction (strategic intent and mission), situation analysis, statements of strengths/weaknesses and opportunities/threats, strategy formulation, and implementation plan. These sections, which can be completed only through use of the two types of thinking featured in Exhibit 3, are described in the following discussion. Familiarity with the contents of this book's 13 chapters is helpful because the general outline

---

EXHIBIT 3 Types of Thinking in Case Preparation: Analysis and Synthesis

ANALYSIS

External environment

General environment
Industry environment
Competitor environment

Internal environment

Statements of strengths, weaknesses, opportunities, and threats

Alternatives
Evaluations of alternatives
Implementation

SYNTHESIS

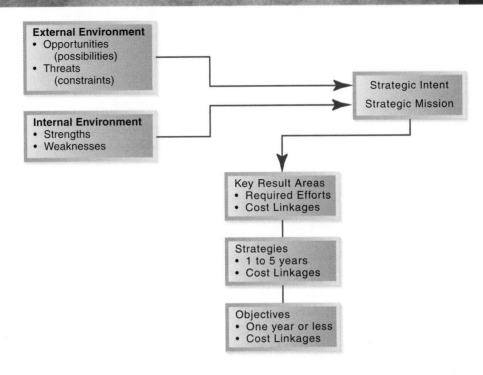

- *Strategic planning* is a *process* through which a firm determines what it seeks to accomplish and the actions required to achieve desired outcomes
  - ✓ *Strategic planning*, then, is a *process* that we use to determine *what* (outcomes to be reached) and *how* (actions to be taken to reach outcomes)
- The effective *strategic plan* for a firm would include statements and details about the following:
  - ✓ *Opportunities* (possibilities) and *threats* (constraints)
  - ✓ *Strengths* (what we do especially well) and *weaknesses* (deficiencies)
  - ✓ *Strategic intent* (an indication of a firm's ideal state)
  - ✓ *Strategic mission* (purpose and scope of a firm's operations in product and market terms)
  - ✓ *Key result areas* (KRAs) (categories of activities where efforts must take place to reach the mission and intent)
  - ✓ *Strategies* (actions for each KRA to be completed within one to five years)
  - ✓ *Objectives* (specific statements detailing actions for each strategy that are to be completed in one year or less)
  - ✓ *Cost linkages* (relationships between actions and financial resources)

for an oral or a written strategic plan shown in Exhibit 5 is based on an understanding of the strategic management process detailed in these chapters.

EXTERNAL ENVIRONMENT ANALYSIS

As shown in Exhibit 5, a general starting place for completing a situation analysis is the external environment. The *external environment* is composed of outside (exter-

nal) conditions that affect a firm's performance. Your analysis of the environment should consider the effects of the *general environment* on the focal firm. Following that evaluation, you should analyze the *industry and competitor environmental* trends.

These trends or conditions in the external environment shape the firm's strategic intent and mission. The external environment analysis essentially indicates what a firm *might choose to do.* Often called an *environmental scan,* an analysis of the external environment allows a firm to identify key conditions that are beyond its direct control. The purpose of studying the external environment is to identify a firm's opportunities and threats. *Opportunities* are conditions in the external environment that appear to have the potential to contribute to a firm's success. In essence, opportunities represent *possibilities.* *Threats* are conditions in the external environment that appear to have the potential to prevent a firm's success. In essence, threats represent potential *constraints.*

When studying the external environment, the focus is on trying to *predict* the future (in terms of local, regional, and international trends and issues) and to *predict* the expected effects on a firm's operations. The external environment features conditions in the broader society *and* in the industry (area of competition) that influence the firm's possibilities and constraints. Areas to be considered (to identify opportunities and threats) when studying the general environment are listed in Exhibit 6. Many of these issues are explained more fully in Chapter 2.

Once you analyze the general environmental trends, you should study their effect on the focal industry. Often the same environmental trend may have a significantly different impact on separate industries. Furthermore, the same trend may affect firms within the same industry differently. For instance, with deregulation of the airline industry, older, established airlines had a significant decrease in profitability, while many smaller airlines such as Southwest Airlines, with lower cost structures and greater flexibility, were able to aggressively enter new markets.

Porter's five forces model is a useful tool for analyzing the specific industry (see Chapter 2). Careful study of how the five competitive forces (i.e., supplier power, buyer power, potential entrants, substitute products, and rivalry among competitors) affect a firm's strategy is important. These forces may create threats or opportunities relative to the specific business-level strategies (i.e., differentiation, cost leadership, focus) being implemented. Often a strategic group's analysis reveals how different environmental trends are affecting industry competitors. Strategic group analysis is useful for understanding the industry's competitive structures and firm constraints and possibilities within those structures.

Firms also need to analyze each of their primary competitors. This analysis should identify competitors' current strategies, strategic intent, strategic mission, capabilities, core competencies, and a competitive response profile. This information is useful to the focal firm in formulating an appropriate strategic intent and mission. Sources that can be used to gather information about a general environment, industry, and companies

with whom the focal firm competes are listed in Appendix I. Included in this list is a wide range of websites; publications, such as periodicals, newspapers, bibliographies, and directories of companies; industry ratios; forecasts; rankings/ratings; and other valuable statistics.

INTERNAL ENVIRONMENT ANALYSIS

The *internal environment* is composed of strengths and weaknesses internal to a firm that influence its strategic competitiveness. The purpose of completing an analysis of a firm's internal environment is to identify its strengths and weaknesses. The strengths and weaknesses in a firm's internal environment shape the strategic intent and strategic mission. The internal environment essentially indicates what a firm *can do.* Capabilities or skills that allow a firm to do something that others cannot do or that allow a firm to do something better than others do it are called strengths. *Strengths* can be categorized as something that a firm does especially well. Strengths help a firm take advantage of external opportunities or overcome external threats. Capabilities or skill deficiencies that prevent a firm from completing an important activity as well as others do it are called weaknesses. *Weaknesses* have the potential to prevent a firm from taking advantage of external opportunities or succeeding in efforts to overcome external threats. Thus, *weaknesses* can be thought of as something the firm needs to improve.

Analysis of the primary and support activities of the value chain provides opportunities to understand how external environmental trends affect the specific activities of a firm. Such analysis helps highlight strengths and weaknesses (see Chapter 3 for an explanation of the value chain). For purposes of preparing an oral or written presentation, it is important to note that strengths are internal resources and capabilities that have the potential to be core competencies. Weaknesses, on the other hand, have the potential to place a firm at a competitive disadvantage relative to its rivals.

When evaluating the internal characteristics of the firm, your analysis of the functional activities emphasized is critical. For instance, if the strategy of the firm is primarily technology-driven, it is important to evaluate the firm's R&D activities. If the strategy is market-driven, marketing functional activities are of paramount importance. If a firm has financial difficulties, critical financial ratios would require careful evaluation. In fact, because of the importance of financial health, most cases require financial analyses. Appendix II lists and operationally defines several common financial ratios. Included are exhibits describing profitability, liquidity, leverage, activity, and shareholders' return

Technology	• Information technology continues to become cheaper and have more practical applications
	• Database technology allows organization of complex data and distribution of information
	• Telecommunications technology and networks increasingly provide fast transmission of all sources of data, including voice, written communications, and video information
Demographic Trends	• Computerized design and manufacturing technologies continue to facilitate quality and flexibility
	• Regional changes in population due to migration
	• Changing ethnic composition of the population
	• Aging of the population
	• Aging of the "baby boom" generation
Economic Trends	• Interest rates
	• Inflation rates
	• Savings rates
	• Trade deficits
	• Budget deficits
	• Exchange rates
Political/Legal Environment	• Anti-trust enforcement
	• Tax policy changes
	• Environmental protection laws
	• Extent of regulation/deregulation
	• Developing countries privatizing state monopolies
	• State-owned industries
Sociocultural Environment	• Increasing number of women in the workforce
	• Awareness of health and fitness issues
	• Concern for the environment
	• Concern for customers
Global Environment	• Currency exchange rates
	• Free trade agreements
	• Trade deficits
	• New or developing markets

ratios. Other firm characteristics that should be examined to study the internal environment effectively include leadership, organizational culture, structure, and control systems.

IDENTIFICATION OF STRATEGIC INTENT AND MISSION

Strategic intent is associated with a mind-set that managers seek to imbue within the company. Essentially, a mind-set captures how we view the world and our intended role in it. Strategic intent reflects or identifies a firm's ideal state. Strategic intent flows from a firm's opportunities, threats, strengths, and weaknesses. However, the major influence on strategic intent is a firm's *strengths*. Strategic intent should reflect a firm's intended character and reflects a commitment to

"stretch" available resources and strengths in order to reach what may seem to be unattainable strategies and objectives in terms of key result areas (KRAs). When established effectively, strategic intent can cause each employee to perform in ways never imagined possible. Strategic intent has the ability to reflect what may be the most worthy goal of all: to unseat the best or to be the best on a regional, national, or even international basis. Examples of strategic intent include:

- The relentless pursuit of perfection (Lexus).
- It's our strategic intent that customers worldwide view us as their most valued pharmaceutical partner (Eli Lilly).
- To be the top performer in everything that we do (Phillips Petroleum).

- To become a high performance multinational energy company—not the biggest, but the best (Unocal Corporation).
- We are dedicated to being the world's best at bringing people together (AT&T).
- Ben & Jerry's is dedicated to the creation and demonstration of a new corporate concept—linked prosperity.
- Our intent is to be better than the best (Best Products).
- The Children's Defense Fund exists to provide a strong and effective voice for the children of America who cannot vote, lobby, or speak for themselves.
- We build homes to meet people's dreams (Kaufman & Broad).
- We will be a leader in the emerging energy services industry by challenging conventional wisdom and creating superior value in a safe and environmentally responsible manner (PSI Energy, Inc.).
- We intend to become the single source of information technology for the home (Dell Computer Corporation).
- To be a premier provider of services and products that contribute to the health and well-being of people (MDS Health Group Limited).
- We seek to set the standard for excellence, leadership and integrity in the utility industry (New York State Electric & Gas Corp.).

The strategic mission flows from a firm's strategic intent; it is a statement used to describe a firm's unique intent and the scope of its operations in product and market terms. In its most basic form, the strategic mission indicates to stakeholders what a firm seeks to accomplish. An effective strategic mission reflects a firm's individuality and reveals its leadership's predisposition(s). The useful strategic mission shows how a firm differs from others and defines boundaries within which the firm intends to operate. Examples of strategic missions include:

- To make, distribute, and sell the finest quality all-natural ice cream and related products in a wide variety of innovative flavors made from Vermont dairy products (Ben & Jerry's).
- To serve the natural and LP needs of the customers in the Clearwater and surrounding Florida Sun-Coast area in the most safe, reliable and economical manner possible while optimizing load growth, customer satisfaction, financial return to the City of Clearwater and the equity value of the Clearwater Gas System (Clearwater Gas System).
- Public Service Company of Colorado is an energy company that primarily provides gas, electricity and related services to present and potential markets.

- Our mission is to understand and satisfy customer expectations for quality and energy and energy-related products and services and profitably serve Oklahoma markets (Public Service Company of Oklahoma).
- Children's Hospital Medical Center is dedicated to serving the health-care needs of infants, children, and adolescents and to providing research and teaching programs that ensure delivery of the highest quality pediatric care to our community, the nation, and the world (Children's Hospital Medical Center).
- To provide services and products which will assist physicians, health care institutions, corporations, government agencies, and communities to improve the health and well-being of the people for whom they are responsible (MDS Health Group Limited).
- The William Penn Foundation is a private grant making organization created in 1945 by Otto Haas and his wife, Phoebe. The principal mission of the Foundation is to help improve the quality of life in the Delaware Valley (William Penn Foundation).

KEY RESULT AREAS (KRAS)

Once the strategic intent and mission have been defined, the analysis can turn to defining KRAs to help accomplish the intent and mission. *Key result areas* are categories of activities that must receive attention if the firm is to achieve its strategic intent and strategic mission. A rationale or justification and specific courses of action for each KRA should be specified. Typically, a firm should establish no more than six KRAs. KRAs should suggest (in broad terms) a firm's concerns and intended directions.

Flowing from the nature of a firm's KRAs, *strategies* are courses of action that must be taken to satisfy the requirements suggested by each KRA. Strategies typically have a one-, two-, or three-year time horizon (although it can be as long as five years). Strategies are developed to describe approaches to be used or methods to follow in order to attain the strategic intent and strategic mission (as suggested by the KRAs). Strategies reflect a group's action intentions. Flowing from individual strategies, *objectives* are specific and measurable statements describing actions that are to be completed to implement individual strategies. Objectives, which are more specific in nature than strategies, usually have a one-year or shorter time horizon.

Strategic planning should also result in cost linkages to courses of action. Once key cost assumptions are specified, these financial requirements can be tied to strategies and objectives. Once linked with strategies and objectives, cost or budgetary requirements can be related back to KRAs.

HINTS FOR PRESENTING AN EFFECTIVE STRATEGIC PLAN

There may be a temptation to spend most of your oral or written case analysis on results from the analysis. It is important, however, that you make an equal effort to develop and evaluate KRA alternatives and to design implementation for the chosen alternatives. In your presentation, the *analysis* of a case should not be overemphasized relative to the *synthesis* of results gained from your analytical efforts (see Exhibit 3).

STRATEGY FORMULATION: CHOOSING KEY RESULT AREAS

Once you have formulated a strategic intent and mission, choosing among alternative KRAs is often one of the most difficult steps in preparing an oral or written presentation. Each alternative should be feasible (i.e., it should match the firm's strengths, capabilities, and especially core competencies), and feasibility should be demonstrated. In addition, you should show how each alternative takes advantage of the environmental opportunity or avoids/buffers against environmental threats. Developing carefully thought out alternatives requires synthesis of your analyses and creates greater credibility in oral and written case presentations.

Once you develop strong alternative KRAs, you must evaluate the set to choose the best ones. Your choice should be defensible and provide benefits over the other alternatives. Thus, it is important that both the alternative development and evaluation of alternatives be thorough. The choice of the best alternative should be explained and defended.

KEY RESULT AREA IMPLEMENTATION

After selecting the most appropriate KRAs (that is, those with the highest probability of enhancing a firm's strategic competitiveness), you must consider effective implementation. Effective synthesis is important to ensure that you have considered and evaluated all critical implementation issues. Issues you might consider include the structural changes necessary to implement the new strategies and objectives associated with each KRA. In addition, leadership changes and new controls or incentives may be necessary to implement these strategic actions. The implementation actions you recommend should be explicit and thoroughly explained. Occasionally, careful evaluation of implementation actions may show the

strategy to be less favorable than you originally thought. A strategy is only as good as the firm's ability to implement it effectively. Therefore, expending the effort to determine effective implementation is important.

PROCESS ISSUES

You should ensure that your presentation (either oral or written) has logical consistency throughout. For example, if your presentation identifies one purpose, but your analysis focuses on issues that differ from the stated purpose, the logical inconsistency will be apparent. Likewise, your alternatives should flow from the configuration of strengths, weaknesses, opportunities, and threats you identified through the internal and external analyses.

Thoroughness and clarity also are critical to an effective presentation. Thoroughness is represented by the comprehensiveness of the analysis and alternative generation. Furthermore, clarity in the results of the analyses, selection of the best alternative KRAs, and design of implementation actions are important. For example, your statement of the strengths and weaknesses should flow clearly and logically from the internal analyses presented.

Presentations (oral or written) that show logical consistency, thoroughness, and clarity of purpose, effective analyses, and feasible recommendations are more effective and will receive more positive evaluations. Being able to withstand tough questions from peers after your presentation will build credibility for your strategic plan presentation. Furthermore, developing the skills necessary to make such presentations will enhance your future job performance and career success.

NOTES

1. 2000, M. A. Lundberg, B. B. Levin, & H. I. Harrington, *Who Learns What From Cases and How? The Research Base for Teaching and Learning with Cases* (Englewood Cliffs, New Jersey: Lawrence Erlbaum Associates).

2. 1994, L. B. Barnes, A. J. Nelson, & C. R. Christensen, *Teaching and the Case Method: Text, Cases and Readings* (Boston: Harvard Business School Press); 1993, C. C. Lundberg, Introduction to the case method, in C. M. Vance (ed.), *Mastering Management Education* (Newbury Park, Calif.: Sage); 1989, C. Christensen, *Teaching and the Case Method* (Boston: Harvard Business School Publishing Division).

3. 1993, C. C. Lundberg & E. Enz, A framework for student case preparation, *Case Research Journal*, 13 (Summer): 133.

4. 1971, J. Solitis, John Dewey, in L. E. Deighton (ed.), *Encyclopedia of Education* (New York: Macmillan and Free Press).

5. 1987, F. Bocker, Is case teaching more effective than lecture teaching in business administration? An exploratory analysis, *Interfaces*, 17(5): 64–71.

APPENDIX I: SOURCES FOR INDUSTRY AND COMPETITOR ANALYSES

Strategic Management Websites

Search Engines (may be the broadest sources of information on companies and industries)

Alta Vista—*http://www.altavista.digital.com*

Excite—*http://www.excite.com*

InfoSeek—*http://www.infoseek.com*

Lycos—*http://www.lycos.com*

WebCrawler—*http://www.webcrawler.com*

Yahoo!—*http://www.yahoo.com*

Professional Societies

Academy of Management <*http://www.aom.pace.edu*> publishes *Academy of Management Journal, Academy of Management Review, and Academy of Management Executive,* three publications that often print articles on strategic management research, theory, and practice. The Academy of Management is the largest professional society for management research and education and has a large Business Policy and Strategy Division.

Strategic Management Society <*http://www.smsweb.org*> publishes the *Strategic Management Journal* (a top academic journal in strategic management).

Government Sources of Company Information and Data

Census Bureau <*http://www.census.gov*> provides useful links and information about social, demographic, and economic information.

Federal Trade Commission <*http://www.ftc.gov*> includes discussion on several antitrust and consumer protection laws useful to businesses looking for accurate information about business statutes.

Free EDGAR <*http://www.freeedgar.com*> provides free, unlimited access to real-time corporate data filed with the Securities and Exchange Commission (SEC).

Better Business Bureau <*http://www.bbb.org*> provides a wide variety of helpful publications, information, and other resources to both consumers and businesses to help people make informed marketplace decisions.

Publication Websites

Business Week <*http://www.businessweek.com*> allows search of *Business Week* magazine's articles by industry or topic, such as strategy.

Forbes <*http://www.forbes.com*> provides searching of *Forbes* magazine business articles and data.

Fortune <*http://www.fortune.com*> allows search of *Fortune* magazine and other articles, many of which are focused on strategy topics.

Financial Times <*http://www.ft.com*> provides access to many *Financial Times* articles, data, and surveys.

Wall Street Journal <*http://www.wsj.com*> *The Wall Street Journal Interactive* edition provides an excellent continuing stream of strategy-oriented articles and announcements.

Abstracts and Indexes

Periodicals

ABI/Inform
Business Periodicals Index
InfoTrac (CD-ROM computer multidiscipline index)
Investext (CD-ROM)
Predicasts F&S Index United States
Predicasts Overview of Markets and Technology (PROMT)
Predicasts R&S Index Europe
Predicasts R&S Index International
Public Affairs Information Service Bulletin (PAIS)
Reader's Guide to Periodical Literature

Newspapers

NewsBank
Business NewsBank
New York Times Index
Wall Street Journal Index

	Wall Street Journal/Barron's Index
	Washington Post Index
Bibliographies	*Encyclopedia of Business Information Sources*
	Handbook of Business Information
Directories	
Companies—General	*America's Corporate Families and International Affiliates*
	Hoover's Handbook of American Business
	Hoover's Handbook of World Business
	Million Dollar Directory
	Standard & Poor's Corporation Records
	Standard & Poor's Register of Corporations, Directors, and Executives
	Ward's Business Directory
Companies—International	*America's Corporate Families and International Affiliates*
	Business Asia
	Business China
	Business Eastern Europe
	Business Europe
	Business International
	Business International Money Report
	Business Latin America
	Directory of American Firms Operating in Foreign Countries
	Directory of Foreign Firms Operating in the United States
	Hoover's Handbook of World Business
	International Directory of Company Histories
	Moody's Manuals, International (2 volumes)
	Who Owns Whom
Companies—Manufacturers	*Manufacturing USA: Industry Analyses, Statistics, and Leading Companies*
	Thomas Register of American Manufacturers
	U.S. Office of Management and Budget, Executive Office of the President, *Standard Industrial Classification Manual*
	U.S. Manufacturer's Directory
Companies—Private	*Million Dollar Directory*
	Ward's Directory
Companies—Public	Annual Reports and 10-K Reports
	Disclosure (corporate reports)
	Q-File
	Moody's Manuals:
	Moody's Bank and Finance Manual
	Moody's Industrial Manual
	Moody's International Manual
	Moody's Municipal and Government Manual
	Moody's OTC Industrial Manual
	Moody's OTC Unlisted Manual
	Moody's Public Utility Manual
	Moody's Transportation Manual
	Standard & Poor Corporation, *Standard Corporation Descriptions*:
	Standard & Poor's Handbook
	Standard & Poor's Industry Surveys
	Standard & Poor's Investment Advisory Service
	Standard & Poor's Outlook
	Standard & Poor's Statistical Service
Companies—Subsidiaries and Affiliates	*America's Corporate Families and International Affiliates*
	Ward's Directory
	Who Owns Whom
	Moody's Industry Review
	Standard & Poor's Analyst's Handbook
	Standard & Poor's Industry Report Service
	Standard & Poor's Industry Surveys (2 volumes)
	U.S. Department of Commerce, *U.S. Industrial Outlook*

Industry Ratios	Dun & Bradstreet, *Industry Norms and Key Business Ratios* *Robert Morris Associates Annual Statement Studies* *Troy Almanac of Business and Industrial Financial Ratios*
Industry Forecasts	International Trade Administration, *U.S. Industrial Outlook* *Predicasts Forecasts*
Rankings & Ratings	Annual Report on American Industry in *Forbes* *Business Rankings and Salaries* *Business One Irwin Business and Investment Almanac* *Corporate and Industry Research Reports (CIRR)* *Dun's Business Rankings* *Moody's Industrial Review* *Rating Guide to Franchises* *Standard & Poor's Industry Report Service* *Value Line Investment Survey* *Ward's Business Directory*
Statistics	*American Statistics Index (ASI)* Bureau of the Census, U.S. Department of Commerce, *Economic Census Publications* Bureau of the Census, U.S. Department of Commerce, *Statistical Abstract of the United States* Bureau of Economic Analysis, U.S. Department of Commerce, *Survey of Current Business* Internal Revenue Service, U.S. Treasury Department, *Statistics of Income: Corporation Income Tax Returns* *Statistical Reference Index (SRI)*

APPENDIX II: FINANCIAL ANALYSIS IN CASE STUDIES

EXHIBIT A-1 Profitability Ratios

Ratio	Formula	What It Shows
1. Return on total assets	$\dfrac{\text{Profits after taxes}}{\text{Total assets}}$ or $\dfrac{\text{Profits after taxes + interest}}{\text{Total assets}}$	The net return on total investment of the firm or The return on both creditors' and shareholders' investments
2. Return on stockholders' equity (or return on net worth)	$\dfrac{\text{Profits after taxes}}{\text{Total stockholders' equity}}$	How effectively the company is utilizing shareholders' funds
3. Return on common equity	$\dfrac{\text{Profit after taxes} - \text{preferred stock dividends}}{\text{Total stockholders' equity} - \text{par value of preferred stock}}$	The net return to common stockholders
4. Operating profit margin (or return on sales)	$\dfrac{\text{Profits before taxes and before interest}}{\text{Sales}}$	The firm's profitability from regular operations
5. Net profit margin (or net return on sales)	$\dfrac{\text{Profits after taxes}}{\text{Sales}}$	The firm's net profit as a percentage of total sales

Ratio	Formula	What It Shows
1. Current ratio	$$\frac{\text{Current assets}}{\text{Current liabilities}}$$	The firm's ability to meet its current financial liabilities
2. Quick ratio (or acid-test ratio)	$$\frac{\text{Current assets} - \text{inventory}}{\text{Current liabilities}}$$	The firm's ability to pay off short-term obligations without relying on sales of inventory
3. Inventory to net working capital	$$\frac{\text{Inventory}}{\text{Current assets} - \text{current liabilities}}$$	The extent of which the firm's working capital is tied up in inventory

Ratio	Formula	What It Shows
1. Debt-to-assets	$$\frac{\text{Total debt}}{\text{Total assets}}$$	Total borrowed funds as a percentage of total assets
2. Debt-to-equity	$$\frac{\text{Total debt}}{\text{Total shareholders' equity}}$$	Borrowed funds versus the funds provided by shareholders
3. Long-term debt-to-equity	$$\frac{\text{Long-term debt}}{\text{Total shareholders' equity}}$$	Leverage used by the firm
4. Times-interest-earned (or coverage ratio)	$$\frac{\text{Profits before interest and taxes}}{\text{Total interest charges}}$$	The firm's ability to meet all interest payments
5. Fixed charge coverage	$$\frac{\text{Profits before taxes and interest} + \text{lease obligations}}{\text{Total interest charges} + \text{lease obligations}}$$	The firm's ability to meet all fixed-charge obligations including lease payments

EXHIBIT A-4 Activity Ratios

Ratio	Formula	What It Shows
1. Inventory turnover	$\dfrac{\text{Sales}}{\text{Inventory of finished goods}}$	The effectiveness of the firm in employing inventory
2. Fixed assets turnover	$\dfrac{\text{Sales}}{\text{Fixed assets}}$	The effectiveness of the firm in utilizing plant and equipment
3. Total assets turnover	$\dfrac{\text{Sales}}{\text{Total assets}}$	The effectiveness of the firm in utilizing total assets
4. Accounts receivable turnover	$\dfrac{\text{Annual credit sales}}{\text{Accounts receivable}}$	How many times the total receivables have been collected during the accounting period
5. Average collection period	$\dfrac{\text{Accounts receivable}}{\text{Average daily sales}}$	The average length of time the firm waits to collect payments after sales

EXHIBIT A-5 Shareholders' Return Ratios

Ratio	Formula	What It Shows
1. Dividend yield on common stock	$\dfrac{\text{Annual dividends per share}}{\text{Current market price per share}}$	A measure of return to common stockholders in the form of dividends.
2. Price-earnings ratio	$\dfrac{\text{Current market price per share}}{\text{After-tax earnings per share}}$	An indication of market perception of the firm. Usually, the faster-growing or less risky firms tend to have higher PE ratios than the slower-growing or more risky firms.
3. Dividend payout ratio	$\dfrac{\text{Annual dividends per share}}{\text{After-tax earnings per share}}$	An indication of dividends paid out as a percentage of profits.
4. Cash flow per share	$\dfrac{\text{After-tax profits + depreciation}}{\text{Number of common shares outstanding}}$	A measure of total cash per share available for use by the firm.

Name Index

Name Index

Company Index

A

Aaon, 127
Abercrombie & Fitch, 109
ABN AMRO, 278, 280
Accenture, 50
Acme, 222
Acura, 9
Adams, 155–156
Advanced Micro Devices, 158, 283
Aerospace Industrial Development Corporation, 286
AgustaWestland, 286
Ahold NV, 330, 391, 393
Air Canada, 275
Air France, 275, 281
Airborne Inc., 206, 242
Airbus, 56, 58, 59, 253, 357
AirTran Airways, 54
Albertson's Inc., 84
Alderwoods Group, 217
Alfa Romeo, 176
Alitalia, 275
All Nippon Airways, 281
Alliance Data, 273
Altria Group Inc., 20, 122, 208, 214
AM General, 271
Amaze Entertainment, 339–340
Amazon.com, 42, 79, 106, 107
AmBev, 214
American Airlines, 7, 18, 51, 86, 138, 275, 281
American Express, 219, 373
American Home Mortgage Holdings Inc. (AHMH), 150
American Household, 317
American International Group (AIG), 274
American Services Group Inc. (ASG), 123
Amurol Confections, 155
Anheuser-Busch, 140, 214, 238, 243, 322
Ann Taylor, 273
AOL, 60, 61, 201–202, 213, 280–281
AOL Time Warner, 60, 61, 169, 182, 186, 188, 191, 201–202, 203, 213

Aozora Bank, 220
Apple Computer, 21, 60, 180, 289, 290, 322, 412
Applied Materials Inc., 138, 160, 373, 375
ApproTEC, 410
Aravon, 124
Arcadia, 204
Arrow, 252–253
ArvinMeritor, 324
Asda, 204
Asea Brown Boveri (ABB), 255, 326
Aston Martin, 12
AstraZeneca, 32
Atlantic Health Systems (AHS), 420
AT&T, 60, 407
Audi, 145
Austrian Airlines, 275
Aviall, 129–130
Avis Rent A Car System, 177
Avnet, 252–253
Avon Products, 372, 373, 378

B

Bad Boy Entertainment, 277
Bain Capital, 222
Bank of America, 50
Bank One, 41, 222
Barnes & Noble, 107
BASF, 241
Bayerische Motoren Werke (BMW), 8, 9, 63, 124, 328
BBAG, 214
BearingPoint, 420
Beijing Automotive Industry Holding Co., 278
Bell Canada, 278
Bell Helicopter, 286
BellSouth, 269, 278, 279
Ben & Jerry's, 252, 350
Beneficial, 208
Benefit Consultants, 177
Benetton, 236
Bentley, 145
Berkshire Hathaway, 218, 219
Bertelsmann AG, 60, 169, 188–189, 202
Bestfoods, 350, 359–360
Bethlehem Steel, 222

Big Dog Motorcycles, 125–126
Big Issue, 410
Big Lots, 115
Blockbuster Inc., 252, 423
BMG, 290
BMW, 8, 9, 63, 124, 328
Boeing Corp., 51, 56, 58, 59, 93, 147, 253, 275, 357
Boise Cascade Office Products, 420
Booz Allen Hamilton, Inc., 273
Borders, 79
Bose, 121
Boston Beer Company, 57
Breyers, 252
Bristol-Myers Squibb, 32
British Airways, 51, 275, 281
British Petroleum (BP), 204, 285
Bucyrus-Erie, 250
Budget Car and Truck Rental, 177
Bugatti, 145
Buick, 9
Building Materials Holding Company (BMHC), 126
Burger King, 142, 222
Burlington Industries, 222

C

Cadillac, 9
Callaway Golf Company, 122
Campbell Soup, 173
Carling Brewery, 214
Carlsberg, 214
Carrefour, 144
Carrier Corporation, 210, 357
Cartoon Cuts, 125
Casketfurniture.com, 123, 125, 346
Caterpillar, 70, 71–72, 83, 119, 250
CBS, 202
CBS Records, 206
Cemex SA, 13, 107, 244, 246
Cendant Corporation, 173, 177–178, 179, 284, 317, 319
Cendant Mobility, 177
Century 21, 177, 284

Chaparral Steel, 83, 87
CheapTickets.com, 177, 178
China Construction Bank, 287
China National Offshore Oil Corporation (CNOOC), 251, 282–283
Christopher & Banks, 109
Chrysler, 190
Chrysler Corporation, 12, 204, 208, 245
Chubb PLC, 210, 357
Cigna, 142
Cinemex, 386
Cinergy Corp., 305
Cisco Systems Inc., 7, 22, 23, 25, 26, 149, 210–211, 258–259, 291, 309, 322, 364, 366, 420
Citibank, 213
Citigroup Inc., 76, 272, 319
Clear Channel Communications, 3–4, 56, 62, 63, 203
Coca-Cola Company, 54, 88, 138, 147, 148, 219
Coldwell Banker, 188
Coldwell Banker Commercial, 177
Columbia Pictures, 169, 206
Comcast, 60, 269, 279
Commerzbank, 327
Compaq Computer Corp., 4, 155, 175–176, 345, 383, 392
Computer Associates (CA), 217–218, 316
Conseco, 50
Consolidated International, 115
Continental Airlines, 112, 220, 224, 281
Coopers Industries, 178
Coors, 214
Corus, 216–217
Cosi, Inc., 43
Costco, 132
Crate & Barrel, 83
Credit Suisse First Boston, 213
CUC International, 177, 178–179
Cummins Engine, 250
CVS Corp., 142–143, 144

Subject Index